# ACTA MEDICINÆ LEGALIS

Vol. XLIV

**1994**

P. Mangin B. Ludes (Eds.)

Springer
*Berlin*
*Heidelberg*
*New York*
*Barcelona*
*Budapest*
*Hong Kong*
*London*
*Milan*
*Paris*
*Tokyo*

P. Mangin B. Ludes (Eds.)

# ACTA MEDICINÆ LEGALIS

Vol. XLIV

1994

XVIth Congress of the International Academy
of Legal Medicine and Social Medicine
Strasbourg, France, 31 May - 2 June, 1994

XVIème Congrès de l'Académie Internationale
de Médecine Légale et de Médecine Sociale
Strasbourg, France, 31 mai-2 juin 1994

Springer

Professor Dr. Patrice Mangin
Université de Strasbourg
Institut de Médecine Légale
11, rue Humann
F-67085 Strasbourg

Dr. Bertrand Ludes
Université de Strasbourg
Institut de Médecine Légale
11, rue Humann
F-67085 Strasbourg

*The authors would like to thank Ms Anne Tricot for her help in the production of the book.*

ISBN-13:978-3-540-58847-4 e-ISBN-13:978-3-642-79523-7
DOI: 10.1007/978-3-642-79523-7

CIP data applied for



SPIN: 10482610 19/3130- 5 4 3 2 1 0 – Printed on acid-free paper

# Preface

**Professor Patrice MANGIN**
**President of the XVIth Congress of the International Academy of Legal Medicine and Social Medicine**

The International Academy of Legal Medicine and Social Medicine was founded in 1938 in Bonn. The motive for founding the Academy was to promote associating and confronting on an international background the scientific research work produced in the various domains dealing with the Legal and Social Medicine. As first president of the International Academy of Legal Medicine and Social Medicine, Professor Knud Sand from Copenhagen, assisted by colleagues of the Praesidium appointed as national representatives, succeeded in gathering together nearly the whole academic people involved in Legal and Social Medicine. Thus one year later, in 1939, The Academy became a worldwide institution of 450 members from thirty nations. After the war, what had been before of considerable interest for the progress of the knowledge and techniques in Legal Medicine remained again a pressing necessity leading to the second meeting of the Academy in 1947 in Brussels under the presidency of Professor De Laet. Since then the meetings of the Academy followed one another every three years. At this point, I would like to thank all the past presidents of the Academy and in particular Professor Roche and Professor André for their contribution without which the Academy would not be what it is presently. In the meantime, it must be also admitted that the worldwide audience of the Academy at the beginning has declined progressively year after year to become restricted to Europeans and even to a certain extent to people from southern European nations while scientists belonging to English speaking, German or Scandinavian countries would rather attend the meetings of the powerful and attractive International Association of Forensic Sciences more recently founded on the basis of a multidisciplinary approach of the Forensic Sciences. Even so, due to its broad spectre of interest, the International Association of Forensic Sciences itself has to compete now with the apparently non reversing trend towards specialization that each of us can observe with the emergence of unidisciplinary societies or associations such as TIAFT or IFSH which are gaining each year more in popularity and importance. In this respect, I express the wish that the Academy could regain possession in the domains of the Legal Medicine and sciences directly connected with the leadership for which it has been founded more than fifty years ago. This objective does not seem unrealistic provided that each member accept to act with full knowledge of the case. It is the merit of Professor Enrique Villanueva to have initiated this reflection under his presidency. It will be without any doubt the expected role of Professor Bernd Brinkmann, his successor, to act up the fruit of this reflection.

Legal Medicine is taught in Strasbourg for exactly two hundred years. In 1794, the French Revolution decided to create simultaneously three Schools of Medicine in Paris, Montpellier and Strasbourg. Immediately after its creation, the School of Medicine of Strasbourg endowed a chair of Legal Medicine which has been occupied by very famous professors such as Fodéré, Tourdes or Simonin. As you can see, the Legal Medicine in Strasbourg is an old and venerable institution which succeeded to pass through the vicissitudes of the history without losing strength but on the contrary in drawing benefits from the alternations of the French and German cultures. In 1990, I enjoyed the privilege of succeeding Professor André Chaumont who was occupying the chair since 1962 after Professor Simonin retired. I would like to take the opportunity which is offered to me today to express publicly to Professor Chaumont my deep gratitude for having chosen me to take in hand the destiny of the Institute of Legal Medicine.

Organizing this meeting was hard work and successful. I would like to express deeply my thanks to the Praesidium of the International Academy and in particular to its president Professor Enrique Villanueva for having chosen Strasbourg as the seat of the XVIth Congress.

It is also a pleasure for me to express sincere appreciation to the guest speakers and to the participants in the different scientific sessions, worshops and seminars that should form the basic structure of the meeting. I am also grateful to my collaborators who did a great job, to the sponsoring companies whose names are listed on the programme book, the European Council for its support in financing the coming of colleagues belonging to eastern European countries, the Ville de Strasbourg, the Conseil Général du Bas-Rhin and the Conseil Régional d'Alsace for providing support and all those who helped us by some means or other.

Finally, the publication of the proceedings of the XVIth Congress constitutes the continuation of the „Acta Medicinae Legalis" previously „et Socialis" which offers to each member of the IALM a compilation of the main scientific contributions presented during this event.

# Speech of Professor Giacomo Canepa at the Opening Ceremony

of the XVIth Congress of the International Academy of Legal Medicine and Social Medicine, Strasbourg, May 30, 1994

Messieurs les Présidents,
Mesdames, Messieurs, et Chers Collègues,

Je suis très heureux de prendre la parole pour remercier les organisateurs de ce Congrès de notre Académie Internationale et pour rendre hommage à tous ceux qui, avec le Professeur Chaumont et le Professeur Mangin, ont travaillé pour réaliser cette manifestation internationale, dont le programme confirme l'importance et l'efficacité de l'activité scientifique et pratique de notre discipline, la médecine légale.

Je m'adresse à vous avec mes compliments très sincères et avec mes meilleurs voeux pour le déroulement des travaux du Congrès, non seulement en ma qualité de vice-président du Praesidium actuel de l'Académie, mais surtout en tant que délégué officiel de deux Sociétés Internationales :

1) la Société Internationale de Défense Sociale, qui doit ses origines à l'initiative d'un professeur de Droit, Filippo Gramatica, en 1947 dans ma ville de Gênes et qui actuellement a son siège social à Paris, où, après la présidence de Gramatica et d'Ancel, la Société est actuellement présidée par Madame Simone Rozès, ancien premier président de la Cour de Cassation. Aussi, au nom de la présidence, ainsi que du secrétaire général M. Adolfo Beria Di Argentine, je formule mes meilleurs voeux pour le succès du Congrès ;

2) la Société Internationale de Criminologie, qui a son siège à Paris et dont j'ai été le président pour cinq années (actuellement le président est le Professeur Rees de l'Université de Yale, USA). Le secrétaire général de cette Société, le Professeur Georges Picca, m'a écrit ce qui suit : „nous serions très heureux que vous acceptiez à cette occasion, et en votre qualité de président honoraire de la Société Internationale de Criminologie, de représenter officiellement notre organisation. ainsi que vous le savez, nous portons en effet un vif intérêt à l'évolution scientifique de la Médecine Légale, qui n'est pas sans relation avec nos activités".

Les deux Sociétés que je représente ici, avec deux autres Sociétés, l'Association Internationale de Droit Pénal (Président le Professeur Bassiouni de Chicago) et la Fondation Internationale Pénitenciaire, présidée par le Professeur De Figueiredo Dias de Coimbra (on les appelle les „Quatres Soeurs"), sont dotées du statut consultatif auprès des Nations Unies et du Conseil de l'Europe. Nous allons préparer un rapport des Quatre Sociétés pour le „Congrès de l'ONU sur la prévention du crime et le traitement des criminels", qui aura lieu à Tunis en avril 1995.

Je souhaite enfin qu'à l'avenir, notre Académie Internationale de Médecine Légale puisse entretenir les mêmes liaisons très étroites avec l'ONU et le Conseil de l'Europe.

Dans cette perspective, je vous souhaite un bon travail et je vous remercie.

# Contents

## 3. Ethics and Forensic Psychiatry



## 4. Post Mortem Chemistry

## 5. Toxicology



## 6. Jurismedicine

## 7. Pathology

## 10. Bodily Damage Evaluation in Europe



## 11. Time of Death Estimation



## 12. Interpretation of Post Mortem Toxicological Data

## 13. Mass Disasters



## 14. Systematic Toxicological Analysis

## 15. Forensic Aspects of Drug Addiction



## 16. Entomology

# Index of Senior Authors

# 1. Plenary Session

# *LEGAL MEDICINE IN EUROPE*

*A. Busuttil*

*It has often been stated by historians and politicians that it is our past that illuminates the present and moulds our future.*

## *PAST HISTORY*

*In a 'whistle-stop' tracing back of the origins of Legal Medicine, several distinct well-rehearsed historically-rich strands have to be unravelled and followed-up. These lead our investigation towards the earliest of civilisations - into Babylon, Ancient China, into Sumeria and Mesopotamia, and later into Pharaonic Egypt; provisions were in force in all these cultures to call on the priests, in their ancillary role of physicians, to help arbitrate in matters of disease and death.*

*The advent of the philosophies and ethical concepts of the Greco-Roman era and of the codified rules laid down by the established Judaic, Christian and Islamic religions, followed on the decline of the Roman Empire and further moulded both legal and medical concepts. In the ambit of the next ten centuries these had percolated deeply into the very roots of European jurisprudence and court practice, and established the foundations of sound medico-legal principles into legislation. These origins, together with so-called 'Common Law', has shaped most European criminal and civil legal frameworks. Eventually these were exported to the many other forensic systems world-wide that have been generated from or were affiliated to the European systems through colonisation and trade; identical basic medico-legal concepts are thus to be found in many other countries in Asia and Africa, as well as in North and Latin America and in Australia.*

*In all the civilisations which have come and gone on the face of this planet, the forensic impact of the medical profession lay in the provision of specialised assistance through the evidence of the doctor on matters with which he was professionally familiar and clinically experienced, as and when this was required by the courts for the fair administration of justice. Therefore the doctor's role has always been sought in the interpretation of injuries, in the investigation of sudden and unexpected death particularly when this was overtly violent or suicidal, in allegations related to sexual misconduct, in abortion and suspected infanticide, in assessing the intrinsic culpability and direct criminal responsibility of the perpetrator.*

## *THE MEDICO-LEGAL SPECIALITY*

*The integrity and the assumed lack of bias of the doctor's expertise and professionalism were sought as safeguards for the fair and sound administration of the ' divine prerogative ' of justice, thereby ensuring that the party who was actually guilty is convicted and punished, and that the innocent are exonerated and acquitted, protected or compensated. A mantle of integrity, sound judgement and carefully considered opinion has fallen on to the doctor is his role as the forensic 'expert witness'.*

*Originally any qualified doctor was thought to have sufficient qualification and expertise to fulfil this role, but as medical specialisms began to evolve, the court medical expert became established as a separate entity. Arguably, Europe also holds the primacy for the establishment and evolution of Legal Medicine as a respected and well-established ' stand-alone ' medical speciality. Through the centuries this formal enshrinement of the medico-legal 'peritus' into European courts of law was brought about and gradually enhanced through the activity of jurists and law makers, who demanded and defined the specific expertise and qualities that were deemed to be essential attributes of the courts' medical expert witness. Eminent forensic doctors have consolidated these demands through the soundness, integrity and probity of their valuable contributions to the courts.*

## *HISTORICAL BACKGROUND*

*To cite just a few examples in twelfth century the crusader king Godfrey de Bouillon established the direct involvement of physicians, surgeons and apothecaries in matters pertaining to personal injury or illness caused by another party. In 1276 in Britain the office of the 'Crowner' - now H. M. Coroner - was instituted by law in the enactment of ' De Officio Coronatoris '; this 'gentleman' had allocated to him a specified investigatory role in sudden unexpected death. In 1249 Hugo de Lucca is documented to have given evidence on oath in a ecclesiastical tribunal on an abortion case after being asked to perform a clinical examination of the woman concerned.*

*The Popes - particularly Innocent III, Gregory IX, John XXII and Gregory XII - further shaped the forensic role for the medical expert through pronouncements, bulls and enactments in 'canon law'. In 1532 Charles V introduced the ' Constitutio Criminalis Carolinae ' in which such matters as abortion, homicide, suicide, personal injury were raised; these were to be followed on later by similar codes in France and other European States. It is however to Paulo Zacchia, a native of Sicily and personal physician to the Popes Innocent X and Alexander VII that through the publication of first of his books entitled ' Quaestiones Medico-Legales ' in 1621 the basis of the speciality was unshakeably established.*

## *LEGAL MEDICINE AS AN ACADEMIC SUBJECT*

*This court-centred respectability became further consolidated when Medical Jurisprudence and Public Health Medicine started to be taught jointly as a specific subject throughout the European seats of learning and became an integral part of the medical curriculum. In my own city of adoption, Edinburgh no less than the monarch himself, George III was prevailed upon to institute the first chair of 'Medical Jurisprudence and Medical Police' in 1807 endorsing the trend in all the other major European medical schools such as Holland, France, Italy and Germany: this 'regius chair' has managed to survive the various vicissitudes of academic politicking.*

*As was to be expected, the role of the forensic medical expert in each individual country has been moulded and shaped over the years in accordance with the requirements and specific nuances of prevailing and often disparate legal systems.*

*The ever-expanding knowledge of scientific and medical matters has led appropriately, to the devolvement of certain aspects of the subject to scientists, to law enforcement agencies and to other medical specialists. In the appropriate cases medical expert evidence became a 'sine qua non' but territorial and cultural frontiers and nationalistic trends have tailored the role and duties of the medical forensic expert to the requirements of individual national courts with variability in style, format of presentation, accreditation to the courts, etc.*

## *UNIFICATION OF EUROPE*

*Since the end of World War II, as the ease and accessibility of travel improved and communication facilities expanded, as education became more universally sought, politicians were faced with the concept of Europe's transformation into a supranational community with an undercurrent of unification, democracy and harmonisation and a major trend towards a closer union in economic and political terms. More than ever in the light of the turbulent history of the first four decades of this century, the upholding of human rights and the quest for a lasting peace within Europe became the goals and ideals to strive for, by every European politician.*

*Individual and collective ethics and positive public action in support of human rights became the driving force in developing national and international codes of law, particularly since no country could claim to be immune from violations of human rights, some of which were even state-sanctioned. A major drive was also in progress to achieve political unity and thereby to contain extreme ideologies.*

*Simultaneously crime has also spread across frontiers: drug smuggling and abuse, child pornography and abuse, international terrorism and fraud, have all become, and remain, trans-European problems. Major natural and man-made disasters became more frequent and often involved larger numbers of casualties and fatalities which are frequently of multi-national origins. All these factors had to be taken into the fullest consideration when the continued pan-European development of Legal Medicine is being considered.*

## *THE COUNCIL OF EUROPE*

*When on May 5 th 1949 the Statute of the Council of Europe was signed in London on behalf of ten European States, they solemnly pledged their endorsement to the upholding of the ' spiritual and moral values which are the common heritage of their people and the true source of individual freedom, political liberty and the rule of law, principles which form the basis of all genuine democracy' . In the original plan of Robert Schuman the setting up of a European international court of justice had been envisaged and in due course this also came to pass and remains established.*

*The ' European Convention for the Protection of Human Rights and Fundamental Freedoms ' can be described as one of the greatest achievements of the Council of Europe. This 'Convention' signed first in 1950, and now in force, to some extent or another, in most of the member countries of the Council, is held as a standard of achievement in its own right of a unifying Europe. More than 240 million persons in Europe may bring before the European Commission of Human Rights allegations that their rights have been violated after exhausting the remedies which their own State provides and many have done and will continue to do so.*

*These sentiments are well expressed in NOLD case, heard before the court in 1974 when the Court stated: '.....and it cannot therefore, uphold measures which are incompatible with fundamental rights recognised and protected by the Constitutions of those States......similarly, international treaties for the protection of human rights, on which Member States have collaborated or of which they are signatories, can supply guidelines which should be followed within the framework of Community law.'*

*TREATY OF ROME*

*A few years later, in 1957, the six members of the ' European Coal and Steel Community ' signed in Rome the Treaties establishing the 'European Economic Community' and 'European Atomic Energy Committee' These treaties which were essentially economic in nature are regarded as the foundation of the European Community i.e. the 'European Union', as designated in the Treaty of Maastricht Treaty, signed on the 7 th. February 1992.*

*Article 7 established that within Europe there would be no discrimination on grounds of nationality while freedom of movement was secured by Articles 48 - 52 of the same treaties. Article 164 requires the European court to ensure that in the interpretation and application of the treaty the 'law' is observed.*

*HUMAN RIGHTS*

*As this rapprochement and European ' entente ' were developing on the political scene and were accompanied by an expressed solidarity in the safeguarding of human rights, several adverse changes could also be observed on other fronts. On the academic front, there had been with a gradual erosion in the teaching of Legal Medicine to undergraduates within the medical schools and colleges of the European states. Modern subjects such as molecular biology, genetics, transplantation studies were introduced at the expense of teaching of 'Legal Medicine'. Furthermore there also appeared to be discrepancies between the standards of court medical expertise acceptable to individual country and levels of acceptable standards of practice. The training and experience requirements of the forensic expert varied widely between different European States.*

*A less than equitable and harmonious exchange of information and closeness of co-operation between the practitioners of this speciality throughout Europe was noted and in some instances this amounted to frank hostility. Another flaw in the system was the dubious independence of some medical forensic experts from the law enforcement agencies leaving the door wide open to allegations of bias and dubiety about the integrity and credibility of the medico-legal expert.*

*THE ' SEVILLE WORKING PARTY '*

*This called for an initiative in harmonisation, - for a stock-taking initiative and for an expression of mutual trust and common purpose. It was thanks to Professor Don Luis Frontela Carreras of Seville who, so to speak, personally took the bull by the horns and at his own initiative and expense brought together representatives from Spain, Belgium, Netherlands, France, Denmark, West Germany, Great Britain, Ireland, Greece, Italy, and Portugal. This meeting resulted in the formation of the 'Seville Working Party', and culminated in the signing of the 'Seville Manifesto' on the 6 th September 1986.*

*In outline, this declaration highlighted the requirement for the speciality of Legal Medicine to attain a higher profile both politically and academically; it was suggested that Legal Medicine could no longer limit itself solely to its involvement with the criminal code but should involve itself with all medical matters that any law, in whatever sector of society, brought to the fore. This would include such matters as disputed paternity, personal injury and infirmity, injuries at work and invalidity as a consequence, chronic alcohol and drug abuse and so on.*
*The document also strongly advocated the compulsory instruction in this subject of medical undergraduates with the suggestion that such a syllabus should encompass clinical forensic medicine, thanatology, forensic toxicology, haemogenetics, medical rights and duties, and medical ethics. It recommended that such training should also be extended to trainee practitioners of dentistry and nursing, and to colleagues in the judiciary and the law enforcement agencies.*
*The seed planted in the fertile soil of Spain gradually grew and ramified not least through the unabating zeal and enthusiastic commitment of Dr Barend Cohen, the Honorary Secretary of the Seville Working Party. It also bore fruit in that the Seville Manifesto did raise the profile of Legal Medicine throughout the signatory countries. Scotland, Luxembourg joined the S W P, corresponding membership status was accorded to other Eastern European states, a joint consensus European document was produced outlining harmonisation of autopsy protocols particularly in major disasters - later adopted through Mr. Morris a member of the European Parliament as a European Council recommendation. A retrospective study on deaths from drugs was conducted and reported on. The Working Party also met and corresponded regularly, and thereby relations between individual specialists from different countries were fostered on a personal level.*
*An official and specific voice in the official European committees on medical education and accreditation, such as U E M S was however still lacking. In July 1991 in an attempt to unblock this log-jam, under the aegis of Professor Bernd Brinkmann, the President-elect of this Academy, representatives from the European Council Member countries in which the speciality of Legal Medicine was well-established in its academic and legal system were brought together in Monaco of Bavaria; these were in addition to Germany, Italy, Greece and Spain. As a consequence of this Monaco meeting, a joint document was signed which further assisted in keeping up the momentum and applying pressure at the right quarters.*

### *PERUGIA MEETING*

*Later on in that year the scene shifts to Perugia where between the 9 and 12 October 1991, through the magnanimous generosity of Professors Franco Fabbroni and Gian Aristide Norelli, a major international conference was held in Perugia under the banner of 'De rebus Medicinae sub specie juris ' and with the title of " La medicina legale nell' Europa communitaria '. The S W P party members were specifically invited to this congress and contributed to the proceedings. Towards the latter part of this meeting, attenders from established academic departments got together in an impromptu fashion and the document entitled ' The Teaching of Legal Medicine to Medical Undergraduates ' was preliminarily forged.*
*Professor Brinkmann in a valiant attempt to consolidate this initiative, with the co-operation and participation of the President of the International Academy, Professor Enrique Villaneuva, the generous co-operation of the German Medico-*

*Legal Society and the kind hospitality of the Professor Stak, organised a further general meeting of representatives from all E C members countries which was held in Cologne, Germany. At this meeting the 'European Council of Legal Medicine', the E C L M , was founded, and after two days of hard work, its Statutes were duly agreed to. An 'interim steering committee' was elected to found the first Executive Council. The statutes were duly notarised in the German Civil Courts and the final version of the Perugia Document also ratified and later printed under the auspices of the E C L M.*

***THE 'EUROPEAN COUNCIL FOR LEGAL MEDICINE'***

*The ' General Assembly ' of the Council met for the first time in Dusseldorf last summer with thanks to Professor W, Bonte. At this meeting were representatives from all E C countries and all countries that had subscribed to E F T A ( European Free Trade Agreement ) . The first official Executive Committee of the Council was elected and it was indeed a pleasure to note that quite a large number of members of the S W P were voted on to this executive; indeed those who had not been elected were later offered ' observer status ' to enable the E C L M to benefit form their expertise.*

*At this meeting two further documents were tabled and discussed in their preliminary state. The first is an 'autopsy protocol' and the second was a 'syllabus for post-graduate specialisation for a European practitioner of Legal Medicine. The intention of the 'autopsy protocol' is to set down the ground rules of good practice in the performance of post-mortem examinations. The scope of the 'post-graduate syllabus' is to provide a framework for the level, depth and range of expertise to be expected from a specialist in Legal Medicine ~ a 'least common denominator' to be effective throughout Europe*

*It was also reported at this meeting that ' observer status ' was sought and accorded to a representative of the E C L M Council on the monospeciality subcommittee in Pathology of the U E M S.*

***THE FUTURE***

*That is the story so far but hopefully there will be several more exciting and fulfilling chapters that will be added to it in the proximate forthcoming months.*

*The future of Legal Medicine as speciality in Europe needs to be consolidated even further and in the furtherance of this, I wish to propose to you a nine point plan:*

*1. Let us keeping conversing with one another throughout Europe, exploring to the fullest potential all the matters which unite us and thus consolidating a base of mutual agreement: let us put to one side institutional differences and nuances of practice. Meeting each other regularly has many benefits to the discipline and to ourselves, but our unifying thoughts and words will have to be translated into action.*

*2. We need to continue to strive to re-institute ' Legal Medicine ' fully into its rightful niche within the medical undergraduate curriculum of each of our countries; if all doctors have acquired by the time that they qualify a modicum of Legal Medicine in their background, our role as medico-legal specialists is better defined and our future would be better assured.*

*3. There is much further scope for trans European harmonisation of training programmes and standardisation of the practice of Legal Medicine whilst maintaining high basic standards; colleagues in other disciplines have managed to do this why not us ?*

*4. High standards of good practice require a sound postgraduate specialisation and perhaps the one way of achieving this would be through some form of unified and communal continental form of accreditation in the manner of an European 'Board 'of Legal Medicine.*

*5. We have to continue to lobby our political colleagues and masters individually but on matters of international importance this should be done through one collective but representative voice and not just as individuals; we require to make our impact felt, and to speak up and be counted, on each and every occasion where we feel that this intervention is merited, and as such we have to be pro-active in putting the speciality forward.*

*6. We should encourage many more trans-European joint research projects and exchange of graduates in the spirit of the Treaties of Rome and Maastricht.*

*7. We need to keep fully abreast of and foster developments in all branches of forensic science and other forensically orientated subjects, and we need to work closely with colleagues in allied disciplines and preferably under the same roof and in the same institutes, offices and departments with them.*

*8. Whatever pressures are brought to bear on us, our ideals of unyielding honesty, untainted integrity and professional independence will have to be maintained whichever and whenever our involvement.*

*9. An air of courteous and friendly camaraderie is to be fostered and our colleagues should always be accorded our fullest co-operation within the limits allowed by our individual legal systems.*

*These, I believe , are eminently achievable ideals and in this vein I would like to propose and recommend heartily to you all as the official toast of this prestigious medicolegal event: ' Floreat res medica legalia europea'.*

**Who is Who in Forensic Sciences - Suggestion of a biographical archive for common benefit**

R. Klaus Mueller, Leipzig (Germany)
Institute of Forensic Medicine, Leipzig University

Forensic Sciences in total and Legal Medicine in itself are multidisciplinary, they represent a variety of areas.
Scientists working in these fields therefore even more than colleagues of other areas feel the crucial importance of co-operation, mutual exchange and consultation.

Information about specialisation and main interests, topics of research or individual experiences might be helpful in seeking co-operation or advice or in simply looking for contacts, beyond the mere knowledge of addresses and telecommunication numbers.

Data of personal scientific backgrounds or curricula vitae might can become relevant for various reasons.
Not only, when someone should perhaps be selected for an honour or award, should be taken into consideration for an election to a board, committee, academy etc., it will turn out that the mere name, address and professional field provide only very sober information, and personal suggestions by others are always fairly subjective or even biased.

If one is interested in the history and development of science, she or he will soon find another reason for the collection of personal data already during the lifetime of individuals, as we did.

When looking for the life and work of the famous German-Jewish toxicologist Louis LEWIN (1850 - 1929) a few years ago, we came across startling mistakes only a few decades after his death. He was one of the most well-known scientists of the last century, having written about 300 papers and a whole series of books, some of them being reprinted even quite recently. Nevertheless, we found several birthdays and birthplaces, a wrong residence address, a wrong doctoral thesis and wrong papers associated to him, wrong workplaces and journeys among a variety of correct data undoubtedly identifying the right person.

What possibilities of error might occur, if the historical reflection is begun with greater delay?
Or imagine how time-consuming the compilation of an individual bibliography will become, if someone else has to do this retrospectively.

There are numerous well-known biographical dictionaries throughout the world, which will certainly remain their value for various purposes. But they are far too voluminous and widespread to be used for such a special professional field, and they cannot at all provide the detailed information outlined above.

On the other hand, the existing national or regional information systems or periodicals like INFORM, or the journals of national societies, or even the Newsletters of our International Academy have different aims and do not provide biographical and bibliographical data in such a general way.

With these contemplations in mind, we have already started some years ago to compile a Biographical and Bibliographical Archive of Forensic Toxicology. Including some historical, but mainly living personalities, it comprises about 100 biographies and bibliographies at present, most of them voluntarily provided by the biographees themselves.

We would now like to propose

- to extend this biographical endeavour to the whole area of Legal Medicine and Forensic Sciences and
- to envisage a periodical book edition of the kind of a "Who is Who in Forensic Sciences" on this base.

There will certainly be some difficulties.

Who should be included?
This had perhaps to be discussed, but possibilities would be:
- Senior staff of reputed institutions in the field, qualified by responsibility and experience and/or by scientific publications
- members of executive boards, advisory or editory committees of scientific societies or journals
- university or college teachers of relevant disciplines.

How far aspects of data protection had to be observed?

The included information should be provided individually and deliberately, so that question should not arise. Any detail had to be proven by the biographee, so that the privacy would remain under individual control, and in addition accuracy would be guaranteed. If one later would become interesting from the standpoint of the history of our science, at least the personal data would be correctly stored and accessible.

All bibliographic titles will already have been published before, so that they cannot be a matter of privacy.

In addition, it would certainly be possible to distinguish between data only for inclusion into an archive and others to be printed in a periodical dictionary.

A rather serious problem would certainly be the completeness / incompleteness of such an archive or book.
But it would improve when growing, becoming more and more a complete survey and source of information. Even at the beginning, an incomplete attempt will be more than nothing.

And finally - the development and success will depend on our scientific community - at first on the members of our International Academy of Legal Medicine and Social Medicine.

Adress of the author:

Prof. Dr. R. Klaus Müller
Institute of Forensic Medicine, Leipzig University
and Institute of Doping Analysis Kreischa near Dresden
Johannisallee 28
D-04103 L E I P Z I G

## Who is Who in Forensic Sciences

Name
Profession
Title(s)
Birthday, -place
Address Office
Phone | Fax | Telex
Address private [1]
Phone | Fax
Main topics of work / interest

Education

Memberships

Avocations [1]

Main publications (please select up to 10 of your own choice)

Publication list (to be attached voluntarily)

---

[1] Even if the personal data are provided for inclusion into the Biographical Archive and Dictionary of Personalities in Forensic Sciences, special data categories might be omitted.

# 2. Advances in DNA technology

# PCR-BASED ANALYSIS FROM FORMALIN-FIXED AND PARAFFIN-EMBEDDED TISSUES

*A Alonso*, P Martín*, C Albarrán*, B Aguilera**, H Oliva** and M sancho*.*
* Sección de Biología. Instituto Nacional de Toxicología. Mº de Justicia. Madrid. SPAIN.
** Fundación Jimenez Díaz. Departamento de Anatomía Patológica. Madrid. SPAIN.

## Introduction

The PCR has extends DNA typing to a significant proportion of biological evidence that contains highly degraded DNA. Formalin-fixed, paraffin-embedded tissues are good examples of surgical specimens with highly degraded DNA that are being analyzed increasingly via PCR at the forensic laboratory.
Here, we present the analysis of sequence polymorphisms (HLA-DQA1, LDLR, GYPA, HBGG, D7S8 and GC), VNTR polymorphism (D1S80) and STR polymorphisms (HUMTH01, HUMFABP and HUMVWA) from formalin-fixed, paraffin-embedded fetal tissue blocks in two paternity studies.
On the other hand, we report preliminary results on the analysis of the above mentioned DNA polymorphisms using as a template of amplification the DNA extracted from paired formalin-fixed, paraffin-embedded tumor and normal tissue blocks corresponding to three individuals.

## Material and methods

### *Samples and DNA extraction*

Two formalin-fixed and paraffin-embedded fetal tissue blocks (FT1 and FT2) and four EDTA-blood samples corresponding to two paternity studies as well as six paired formalin-fixed and paraffin-embedded tumor and normal tissue blocks (N1, N2, N3, T1, T2 and T3) corresponding to three individuals were analyzed.

***Table 1.*** Characteristics of the formalin-fixed and paraffin-embedded tissue blocks and type of investigation.

| Sample nomenclature | FT1 | FT2 | N1 | T1 | N2 | T2 | N3 | T3 |
|---|---|---|---|---|---|---|---|---|
| Type of tissue blocks | Chorionic villi mixed with maternal tissue proceeding from an abortion | Different fetal tissues proceeding from a lifeless newborn | Normal tissue of patient 1 | Gastric adenocarcinoma of patient 1 | Normal lung tissue of patient 2 | Pulmonary adenocarcinoma of patient 2 | Normal tissue of patient 3 | Gastric adenocarcinoma of patient 3 |
| Time of storage at room temperature | 6 months | 4 years | 5 years | 5 years | 4 years | 4 years | 5 years | 5 years |
| Type of investigation | Paternity investigation for the identification of a rapist | Paternity investigation to discard the possibility of a newborn change at the maternity service of a hospital | Comparison of DNA polymorphisms in paired normal and tumor tissue blocks | | | | | |

DNA was extracted from formalin-fixed and paraffin-embedded tissue blocks by the following procedure:

- Deparaffinization of the minced tissue pieces with xilene followed by ethanol rinses.
- Proteolitic digestion with proteinase K in the presence of SDS and DTT.
- Phenol / Chloroform extraction.
- Washing and concentration of the DNA extracts by ultrafiltration (Centricon-100 concentrator).

DNA was extracted from EDTA-blood samples by the standard phenol/chloroform extraction procedure [1].

***PCR amplification and Typing***

The PCR amplification and typing of the HLA-DQA1 locus were performed using the Amplitype HLA-DQA1 Forensic DNA Amplification and Typing Kit (Perkin-Elmer).

The simultaneous PCR amplification of LDLR, GYPA, HBGG, D7S8 and GC loci and subsequent typing were performed using the Amplitype PM PCR Amplification and Typing Kit (Perkin-Elmer).
The D1S80 locus was PCR amplified using the primer sequences and PCR time-temperature profiles previously described [2]. D1S80 PCR-products were analyzed by discontinous (Tris-glycine/Tris-chloride) polyacrylamide gel electrophoresis followed by silver stain [3].
The STR loci (HUMTH01, HUMFABP and HUMVWA) were amplified using the primer sequences and time-temperature profiles previously described [4,5]. The PCR-products were analyzed by denaturing polyacrylamide gel electrophoresis followed by silver stain.

**Results**

**<u>PATERNITY CASE Nº 1</u>: A paternity investigation for the identification of a rapist.**

| | | GENETIC TYPING RESULTS | | | | | | | | | |
|---|---|---|---|---|---|---|---|---|---|---|---|
| **Sample** | **Type of sample** | **DQA1** | **D1S80** | **LDLR** | **GYPA** | **HBGG** | **D7S8** | **GC** | **TH01** | **FABP** | **VWA** |
| F1 | alleged father's blood | 4,4 | 22,>40 | AA | BB | AA | AB | AC | 9,9.3 | 11,13 | 18,20 |
| FT1 | paraffin block (chorionic villi mixed with maternal tissue) | 4,4 | 18,24, > 40 | A (B) | B (A) | AB | B (A) | AC (B) | 9,9.3, (7) | 11,13, (10) | 16,18, (15) |
| M1 | mother's blood | 4,4 | 18,24 | AB | AB | BB | AB | AB | 9,7 | 10,11 | 15,16 |

NO EXCLUSION OF PATERNITY
PROBABILITY OF PATERNITY : 99,78 %

**<u>PATERNITY CASE Nº 2</u>: A paternity investigation to discard the posibility of a newborn change at the maternity service of a hospital**

| | | GENETIC TYPING RESULTS | | | | | | | | | |
|---|---|---|---|---|---|---|---|---|---|---|---|
| **Sample** | **Type of sample** | **DQA1** | **D1S80** | **LDLR** | **GYPA** | **HBGG** | **D7S8** | **GC** | **TH01** | **FABP** | **VWA** |
| F2 | alleged father's blood | 3,4 | — | BB | BB | AB | AB | CC | 7,9 | 10,10 | 16,17 |
| FT2 | paraffin block (fetal tissue of a newborn) | 2,4 | — | AB | BB | AB | AA | BC | 9,10 | 10,10 | 16,17 |
| M2 | alleged mother's blood | 1.2,2 | — | AB | AB | BB | AA | AB | 9,10 | 10,10 | 17,20 |

NO EXCLUSION OF PATERNITY/MATERNITY
PROBABILITY OF PATERNITY/MATERNITY : 99,98 %

## COMPARISON OF DNA POLYMORPHISMS IN PAIRED NORMAL AND TUMOR BLOCKS

| Sample | Type of sample | GENETIC TYPING RESULTS | | | | | | | | |
|---|---|---|---|---|---|---|---|---|---|---|
| | | DQA1 | LDLR | GYPA | HBGG | D7S8 | GC | TH01 | FABP | VWA |
| N1 | Normal tissue of patient 1 | 1.1,4 | AA | AA | AA | AB | CC | 7,9 | 11,13 | 15,19 |
| T1 | Gastric adenocarcinoma of patient 1 | 1.1,4 | AA | AA | AA | AB | CC | 7,9 | 11,13 | 15,19 |
| N2 | Normal lung tissue of patient 2 | 1.2,2 | AA | AA | AA | AB | CC | 6,9.3 | 10,13 | 16,17 |
| T2 | Pulmonary adenocarcinoma of patient 2 | 1.2,2 | AA | AA | AA | AB | CC | 6,9.3 | 10,13 | 16,17 |
| N3 | Normal tissue of patient 3 | 1.2,2 | AA | BB | AB | AA | AC | 9,9.3 | 11,13 | 17,17 |
| T3 | Gastric adenocarcinoma of patient 3 | 1.2,2 | AA | BB | AB | AA | AC | 9,9.3 | 11,13 | 17,17 |

### Concluding remarks

The PCR-amplification of six sequence polymorphisms (HLA-DQA1, LDLR, GYPA, HBGG, D7S8 and GC) and three STRs (HUMTH01, HUMFABP and HUMVWA) using as a template of amplification the DNA extracted by phenol-chloroform / Centricon-100 from eight formalin-fixed, paraffin-embedded tissue blocks has worked very efficiently in all cases. In contrast, no amplifiation products were generated at locus D1S80, but one case.
Once again, these results reflect the high efficiency of STR and short sequence DNA polymorphisms (size range 300 - 100) to be amplified from very degraded samples.
Two examples of paternity investigations performed on formalin-fixed, paraffin-embedded fetal tissue blocks are given to illustrate the strength of the genetic evidence provided by the DNA polymorphisms analyzed.
On the other hand, no discrepancies were found in the comparative analysis of DNA polymorphisms (HLA-DQA1, LDLR, GYPA, HBGG, D7S8, GC, HUMTH01, HUMFABP and HUMVWA) performed from paired formalin - fixed, paraffin - embedded tumor and normal tissue blocks corresponding to three individuals. However, these are very preliminary results and it is necesary to study a larger sample to evaluate the impact that the recently reported genetic unstability of repeated sequences in human cancers [6,7], could have in some forensic DNA studies (paternity testing from tumor biopsies,...).

### References


[1]-Smith JC, Newton CR, Alves A, Anwar R, Jenner D and Markham AF (1990). J Forensic Sci Soc. 30:3-18.
[2]-Budowle B, Chakraborty R, Giusti AM, Eisenberg AJ and Allen RC (1991). Am J Hum Genet. 48: 137-144.
[3]-Alonso A, Martin P, Albarrán C and Sancho M (1994). Adv in Forensic Haemogenetic 5 (in press).
[4]-Edwards A, Civitello A, Hammond MA and Caskey CT (1991). Am J Hum Genet. 49: 746-756.
[5]-Kimpton CP, Walton A and Gill P (1992). Hum Mol Gen. 1: 28.
[6]-Wooster R, Cleton-Jansen AM, Collins N, Mangion J, Cornelis RS, Cooper CS, Gusterson BA, Ponder BAJ, Von Deimling A, Wiestler OD, Cornelisse CJ, Devilee P and Stratton MR (1994). Nature Genetics. 6: 152-156.
[7]-Shibata D, Peinado MA, Ionov Y, Malkhosyan S and Perucho M (1994). Nature Genetics. 6: 273-281.

# Past, Present and Future Trends in Forensic DNA Technologies in Europe

W. Bär

Institute of Legal Medicine, University of Zürich-Irchel, Winterthurerstrasse190, CH-8057 Zürich

The concept of using polymorphic markers to solve forensic problems is far from new since in all times people tried to find matches by comparing similarities or dissimilarities to consequently include or exclude a person as a perpetrator. The limited availability of useful marker systems was however a serious drawback for such work. Even the smell and odour of blood stains were investigated in the 19th century by the Frenchman Barruel[1] who claimed to be able to distinguish human from animal species and among human stains between male and female origin.

The systematic application of genetic markers of established heritage, e.g. the blood group markers has been known since the beginning of this century[2]. The concept of applying genetically based polymorphic markers like ABO was largely extended to other systems to finally reach a considerable number of genetic marker systems. But some of the more serious drawbacks like modest levels of polymorphism and therefore low statistical evidentiary value and poor stability with rapid deterioration and occasional transformational artefacts[3] leading to false exclusions reduced the value of these systems. Furthermore, most of the markers are only present in blood and the investigation of body tissues is usually not possible.

Recent advances - although now ten years old - have made it possible to directly investigate the genetic material at the DNA level by relatively simple technical means. While most of the DNA shows modest variation between individuals, there exists regions called minisatellites or VNTRs that can exhibit an extraordinary level of length variation[4]. This variation is based on regions of repeatedly arranged almost identical short DNA sequences which vary only in number of elements at a given locus and as a result some of these minisatellites can show hundreds of length states which provide marker systems of previously unimaginable variability. It was called DNA-fingerprinting by its inventor Alec Jeffreys[5].

DNA fingerprinting is a complex and technically rather demanding process. Although a DNA fingerprint is remarkable stable, irrespective of its source, reproducibility cannot always be achieved due to rather delicate conditions of hybridisation. Furthermore, the amount of stain material necessary for successful typing is considerable and we showed already in 1988 that degradation of DNA leads to the gradual loss of the longer fragments[6]. The multi-loci-origin of the DNA-Fingerprint pattern is another drawback since the statistical elucidation of the results especially in paternity investigations is demanding and complex[7,8] not only in cases with involving relatives[9]. The patterns - albeit very pictorial and easy to compare by the naked eye - proved to be rather refractory to computer analysis and data basing and therefore inter laboratory data exchange was hardly possible.

The appearance of much simpler DNA profiles in 1986[10,11] usually two-banded patterns detected by the so-called Single Locus Probes, soon proved to be the appropriate tools for the forensic society. The loss of individual specificity of a single system was by far outbalanced by the availability of different independent probes, the reproducibility of the patterns, the increase in sensitivity and the detectability of stain mixtures so important in forensics. Inter laboratory exchange of data now became reality. The European DNA Profiling Group EDNAP was founded in 1988 on the initiative of our English Colleagues with the aim to achieve uniformity in Europe. Although this goal was not realised the aim to standardise and to recommend a few reliable systems for common use throughout Europe proved to be very important also to consolidate the confidence in DNA profiling by the Law enforcement agencies. It was shown that comparability of DNA profiles can be obtained provided that a minimal standardisation is followed, mainly by using the same buffer and the same DNA length marker[12]. It was also shown that the inter laboratory variation was relatively small but greater for probes displaying the bands in the high molecular range.

The successful application of single locus probe technique to stain analysis and paternity testing motivated us to rapidly introduce these systems into routine casework and by the end of the first quarter of 1991 all conventional blood group systems were replaced by DNA based systems. We perform every analysis of paternity independently twice and exclusions are investigated even for a third time. The increase in performance in paternity investigations can be demonstrated by both the extreme mean value of the chance of exclusion of a non-father - more than 99.99989% for 4 SLPs as well as the increase of the W-value above the necessary level in Switzerland of 99.8 %. DNA analysis is also extremely suitable for the analysis of difficult filiation cases involving relatives and missing persons. Additionally, prenatal paternity diagnosis is possible either with cultured amniotic fluid cells or chorionic tissue or abortion material, for instance after termination of pregnancy following rape[13].

DNA analysis of biological stain material in criminal cases can and does usually provide very powerful evidence to a court and it is therefore extremely important to always stress that the identification of a stain donator by DNA evidence may, but does not by itself, identify him as the perpetrator. The more powerful our analytical tools the more it is mandatory to document the exact origin of the stain at the scene of the crime. Other properties of a stain, for instance its micromorphological aspect should also be very carefully recorded and properly interpreted by the expert[14]. Poor quality of the DNA evidence or band shifts have to be openly described and it is better to leave a doubtful result inconclusive rather than giving an over interpretation.

There has been a considerable discussion about the value of matching criteria[15,16]. Visual matching by side-to-side comparison preferably confirmed by a computer-assisted band-measurement is sufficient and reliable. The sequential application of several single locus probes is by far the safest way to confirm true exclusions. The redundancy of a battery of four to five single locus probes in routine case work is impressive. The application of adequate frequencies to calculate probabilities is of importance in every case but may not always be forensically significant since experience shows that it would be permissable to consider identification as successfully proven, if a non-exclusion of an individual in at least four single locus probe patterns was observed - irrespective of the ethnic origin of the accused. Similarly, in a simple trio case of paternity it would be permitted to always conclude for paternity if a set of four probes displays the paternal allele in the patterns of the child. However, adequate band frequencies are of prime importance in cases where a close relative of the perpetrator or of the non-excluded man in paternity must be considered as being involved. The same holds for deficient paternity cases with missing persons where a genetic exclusion will never be possible. Applying incorrect frequency data usually leads to an overestimation of the evidence since common traits in other ethnic groups are usually rare in ours and vice versa. However, the use of several polymorphic DNA systems frequently compensates for such inadequacies.

The consideration of close kinship is relevant, but the more distant the kinship of a possibly involved relative with the accused the less the plea effects the probability of the accused. The objection of an involved brother does however substantially affect the probability of identity of the accused[17]. Further investigations with additional probes or PCR-systems are needed to solve these cases. However, an alleged involvement of another relative like the father or a cousin can usually be ruled out on a statistical basis.

The need for greater sensitivity, greater speed and of the typing of degraded material cannot fully be met by the DNA profiling techniques. The discovery and the rapid introduction and availability of several PCR-based[18] DNA systems comprising discrete allelic products very favourably satisfies this demand. Indeed quite a high proportion of forensic stain material is either of poor quality or the DNA yields are insufficient for DNA profiling. Although the theoretical goal of typing one single cell has not been reached so far, typing with identification of previously intractable samples like urine, saliva, teeth, hair, nail clippings and skeletal remains has become a reality. AMFLP'S like D1S80, sequence specific oligonucleotide probes like HLA DQ$\alpha$ and more recently the so-called STRs are already in wide use and it seems quite obvious that these systems have the potential to and will eventually replace the DNA profiling systems[19].

The STRs consist basically of tandemly repeated sequences composed of 2, 3 or 4 bases[20]. Their polymorphisms are with a few exceptions, e.g. of SE33[21] much smaller but they display alleles of precise length detectable with complete precision. EDNAP recommends the use of the two common systems HumTH01 and HumVWA[22]. Typing with semi-automated devices using fluorescent labelled primers greatly favours reproducibility and the investigation of large numbers of stains as well as efficient multiplexing[23].

The absence of common nomenclatures for many of these STR-systems is hindering the interlaboratory exchange of STR data. The propositions for nomenclatures by the DNA Commission of the International Society for Forensic Haemogenetics are relatively simple and are based on a decimal system comprising the number of repeats present in a allele. Incomplete repeats are added as a decimal to a full repeat according to the number of bases present[24]. Sequenced ladders will represent important references but their actual non-availability is delaying the proposition of a universally applicable standard nomenclature. However the lack of a common nomenclature does not slow down the spreading use of these systems in the forensic community since laboratory internal ladders will do for the local application of these systems. Some of the STRs are far more complex than anticipated. DNA sequence data recently published by two groups[25,26] opens an insight into a fascinating world of structural microheterogeneity of these STRs. This kind of data will help to better understand the observation of migration differences of alleles of equal length but slightly different base compositions submitted to different electrophoretic procedures as well as the evolution of the STRs.

Digital DNA Typing as invented by Alec Jeffreys and displayable by a relatively simple PCR assay can produce an unambiguous digital code derived from the two alleles of either the MS32-[27] or the MS31-locus. These codes would indeed be ideal for data basing and identifying forensic samples but to my knowledge the system has for various reasons not gained widespread acceptance in the forensic community.

Mitochondrial DNA present in high copy numbers even in very degraded material shows extensive variation particularly in a segment called the control region[28]. Amplification and sequencing of this region with a rather sophisticated system of nested PCR as shown by Sullivan et al.[29] reveals a considerable amount of variation. Since mitochondrial DNA is mainly of maternal origin, it cannot however be used for paternity testing nor to distinguish between matrilineal related persons. It can be very useful for hair analysis although there is need for systems for the rapid screening of larger quantities of hairs to quickly exclude hairs not relevant for the case from the costly and time-consuming procedure of mitochondrial DNA sequencing.

Future developments apart from the accumulation of large numbers of polymorphic DNA systems will most probably concern the process of automation and acceleration of the analytical procedures. Capillary electrophoresis may have the potential of considerably accelerating the DNA typing and multichannel devices can also meet the demand for the increase of the analytical capacity. DNA "chip technology" has a great potential for the complete automation of DNA analysis since it is already technically possible to place about 64000 probes on a chip of a surface of about 1 square centimetre[30]. Ultra fast laser detection of a very great number of loci displaying modest to low polymorphism together with a computer-assisted evaluation of these codes can make identification possible in the time of a snap of a finger.

The potential of genetic analysis is of course much greater than by just looking for non-coding sequences in the human genome. Since quite a few of the individualised stains in case work cannot be placed due to the lack of a suspect it would of course be attractive for the investigator to be provided with data phenotypically more relevant , like the gender, the physical appearance, the ethnic origin and maybe the disease status of the unknown donor of a stain. It is already possible to type the gender[31] and it will probably also be possible to detect other traits in the future. However nowadays it is not even known where these traits are genetically located. I am also quite sure that the social and political implications of such DNA applications will be quite important and it might well be that this kind of analysis would be totally forbidden or restricted to only a very selected number of cases.

---

[1]Barruel JP (1829) Mémoire sur l'existence d'un principe propre à caractériser le sang de l'homme et celui des diverses espèces d'animaux. Ann Hyg Publique Med Leg 1:267-277

[2]Landsteiner K (1901) Über Agglutinationserscheinungen normalen menschlichen Blutes. Wiener Klin Wschr 14:1132-1134

[3]Sensabaugh GF, Blake ET and Northey DH (1980) Genetic markers in semen.III: alteration of phosphoglucomutase isozyme patterns in semen contaminated with saliva. J Forens Sci Soc 25:470-478

[4]Jeffreys AJ, Wilson V and Thein SL (1985) Hypervariable "minisatellite" regions in human DNA. Nature 314:67-73

[5]Jeffreys AJ, Wilson V and Thein SL (1985) Individual-specific fingerprints of human DNA. Nature 316:76-79

[6]Bär W, Kratzer A, Mächler M, Schmid W (1988)Postmortem stability of DNA. Forens Sci Intern 39:59-70

[7]Evett IW, Werrett DJ, Buckleton JS (1989) Paternity calculations from DNA multilocus profiles. J Forens Sci Soc 29:249-254
[8]Hummel K, Fukshansky N, Bär W, Zang K (1990) Biostatistical approaches using minisatellite DNA patterns in paternity cases (mother-child-putative-father trios). Advances Forens Haemogenetics 3:17-19
[9]Hummel K, Fuksahansky N, Bär W (1990)Kinship plausibilities from DNA fingerprints. Advances Forens Haemogenetics 3:20-22
[10]Wong Z, Wilson V, Jeffreys AJ, Thein SL (1986) Cloning a selected fragment from a human DNA "Fingerprint": isolation of a extremly polymorphic minisatellite. Nucl Acid Res 14:4605-4616
[11]Nakamura Y, Leppert M, O'Connel P, Wolff R, Holm T, Culver M, Martin C, Fujimoto E, Hoff M, Kumlin E, White R (1987) Variable number of tandem repeat (VNTR) markers for human gene mapping. Science 235:1616-1622
[12]Gill P, Woodroffe S, Bär W, Brinkmann B, Carracedo A, Eriksen B, Jones S, Kloosterman AD, Ludes B, Mevag B, Pascali VL, Rudler M, Schmitter H, Schneider PM, Thomson JA (1992) A Report of an international collaborative experiment to demonstrate the uniformity obtainable using DNA profiling techniques. Forens Sci Intern 53:29-43
[13]Bär W, Kratzer A (1992) Paternity investigations based on DNA-analysis only. Advances Forens Haemogenetics 4:123-125
[14]Brinkmann B, Madea B, Rand S (1986) Zu den Einflussfaktoren auf die Morphologie der Blutspur. Beitr gerichtl Med 44: 67-73
[15]Evett IW, Werrett DJ, Gill P (1989) DNA fingerprinting on trial. Nature 340:435
[16]Eriksen B Svensmark O (1993) DNA-Profiling of stains in criminal cases: analysis of measurement errors and band-shift. Discussion of match criteria. Forens Sci Intern 61: 21-34
[17]Hummel K, Bär W (1993) Probability of identity of DNA evidence of biological stains in special situations. 13th Meeting of IAFS, Düsseldorf, p. A124
[18]Saiki RK, Gelfand H, Stoffel S, Scharf SJ, Higuchi R, Horn GT, Mullis KB, Erlich HA (1988) Primer-directed enzymatic amplification of DNA with a thermostable DNA polymerase. Science 239:487-491
[19]Brinkmann B (1993) The use of STRs in stain analysis. In: Proceedings from the third International Symposium on Human Identification. Promega Corporation, Madison, USA, pp. 357-373
[20]Edwards A, Civitello A, Hammond HA, Caskey CT (1991) DNA typing and genetic mapping with trimeric and tetrameric tandem repeats. Amer J Hum Genet 49:746-756
[21]Polymeropoulos MH, Rath DS, Xiao H, Merril CR (1992) Tetranucleotide repeat polymorphism at the human beta-actin related pseudogene H-beta-Ac-psi-2 (ACTBP2). Nucleic Acids Res 20:1432
[22]Gill P, Kimpton C, D'Aloja, Andersen JF, Bär W, Brinkmann B, Holgersson S, Johnsson V, Kloosterman AD, Lareu MV, Nellelmann L, Pfitzinger H, Phillips CP, Schmitter H, Schneider PM, Stenersen M (1994) Report of the European DNA profiling group (EDNAP) - towards standardisation of short tandem repeat (STR) loci. Forens Sci Intern 65: 51-59
[23]Kimpton CP, Gill P, Walton A, Urquhart A, Millican ES, Adams M (1993) Automated DNA profiling employing multiplex amplification of short tandem repeat loci. PCR Methods Applic 3:13-22
[24]DNA recommendations (1992)1992 report concerning recommendations of the DNA Commission of the International Society for Forensic Haemogenetics relating to the use of PCR-based polymorphisms. Int J Leg Med 105:63-64
[25]Urquhart A, Kimpton CP, Gill P (1994) Sequence variability of the tetranucleotide repeat of the human beta-actin related pseudogene H-beta-Ac-psi-2 (ACTBP2) locus. Hum Genet 92:637-638 (1993)
[26]Möller A, Brinkmann B (1994) Locus ACTBP2 (SE33). Sequence data reveal considerable polymorphism. Int J Leg Med 106:262-267
[27]Jeffreys AJ, MacLeod A, Tamaki K, Neil DL and Monckton DG (1991) Minisatellite repeat coding as a digital approach to DNA typing. Nature 354: 204-209
[28]Greenberg BD, Newbold JE, Sugino A (1983) Intraspecific nucleotide-sequence variability surrounding the origin of replication in human mitochondrial DNA. Gene 21:33-49
[29]Sullivan KM, Hopgood R, Gill P (1992) Identification of human remains by amplification and automated sequencing of mitochondrial DNA. Int J Leg Med 105:83-86
[30]Weissmann Ch: Personal Communication
[31]Gill P (1987) A new method for sex determination of the donor of forensic samples using recombinant DNA probe. Electrophoresis 8: 35-38

## Evaluation of an Automated DNA-Extractor for DNA-Profiling

Bartel, J., Koegel, W., Weizenegger, M. and Pampel, Ingelore.

Labor Dr. Limbach und Partner, Im Breitspiel 15, 69126 Heidelberg, Germany

XVIth Congress of the International Academy of Legal Medicine and Social Medicine, Strasbourg, 31 may - 2 june 1994.

**Introduction :**

Manual DNA extraction procedures for profiling purposes are still laborious, time consuming and hazardous when phenol/ chloroform protocols are used.

We therefore tested an automated instrument (Autogen 540, Integrated Separation Systems) for DNA extraction from whole blood samples. This instrument combines a centrifuge with a pipetting device and is able to handle up to 12 different reagents.

**Materials and methods :**

Standard phenol/chloroform extraction after proteinase K digestion was compared with the automated procedure.

Briefly, the instrument isolates white cells by performing three washing steps. Lysis of leukocytes is achieved by vigorous mixing of the pellet in an SDS buffer. DNA extraction is done by vigorous mixing with phenol/chloroform. After a centrifugation step the DNA containing aqueous phase is transferred by the pipetting device to the next tube and the DNA is precipitated by adding 3-propanol.

To investigate the quality of the resulting DNA for profiling purposes, blood from different individuals with alleles from 1.7 kb up to 14.3 kb at the locus D7S22 was extracted 20 times with the Autogen extractor and with the manual standard procedure.

The resulting DNA samples were restricted with HINF 1 and run on 20 different agarose gels (0.7 %), the membranes were hybridised with the NICE-probe g3 (Cellmark).

For calibration the GIBCO BRL ladder was used, and the sizes of the restriction fragments were determined with a video system (Bioprofil, Vilber Lourmat).

**Results :**

In general, the yield of DNA using the automated procedure was comparable to manual DNA extraction (between 10 and 20 μg/sample).

The fragment sizes obtained by the automated procedure were identical to those of the manual technique, and the imprecision of both methods was very comparable with variation coefficients between 0.6% for small fragments and 1.2% for larger fragments (Fig.1) for the entire procedure.

Using the multilocus probes MS33.6 and MS33.15 (data not shown) identical fingerprinting patterns could be generated with both methods.

Furthermore, in fifty cases with established mother-child-father trios we have not seen any significant difference between the manual and the automated DNA extraction method.

**Conclusion :**

The Autogen 540 DNA extractor is a suitable instrument for isolating DNA from whole blood samples in an automated manner. The quality and the yield of the resulting DNA are identical to that obtained by manual methods.

We therefore conclude, that the Autogen 540 DNA extractor can act as a powerful tool in the automated DNA laboratory.

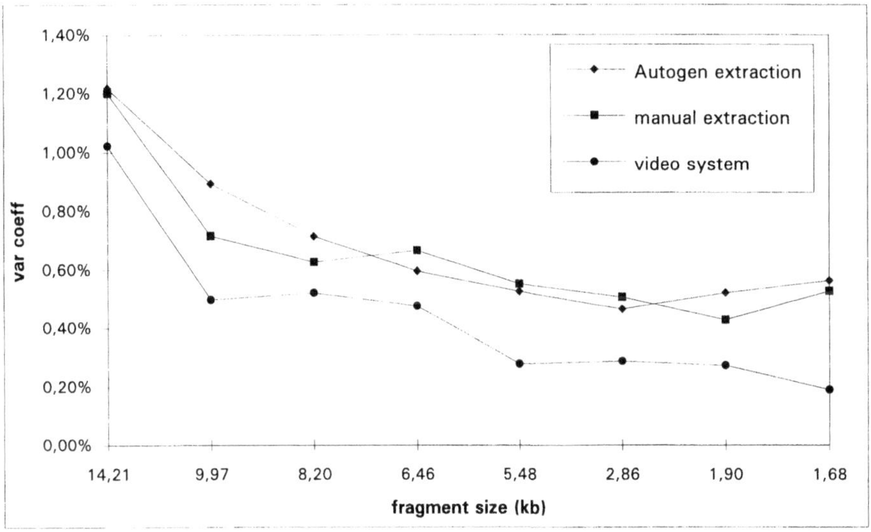


***Fig. 1 :*** *Variation coefficients of DNA profiling for different fragment sizes using either the automated DNA extraction instrument (—◆—) or the standard manual method (—■—). The coefficients of the whole process are compared with the coefficients of the video analysis (—●—) alone.*

# DEFICIENCY CASES IN DISPUTED PATERNITY

**C. Brandt-Casadevall, N. Dimo-Simonin**
Institut de Universitaire de Médecine légale, Bugnon 21, 1005 Lausanne, Switzerland

Nowadays, paternity testing in Switzerland relies on the determination of the VNTR-DNA polymorphisms. In the standard case of the mother-child-presumed father trio, the study of four loci is sufficient to prove exclusion. When there is no exclusion, we calculate the probability of paternity according to the method of Essen-Möller taking into account the frequency of bands in the Swiss-population. By studying four VNTR loci we often exceed a probability of paternity of 99.8% which correspond to the minimal value set by the Federal Tribunal to conclude that paternity is pratically verified.

Occasionally, we encounter cases in which one of the progenitors is missing which requires that examination be performed on other family members. Situations that may be problematic are those when the missing progenitor is the father. However thanks to their strong capacity to discriminate individuals, VNTR polymorphims analyses usually make it possible to solve such cases. Nevertheless, in some instances problems remain. We present here two such cases.

The first one involves a paternity testing for an extramarital child whose presumed father is deceased. The examination was carried out on the presumed grandparents. In this case polymorphism was studied for D7S22, D5S43, D16S309, D12S11, D2S44 and D7S21 loci. Of the seven loci studied, the analysis of six loci led to the exclusion of the grandmother and the grandfather. Indeed, only with the probe MS43a did the child and the grandmother exhibit a common band. Importantly, this band is also present in about 9% of the population, representing the highest percentage that can be obtained with this probe.

We carried out a number of blood group analysis and found an exclusion on the erythrocyte acid phosphatase phenotype. Indeed, the child exhibites a C characteristic that could only have been inherited from the father. At the same time, neither presumed grandparent present this caracteristic (Table 1).

| Blood Groups | Mother | Child | Putative Grandmother | Putative Grandfather |
|---|---|---|---|---|
| ABO | A | A | O | O |
| PGM | a4-a2 | a2-a1 | a2 | a2-a1 |
| EAP | AB | AC | B | A |
| ESD | 1 | 1 | 2-1 | 1 |

**Table 1.** Determination of some blood groups.
An exclusion is present in the EAP system : C characteristic in the child must come from the father.

We have also carried out a number of PCR analysis. We found no exclusions for any of the systems analyzed.

Our conclusion communicated to the Court was the following : the presumed father could not have been the father of the child providing that the two individuals whose blood was analyzed were indeed the progenitors of this man. Clearly, we could exclude the grandparents strictly as a couple, but not the grandmother as an individual since she could have had her child with another man than the one whose blood was analyzed.

The second case also concerned a paternity testing for an extramarital child whose presumed father is deceased. Examination was carried out with other children that the father may have had with another woman. Because of the necessity to know characteristics each child received from each progenitor, the two mothers also had to participate in the testing.

The deceased presumed father had been married and three children were born thanks to this union (Fig 1).

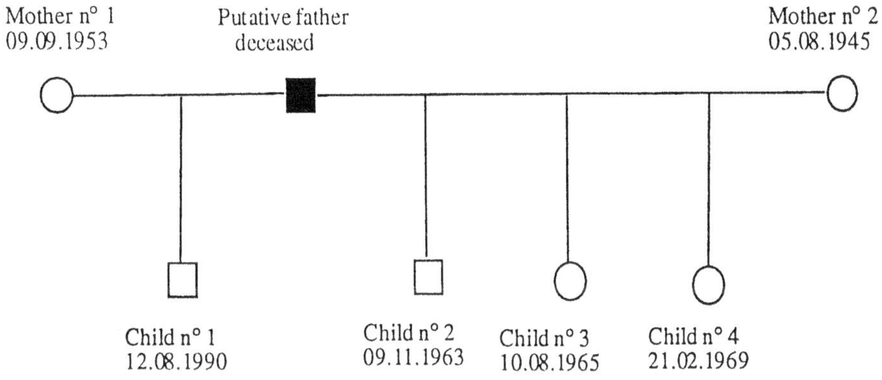


**Fig 1**. Genealogic tree.

We present in Table 2 the results obtained in the form of the report that we use to send to the Court. The bands are examined starting with the highest number of Kilobases, in a descending order. The presence of a band is scored as a plus and the absence of a band is scored as a minus.

From our results, child n° 4 (the third child of the "legitimate" couple) consistently failed to show a band in common with his brother and sister. Moreover, the results from probes MS8 and MS205 generated different bands in the brother and the sister, resulted in yet another, different set in this child.

Accordingly it can be yet excluded that his biological father is the same than that of his brother and sister. On the other hand, in four out of the seven probes, child n° 1 exhibited a band also found either in one or both brother and sister. Even though we were at that point convinced of the outcome of our tests we carried our analyses further to confirm our belief.

| Probe | Locus | Mother n° 1 | Child n° 1 | Mother n° 2 | Child n° 2 | Child n° 3 | Child n° 4 |
|---|---|---|---|---|---|---|---|
| MS43a | D12S11 | - | + = 4% | + | + = 4% | + = 4% | + |
| (HinfI) | | - | - | - | - | - | + = 5% |
| | | + | - | - | - | - | - |
| | | + | + | - | - | - | - |
| MS31 | D7S21 | + | + | - | - | - | - |
| (HinfI) | | + | - | - | - | - | - |
| | | - | - | + | - | - | + |
| | | - | - | - | - | - | + = 8% |
| | | - | - | + | + | + | - |
| | | - | + = 2% | - | - | - | - |
| | | - | - | - | + = 1% | + = 1% | - |
| g3 | D7S22 | - | - | + | + | - | + |
| (HinfI) | | - | - | - | - | - | + = 2% |
| | | + | - | - | - | - | - |
| | | - | + = 2% | - | + = 2% | + = 2% | - |
| | | + | + | - | - | - | - |
| | | - | - | + | - | + | - |
| YNH24 | D2S44 | - | - | - | + = 3% | + = 3% | - |
| (HinfI) | | - | - | + | + | + | - |
| | | - | + = 5% | - | - | - | + = 5% |
| | | + | + | - | - | - | - |
| | | + | - | - | - | - | - |
| | | - | - | + | - | - | + |
| MS1 | D1S7 | - | - | + | + | - | + |
| (HinfI) | | + | - | - | + = 2% | + = 2% | - |
| | | - | + = 3% | - | - | - | - |
| | | - | - | - | - | - | + = 3% |
| | | + | + | - | - | - | - |
| | | - | - | + | - | + | - |
| MS8 | D5S43 | - | - | - | - | - | + = E |
| (HinfI) | | - | - | - | + | - | - |
| | | - | - | + | + | - | + |
| | | + | + = 15% | - | - | + = 15% | - |
| | | + | - | - | - | - | - |
| | | - | - | + | - | + | - |
| MS205 | D16S309 | - | - | - | - | - | + = E |
| (HinfI) | | + | + | - | - | - | - |
| | | + | - | - | - | - | - |
| | | - | - | + | + | - | - |
| | | - | - | - | + | - | - |
| | | - | - | + | - | + | + |
| | | - | + < 1% | - | - | + < 1% | - |

**Table 2.** VNTR-polymorphisms.
The (+) scores the presence of a band; the (-) scores the absence of a band.
E = Exclusion / % = frequence of the band in the population.

The analysis of several PCR systems yielded interesting results which are shown in Table 3. Based on the results obtained with the two first legitimate children, in the DQalpha, TC11 and APOB systems, the father must have had a genotype that excluded the child n° 4, but not the child born out of weddlock. In the FES system, the estimated genotype of the father is 8 and either 10 or 12, but certainly not allele 11 carried by child n° 4, a finding which also leads to exclusion. The only PCR system that didn't lead to the exclusion of child n° 4 is D1S80. Indeed, here child n° 4 inherited allele 24 from the father, the same allele present in the other children. However, it is important to note that this allele is the most frequent one in the D1S80 system: it is present in 36% of the population.

| PCR systems | Mother 1 | Child 1 | Mother 2 | Child 2 | Child 3 | Child 4 |
|---|---|---|---|---|---|---|
| **DQa** | 1.1 , 4 | **1.1 , 4** | 1.2 , 4 | **1.1** , 1.2 | **4** | 1.2 , **2*** |
| **TC11** | 7 - 9 | **7 - 9** | 7 - 9.3 | **7 - 9** | **7** - 9.3 | **8*** - 9.3 |
| **APOB** | 29 - 37 | 35 - 37 | 37 - 49 | 49 - **51** | **35** - 37 | **37*** |
| **FES** | 10 - 11 | **8** - 11 | 10 - 12 | **8** - 10 | **10 - 12** | 10 - **11*** |
| **D1S80** | 29 - 30 | **18** - 29 | 18 - 31 | **24** - 31 | **24** - 31 | 18 - **24** |

**Table 3.** Determination of five PCR systems.
In bold the alleles that children inherited or could inherited from their father.
*) Alleles that determine an exclusion.

We were faced with a major problem in interpreting this case : we had convinced ourselves that the so-called "legitimate" third child did not have the same father as the two other children. On the other hand, not only was child n° 1 not excluded, but the probability of paternity of the deceased man was significantly higher than 99.8%.

The problem we had to solve was moral and humane in nature. Indeed, the assignment given to us by the Court was to exclude or affirm the paternity of the presumed father in relation to the extramarital child, but certainly not to provide evidence jeopardizing the paternity of the deceased in relation to one of the other children.

We contacted the Court and exposed this problem. We explained what consequences this may have on the third child who, as an adult, would learn that his father was not his actual father. The Court decided to consult with the lawyer of the demanding party, who still had the option to withdraw their request and simply recognise the extramarital child. As this was refused, we were summoned to a meeting between the President of the Tribunal and the lawyers representing each party. The goal was to decide what further action should be taken. We explained how we reached our conclusions. It was finally decided that the Institute of Forensic Medicine would only provide a concise answer to the following questions : "Could Mr X be the father of child Y? If so, what is the probability of paternity?". This is exactly what we did.

# APPLICATION OF PCR TO A FORENSIC CASEWORK: IDENTIFICATION OF BURNED HUMAN REMAINS

**Nicoletta Cerri and Francesco De Ferrari**

*Institute of Forensic Medicine - University of Brescia - Spedali Civili - P.le Spedali Civili, 1 - 25100 Brescia - Italy*

We report the description of a judicial event that was performed by our Institute of Forensic Medicine some time ago.

We were charged by the authority to try to identify some remains that were found in an industrial shed where was located a furnace whose functional temperature was about 1000 °C.

Particularly these remains were composed by a totally carbonized fragment of skull, small bits of burned flesh and a fragment of brain; with histological analysis and species' diagnosis we confirmed that these remains were human remains.

From the reconstruction of the event it was presumed that they belonged to a man who had been thrown into the furnace: the difference of the temperature between the body of the man and the liquid of the furnace caused an explosion with consequent projection of these remains at distance. The rest of the body was never recovered.

Nearby the furnace some small stains, later on identified as bloodstains; had also been recovered, moreover sticked to the furnace wall had been found mineral deposits containing bloodstains too.

Finally, in a house, not far from the furnace, further small bloodstains were identified too.

The first analysis performed on these remains were carried out with the technique of the Polymerase Chain Reaction; particularly we studied the DQalpha locus, a marker that routinarly had been utilized in our laboratory by using the Perkin Elmer Forensic Kit.

DNA was extracted with Chelex method according to Walsh et al.(1991) and the amplification was carried out according to the kit's protocol with the use of 20 microlitres of Chelex extraction's product.

The results of the typification showed in all the remains and the bloodstains the same genetic profile: 2:4; instead the fragment of skull, gave us no result.

At this point with the results of the investigation it was presumed that bloodstains and human remains belonged to the owner of the furnace.

So, in order to allow the identification, some personal belongings (hair brush, razors, a crash-helmet) were analyzed to find eventual hair.

Even in these case the analysis were performed by studying DQalpha locus, according to the Walsh DNA protocol of extraction.

The results of these group of analysis showed that the found hair had different genetic profile: 1.1;1.2 - 1.1;4 - 1.2;4, but one single hair, taken from the crash-helmet (certainly used by the man), resulted of 2;4 genotype.

According to further investigation the before demonstrated genetic profile were found compatible with relative's genetic profile.

At this point the results of the exams performed on the remains were compared with the data obtained by the blood analysis of the four children and of the wife of the suspected deceased.

At that time we studied DQalpha locus and the VNTR system D1S80 with the commercial forensic kit and after even the STR system HumTH01 according to the Edwards protocol with small modifications.

DNA was extracted with Chelex protocol and the conditions of amplification and resolution were:

DQalpha:

| | | |
|---|---|---|
| 32 cycles | Den. 94°C 1 min. | |
| | Ann. 60°C 30 sec. | + 7 Min. at 72°C |
| | Ext. 72°C 30 sec. | |

Resolution: Reverse Dot Blot

D1S80:

| | | |
|---|---|---|
| 30 cycles | Den. 94°C 1 min. | |
| | Ann. 65°C 1 min. | +10 Min. at 72°C |
| | Ext. 72°C 1 min. | |

Resolution: Agarose gel electrophoresis containg ethidium bromide

HumTH01:

| | | |
|---|---|---|
| 26 cycles | 1°C.Den. 95°C 3 min. | |
| | Ann. 64°C 1,5 min. | |
| | Ext. 70°C 1,5 min. | |
| | | |
| | 9 C.Den. 94°C 1 min. | |
| | Ann. 64°C 1 min. | |
| | Ext. 70°C 1,5 min. | |
| | | |
| | 16 C.Den. 90°C 1 min. | |
| | Ann. 64°C 1 min. | + 3,5 min. at 70°C |
| | Ext. 70°C 1,5 min. | |

Resolution: PAGE (T=8% - C=5%) + silver staining

The results of the study are resume in the Figure N.1

For DQalpha system we can see that the children have a 1.1 and 1.2 allele from the mother, the remaining allele is compatible with the suspected father.
Same result can be obtained by the study of D1S80: 29 and 32 alleles from the mother, 24 and 29 compatible with the father.
Identical results with TH01 system: allele 10 from the mother, 7 and 8 alleles from the father.
The use of PCR techniques has so permitted the resolution of this forensic casework.

## REFERENCES


1. Walsh P.S., Metzeger D.A., Higuchi R.(1991) Chelex 100 as a medium extraction of DNA for PCR-based typing from forensic material. BioTechniques 10: 506-513.
2. Edwards A., Hammond H.A., Jin Li, Caskey C.T., Chakrabosky R. (1992) Gentic variation of five trimeric and tetrameric tandem repeat loci in four human population groups. Genomics 12: 241-253.


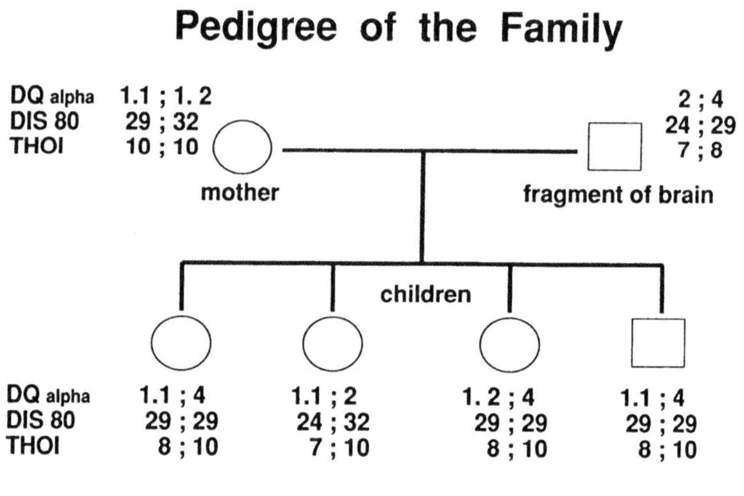


FIGURE N°1

**Cadaveric DNA Extraction Protocol Based on Cetyl Trimethyl Amonium Bromide (CTAB).**

**Daniel Corach, Gustavo Penacino and Andrea Sala. Servicio de Huellas Digitales Genéticas,Facultad de Farmacia y Bioquímica, Universidad de Buenos Aires, Junín 956, (1113)-Buenos Aires, Argentina.**

## Introduction

DNA extraction from fresh tissues is a straightforward process that can be accomplished by a wide variety of procedures. Such techniques are usually employed efficiently in DNA typing laboratories. However, in forensic DNA analysis the extraction protocol is the limiting factor that determines the success of a molecular investigation. In this field, blood and semen stains and vaginal and oral swabs required the development of suitable and highly efficient protocols.

The combination of proteolityc enzymes (e.g. Proteinase K, Pronase, etc.) and caotropic agents (Sodium Lauryl Sulfate, Sodium N-Lauryl Sarcosine, etc.) followed by organic solvent extraction (1, 2, 3) or by salting-in procedures (4), are the most often used strategies for DNA extraction. Further purification is commonly required.

The extraction of DNA samples from small fragments of badly decayed cadaveric remains constitues a serious challenge and suitable protocols should be used to overcome the constrains imposed by the reduced amount and the degradation of the DNA that may be recovered from such materials.

The aim of this work is to describe a DNA extraction protocol based on the quaternary amonium salt detergent: Cetyl Trimethyl Amonium Bromide (CTAB), that is qualified to be used for DNA recovery from cadaveric material.

## Protocol

The presented protocol, being currently used in our laboratory, is based on the ammonium quaternary detergent Cetyl Trimethyl Ammonium Bromide (CTAB) Sigma H-5882, Fluka Cat.# 52370 or Carlo Erba Code 489 833., followed by multiple Chloroform/Iso-Amyl alcohol extraction and finally precipitated with Iso-Propyl alcohol (5).

Homogenization Buffer: CTAB 2% (w/v). NaCl 1.4 M. 2-mercaptoethano 0.2% (v/V). EDTA 20 mM. Tris/HCl (pH=7.5) 100 mM. Organic Solvents: Chloroform/Isoamyl alcohol 24/1 (v/v). Alcohols: Iso-Propyl Alcohol.

All chemicals used are Pro-analysis,and the plasticware (polypropilene) new, sterile and disposable.

Tissue amounts to be used: Skin: 1 square centimeter, Muscle a volume equivalent to 5 g., Bone a Metarsum or Metacarpum. Teeth one or two molars providing no caries are evident.

Tissue Treatment

According to the tissues to be employed for DNA extraction,different treatments should be used. Tissues can be grouped into two major groups: hard tissues and soft tissues.

1- Those included in the former group can be throughly cleaned by tap water washes, in order to remove all soft remains, then, immersion in a 10 % bleach/water solution, with agitation for two hours, rinse the tissues with sterile destileted water, and immerse them in a 70 % ETOH/water solution for one hour with agitation, finally at least five washes with sterile distilated water are performed.

Teeth are covered with a thick but flexible plastic sheet and broken with a hammer, powdered tissue is collected in a 4.5 ml polypropilene tube.

Bones are sawed sagitally, the marrow area is scratched with a disposable scalpel, the powdered tissue is collected in a 4.5 ml polypropilene tube.

2-Within the second group, skin and muscle are the preferred tissues. The pieces choosen as DNA source should be selected properly, avoiding all possible exogenous human DNA contamination.

Selected fragments must be washed in sterile double distilled water three times, then blotted dry on paper towels, placed in a petri dish and cut into very small pieces and finally reduced to powder in a mortar with liquid nitrogen. The tissue is then placed in a 4.5 ml polypropilene tube.

DNA extraction

1.5 ml of the homogenization buffer are added to the 4.5 ml tubes containing the mechanically reduced samples. Homogenization buffer should be prewarmed at 60 degrees Celsius before use. Samples should be incubated at 60 degrees Celsius for three hours, and vigorous agitation should be performed after 30 minutes periods.

About 2 mls of saturated chloroform/isoamyl alcohol are added to the tubes. Vigorous agitation should be performed in order to obtain an homogeneous emulsion, for 10 minutes.- Organic and aqueous phases are separated by means of centrifugation at 8,000 rpm (SS-34 Sorvall rotor) for 10 minutes. Aqueous phase is transferred to a fresh tube and re-extracted as many times are required to eliminate proteic interphase. -

Finally DNA is precipitated by adding 2/3 volumes of isopropyl alcohol (for an aqueous solution of 2 ml, 1.66 ml of iso-propyl alcohol should be added). Carefull agitation must be performed until a precipate is evident, if DNA is highly degraded it may appear like powder. Centrifugation, as above will allow us to recover a pellet that should be washed with EtOH 70% + 10 mM Amonium Acetate (pH=7.5). After a brief centrifugation the alcoholic liquid is drained off by pipetting and the pellet dried a 37 degrees. DNA is resupended in 200 ml of distilled sterile water or TE .

Further Purification.

In some cases DNA obtained is unable to be digested or amplified, because of contaminants that may arise during the putrification process. In these cases it is advisable to purify the obtained DNA samples by two different procedures according to the methodological requirements to be followed. On one hand, if samples are required for use in Southern Blot based typing it is advisable to use purification systems such as Gene Clean II or Glass-Max (BRL), that may yield a high molecular weight doble stranded DNA sample. On the other hand if PCR amplification based typing is required, DNA samples can be purified by means of Chelex P-100 (Bio-Rad) procedures. In most cases further purifications are not required, however the specimens to be investigated will determine the best startegy to be followed.

References

1- Hochmeister, M. N.; Budowle, B.; Borer, U.; Eggman, U.; Comey, C. and Dirnhofer, R. (1991). Typing of DNA extracted from compact bone from human remains. Journal of Forensic Science 36: 1649-1661.

2- Jung, J.; Comey, C.; Baer, D. B. and Budowle, B. (1991). Extraction strategy for obtaining DNA from bloodstains for PCR amplification and typing of the HLA-DQalpha gene. Int. J. of Legal Medicine 104: 145-148.

3- Laber, T.; O'Connor, J.; Iverson, J.; Liberty, J. and Bergman, D. (1992) Evaluation of four DNA extraction protocols for DNA yield and variation in RFLP sizes under varying gel conditions. J. For. Sci. 37: 404-424.

4- Miller, S.; Dykes, D. and Polesky, H. F. (1988) A simple salting out procedure for extracting DNA from human nucleated cells. N. Acid Research 16 (3): 1215.

5- Corach, D. (1991) A reliable, rapid and simple method for DNA extraction from frozen sperm cells. Fingerprint News 3: 13.

# POLYMARKER AND HLA DQA1 GENETIC MARKERS IN FORENSIC CASEWORK

R. Espinheira[1], T. Ribeiro[1], H. Geada[2] and L. Reys[1,2]

Institute of Legal Medicine, Lisbon[1]
Department of Legal Medicine, Faculty of Medicine, Lisbon[2], Portugal

## INTRODUCTION

Polymarker and HLA DQA1 systems offer new tools for forensic analysis both in identification and in paternity investigation. Polymarker (PM) includes five genetic loci: Low Density Lipoprotein Receptor (LDLR), Glycophorin A (GYPA) and D7S8, each containing two alleles and Hemoglobin G Gammaglobin (HBGG) and Group Specific Component (GC), each containing three alleles. HLA DQA1 polymorphism reveal six major allelic types - DQA1.1, DQA1.2, DQA1.3, DQA2, DQA3 and DQA4.
We present data on PM and HLA DQA1 genotype and allele frequencies in a Portuguese Population sample. Validation studies for application to forensic casework were also performed with hair and blood.

## MATERIAL AND METHODS

Unrelated individual blood samples from paternity cases were studied for population analysis - 121 samples for Polymarker and 234 samples for HLA DQA1. These samples mainly from the South of the Country include Continental as well as Madeira and Açores Islands inhabitants. Fifteen samples of hairs, eye-brows, pubic hairs and the correspondent blood were also studied.
DNA was extracted from bloodstains and hair using Chelex 100. DNA amplifications were performed according to PCR Amplification and Typing Kit protocols - AmpliType$^R$ HLA DQ$\alpha$ and AmpliType$^R$ PM (Perkin Elmer - Roche). The PM alleles and the HLA DQA1 alleles were typed on separate strips by reverse dot blot technology.

## RESULTS AND DISCUSSION

A Portuguese population data for PM and HLA DQA1 genetic markers was obtained. The observed and expected genotypes of HLA DQA1 and of four PM loci (LDLR, GYPA, HBGG and GC) showed no significant departure from Hardy- Weinberg equilibrium.
For D7S8 locus there was deviation from the Hardy-Weinberg equilibrium with our 121 Portuguese Population sample, which could suggest a mixed population sample. Blood samples only from South Portugal gave a good agreement between observed and expected values for D7S8 locus ($x^2$=1.94, df=1, 0.10< p <0.20). These results can be used for forensic analysis due to the power of discrimination of 0.8925 for all five PM loci and of 0.9283 for HLA-DQA1 locus.
The results obtained from different hair type analysis indicate that these loci are suitable for forensic hair identification. All samples gave very good typing results when performing the six genetic loci analysis involving hair specimens and the corresponding blood samples.
In conclusion, PM and HLA DQA1 results obtained by population studies and comparative hair analysis validate these systems for forensic application.

TABLE 1. Distribution of HLA DQA1 Genotypes and Allele Frequencies in a Portuguese Population, mainly from the South

| Genotype | Observed n | % | | n | % | | n | % |
|---|---|---|---|---|---|---|---|---|
| 1.1-1.1 | 5 | 2.13 | 1.2-1.3 | 5 | 2.13 | 1.3-4 | 16 | 6.84 |
| 1.1-1.2 | 11 | 4.70 | 1.2-2 | 11 | 4.70 | 2-2 | 5 | 2.14 |
| 1.1-1.3 | 10 | 4.27 | 1.2-3 | 8 | 3.42 | 2-3 | 13 | 5.56 |
| 1.1-2 | 12 | 5.13 | 1.2-4 | 20 | 8.55 | 2-4 | 21 | 8.97 |
| 1.1-3 | 9 | 3.85 | 1.3-1.3 | 0 | 0.00 | 3-3 | 3 | 1.28 |
| 1.1-4 | 38 | 16.24 | 1.3-2 | 8 | 3.42 | 3-4 | 9 | 3.85 |
| 1.2-1.2 | 6 | 2.56 | 1.3-3 | 8 | 3.42 | 4-4 | 16 | 6.84 |
| Total | 234 | 100.00 | | | | | | |

HLA DQA1.1 = 0.1923; HLA DQA1.2 = 0.1432; HLA DQA1.3 = 0.1004;
HLA DQA 2 = 0.1603; HLA DQA 3 = 0.1132; HLA DQA 4 = 0.2906
$X^2$=18.72; df = 15; $0.20 < p < 0.30$; CE = 0.55; Pd = 0.9283

TABLE 2. Polymarker Genotypes and Allele Frequencies in a Portuguese Population, mainly from the South.

| Locus | Genotypes | Observed n | % | Expected n | % | Allele Frequencies |
|---|---|---|---|---|---|---|
| | | | | | | A=0.3843 |
| LDLR | AA | 14 | 11.57 | 17.87 | 14.77 | B=0.6157 |
| | AB | 65 | 53.72 | 57.26 | 47.32 | $X^2$=2.21 df=1 |
| | BB | 42 | 34.71 | 45.87 | 37.91 | $0.10 < p < 0.20$ |
| | | 121 | 100.00 | 121.00 | 100.00 | CE = 0.1806 |
| | | | | | | Pd = 0.5776 |
| | | | | | | A=0.5331 |
| GYPA | AA | 31 | 25.62 | 34.38 | 28.42 | B=0.4669 |
| | AB | 67 | 55.37 | 60.24 | 49.78 | $X^2$=1.52 df=1 |
| | BB | 23 | 19.01 | 26.38 | 21.80 | $0.10 < p < 0.20$ |
| | | 121 | 100.00 | 121.00 | 100.00 | CE=0.1869 |
| | | | | | | Pd=0.5917 |
| | | | | | | A=0.5165 |
| | | | | | | B=0.4628 |
| HBGG | AA | 29 | 23.97 | 32.28 | 26.68 | C=0.0207 |
| | AB | 65 | 53.72 | 57.85 | 47.81 | $X^2$=2.19 df=3 |
| | AC | 2 | 1.65 | 2.58 | 2.13 | $0.50 < p < 0.70$ |
| | BB | 22 | 18.18 | 25.92 | 21.42 | CE=0.2129 |
| | BC | 3 | 2.48 | 2.31 | 1.91 | Pd=0.6200 |
| | CC | 0 | 0.00 | 0.05 | 0.04 | |
| | | 121 | 100.00 | 121.00 | 100.00 | |
| | | | | | | A=0.5620 |
| | | | | | | B=0.4380 |
| D7S8 | AA | 45 | 37.19 | 38.22 | 31.58 | $X^2$=6.28 df=1 |
| | AB | 46 | 38.02 | 59.57 | 49.23 | $0.05 > p > 0.01$ |
| | BB | 30 | 24.79 | 23.21 | 19.19 | CE=0.1855 |
| | | 121 | 100.00 | 121.00 | 100.00 | Pd=0.6557 |
| | | | | | | A=0.3099 |
| | | | | | | B=0.1570 |
| GC | AA | 15 | 12.40 | 11.62 | 9.61 | C=0.5331 |
| | AB | 12 | 9.92 | 11.78 | 9.73 | $X^2$=2.87 df=3 |
| | AC | 33 | 27.27 | 39.98 | 33.04 | $0.30 < p < 0.50$ |
| | BB | 2 | 1.65 | 2.98 | 2.47 | CE=0.3155 |
| | BC | 22 | 18.18 | 20.26 | 16.74 | Pd=0.7736 |
| | CC | 37 | 30.58 | 34.38 | 28.42 | |
| | | 121 | 100.00 | 121.00 | 100.00 | |

# STUDIES ON HLA DQ ALPHA GENOTYPES CARRIED OUT FROM DENTAL MATERIAL DISCOVERED SUBSEQUENTLY ON THE SCENE OF THE AIRCRASH OF FLIGHT IT 5148.

F. Gaillard, B. Ludes, J. M. Hutt, H. Pfitzinger, P. Mangin.
Institut de Médecine Légale-Laboratoire Codgène,
11 rue Humann 67085 Strasbourg Cedex.

## INTRODUCTION:

The medico-legal examination carried out after the crash on 20 january 1992 of the flight Lyon-Strasbourg allowed the identification of 85 out of 87 victims. We have tried to find some biological elements of the two missing victims though the analysis of fragments of the maxillary bones still carrying teeth found on the area of the crash a few days after the accident.
We referred to the research of Lawton *et al.*, Menard *et al.*, Pötsch *et al.* who have exploited tooth DNA as well as Schwartz's et al. who have displayed the possibility of obtaining DNA from teeth subjected to environnemental insults.
An amplification of the locus HLA DQ alpha has been carried out in order to compare the genotypes of the teeth with the genotypes of the relatives the two missing persons and to compare teeth genotypes with those of tissues with the same reference.

## MATERIALS AND METHODS:

The fragments of the maxillary bones and of the scattered teeth have been preserved at a temperature of -10°C.
Fourteen teeth of wHich four were carbonized have been extracted from these fragments and classified according to the area where they were found.
We carried out a scrupulous cleaning of each tooth: the remains of tissues attached to the root(s) have been mechanically eliminated, the traces of blood still remaining washed with a cold water spray, the cleaned tooth has immersed in $H_2O_2$ (30 volumes). Tissue degradation particulary that of the alveolar bone attached to the roots, made the manipulation rather difficult.
After having obtained absolutely clean hard dental tissues (free of any organic traces) a cut was made in occluso apical direction with a fissure drill and finished with a knife and hammer . The pulp was extracted with a pincer and placed in an Eppendorf micro-tube.
The hard tissues were crushed to a fine powder under liquid nitrogen .
The pulp has placed in 400 $\mu$l of buffer (containing 12 $\mu$l of proteinase K) for 12 hours and the DNA extracted by 2 consecutive phenol chloroform and one isoamyl chloroform phases.
For the hard tissues we utilized a Chelex® extraction (2 ml of Chelex® for 18 h at 56°C , boiling for 8 min and centrifugation).
The DNA was precipitated with cold absolute ethanol (2 volumes) overnight.
The quantity of DNA extracted was estimated on yield gels for pulp samples and on a slot blot for the hard tissues.
Following the kits protocols (Cetus Perkin Elmer ®) we have amplified the DNA for 32 cycles (1 min at 94°C, 30 s at 60°C, 30 s at 94°C).

The genotype of each sample was revealed following hybridization on strips.

## RESULTS:

On the yield gels, we visualise a significant degradation of the DNA for all the samples. The quantity of the high molecular weight DNA was however sufficient for HLA DQ alpha analysis in the majority of cases;
We could read on the strips 13 HLA DQ alpha genotypes out of 14 pulp samples. On the other hand only 1 hard tissue sample out of 8 gave a positive result. In this last case we can see that the response remained very weak.
Remark: We have made restriction fragment lengh polymorphism analysis from the pulp samples and we have obtained only one genetic fingerprint out of fourteen.

## DISCUSSION AND CONCLUSION.

This study shows that it is possible to utilise dental tissue and more precisely the pulp as a source of DNA. This source seems the more interesting since it is possible to extract the DNA from partially burnt dental tissue . We have obtained positive genotype results for 3 out of 4 teeth.

**Two reasons can explain this result: the teeth are more protected from physical aggression by the muscle of the cheek and jawbone and the hard tissues of the tooth are the hardest in the body and are more resistant to fire.**

Although this work didn't allow the identification of the two missing victims, they nevertheless pointed out the lacunae that existed when collecting human fragments. In fact the comparison HLA DQ alpha the genotypes of these dental samples with genotypes obtained from other tissues showed identical references show differences between the results.

## REFERENCES :

Lawton M.E., Stringer P., Churton M. DNA profiles from dental pulp. Forensic aspect of DNA analysis. Proceedings of International Sympsium of the FBI Academy. Quantico, Virginia; 19-23 June 1989.

Ludes B., Mangin P. Les empreintes génétiques en Médecine Légale, 1e éd. Paris, Tec. & Doc. Lavoisier, 1992.

Menard R., Ossenkop V., Witucki R., Wuensch C. Extraction, quantification, and RFLP analysis of DNA from dental pulp. Communication at the second Symposium on the forensic aspect of DNA analysis. Forensic Science Research and Training Center FBI Academy, Quantico Virginia, 29-03-1993; 02-04-1993.

Pötsch L., Meyer U., Rothschild S., Schneider P.M., Rittner Ch. Application of DNA techniques for identification using dental as a source of DNA. Int. J. Leg. Med., 105: 139-143, 1992.

Schwartz T.R., Schwartz E.A., Mieszerski L., McNally L., Kobilinsky L., D. Ph.. Characterization of deoxyribonucleic acid (DNA) obtained from teeth subjected to various environmental conditions. Journal of Forensic Sciences, JFSCA, 1991; 36, 979,990.

**Allele frequencies of HLA-DQA1, LDLR, GYPA, HBGG, D7S8 and GC in the resident population of the Basque Country**

O. García[1], P. Martín[2], C. Albarrán[2], A. Alonso[2]
[1]Laboratorio UTAP, Departamento de Interior, Gobierno Vasco, C/ María Díaz de Haro, 3 - 2ª Planta, 48013 Bilbao (Spain)
[2]Sección de Biología, Instituto Nacional de Toxicología, Madrid (Spain)

Before a new marker system can be introduced in forensic casework, a population database for the relevant population must be established for statistical evaluation of forensic evidence. In conformity with this guideline, the allele and genotype frequencies of 6 different PCR-systems (HLA-DQA1, LDLR, GYPA, HBGG, D7S8 and GC) were determined for a Basque Country resident population sample of 212 unrelated individuals (Tables 1-6). The power of discrimination (PD) values calculated for these genetic markers are given in Table 7.

DNA was extracted by the chelex method (Singer-Sam et al., 1989). The PCR products were analysed by agarose gel electrophoresis (5% Metaphor in TAE). The amplification by PCR and the typing by reverse dot-blot methodology using allele specific oligonucleotide (ASO) probes were performed according to the AmpliType HLA DQα and AmpliType PM PCR Amplification and Typing kit protocol provided by the manufacturer (Perkin-Elmer Cetus).

The allele frequencies profiles obtained were consistent with those previously reported in other caucasian populations. In all six systems, the genotype frequencies are in accordance with Hardy-Weinberg expectations. The six investigated polymorphism systems are reliable and sensitive marker systems that are well suited for use in forensic casework.

**Table 1. HLA-DQA1 gene frequency**

| Type | Gene Frequency |
|---|---|
| HLA-DQA1*1.1 | 0.156 |
| HLA-DQA1*1.2 | 0.184 |
| HLA-DQA1*1.3 | 0.087 |
| HLA-DQA1*2 | 0.158 |
| HLA-DQA1*3 | 0.153 |
| HLA-DQA1*4 | 0.262 |

**Table 2. LDLR gene frequency**

| Type | Gene Frequency |
|---|---|
| LDLR *A | 0.439 |
| LDLR *B | 0.561 |

**Table 3. GYPA gene frequency**

| Type | Gene Frequency |
|---|---|
| GYPA *A | 0.514 |
| GYPA *B | 0.486 |

**Table 4. HBGG gene frequency**

| Type | Gene Frequency |
|---|---|
| HBGG *A | 0.535 |
| HBGG *B | 0.458 |
| HBGG *C | 0.007 |

**Table 5. D7S8 gene frequency**

| Type | Gene Frequency |
|---|---|
| D7S8 *A | 0.575 |
| D7S8 *B | 0.425 |

**Table 6. GC gene frequency**

| Type | Gene Frequency |
|---|---|
| GC *A | 0.302 |
| GC *B | 0.113 |
| GC *C | 0.585 |

**Table 7. Power of discrimination**

| | |
|---|---|
| HLA-DQA1 | 0.9409 |
| LDLR | 0.6211 |
| GYPA | 0.6248 |
| HBGG | 0.6341 |
| D7S8 | 0.6191 |
| GC | 0.7275 |
| Combined | 0.9997 |

**Figure 1. Detection of amplification**

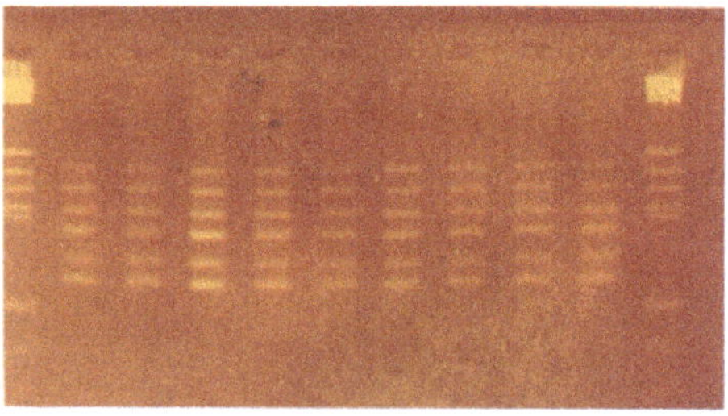

Figure 2. Detection of HLA-DQA1

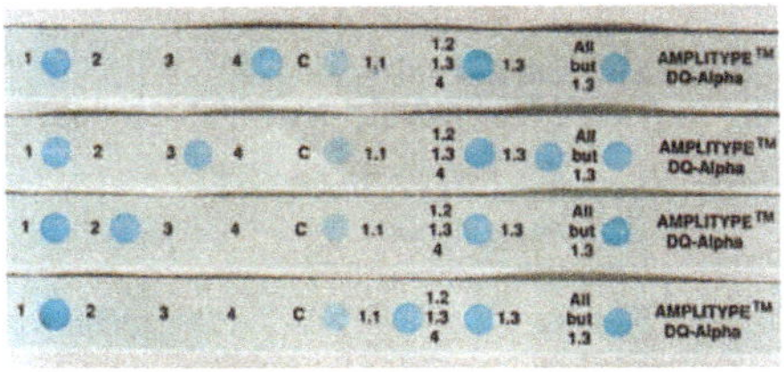


Figure 3. Detection of Polymarker

## REFERENCES

Singer-Sam J, Tanguay R L, Riggs A (1989) Use of Chelex to improve the PCR signal from a small number of cells. Amplifications 3:11

Amplitype User Guide - Version 2 (1990) Cetus Corporation, Emmeryville, CA, USA

# HUMTH01 (TC11) and HUMFESFPS (FES) alleles distribution in a South West Swiss population

Grange F., Dimo-Simonin N., Brandt-Casadevall C.
Institut Universitaire de Médecine Légale, Bugnon 21, Lausanne, Switzerland

## INTRODUCTION

DNA typing of Short Tandem Repeat (STR) by Polymerase Chain Reaction (PCR) is a powerful tool in forensic medicine. However, it is essential that the distribution of STR's alleles be studied throughout a variety of sub-populations to discover possible variations.
In this study we report the allele and genotype frequencies of HUMTH01 (TC11) and HUMFESFPS (FES) in a population from South-Western Switzerland and we compare our allele frequency distribution with other Swiss and Caucasian populations.

## MATERIALS AND METHODS

Blood samples were obtained from 137 unrelated individuals of known origin. These samples were saline extracted. The remaining samples (68 for TC11 and 62 for FES) were buccal swabs of unrelated university personnel obtained after verification of their origin. In those samples the DNA was extracted by chelex.

### PCR amplification

For both HUMTH01 (TC11) and HUMFESFPS (FES) the reaction mixture contained : 1 to 20ng template DNA, 50 mM KCl, 10 mM Tris-HCl (pH 9.0 at 25 °C), 1% Triton X-100, 1.5 mM $MgCl_2$, 0.1 mM each dNTP, 4 mM each primer, 1U Taq DNA polymerase and 8 ug albumin. The reaction mixture was overlayed with a drop of oil. The primers used were those reported by Edwards [1] for TC11 and Kimpton [2] for FES.
The amplification was performed with the thermocycler Biometra, triothermoblock, according to the following protocols: TC11 : 94 °C, 5 min; 94 °C, 45 sec; 60 °C, 30 sec; 72 °C, 30 sec (30 cycles); 72 °C, 7 min. FES : 94 °C, 5 min; 94 °C, 45 sec; 58 °C, 30 sec; 72 °C, 30 sec (30 cycles); 72 °C, 7 min.

### Detection of amplified products

For each sample the amplification product from both systems were mixed and then separated on a vertical electrophoresis apparatus using a 10% Hydrolink Long Ranger gel and a discontinuous glycine/chloride buffer system, followed by silver staining. Their identification was done by comparison with an allelic ladder obtained by mixing the amplified products of known samples provided to us by Prof. Baer of the Institute of Legal Medicine in Zurich, where the samples had been typed on an Applied Biosystems Automated DNA Sequencer (ABI).

## RESULTS

### Alleles and genotypes distribution

Seven discrete alleles were observed for TC11 and five for FES. As expected, TC11 demonstrated better polymorphism than FES with five of the seven alleles well distributed among the population, while only three of the FES alleles were found to be common. The alleles distribution observed correlates well with other Caucasian populations [1, 3, 4, 5, 6] except for the increased number of the FES allele 8 seen in the USA population [6].

The Hardy-Weinberg formulation was calculated by comparing observed and expected genotypes; we pooled all classes of genotypes containing one of the less common alleles (5 or 10 for TC11; 8 or 13 for FES), which generally corresponded to the classes with less than four events. No deviation from Hardy-Weinberg law was observed for either TC11 or FES.

HUMTH01 (TC11) alleles distribution in four caucasian populations

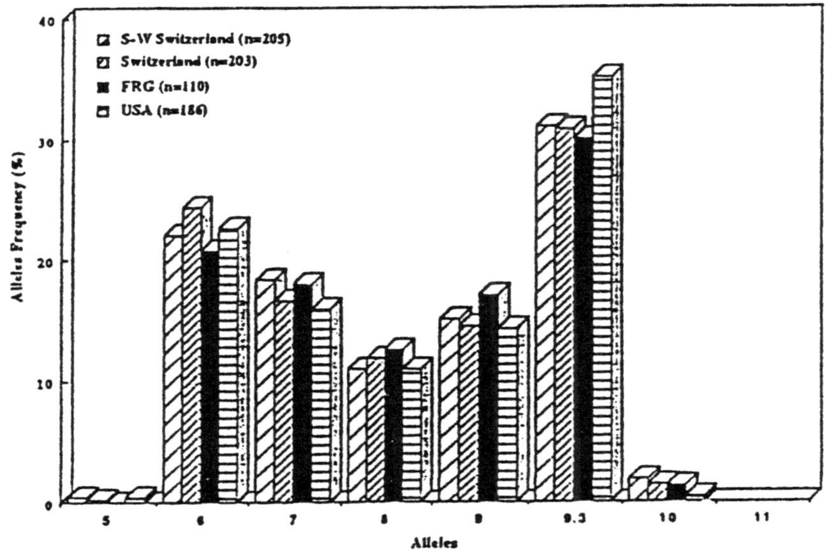


HUMTH01 genotypes distribution in a population from South-West Switzerland

| Genotypes | Frequency observed | Frequency expected |
|---|---|---|
| 5-5 | 0 | 0 |
| 5-6 | 0 | 0.4 |
| 5-7 | 0 | 0.4 |
| 5-8 | 0 | 0.2 |
| 5-9 | 1 | 0.3 |
| 5-9.3 | 1 | 0.6 |
| 5-10 | 0 | 0 |
| 6-6 | 13 | 9.9 |
| 6-7 | 17 | 16.5 |
| 6-8 | 11 | 9.9 |
| 6-9 | 18 | 13.6 |
| 6-9.3 | 18 | 28.1 |
| 6-10 | 1 | 1.8 |
| 7-7 | 5 | 6.9 |
| 7-8 | 4 | 8.2 |
| 7-9 | 14 | 11.3 |
| 7-9.3 | 30 | 23.4 |
| 7-10 | 0 | 1.5 |
| 8-8 | 4 | 2.5 |
| 8-9 | 6 | 6.8 |
| 8-9.3 | 15 | 14.1 |
| 8-10 | 1 | 0.9 |
| 9-9 | 3 | 4.7 |
| 9-9.3 | 15 | 19.4 |
| 9-10 | 1 | 1.2 |
| 9.3-9.3 | 23 | 20 |
| 9.3-10 | 3 | 2.5 |
| 10-10 | 1 | 0.1 |
| Total | 205 | |
| Chi2 | 15.32 | |
| P | 0.5-0.7 (df = 16) | |

HUMFESFPS (FES) alleles Distribution in four caucasian populations

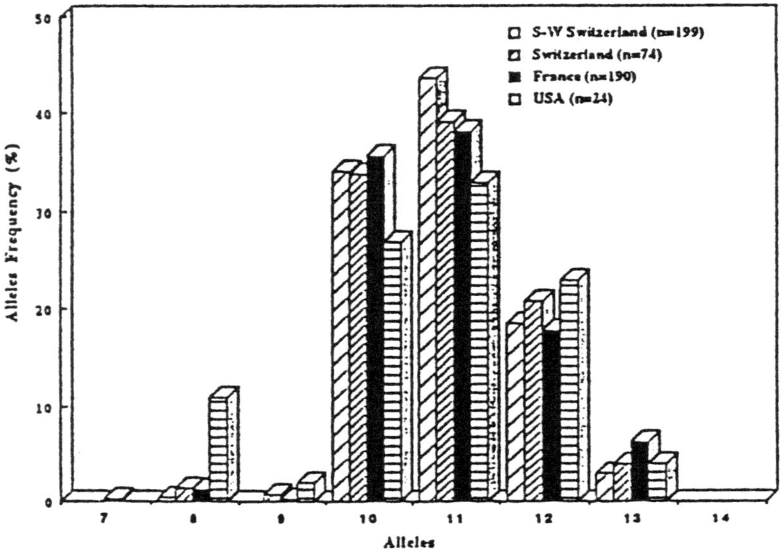


HUMFESFPS genotypes distribution in a population from South-West Switzerland

| Genotypes | Frequency observed | Frequency expected |
|---|---|---|
| 8-8 | 0 | 0 |
| 8-10 | 0 | 0.7 |
| 8-11 | 2 | 0.9 |
| 8-12 | 0 | 0.4 |
| 8-13 | 0 | 0.1 |
| 10-10 | 20 | 23.2 |
| 10-11 | 64 | 59.5 |
| 10-12 | 28 | 25.3 |
| 10-13 | 4 | 4.1 |
| 11-11 | 33 | 38.0 |
| 11-12 | 33 | 32.4 |
| 11-13 | 4 | 5.3 |
| 12-12 | 3 | 6.9 |
| 12-13 | 2 | 2.2 |
| 13-13 | 1 | 0.2 |
| Total | 159 | |
| Chi2 | 4.94 | |
| P | 0.5-0.7 (df = 6) | |

# CONCLUSION

We found a good correlation between our population and other Caucasian populations for both TC11 and FES. As expected, TC11 demonstrated better polymorphism than FES.

## REFERENCES

1) Edwards A, Hammond HA, Jin L, Caskey CT, Chakraborty (1992) Genetic variation at five trimeric and tetrameric tandem repeat loci in four human population groups. Genomics 12:241-253
2) Kimpton CP, Gill P, Walton A, Urquhart A, Millican ES, Adams M (1993) Automated DNA profiling employing multiplex amplification of Short Tandem Repeat loci. PCR Methods and Applications 3:13-22
3) Kratzer A, Gränacher A, Jamnicki M, Bär W (1993) Swiss population data for 3 STR-systems (SE33, HUMTH01, D21S11), HLA DQa and D1S80. In: 15th International Congress, International Society of Forensic Haemogenetics, Venezia
4) Kratzer A, Bär W (1993) personnal communication
5) Pfitzinger H (1994) Poster presented at the American Academy of Forensic Sciences, 46th Annual Meeting
6) Wiegand P, Budowle B, Rand S, Brinkmann B (1993) Forensic validation of the STR systems SE33 and TC11. International Journal of Legal Medicine 105:315-320

**Acknowledgments** : This project was supported by a grant from: Service des Hospices Cantonaux, Département de l'Intérieur et de la Santé Publique, Etat de Vaud, Suisse.
The authors wish to thank Mrs C. Besançon and A. Grini for their assistance.

# GENETIC TYPING OF BIOLOGICAL EVIDENCE USING PCR

**F. Heidorn, G. Wrobel, V. Schneider, H. Pöche.**
**Institut für Rechtsmedizin, Freie Universität Berlin, Hittorfstraße 18, D-14 195 Berlin**
**Correspondence to: Dr. Hubert Pöche, Institut für Rechtmedizin, Freie Universität Berlin, Hittorfstraße 18, D-14 195 Berlin, Germany**

## Introduction

In three separate crime cases identification was achieved using three different PCR systems D1S80 (Budowle et al., 1991), TC11 (Edwards et al., 1992) and SE33 (Polymeropoulos et al., 1992). Although more than 27 alleles are known in the D1S80 system the value of the findings is limited, because of the high frequency of the alleles 18 and 24.

The TC11 system has, in our experience, proved to be very sensitive and is therefore used particularly in complicated trace investigation cases. However, the significance of the results is also limited, because only 7 different types of allele exist with 5,6,7,8,9 and 10 complete repeat-sequences as well as 9 repeats with 3 bases (called 9.3 as suggested by the Münster-working group). This allele 9.3 has a very high frequency in the Caucasian population. The highest value of the findings is achieved with the SE33 system, because there is a great variety of alleles and the distribution of the allele frequency is more evenly spread.

The separation of the alleles requires a greater outlay and effort than would be nescessary with D1S80 and TC11, because the alleles do not comprise only complete repeat sequences, there are also a great number of inter-alleles, which differ by only two bases. Thus a quick separation by horizontal polyacrylamide gel electrophoresis and subsequent detection by silver staining, which we are using for the two other methods, is not of sufficient value. In the SE33 system we are working with Digoxigenin-labelled primers. In a direct blotting procedure the labelled PCR fragments were blotted onto a moving nylon-membrane during the running of the gel. After crosslinking the DNA on the membrane by UV-light, a detection followed by using an anti-digoxigenin-antibody-alkaline-phosphatase-complex and the dye NBT. Based on this method all the fragments have the same length of separation. Consequently the length of running on the membrane is linear to the length of the fragments, which makes possible a relatively accurate interpolation of allele types which are not an element of the reference ladder.

## Results and Discussion

In the first case we had to examine biological material found on the necks of two bottles. The question was, if these bottles had been used in a sexual act. We obtained blood from the victim as reference and isolated DNA from the material on the necks of the bottles. From one of these, a "vodka bottle" , we could isolate a single hair, which we tried to amplify directly in the D1S80 system at first.

In Fig. 1a it can be seen that the alleles from the sample of the hair and the material from both bottles were identical with those of the victim. We took 20 µl of the

D1S80 amplification product from the hair and amplified this again in the TC11 system, where we obtained identical results ( Fig. 1b). We amplified 5 µl of the D1S80 amplification product of the hair in the SE33 system as well and, as shown in Fig. 1c, the alleles of the victim and the material from the bottles corresponded. By interpolation we established a length for the alleles of 275 bp and 329 bp.
A single hair plays an important role in the next crime investigation too. An Asian man sitting in the rear of a car was shot dead. Another one was injured by a bullet in the neck. This man maintained that he was sitting in the front of the car at the time of the shooting. However, the person who fired the gun from outside the car claimed that this second person was also outside the car and attacking him and his friend, thus the shot was fired in self-defence.
It was possible to recover a fragment of a bullet from the rear seat, which carried a single hair and a trace of blood. The ballistic investigation concluded that this fragment could probably have injured the Asian in the neck if he had been sitting in the front of the car. We separated the single hair and amplified it, as in the case before, in all systems. DNA was isolated from the remnants of blood and amplified as well. This amplification was unsuccessful, but the hair gave clear results:
In the D1S80 system the alleles of the injured person sitting in the front were identical with those of the hair while the alleles of the murdered person were different (Fig.2 a). In order to get a higher probability we amplified this again in the TC11 system. Unfortunately the two Asian people had the same alleles -7 and 7- (Fig.2 b). This can be put down to the high frequency of the alleles 7 and 9 among the Asian population. To acquire a higher probability we had to rely on the SE 33 system. In this way we identified the alleles with 251 bp and 313 bp for the isolated hair, which corresponded with the alleles of the injured person, while the victim showed alleles with 263 bp and 301 bp (Fig.2 c). So with a high probability it was clear that the injured person was sitting in the front of the car at the time of shooting.
In the third case a Turkish man stood accused of murdering his mistress and a female friend of hers who had witnessed the shooting. Cigarette ends found at the scene of the crime were first identified in the D1S80 system. The defendant´s brother, though not a likely suspect, was also investigated since he had access to the victim´s appartment. The isolated samples from the cigarettes revealed alleles corresponding with those of the accused. In this system the brother also showed identical alleles (Fig. 3a).
Three days before the trial we were informed by the public prosecutor`s office that the defendant was maintaining that his brother had been in the flat and had been smoking. Thus in the shortest time possible we had to conduct an investigation using an alternative system, in the hope that it would reveal different alleles for the accused and his brother. We achieved this objective using the TC 11 system (Fig. 3b): the defendant displayed the alleles 9 and 9.3 corresponding to those isolated from the cigarettes, while the brother showed the alleles 8 and 9.3, thus eliminating him from the inquiry. Later we subjected the samples to

analysis by the SE33 system (Fig. 3c). As for D1S80, the defendant and brother displayed identical alleles. As before, the cigarettes showed a positive match.

**Conclusion**

This last case demonstrates the necessity of using different PCR systems in the investigation of crime cases - particularly where related persons are involved. The clustered allele frequency in the systems D1S80 and TC 11 often means you cannot make an unequivocal statement with just these systems.

On the other hand, these systems permit relatively quick and easy separation and detection, an advantage over the SE33 system when results must be obtained promptly.

**Budowle B, Chakraborty R, Giusti AM, Eisenberg AJ, Allen RC** (1991) Analysis of the VNTR locus D1S80 by the PCR followed by high-resolution PAGE. Am. J. Hum. Genet. 48:137-144

**Edwards A, Hammond H A, Jin L, Caskey T, Chakraborty R** (1992) Genetic variation at trimeric and tetrameric tandem repeat loci in four human population groups. Genomics 12:241-253

**Polymeropoulos M H, Rath DS, Xiao H, Merill C R** (1992) Tetranucleotide repeat polymorphism at the human beta-actin related pseudogene H-beta-Ac-psi-2 (ACTBP2). Nucleic Acids Research, Vol 20, No. 6: 1432 (1992).

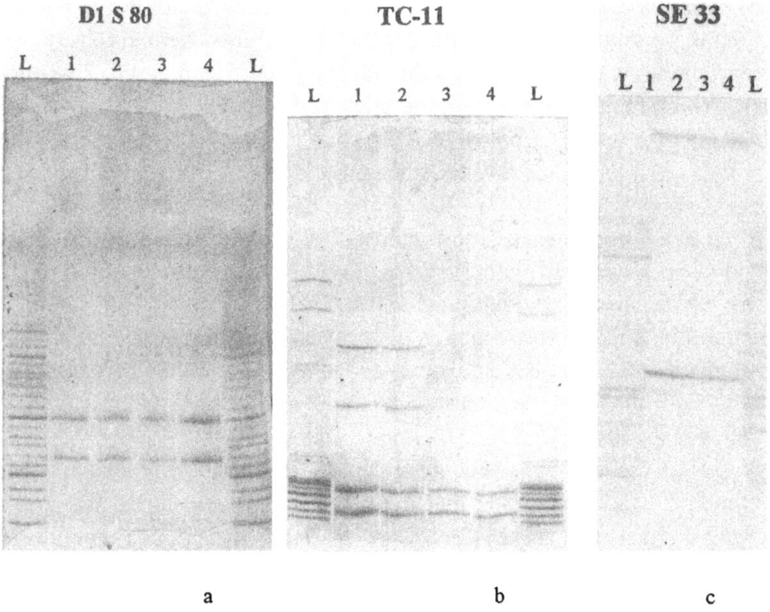


**Fig. 1**: L: reference ladder; 1: victim; 2: sample of hair taken from the rim of the bottle; 3: material taken from the neck of the vodka bottle; 4: material taken from the neck of the liqueur bottle. a: alleles 20/24; b: alleles 6/9; c: 275 bp/ 329 bp (interpolated).

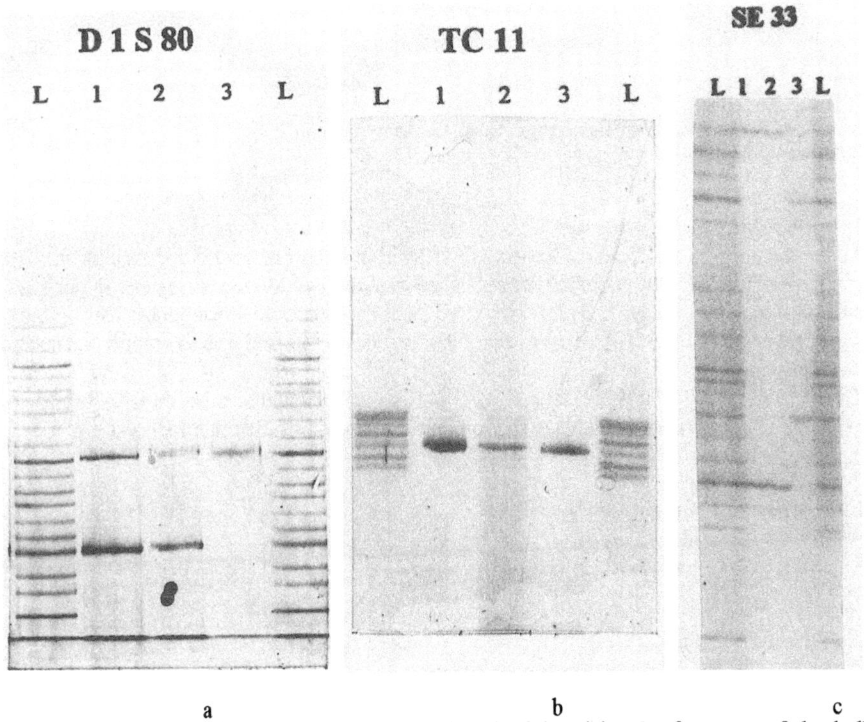


**Fig 2**: L: reference ladder; 1: person presumed to be injured by the fragment of the bullet; sample of hair taken from the fragment of the bullet; 3: victim of the shooting. **a**: alleles 18 / 24 (1;2) and 24/31 (3); **b**: alleles 7/7; **c**: 251 bp/ 313 bp (1;2) and 263 bp/301 bp (3).

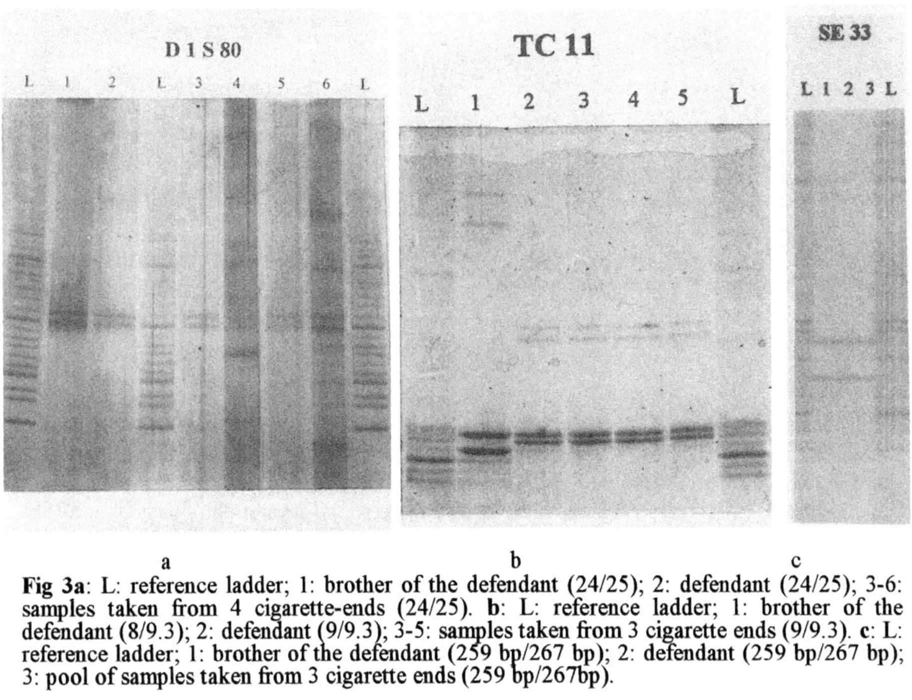


**Fig 3a**: L: reference ladder; 1: brother of the defendant (24/25); 2: defendant (24/25); 3-6: samples taken from 4 cigarette-ends (24/25). **b**: L: reference ladder; 1: brother of the defendant (8/9.3); 2: defendant (9/9.3); 3-5: samples taken from 3 cigarette ends (9/9.3). **c**: L: reference ladder; 1: brother of the defendant (259 bp/267 bp); 2: defendant (259 bp/267 bp); 3: pool of samples taken from 3 cigarette ends (259 bp/267bp).

## Suitability Of Short Tandem Repeats In Forensics: A Comparison Of 7 Loci

P. Huber and J. Holtz
Institute of Forensic Medicine, University of Bonn, Germany
Stiftsplatz 12 D- 53111 Bonn

### Introduction

Today the use of Short Tandem Repeats (STR's) is an important tool in forensic identification and paternity cases. But not all of the published loci fulfill all forensic demands. In our study we investigated 7 of these loci and conducted a comparison of their usefulness for routine work, especially of their robustness - that means: success rate and bias to amplify the specific products.
The loci ACTBP2 ( SE33), PLA2 and APO C II are still used in connection with forensic genetic analysis. To our knowledge the forensic application of the other loci was not described till now.

### Characteristics of the investigated loci

| Locus | Chromosomal Location | Number of Alleles | Polymorphic Repeat | Range of Allele size | Maximal Frequency | Maximal Annealing Temperature* [C°] |
|---|---|---|---|---|---|---|
| D8S320 | Chromosome 8 q | 11 | [AAAG] | 386-426 bp | 0,21 | 64 |
| ACTBP2 (SE33) | Chromosome 6 | 26 | [AAAG] | 226-330 bp | 0,092 | 64 |
| AR | Chromosome Xq 11-12 | 15 | [CAG] | 193-238 bp | female: 0,16<br>male: 0,27 | 64 |
| PLA2 | Chromosome 12 | 6 | [TTA] | 122-137 bp | 0,33 | 62 |
| D6S366 | Chromosome 6q 21 | 9 | [AAT] | 138-162 bp | 0,26 | 62 |
| APO C II | Chromosome 19q 12-13 | 15 | [CA] | 127-171 bp | 0,26 | 64 |
| CTLA4 | Chromosome 2q 33 | 17 | [AT] | 130-92 bp | 0,13 | 64 |

* for our special PCR conditions

In routine work we decreased the maximal annealing temperatures about two degrees, to increase the yield and thereby success rate.

### Discussion of the single loci

#### D8S320[1)]

This tetra repeat is an excellent marker system. We got a success rate over 98 % and no extra bands in most of the cases. The limit of detection is about 25 pg DNA. We did not find any mutation in 24 trios.
A disadvantage of the system is the difficult electrophoretical separation of neighbour alleles.

**AR[2)]**

The trinucleotide polymorphism at the androgen receptor gene, located on the X-chromosome, is a high polymorphic locus with a balanced distribution (we found 15 alleles [published till now: 11 alleles [2)]], maximal frequency in a female population sample: 0,16). More than 95 % of the samples could be typed unequivocally.
Because of its location on the X-chromosome and the observed mutations (we found 2 in 38 trios) we use this system for identification cases exclusively.

**ACTBP2 (SE33)[3)]**

The tetra repeat ACTBP2 (SE33), which is introduced in many laboratories, is one of the most polymorphic STR's in forensic analysis; but it is a problematic system. The irregular repeat structure complicates exact allele determination by comparison with allelic ladders. Successful amplification of the system requires well prepared DNA. We experienced that the use of Chelex extracts often yielded no products, although the same extracts gave well defined products at the loci D8S320 and AR. As we used standard extraction methods (phenol/chloroform, ethanol precipitation), we got a success rate of about 85 %.

**PLA2[4)]**

The system is low polymorphic (6 alleles). Mendelian inheritance was observed in all cases. The system is suitable for typing DNA in high degraded condition because of the small fragment size. We often got extra bands, the success rate was about 80 %.

**APO C II[5)]**

Amplification of slippage bands is typical for dinucleotide repeats, so for the APO C II locus. By using high stringent PCR conditions these bands were nearly avoided, but on the other hand the success rate decreased. We use the system only in one of our multiplex systems and for locus specific amplification after pretreatment with PEP.

**D6S366[6)] and CTLA4[7)]**

These loci gave no interpretable results in most of the cases, although we made many experiments to optimize the systems.

**Multiplex Amplification of STR's**

We combined the loci ACTBP2-AR-APO C II and D8S320-ACTBP2-AR.
The criteria for the selection of these loci were compatibility of the primer sets, chromosomal location and non overlapping fragment sizes to detect the products by silver staining after simultanous run on a PAA-gel (in rare cases overlapping of very small ACTBP2 respectively very big AR alleles is possible; this requires single typing of each locus).

**Preamplification with random primers - Primer extension Preamplification (PEP)**

By application of this procedure, first described by Zhang et al.[8)], we were able to type samples,which were otherwise unamplifiable because of the minute amount of template DNA[9)], for example a cigarette butt or single hair shafts. The STR's, which could be amplified successfully after PEP were: D8S320, ACTBP2 and APO C II.

## Conclusions

Our study demonstrates the differences of the loci concerning the robustness in routine work. In the following figure the systems are sorted according to decreasing robustness:

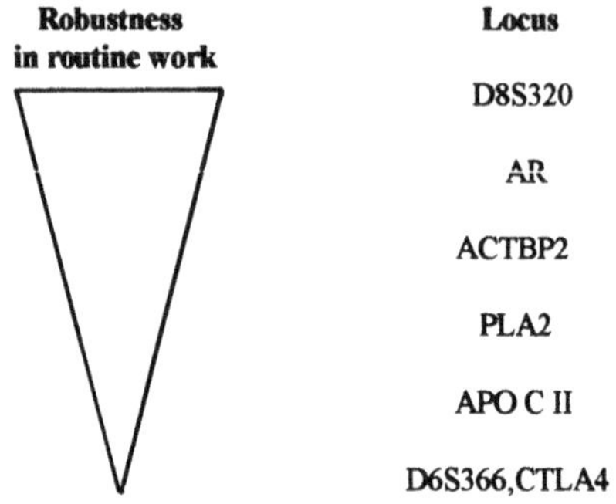


For choosing efficient marker systems in forensic casework a lot of criteria have to be considered, for example reliability and specifity of amplification, degree of polymorphism and allelic distribution, optimal extraction and electrophoretical seperation methods.
Multiplex amplification of several loci achieves enhancement of probability in one working process. The PEP procedure is an alternative in case of otherwise unamplifiable specimens.

## References

1) Riley R, Nelson L, Lu J, Robertson M, Ballard L, Connolly J, Ward K (1993) Tetranucleotide repeat polymorphism at the D8S320 locus. Hum Mol Genet 2: 1512

2) Sleddens HFBM, Oostra BA, Brinkmann AO, Trapman J (1992) Trinucleotide repeat polymorphism in the androgen receptor gene (AR). Nucl Acids Res 20: 1427

3) Wiegand P, Budowle B, Rand S, Brinkmann B (1993) Forensic validation of the STR systems SE33 and TC11. Int J Leg Med 105: 315-320

4) Polymeropoulos MH, Rath DS, Xiao H, Merril CR (1990) Trinucleotide repeat polymorphism at the human pancreatic phospholipase A-2 gene (PLA2). Nucl Acids Res 18: 7468

5) Weber JL, May PE (1989) Abundant class of human DNA polymorphisms which can be typed using the polymerase chain reaction. Am J Hum Gen 44: 388-396

6) Panzer SW, Hammond HA, Stephens L, Chai A, Caskey CT (1993)Trinucleotide repeat polymorphism at D6S366. Hum Mol Genet 2: 1511

7) Polymeropoulos MH, Xiao H, Rath DS, Merril CR (1991) Dinucleotide repeat polymorphism at the human CTLA4 gene. Nucl Acids Res 19: 4018

8) Zhang L, Cui X, Schmitt K, Hubert R, Navidi W, Arnheim N (1992) Whole genome amplification from a single cell: implications for genetic analysis. Proc Natl Acad Sci 89: 5847-5851

9) Huber P, Holtz J (in press) Random priming and multiplex PCR with three short tandem repeats in forensic casework. In: Rossi U (ed) Advances in forensic haemogenetics, vol 5. Springer, New York, Berlin, Heidelberg

# Detection of sex specific DNA fingerprint bands in Peregrine falcon using non radioactive 33.6 and 33.15 human probes

C. Keyser [1], B. Ludes [2], H. Pfitzinger [1], P. Mangin [2]
[1] Laboratoire Codgène, 11 rue Humann, 67000 Strasbourg, FRANCE
[2] Institut de Médecine légale, 11 rue Humann, 67000 Strasbourg, FRANCE

Although originally developed for humans, DNA fingerprinting is now widely applied in animal species. Potential applications of this technique in the study of wild and domesticated animals are multiple and diversified and the human minisatellite probes 33.6 and 33.15 (1) have been used to generate informative DNA banding patterns from a wide range of animal species. The advent of non-isotopically labelled probes made their use into routine technique more convenient (2). We have investigated the application of the probes 33.6 and 33.15, labelled with alkaline phosphatase and detected by chemiluminescence for individual identification and parentage analysis within raptor species. Besides detecting numerous autosomal loci, each probe allowed the detection of a DNA fragment present only in DNA profiles obtained from female peregrine falcons and transmitted to female offspring only.

We analysed birds of prey of known sex including 31 peregrine falcons (*Falco peregrinus*), among which three chicks and their parents, 2 lanner falcons (*Falco biarmicus*), 4 gyrfalcons (*Falco rusticolus*), 4 laggar falcons (*Falco jugger*) and 3 hybrids produced in captivity by artificial insemination (2 *F. peregrinus/rusticolus* hybrids and 1 *F. cherrug/ rusticolus* hybrid).

DNA extracted from bird blood samples were digested with the *Hae*III endonuclease. DNA restriction fragments were separated by electrophoresis on agarose gels (30 cm long, 0.7%) and transferred onto nylon membranes by standard capillary Southern blotting. Blots were hybridized successively with non-isotopic chemiluminescent enhanced (NICE) 33.6 and 33.15 probes from ICI Cellmark Diagnostics (UK) according to the manufacturer's protocol.

Both Jeffreys' 33.6 and 33.15 probes gave specific DNA fingerprint patterns for the different falcon specimens studied. Moreover, the probe 33.6 revealed a single band at about 5.1 kb that was shared by all female peregrine falcon DNA patterns examined and absent from the male peregrine falcon DNA patterns (a sample of which is reported in Fig. 1). This 5.1 kb DNA fragment was detected in a female peregrine/gyrfalcon hybrid DNA profile but neither in a female gyrfalcon DNA profile nor in a female laggar falcon DNA profile thus appearing to be species specific.

The autoradiographs produced using the 33.15 probe revealed a very weak 11.7 kb DNA fragment solely observed in female peregrine falcon DNA profiles. This fragment was more than twice bigger than the female specific fragment observed with the probe 33.6 but its intensity was strongly reduced (Fig.2).

The pedigree analysis of a small family (three chicks and their parents) showed that the maternal specific bands observed with both 33.6 and 33.15 probes were transmitted to the female chick only and testified the Mendelian inheritance of the two sex-linked DNA fragments.

The application of non-radioactive DNA fingerprinting provides a more sensitive and more convenient alternative to $^{32}$P-based systems and facilitates the use of DNA fingerprinting in routine analyses. This is of particular interest in the control of the illegal trade of birds of prey where definitive proof of bird's identities is required. Parentage analysis can exclude from a captive breeding an individual took illegally from the wild and thus allows to convict dealers (3).

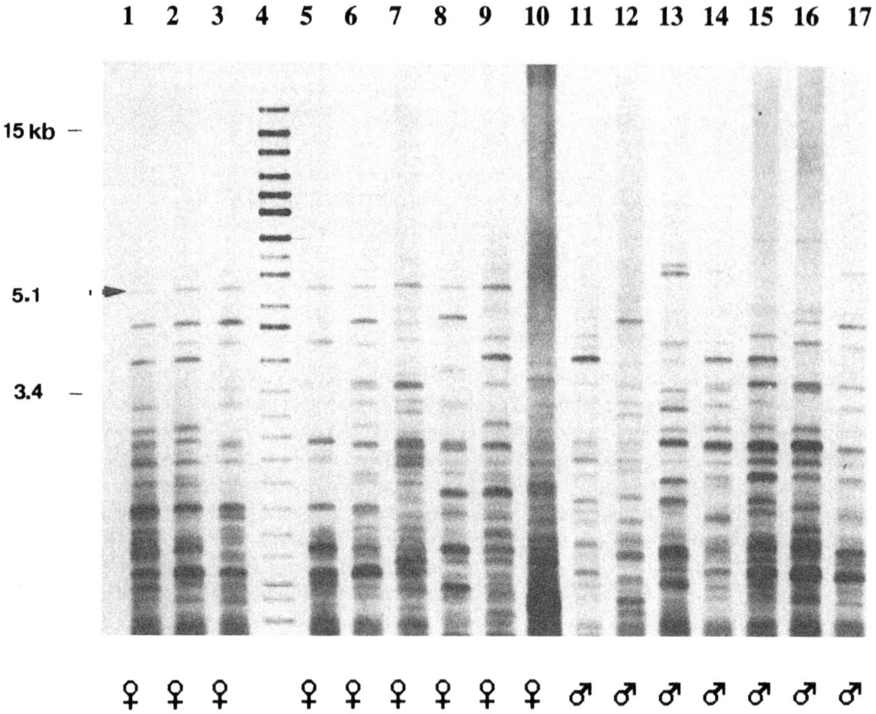


**Figure 1**. DNA fingerprints of falcon individuals obtained with the non isotopic 33.6 NICE probe. Lanes 1-3, 5-9, 11 and 13-17 are peregrine falcons DNA samples, lane 10 is a laggar falcon DNA sample and lane 12 corresponds to a peregrine-gyrfalcon hybrid. The MW100 molecular weight marker from Gibco BRL is present on lane 4. The arrow indicates the female specific DNA fragment of 5.1 kb.

The use of the human 33.15 probe as a method of sex-determination has been reported in several avian species (4, 5, 6). Bird sex-specific fragments are less frequently found with the 33.6 probe. No coexistence of cross hybridization of 33.6 and 33.15 to female-specific fragments have yet been found in bird DNA fingerprints.

Adult peregrine falcons exhibit sexual dimorphism, there is consequently no need to determine gender for adults through laboratory tests, but this could be advantageous for immature individuals. Moreover, the species-specific sex-linked fragments could represent useful molecular markers for investigating phylogenetic relationships among the Falconidae family (7) and may provide evidences for the parental origin of hybrid birds.

There is obvious interest if similar markers could be found in species whose gender is not easily determined such as other Falconiformes (*Sarcorhamphus papa* or *Aegypius monachus* for example) and most of the Psittacidae. Through the 33.6 probe, we have probably revealed such a sex-specific fragment in the African grey parrot (*Psittacus erithacus*) which is a monomorphic bird, but this result must be confirmed on a larger number of samples.

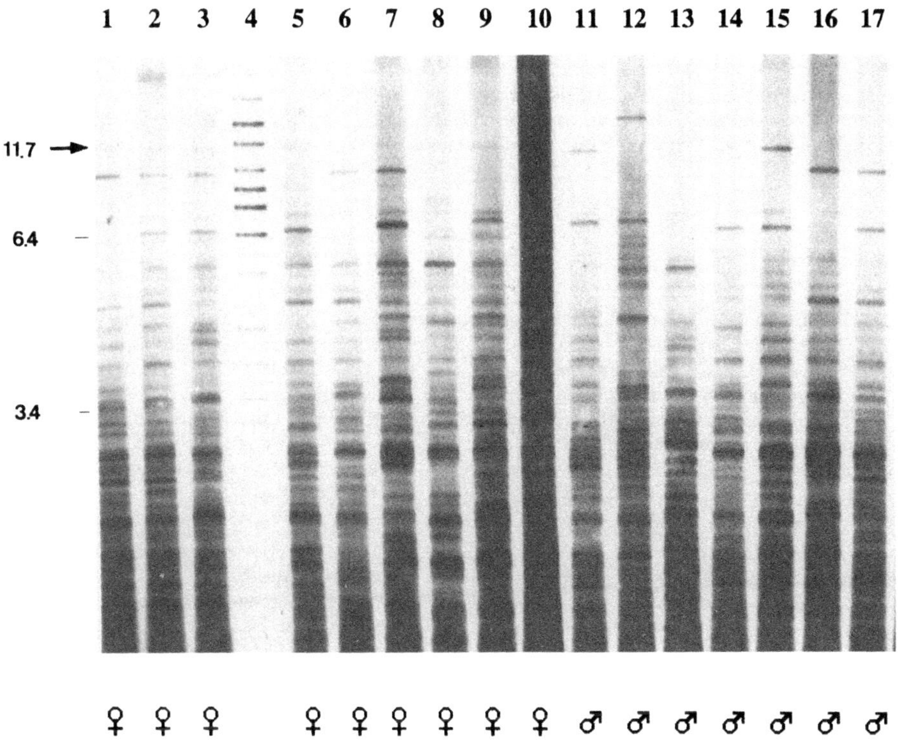


**Figure 2.** Autoradiography of the membrane shown in Fig.1 and hybridized with the 33.15 NICE probe. The arrow indicates the female specific DNA fragment of 11.7 kb .

## REFERENCES


1. Jeffreys AJ, Wilson V, Thein SL (1985) Hypervariable 'minisatellite' regions in human DNA. Nature 314:67-73
2. Giles AF, Booth KJ, Parker JR, Garman AJ, Carrick DT, Akhavan H, Schaap AP (1990) Rapid, simple, non-isotopic probing of southern blots for DNA fingerprinting. Adv in For Haemogenetics 3:40-42
3. Máthé JC, Eisenmann A, Seitz (1993) Paternity testing of endangered species of birds by DNA fingerprinting with non-radioactive labelled oligonucleotide probes. In: Pena SDJ, Chakraborty R, Epplen JT (eds) DNA fingerprinting : State of the Science. Birkhäuser Verlag, Basel, pp.387-393
4. Rabenold PP, Piper WH, Decker MD, Minchella DJ (1991) Polymorphic minisatellite amplified on avian W chromosome. Genome 44:489-493
5. Miyaki CY, Hanotte O, Wajntal A, Burke T (1992) Sex typing of *Aratinga* parrots using the human minisatellite probe 33.15. Nucleic Acids Res 19:5235-5236
6. May CA, Wetton JH, Parkin DT (1993) Polymorphic sex-specific sequences in birds of prey. Proc R Soc Lond B 253:271-276
7. Longmire JL, Ambrose RE, Brown NC, Cade TJ, Maechtle TL, Seegar WS, Ward FP, White CM (1991) Use of sex-linked minisatellite fragments to investigate genetic differentiation and migration of north american populations of the peregrine falcon (Falco peregrinus). In: Burke T, Dolf G, Jeffreys AJ, Wolff R (eds) DNA Fingerprinting: Approaches and Application. Birkhäuser Verlag Basel, Switzerland, pp.217-229

# GENETIC ANALYSIS OF FLUORESCENT LABELED AMPLIFIED DNA USING SERIES OF OLIGONUCLEOTIDE PROBES COVALENTLY BOUND TO MEMBRANES

I.A. Kozlov, N.A. Naryshkin, K.I. Ivanov, I.V. Lebedeva, M.G. Ivanovskaya, Z.A. Shabarova
A.N. Belozersky Research Institute of Physico-Chemical Biology, Moscow State University, Moscow, 119899, Russia, FAX: 0107 095 9393181

**INTRODUCTION.** Recently proposed reverse hybridization method is very convenient for simultaneous detection of a set nucleotide sequences in a DNA fragment of interest (1,2). The main idea of this method is immobilization of an oligonucleotide probes set on a solid support and their hybridization with the labeled DNA fragment. Here we report on an improved non-radioactive reverse hybridization method and provide an example of its application for testing point mutations responsible for β-thalassemia.

**EXPERIMENTAL PROCEDURES.** To obtain a conjugate of oligonucleotide with reduced glutathione N-hydroxybenzotriazole activation of the phosphate group was employed as described in (3). Immobilization of the oligonucleotide conjugate on nylon membrane "Biodyne B" carrying amino groups was performed under the action of 0.5M water-soluble 1-ethyl-3-(3'-dimethylaminopropyl)carbodiimide (EDC) in 0.5M MES-buffer, pH 4.25. Introduction of fluorescent labels - 5-carboxyfluorescein (FAM) and 6-carboxytetramethylrodamine (TAMRA) - at the 5' end of the oligonucleotide was carried out as previously described (4). Obtained fluorescently labeled primers were introduced in PCR to obtain β-globin gene fragment carrying non-radioactive label in conditions provided in (5). Hybridization of the immobilized oligonucleotides with the amplified fragment of β-globin gene was performed in 1 ml of a hybridization buffer, pH 7.2, containing 0.9M NaCl, 0.09M sodium citrate, 0.1% SDS, 0.1% Ficoll-400, 0.1% polyvinylpyrrolidon, 0.1% bovine serum albumin, 10 μg of DNA of salmon sperm sonicated, 12 hours at 42. Before hybridization the membrane was pre-hybridized in the hybridization buffer for 1 hour at 42.

**RESULTS AND DISCUSSION.** We proposed a novel method for immobilization of the conjugate of oligonucleotide with reduced glutathione at oligonucleotide's terminal phosphate on the nylon membrane carrying amino groups. The immobilization was performed with the aid of EDC during 2 hours at pH 4.25 as shown on the next page.

The efficiency of the immobilization was 85%, maximal quantity of the oligonucleotide in a single dot being 50 pmol. Immobilized oligonucleotides were used as probes for detection of point mutation in β-globin gene responsible for β-thalassemia.

The mutation in position 110 of β-globin gene small intron from β-thalassemia patients in Azerbajan was chosen as an object of investigation. Two 19-membered oligonucleotides were immobilized on the membrane, one of them being complementary to corresponding regions of the normal DNA and the other one - to the mutant DNA respectively. Sequences of the oligonucleotides were designed so that the nucleotide pair being tested was in the central region of the probe (5).

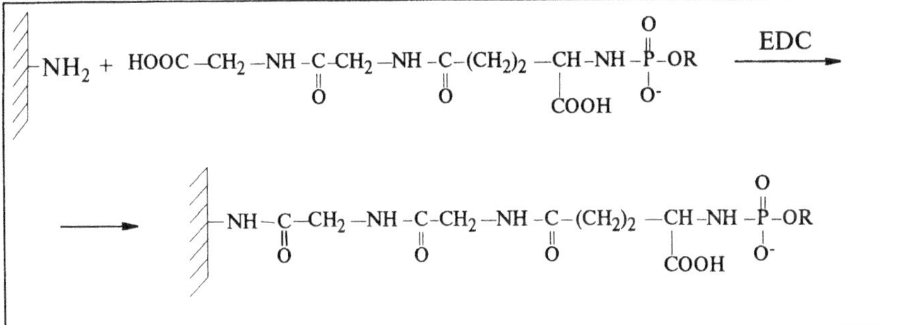


**R - OLIGONUCLEOTIDE RESIDUE, EDC** — $C_2H_5-N{=}C{=}N-(CH_2)_3-\overset{+}{N}H(CH_3)_2\ Cl^-$

Fluorescently labeled DNA fragment of β-globin gene (469 b.p.) was obtained through PCR in conditions as described in (5) with the aid of fluorescently labeled oligonucleotide primers. DNA fragment obtained was introduced without isolation into 1 ml of hybridization buffer. The hybridization was carried out 12 hours at 42°C. After that the membranes were washed out during 1 minute 6 times in 6xSSC. Availability of the mutation in a sample under investigation can be detected in UV light, wave length - 254 nm. Under UV irradiation DNA strand labeled with TAMRA produces yellow light and the one labeled with FAM - red light.

Sensitivity in our experiments was 0.3 pmol of DNA. We suppose that such a modest value was determined by the usage of total amplified ds-DNA for hybridization. Our control experiments showed that ds-DNA was in one order of magnitude worse than ss-DNA. Now we are working at some improvements of our method making use of preliminary strands separation.

Hence, the described method allow one to handle rapidly and efficiently non-radioactive examination not of a series of mutations responsible not only for β-thalassemia but also for various hereditary diseases.

**REFERENCES**

1. Saiki RK, Walsh PS, Levenson CH, Erlich HA (1989) Genetic analysis of amplified DNA with immobilized sequence-specific oligonucleotide probes. Proc Natl Acad Sci USA 86:6230-6234
2. Zhang Y, Coyne MG, Will SG, Levenson CH, Kawasaki ES (1991) Single-base mutational analysis of cancer and genetic diseases using membrane bound modified oligonucleotides. Nucl Acids Res 19:3929-3933
3. Ivanovskaya MG, Gottikh MB, Shabarova ZA, Prokofiev MA (1987) Active oligonucleotide esters - novel type of phosphorylating agents in aqueous medium. Doklady Academii Nauk USSR 293:477-481
4. Farid FC Kan YW (1989) Detection of specific DNA sequences by fluorescence amplification: A color complementation assay. Proc Natl Acad Sci USA 86:9178-9182
5. Lebedeva IV, Ivanovskaya MG, Fedorov AN, Limborskaya SA, Shabarova ZA (1994) New method of non-radioactive labeling of oligonucleotides and their use as allele-specific probes for b-thalassemic diagnosis. Molecularnaya Biologya 4:796-804

# P.C.R. AMPLIFICATION OF D.N.A. FROM AMNIOTIC FLUID IN A PATERNITY STUDY FOLLOWING A RAPE

Jose A. LORENTE M.D.,Ph.D, Miguel LORENTE M.D., Ph.D.,
J. Carlos ALVAREZ B.S. & Enrique VILLANUEVA M.D.,Ph.D.

Department of Legal Medicine,University of Granada,
Av. Madrid 11 - 18012 - Granada, Spain

## INTRODUCTION

In June 1993, a 18-year old woman was raped and became pregnant. She was under psychiatric treatment because of some schizophrenic disorders associated with mental retardartion (IQ = 55). She was living with her family (parents, one brother, one sister and two maternal uncles), but nobody realized that she was pregnant until the begining of the fourth month. According to the Spanish Penal Law, this was a rape case; among other cases, having sexual intercourse with a woman who cannot give valid consent is classified as "rape".

We were requested to perform a paternity investigation by using amniotic fluid, that was taken at the begining of the fourth month of pregnancy.

## MATERIALS & METHODS

- 4 ml of amniotic fluid obtained throw amniocentesis.
- 3 ml of peripheral blood from the mother.
- 3 ml each of peripheral blood from the four suspects, as follows: Uncle #1 (brother of victim's mother). Uncle #2 (brother of victim's mother). Brother and Father.

D.N.A. was extracted with phenol:chloroform (organic extraction) and quantitated by slot-blot.

Because of the small amount of genetic material obtained from the amniotic fluid, PCR was considered as the only technical approach. Five different loci were amplified: HLA-DQA1, D1S80, HUMTH01, HUMVWA and D21S11.

## RESULTS AND DISCUSSION

Results are shown in the table at the next page. According to these results,

Uuncle #1 was excluded with HUMTH01, D21S11 and VWA; Uncle 2 was excluded with D1S80, D21S11 and VWA; her brother was excluded with HUMTH01 and VWA, and finally her father was excluded with HUMTH01 and VWA.

| | HLA-DQx | D1S80 | HUMTH01 | D21S11 | VWA |
|---|---|---|---|---|---|
| VICTIM | 1.2,4 | 21,24 | 6,7 | 6,6 | 14,14 |
| FETUS | 1.2,4 | 18,24 | 6,6 | 6,8 | 14,15 |
| UNCLE #1 | 1.2,1.3 | 18,29 | 7,9 | 5,6 | 16,17 |
| UNCLE #2 | 1.3,4 | 21,29 | 6,9 | 5,6 | 17,18 |
| BROTHER | 1.3,4 | 21,24 | 7,9 | 4,6 | 14,15 |
| FATHER | 4,4 | 24,24 | 7,7 | 4,6 | 14,15 |

Amplification of all loci gave good results. This is logical considering the sources of DNA. There was no contamination and no degradation.

The overall results, as seen in this table, excluded all the suspects at least in two loci. This case was initially very difficult because all the suspects were relatives of the mother and they could have shared some of the alleles.

Some results warrant further emphasis. For instance, the locus *D21S11* excludes ALL THE SUSPECTS, while the high polymorphic *HLA-DQx*, DOES NOT EXCLUDE any suspect.

*D1S80* excludes only one suspect out of four, probably because these alleles that they all have are the most common in Caucasian populations (#18, #21, #24).

*HUMTH01* excludes all but one of the suspects and *HUMVWA* excludes two out of four.

Of course, the victim and her brother share at least one allele at each locus, which comes from one of the another suspects (father).

In conclusion, many cases, especially in criminalistics, will be able to be excluded by using appropiate loci. Analysis must include at least 4 loci. Two of them should be STRs.

**REFERENCES**


Lorente JA, Lorente M, Budowle B, Villanueva E (1992) Analysis of the HLA-DQx allele frequencies in the Spanish population. Proceedings of the III Symposium on Human Identification. Promega Corporation.

Lorente JA, Lorente M, Budowle B, Wilson MR, Villanueva E Analysis of the HUMTH01 allele frequencies in the Spanish population. (1994) J For Sci 39: 1270-1274

Lorente JA, Lorente M, Budowle B Wislon MR, Villanueva E Analysis of the Short Tandem Repeat (STR) HUMVWA in the Spanish population. (1994) Forensic Sci Int 65: 169-175

Sharma V, and Litt M. Tetranucleotide repeat polymorphism at the D21S11 locus (1992) Hum Mol Gen, 1: 67

# P.C.R. GENERATED ALLELE FREQUENCIES IN THE SPANISH POPULATION

Miguel LORENTE[1] M.D.,Ph.D., Jose A. LORENTE[1] M.D.,Ph.D, Bruce BUDOWLE[2] Ph.D., J.C. ALVAREZ[1] B.S., Mark R. WILSON[2] M.S. & E. VILLANUEVA[1] M.D.,Ph.D.

1) Department of Legal Medicine. University of Granada.
Av. Madrid 11 - 18012 Granada, Spain
2) Forensic Science Research. Laboratory Division, FBI Academy.
Quantico, VA 22135, USA

## INTRODUCTION

Amplification by polymerase chain reaction (PCR) and subsequent electrophoresis of the amplified products has become a useful approach for typing variable number of tandem repeats (VNTR) loci. One of these STR loci, called *M.B.P. (Mielin Basic Protein)* [3], chromosomal location 18q23-pter, is rather polimorphic and could be robust enough for forensic analysis. This locus is peculiar because two intron polymorphisms are simultaneously amplified (called Locus A and Locus B) using one pair of primers.

In any case, for M.B.P. to be useful for forensic identity testing, some population data are desirable. This poster describes frequency data of the alleles of the **Locus B** of the **M.B.P. (MBP-B)** from a Spanish sample population.

*Population:* 120 unrelated Spanish Caucasians from Andalucía (southern Spain).

*DNA isolation:* organic extraction.

*DNA quantitation:* slot-blot + probe D17Z1

*Primer sequences:* 5'- GCA CCT CGT GAA TTA CAA TC-3'
5'- ATT TAC CTA CCT GTT CAT CC-3'

*ANALYTICAL CONDITIONS*

**1. PCR reaction (final volume: 50 $\mu$l)**

5 ng DNA, 1 $\mu$l dNTPs each (0.2 $\mu$M concentration each), 5 $\mu$l 10X Taq polymerase buffer, 1 $\mu$l Primer A (from 20 $\mu$M stock), 1 $\mu$l Primer B (from 20 $\mu$M stock), 0.5 $\mu$l Taq polymerase (2.5 UI), Qs $H_20$ to 50 $\mu$l

**2. Thermal Cycler (Perkin Elmer 9600)**

[95°C x 30 sec + 64°C x 30 sec. + 72°C x 30 sec.] x 27 cycles

**3. Gel Conditions:**

Discontinuous horizontal polyacrylamide gel (8.5%T, 3.5% C , PDA as cross-linker), 60 mM Tris-formate pH 9.0. Electrode Buffer: 0.28 M Tris-borate, pH 9.0
5 $\mu$l of PCR-product were placed on fiber glass application tabs at 1 cm from the cathode.

**4. Electrophoresis:**
Settings: 600 V - 20 mA - 10 W - Temp. 15°C

## RESULTS AND DISCUSSION

Allele numbers at the Locus B were assigned after comparison with an allelic ladder and designated from allele #1 to #6.

Allele frequencies obtained in our sample of 120 unrelated Spanish Caucasians are shown in Figure 1. We observed 5 different alleles, with frequencies ranging from 0.305 (allele #5) to 0.052 (allele #3). There were 3 common alleles (#1, 5, & 6) with frequencies over 0.25, and 3 uncommon alleles (#3 & 4) with frequencies under 0.05. Allele #2 was not observed in our population sample. The observed heterozygosity was 85.50%

The genotype distribution observed in this sample of the Spanish gene pool met Hardy-Weinberg expectations as judged by three currently employed test criteria. First, the test based on total number of heterozygotes and homozygotes gives a chi-square value of 0.36 with 1 df, which is not significant ( $P < 0.54$). Second, comparison of the frequencies of each specific genotypes with their expectations under the Hardy-Weinberg assumptions yields a log likelihood ratio of 32.467, which is also statistically not significant ( $P = 0.255$).

Third, Guo and Thompson's Exact Test with 1.000 replication of permutation of alleles yields an empirical probability of 0.115, greater than 0.05 (at which level we would have concluded a departure from the Hardy-Weinberg expectations).

In ***conclusion***, the Locus B of the **MBP** appears to be an informative genetic marker for identity testing purposes in the Spanish population. Since as little as 1 ng of human genomic DNA is required for PCR, it would appear that sensitivity of detection will not be a serious concern for typing this locus.

## REFERENCES

Polymeropoulos MH, Xiao H, Merrill CR (1992) Tetranucleotide repeat polymorphism at the human myelin basic protein gene (MBP). Human Molecular Genetics 1:658

Möller A, Wiegand P, Grüschow C, Seuchter SA, Baur MP, Brinkmann B (1994) Population data and forensic efficiency values for the STR systems HumVWA, HumMBP and HumFABP Int J Legal Med 106:183-189

Nei M (1978) Estimation of average heterozyfosity and genetic distance from small number of individuals. Genetics 89:583-590.

Weir BS (1992) Independence of VNTR alleles defined by fixed bins. Genetics 130:873-887.

Guo SW, Thompson EA (1992) Performing the exact test of Hardy-Weinberg proportion for multiple alleles. Biometrics 48:361-372

# POSITIVE IDENTIFICATION OF A COUPLE OF FLOOD VICTIMS BY AUTOPSY DATA AND PCR INVESTIGATION

Armando MANNUCCI PhD, Lucia CASARINO PhD, Gianlorenzo BRUNI MD, Andrea LOMI MD and Francesco DE STEFANO MD
*Istituto di Medicina Legale e delle Assicurazioni dell' Università di Genova - Via De Toni 12 - 16132 GENOVA - ITALY*

In September 93, the 23rd, four people disappeared because of a flood in Genoa. Among them an elderly couple was wiped away from his house.

Four days later, on the 27th, a floating body was found some hundred meters from the coastline. At the external examination, the body was of a decomposed, partially skeletonized, white male. Maxillary alveoli were destroyed and the lower jaw was absent. The right arm was missing, disarticulated at the shoulder joint; the left arm was partially skeletonized. Both legs were cut off below the knees and a xiphoid-ombelical scar was present. A total body X-ray examination was performed but only traumatic lesions and no useful data for identification were found. No identification by dental records was possible, due to the absence of teeth, mandibula and maxillary alveoli.

The autopsy was performed, and showed mild to severe decomposition of the internal organs, a partial gastrectomy and a small nodular prostate gland.

All these data were consistent with the medical history of the man of the elderly couple, who received surgery in the past (partial gastrectomy due to gastric ulcer and trans-urethral prostatectomy due to adenoma of the prostate gland), but positive identification was not possible by mean of morphological data.

As paraffin embedded tissue from the trans-urethral prostatectomy was supplied from the hospital where the surgery was performed, our laboratory was charged for attempting DNA identification. One of the ileopsoas muscle was sampled at the autopsy table and DNA extracted by employing the usual protocols (1). Extraction from the paraffin embedded gland was performed employing the procedure described by Goelz et al. published protocol (2). Quality of the extracted DNA was tested by 0.8% agarose gel, quantification was obtained fluorometrically by TKO 100 Mini Fluorimeter with Hoechts dye.

On October 10th 1993, another decomposed body of a white elderly female was found under a layer of debris at the outlet of the river which wiped away the couple. At the external examination, a surgical thyroidectomy scar was noted. At the autopsy, severe decomposition and multiple fractures were observed and the thyroid was absent. No clinical data were available and the son gave no confidence in identification by visual data, so a sample of ileopsoas muscle was taken and DNA extracted for furher examination. As circumstances indicated that body pertained to the woman of the elderly couple, their son was called and blood sampled in order to perform a maternity test, combining data from the DNA profile of the two bodies, the paraffin embedded prostate and the putative sibling. All the extractions were carried out simultaneously.

We amplified a total of 11 loci, using about 10 ng of DNA for each reaction. Bovine Serum Albumine was added to sample extracted from paraffin embedded tissue to enhance results (3). Commercial kits from Perkin Elmer were used for D1S80, HLA-DQA1 and Polymarker. Published sets of primers and conditions were applied for HUMFES/FPS, HUMCD4, HUMTH01 and ApoB (4; 5; 6; 7). Amplification products were analised by reverse dot-blot for Polymarker and HLA-DQA1, GeneAmp detection gel for D1S80, 8% denaturing polyacrilamide denatutring gel (PAGE) for HUMTH01, 8% PAGE for HUMCD4, 12% PAGE for HUMFES/FPS and 2% agarose gel for ApoB.

Table 1 shows the genotype profile matched for the eleven examined loci (D1S80, APOB, GYPA, GC, HLA-DQA1, D7S8, HBGG, HUMTH01, HUMCD4, HUMFES/FPS, LDLR) between the white male body and the paraffin embedded gland. The final casual genotype sharing was calculated as $1.46x10^{-8}$.

So, after the identification of the man, his profile, the one from his son and from the female body were matched to achieve the woman identification. No exclusions were found and casual allelic sharing in maternity identification was computed as $1.15x10^{-4}$.

In this way, by crossing data from autopsy and circumstances, the laboratory carried out the positive identification of two of the victims of the flood by DNA profiling. One time more, this example shows that DNA is a powerful tool to achieve aims in forensic investigations conceirning personal identity. Vice versa, DNA results need correlate informations from circumstances and post mortem examination for giving useful and certain answers to proposed questions.

**REFERENCES**

1) Sambrook, Fritsch, Maniatis (1989) Molecular Cloning, Cold Spring Laboratory Press. 3:E3-E4.
2) Goelz S.E., Hamilton S.R., Vogelstein B. (1985) Purification of DNA from formaldehyde fixed and paraffin embedded human tissue. Biochem. Biophys. Res. Comm.130, 1: 118-126.
3) Hochmeister M.N., Budowle B., Jung J., Borer U.V., Comey C.T., Dirnhofer (1991) PCR-based typing of DNA extracted from cigarette butts. Int. J. Leg. Med. 104:229-233.
4) Polymeropoulos M.H., Rath D.S., Xiao H., Merril C.R.. (1991) Tetranucleotide repeat polymorfism at the human c- fes/fps proto-oncogene (FES). NAR vol 19 n 14: 4018.
5) Edwards M.C., Clemens P.R., Tristan M., Pizzuti A., Gibbs R.A. (1991) Pentanucleotide repeat lenght polymorphism at the Human CD4 locus. NAR vol 19 n 17: 4791.
6) Polymeropoulos M.H., Xiao H., Rath D.S., Merril C.R. (1991) Tetranucleotide repeat polymorfism at the human tyrosine hydroxilase gene (TH). NAR vol 19 n 13: 3753.
7) Boerwinkle E., Xiong W., Fourest E., Chan L. (1989) Rapid typing of tandemly repeated hypervariable loci by the polymerase chain reaction: Application to the apolipoprotein B 3' hypervariable region. Proc. Natl. Acad. Sci. USA 86: 212-216.

| System | MALE BODY | P.E. | SIBLING | A.M. |
|---|---|---|---|---|
| D1S80 | T24/T24 | T24/T24 | T24/T24 | T24/T24 |
| ApoB | 37/37 | 37/37 | 37/37 | 37/37 |
| GYPA | B/B | B/B | B/B | A/B |
| GC | A/C | A/C | A/A | A/B |
| HLA-DQA1 | 1.2/3 | 1.2/3 | 1.2 | -/- |
| D7S8 | A/B | A/B | A/B | B/B |
| HBGG | A/B | A/B | B/B | B/B |
| HUMTH01 | 9.3/9.3 | 9.3/9.3 | 9.3/9.3 | 9.3/9 |
| HUMCD4 | 10/5 | 10/5 | 10/5 | 10/6 |
| HUMFES/FPS | 12/11 | 12/11 | 11/11 | 12/11 |
| LDLR | A/B | A/B | A/B | A/B |

**Table**

INDIVIDUAL IDENTIFICATION OF THE MALE BODY BY DIRECT MATCH TO THE PARAFFIN EMBEDDED GLAND AND MATERNITY INDICATION OF THE FEMALE BODY.

P.E. = PARAFFIN EMBEDDED PROSTATIC GLAND; A.M. = ALLEGED MOTHER.

CASUAL GENOTYPE SHARING IN MALE BODY-PARAFFIN EMBEDDED TISSUE IDENTITY $1.46 \times 10^{-8}$

CASUAL ALLELIC SHARING IN MATERNITY IDENTIFICATION $1.027 \times 10^{-4}$

# AMPLIFIED FRAGMENT LENGTH POLYMORPHISM ANALYSIS OF THE VNTR LOCUS D1S80 IN ASTURIAS (NORTH-WEST SPAIN).

MARTINEZ-JARRETA B, ALMUZARA I, *HINOJAL R, CASTELLANO M

LABORATORIO DE MEDICINA LEGAL Y TOXICOLOGIA. UNIDAD DOCENTE DE MEDICINA LEGAL Y TOXICOLOGIA. FACULTAD DE MEDICINA. ZARAGOZA. ESPAÑA.
*CATEDRA DE MEDICINA LEGAL Y TOXICOLOGIA. FACULTAD DE MEDICINA. OVIEDO. ESPAÑA.

## INTRODUCTION

Analysis of variable number of tandem repeats (VNTR) loci is widely used for individualization at the DNA level in forensic testing (1).The VNTR locus D1S80 was first isolated and identified by Nakamura et al (2) and successfully amplified by the PCR (3).This is probably one of the most commonly used PCR systems in forensic laboratories and so more population data are available (4, 5, 6, 7, 8, 9, 10, 11).

In the present study, the distribution of D1S80 alleles in the Asturian population was examined and compared with allelic data from other ethnic groups.

## MATERIAL AND METHODS

***Samples:****Whole blood was collected in EDTA tubes by venipuncture from healthy unrelated individuals living in Asturias and DNA was extracted by the Chelex method suggested by Walsh et al .[12).*

***Amplification:*** *Amplification of D1S80 was performed with the following primers sequences (3) and conditions:*

*5' GAAACTGGCCTCCAAACACTGCCCGCCG 3' and 5' GTCTTGTTGGAGATGCACGTGCCCCTTGC 3'. Temperature: 94/65/72 °C; Time: 1 / 1 / 1 min; Cycles: 30 (After the last cycle and additional extension at 72°C for 10 min was performed). Each amplified sample contained 1-10 ng DNA, 10 mM Tris-HCl (pH 8.3), 50 mM KCl, 1,5 mM $MgCl_2$, 0,01% gelatin, 2.5 units of Amplitaq DNA Polymerase, 1 μM of each primer and 200 μM of each dNTP, in a total volume of 50 μl.*

***Typing:****D1S80 (MCT 118) was performed using Phast-gels 10-15 (Pharmacia LKB) and silver staining with the conditions described by Barros et al. (13).*

## RESULTS AND DISCUSSION

The distribution of genotypes for D1S80 in a population sample of 178 unrelated individuals living in Asturias (N-W Spain) are shown in Table 1 and D1S80 allele frequencies in Table 2. 21 different alleles were distinguished, ranging between 14 and 37 repeats. The alleles: 24 (f=0,3824) and 18 (f=0,2390) were the most common in our sample. Consequently, the most common genotypes observed were the combinations of these 2 alleles, e.g., 18-18 (f: 0,0786); 18-24 (f: 0,1685); and 24-24 (f: 0,1460). All other alleles showed frequences of less than 0,100.

Because of the relatively small population sample, a reliable estimation of derivations from the Hardy-Weinberg equilibrium is not possible using each separate allele. Alleles were therefore categorized into 4 allele groups and calculations were carried out using these models. The $\chi^2$ value showed no significant deviation between expected and observed values (Table 3).Other statistic of genetic and medico-legal interest : the discrimination power (DP) (0,93) and the allelic diversity (h) (0,79) were the similitar to the other populations studied (9). Comparative studies were carried out with other populations studied up to date for D1S80 (Fig.1). No significant differences were observed between the population of Asturias and Portugal ($\chi^2$ = 11,10; p= 0,8511) (9), Central Spain ($\chi^2$ = 3,95; p= 0,9995) (10), Galicia ($\chi^2$ = 6,602; p= 0,9881) (9), Holland ($\chi^2$ = 10,72; p= 0,8711) (6). However we found differences between our results and those reported for no-Caucasians populations as Japanese ($\chi^2$ = 34,95; p= 0,0063) (11).

**TABLE 1.** DISTRIBUTION OF D1S80 GENOTYPES

| GENOTYPE | OBSERVED N | OBSERVED % | GENOTYPE | OBSERVED N | OBSERVED % |
|---|---|---|---|---|---|
| 14 - 18 | 1 | 0,56 | 23 - 25 | 1 | 0,56 |
| 17 - 18 | 1 | 0,56 | 23 - 29 | 1 | 0,56 |
| 18 - 18 | 4 | 7,66 | 23 - 32 | 1 | 0,56 |
| 18 - 20 | 3 | 1,68 | 23 - 34 | 1 | 0,56 |
| 18 - 21 | 3 | 1,68 | 24 - 24 | 26 | 14,61 |
| 18 - 22 | 4 | 2,24 | 24 - 25 | 3 | 7,30 |
| 18 - 24 | 30 | 16,85 | 24 - 26 | 4 | 2,24 |
| 18 - 25 | 4 | 2,24 | 24 - 27 | 2 | 1,12 |
| 18 - 27 | 2 | 1,12 | 24 - 29 | 12 | 6,74 |
| 18 - 28 | 1 | 0,56 | 24 - 31 | 13 | 7,30 |
| 18 - 29 | 4 | 2,24 | 24 - 36 | 1 | 0,56 |
| 18 - 31 | 2 | 1,12 | 24 - 37 | 1 | 0,56 |
| 18 - 34 | 1 | 0,56 | 25 - 29 | 2 | 1,12 |
| 18 - 37 | 1 | 0,56 | 26 - 26 | 1 | 0,56 |
| 19 - 22 | 2 | 1,12 | 26 - 30 | 1 | 0,56 |
| 19 - 30 | 1 | 0,56 | 26 - 31 | 1 | 0,56 |
| 20 - 22 | 1 | 0,56 | 26 - 34 | 1 | 0,56 |
| 20 - 24 | 1 | 0,56 | 27 - 31 | 1 | 0,56 |
| 22 - 24 | 3 | 1,68 | 27 - 32 | 1 | 0,56 |
| 22 - 28 | 1 | 0,56 | 28 - 29 | 1 | 0,56 |
| 22 - 29 | 1 | 0,56 | 29 - 29 | 2 | 1,12 |
| 22 - 30 | 1 | 0,56 | 29 - 31 | 2 | 1,12 |
| 22 - 36 | 1 | 0,56 | 31 - 33 | 1 | 0,56 |
| 23 - 23 | 1 | 0,56 | | | |

**TABLE 2.** D1S80 ALLELE FREQUENCIES IN THE POPULATION OF ASTURIAS (N-W SPAIN).

| ALLELE (Repeat No) | FREQUENCY |
|---|---|
| 14 | 0,0028 |
| 17 | 0,0028 |
| 18 | 0,2390 |
| 19 | 0,0084 |
| 20 | 0,00225 |
| 21 | 0,0112 |
| 22 | 0,0393 |
| 23 | 0,0168 |
| 24 | 0,3824 |
| 25 | 0,0561 |
| 26 | 0,0252 |
| 27 | 0,0168 |
| 28 | 0,0084 |
| 29 | 0,0760 |
| 30 | 0,0084 |
| 31 | 0,0562 |
| 32 | 0,0056 |
| 33 | 0,0028 |
| 34 | 0,0056 |
| 36 | 0,0084 |
| 37 | 0,0056 |

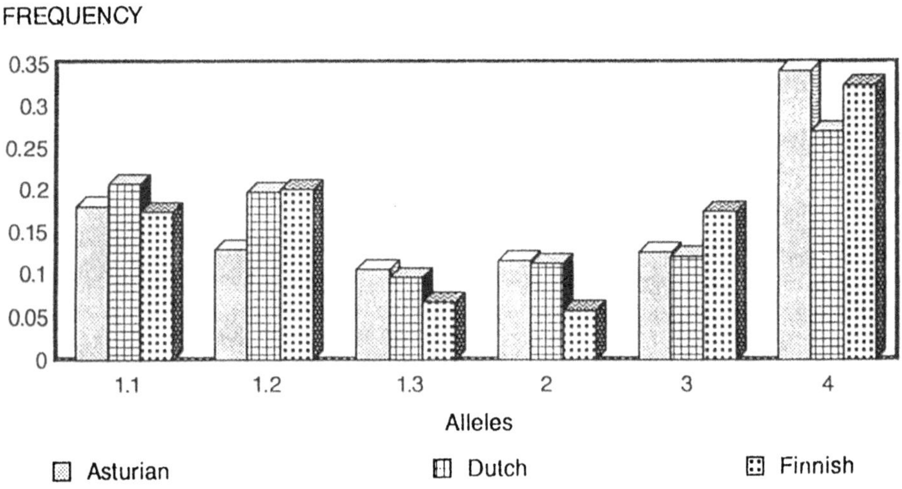


**FIG.1.Comparison of D1S80 allele frequencies in 178 unrelated individuals from Asturias with that from other populations (Dutch and Japanese).**

**TABLE 3.**CHECK FOR HARDY-WEINBERG EQUILIBRIUM

| ALLELE GROUPS | 4 ALLELE MODEL |
|---|---|
| GROUP I | ALLELES 14-23 |
| GROUP II | ALLELES 24 |
| GROUP III | ALLELES 25-29 |
| GROUP IV | ALLELES 30-27 |

| | Observed | | Expected | |
|---|---|---|---|---|
| | N | % | N | % |
| I - I | 30 | 16,85 | 20,90 | 11,74 |
| I - II | 38 | 21,35 | 46,60 | 26,20 |
| I - III | 15 | 8,43 | 22,27 | 12,51 |
| I - IV | 9 | 5,07 | 11,30 | 6,35 |
| II - II | 26 | 14,60 | 25,97 | 14,60 |
| II - III | 31 | 17,41 | 24,83 | 13,95 |
| II - IV | 15 | 8,43 | 12,60 | 7,08 |
| III - III | 6 | 3,37 | 5,93 | 3,34 |
| III - IV | 7 | 3,93 | 6,02 | 3,38 |
| IV - IV | 1 | 0,56 | 1,52 | 0,85 |
| TOTAL | 178 | 100 | 178 | 100 |
| $\chi 2$ = 10,67 | d.f. =6 | 0,2>p>0,05 | | |

**REFERENCES**


1.- Lewotin RC; Hartl DL (1991) Population genetics in forensic DNA typing. Science 254: 1745-1750

2.- Nakamura Y, Carlson M, Krapcho K, White R (1988) Isolation and mapping of a polymorphic DNA sequences pMCT 118, on chromosome 1p (D1S80). Nucleic Acids Res 16: 9364

3.- Kasai K, Nakamura Y, White R (1990) Amplification of a variable number of tandem repeats (VNTR) locus (pMCT 118) by the polymerase chain reaction and its application to forensic science. J Forensic Sci 35: 1196-1200

4.- Rand S, Puers C, Skowasch K, Wiegand P, Budowle B, Brinkmann B (1992) Population genetics and forensic efficiency data of 4 AMPFLP's. Int J Leg Med 104: 329-333

5.- Skowasch K, Wiegand P, Brinkmann B (1992) pMCT 118 (D1S80): a new allelic ladder and an improved electrophoretic separation lead to the demonstration of 28 alleles. Int J Leg Med 105: 165-168

6.- KLoosterman AD, Budowle B, Daselaar P (1993) PCR-amplification and detection of the human D1S80 VNTR locus. Int J Leg Med 105: 257-264

7.- Budowle B, Chakraborty R, Giusti AM, Eisenberg AJ, Allen RC (1991) Analysis of the VNTR locus D1S80 by the PCR followed by high-resolution PAGE. Am J Hum Genet 48: 137-144

8.- Eisenberg AJ, Maha G (1991) AMPFLP analysis in parentage testing. In: Proceedings from the Second International Symposium on Human Identification, Promega Corporation, Madison, P 129-154

9.- Lareu, MV, Muñoz I, Pestoni C, Rodriguez MS, Vide C, Carracedo A (1993) The distribution of HLA-DQA1 and D1S80 (pMCT118) alleles and genotypes in the populations of Galicia and Central Portugal. Int J Leg Med 106: 124-128

10.-Alonso A, Martin P, Albarran C, Sancho M (1993) Amplified fragment length polymorphism analyses of the VNTR locus D1S80 in Central Spain. Int J Leg Med 105: 311-314

11.- Sugiyama E, Honda K, Katsuyama Y, Uchiyama S, Tsuchikane A, Ota M, Fukushima H (1993) Allele frequency distribution of the D1S80 (pMCT118) locus polymorphism in the Japanese population by the polymerase chain reaction. Int J Leg Med 106: 111-114

12.- Walsh PS, Metzger DA, Higuchi R (1991) Chelex 100 as a medium for simple extraction of DNA for PCR-base typing from forensic material. Biotechniques 10: 506-513

13.- Barros F, Vide MC, Lareu MV, Carracedo A (1992) SDS-PAGE typing of HLA-DQA1 and pMCT118 after PCR amplification. In: Rittner CH, Schneider P(eds) Advances in Forensic Haemogenetics 4. Springer-Verlag, Berlin, Heidelberg, P 64-66

# FREQUENCY DATABASE FOR THE D2S44 LOCUS USING DIG-LABELED YNH24 PROBE IN THE BASQUE COUNTRY POPULATION

Fernández-Fernández I., Castro A., Alonso S., Gómez de Cedrón M., Barbero C., García-Orad A., Tamayo G., M. de Pancorbo M.

Dpto. de Biología Celular e Instituto Vasco de Criminología. Universidad del País Vasco. 48940. Leioa, Bizkaia. SPAIN.

## INTRODUCTION

Locus D2S44 shows a VNTR polymorphism whose heterozygosity and mendelian inheritance make it a suitable tool for identity and relationship purposes (Nakamura et al., 1987). So, the objective of this work was to obtain the frequency distribution of this locus, as well as some parameters of interest in Legal Medicine such as the "A Priori Probability of Exclusion" and "Index of Discrimination", to apply this system in the Basque Country casework.

## MATERIALS AND METHODS

The population study was based on a sample of 200 unrelated individuals, residing in the Basque Country. Aliquots of 700µl of whole blood were extracted by the phenol-cloroform-isoamylalcohol (25:24:1) method.

The combination Hinf I/ YNH24 was used in this work. The probe was labelled by random priming with DIG-11-dUTP and further purified by a Sephadex G-50 column. The efficiency of the labelling method was estimated through an slot blot containing 3ng, 30pg and 300pg of DIG-labelled control pBR328 as well as 1.5 ng of DIG-labelled YNH24.

Varying amounts (5, 2.5 and 1.5 µg) of human DNA from 6 unrelated individuals were digested with 10 units/µg of Hinf I and loaded onto 0.7% agarose gels, which were run with TBE 1X as buffer and 3 V/cm during the time required for the 2.3 Kb Lambda Hind III band to migrate 15 cm from the origin.

Fragments were transferred onto positively charged membranes using the Southern method. Membranes were prehybridized at 50°C for 45 min in 0.5 M $Na_2HPO_4$ pH 7.2, 1% SDS, and 2% ICI blocking reagent. Hybridization was carried out in 0.04 ml/cm$^2$ of prehybridization solution and 8 ng of DIG-labelled YNH24 probe/ml at 62°C overnight. In order to remove an excess of the probe, membranes were washed twice in 0.01 M $Na_2HPO_4$ pH 7.2 and 0.1% SDS at 50°C for 10 min, followed by 2 washes in 0.1 M maleic acid, 0.15 M NaCl, pH 7.5 for 5 min at RT. Chemiluminescent detection was carried out as recommended by Boehringer Mannheim, but the blocking reagent was increased to 5%.

Fragments size was estimated following Elder and Southern's reciprocal method (Elder and Southern, 1983), using as reference the size marker NICE DNA Analysis Ladder (BRL) in combination with the DIG labeled probe (BRL DNA Analysis system).

To obtain the frequency distribution, fragment sizes were grouped in fixed bins based on the K562 control cell line standard deviations, which were previously calculated from 35 gels using MS1, MS31, MS43A and YNH24 probes.

## RESULTS AND DISCUSSION

The population analyzed displays a bimodal allele frequency distribution, ranging in size from 2.1 to 7.8 Kb, distributed in 32 bins, with two peaks at 2.7 and 4 Kb (Fig. 1), which shows great similarity to other Caucasian population distributions. (Domenici et al., 1992; Valverde et al., 1992).

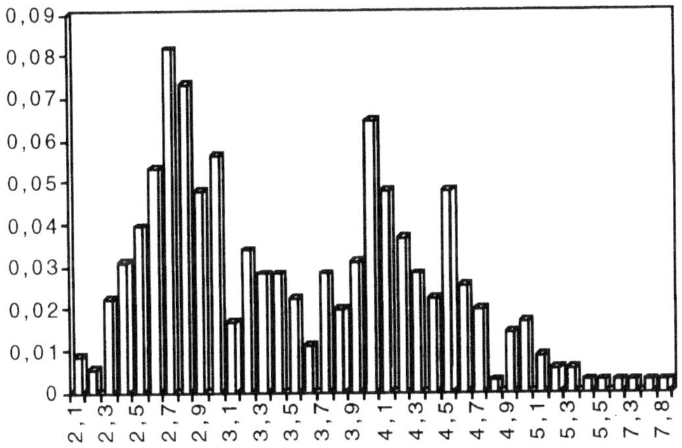


Fig 1. Allele frequency distribution for D2S44 in The Basque Country population.

The sample heterozygosity was estimated by the method of Nei (1978) as 0.96±0.002. No mutations were observed in 25 mother-child pairs, which indicates that the mutation rate per gamete may be lower than 0.04. Some calculated parameters of interest in Legal Medicine were PEX, the "A Priori Probability of Exclusion" (Smouse et. al. 1986), 0.914 and ID, the "Index of Discrimination" (Wong et al., 1987), 0.032. The great variability detected with this system, its relatively low mutation rate, and its conservative allele frequency distribution, at least in Caucasian populations, seem to validate this locus for paternity and forensic casework.

**LITERATURE**

Domenici R, Spinetti I, Nardone M, Pistello N, Ceccherini-Nelli L (1992) Distribution of variable number of tandem repeats (VNTR) DNA polymorphism at D2S44 locus in Tuscany (Italy). In: Rittner C, Schneider PM (eds) Advances in Forensic Haemogenetics, vol 4. Springer-Verlag, Berlin Heidelberg, pp 243-245

Elder JK, Southern EM (1983) Measurement of DNA fragment length by gel electrophoresis. Anal. Biochem. 128:227-231

Nakamura Y, Leppert M, O`Connell P, Wolff R, Holm T, Culver M, et al. (1987) Variable number of tandem repeats (VNTR) markers for human gene mapping. Science 235:1616-1622

Nei M. (1978) Estimation of average heterozygosity and genetic distance from a small number of individuals. Genetics 89:583-590

Smouse PE, Chakraborty R (1986) The use of restriction fragment length polymorphisms in paternity analysis. Am. J. Hum. Genet. 38:918-939

Valverde E, Cabrero C, Diez A, Carracedo A, Borras T (1992) Allele frequency in the population of Spain using several single locus probes. In: Rittner C, Schneider PM (eds) Advances in Forensic Haemogenetics, vol 4. Springer-Verlag, Berlin Heidelberg, pp 187-189

Wong Z, Wilson V, Patel I, Povey S, Jeffreys AJ (1987) Characterization of a panel of highly variable minisatellites cloned from human DNA. Ann. Hum. Genet. 51:269-288

# INVESTIGATION OF D1S80 VNTR LOCUS IN A POLISH POPULATION

**Danuta Miścicka-Śliwka, Anna Syroczyńska, Karol Śliwka and Jarosław A. Berent**

**Forensic Medicine Institute, The Ludwik Rydygier's University School of Medical Sciences in Bydgoszcz, ul. Skłodowskiej-Curie 9, 85-094 Bydgoszcz, Poland**
**tel/fax ++48 52 41 12 49**

**Key words**
DNA Polymorphism, VNTR, AMPFLP, D1S80, PCR, Population Genetics, Polish Population

**Introduction**

The D1S80 locus contains repetitive DNA sequences that are arranged as tandem repeat units (VNTR). The D1S80 tandem repeat unit defined by Nakamura et al. [4] is 16 base pairs in length repeated from 14 to over 41 times for each allele. The D1S80 locus has been localized to the distal end of chromosome 1p and shows codominant autosomal segregation [1-5].

The aim of this paper was to estimate frequencies and distribution of genotypes in a population sample from the Pomerania-Kujawy region of Poland.

**Materials and methods**

Blood samples were obtained from 100 unrelated persons and 26 mother-child pairs. DNA for PCR analysis was isolated from blood by phenol-chloroform extraction. The extracts were normalized to a concentration of 1 ng/µl. Amplification of D1S80 was achieved using the AmpliFLP D1S80 Amplification Kit (Perkin-Elmer) and GeneAmp PCR System 9600 (Perkin-Elmer) and manufacturers procedure. PCR products and the allelic ladder consisting of 15 or 27 D1S80 alleles were separated by electrophoresis in a discontinuous buffer system using ultra thin layer polyacrylamide gels (12%T, 3%C) with DATD as a crosslinker. Gels containing 60 mM Tris formate buffer pH 9.0 were cast using flap technique. The 2% agarose plugs containing 0.01% bromophenol blue were used as a visual marker. The trailing ion was 0.28 M Tris-borate buffer pH 9.0. The distance between the electrodes was 16 cm. A sample of 5 µl of the PCR mixture was applied to the gel surface 1 cm from the cathode. Electrophoresis was performed on the 2117 Multiphor unit (LKB) at constant temperature of 10 °C and constant current 15 mA. Following electrophoresis the gels were stained with silver [1].

**Results and discussion**

Fig. 1 shows the amplified fragment length polymorphism (AMP-FLP) of D1S80. Each band of the allelic ladder was completely separated. Allele determination was carried out by comparision with an allelic ladder. The distribution of D1S80 genotypes is shown in table 1. The allele frequencies were calculated from the number of each genotype (table 2). The observed genotypes were in agreement with the expected genotypes and confirmed the Hardy-Weinberg's equilibrium expectation. A qualitative comparision between different populations showed that allele frequencies were quite similar.

Analyse of child-mother pairs shows that in all cases a maternal allele was found in the phenotype of the child. No mutations were observed. Samples from mother and her child were analyzed in neighbouring lanes on the same gel and the shared bands always showed the same migration distance.

**Conclusion**

A genomic locus D1S80 determination by DNA amplification is a powerful tool for application in forensic case analysis.

Table 1. DISTRIBUTION OF D1S80 GENOTYPES IN POLISH POPULATION

| Genotype D1S80 | Observed (expected) number | Frequency |
|---|---|---|
| 18/18 | 10 (4.20) | 0.10 |
| 18/21 | 1 (0.41) | 0.01 |
| 18/22 | 1 (0.62) | 0.01 |
| 18/24 | 9 (11.89) | 0.09 |
| 18/25 | 4 (4.31) | 0.04 |
| 18/26 | 1 (0.82) | 0.01 |
| 18/30 | 1 (1.44) | 0.01 |
| 18/31 | 2 (2.87) | 0.02 |
| 18/34 | 1 (0.21) | 0.01 |
| 18/37 | 1 (0.41) | 0.01 |
| 19/21 | 1 (0.03) | 0.01 |
| 19/24 | 1 (0.87) | 0.01 |
| 19/31 | 1 (0.21) | 0.01 |
| 20/24 | 1 (1.16) | 0.01 |
| 20/27 | 1 (0.14) | 0.01 |
| 20/29 | 1 (0.18) | 0.01 |
| 20/32 | 1 (0.14) | 0.01 |
| 22/24 | 1 (0.87) | 0.01 |
| 22/27 | 1 (0.11) | 0.01 |
| 23/23 | 1 (0.16) | 0.01 |
| 23/27 | 1 (0.28) | 0.01 |
| 23/28 | 1 (0.16) | 0.01 |
| 23/29 | 2 (0.36) | 0.02 |
| 23/31 | 1 (0.56) | 0.01 |
| 23/33 | 1 (0.04) | 0.01 |
| 24/24 | 10 (8.41) | 0.10 |
| 24/25 | 7 (6.09) | 0.07 |
| 24/26 | 1 (1.16) | 0.01 |
| 24/28 | 1 (1.16) | 0.01 |
| 24/29 | 2 (2.61) | 0.02 |
| 24/30 | 6 (2.03) | 0.06 |
| 24/31 | 6 (4.06) | 0.06 |
| 24/36 | 2 (0.87) | 0.02 |
| 24/30 | 1 (0.29) | 0.01 |
| 25/25 | 2 (1.10) | 0.02 |
| 25/27 | 2 (0.74) | 0.02 |
| 25/28 | 1 (0.42) | 0.01 |
| 25/31 | 1 (1.47) | 0.01 |
| 25/32 | 2 (0.74) | 0.02 |
| 26/28 | 1 (0.08) | 0.01 |
| 26/36 | 1 (0.06) | 0.01 |
| 27/32 | 1 (0.25) | 0.01 |
| 27/37 | 1 (0.07) | 0.01 |
| 29/31 | 2 (0.63) | 0.02 |
| 29/32 | 2 (0.32) | 0.02 |
| 31/32 | 1 (0.49) | 0.01 |

Hardy-Weinberg equilibrium expectation:
$chi^2 = 7.6$ ( df=3) $p > 0.05$
Heterozygosity: 77%
Expected heterozygosity: 79% +/- 3%
Power of discrimination (PD): 0.9516

Table 2. D1S80 ALLELE FREQUENCIES IN POLISH POPULATION.

| Allele | Number | Frequency |
|---|---|---|
| 18 | 41 | 0.205 |
| 19 | 3 | 0.015 |
| 20 | 4 | 0.020 |
| 21 | 2 | 0.010 |
| 22 | 3 | 0.015 |
| 23 | 8 | 0.040 |
| 24 | 58 | 0.290 |
| 25 | 21 | 0.105 |
| 26 | 4 | 0.020 |
| 27 | 7 | 0.035 |
| 28 | 4 | 0.020 |
| 29 | 9 | 0.045 |
| 30 | 7 | 0.035 |
| 31 | 14 | 0.070 |
| 32 | 7 | 0.035 |
| 33 | 1 | 0.005 |
| 34 | 1 | 0.005 |
| 36 | 3 | 0.015 |
| 37 | 2 | 0.010 |
| 40 | 1 | 0.005 |

Alleles not observed were omitted from the table

Figure 1. Phenotypes of D1S80

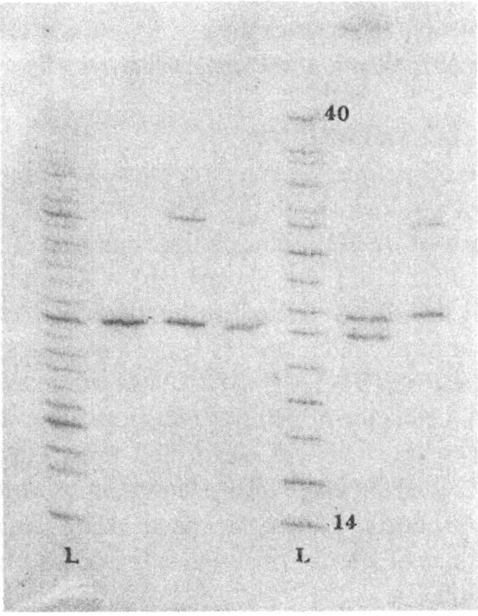


## References

1. Allen RC, Graves G and Budowle B (1989) Polymerase chain reaction amplification products separated on rehydratable polyacrylamide gels and stained with silver. Biotechniques 7:736-744
2. Kasai K, Nakamura Y and White R (1990) Amplification of variable number tandem repeats (VNTR) locus (pMCT 118) by the polymerase chain reaction (PCR) and its application to forensic science. J Forensic Sci 35:1196-1200
3. Kloosterman AD, Budowle B and Daselaar P (1993) PCR-amplification and detection of the human D1S80 VNTR locus. Amplification conditions, population genetics and application in forensic analysis. Int J Leg Med 105:257-264
4. Nakamura Y, Carlson M, Krapcho K and White R (1988) Isolation and mapping of polymorphic DNA sequence (pMCT 118) on chromosome 1p (D1S80). Nucl Acids Res 16:9364
5. Thymann M, Neuermann LJ, Masumba G, Irgens-Moller L and Morling N (1993) Analysis of the locus D1S80 by amplified fragment length polymorphism technique (AMP-FLP). Frequency distribution in Danes. Intra and inter labolatory reproducibility of the technique. Forensic Sci Int 60:47-56

# USEFULNESS OF D1S80 SYSTEM IN PATERNITY INVESTIGATION

Danuta Miścicka-Śliwka, Karol Śliwka, Anna Syroczyńska and Jarosław A. Berent

Forensic Medicine Institute, The Ludwik Rydygier's University School of Medical Sciences in Bydgoszcz, ul. Skłodowskiej-Curie 9, 85-094 Bydgoszcz, Poland
tel/fax ++48 52 41 12 49

**Key words**
DNA, VNTR, D1S80, paternity

**Introduction**

Before the developement of DNA polymorphism the most cases of disputed paternity were solved by testing blood groups, serum proteins, erythrocyte enzymes and additionally HLA. Nevertheless in cases of only one system exclusion, especially homozygotic ones, or silent genes the further extension of surveys, family investigations or finally investigation of the enzyme activity has been required. Those cases have been suggested by some authors to be resolved using the DNA technique [4,7,8,10]. Since Nakamura et al. [9] had reported the polymorphic region - VNTR locus D1S80 and Kasai et al. [3] had sequenced it the new approach caused by the introduction of D1S80 into disputed paternity investigation has been used.

It seemed to be interesting to see what effect the introduction of the VNTR D1S80 has on the practical application to forensic surveys of paternity testing.

**Materials and methods**

The 38 paternity cases investigated in our Institute during 1993/1994 have been analysed. During serological surveys AB0, MN, RhCcDEe, Kell, Gm, Hp and acid phospatase (ACP), esterase D (ESD), phosphoglucomutase 1 (PGM1), glyoxalase I (GLOI), group specific component (GC) and phosphoglycolate phosphatase (PGP) were studied in the routine way. PGM1 and GC were isoelectrophocused. The probability of paternity (P) was calculated by the method of Szczotka et al. [11] in all the cases without exclusion of the disputed man.

Afterwards VNTR D1S80 investigation was performed. DNA was isolated from blood using phenol-chloroform method with proteinase K according to the protocol of Kunkel et al. [5]. The amplification was performed using AmpliFLP D1S80 Amplification Kit and GeneAmp PCR System 9600 (Perkin Elmer Cetus) and manufacturer's procedure with small alterations. PCR products were separated using high-resolution PAGE technique according to the procedure of Kloosterman et al. [6] with some modifications. The gels were stained with silver after Allen et al. [1].

**Results and discussion**

There were 19 exclusions from the 38 cases after serological examination, 8 of them in two and more systems and 11 of them in only one system. The 6 cases from the group of single exclusion were based on opposite homozygosity.

In the remaining cases no exclusion was observed. In this group the probability of paternity for 14 cases was $P>0.91$ and for 5 cases $P<0.90$. Only 1 exclusion in D1S80 occurred. The detailed results are showed in Tab. 1 and Tab. 2. The presented results show the practical meaning of VNTR D1S80 system, which is equal to the full set of serological investigation (called 1$^{st}$ degree serological expertise).

**Table 1.** Analysis of D1S80 after serological examination without exclusion.

| | Probability of paternity (P) | n | D1S80 exclusion | D1S80 no exclusion |
|---|---|---|---|---|
| no exclusion after serological examination | P > 0.91 | 14 | 1 | 13 |
| | P < 0.90 | 5 | 0 | 5 |
| Total | | 19 | 1 | 18 |

**Table 2.** Analysis of D1S80 after serological examination with exclusion

| | serological examination | D1S80 exclusion | D1S80 no exclusion |
|---|---|---|---|
| exclusion in 1 system | 5 | 5 | 0 |
| opposite homozygotic exclusion in 1 system | 6 | 6 | 0 |
| 2 and more system exclusions | 8 | 8 | 0 |
| Total | 19 | 19 | 0 |

The results of our study and earlier published works have pointed out that the D1S80 system is worth including into disputed paternity investigation.

## References


1. Allen RC, Graves G and Budowle B (1989) Polymerase chain reaction amplification products separated on rehydratable polyacrylamide gels and stained with silver. Biotechniques 7:736-744
2. Basler M, Sprecher W, Rink M and Saternus KS (1992) The application of DNA polymorphisms in paternity testing. In: Advances in Forensic Haemogenetics, Vol 4. Springer Verlag, Berlin, Heidelberg, P 184
3. Kasai K, Nakamura Y and White R (1980) Amplification of variable number tandem repeats (VNTR) locus (pMCT 118) by the polymerase chain reaction (PCR) and its application to forensic science. J Forensic Sci 35:1196-1200
4. Kishida T, Fukuda M and Tamaki Y (1992) Application of DNA Fingerprinting to problematical paternity cases. In: Advances in Forensic Haemogenetics Vol 4. Springer Verlag, Berlin, Heidelberg, P 222
5. Künkel LM, Smith KD, Boyer SH et al (1977) Analysis of human Y chromosome - specific reiterated DNA in chromosome variants. Proc Natl Acad Sci USA 74:1245-1249
6. Kloosterman AD, Budowle B and Daselaar P (1993) PCR-amplification and detection of the human D1S80 VNTR locus. Amplification conditions, population genetics and application in forensic analysis. Int J Leg Med 105:257-264
7. Lincoln PJ, Phillips CP, Syndercombe D et al (1992) Application of conventional polymorphism and single locus DNA probes in cases of disputed paternity. In: Advances in Forensic Haemogenetics Vol 4. Springer Verlag, Berlin, Heidelberg, P 215
8. Mauff G, Pulverer G, Muhlenbrock E et al (1992) Comparision of minisatellite DNA probes and blood group protein and enzyme markers in paternity cases. In: Advances in Forensic Haemogenetics Vol 4. Springer Verlag, Berlin, Heidelberg, P 198
9. Nakamura Y, Carlson M, Krapcho K and White R (1988) Isolation and mapping of polymorphic DNA sequence (pMCT 118) on chromosome 1p (D1S80). Nucl Acids Res 16:9364
10. Perke L and Balazs J (1992) Validation of the use of DNA amplification for the analysis of forensic samples by comparision with tests using non-amplified DNA polymorphism. In: Advances in Forensic Haemogenetics Vol 4. Springer Verlag, Berlin, Heidelberg, P 57
11. Szczotka H and Schlesinger D (1980) Tablice do obliczania prawdopodobieństwa ojcostwa w populacji polskiej. Materiały i Prace Antropologiczne 98:3-51

# DETECTION OF A NEW LARGE ALLELE AT THE D17S5 (YNZ22) LOCUS

S.Pelotti*, P. Degli Esposti°, V. Mantovani**, E. Collina**, G. Pappalardo*
* Institute of Legal Medicine, University of Bologna, Italy
° Institute of Anthropology, University of Bologna, Italy
** Tissue Typing Laboratory Malpighi Hospital, Bologna, Italy

## INTRODUCTION

The variable number of tandem repeat regions (VNTRs) are a great source of polymorphism in the human genome. VNTR alleles have been identified initially by Southern blotting analysis . To date, as the sequences surrounding the polymorphic region have been defined, rapid typing of VNTRs polymorphism has been performed using PCR. PCR-based assay is rapid and can offer DNA typing also when the amount of DNA is too small to be typed with Southern blotting.

D17S5 (YNZ22) is an informative VNTR locus localized to chromosome 17. The complete sequence of YNZ22 has been determined by Wolff et al. (1988) and the polymorphism is due to the repetition of a 70 bp core unit. Horn (1989) analyzed this polymorphism using PCR and detected 11 alleles with a Mendelian pattern of inheritance. To date other authors have studied the variation at this locus and some technical problems have been pointed out especially the preferential amplification of small alleles when present in a heterozygous feature with a large allele and the presence of amplification artifacts visible as faint extra bands. (Batanian et al. 1990, Gécz 1991, Deka et al. 1992).

In order to overcome both difficulties we have optimized the PCR protocol and developed a rapid method to distinguish real alleles from non- specific amplification products.

## MATERIALS AND METHODS

### DNA extraction

Genomic DNA was obtained from peripheral blood cells by the fast protocol Genomix method (CellBio).

### PCR amplification

Thirty cycles of PCR amplification were completed with 100 ng of DNA in 50 μl reaction volume containing 50 mM KCl, 10 mM Tris- HCl, 0.5 mM $MgCl_2$, 100 μM each dNTP, 0.1%Triton X-100, 0.2 μM each primer (Horn 1989) and 1.25 U Taq polymerase (Promega). Each cycle consisted of 95°C denaturation for 1 min, 55°C annealing for 30 sec and 72°C extension for 4 min. Before amplification a manual hot start, consisting of 95°C for 7 min, was carried out.

### Electrophoresis and hybridization

Aliquots of 8 μl of the PCR product were electrophoresed in 2% agarose gels, containing 1 μg/ml ethidium bromide, in 1x TBE at 90 V for 2 h. DNA fragments were denatured for 30 min in 0.5 M NaOH/1.5M NaCl, for 30 min in 0.5 M Tris-HCl/1.5 M NaCl, and transferred to a nylon membrane by the capillary method in 20x SSC overnight and UV cross-linked.

The oligoprobe Z22 (5'-CCTTACAGAAGCAATGAG-3') was 5' end-labeled with $^{32}$P-dATP and used to hybridize the membrane by using the tetramethylammonium chloride method ( Wood et al. 1985). The filter was exposed to Kodak XAR-5 at -70°C for 2-12 h.

## RESULTS AND DISCUSSION

In a large panel of unrelated healthy individuals screened in our laboratory for the D17S5 locus, we have encountered the previously described technical problems: i.e. the preferential amplification of the smaller allele when a large allele is simultaneously present, the presence of amplification artifacts visible as faint extra bands. The optimization of the PCR protocol enabled us to obtain the amplification of the large alleles and to improve the specificity of the reaction, avoiding artifacts (Pelotti et al. 1994).

In addition, we found in a man aged 49 the allele 3 together with a fragment between 1230 bp and 1353 bp, compatible with 17 repeat units in length. Our hybridization method enabled us to detect the presence of the repeat unit sequence in this fragment, confirming the existence of a large allele which was not yet described and the heterozygous genotype of the subject. The study of Mendelian inheritance was inconclusive: both parents of the *propositus* were deceased and the two brothers and the only son did not show the new allele.

The illustrated procedure can be applied directly on the amplification products, avoiding the RFLP analysis requiring high amount of genomic DNA and is a powerful tool for forensic applications.

## REFERENCES


Batanian JR, Ledbetter SA, Wolff RK, Nakamura Y, White R, Dobyns WB, Ledbetter DH (1990) Rapid diagnosis of Miller-Dieker syndrome and isolated lissencephaly sequence by the polymerase chain reaction. Hum. Genet. 85: 555-559.

Deka R, De Croo S, Yu LM, Ferrel RE (1992) Variable number of tandem repeat (VNTR) polymorphism at locus D17S5 (YNZ22) in four ethnically defined human populations. Hum. Genet. 90: 86-90.

Gécz J (1991) PCR amplification of large VNTR alleles of D17S5 (YNZ22) locus. Nucl. Acids Res. 19: 5806.

Horn GT, Richards B, Klinger KW (1989) Amplification of a highly polymorphic VNTR segment by the polymerase chain reaction. Nucl. Acids Res. 17: 2140.

Pelotti S, Degli Esposti P, Mantovani V, Collina E, Pappalardo G (1994) Study of D17S5 (YNZ22) locus polymorphism in an italian population sample. XVI th Congress of the International Academy of legal medicine and social medicine. Strabourg 31 may-2 june 1994.

Wolff RK, Nakamura Y, White R (1988) Molecular characterization of a spontaneously generated new allele at a VNTR locus: no exchange of flanking DNA sequence. Genomics 3: 347-351.

Wood W, Gitschier J, Lasky LA, Lawn MR (1985)Base composition-independent hybridization in tetramethylammonium chloride: a method for oligonucleotide screening of highly complex gene libraries. Proc Natl Acad Sci USA 82: 1585-8.

# PCR APPLICATIONS OF GENOTYPING IN BORDERLINE CASEWORK

**ALAIN PENEAU, JEAN-LUC ROLLAND, CHRISTINE TESSON, JEAN-PAUL MOISAN, OLIVIER PASCAL.**
Laboratoire de Génétique Moléculaire, Plateau technique de l'Hotel-Dieu,
Centre Hospitalier Régional et Universitaire, 44035 NANTES cedex, FRANCE.
Phone : (33) 40 08 40 22 - Fax : (33) 40 08 41 14

In routine casework, laboratories performing genotyping in forensic applications have often to deal with samples containing little and/or badly preserved DNA. We present here the results obtained in our laboratory under such difficult situations.

## I) Cigarette butts

DNA analysis from cigarette butts have been first reported by M. Hochmeister et al. (1) and is now widely used.

We tested in our laboratory 36 butts according to the Hochmeister protocol (1). The DNA yield ranged from 1 ng to 150 ng. Genotyping was then performed by PCR on the markers D1S80, von Willebrand Factor, TC11, YNZ 22, HLADQ$\alpha$ and Apo B.

The first experiments were quite disappointing, since we only had a 50 - 60 % rate of success in obtaining amplification. This rate reached over 90 % just by adding BSA in the PCR reaction mix. Therefore, we would advise laboratories starting analysis on butts to systematically use BSA which neutralizes inhibitors coextracted with DNA.

## 2) Bottles and Cans

We recently received from police investigators bottles and cans which have been found at crime scenes. We decided to test whether we could find DNA coming from mouth or lips cells remaining on the bottles necks or on the cans.

DNA was extracted by wiping the area of the can or of the bottle with a swab where the lips are assumed to be in contact. The swab was then processed by proteinase K and phenol/chloroform extraction. After DNA precipitation in ethanol, PCR experiments can be performed.

We tested 10 samples and the DNA yield ranged from 5 - 50 ng allowing genotyping by several markers.

For example, we tested two bottles, one bottle of wine and one bottle of "bitter lemon", on which we had quite informative results. For the wine bottle, we obtained 20 ng of extracted DNA, and we could perform PCR on the following markers : TC11, D1S80, von Willebrand factor and HLADQ$\alpha$. The genotype obtained from these four markers had a frequency of 1 in 1.2 million in the French population. With the second bottle we extracted 30 ng of DNA and could investigate the same markers and in addition, markers YNZ 22 and Apo B, providing a genotype with a frequency of 1 in 150 million.

Lip and mouth cells are a good source of DNA on bottles and cans which can provide very useful information. Indeed, on 10 samples which have been tested, we obtained DNA with all of them. Furthermore, the DNA quality is quite good since bottles and cans usually possess no inhibitors and DNA extraction with chelex and centricon columns are not necessary. We think that Southern blotting could be performed when the DNA yield is sufficient.

### 3) Bone remains

We had to deal with four identifications of bone remains. In each case, DNA was extracted from bones according to the protocol of Höss and Pääbo (2). Then, PCR experiments were performed for TC11 and von Willebrand factor markers (providing low molecular weight allelic fragments) and mitochondrial DNA. In the latter case we amplified the D loop region according to the protocol of Sullivan et al. (3).

Case 1 : a bone sample was compared to a putative mother and exclusions could be found on the following data :

- Mitochondrial DNA showed two nucleotides of difference including a nucleotide insertion,
- For the TC 11 marker, no common allele could be observed between the bone and the putative mother.

Case 2 : a bone sample was compared to a putative mother and a putative brother. Here again exclusion could be assessed on the basis of :

- one nucleotide of difference on mitochondrial DNA,
- no common alleles between allegued mother and bone sample were observed with marker von Willebrand factor.

Case 3 : a bone sample was compared to the putative mother and father. We could link the bone remains to this couple because :

- von Willebrand factor and HLADQ$\alpha$ markers were in agreement with paternity and maternity,
- bones and putative mother presented the same mitochondrial DNA, including the same two mutations (by comparison to the Anderson sequence (4)).

Case 4 : a bone fragment was compared to a putative mother. No amplification could be obtained with markers TC11, von Willebrand factor or HLADQ$\alpha$. The mitochondrial DNA data showed one nucleotide of difference between bone and putative mother. This result has been confirmed by several sequences from two different DNA extractions. At this point of our analysis, we have not concluded an exclusion since one point mutation can be observed between mother and child. Furthermore, no available data can yet give us an estimation of such events.

Mitochondrial DNA analysis can provide very useful information for identification of bone remains. However, as illustrated in our experience, the possibility to investigate Short Tandem Repeats (STR) is very important for making a decision of inclusion or exclusion. As it can be sufficient by itself, we suggest to test STRs in the first instance, or at minimum to test these markers systematically with mitochondrial DNA.

REFERENCES

1- Hochmeister M.N. et al. Int. J. Leg. Med. (1991) PCR - based typing of DNA extracted from cigarette butts. 104 : 229-233

2- Höss M. and S. Pääbo (1993) DNA extraction from pleistocene bones by silica - based purification method. Nucleic Acids Res. 21 : 3913-3914

3- Sullivan K.M. et al. (1992) Identification of human remains by amplification and automated sequencing of mitochondrial DNA. Int. J. Leg. Med. 105 : 83-86

4- Anderson et al (1981) Sequence and organization of the human mitochondrial genome. Nature 290 : 457-465

# USE OF THE AMPLITYPE PM COAMPLIFICATION SYSTEM ON FORENSIC ANALYSIS

*Pinheiro MF; Pontes ML; Pinto da Costa J*

Medico-legal Institute, Biomedical Sciences Institute "Abel Salazar", Faculty of Medicine, University of Oporto; Faculty of Law, Universidade Portucalense "Infante D. Henrique"; Jardim Carrilho Videira 4000, Porto, Portugal

## INTRODUCTION

DNA profiling has rapidly become a routine technique in forensic laboratories worldwide since its introduction in 1985. Recently a commercially available product appeared for forensic cases based on reverse dot-blot technology - Amplitype PM. We report here the allele frequencies for those 5 markers (LDLR, GYPA, HBGG, D7S8 and Gc) in a population from north Portugal.

## MATERIALS AND METHODS

Blood samples were taken from 1 15 unrelated individuals of 54 routine paternity cases. These trios were analysed using conventional markers and other DNA polymorphisms that confirmed the results obtained with the Amplitype PM.

DNA extraction was achieved using phenol-chloroform-isoamyl alcohol or Chelex.

PCR amplification and typing was performed using the Amplitype PM kit (Perkin-Elmer) and the protocols provided by the manufacturer. The cycling reaction was done in a programmable heat block (TC 480 Perkin-Elmer).

## RESULTS

The allele frequencies are shown below (Table l).

The genotype distribution were in Hardy-Weinberg equilibrium for the five loci (Table 2).

The test for the HWE was also conducted using the proportion of heterozygous individuals observed versus those expected, suggesting that there is no deviation from the Hardy-Weinberg equilibrium.

**Table l**. Allele Frequencies of Amplitype PM in the population of the North of Portugal.

| Locus | Allele | Allele frequencies |
|---|---|---|
| LDLR | A | 0.4696 |
| | B | 0.5304 |
| GYPA | A | 0.5130 |
| | B | 0.4870 |
| HBGG | A | 0.5043 |
| | B | 0.4793 |
| | C | 0.0217 |
| D7S8 | A | 0.5913 |
| | B | 0.4087 |
| Gc | A | 0.2870 |
| | B | 0.1304 |
| | C | 0.5826 |

**Table 2**. Genotype distribution for the five loci of the Amplitype PM

| Locus | Genotype | Observed | Expected | |
|---|---|---|---|---|
| LDLR | AA | 26 | 25.3565 | $X^2$=0.580 |
| | AB | 56 | 57.2870 | d.f. = 1 |
| | BB | 33 | 32.3565 | P > 0.805 |
| GYPA | AA | 26 | 30.2695 | $X^2$=2.5397 |
| | AB | 66 | 57.4609 | d.f. = 1 |
| | BB | 23 | 27.2696 | P > 0.110 |
| HBGG | AA | 30 | 29.2522 | |
| | AB | 52 | 54.9739 | $X^2$=2.0751 |
| | AC | 4 | 2.5217 | d.f. = 3 |
| | BB | 28 | 25.8283 | P > 0.557 |
| | BC | 1 | 2.3696 | |
| | CC | 0 | 0.0543 | |
| D7S8 | AA | 40 | 40.2087 | $X^2$=0.0650 |
| | AB | 56 | 55.5826 | d.f. = 1 |
| | BB | 19 | 19.2087 | P > 0.935 |
| Gc | AA | 9 | 9.4695 | |
| | AB | 5 | 8.6087 | $X^2$=3.2015 |
| | AC | 43 | 38.4522 | d.f. = 3 |
| | BB | 2 | 1.9565 | P > 0.361 |
| | BC | 21 | 17.4783 | |
| | CC | 35 | 39.0348 | |

The heterozygosity index (HI) power of discrimination (PD), " a priori" chance exclusion (CE) and Essen-Möller value (EM) are shown in Table 3.

**Table 3**. Statistical parameters

| | LDLR | GYPA | HBGG | D7S8 | Gc |
|---|---|---|---|---|---|
| HI (%) | 48.70 | 57.39 | 49.56 | 48.69 | 60.00 |
| PD (%) | 62.41 | 62.48 | 65.54 | 61.62 | 73.72 |
| CE (%) | 18.70 | 18.74 | 21.44 | 18.33 | 29.25 |
| EM | 9.89 | 9.89 | 9.85 | 9.89 | 9.79 |

## DISCUSSION

These systems are useful in paternity testing as the accumulated " a priori" chance exclusion value is relatively high (70,01%).

We have also successfully used the Amplitype PM to analyse samples containing minute amounts of human and old DNA (blood and semen stains and hair) which proved to be helpful in criminal cases.

## REFERENCES


- Fildes N, Alavaren M, Varlaro J, Reynolds R (1993) Validation of the Amplitype PM Coamplification System for use on forensic casework samples. In press.
- Saiki RK, Bugawan GT, Horn GT, Mullis KB, Erlich HS (1986) Analysis of enzymatically amplified β-globin and HLA DQα DNA with allelic-specific oligonucleotide probes. Nature 324: 163-166.
- Westwood SA, Werrett DJ (1990) An evaluation of the polymerase chain reaction method for forensic applications.Forensic Sci Int 45: 201-215

# French Caucasian Population Data for HUMTH01 and HUMFESFPS Short Tandem Repeat (STR) systems

**H. Pfitzinger, F. Rousselet, B. Ludes, P. Kintz, A. Tracqui and P. Mangin**

**Institut de Médecine Légale - Faculté de Médecine - 11 Rue Humann 67085 Strasbourg France.**

## Introduction

The recently developed technology of amplification of DNA sequences by the polymerase chain reaction (1) has already proved to be a very useful tool for the analysis of variable number of tandem repeat (VNTR or minisatellites) loci for forensic purposes (2). Trimeric and tetrameric short tandem repeat (STR or microsatellites) DNA sequences are other highly polymorphic markers distributed throughout genic and extragenic regions of the human genome (3, 4). STR loci appear to be informative and promising PCR based identification systems. In fact, DNA typing based on amplification of STRs is very sensitive and allows to overcome major problems encountered in forensic practice, such as typing of minute amounts of DNA, highly degraded DNA, or mixtures of DNA from more than one individual. The high sensitivity and the increased speed of the PCR technique are two important properties for forensic analyses.

## Material and Methods

The PCR reactions were performed on DNA extracted from whole blood samples of randomly selected and unrelated french caucasian individuals. The 50 $\mu$l reaction mixture contained : 10 ng of DNA, 0.25 $\mu$M of each primer, 200 $\mu$M of each dNTP, 10 mM Tris HCl pH 8.3, 50 mM KCl, 1.5 mM MgCl2, 0.1 % gelatine, and 1.25 U Taq DNA polymerase (BRL or Perkin Elmer).

Thirty PCR thermal cycles were carried out in a Perkin Elmer Gene Amp$^{TM}$ PCR system 9600, as follows : 94°C - 45 s ; 54°C - 30 s ; 72°C - 30 s for the HUMFESFPS locus. The annealing step was achieved at 60°C for the HUMTH01 locus.

The alleles were identified by loading 6 $\mu$l aliquots on 6 % Hydrolink Long Ranger gels (AT Biochem) using silver staining.

The allele designation used was based on the number of repeat units present in the amplified allelic fragments as already proposed (3, 4).

## Results

. **HUMTH01 LOCUS** : it consists of variable numbers of tetranucleotide repeat units $(AATG)_n$ located on chromosome 11 (3, 5). The primers used are already described by Kimpton et al. (1993) (6). Our study was performed on 194 unrelated individuals, and the alleles were identified against an allelic ladder consisting of 7 human alleles (5, 6, 7, 8, 9, 10-1 and 11) prepared from DNA of known genotypes. We identified 6 different alleles ranging from 154 to 178 bp in our population. The smallest allele observed migrated as allele 5 present in the allelic ladder. The largest allele observed was the variant allele 10-1 (7) whereas allele 11 was not identified in our population sample. Furthermore, allele 10 never identified in our population sample and rare in other population samples (4, 7 and 8) may have been mis-typed as allele 10-1 : population data were therefore established by grouping allele 10-1 and 10 for frequency purposes. The two most frequent alleles were allele 6 (25 %) and allele 10-1 (30.67 %) as already observed (3, 4, 6 and 8).

Our allele frequencies distribution was shown, using a RXC contigency table, to be similar to that observed for a German caucasian sample (8) : $X^2 = 4.68$ ; df = 5 ; $0.3 < p < 0.5$ and also similar to that observed for an American caucasian sample. (4) : $X^2 = 3.35$ ; df = 5 ; $0.5 < p < 0.9$. All classes with less than 5 observations were pooled.

The distribution of the HUMTH01 genotypes is in Hardy Weinberg equilibrium (HWE) : $X^2 = 4.54$ ; df = 13 ; $p > 0.9$. Calculations have been carried out using a 5 allele model by comparing observed and expected genotypes (observed heterozygosity = 77.32 ; allelic diversity, h = 0.77 ; discrimination power, Pd = 0.91). The homogeneity of HUMTH01 genotype frequencies for our french caucasian population sample was tested with the German caucasian sample (8) (all classes with less than 3 observations were pooled) and no significant differencies appeared : $X^2 = 11.38$ ; df = 12 ; $0.3 < p < 0.5$.

. **HUMFESFPS LOCUS** : it consists of variable number of tetranucleotide repeat units $(ATTT)_n$ located on chromosome 15 (9) and the primers used were already described (6).Our study was performed on 190 unrelated individuals and the alleles were identified against an allelic ladder consisting of 7 known HUMFESFPS alleles (8, 9, 10, 11, 12, 13 and 14) (6). We identified 7 different alleles ranging from 209 to 238 pb, in our population. The smallest allele observed migrated as a 7 repeat allele and has never been reported before (6). The largest allele observed was allele 13, and allele 14 was not identified. The two most frequent alleles were allele 10 (35.8 %) and allele 11 (38.2 %). The allele frequencies distribution appears similar to that observed by Kimpton et al., 1993 (6) : alleles 10, 11 and 12 are the most frequent alleles and allele 14 is not represented. Moreover, we observed an additionnal allele not reported for an English caucasian population sample (6) and appearing as an allele containing 7 repeats. The HWE was tested for HUMFESFPS genotypes and calculations have been carried out using a 5 allele model : no significant deviations were found between observed and expected genotypes : $X^2 = 5.46$ ; df = 9 ; $0.5 < p < 0.9$ .

## Conclusion

Both HUMFESFPS and HUMTH01 tetranucleotide STR loci were easily amplified using the PCR method and allowed us to gather population data for a sample of 190 and 194 French caucasian individuals respectively. The HUMTH01 and the HUMFESFPS genotype distributions were in Hardy Weinberg equilibrium. Genotype and allele frequencies were also similar to that already observed for other caucasian population samples (3, 4, 6, 7, 8). In our HUMFESFPS population sample we observed an additionnal allele not reported by Kimpton et al. (1993) (6) and migrating as allele 7.
However, HUMTH01 and HUMFESFPS PCR based STR systems were studied for a French caucasian population sample for forensic purposes and as they require a greater number of systems to be run in order to reach the equivalent DNA discrimination obtainable with conventional RFLP VNTR systems (6), population data for other STR systems (HUMVWA31 and HUMF13A1) (6) are developed.
Furthermore, multiplex reactions testing simultaneously several systems are investigated by the use of different fluorescent dyes in conjunction with the Applied Biosystems automated DNA sequencer (model 373A). The use of denaturing gels will also provide us an improved gel system allowing single base resolution and the detection of rare alleles differing by only one base-pair.

## Bibliography

**1.** Saiki et al. (1986) Analysis of enzymatically amplified B-globin and HLA-DQ-Alpha DNA with allele specific oligonucleotide probe. Nature 324 : 163-166
**2.** Budowle et al. (1991) Analysis of the VNTR locus D1S80 by the PCR followed by high-resolution PAGE. Am. J. Hum. Gen. 48 : 137-144.
**3.** Edward et al. (1991) DNA typing and genetic mapping with trimeric and tetrameric tandem repeats. Am. J. Hum. Gen. 49 : 746-756.
**4.** Edwards et al. (1992) Genetic variation at five trimeric and tetrameric tandem repeat loci in four human population groups. Genomics 12 : 241-253.
**5.** Polymeropoulos et al. (1991) Tetranucleotide repeat polymorphism at the human tyrosine hydroxylase gene (TH). NAR 19 : 3753.
**6.** Kimpton et al., (1993) Automated DNA profiling employing multiplex amplification of short tandem repeat loci. PCR Method and applications : 3 : 13-22.
**7.** Puers et al. (1993) Identification of repeat sequence heterogeneity of the polymorphic short tandem repeat locus HUMTH01 $(AATG)_n$ and reassignement of alleles in population analysis by using a locus-specific allelic ladder. Am. J. Hum. Gen. 53 : 953-958.
**8.** Wiegand et al. (1993) Forensic validation of the STR systems SE 33 and TC 11. Int. J. Leg. Med. 105 : 315-320.
**9.** Polymeropoulos et al. (1991) Tetranucleotide repeat polymorphism at the human c-fes/fps proto oncogene (FES). NAR 19 : 4018.

# APPLICATION OF THE AMPLITYPE PM COAMPLIFICATION SYSTEM TO FORENSIC CASEWORK.

Sanz P, Prieto V.
Instituto Nacional de Toxicología, Sevilla, Spain.

## INTRODUCTION

For the last two years our laboratory has included PCR amplification techniques in paternity tests and in forensic casework as a supplement to traditional diagnostic procedures. Up to this moment the following genetic markers have been used: DQA1, D1S80, when required DYZ3 for sex determination, and more recently the amplitype PM amplification system from Perkin Elmer. This system coamplifies the following loci: low density lipoprotein receptor (LDLR), glycophorin A (GYPA), hemoglobin G gammaglobin (HBGG), D7S8 linked to cystic fibrosis locus, and Group specific Component (Gc). PM success rates versus DQA1 and D1S80 and a selection of the most representative cases where PM amplification was included, are reported.

## MATERIALS AND METHODS

Our Institute is located in southern Spain and covers about one third of the country and the Canary Islands. Paternity samples: blood samples are usually taken by venipuncture at our laboratory. Occasionally (i.e. from Canary Islands) they are sent according to a preestablished protocol. Forensic samples: they are sent to the laboratory by different transport means.

DNA extraction: In general extraction protocols have been taken from the AmpliType user guide, Version 2 (Cetus Corporation)
Blood and blood stains: Chelex extraction.
Semen stains and swabs: Phenol extraction followed by Centricon concentration.
Spermatozoa were recovered from non-stained or stained slides according to Wiegand et al. (1993).
Cigarette ends: as previously described (Sanz and Prieto, 1993)
Hair roots: Rapid DNA extraction.
Amplification and typing: Perkin Elmer Cetus 480
DQA1: Amplitype HLADQA1 Forensic DNA Amplification and Typing kit (Perkin-Elmer) PCR Product Detection: hybridisation with allele specific oligonucleotide probes
D1S80: The D1S80 DNA Amplification Reagent Set (Perkin Elmer). PCR Product Detection: flat bed SDS-PAGE. Gel: 8-18% SDS PAA. Gel Buffer: 0.12 M Tris-Acetate, 1 g/L SDS, pH 6.4. Electrode Buffers: Anode: 0.3 M Tris-Acetate, 4 g/L SDS, pH 6.4. Cathode: 0.08 M Tris, 0.8 M Tricine, 4 g/L SDS, pH 7.1. Electrophoretic conditions: 400V, 100 mA, 30 W, 50-55 min. Silver Stain
PM: Amplitype PM PCR coamplification kit (Perkin Elmer). PCR Product Detection: Simultaneous hybridisation with allele specific oligonucleotide probes.

## RESULTS

We comment here on the results obtained from 21 forensic cases and 7 paternity tests where the PM amplification system was applied.
PATERNITY TESTING: Our routine test battery at the present time includes conven-

tional genetic markers: ABO, Rh, MNSs, AcP, EsD, PGM1, Tf, Hp, Gc, AAT. PCR: DQA1, D1S80. SL: D2S44, D12S11, D7S21, occasionally D7S22, D7S21, D5S43 The PM coamplification system was included only in conflicting cases: insufficient blood sample for SL or degradated DNA. Conventional markers not possible (embryo, exhumed tissue from alleged father, etc.). Anomalous results in some markers that make genetic interpretation difficult. Success rate was 100%

FORENSIC CASES

Success rate versus total analysed samples: DQA1 83.83%, D1S80 58.10%
The success of DQA1 and D1S80 was mainly related to the correct collection and preservation of samples. Wet conditions were the first cause of failure, followed by the adsorption characteristics of some supporting materials (soil, stones, bricks). We never obtained positive results with D1S80 when DQA1 was unsuccessful so, routinely DQA1 was always done first (Sanz and Prieto, 1993).
PM 92.13% but this result is biased because samples had been carefully preselected.In 8.98% of the samples only PM was done. Success rate versus DQA1 was 97.53%.
In one case (partially mummified muscle tissue from a corpse exhumed one year after burial), amplification on some loci of the PM system failed: LDLR and GYPA, and the dot blot signal was faint with the remaining loci (HBGG, D7S8 and Gc)

SELECTED EXAMPLES FROM CASEWORK

CASE N°1. Sexual assault. Samples: One single stained microscopie slide, stain: May-Grünwal Giemsa, Spermatozoa: about 100; blood from the victim and one suspect
PM confirmed and increased exclusion power in the identification of the suspect.

CASE n°2. Criminal assault. Samples: blood stains: blue jeans from the suspect, knife and its sheath; blood from the victim and the suspect.
PM permitted the identification of the suspect.

CASE n°3. Criminal assault. Samples: Cigarette ends and hairs found at the scene of the crime; blood from the victim; cigarette end smoked by the suspect.
Only PM was carried out. All the hairs coincided with the characteristics of the victim. In the cigarette ends, 3 different individuals were detected. The characteristics of one of them coincided with the suspect.

CASE n°4. Individual identification. Samples: Rectal device for drug transport; blood from two suspected drug dealers
PM confirmed and increased exclusion power in the identification of one of the drug dealers and the exclusion of the other.

REFERENCES

Cetus Corporation (1990) AmpliType User Guide, Emeriville

Sanz P, Prieto V (to be published) Use of PCR in forensic case work in southern Spain. In: Advances in Forensic Haemogenetics, vol 5. Springer Verlag, Berlin

Sanz P, Prieto V (to be published) Use of PCR for forensic analysis of DNA in cigarette ends. In: Advances in Forensic Haemogenetics, vol 5. Springer Verlag, Berlin

Wiegand P, Schürenkamp M, Brinkmann B (to be published) Investigation of vaginal cell/sperm mixtures from microscopical slides. In: Advances in Forensic Haemogenetics, vol 5. Springer Verlag, Berlin

# Application of DNA polymorphisms to postmortem paternity cases

Akiko Sawaguchi, Shigeki Nakamura, Toshiko Sawaguchi

Department of Legal Medicine, Tokyo Women's Medical College, Tokyo 162, Japan

## Introduction

Most cases of disputed paternity can be adequately resolved by testing conventional systems including HLA. In some cases such as the postmortem paternity cases, the probability of fatherhood according to Essen-Möller is lower than 99.80%. The analysis of DNA polymorphisms is a very useful additional system for providing convincing evidence in favor of paternity in cases of non-exclusions. The purpose of this presentation is to report the results from the postmortem paternity cases in our laboratory in which the analysis of DNA polymorphisms greatly helped clear up the paternity.

## Materials and methods

### Paternity testing

Seventeen postmortem paternity cases were analysed by 28 conventional systems and DNA profiling.

Routine paternity testing consisted of the conventional serological analysis of the red cell antigen systems ABO, MNSs, Rhesus, P, Duffy, Kidd and Lewis, the serum proteins GC, HP, BF, IF, C1R, C2, C6, C7, C81, F13A, F13B and PLG, the red cell enzymes ACP, PGM1, ESD, GPT and PGD, and leucocyte antigens HLA-A, -B, -C by means of standard techniques. DNA was extracted from 5 ml EDTA treated blood samples by phenol-chloroform extraction. DNA fingerprinting with minisatellite probe MZ1.3 (Biotest AG, Dreieich, FRG), single locus probe YNH24 (Promega, Madison, USA), VNTR loci D1S80 (AmpliFLP D1S80 PCR Amplification Kit Perkin Elmer, USA) and HLADQ$\alpha$ (AmpliType HLADQ$\alpha$ PCR Amplification and Typing Kit, Perkin Elmer, USA) were carried out according to the manufacturer's instructions.

### Case summary

The numbers of parties concerned in 17 postmortem paternity cases are shown in table 1. Paternity testing in case 2 and 4 was performed with preserved blood samples of the deceased putative father. Case 5 was a postmortem paternity case between child and 2 legitimate children, and case 9 was a postmortem maternity case.

## Results and discussion

### Results of paternity testing with conventional systems

Figure 1 shows the probabilities of fatherhood (W) according to Essen-Möller in 17 postmortem paternity cases. The paternity in cases 2 and 4 was excluded with conventional systems. The probabilities of fatherhood (W) in the other cases were calculated as 20.10% - 99.9994%. Inconclusive results were obtained in cases 12 and 16. The probability of fatherhood in case 5 was 20.10%, which was too low to establish paternity.

## Results of DNA profiling

The band sharing rates of MZ1.3 for the combinations between child and legitimatechildren and siblings of putative father in the present study are indicated in Fig. 2. The band sharing rate was calculated as follows: RAB = N / 2 X ( 1 / a + 1 / b ) X 100 (%) (N=Number of common bands, a, b = Total number of bands in individuals A and B)[1]. It has already been reported that the mean band sharing rate between parent and children was estimated as 61.8 ± 7.6%, and 30.1 ± 6.1% was obtained among unrelated individuals[2]. The mean band sharing rate of 44.8 ± 6.9% may indicate a possible second degree relationship. The mean band sharing rates (R) in child/legitimate children of deceased putative father in case 5 were calculated as R=31.4%. So, the paternity was excluded. The paternity in cases 2 and 4 was also excluded. In the other cases, the deceased man has highly likely to have been the father of the children. These results suggested that the band sharing information is useful in postmortem paternity cases by including parents, legitimate children, siblings of a deceased putative father into the analysis. The results of DNA testing in 17 postmortem paternity cases are summarized in table 2. In all the cases, paternity were not excluded with YNH24, D1S80 and HLADQα. In each case an unequivocal conclusion was obtained after DNA analysis.

## References

1) Schneider PM, Fimmers R, Bertrams J, Brikner P, Braunbech K, Bulnheim U,Feuerbach M, Henke L, Iten E, Osterhaus E, Prinz M, Simeoni E, and Rittner C (1992) Biostatistical basis of individualization and segregation anlysis using the multilocus DNA probe MZ1.3: Results of a collaborative study. Forensic Sci Int, 55: 45-58

2) Nakamura S. Sawaguchi T, Nakada N, Ohue O, Ogasawara T, Sawaguchi A (1994) Application of DNA polymorphism to paternity test (III). Jpn J Legal Med, 48, Supplement, 53

Table 1 Postmortem paternity cases in our laboratory

| Numbers of parties concerned | | | | | |
|---|---|---|---|---|---|
| | | | Families of deceased putative father | | |
| 1 | Child | | Spouse | 2 legitimate children | |
| 2 | Child | | | 1 legitimate child | 2 siblings * |
| 3 | Child | Mother | | | 6 siblings |
| 4 | Child | Mother | | 1 legitimate child | * |
| 5 | Child | | | 2 legitimate children | |
| 6 | Child | Mother | Spouse | 3 legitimate children | |
| 7 | Child | Mother | Spouse | 2 legitimate children | |
| 8 | Child | Mother | Spouse | 2 legitimate children | |
| 9 | Child | Father | | | 5 siblings |
| 10 | Child | Mother | Spouse | 5 legitimate children | |
| 11 | Child | Mother | Spouse | 4 legitimate children | |
| 12 | Child | Mother | Spouse | 1 legitimate child | 4 siblings |
| 13 | Child | Mother | Father | | 1 sibling |
| 14 | Child | Mother | Spouse | 3 legitimate children | |
| 15 | Child | Mother | Spouse | 2 legitimate children | 3 siblings |
| 16 | Child | Mother | Spouse | 1 legitimate child | |
| 17 | Child | Mother | | 2 legitimate children | |

* Blood samples of putative father were preserved.

Table 2 Results of DNA testing in 17 postmortem paternity cases

| | 28 Conventional genetic markers | YNH24 / D1S80 / HLADQ$\alpha$ | MZ1.3 | Conclusion after DNA testing |
|---|---|---|---|---|
| 1 | no exclusion | no exclusion | no exclusion | paternity confirmed |
| 2 | exclusion | " | exclusion | paternity excluded |
| 3 | no exclusion | " | no exclusion | paternity confirmed |
| 4 | exclusion | " | exclusion | paternity excluded |
| 5 | no exclusion | " | " | " |
| 6 | " | " | no exclusion | paternity confirmed |
| 7 | " | " | " | " |
| 8 | " | " | " | " |
| 9 | " | " | " | " |
| 10 | " | " | " | " |
| 11 | " | " | " | " |
| 12 | " | " | " | " |
| 13 | " | " | " | " |
| 14 | " | " | " | " |
| 15 | " | " | " | " |
| 16 | " | " | " | " |
| 17 | " | " | " | " |

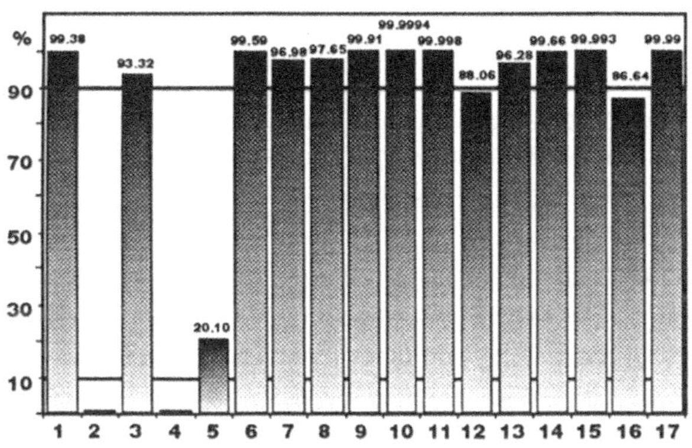


Fig. 1. The probabilities of fatherhood(W) in 17 postmortem paternity cases in our laboratory.

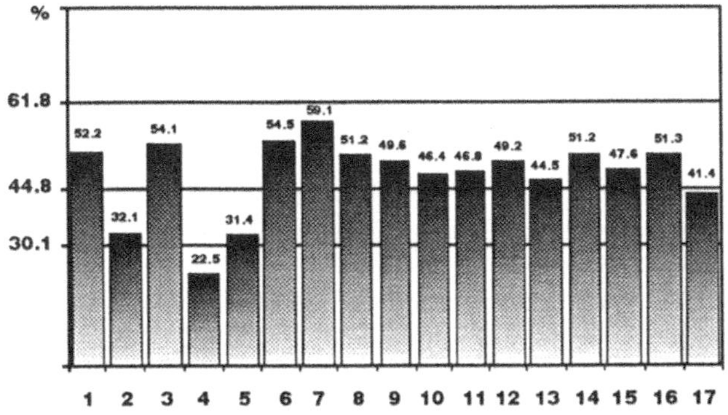


Fig. 2. The mean band sharing rates among 17 postmortem paternity cases.

# COMPARISON BETWEEN THE CONSANGUINITY DETERMINATION BY A MULTI-LOCUS PROBE AND THREE SINGLE-LOCUS PROBES

**L.E. Schwarz, E. Kattner*, V. Mauer, V. Schneider, H. Pöche**
**Institut für Rechts-medizin, F U Berlin, Hittorfstraße 18, D-14195 Berlin**
***Krankenhaus Wandsbek, Alphonsstraße 14, D-22043 Hamburg**

**Introduction**

Two main types of genomic RFLP-analysis are used today. Single-Locus-Probes (SLP) and Multi-Locus-Probes (MLP). Both are equally informative, but the quantification of the MLP results is not generally accepted. The overall transmission probability of the bands calculated by the method of Evett and co-workers is slightly greater than expected by the Mendelian model, indicating that not every band represents only one allele. This leads to the fact that the Single-Locus-Probes are much more used than the MLP in uncomplicated paternity cases, even if one MLP is as informative as three or four SLPs combined.

**Material and Methods**

The DNA was prepared in accordance with the extraction protocols of our laboratory and hybridised on the same membrane with the probes, MS 31, MS 43 a, G3 and (GTG)5 according to Pöche et al. (1993).

**Results**

50 families were included in our studies. Every family was analysed with the above mentioned probes. The probability of paternity was calculated according to the method of Charles Brenner (LA) and determined to be more than 99,9% for all the cases with SLP.

In the MLP the mean father/child bandsharing rate was 0,62; to be mean bandsharing rate between unrelated individuals (mother and father in every case) was 0,144 and the mutation rate for (GTG)5 was calculated taking the appearance rate of the - + - constellation to be 0,002. The probability of paternity calculated according to the formula shown below, was also more than 99,9% in all the cases.

The most interesting case in our study were quadruplets from a pregnancy after hormone treatments, there were one male and three female babies. Because two of the female babies showed severe intrauterine growth retardation, it was speculated that this might be due to a twin to twin transfusion, only possible in monozygotic twins. It could be proven that the two small girls were monozygotic twins (Fig.1), a quite unusual event in a multiple pregnancy, induced by hormones.

According to the actual hypothesis one band can be formed (Fig.2) either by one allele, two homozygous alleles, two or more equal sized alleles from different loci, or due to mutation (Jeffreys et al. 1985).

Transition (mutation) is produced by an existing parental band in the low resolution zone of the gel, increasing its number of tandem repeats by unequal crossing-over during meiosis, or by a point-mutation in a restriction site.

For calculating t [the overall transmission rate of the bands, according to Evett et al. (1989)] the influence of the parameter m („mutation" depending of the increase of the number of tandem repeats in one low molecular weight allele) (Fig.3) was eliminated from the final result by calculating it separately. This leads to the formula shown below, which was used in the paternity calculation. The parameter t calculated in this way is also a good indicator for the proportion of comigrating alleles in each Multi-Locus-Fingerprint.

E.g. The probability of appearance of a child's band at the given parental configuration + + is:

**P= 2 [t (1-t)(1-m)(1-m)]** (Probability of a transmission from one of the parents, without appearance of a mutation) + **$t^2$ (1-m)(1-m)** (Probability of the band being transmitted from both parents simultaneously, without appearance of a mutation) + 4[t(1-t) m (1-m)] (Probability of one transmission and one mutation, either both on the same parent or one in each) + **2[t(1-t) $m^2$ ]** (Probability of one transmission and two mutations) + **2[ $t^2$ (1-m) m]** (Probability of one mutation and two transmissions) + **$t^2$ $m^2$** (Probability of two transmissions and two mutations) + **2[(1-t)(1-t)m(1-m)]** (Probability of one mutation and no transmission) + **(1-t)(1-t) $m^2$** (Probability of two mutations and no transmission).

The total probability of the child to show a band at a given position is:

$$P = - p^2 t^2 m^2 + 2 p^2 t^2 m - p^2 t^2 + 2pt m^2 - 4ptm + 2pt - m^2 + 2m$$

Which according to Evett and coworkers equals the general probability **p** of band appearance in the population. The formula can be simplified to:

$$p= p^2 t^2 (-m^2 + 2m -1) - 2pt (-m^2 + 2m -1) - m^2 +2m$$

Which given the appearance rate of - + - = **m (1-m) + (1-m) m + $m^2$ = $-m^2$ + 2m = K** results in: **$p = p^2 t^2 (K-1) - 2pt (K-1) + K$** with K being 0,002 for $(GTG)_5$

The parameter t calculated from our series according to this method is 0,513, which shows no relevant deviation from the transmission rate of 0,5 given by the Mendelian model and assumed for the SLP.

## Conclusion

There is no reason for not using $(GTG)_5$ even in routine cases because the gained results are absolutely compatible to SLP.

**Evett IW, Werrett DJ, Buckleton JS** (1989) Paternity calculations from DNA multilocus profiles. J. Forensic Sci. Soc. 29:249-254

**Jeffreys A., Wilson V., Thein SL** (1985) Individual-specific "fingerprints" of human DNA. Nature 316:76-79

**Pöche H, Schmidt V, Mauer V, Wandelt S, Schneider V** (1993) Individualisierung und Identifizierung durch Schiffsschraubenkontakt zerstückelter Leichenteile mittels DNA-Technologie. Pathologe 14:193-198

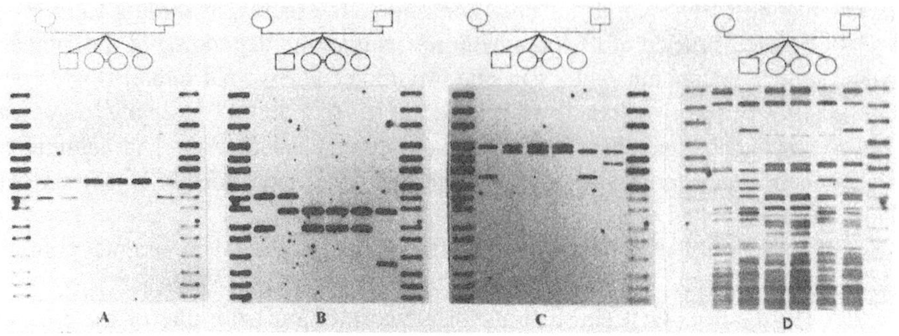


**Fig. 1**: Determination of zygosity in quardruplets with the Single-Locus-Probes MS 43 (A), MS 31 (B), G3 (C) and the Multi-Locus-Probe $(GTG)_5$ (D).

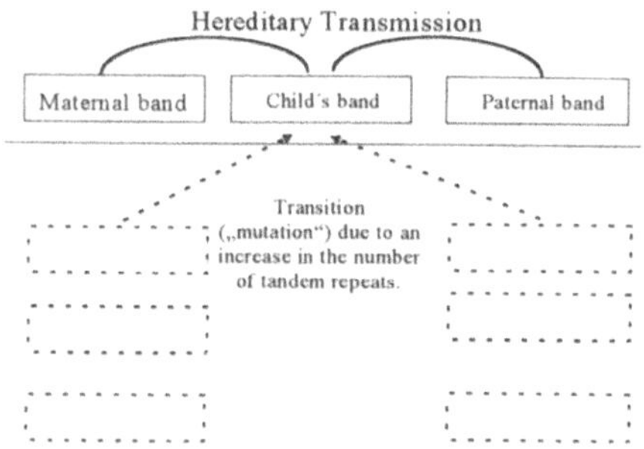


**Fig.2**: Different possible origins of a child`s band in a Multi-Locus-Fingerprint as taken into account.

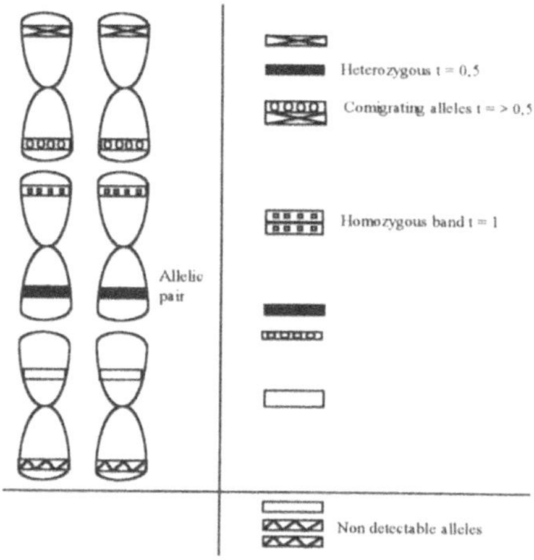


**Fig.3**: Possible allele combinations in Multi-Locus-Fingerprints with their bandtransmission probability t according to the Mendelian model.

# TYPING OF MUCOID CELL STAINS AT BITE MARKS ON VICTIMS OF SEXUAL HOMICIDE CRIMES

SZIBOR, R., SCHÖNING, R., PLATE, INES., KRAUSE, D.:

Institut für Rechtsmedizin der Otto-von-Guericke-Universität Magdeburg, Leipziger Strasse 44, 39120 Magdeburg, Germany

## Case work:

After a party, which included 3 males and 4 females, one of the females was found dead in an adjoining room. The corpse was clothed in a nightie, which was pulled up to the neck. The cause of death was strangulation. Although the age of the dead person was 60 years and no sperma was found, the offence is believed to have been sexualy motivated. Five bite marks were found at the upper part of the arms(2x), at the tummy (1x) and at the bottom.
The examination by the police revealed that a lot of alcohol was drunk at the party. None of the people concerned confessed the offence and all pretended that they did not remember details. Considering the fact that there was no evidence for the identity of the party having caused the bites and the homocide, comparing the bite marks with each of the defendants was of high interest for the inquiries.
Discrimination between the possible offenders was complicated by the fact that two persons were brothers and one of the possible offenders was the son of the victim.
We report on DNA typing and matching results using mucoid cell stains in the bite marks and blood specimens of the possible offenders.

## Materials and methods:

About 12 hours after death the first forensic examination was done. Mucoid cell stains were taken from two areas of bite marks using prewetted Q-tips:

1. area of teeth marks
2. area of tongue attachment

The methodical study performed later considered 2 additional areas:

3. area of lips' attachment
4. blank outside the bite marks

## DNA extraction was done using chelex method:

Q-tips were used for saving stain material.
Q tips were rinsed in 500 µl 0.9 % NaCl.
Cells were sedimented at 12 000 g.
30 µl cell suspension was mixed with 400µl 5% chelex (Bio-Rad) and 30µl Proteinase K (5 mg/ml) and incubated for 20 min at 55°C. After vortexing the mixture was boiled for 8 min.
After vortexing again 15 µl supernantant were used for establishing 25 µl PCR mix.
PCR and native PAGE were carried out in the systems TC11(2), MBP(3), SE33, vWA using standard protocols. On account of incomplete amplification success in the STRs SE33 and vWA these systems did not support the identification process.
Visualisation of DNA fragments in PAGE was done by silver staining.
Mitochondrial D-loop CA repeat polymorphism was amplified and separated after Bodenteich et al. (1).

## Results and discussion:

Using Q-tips mucoid cell stains were taken from bite marks of the body some hours after death. Two bite mark areas were distinguished by the investigators: Area of teeth marks and area of tongue attachment. All specimens were marked with regard to be documented number of bite marks and bite mark area.
Although all Q-tips were extracted in the same manner not all specimens gave good results after chelex DNA extraction. However, non regularity was recognised in regard to a supposed relationship between bite mark area and DNA extraction success.
Therefore a methodical study to optimize stain removal was undertaken (see below).
In the actual case PCR was carried out with sufficient success in at least 3 systems: TC11, MBP and mitochondrial D-loop CA repeat polymorphism. In the SE33 and vWA systems amplification success was not sufficient, thus these systems did not contribute to the results for identification in this special case (data not shown).
Silver-stained electropherograms of TC11 are depicted in fig.1. These results are sufficient to rule out 5 of the 6 possible offenders (see table 1)
Results in MBP ( electropherograms not shown) were suitable to rule out 2 of 4 possible offenders (see table 1).
As demonstrated in table 1 the discrimination power of the mitochondrial D-loop CA repeat polymorphism is fairly low (electropherograms not shown). However, an advantage of this system is its high sensitivity. For discrimination of the offenders in the actual case this polymorphism can contribute to a second exclusion for possible offender 1.

## Results of the methodical study for optimizing mucoid cell stain removal from bite marks:

Three test persons from the laboratory staff gave themselves bite marks on their arms. Ten min later mucoid cells were gathered using prewetted Q-tips from 3 areas (lip attachment, teeth marks, and tongue attachment) A 4th Q-tip was used for establishing a blank preparation from an outside area.
Good amplification success for specimens of all bite mark areas using system TC11 has been found (see fig.2). No DNA was extracted from blank outside the bite mark.

**Table 1:**

**Identification of the possible responsible party of bite marks by matching PCR patterns in 3 polymorphisms. Only the pattern of offender 6 completly matches the bite mark pattern**
**(offender 1 is the son of the victim; offenders 5 and 6 are brothers).**

| | | TC 11 | MBP (locus B) | D-loop repeat |
|---|---|---|---|---|
| possible offender 1 | (blood) | 11 / 11 | **6 / 6** | 132 bp |
| possible offender 2 | (blood) | 7 / 10 | – | **134 bp** |
| possible offender 3 | (blood) | 8 / 11 | 2 / 6 | **134 bp** |
| possible offender 4 | (blood) | 7 / 10 | – | **134 bp** |
| possible offender 5 | (blood) | 7 / 10 | 4 / 6 | **134 bp** |
| **possible offender 6** | **(blood)** | **8 / 10** | **6 / 6** | **134 bp** |
| victim | muscle | 8 / 8 | 1 / 6 | 132 bp |
| **bite marks** | | **8 / 10** | **6 / 6** | **134 bp** |

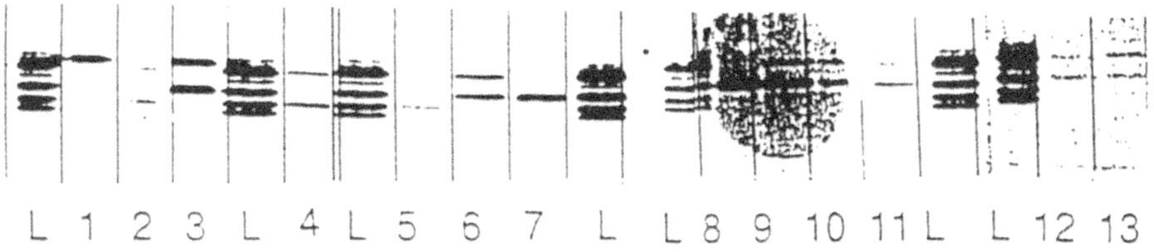


Fig. 1:

Electrophoretic pattern in the TC11 polymorphism of 6 possible offenders, the victim and 5 mocoid cell stains of bite marks:

| | | alleles: |
|---|---|---|
| lane: L: allelic ladder | | |
| lane: 1: possible offender 1 | (blood) | 11 / 11 |
| lane: 2: possible offender 2 | (blood) | 7 / 10 |
| lane: 3: possible offender 3 | (blood) | 8 / 11 |
| lane: 4: possible offender 4 | (blood) | 7 / 10 |
| lane: 5: possible offender 5 | (blood) | 7 / 10 |
| **lane: 6: possible offender 6** | **(blood)** | **8 / 10** |
| lane: 7 and 8: victim | (muscle) | 8 / 8 |
| **lane: 9 - 13: bite marks** | | **8 / 10** |

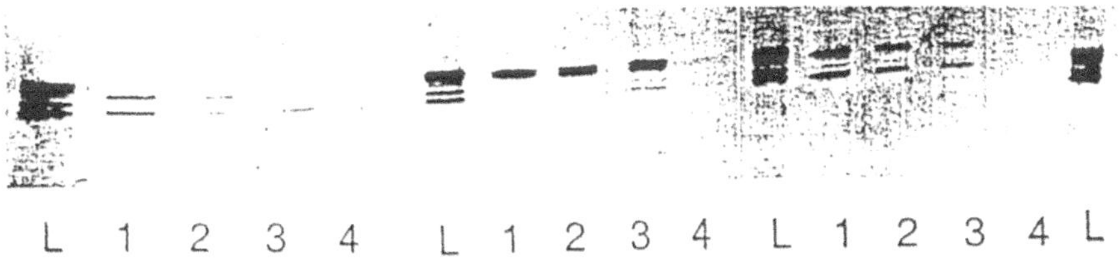


Fig 2:

**TC11 amplification of stain DNA drawn from experimental bite marks of laboratory stuff:**

1. area of teeth marks
2. area of tongue attachment
3. area of lips' attachment
4. blank outside the bite marks

References


1. Bodenteich A, Mitchell LG, Polymeropoulos MH, Merril CR (1992) Dinucleotide in the human mitochondrial D-loop. Hum Mol Genet 1:140.
2. Edwards A, Civitello A, Hammond HA, Caskey CT (1991) DNA typing and genetic mapping with trimeric and tetrameric tandem repeats. Am J Hum Genet 49: 746-756
3. Polymeropoulos MH, Xiao H, Merril CR (1992) Tetranucleotid repeat polymorphism at the human myelin basic protein gen (MBP). Hum Mol Genet 1: 658

# FORENSIC APPLICATION OF TWO SHORT TANDEM REPEAT SYSTEMS: HUMTH01 AND HUMvWA31.

*A. Tagliabracci, L. Buscemi, N. Cucurachi and S.D. Ferrara
*Istituto di Medicina Legale e delle Assicurazioni, Università di Ancona, Italy.
Istituto di Medicina Legale e delle Assicurazioni, Università di Parma, Italy.

## INTRODUCTION

Over the past few years many laboratories worldwide have introduced analysis of DNA polymorphisms as a routine method for forensic purposes. In particular, VNTRs, investigated by PCR, have reached an important position after considerable development. At present laboratories are studying a further series of highly polymorphic loci whose polymorphism derives from a dimeric-trimeric-tetrameric tandem repeated core sequence, named short tandem repeats (STRs) (Weber and May 1989; Edwards et al.1991). The aim of the present study was to investigate two of these STRs, HUMTH01 (Edwards et al. 1992) and HUMvWA31 (Kimpton et al. 1992) to evaluate:1) allele frequencies in an Italian population sample, and 2) their efficiency for personal identification on aged bloodstains from various substrates.

## MATERIALS AND METHODS

***Stain preparation*** : a series of stains prepared from 3, 6,10 and 20 μl of whole fresh blood obtained from six subjects was collected on paper, white cotton and glass and were stored for 3 years at room temperature.
***DNA extraction***: extracted from the fresh blood of unrelated healthy subjects (HUMTHO1 n= 288; HUMvWA31 n=211) and from 72 bloodstains using phenol-chloroform (Budowle and Baetchel 1990) and chelex (Walsh el al. 1991) methods.
***PCR amplification***: according to Brinkmann et al. (1993a) for HUMTH01 and Wiegand et al. (1993) for HUMvWA31 with the primers proposed by Edwards et al. (1991) for HUMTH01 and by Kimpton et al. (1992) for HUMvWA31.
***Electrophoresis***: separation by high-resolution PAGE (Budowle et al. 1991) for HUMTH01 and denaturing PAGE for HUMvWA31 using a discontinuous buffer (Allen et al. 1989). Bands were visualised by silver staining (Budowle et al. 1991) and phenotyped by side-to-side comparison with an allelic ladder (Fig. 1 a,b,c).

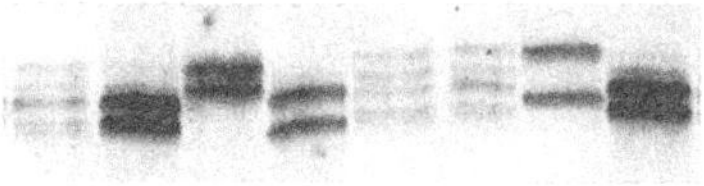

a)

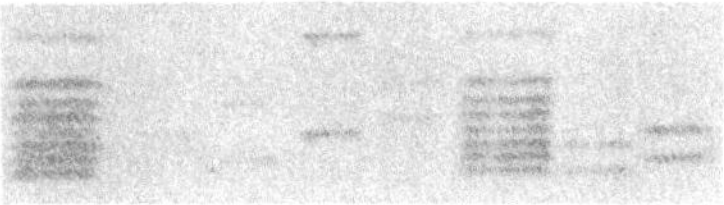

b)

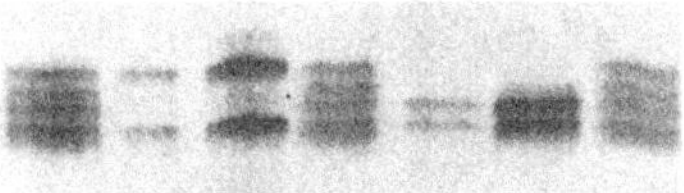

c)

**Fig. 1 (a,b,c)** Amplified DNA fragments in HUMTH01 and HUMvWA31 systems using polyacrylamide gels and silver staining.
a) HUMTH01: from left to right: allele ladder is in lanes 1,5,6; HUMTH01 phenotypes: lane 2: 8-9.3; lane 3: 6-7; lane 4: 8-10; lane 7: 6-9; lane 8: 8-9.3.
b) HUMvWA31: from left to right: allele ladder is in lanes 1,6; HUMvWA31 phenotypes: lane 2: 17-18; lane 3: 15-19; lane 4: 11-17; lane 5: 14-16; lane 7: 18-20; lane 8: 17-19.
c) HUMTH01: from left to right: allele ladder is in lanes 1,4,7: lanes 2 and 3: 6-9.3 phenotypes from 3 and 20 μl aged bloodstains; lanes 5, 6: 8-9.3 phenotypes from 3 and 20 μl aged bloodstains.

## RESULTS AND DISCUSSION

Six alleles for HUMTH01 (183-207 bp) and 7 for HUMvWA31 (138-162 bp) were observed. A new allele located on the anodic side of allele HUMvWA31*14 was found (temporarily designated as HUMvWA*11). The frequency distribution of HUMTH01 and HUMvWA31 alleles is shown in figure 2 a,b. Observed and expected genotypes were compared by assuming the Hardy-Weinberg law (HUMTH01 $\chi^2$ = 9,40 0.80< P <0.90; 15 d.f.- HUMvWA31 $\chi^2$= 22.166 0.75< P <0.90; 28 d.f.). The power of discrimination (PD) and chance of exclusion were, respectively, 0.92 and 0.57 for HUMTH01 and 0.93 and 0.61 for HUMVWA31, suggesting that these STR systems may be a powerful tool in forensics. Table 1 summarizes the results expressed as percentages of amplification and typing from aliquoted bloodstains on various substrates, using two extraction methods (phenol-chloroform vs chelex). The results show that: a) 3 μl are sufficient to obtain positive amplification; b) paper and glass are better substrates than white cotton; c) in our bloodstain storage conditions, phenol-isoamyl alcohol was better than the chelex method.

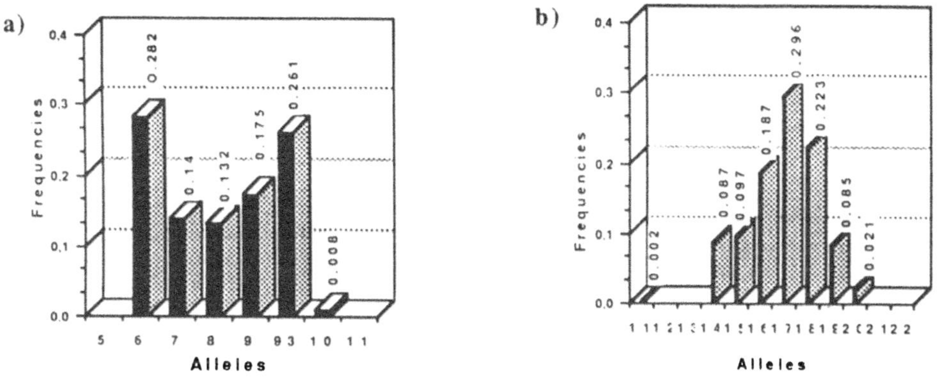


**Fig. 2 (a,b)** Frequency distribution of HUMTH01 (a) and HUMvWA31(b) system alleles in an Italian population sample.

| | PAPER | | WHITE COTTON | | GLASS | |
|---|---|---|---|---|---|---|
| SIZE | HUMTH01 %<br>*a* *b* | HUMvWA31 %<br>*a* *b* | HUMTH01 %<br>*a* *b* | HUMvWA31 %<br>*a* *b* | HUMTH01 %<br>*a* *b* | HUMvWA31 %<br>*a* *b* |
| 20 mcl | 100 (33.3) | 100 (16.7) | 16.7 (66.7) | 66.7 (66.7) | 100 (66.7) | 100 (33.3) |
| 10 mcl | 100 (33.3) | 100 (16.7) | 16.7 (66.7) | 50 (50) | 100 (66.7) | 100 (33.3) |
| 6 mcl | 100 (33.3) | 83.3 (16.7) | 16.7 (66.7) | 50 (50) | 83.3 (50) | 83.3 (16.7) |
| 3 mcl | 83.3 (33.3) | 66.7 (16.7) | 83.3 (50) | 16.7 (16.7) | 66.7 (33.3) | 83.3 (16.7) |

*a) phenol-chloroform; b) chelex*

**Table 1**. Amplification and typing of HUMTH01 and HUMVWA 31 from bloodstains of different sizes on various substrates using two extraction methods

## REFERENCES

Allen RC, Graves G, Budowle B (1989) Polymerase chain reaction amplification products separated on rehydratable polyacrylamide gels and stained with silver. Bio Tech 7: 736-744

Brinkmann B, Rand S, Bajanowsky T (1992) Forensic identification of urine samples. Int J Leg Med 105: 59-61

Budowle B, Baechtel FS (1990) Modifications to improve effectiveness of restriction fragment length polymorphism typing. Appl Theor Electrophor 1:181-187

Budowle B, Chakraborty R, Giusti AM, Eisenberg AJ, Allen RC (1991) Analysis of the variable number of tandem repeats locus D1S80 by the polymerase chain reaction followed by high resolution polyacrylamide gel electrophoresis. Am J Hum Genet 48: 137-144

Edwards A, Civitello A, Hammond HA, Caskey CT( 1991) DNA typing and genetic mapping with trimeric and tetrameric tandem repeats. Am J Hum Genet 49: 746-756

Edwards A, Hammond HA, Jin L, Caskey CT, Chakraborty R (1992) Genetic variation at five trimeric and tetrameric tandem repeat loci in four human population groups. Genomics 12: 241-253

Kimpton C, Walton A, Gill P (1992) A further tetranucleotide repeat polymorphism in the vWF gene. Hum Mol Genet 1:287.

Walsh PS, Metzger DA, Higuchi R (1991) Chelex 100 as a medium for simple extraction of DNA for PCR-based typing from forensic material. Biotechniques 10: 506-513

Weber J L and May P E (1989) Abundant class of human DNA polymorphisms which can be typed using the polymerase chain reaction. Am J Hum Genet 44: 388-396

Wiegand P, Bajanowski T, Brinkmann B (1993) DNA typing of debris from fingernails. Int J Leg Med 106: 81-83

# 3. Ethics and Forensic Psychiatry

# THE ONTOGENY OF PATHOLOGICAL SEXUALITY

V. ASTĂRĂSTOAE, C. SCRIPCARU

Medico-legal Institute, Iasi, Rumania

The evolution of the sexuality of mankind was produced by a continuous and parallel process together with humanization and urbanism. This is why human sexuality overcame the natural instinct of perpetuation of species and obtained a more important psychological and social component (society is the only body to define the limits between normal and pathological behaviour). Depending on the socio-cultural and moral factors, sexual instinct (sexual motivation) having a strong heredity component and also an affective one, could be defeated, sublimated or deviated.

This is why sexual liberty and inviolability, which became attributes of human personality, had to be protected not only by the community social relations but also by law. Therefore, the Rumanian laws condemn - not only sexual violence - but also sexual perversions.

Rape as the expression of sexual assault, it is considered by the Rumanian law as the most dangerous sexual violence. It is more serious when the victim is under 14 years old, if it was committed by a group of aggressors, the victim was under the protection, care or treatment of the author, if it caused to the victim a serious physical trauma or led to the death of the victim or suicide.

Sexual perversions, the second group of pathological sexuality condemned by law, represent sexual alerrations which caused public scandal. As a consequence, the law punished all unsual sexual bahavior which, since 1993, is punished only if it causes public scandal. The condemnation of sexual perversion is not only for the protection of a normal sexual life, but also for the protection of modesty and decency in sexual relations. Because of this, we proposed this study to be a research of the correlation between the state of social anomy and pathological sexual states such as sexual violence and sexual perversions with legal consequences.

MATERIAL AND METHODS

The lot was composed of 309 cases, investigated at the Medico-Legal Institute of Iasi, between 1991 and 1993. 279 of them (90,29%) appeared as sexual aggressions, in or outside the family, and 10 cases (9,71%) as modifications of normal sexual behaviour. The investigation of the cases was done with the hepl of a complex methodology which included biomedical and psychosociological exploring. The ***biomedical*** exploring had to establish the role af biological factors in the genesis of deviant reactions. The history, the study of medical documents, the family investigations, were done to find some traumatic factors ambient or genetic) with biological response, capable of modifying the psycho-comportamental normal behaviour. The ***psycho-sociological*** investigations consisted in the WAIS/WISE or RAVEN tests for the determination of intellectual development, the verbo-notional rhytm test (3') the W-M and CATTELL tests for detecting personality changes and anxiety, the SZONDY method for some obscure elements in the structure of personality and social investigation.

The purpose of these tests was to establish the level of development and intellectual efficiency, the affective and behavioural degree of maturation, the specific attitudes and hierarchy of interests, sexual impulse, etc.

RESULTS AND DISCUSSION

Age constitutes an important factor. The age of the aggressors ranged from 15 to 64 years, wuth a maximum level between 17 and 25 years (82,84%). In all the 25 cases of group rape (8,09%), ages ranged from 15 to 18 years old. The victim were - in 10% of the cases - under 12 years old. In 43% of the cases, the victims were between 12 and 18 years old in 5% they were women over 60 years old. In 60% of the cases we found body trauma and in 50% of the cases, there lesions were more than 3 days old, which led us to understand that the victims preffered to remain silent about the rape. In 16 cases (5,17%), the victims were obliged to submit also to sexual perversions such as anal penetration. The study of the intellectual development showed a medium Q.I. of the group of 97. On this occasion, we found that in 94 of the cases (30,42%), the victims were under the Q.I. of 70. which corresponds to mental debility in comparioson to the aggressors, where this level of Q.I. was found only in 36 cases (11,65%). The psychological investigations showed a huge variety of disturbances, especially in the emotional field. We found lack of affection, affective liability, emotional insensibility, psycho-physical instabiliyy, anger, amplified sexual impulse. At the same time as some emotional and aducational disturbances produced by the noxious families, people may develop behavioural disturbances and special sexual dysfunctions.

The evident coexistence of sexual dysfunctions together with personality disturbances in over 60% of the cases, make us consider them as a symptom of psychopathy and name it as "sexopathy". This is proved also by the fact that in only 12% of the cases, sexophony was only a symptom of psychosis.

From a victimological pont of view, we found a nondifferentiated sexual motivation, consumed in conditions of fragile personality, infantile credulity and alcohol consumation, which led to the well known ambivalence and liability of the led to the well known ambivalence and liability of the opposition to aggression.

We were very interested in the ontogeny of sexual perversions and their risk of becoming permanent in adults, by fixation and pathological conditioning. Starting from Freud's concept of "polymorphous perversions of childhood", we may admit that the first negative sexual experiences, risk to be permanent and produce a non-harmonic integration of personality, as we saw frequently in adults with habitual sexopathies. The lack of sentiments of guilt, erotical-effective dissociation, etc, dyssharmonic personality, appear after a long evolution as a consequence of the absence of infantile cleavage and of the dedublation of personality. In this context, perversion is not only natural so it does not always justify the severity of law, but more frequent, it is an antithetical consequence of profound individual impulses and of the replacement of biological reality with a pathological imagination.

CONCLUSIONS

Sex behaviour in adults may be the epiphenomenon pf a deficient ontogeny concerning sexual integration in individual personality.

In thisontogeny and affective trauma, pathological family conditions, negative induction, etc., may play a very important role.

# Violation of human rights by the Soviet regime in Latvia. Medico-legal aspects.

U. Berzins

Department of Legal Medicine, Medical Academy of Latvia

Violence against an individual, if it grows into a system, acquires a mass-scale character and, if it is carried out (usually in an obscure way) by political, economic or military structures, it turns into genocide. This is the recent history of the Baltic States. Latvia gained its independence in 1918, and after 22 years of existence it fell a victim to the regime, that was ambitious for power, and in 1940 Latvia was occupied by the Red Army. Self-confidence of the freedom-loving and self-respecting nation hindered the Soviet regime to fulfill its geopolitical ambitions. It had to carry out systematic, well-planed and rafined complex of various actions. To make it short, the scheme for action was as follows - to exterminate the Latvian nation in its ethnic, historic territory on the coast of the Baltic Sea, by mass-scale deportations to other regions, thus submitting them to perish. At the same time, masses of aliens were let in by implementing a corresponding economic policy. It was explained to be an immense gift to the Latvian people. But what was in the background of all this? Here are the data of demographic statistics : the number of Latvians in 1939 was 75% ; in 1989 - 50 years later - 52%. The nation was on the verge of extinction. Even nowadays, 65% of the inhabitants in Riga, the capital of Latvia, are aliens. By the way, the western European countries feel threatened and alarmed, if the number of foreigners exceeds 5%. The extent of genocide in Latvia is characterized by the following data. During the first stage of deportations, about 21000 Latvian citizens were transferred to Siberia. The next mass extermination took place in 1949 when, according to a similar scenario, about 40000 Latvian citizens were deported. Apart from these mass actions, continuous "work" was going on to separate individuals or groups of people. In the 1945-1953 period, which is considered as the darkest period of Stalinism terror, about 160000 Latvian citizens, as if by political motives, were again deported, arrested and put to death.

The programme, how to destroy physical and mental potentials of the Latvian nation, was implemented with the help of the various state institutions, whose activities were coordinated by the leading highranking authorities of the Communist Party and of the Soviet government. The State Security Committee (SSC) must be mentioned as one of the most important sectors in the network of the existing system. The many branched SSC apparatus and the network of its agents spied on everybody. Countless testimonies published now, give evidence, that all means were acceptable to acquire information and to make people confess. Any physical and mental violence was exerted, starting with the most primitive and most cruel ones, such as torturing by means of mechanical, thermal or electric appliances, with a purpose to threaten and humiliate people. No one was called to account for the consequences of these deeds, because usually the way out from institutions headed straight to places of confinement or to a cemetary. However, just after 1953, the Soviet SSC tried to make their coercion activity methods more

liberal and humane in the world's eyes, substituting physical violence by psychic methods.
We must also speak about violence done by warders and criminals in the places of imprisonment. In those rare cases when violence resulted in death, and forensic medical expertises were done, these facts were let out. Yet, the exact data of the lethal cases are not exactly known. Causes of death were attributed to various diseases, people were either cremated or buried.
Another example of violence - service in the Soviet army. As a rule, the youth from the Baltic States, who served in the Soviet army, were sent far away from their homes. Service in the army was hard in general, but the attitude towards soldiers from the Baltic regions was especially bad because of their nationality. Physical abuse of young people done in this way was another means to destroy the genetic fund of the Latvian nation. According to rough estimates, we have information that about 20 young people perished in the eighties, but about 300-400 had been mutilated physically. As to moral violence done, we have only an approximate idea. One cannot neglect the demoralizing consequences resulting from homosexual abuse, observed in Soviet army.

Also psychiatry in the Soviet Union was applied as a repressive measure against those whose opinions differred. Many people who worked in the field of culture, politics or social sphere at time were isolated from the society. They were told to be mentally ill and were submitted to compulsory treatment in mental clinics. It is considered as extremely severe violence according to international conventions and condemned by people all over the world.

What reported above is quite true about the recent past. These facts must never be forgotten. And yet we should not forget that in the centre of all these ethical and legal aspects of the problem, there are the people who suffered from the consequences of violence. A special commission, which is set up in the parliament, is going to investigate the crimes committed by the totalitarian regime. The commission has not said its last word as yet, because there is much work to do. Another commission at the Ministery of the Interior must look through 77000 files of the repressed Latvian citizens. How many of them need medical and psychological rehabilitation - these are the facts to be found out. Wounds, inflicted by physical violence, have healed by now. Yet, we cannot say the same about the mental damage done.

Mental rehabilitation of the repressed, as well as the rehabilitation of the whole Latvian nation, is greatly troubled by complicated and uncertain political situation in the Baltic region. An atmosphere of nervousness and irritability is maintained by covetings of the now fallen apart Soviet empire, which still is claiming its right and privileges. One proof of it is the unwillingness of the Soviet military forces to withdraw their troops, inventing various pretences.

The heritage of the former empire is the high level of criminal offenses. The mass of aliens, who have flooded the Republic, do whatever they like, not respecting the laws. This is a good soil for all kinds of violence, which in some cases turns into torture. There are cases, when elements of torturing are part of the activities of individual policemen, who cannot get rid of the old style of work.

# THE CONSENT OF THE MINOR AS BONE MARROW DONOR IN EUROPEAN COMMUNITY COUNTRIES

**Fabio BUZZI, M. Cristina OPPEZZO**
**Institute of Legal Medicine - University of Pavia (Italy)**

Marrow transplantation frequently requires minor donors, patients' siblings especially, thus causing several problems for doctors in getting an ethical and legally valid informed consent.

This transplantation, often the only therapy against many haematological diseases with serious prognosis, has had a growing diffusion thanks to improvement of immuno-suppression and, recently, even through the HLA typification of marrow data banks. In fact, the 15th and last edition of Bone Marrow Donors Worldwide contains almost 2 million donors, available from 31 registries in 27 countries. This means an increasing chance to apply to non consanguineous donors.

Moreover, in the EC area, the organs and tissues exchange and the free access to health services (transplantation included) are today current procedures: thus the reason to adopt uniform rules in this matter. Until now we understand that only France and Spain have adopted formal procedures to obtain the minor donor's consent in this matter.

About fifteen years ago, the European Council had already adopted the Resolution, of May 29-11, 1978 on the member countries legislations harmonization about removal and transplantation of human organs. It was formally suggested to member countries that they conform to it within five years, i.e. May 1983, more than ten years ago.

The Resolution stated that:

1) the donor or, in case of a minor, his legal guardian, must be informed, in an adequate way, about the possible medical, social and psychological effects of the removal, as well as the benefits for the recipitent;

2) a written consent is required for the removal of regenerative tissues that may involve risks to the donor's health, and for the removal of non-regenerating tissues;

3) in case of legally incapable subjects, regenerative tissues removal must be exceptional; it can be performed with the legal guardian's consent only, except for an opposition of the subject himself;

4) if the removal may be risky for the legally incapable subject, a special authorization is necessary;

5) the removal of non-regenerative tissues from legally incapable subjects are forbidden, except if the subject can understand the situation and give his consent, along with authorization of the legal guardian and of an appropriate Authority, anyhow assuming that donor and recipient are consanguineous.

Later, the European Council published the text of the third Conference of Health Service European Ministers, held in Paris on November 16th and 17th, 1987.
This text stated that removal from legally incapable subjects is not permitted, except in the case of regenerative tissues, and only withe the consent of the subject or of his legal guardian; it was then underlined the care of limiting the donor's risks as

much as possible, and the absolute ban of any commercialization in this matter.
Genetic link was requested for kidney donation. Many EC countries require it for removal of regenerative tissues, from minors as well. This is the condition for removal of paired organs, or parts of them, or of regenerative tissues (blood excepted) in EC countries:

| | from donors legally capable to consent | from minors as well |
|---|---|---|
| Belgium | yes, if the recipient's life is in danger | consanguineous only |
| Denmark | yes | yes |
| France | yes | consanguineous only |
| Great Britain | yes | yes |
| Greece | yes | consanguineous only |
| Ireland | yes | consanguineous only |
| Italy | yes (kidney consanguineous only) | yes (marrow only) |
| Luxembourg | yes | consanguineous only |
| Netherlands | yes | yes |
| Portugal | yes | yes |
| Germany | yes | yes |
| Spain | yes | consanguineous only |

As far as marrow is concerned, genetic link is justified by the consanguineous donation opportunity, especially among siblings, but it seems very restrictive in the perspective of wider transplant possibilities through marrow data banks, where in future minors able to understand (especially if older than 12-14) could be accepted, as donors or as recipients.
The International Convention of Children Rights, held in New York on November 20th, 1989, stated (Art. 12) that the minor has the right to freely express his opinion on every matter he is involved in, and that his opinions must duly be taken into consideration.
Apropos, even in case of consanguinity in the majority of EC Countries, it is necessary to inform the minor about medical procedures and to consider his possible refusal.

| | request of parents or consent of legal representative | intervention of ethical committee (*), jurisdictional organ (**) or witness (***) | information to the minor able to understand and consideration of his possible refusal |
|---|---|---|---|
| Belgium | yes | *** | yes |
| Denmark | yes | --- | yes |
| France | yes | * | yes |
| Great Britain | yes | * | yes |
| Greece | yes | --- | --- |
| Ireland | yes | --- | --- |
| Italy | yes | ** | --- |
| Luxembourg | yes | * | yes |
| Netherlands | yes | --- | yes |
| Portugal | yes | --- | yes |
| Germany | yes | --- | yes |
| Spain | yes | * | yes |

Some European Countries provide for the intervention of an ethical committee, to ensure the greatest neutrality in obtaining the minor's acceptance. In fact it is arguable that this situation may condition his will, because of the ineluctably strong influence of parents upon their own sons. In Germany, in the extreme situation of a parent recipient, a jurisdictional guaranty in expressly required, in order to avoid the peculiar overlap of rules and interests.

Outside EC, Sweden and Finland have model rules in this matter and national advisory committees, charged also to validate parents and minor consent, upon analysis of the peculiar aspects of every case.

We would like to stress the importance of a neutral and authoritative intervention, such as that of an ethical committee. We think this advisory organ could give the best guardianship of any interest involved in information procedures, donor consent gathering and, especially, ethical validation of the removal from a minor incapable of giving a valid consent.

This condition needs a peculiar legal and ethical consideration, founded not only upon the parents' will: two cases have been reported of birth on purpose to obtain marrow for a member of the family (and theoretically, this member could even be one of the parents) and one case of refusal of typing by a mother of a two step-siblings, born out of wedlock, in favour of a legitimate one, who was dying of leukemia.

Incidentally, the third World Medical Assembly, held in Madrid October 1987, stated that both donor and recipient are considered as patients and that their rights must be likewise protected; moreover, the organ transplantation project must be discussed between them, or the parents or the legal representatives of minor donors, explaining carefully the procedures, known risks, potential dangers and any other possible alternative.

It follows the ample usefulness of the intervention of an ethical committee, in this matter necessarily including an evolutive age psychologist, to test the competency of the minor to understand this kind of request and to give his valid consent or not.

At the moment, in European Countries, formalities to inform and to obtain the consent of minor donors are very different:

| | |
|---|---|
| **BELGIUM** | **Married donor under 21: consent of the adult who allowed the marriage. From 15 to 18: written consent in the presence of a witness, countersigned by the legal guardian and endorsed by a doctor.** |
| **DENMARK** | **Minors under 21: written consent of the donor and of parents or of the legal guardian.** |
| **FRANCE** | **Minor opinion gathered from an «ad hoc» committee (L. 76-1181/1976), that must inform him about the operation consequences and respect his will; the committee must also obtain the consent of parents or of the legal guardian.** |
| **GREAT BRITAIN** | **Ordinary procedure of consent extablished by the N.H.S. circular (1/8/93). From 16 to 18 written consent of the donor. Minors under 16 may consent if capable of understanding; if not, the consent of the parents or of the legal guardian is required.** |
| **GREECE** | **Written consent of the legal guardian.** |
| **IRELAND** | **Written consent of the legal guardian.** |
| **ITALY** | **No rules established.** |
| **LUXEMBOURG** | **Written consent together with an authorization of three experts (two doctors) appointed by the Health Department. If donor is minor, the consent of the legal guardian is also required.** |
| **NETHERLANDS** | **Written consent of the legal guardian.** |
| **PORTUGAL** | **Verbally expressed consent of the legal guardian and assent of the mentally capable minor.** |
| **GERMANY** | **Written consent of the legal guardian. When the receiver is a parent, consent of an «ad hoc» legal guardian. If minor is over 14, he is considered capable of expressing a valid consent.** |
| **SPAIN** | **Written consent of the parents, endorsed by a state authority and countersigned by a doctor.** |

Owing to these differences, we propose a simple and quite warrantable procedure, with regard to the following items:

1) Activation of an ethical committee including a psychologist of the evolutive age;

2) Ascertainment, by this ethical committee, of the mental competence of minor donor to understand the situation and to express a valid consent;

3) Obtaining, at separate sessions, of the parents' or legal guardian's consent; not binding in case of parental disagreement, or of different choice from that of the minor, judged mentally capable;

4) Statement by the committee of removal feasibility from the ethical point of view.

Finally, transplantion being a procedure that requires an high degree of unselfishness and solidarity from donors, and that has remarkable positive effects on other people's health, with some risks for the donor's health (even if statisticaily slight), it seems quite right to provide specific measures of compensation for eventual damages. At the moment, such measures exist only in Spain and Portugal.

# INTRODUCTION A L'ETUDE DES PROBLEMES DE L'ETHIQUE EN PSYCHIATRIE MEDICO-LEGALE

GIACOMO CANEPA

Professeur à l'Institut de Médecine Légale
Via de Toni 12, Université de Gènes, Italie

## 1. Considérations préliminaires

On constate actuellement une certaine confusion dans le domaine des problèmes concernant les règles de conduite à suivre dans le domaine bio-médical. A ce propos, il faut présenter les définitions ou précisions suivantes :

1) l'éthique, en général coincide avec la philosophie morale, qui étudie l'action humaine et particulièrement les facteurs étiologiques de cette action, les finalités, ainsi que les règles et les valeurs qui sont à la base de l'action même. Dans ce cadre général on peut considérer :

- la bio-éthique, qui concerne plus spécifiquement les problèmes susdits dans le domaine de l'action biomédicale, et dans le cadre des activités qui se développent par les études scientifiques (Canepa, Lagazzi, 1988) sur l'être humain et qui ne sont pas encore, dans plusieurs Etats, l'objet de codification légale (par exemple l'euthanasie, l'insémination artificielle, etc.).
- l'éthique médicale, concernant les règles de conduite qui se posent, pour les médecins, dans le domaine des études scientifiques susdites afin de donner à ces règles une valeur légale par leur introduction dans la législation future ;

2) la déontologie médicale concerne l'ensemble des normes qui règlent la conduite professionnelle des médecins dans leur activité pratique, établies surtout par les lois déjà en vigueur, et aussi par les normes culturelles et sociales qui sont propres à la tradition de chaque pays.

Sur la base de ces distinctions préliminaires (éthique médicale et déontologie médicale) il faut considérer spécifiquement les problèmes de la psychiatrie médico-légale.

2. La psychiatrie médico-légale et ses problèmes du point de vue éthique et déontologique

Etant donné la quantité énorme des problèmes qui se posent dans ce domaine (Rasch), je présenterai une liste de sujets (qui seront, j'espère, l'objet d'approfondissement au moment de la discussion) :

1) l'humanité, le respect des droits humains et la "sympathie" affective (suivant la signification étymologique de ce mot) en tant que principes communs à l'activité psychiatrique, soit clinique, soit médico-légale (Canepa, 1983 ; Gayda) ;
2) le problème du consentement en psychiatrie clinique et en psychiatrie médico-légale : affinités et différences dans le domaine des devoirs et des pouvoirs ;
3) la défense de l'utilisation de techniques diagnostiques qui peuvent exposer à un danger (p. exemple TC cérébrale avec moyens de constraste) en psychiatrie médico-légale ;
4) le droit du malade mental d'avoir une copie de son dossier, après la période d'internement, en psychiatrie clinique et en psychiatrie médico-légale ;
5) les entrevues ou colloques en psychiatrie médico-légale et le problème de considérer les déclarations spontanées de la part du patient à son psychiatre traitant (et de l'expertisé à l'expert en psychiatrie médico-légale), concernant sa culpabilité et non sa personnalité ;
6) les traitements psychiatriques obligatoires (y compris l'hospitalisation sans consentement) en psychiatrie clinique et en psychiatrie médico-légale (Conseil de l'Europe, 1983, 1986 ; Canepa, 1992, 1993 ; De Guevara, Moya Pueyo) ;
7) le problème de la responsabilité professionnelle du psychiatre expert, c'est-à-dire du médecin légiste psychiatre. Sur ce point il faut faire une distinction préalable :
- les problèmes concernant la psychiatrie légale, dans les pays où le psychiatre expert a aussi la tâche de soigner ou traiter (Bean ; Beyaert) le malade mental délinquant, se rapportent aussi à la psychiatrie clinique, suivant une extension plus élargie ;
- dans les autres pays la tâche du psychiatre expert est limitée à l'évaluation médico-légale et, par conséquent, les problèmes qui se posent dans ces cas peuvent être examinés dans le cadre des précédents points énumérés. Etant donné le temps

limité de ce rapport introductif, je souhaite que tous les problèmes énumérés soient examinés et approfondis au cours de la discussion qui suivra, ainsi que des communications, objet de notre workshop.

3. Conclusions

J'ai cherché à éclaircir, au début de ce rapport, la définition, la tâche et l'importance de :

1) l'éthique médicale ;

2) la déontologie médicale.

Cette distinction correspond exactement aux deux parties essentielles de la médecine légale :

1) la médecine légale judiciaire, correspondnt à l'activité du médecin légiste qui collabore avec le magistrat pour l'application de la loi en vigueur ;

2) la médecine légale juridique, qui concerne l'activité du médecin légiste qui collabore avec le législateur (national ou régional) pour la promulgation de lois nouvelles ou pour la réforme des lois existantes qu'il faut modifier.

Il s'ensuit que :

1) l'activité du médecin légiste est nécessaire et de première importance dans les comités déontologiques (et non d'éthique), dont le but essentiel est de formuler des avis aux médecins pour ce qui concerne la conduite professionnelle, compte tenu des normes et des lois en vigueur ;

2) l'activité du médecin légiste est nécessaire, même si non de première importance, au niveau des comités éthiques, qui doivent fonctionner au niveau national et régional pour l'étude de problèmes non encore codifiés dans le système législatif en vigueur.

Je pense, que dans cette perspective, on doit bien préciser l'activité pratique du médecin légiste, au sujet des problèmes de psychiatrie clinique et de psychiatrie médico-légale, dans le cadre des comités déontologiques et des comités d'éthique.

# Références bibliographiques

**Bean P.** (1986) Mental disorder and legal control. Cambridge University Press, Cambridge

**Beyaert F.** (1990) Dutch forensic psychiatry and Pieter Baan Center Utrecht. In: Bluglass R and Bowden P (ed) Principles and practice of forensic psychiatry, Churchill Livingstone, Edinburgh, P 1339

**Canepa G.** (1983) Note introduttive allo studio della responsabilità professionale dello psichiatra in ambito ospedaliero. Rivista Italiana di Medicina Legale, 5:19-28

**Canepa G., Lagazzi M.** (1988) Les problèmes éthiques et déontologiques des nouvelles technologies génétiques. Persception sociale et prescriptions normatives dans une perspective européenne. Les cahiers des recherches criminologiques, 9:579, Université de Montréal

**Canepa G.** (1992) Les droits du malade mental. Hospitalisation sans consentement du patient. Evaluation des expériences de libération. Rapport d'introduction. Rapport de synthèse. Comptes-rendus du XVe Congrès de l'Académie Internationale de Médecine Légale et de Médecine Sociale (Zaragoza, 27-31 mai 1991), Libreria General, Zaragoza, P 223, P 231

**Canepa G., Montolivo A., Salvi M.** (1993) La protection du malade mental en Europe. Actes des Xèmes Journées Méditerranéennes de Médecine Légale (Montpellier 13-17 septembre 1992). Imp. Presses du Midi, Saint-Jean-de-Védas, P 510

**Conseil de l'Europe** (1983) Protection Juridique de personnes atteintes de troubles mentaux et placées comme patients involontaires. Recommandation n. R (83)2. Affaires Juridiques, Strasbourg

**Conseil de l'Europe** (1986) Etudes sur la responsabilité pénale et le traitement psychiatrique des délinquants malades mentaux. Etudes relatives à la recherche criminologique, 24, Affaires Juridiques, Comité Européen pour les problèmes criminels, Strasbourg

**Conseil de l'Europe** (1986) Mesures visant à promouvoir l'intégration sociale des personnes handicapées mentales. Accord partiel. Conseil de l'Europe, Strasbourg

**De Guevara J.L., Moya Pueyo V.** (1988) Problèmes de l'internement psychiatrique en Espagne. Acta Medicinae Legalis et Socialis, 32/2:203

**Gayda M.** (1991) Les droits et la protection des personnes hospitalisées en raison de troubles mentaux et de leurs conditions d'hospitalisation. Journ. de Méd. Lég. Dr. Méd., 34:339

**Rasch W.** (1982) Current issues of forensic psychiatry in the Federal Republic of Germany. Acta Crim. Japon., 48:135-144

# CAUSAL EXPLANATION AND UNDERSTANDING IN PSYCHIATRIC FORENSIC EXAMINATION

AUTHORS: Prof. Dr. Virgil T. Dragomirescu, Dr. Octavian Buda

National Institute of Legal Medicine "Mina Minovici"
Sos. Vitan-Birzesti 9, 75669 Bucharest - ROMANIA

The Causal Interpretation Method may be extended from the traumatology examination field into the psychiatric examination branch in order to determine the proper connections which exist between personality, behaviour, transgression (nature, motive, motivation, realization, attitude before and after the action was done, etc). One the other hand the nature of responsibility or of irresponsibility must be determined.

The paper endeavours to present a general interdisciplinary criteriology definition for an individual interpretation of facts and responsibility; this may be useful for a harmonized forensic psychiatric methodology in all European countries and to link the Forensic Causal Interpretation with socio-juridical causality, using psycho-social facts determination.

In forensic psychiatric theory and practice, the philosophical notion of causality represents both a fundamental principle and a practical method. A principle because it is tied to the necessity of a determinist integration in social bio-medico-psychical life, particularly into the legal and social causality report. A method because it represents the main tool in searching the objectives of the examination in order to obtain conclusions of scientific quality.

Causality must not be considered synonymous with aetiology or aetiopathology (but can be sufficient for an analogical analysis), for the same reason cause and aetiological agent "have different" meanings.

The German psychiatrist and philosopher Karl Jaspers (1883-1969) has introduced, between the bio-medical level and the psychological level of the psychopathological approach, a methodological dichotomy that considerably influenced psychiatry and related sciences, including forensic psychiatry. He devised the terms *"explanation"* and *"understanding"*. The aim of the bio-medical sciences is to explain; the aim of psychology is "par excellence" to understand. The first method consists, more specifically, in the submission of individual cases under hypothetically assumed general laws of nature (in our case, medical biology) and is aimed at generalisations about reproducible and predictible phenomena. The second method grasps the individual and the unique features of their history. These aspects represent both, fundamental principles and methods of solving the objectives of the main categories of forensic examination which occur in the assistance and socio-judicial probation. As to the practical application of those principles related to causality (explanation being related to the so-called *"external causality"* of bio-medical type, and understanding to the *"internal causality"* of psychological nature) it is limited to the necessity of creating operational schemes which would be not only intelligible, but also translatable in a suggestive way for the medico-judicial assistance, without altering the scientific truth.

We consider that the main objective of an examination is the offender's personality. This must be defined in order to determine individual structures and tendencies. To connect these structures with elements of juridical specific related facts represents the only way to individualise each case.

A borrowed terminology can determine confusion or, even more, diagnosic errors in forensic and judicial practice. To avoid these errors, it is important to use significant, universal validated notions (responsibility, discernment, psycho-physical capacity) avoiding terminological adaptations that can misrepresent the scientific truth. Conflicts between experts still exist. The main controversy lies in accepting terms like culpability or imputability instead of the complex judicial term of responsibility. We consider that determinism is more related to facts than causality, for the same reasons that rule the *"condition"* term to reflect a general and permanent situation and *"circumstance"* term to consider the cause action at a precise moment of time. The forensic psychiatric examination is called to emphasize the existing circumstances in the action moment, in order to establish psychical capacity and responsibility for that moment.

In forensic psychiatric examination there are two main stages for examining and solving the "determinism" concept and the causal relationship:

- to establish the subject's and the offence characteristics and the causal relationships with psychical, penal and exercise capacity (responsibility not reflected by examination conclusions). This is the conscience level that is to be analyzed with the help of the discernment qualitative function correlated to acquired clinical and forensic laboratory tests data (**A**).

- to establish the causal relationship between individual psychological characteristics (mature/immature, borderline/pathological) and main constitutive elements of the offence (nature of the offence, way of achievement, existing circumstances, former and later attitude) (**B**).

**A**. The person's characteristics must reflect the main bio-psycho-social structural components (impulses, tendencies, conscience level) and individual normal and pathological psychological determinants with the help of the study of conflict and motivation nature.

The offence characteristics can offer indirect diagnosis conclusions (aggressiveness quantification, from normal to pathologic, reactivity and antisocial conflictuality).

It is usual to accept that forensic psychiatric examination use psychiatric criteriology in correlation with forensic methodology in order to obtain a correct diagnosis and accurate conclusions.

Causal relation represents a well established truth in forensic traumatology, but forensic psychiatry is not ready to adopt the same attitude. We consider that this criteriology can enhance the expert's ability to establish the author's responsibility. On the other hand it represents the way to increase the evidence value of examination by making it more criminologically oriented. So, we can discuss about a complex - operational norm setter in establishing a causal relation between psychical, judicial and exercise capacity in order to transpose the philosophical notion of determinism to the social life.

**B**. Observing the causal relation between individual, psychological characteristics and main constitutive elements of the offence at a precise moment of time, we have to conclude that all the mentioned factors are concordant with the next items:

- the disease diagnosis (illness or syndrome)
- the nature and intensity of the psychic disturbances (studied at the time of the offence)
- time and intensity of any existing conflict situation
- any existing favour of circumstances (offence, provocation, alcohol ingestion, frustration, physical and physiological status)
- sex, age, environment
- progressive stage of psychic disease, with a focused attention on gradual, cyclic and/or sinuous disease evolution.

As we have already mentioned, in assessing the traumatic prejudice, the causal relation chain is widely operational. The causal relation is accepted as direct (with two sections, unconditioned/conditioned) and indirect causality. This is the main instrument to generate a correct clarification of the offence terms.

A direct unconditioned traumatic prejudice correlated with the primary causes touches is to be defined in respect of the following terms:
- the reality of the trauma
- the reality of the prejudice
- the existence of any antecedent dysfunctions
- any other possible causes generating similar effects.

We have implemented the same causal relationships to the forensic psychiatric examination. In order to reflect the main causal relation characteristics, we have defined some new terms that can reveal the continuity of the philosophical process:

**- Syncronism** - time concordance between existing psychical disorders and the aberrant behaviour (demonstrated by "forensic debut" of psychiatric disorder).

**- Syntonicity** - intensity concordance between psychical disorders and the gravity of the offence (pathologic homicide in a jealousy delirium).

**- Syntendency** - trend concordance between the nature of psychical disorders and the nature of the offence. The mentioned association can amplify or inhibit the nature of the main cause.

**- Syntopicity** - an additional notion, the interval concordance between the nature of psychic troubles and time, place and existing circumstances, that may indicate the concordance between causes, conditions and circumstances location in conditioned causal relation chain.

It must be remembered that there is another indirect causal relation (secondary) developed as a complication of the causal chain (a supplementary event arising from the primary cause able to influence the nature of the offence or to determine secondary effects).

Besides these three main causal relations, we can discuss others, such as: divergent or antagonistic causality, or the term of complex causality (very often considered because of its complexity). The antagonistic causality is to be characterized by the lack of syncronism and syntonicity as well as syntopicity.

The aforementioned causal chain philosophical notions are used in our everyday examination activity and are suitable to be accepted in a harmonized forensic psychiatric methodology, in order to promote a larger evidence value of the examination grounded on scientific truths.

## REFERENCES

DRAGOMIRESCU VT (1994) A criminologic and anthropologic prospective over the Forensic Investigation. Rom J Leg Med 2: 12-17

DRAGOMIRESCU VT (1986) An interdisciplinary approach of causality in Forensic Medicine. Acta Medicinae Legalis et Socialis XXXVI/2:214-224

GLATZEL J (1985) Forensische Psychiatrie. Ferdinand Enke, Stuttgart, 66-69

JASPERS K (1965) Allgemeine Psychopathologie. Springer, Berlin-Heidelberg- New York

THIELE H (1962) Die gutachteliche Beurteilung des ursächlichen Zusammenhang auf der Grundlage von Disposition und Exposition. Dtsch Gesundheitwesen 12: 113-125

WRIGHT GH von (1971) Explanation and Understanding. Routledge and Kegan Paul, London, 4-7

WULFF HR, PEDERSEN SA, ROSENBERG R (1990) Philosophy of Medicine - an introduction. Blackwell Scientific Publications, Oxford-Edinburgh, 162-163

# THE BEHAVIOR CONSEQUENCES IN UNDESIRABLE-CHILD SYNDROME

*Laura Florescu, Cristiana Dragomir*
Orphanage no. 1 - IASI, ROMANIA

The consequence of a restrictive law concerning the abortion is an increasing number of abandoned (undesirable) children. The aim of this study is a watching over their behavior development.

The child with low birth weight represents an important problem both infant mortality/morbidity rate and psychomotor development. Numerous studies show that the maturation degree of newborn infants influences the entire somatic and psychic development during the first 3 years of life.

The environmental conditions in which the child is developing and, also, the way in which adults take care of him influence the activating process of genetic inheritance of the child. In normal conditions, mothers take care of their infants; in time, the rest of the family interferes in educational process, thus, the child is developing spontaneously into his family environment.

Children from Orphanages are developing into an artificial environment that influences the somatic and psychic development, especially due to affectivity frustration of adult-child relation.

The most important purpose in this situation is the education -- a complex process of internalizing the multiple environmental influences and relations.

Following up of psychomotor development, knowing the specific way of evolution of children from orphanages, taking notice of some negative abnormal phenomena are now and remain a permanent concern of the interdisciplinary equip -- physician- psychologist- physiotherapist- logopedist- pedagogue -- which will elaborate prophylactic and therapeutic measures for improvement, compensation and cancellation of any developmental delays.

**Method and materials**

We made a longitudinal study concerning the psychomotor development. We used two groups: group A - 25 children with low birth weight, abandoned in orphanage - and group B (the control group) - 25 children with normal birth weight, also abandoned in orphanage.

The study covers 3 years (1989-1992) and the children were between 3 months and 3 years old at that time.

The children with genetic and neurological disorders were not included in our study.

We used Denver II-test that has 125 items arranged in four behavioral areas: personal-social, fine-motor, gross-motor and language development. The test was performed every three month and the results were statistically analyzed through test "t".

**Results and discussions**

Concerning the global psychomotor development (figure 1), the highest level was found at children from group B (but not reaching normal values for age) in the interval of 0-6 months.

The lowest levels were found for group A children during the entire period of study.

Group B children have a psychomotor age on the right side of intervals until 6 months of life (close to normal values for age).

Group A children have psychomotor ages on the right side of intervals until 4 months of life, and, after that, on the left side of intervals.

The level of psychomotor development is decreasing for both groups and is placed under corresponding intervals, beginning with 12-15 months for group B and beginning with 9-12 months for group A.

Among 0-4 months on both groups we found near to normal values for age; the explanation is that during the first 3-4 months of life, the nutritional and sleeping activities prevail.

The developmental delays are emphasized in time, when mental activities are predominant. The lack of nursing and educational personnel influence negatively the psychomotor development, especially in group A-children.

Monthly assimilation rhythm (figure 2) completes the anterior findings:

- the most increased assimilation rhythm is found from birth until 6-9 months of life, with important differences: 0.79 for group A and 0.85 for group B (table 1);
- assimilation rhythm has an important decrease with age: 0.30 for group A and 0.33 for group B;
- assimilation rhythm is, for entire period of the study 0.38 for group A and 0.43 for group B.

As concerns the psychomotor development on comportamental sections (figure 3) we find the best gross-motor development for both groups and for entire period of study.

The differences as against group B values occur during the second half-year and during the third year of life.

Tests, like "pull to sit-no head lag" and "pull to stand" will be realized later by group A-children and, also "jump up", "broad jump" and "balance each foot" tests - during the third year of life.The explanation may be the lack of movement possibilities (the lack of play-rooms or endowment).

The lowest level was found for language development, in both groups. The significant differences occur after the first year of life. This delay can be explained by the lack of affective adult-child relation and the lack of adult interest in children (all activities are mechanically performed, without speaking with the child).

On the other hand, we must not forget that also in families, where exist the best conditions for children, can appear delays in language development.

**Conclusions:**

The global level of psychomotor development on both groups is considerable diminished as against normal values for age (p=0.001).

Due to the lack of affectionate adult-child relation, the language development is the most affected.

Between 0-9 months of age, the gross-motor development is almost normal for both groups, but an emphasized decreased is shown after that.

The lack of affectivity causes a delay of psychomotor development especially for language development. There are necessary:

- a proper regulation in accord with human rights (about contraception and birth-control);
- an increase of affectivity in Orphanages similar with family conditions;
- modification of personnel standard (a smaller number of children for one nursing person);
- an increase of the number of pedagogues, psychologist, physiotherapist;
- performing tests for audio-visual acuity for finding possible disorders;
- stimulation and precocious recovering of developmental delays.

**References:**

1. Brazeltan, Berej.; *"Children and Mothers. Differences of Development."* Bucharest, 1974.

2. Chiriac Irina, Trifan Livia; *"Neuro-psychic development aspects in 1-12 months old Children as against Birth-weight"*; Pediatrie, no. 3, 1973.

3. Dragomir Cristiana, Ciongradi Mihai, Virginia Scripcaru, Liliana Soroceanu, Sparling J., Alina Bordea; *"Prevention of developmental delays in yammer children in a Romanian orphanage"*; East European Journal, 1, no. 2, 1992.

4. David Miriam; *"Child of 0-2 years of life - affective life-familial problems"*, Eduard privat Ed., 1976.

5. Frankenberg K. W., Jasiah B. Dodds; *"Denver II Screening manual"*, Denver, Colorado-U.S.A., 1990.

6. Scripcaru Virginia, Apostol Stella; *"Contribution in the study of appearance of human capacities in children with low birth weight, from orphanage"*, vol."Psychologic and logopedic elements", Iasi, p. 288-92, 1988.

**Table and figures**

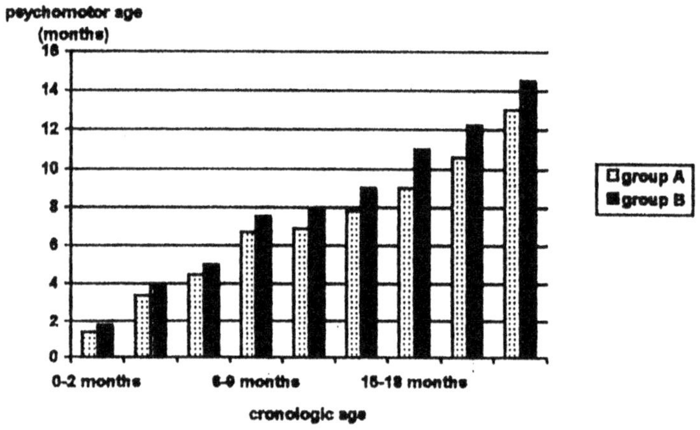


**Figure 1.** Global developing level.

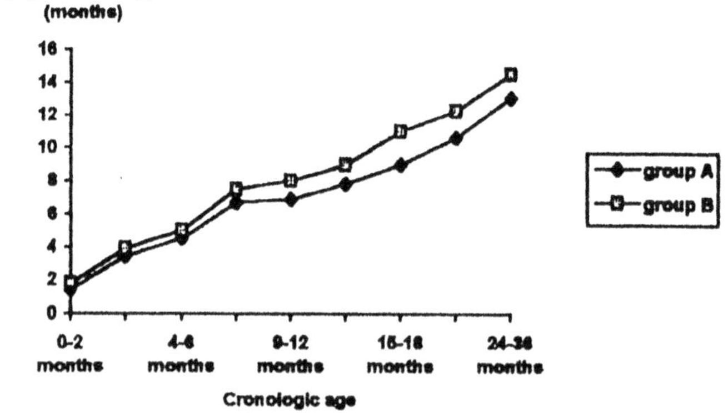


**Figure 2.** Monthly assimilation rhythm.

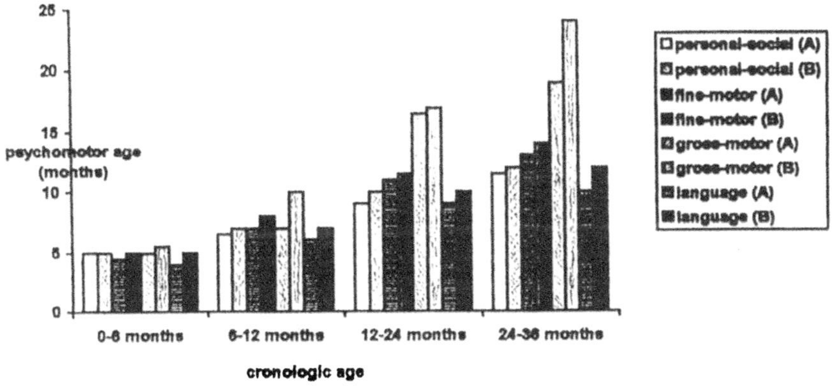


**Figure 3.** Psychomotor development in the four comportamental areas.

| age interval | group A | group B |
|---|---|---|
| 0-2 mo. •6-9 mo. | 0.80 | 0.79 |
| 6-9 mo. •24-36 mo. | 0.30 | 0.33 |
| 0-2 mo. •24-36 mo. | 0.38 | 0.43 |

**Table 1.** Assimilation rhythm.

# Enjeux éthiques des législations nouvelles de santé mentale

Fernand GOFFIOUL

*Président élu de l'Association Mondiale de Psychiatrie et Psychologie Légales*

Au cours des deux dernières décennies, beaucoup de pays ont revu ou sont en train de réaménager leur législation de santé mentale en matière civile, pénale et administrative.
La psychiatrie légale se situe au carrefour des idéologies et des pratiques tant sur les plans médical, philosophique, psychologique, social que juridique.
Au delà de la disparité des systèmes juridiques inspirés de la philosophie des Lumières, du Code Napoléon, du système de Common Law ou d'autres, la démarche législative actuellement évolutive des pays est influencée par des organismes internationaux intergouvernementaux N.-U., O.M.S., Conseil de l'Europe ou non gouvernementaux, O.N.G. à caractère scientifique ou humanitaire.

On peut structurer la réflexion éthique sur les tendances évolutives en psychiatrie légale en considérant des paliers interdépendants : valeurs, attitudes, motivations, besoins.

1° Le construit législatif, reflète une trajectoire et une dynamique socioculturelles est imprégné de **valeurs** que la société accepte et promeut, de façon pas toujours explicite.
De plus, le **rangement des valeurs** fait problème et crée des tensions contraires entre
- la protection de la vie et des intérêts de l'individu authentiquement considéré comme une personne digne de protection et d'aide et ceux de la collectivité,
- la tranquilité publique ou la liberté,
- les moyens sociaux et économiques permettant de maintenir les sujets problèmes dans la vie courante,
- l'autorité publique et le maintien de l'ordre et l'évaluation consciencieuse des risques. L'espace et le temps psychosociaux demandent à être revisités.

2° Les **attitudes**, ou dispositions à l'action sont traduites par les lois, règlements et les moyens effectifs de leur application. Il faut analyser les énoncés dans une perspective lexicographique transdisciplinaire médico-psycho-juridique.

3° Il faut scruter les exposés des motifs des lois qui sont censés éclairer sur les **motivations**. Il faut se méfier de leur attribuer un caractère obvie, tant les déterminants rationnels et irrationnels s'imbriquent et sont difficilement départagés.

4° Les **besoins** vitaux mais aussi les aspirations légitimes, mesurées par référence au standard moyen de la population doivent être pris en compte lors des périodes de liberté restreinte pour des raisons psychiatriques et ultérieurement.

Sur le plan **médical**, la protection de la vie, de l'intégrité physique et psychique, le consentement éclairé dans toute la mesure du possible, les choix thérapeutiques, la confidentialité, le respect de la vie privée sont des **impératifs éthiques fondamentaux que la psychopathologie dont le sujet est porteur n'abolit pas.**
Ils sont, en effet, modulés par une démarche diagnostique reposant sur des standards admis et retravaillés en permanence (ICD 10, DSM IV) par la communauté scientifique internationale mais aussi sur des stratégies thérapeutiques intégratives.

Les points de passage et de complémentarité entre mission d'expert et le rôle de thérapeute lors d'un traitement imposé méritent considération ajustée et soucieuse des Droits de l'Homme.

Les questions de la responsabilité pénale, de la capacité civile, de la dangérosité doivent être considérées en fonction de l'homme situé actuellement ou virtuellement, par rapport à son environnement humain.

La compatibilité sociale et la convivialité sont les fruits d'une attitude désaliénante, c'est-à-dire solidaire.

Il faut rendre plus visibles les débats éthiques de la médecine qui sont spécialement accentués en Psychiatrie Légale. Cette démarche qui rassemble médecins, juristes, sociologues et politiques des pays de tradition démocratique ancienne ou récemment reconquise appelle une action de sensibilisation pédagogique et sociale élargie.

# ACTIVITY OF THE MEDICAL ETHICS COMMITTEE OF THE MARSEILLES UNIVERSITY HOSPITAL CENTRE

G. LEONETTI; F. VAREILLES; M.D. PIERCECCHI; F.CIANFARANI
Unité de Médecine Légale - CHU La Timone MARSEILLES

The Medical Ethics Committee of the Marseilles University Hospital Centre was active from 1979 to 1991. Due to the scientific and ethical qualifications of its members, its large area of pratice extended to the medical region, the number of dossiers it dealt with for ten years (343) with great scientific, legal and ethical rigour, it has acquired wide experience in the field of experimentation on human beings and great notoriety among research centres and pharmaceutical laboratories.

As from the beginning, it enlarged its scope, going beyond examination of protocols to more general problems of ethics.

Moreover, it participated in the creation of a network of Medical Ethics Committees, through its relations with other regional Committees and the National Consultative Committee of Ethics (NCCE).

Voluntarily dissolved when Consultative Committees for the Protection of Persons in Biomedical Research (CCPPRB) were created by the Hurriet Law, its work in the ethical field did not stop, and it became an Ethics Committee no longer responsible for therapeutic test protocols.

In all, it took three kinds of decisions during its ten years activity :

- favourable in 66 % of the cases.
- favourable, given modifications or further elements to the protocol in 18,66 %
- negative in 0,58 %

The following tables resume these results:

| Years | 80 | 81 | 82 | 83 | 84 | 85 | 86 | 87 | 88 | 89 | Total |
|---|---|---|---|---|---|---|---|---|---|---|---|
| Favourable decisions | 0 | 5 | 1 | 0 | 8 | 17 | 13 | 28 | 91 | 110 | 273 |
| Favourable decisions with reservations or with remarks | 2 | 2 | 6 | 1 | 1 | 8 | 7 | 9 | 15 | 13 | 64 |
| Unfavorable decisions | 0 | 0 | 0 | 0 | 0 | 1 | 0 | 1 | 0 | 0 | 2 |
| No decision | 0 | 0 | 0 | 0 | 0 | 0 | 0 | 1 | 2 | 1 | 4 |
| TOTAL | 2 | 7 | 7 | 1 | 9 | 26 | 20 | 39 | 108 | 124 | 343 |

| Years | 80 | 81 | 82 | 83 | 84 | 85 | 86 | 87 | 88 | 89 | Total |
|---|---|---|---|---|---|---|---|---|---|---|---|
| Medicamentous tests | 0 | 4 | 4 | 1 | 6 | 21 | 17 | 30 | 94 | 104 | 281 |
| Multicentric | 0 | 2 | 1 | 0 | 3 | 9 | 5 | 19 | 44 | 55 | 138 |
| Monocentric | 0 | 2 | 3 | 1 | 3 | 12 | 15 | 11 | 50 | 49 | 143 |
| Without comparison group | 0 | 1 | 4 | 0 | 3 | 9 | 8 | 8 | 34 | 40 | 107 |
| Compareted | | | | | | | | | | | |
| Open | 0 | 0 | 0 | 0 | 0 | 0 | 4 | 5 | 17 | 22 | 48 |
| Simple blind | 0 | 0 | 0 | 0 | 0 | 1 | 0 | 1 | 2 | 8 | 12 |
| Double blind | 0 | 3 | 0 | 1 | 3 | 11 | 5 | 16 | 41 | 34 | 114 |
| Against placebo | 0 | 0 | 0 | 1 | 1 | 7 | 1 | 12 | 26 | 23 | 71 |
| Against reference substance | 0 | 3 | 0 | 0 | 2 | 5 | 8 | 10 | 34 | 41 | 103 |

# THE HURRIET LAW AND BIOETHICS COMMITTEES

G. LEONETTI; F. VAREILLES; M.D. PIERCECCHI; F.CIANFARANI
Unité de Médecine Légale - CHU La Timone MARSEILLES

The Consultative Committee for Protection of Persons for Biomedical Rearch" (CCPBRB) institution, led the National Ethics Committee to reconsider its 1988 recommendations pertaining to Ethics Committees, in a new bill dated January 27, 1992.

Former Ethics Committees had four missions :

- evaluation of research protocols
- an advisory role in clinical pratice
- a reflection role upon ethical problems
- a role in information and training

On 20th December 1988, the law made it compulsory to evaluate research protocols by a CCPPRB.

The three other roles of the Ethics Committees, however, are not covered by the CCPPRB. Their role is a local one, of reflection, leading to a national consensus on the ethical problems of society.

The "moral responsability" of the Ethics Committees would be ensured by the National Ethics Committee.

Since the Hurriet law has been in force, some of the ethics committees have disappeared, while others have continued and are carying on their ythree other misions. Such is the case for the Paris Hospitals Ethics Committees which have retained the same structure, and whose co-ordination committee is the Ethics Committee of the A.P.H.P. (Public Assistance of Paris Hospitals).

In Marseilles, early in 1992, the Consultative Commission of Biological and Medical Ethics of Marseilles was created by the A.P.H.P. It is an organisational comittee, dealing with and answering requests made by the members of the Assistance Publique de Marseilles. Its five members were chosen for their experience in the main branches of biomedical research.

The Ethics Commission can turn to specialists for solving certain problems.

The Assistance Publique contacts the Commission before financing a biomedical research project when one is to be carried out in one of its hospitals. After having examined the dossier, the coordinator contacts the representative of the scientific committee of the Medical Faculty for an opinion, then contacts a spevcialist.

The commission meets in a plenary session to give a final decision, which is consultative and is sent to the Assistance Publique. Only one negative decision has been rendered among all the projects examined to date by the commission. The investigator modified his project according to the Commission's recommendations.

The members of the commission whish to enlarge its representation to include new members and, most importantly, to officialize a list of specialists. They also wish to contact the National Ethics Committee in order to coordinate future measures and to benefit from decisions rendered by similar commissions.

This Commission does not wish to take the place of the CCPPRB, but it would be the first to be contacted. If a favourable decision is given (scientific validity, moral rigour) to a project, the investigator would then submit his/her project to the CCPPRB before commencing research.

**MASS MURDERS AND SERIAL KILLINGS :**

**A STUDY OF 43 VICTIMS**

D. Rougé, D. Alengrin, P.M. Bras, N. Telmon, P.A Delpla, L. Arbus

Unité de Médecine Judiciaire, CHU Rangueil, F-31054 Toulouse Cedex, France

## INTRODUCTION

The factor which constitutes the essential difference between mass murders and serial killings is the element of time. Mass murders take place in a relatively short period of time and generally in the same place. Serial killings can be separated by long intervals of time and can take place in locations far from each other.

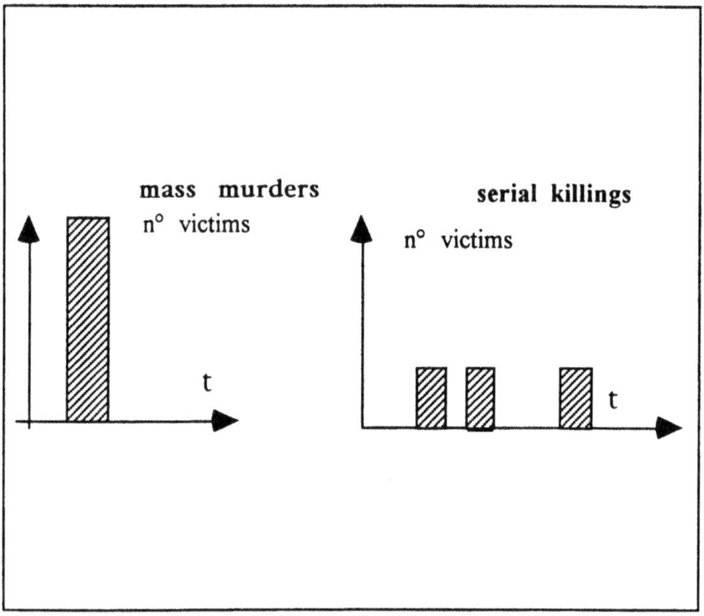


We studied the cases of the medico-legal department between **1981 and 1992**, and found 17 mass murders and two cases of serial killings, accounting for a total of **forty-three deaths.**

## I - SERIAL KILLINGS:

### A - CASES IN THE LITERATURE

Serial killings are less common, but they attract more attention in the media. Infact, they are often the basic element in detective novels. The killer is nearly always a **male** and generally acts **alone**.
The **victims** are usually **young women**. The repetitive and stereotyped nature of the killings is the element which makes it possible to establish a link between them.

| Dates | killer | nationality | n° victims | crime | method of disposal |
|---|---|---|---|---|---|
| **1944** | **PETIOT** | F | 27 ( M,F,Ch) | injections, sequestration, slow death | cremation |
| **1918-19** | **LANDRU** | F | 11 F by marriage advts | strangulation | cremation |
| | HOCH | USA | 24 wives | poison | |
| | BELA KISS | Hungarian | 7 | | fuel tank |
| | SMITH | U.K | 3 F | drowning : bath | |
| **1949** | **HAIGH** | U.K | > 8 | pistol + vampirism | immersion in $H_2SO_4$ |
| **1930** | The Vampire of Düsseldorf | Germany | 9 | ? + vampirism | |
| **1984** | **PAULIN** | F | 18 elderly women | strangulation | |
| **1983** | **NILSEN** | U.K | 15 young M | strangulation with tie | |
| | **SUTCLIFFE** | U.K | 13 F | | |
| | BERKOWITZ | USA | | calibre 44 (20 000 deaths per year, 2/3 of firearms) | |
| | **JACK THE RIPPER** | U.K | 5 Fprostitutes) | knife | dismembering |
| | **BARBEAULT** | F | 8 | 22 L.R | |
| | **DE SALVO** | USA | 13 F | strangulation | |
| | **CHRISTIE** | U.K | 8 | "gassing"+ strangulation | "hidden" in house |
| | **BUNDY** | USA | 16 F | club , rape | |

B - <u>OUR SERIES</u>

There were two cases of serial killings. In the first, four young men aged 21 were responsible for the deaths of four victims : a young woman aged 23 was raped then strangled ; two weeks later, in the same city, two young girls aged 14 and 18 were murdered by knifing and strangulation after sexual assault. The criminals attempted to cover up the crime by burning the bodies in a car. One month later, 600 kilometres away, during a car chase, they shot and killed a man aged 60.

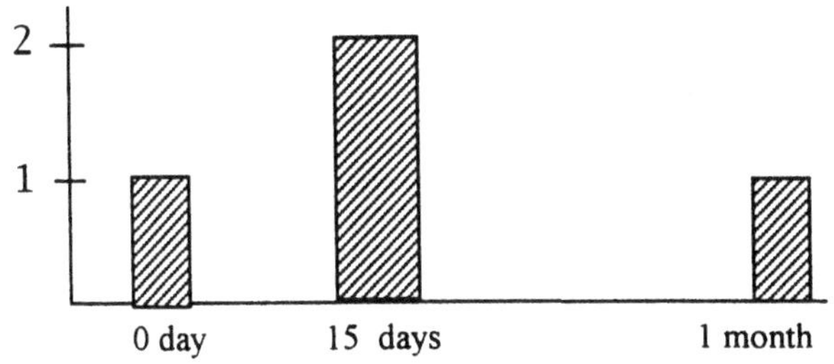


The second serial killer, a young man known as the "assassin in the grey 4CV" killed three persons in succession in two different places.

Towards midday, he shot the proprietor of a café in the abdomen with a pump-gun, and then within the next few hours, three kilometers away, using the same weapon, he shot a young couple in their home, one in the face and the other in the thorax.

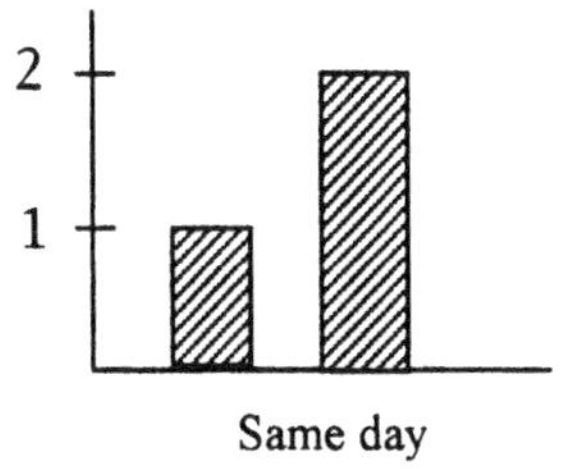

1981 - 1992

| | Killers | Victims | |
|---|---|---|---|
| Serial killer | 2 | 4 (H) | 4 |
| mass muderer extra familial | 5 | 1<br>4 + 4 (M)<br>1 suicide | 3<br>17 |
| intra familial | 12 | 12 ( 10M, 2F)<br>5 suicides | 29 |
| Total | **19** | **25**<br>**6 suicides** | **43** |

table 2

## II MASS MURDERS

Mass murders imply the death of several persons within a short period of time. They can be divided into two categories : a) extra- and b) intra-familial.

a) Those not involving family members are heterogeneous : there is no link between them and they take place in a variety of situations. They are less frequent than intra-familial mass murders. They may be committed during a psychotic episode or under the influence of alcohol. The latter is a factor which is frequently found. In one of our cases, four tramps, chronic alcoholics in a state of inebriety, massacred five of their companions with knives and blunt instruments. In another case, a man aged 45 shot a man and a woman with a 22 long rifle and wounded two other persons.

b) Concerning mass murders within the family, two elements are noteworthy :

- by definition, a blood relationship exists between the perpetrator and the victims,
- in the vast majority of cases, a firearm is the weapon used.

In our series, the exceptions were two mothers who suffocated their children, and knives or daggers were used by only two killers.

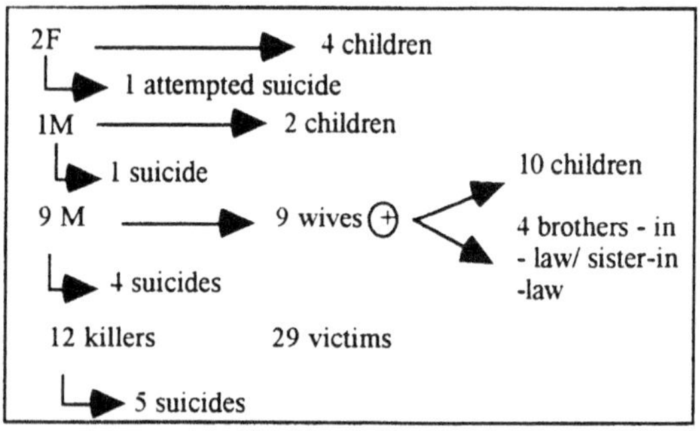


fig. 2

General characteristics of mass murders :

The perpetrators are nearly always young men, and they usually act alone. Their killings are frequently followed by attempted suicide, attempts which usually succeed. They are rarely declared insane (only one killer among our cases was considered to be irresponsible for his acts). The victims are usually women and children, or sometimes children killed by their mothers.

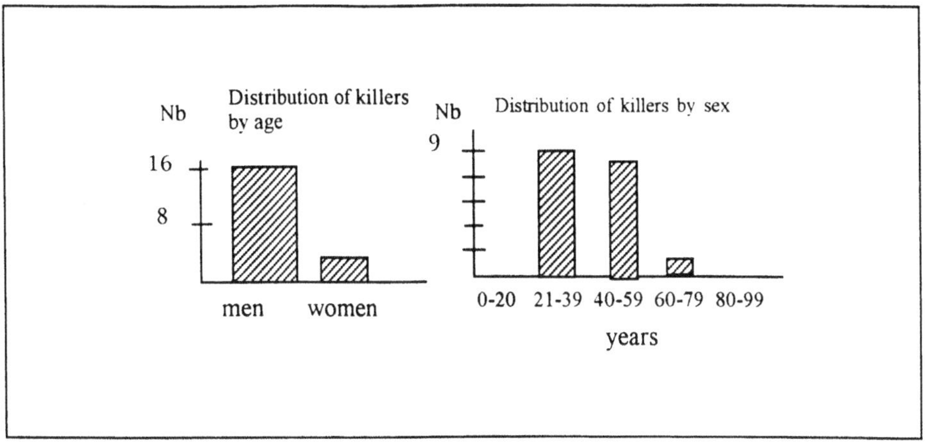
Nb
Distribution of killers by age
16
8
men
women
Nb
Distribution of killers by sex
9
0-20
21-39
40-59
60-79
80-99
years

figure 3

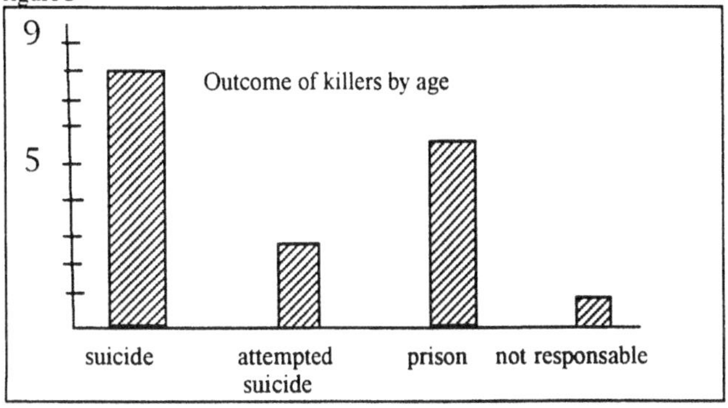
9
5
Outcome of killers by age
suicide
attempted suicide
prison
not responsable

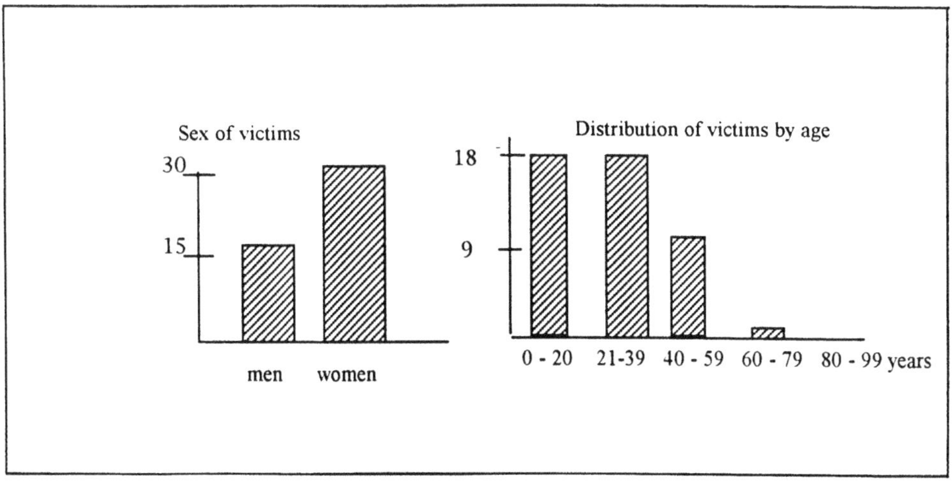
Sex of victims
30
15
men
women
Distribution of victims by age
18
9
0 - 20
21-39
40 - 59
60 - 79
80 - 99 years

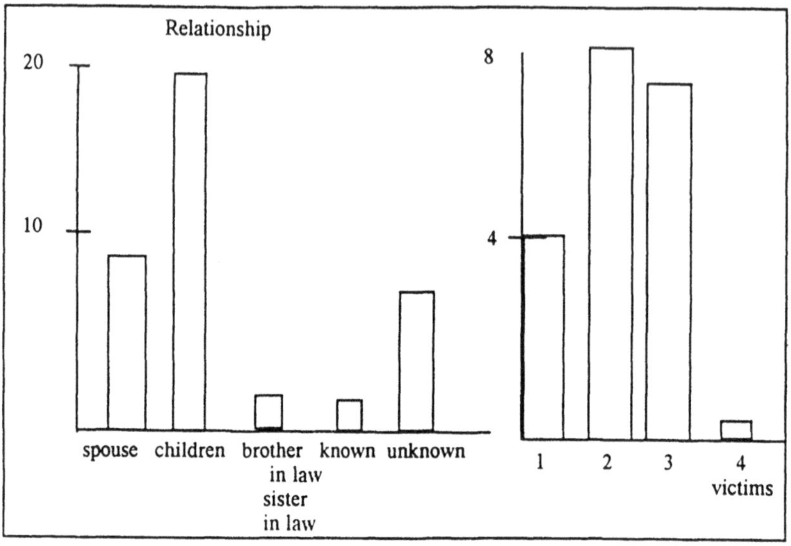


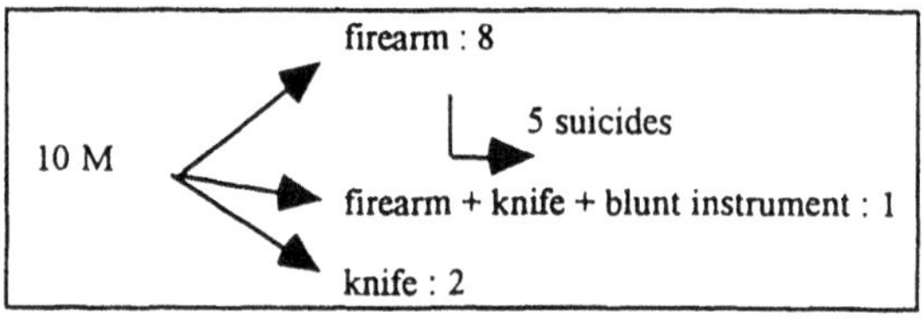


The relationship between killer and victim is often father-daughter or mother-child. There are generally two or three victims.

## CONCLUSION

To sum up, mass murders are fortunately a rarity but they always attract public attention. Intra-familial murders can be difficult to distinguish from collective suicide.

Serial killings, especially when separated in time and distance, raise the problem of establishing the link between the successive murders as quickly as possible. The method of collection, recording and spread of information therefore needs to be standardized and made as efficient as possible.

Mass murders raise the problem of the psychological status of their perpetrator. It is surprising to note that in our series only one killer was considered to be insane and not responsible for his acts. In intra-familial murders, it would also be interesting to try and find out more about the sequence of deaths, to see if there is any link between relationship or position within the family and the sequence.

## SOCIAL ATTITUDES TOWARDS THE LATEST LEGISLATION ON BRAIN DEATH

SALAÇIN S., GÜLMEN M.K., ALPER B., ÇEKIN N., KELLECE L.

Department of Forensic Medicine, Medical School of Çukurova University, Adana, Turkey.

### INTRODUCTION

The first organ donation law in Turkey came out in 1979 (Act.Nr.2238), and was revised in 1982 (Act.Nr.17727). The new legislation on Organ Transplantation Centres came out as Act Nr.21674, on August 20$^{th}$ 1993. The appendix of this act defined the criteria of brainstem death as brain-death, and legally accepted death. The last paragraph of this section describes the procedure for organ donation in brain death-patients as follows; (if the relatives of a brain-death patient, disapprove of organ donation, life-sustaining treatments will be withdrawn.). In this study, we try to investigate the social attitudes towards the concept of brainstem death and the new regulation on consent procedures for post mortem organ donations.

### MATERIAL and METHOD

The questionnaire was given to the professors, research fellows, nurses and to the students of Çukurova Medical School. The sheet of the questionnaires contained no explanation and were picked up immediately to protect impositioning. The questionnaires that had given to the respondents were composed of two requests with three answering choice boxes, as approved, disapproved and uncertain. The requests of the questionnaires as follows;

1) What is your attitude towards the concept of determining the brain-death patient as legally dead ?

2) What is your ethical attitude towards the idea of withdrawing the life-sustaining treatment in a brain death-patient in case of refusal of organ donation by the relatives?

The resulting data were studied statistically by using an IBM compatible PC analyzer system.

### RESULTS

A total of 596 people answered the questionnaires. The ages ranged from 18 to 51, showing a peak in the years 18-30 with no significant difference of male/female ratio (312/284). Occupational distribution of the respondents were: students (49.8%), research fellows (21.0%), nurses (16.3%), professors (12.9%) respectively. 58.22% (347) approved, 34.88% (208) disapproved and 7% (41) were uncertain for the first request, and male/female ratio was not significant. 28.20% (168) approved, 64.42% (384) disapproved and 7.38% (44) were uncertain for the second request, and male/female ratio was not significant in this group either.

## CONCLUSION

The development of transplantation technology has increasingly brought out complex ethical and legal problems. Because of the variety of the parties involved, the subject is more complex. The question of determination of death and of consent procedures in post mortem donation are widely acknowledged. The problem of brain death and organ donations had not yet been solved neither in Turkey nor all over the world. It is well known that, nowadays, using the criterion of brainstem death to define brain death is world wide preferenced procedure [1-10].

In this study, taking into consideration the new legislation, we tried to point out the community values by means of a questionnaire. Our study revealed that people are concerned about the subject with no significant difference in ages and sexes. Majority of the respondents approved the concept of determining the brain death patients as legally death, and disapproved for the second request, related to the ethical attitude towards the idea of withdrawing the life-sustaining treatment in a brain-death patient if there is no organ donation by the relatives.

There is no available previous study on this subject in Turkey. Because of this, there is no opportunity to compare and discuss the results of the present study. A similar study which was planned to point out the social attitutes towards the legal perpectives, was presented last year in Berlin by Japanese colleaques with the similar results[11]. It shows clearly that in traditional countries it is much more conflict problem than the others, with regard to socio-cultural values, and it needs more of a social consensus.

The last paragraph of the appendix of the organ transplantation centres legislation, which was the subject of the second request of this study, had been revised while our study was nearly completed. The last revision of the last paragraph dated October, 31st 1993, now reads as follows; "After the occurence of brain death, the condition will be notified to the relatives of the patient. If the relatives of a brain-death patient, approve organ donation or if the patient's will is so; the donated organs and tissues will be saved for transplantation."

The results of public questionnaires should induce politicians to take into consideration the medical and ethical criteria rather than non-medical ones. It is obvious that open public discussions considered in the light of religion, culture, ethics and jurisprudence are essential.

## REFERENCES

1- Abbing R.H.D.C. Transplantation of organs: A European Perspective. Journal of Law, Medicine & Ethics, 21(1): 54-58, 1993.

2- Miles S.H., Medical Futility. Law, Medicine and Health Care, 20:310-315,1992.

3- Rouse F., Advance Directives: Where Are We Heading after Cruzan? Law, Medicine and Health Care. 18:353-359, 1990.

Miller T.E., Public Policy In the Wake of Cruzan : A case Study of NewYork's Health Care Proxy Law. 18:360-367, 1990.

4- McKnight D.K., Bellis M., Foregoing Life-sustaining Treatment for Adult, Developmentally Disabled, Public Wards: A proposed Statute. American Journal of Law and Medicine. XVIII:203-232, 1992.

5- Link J. Concept and Diagnosis of Brain-death. XIII.th Meeting of the International Association of Forensic Sciences, Düsseldorf, Germany, 22-28 August 1993.

6- de Wachter M.A.M. Active Euthanasia in the Netherlands. JAMA, 262(23): 3316-3319, 1989.
7- Youngner S.J., Landefeld C.S., Coulton C.J., Juknialis B.W., Leary M. 'Brain Death' and Organ Retrieval. A Cross-sectional Survey of Knowledge and Concepts Among Health Professionals. JAMA, 261(15): 2205-2210, 1989.
8- Mason J.K., McCall Smith R.A. The diagnosis of death. Chapter 13, pp 289-299, in Law and Medical Ethics. Third Edition, 1991, Butterworths. London, Dublin, Edinburgh.
9- Wanzer S.H., Federman D.D., Adelstein S.J., Cassel C.K., Cassem E.H., Cranford R.E., et al. The Physician's Responsibility Toward Hopelessly Ill Patients. A Second Look. N Engl J Med. 320:844-849, 1989.
10- Brody B., Special Ethical Issues in the Management of PVS Patients. Law, Medicine and Health Care, 20:104-115, 1992
11- Kurosu M., Haseba T., Ohno Y. Is Brain Death Actual Death Medically Speaking? Opinions of Physicians and Medical or Biological Scientists in Japan. XIII.th Meeting of the International Association of Forensic Sciences, Düsseldorf, Germany, 22-28 August 1993.

Correspondent: Serpil SALAÇIN M.D. Çukurova University, Medical School, Dept. of Forensic Medicine, 01330, Balcalı, Adana - TURKEY.

## CONTRIBUTION au RESPECT des DROITS de L'HOMME par des ECHANGES entre PSYCHIATRES LEGISTES RUSSES et FRANCAIS

En mai 1989, avec une Commission internationale de travail, j'ai rencontré des Psychiatres Légistes et Pénitentiaires d'URSS à Moscou et Douchambe ce qui m'a donné l'opportunité de visiter quelques Centres de Recherche en Psychiatrie Légale, un hôpital pour toxicomanes et un centre de réadaptation pour alcooliques. J'ai pu ainsi comparer leur façon d'expertiser le délinquant et la nôtre. Des discussions sur le fond et la forme se sont instaurées; nos collègues ont pris beaucoup de notes. Ce fut le début de ma contribution au respect des Droits de l'Homme en URSS. Ce fut aussi l'occasion d'établir des relations scientifiques avec nos confrères de l'Est.
En juin 1990, le Pr Tatiana DMITRIEVA accompagné du Pr MILIOKHIN et de leur interprète a participé de façon active à un Congrès de Psychiatrie Légale, présidé par Monsieur le Premier Président de la Cour d'Appel de Toulouse et par les Prs Pierre MORON (chef de file de la psychiatrie à Toulouse) et Louis ARBUS, chef du service de Médecine Légale. Les questions furent nombreuses de part et d'autre. Le Président du Centre de Formation Professionnelle des Avocats nous a reçus et a enrichi les débats par l'apport de son expérience professionnelle et par ses précisions sur certains points de notre Droit et notre Jurisprudence. L'Université des Sciences Sociales de Toulouse a bien voulu accueillir nos confrères et un débat passionné s'est établi avec Monsieur le Président GOUR et le Pr ROUJOU de BOUBEE (Directeur de l'Institut de Criminologie). On a pu apprendre que la Psychiatrie Légale n'était plus sous la tutelle du Ministère d'Intérieur Russe mais était sous l'égide du Ministère de la Santé. La Psychiatrie Pénitentiaire est restée dépendante du Ministère de l'Intérieur.
Du 18 au 22 novembre 1992, dix psychiatres du Sud dont Monsieur le Pr Pierre MORON ont participé à Moscou à un Congrès International de Psychiatrie Générale, Pénitentiaire et Légale. Nous avons, grâce à des confrères interprètes, découvert certains aspects spécifiques aux pratiques russes. De notre côté chacun des 10 Français a fait une communication. Nos collègues russes, ukrainiens et géorgiens nous ont posé de nombreuses questions relatives au droit et aux lois françaises. Par ailleurs, ils nous ont affirmé qu'à la suite de ce qu'ils avaient appris à Toulouse, divers projets de loi venaient d'être déposés visant à faire respecter les droits des accusés et ceux des détenus. La presse toulousaine a bien voulu titrer le 13 janvier 1993: "ETHIQUE, Les psychiatres toulousains font école à Moscou".
Les échanges scientifiques se sont poursuivis.
En mai 1993, j'ai été invité à un Colloque International à Saint-Pétersbourg ce qui m'a permis de visiter l'hôpital psychiatrique de cette ville et de mieux faire comprendre aux Russes notre façon de concevoir le respect des Droits de l'Homme. Nos confrères de l'Est ont bien perçu l'intérêt pour les psychiatres russes de participer, avec l'aide des psychiatres de l'Union Européenne, à l'établissement d'un Etat de Droit dans leur pays.

Le 29 novembre 1993, en présence de Monsieur le Président du Tribunal de Grande Instance dans une salle d'audience du Tribunal de Grande Instance s'est tenue une journée de Psychiatrie Légale à laquelle participaient aussi un Belge, des Russes et un Ukrainien. Les communications françaises et étrangères devaient avoir une qualité certaine puisque le 4 janvier 1994, Monsieur Olivier de BAYNAST, Chef du Bureau de la Coopération de notre Ministère de la Justice m'écrivit: "Je tiens à vous adresser mes plus vifs remerciements pour le compte-rendu de vos travaux du 29 novembre dernier.... Le Service des affaires européennes et internationales de la Chancellerie ne manquera pas de vous aider à mener à bien d'autres projets de coopération avec vos collègues d'Europe de l'Est.

Les échanges se poursuivent et s'intensifient. Des "stagiaires" sont venus passer trois semaines dans différentes structures psychiatriques de Toulouse et sa Région. Grâce à l'amabilité du Tribunal de Grande Instance, ces confrères ont pu visiter notre Maison d'Arrêt. Leurs commentaires furent variés mais l'un d'eux laisse à penser que nos échanges doivent continuer: "Votre prison ressemble un peu, par certains côtés, à certaines de nos maisons de retraite".

D'autres stagiaires russes viendront prochainement à Toulouse et Albi.
Les Ukrainiens, aussi, souhaitent aussi connaître notre droit et notre pratique psychiatrique.
Je terminerai donc cette communication par un extrait de lettre remise par le Ministère de la Justice d'Ukraine: "... Nous vous confirmons que nous souhaitons votre soutien pour l'organisation de journées d'études sur le fonctionnement des institutions judiciaires françaises pour les représentants du Ministère de la Justice d'Ukraine... Le thème de ces journées devant porter sur l'établissement des listes d'Experts nationaux, ainsi que sur la coopération des Instituts de Recherche des Services Judiciaires ... avec la police française, en matière de recherche criminologique..."
Devant un tel succès au niveau des échanges, au niveau de la contribution à la défense des Droits de l'Homme en ex-URSS, je viens donc, avec quelques amis juristes et des confrères experts judiciaires, de créer une association régie par la Loi du 1er Juillet 1901. Cette association s'appelle E.D.E.F.I. **Monsieur le Ministre Délégué à la Santé, le Pr DOUSTE-BLAZY**, a bien voulu accepter d'en être le Président d'honneur. Ceux qui souhaiteraient être associés à nos travaux, travaux qui intéressent aussi notre Ministère de la Justice, notre Ministère de l'Intérieur et notre Ministère des Affaires Etrangères, peuvent se mettre en rapport avec moi.

Dr René TOLLEMER
Psychiatre Expert
en cours de D.E.A. de Sciences Criminelles
83, rue de Bourrassol
F - 31300 Toulouse
France

# PRENDRE en CHARGE les SEXOPATHES, en FRANCE dès 1994

"Le Médecin, au service de l'individu et de la santé publique, exerce sa mission dans le respect de la vie et de la personne humaine." Art. 2 du Code de Déontologie.

La "Défense sociale nouvelle", comme l'écrit Roger MERLE (Pr de Droit Pénal), amène à **restituer au délinquant, lorsqu'il l'a perdu, le sentiment inné de la responsabilité et de la dignité humaine; le délinquant est un mineur que la Justice épanouira**. Rien n'empêche de punir le délinquant en soulignant sa responsabilité, de le plonger dans un décor afflictif, **et de le soumettre dans ce cadre pénal à un traitement moderne approprié aux causes concrètes de sa criminalité propre."**
Partant de la même démarche que les criminologues actuels, nous considérerons que la clé de l'énigme de la criminogénèse se trouve dans l'esprit et dans le mécanisme cérébral de l'Homme.
C'est ce postulat qui permet de prétendre traiter le criminel sexuel que nous appellerons SEXOPATHE comme ceci a été déterminé lors de **la journée de psychiatrie légale du 29 novembre 1993 organisée en présence de Monsieur FOULON Président du Tribunal de Grande Instance de Toulouse, présidée par le Professeur Pierre MORON.**
Les sexopathes sont en particulier concernés par les articles de la Section IV du Code Pénal "Attentats aux Moeurs" (exhibitionnistes, violeurs...).

Henri-Nhi BARTE rappelait qu'à la suite des travaux récents de MARTORELL on peut estimer que les problèmes sexopathiques (agresseurs sexuels, violeurs, transgresseurs...) représentent près de 12% de la population carcérale en France. Il s'avère urgent de traiter ces criminels sexuels. Cependant ce n'est pas simple. Lorsque nous sommes face à un sexopathe existe toujours un certain malaise, ***une inquiétante étrangeté, parce que finalement cet autre, c'est soi-même qu'on regarde*** (H-Nhi BARTE, Toulouse, novembre 1994). Si on considère le sexopathe comme un "étranger", on l'exclut; on ne peut pas le traiter. Il faut donc le considérer comme un homme qui souffre et le prendre en charge avec l'aide d'une équipe soignante multidisciplinaire. Ceci est d'autant plus vrai que l'acte criminel du sexopathe n'est souvent pour lui qu'un moyen de survie (L'acte criminel comme moyen de survie, Simone COURAUD). Aussi aidons le sexopathe à gérer sa libido, en Maison d'Arrêt, en Centrale Pénitentiaire et si possible en ville (avant la prison et/ou après l'enfermement).
Deux questions importantes se posent:
- le milieu carcéral français, même depuis les récentes propositions faites par Mme Simone VEIL, est-il en mesure d'accueillir correctement et de prendre en charge le criminel sexuel? Ne fréquentant les prisons que pour des expertises médico-légales, je ne prétends pas répondre sur ce point;
- quelle signification peut avoir une peine incompressible ou la condamnation à perpétuité pour un sexopathe? (Même en 1994, on peut osciller entre la prison salvatrice et la prison-corruptrice). Cependant reste-t-il une place, alors, pour une prise en charge médicale spécifique? Le crime est une faillite de la nature humaine et d'une civilisation donnée (la norme du moment) ***qui impose à nos consciences une inquiétude fraternelle, et à nos intelligences un effort de compréhension***.
Comme l'écrit MERLE: "Les idéologies qui ont inspiré au cours des âges le choix des sanctions furent certes variées... Mais la gamme des moyens adoptés pour atteindre ces buts... a toujours été monotone et peu étendue. "Ne pourrait-on pas, en France, tendre vers une structure comparable à celle de l'Institut Philippe PINEL à Montréal? Mon ami, H-Nhi BARTE pense que c'est là un rêve. Seul un représentant ministériel pourrait nous le confirmer.
Il faut donc miser sur un réseau de groupes thérapeutiques et la multiplicité des approches thérapeutiques, qu'elles soient comportementalistes, psychanalytiques, chimiothérapiques. Pour permettre au sexopathe à l'occasion de la répression sociale, par le freinage chimiothérapique de ses pulsions, par le déplacement de celles-ci lors de thérapies individuelles ou de groupe, de trouver une

satisfaction et une solution acceptable par la société dans laquelle il évolue, et par lui-même, il semble bien nécessaire d'élaborer au niveau national, en relation avec les différents intervenants, un plan de prévention et un programme de prise en charge du criminel sexuel. Celui-ci souffre et a besoin d'une prise en charge adaptée et d'une aide à la gestion de sa libido (et non de sa sexualité).
Plusieurs unités de prise en charge du sexopathe devraient exister sur tout le territoire français.
Chaque unité pourrait comporter quelques lits mais surtout un personnel important et compétent. Il faudrait envisager l'intervention de psychiatres, de psychologues, d'ergothérapeutes, de psychomotriciens, d'infirmiers et d'une assistante sociale. Le responsable de cette unité devrait être un psychiatre ayant déjà l'expérience de la prise en charge des psychopathes et des sexopathes.

Personnellement, je reçois des sexopathes qui me sont adressés par le Comité de Probation. Je les vois dans deux cas:
- Le sexopathe a bénéficié d'une peine se substituant à la prison;
- Il a fait de la prison mais il a été libéré et placé sous contrôle judiciaire.

J'accepte ce type de "client" car j'estime que la sanction pénale fait partie du traitement. La première vocation de la sanction c'est de punir. La seconde vocation dans l'esprit du condamné devrait être son aspect éducatif et thérapeutique avec pour objectif la réinsertion ou l'insertion. La sanction doit jouer un rôle de déclic et faire adhérer le sexopathe à son traitement.
L'expérience manque du recul suffisant pour en parler plus techniquement. Ce sera probablement l'objet d'une communication lors d'un prochain congrès.

Je voudrais conclure en soulignant que le sexopathe devrait être pris en charge, avant la prison, à la prison, après incarcération, en cabinet, en dispensaire, en milieu hospitalier ou dans un centre spécialisé pour criminels sexuels. L'important c'est que le sexopathe soit pris en charge, et qu'on donne à cet homme la chance de retrouver sa santé et sa dignité. Si un réseau national d'équipes multidisciplinaires acceptait la prise en charge des sexopathes, il paraît sensé d'imaginer que la Justice pourrait faire appel à ce réseau comme elle a pris l'habitude de faire confiance à ses éducateurs de justice et à des associations de contrôle judiciaire.

Dr René TOLLEMER
membre de l'Association Française pour la Formation Continue en Médecine Légale
Psychiatre expert près la Cour d'Appel de Toulouse
83, rue de Bourrassol
F - 31300 Toulouse
France

# PROBLEMES ETHIQUES DANS CERTAINES SITUATIONS LIMITES DE L'EXPERTISE PSYCHIATRIQUE

***VEDRINNE J., SABATINI J. et D. WEBER***
Faculté de Médecine Alexis Carrel - Laboratoire de Médecine Légale
Rue Guillaume Paradin - 69372 Lyon Cédex 08

L'expertise psychiatrique de sujets inculpés de crime est un art souvent difficile, plein d'embuches de toutes sortes émaillant le parcours expertal depuis la réception de la mission jusqu'à la déposition en Cour d'Assises en passant par les rencontres avec le sujet, la lecture du dossier, les confrontations avec les autres experts, la rédaction du rapport, etc...

Ce sont autant d'étapes à la faveur desquelles des problèmes éthiques déjà assez bien étudiés et connus peuvent se poser (ainsi par exemple ceux touchant à la légitimité de certaines questions de la mission, au secret par rapport à certains événements biographiques ou le lancinant problème de la responsabilité et de la dangerosité).

Mais des problèmes nouveaux sont toujours susceptibles de se poser : ainsi à propos de deux expertises de sujets inculpés dans le cadre d'infractions fortement marquées historiquement.

**I - La première concerne l'expertise de Klaus BARBIE** qui nous fut confiée par un magistrat instructeur de Lyon, nous faisant ainsi participer à un processus de jugement d'un sujet accusé d'une qualification criminelle inédite dans notre pays, pour des faits remontant à plus de 40 ans...

Certes notre longue expérience de travail expertal et de déposition devant les Cour d'Assises pour des crimes souvent horribles, barbares, nous avait accoutumés à nous interroger sur l'humain et l'inhumain, sur la nature du Mal, sur la nécessité de maintenir une approche clinique, coûte que coûte.

Mais cette fois nous avions accepté de nous impliquer dans l'élaboration d'un événement jurisprudentiel (bien entendu à un niveau très modeste...) appuyé sur la mise en oeuvre d'une loi (26.12.64) centrée exclusivement sur l'imprescribilité du crime contre l'humanité dont elle renvoyait prudemment la définition à celle des Nations Unies (1946) et du Tribunal de Nuremberg (1945), donc à des instances internationales, ce qui était une première dans notre Droit.

Travailler sur la subjectivité d'un homme accusé des pires horreurs pouvait -cela nous a été renvoyé- paraître scandaleux, ou à tout le moins très discutable : pourquoi dépenser de l'énergie à tenter de comprendre le fonctionnement d'un homme estimé unanimement si coupable, et de quels forfaits ! D'entrée de jeu, on touchait en fait au fond du débat : s'agissait-il d'un homme et allait-on l'aborder "comme les autres" et non pas comme radicalement étranger, d'une autre espèce ? Aussi un premier point d'accord fut-il de considérer que la Justice faisait son travail en soumettant Klaus BARBIE à une procédure expertale somme toute assez ordinaire, dans le cadre d'une qualification criminelle sur la légitimité de laquelle aucun d'entre nous n'a estimé émettre des réserves telles qu'elles auraient pu interférer avec les conditions de la rencontre expertale.

En effet, avant d'accepter cette mission, nous avions eu besoin d'un temps important, individuellement et ensemble, pour que chacun se déprenne de la dimension imaginaire du personnage et de l'affaire elle-même, en élaborant un véritable cadre mental préalable au déroulement de notre travail.

C'est ainsi que nous avons été amenés à mettre au clair notre propre situation en tant qu'héritiers d'une histoire dans laquelle nos aînés ont souffert, et actuellement participants d'un monde qui nous confronte constamment à des idéologies ou contre-idéologies.

Notre consentement à cette mission expertale reposait donc sur le respect des conditions nécessaires pour pouvoir aborder l'inculpé comme un homme parmi d'autres et non comme une créature extraordinaire de sadisme, de violence sanguinaire ou perverse dès lors que nous nous étions assurés de la place de nos propres projections.

Ce travail fut possible, l'inculpé acceptant non seulement le principe des rencontres mais surtout de se livrer, au moins en partie, de s'exposer à la passation de nombreux tests psychologiques et cela suffisamment pour esquisser les grandes lignes de force de son fonctionnement psychique.

Cela nous fait poser la question de savoir si la rencontre expertale a pu faire sens chez Klaus BARBIE en particulier par rapport au chef d'inculpation. La rupture provoquée par sa décision de mise hors le cadre du procès aboutissait à mettre en échec ce que nous pensons devoir être un des objectifs de tout procés : réarticuler le sujet avec le reste de l'humanité, refaire circuler entre lui et les autres une parole qui ne soit pas seulement de justification et de défense. Cela ne peut-être obtenu que s'il existe une ouverture suffisante chez l'inculpé pour qu'il soit véritablement participant à son propre procès, en permettant le déploiement d'un débat sur la signification et la portée du concept de crime contre l'Humanité, et le cheminement individuel au sein d'une organisation collective d'un Etat régi par une logique destructrice et barbare.

A vrai dire, parvenus aux terme de notre travail et en dépit de fugitives ouvertures lors de certaines rencontres, il nous paraissait déjà très improbable, compte-tenu précisément de son fonctionnement mental, qu'il puisse "répondre" véritablement de ses actes pendant une période historique donnée, en acceptant de se soumettre à la loi du groupe. Répondre, non pas dans le sens d'une responsabilité à évaluer mais de l'engagement dans un dialogue ouvrant sur la qualité d'humain avec ses doutes, ses incertitudes, sa tolérance, voire sa souffrance.

**II - La deuxième expertise concerne un des leaders de la branche lyonnaise de l'organisation Action Directe.**

Les experts désignés, contrairement à la situation précédente eurent moins d'hésitation à accepter cette mission. En effet, ils estimèrent que seules deux éventualités étaient possibles : soit le refus pur et simple de la rencontre par l'intéressé, soit son déroulement sur la base du respect d'un espace de parole, d'un espace relationnel dans lequel sont inclus les experts permettant ainsi de témoigner du "comment" les caractéristiques psychologiques de l'inculpé ont pu fonctionner dans la rencontre.

Mais les choses ne se sont pas passées ainsi...

L'inculpé a toujours accepté ces rencontres, mais dans une perspective personnelle, différente de celle des experts ("je ne refuse pas de discuter... de ce que je veux") : pour lui, il ne semble pas exister une grande différence entre l'intérieur et l'extérieur de la prison : il continue à être un militant, quel que soit le lieu où il se trouve et la personne qu'il rencontre, à la fois en cherchant à acquérir de nouvelles connaissances et en témoignant de sa vision du monde et de la société. Entre sa personne et Action Directe, il ne semble pas y avoir de véritable limite ; il s'identifie totalement à ce groupe et, à tout moment, il fait oeuvre de pédagogie et de persuasion ; ainsi s'appliquera-t-il à nous démontrer les tenants et les aboutissants politiques de notre fonction expertale, pour mieux la disqualifier dans la perspective qui est la sienne ; il cherchera aussi à obtenir notre ralliement à sa cause, en nous proposant même d'expertiser les détenteurs actuels du pouvoir. Ce discours n'avait rien à voir avec une logique délirante classique.

Ainsi créé-t-il un malaise chez l'interlocuteur, qui n'a aucune place possible en dehors de celles caractérisées par la condamnation ou l'adhésion.

Son discours constitue un tout, clos sur lui-même, sans faille mais sans nuance et suivant une logique très manichéenne. Il ne laisse jamais s'exprimer le moindre affect et toutes nos interrogations sur sa personne seront éludées. Les rares éléments ou images biographiques qu'il laisse transparaître restent sans suite ; il installe immédiatement un écran très épais qui interdit d'y accéder et qui barre l'accès et la compréhension de sa trajectoire existentielle, en tant que sujet.

Compte-tenu de ce verrouillage de la sphère affective, il est devenu impossible, à la fois sur le plan technique et sur le plan éthique, de tenir compte de tout autre élément d'information concernant son histoire, notamment ce qui figure au dossier d'instruction.

En effet, ces éléments ne peuvent être pris en considération que si la personne expertisée en fait elle-même état au cours de la rencontre expertale (rencontre qui constitue la trame de l'expertise) ou que l'expert estime opportun de les introduire pour mieux travailler sur les liens entre le sujet et son histoire.

Dès lors, la seule latitude laissée aux experts ne pouvait consister qu'à répercuter auprès des magistrats et des juges ses analyses et messages.

Or cette possibilité-là ne relève pas de la fonction de l'expert, qui ne serait ainsi transformé qu'en simple porte-parole.

**En conclusion :**

Bien qu'il ait accepté tous les entretiens que nous lui avons proposés, la mission d'expertise psychiatrique et psychologique de l'inculpé s'est avérée d'accomplissement impossible.

Son attitude de fermeture à tout élément de son histoire comme de sa personne nous a contraints à prendre acte de l'impossibilité d'une rencontre authentique.

Toutefois en nous plaçant dans un registre purement sémiologique, il ne nous est pas apparu de signe laissant supposer qu'il pouvait être en état de démence au moment de l'action, au sens de l'article 64 du Code Pénal.

Nous avons bien conscience que d'autres collègues auraient pu rédiger une expertise "sur pièces" à partir des éléments du dossier volumineux concernant des informations d'un intérêt inégal mais certain, ou encore se livrer à une interprétation du discours manifeste, mais un tel travail ne pouvait guère que déboucher sur une prise de position nosographique incertaine à partir d'éléments sémiologiques fragmentaires. Cette position que nous avons adoptée a d'ailleurs été bien comprise par le magistrat instructeur et également lors de la déposition en Cour d'Assises.

x

x x

Ainsi donc, à partir de deux situations expertales, certes fort différentes, nous pensons avoir respecté les principes de base de l'éthique expertale qui sont centrés sur les éléments suivants :

- acceptation par l'expert de se mettre en situation d'être pris dans la relation en tant que personne, en fonctionnement psychodynamique avec l'expertisé.
- travail sur l'approche de la structure psychologique, c'est-à-dire du jeu des éléments constitutifs de la personne (les invariants) qui persiste chez elle et la maintient tout au long de sa vie (d'où la possibilité de travailler même sur une période de vie ancienne).
- contrôle réciproque dans le cadre d'une dualité voire pluralité d'experts (contrôle entendu non pas comme un examen critique des éléments soumis au regard de l'autre expert mais comme une création d'un espace de parole où l'expert est amené à dire ce qui en lui a fait émotion, sentiment, effet de vie ou de mort).

Ces éléments permettent de comprendre comment un travail expertal a été possible, même si inachevé, dans le cadre de la première mission concernant un sujet inculpé de crimes contre l'Humanité alors que dans le deuxième cas, un tel travail n'a pas été possible.

# LA CONVENTION EUROPEENNE DES DROITS DE L'HOMME ET LA QUESTION DES HOSPITALISATIONS SOUS CONTRAINTE

VEDRINNE J., GHARIB P. et SABATINI J.
Laboratoire de Médecine Légale - Faculté de Médecine Alexis Carrel - Rue Guillaume Paradin - 69008 Lyon - France.

La Convention Européenne des Droits de l'Homme constitue l'une des oeuvres majeures du Conseil de l'Europe. Elle établit un catalogue des droits à respecter et à protéger, au titre des personnes placées sous la juridiction des Etats membres. La Convention est un traité qui a acquis en quarante ans une maturité et une élaboration reconnues sur le plan international. Son importance ne réside pas seulement dans l'étendue des droits à protéger, mais également dans le mécanisme de protection instauré à Strasbourg pour enquêter sur les violations alléguées et assurer le respect des obligations résultant de la Convention.

Un certain nombre d'Etats ont été obligés de modifier leurs législations et pratiques nationales en raison des décisions rendues par les organes de contrôle de la Convention. La jurisprudence qui en est issue est désormais un élément essentiel du patrimoine juridique européen. Son importance est d'autant plus manifeste qu'en se développant, elle a considérablement renforcé les obligations contractées par les Etats.

La portée des articles contenus dans la Convention européenne est générale, puisqu'ils concernent les libertés fondamentales. Certains d'entre eux sont applicables à la situation des malades mentaux internés et ont été à l'origine de la condamnation de certains Etats, dont la législation ou son application ont donné lieu à des abus au regard de la Cour européenne.

Les principaux articles concernant le domaine des hospitalisations sous contrainte sont les suivants :

*Article 5*

*1)* Toute personne a droit à la liberté et à la sûreté. Nul ne peut être privé de sa liberté, sauf dans les cas suivants et selon les voies légales :

*a)* s'il est détenu régulièrement et après condamnation par un tribunal compétent ;
*e)* s'il s'agit de la détention régulière d'une personne susceptible de propager une maladie contagieuse, d'un aliéné, d'un alcoolique, d'un toxicomane ou d'un vagabond ;
*2)* Toute personne arrêtée doit être informée, dans le plus court délai et dans une langue qu'elle comprend, des raisons de son arrestation et de toute accusation portée contre elle.
*4)* Toute personne privée de sa liberté par arrestation ou détention a le droit d'introduire un recours devant un tribunal, afin qu'il statue à bref délai sur la légalité de la détention et ordonne sa libération si la détention est illégale.
*5)* Toute personne victime d'une arrestation ou d'une détention dans des conditions contraires aux dispositions de cet article a droit à réparation.
*Article 6*
*1)* Toute personne a droit à ce que sa cause soit entendue équitablement, publiquement et dans un délai raisonnable, par un tribunal indépendant et impartial, établi par la loi, qui décidera soit des contestations sur ses droits et obligations de caractère civil, soit du bien-fondé de toute acusation en matière pénale dirigée contre elle(...)

A noter que les articles 8 (protection de la vie privée et familiale, du domicile, de la correspondance), 9 (protection de la liberté de pensée, de conscience et de religion) et 10 (protection de la liberté d'expression) s'appliquent également aux hospitalisations sous contrainte.

Si l'on examine la jurisprudence (soit cinq affaires : WINTERWERP contre PAYS-BAS, 24.10.1979 ; X contre ROYAUME-UNI, 05.11.1981 ; LUBERTI contre ITALIE, 23.02.1984 ; ASHINGDANE contre ROYAUME-UNI, 28.05.1985 ; NIELSEN contre DANEMARK, 28.11.1988), un certain nombre d'éléments peuvent être retenus.

Selon la Cour européenne, la loi ne peut définir la maladie mentale, car son approche ne cesse d'évoluer avec les progrès de la recherche et les changements d'attitude de la société à son égard (arrêt Winterwerp). La classification des troubles mentaux tels qu'ils apparaissent dans le Mental Health Act de 1983 ou la référence à la psychose dans la législation danoise apparaissent donc tout à fait inutiles aux yeux de la Cour. La pièce indispensable au placement reste le certificat médical, "seule preuve" attestant la réalité d'une pathologie psychique : tous les Etats membres y ont du reste recours.

Trois éléments sont indispensables pour légitimer le placement d'un malade mental (arrêt Luberti) : l'aliénation doit être établie de manière probante ; le trouble doit avoir une ampleur suffisante ; il doit persister pour que le placement se prolonge valablement.

Dans le cadre de l'urgence, la Cour fait preuve d'une grande tolérance par rapport aux mesures prises par les autorités compétentes : "un examen médical approfondi ne saurait être exigé avant toute décision" ; "l'autorité compétente doit avoir une grande latitude" ; "dans certaines circonstances, les impératifs de la protection publique prévalent sur la liberté individuelle" (affaire X contre Royaume-Uni).

Un délai de six semaines avant l'intervention du juge, dans le cadre d'une procédure d'urgence, a par ailleurs été jugée acceptable (affaire Winterwerp).

La cour ne considère pas non plus qu'un retard de quinze jours dans la procédure, survenu au moment du renouvellement du placement d'un patient, soit une atteinte formelle à sa liberté individuelle, dans la mesure où cette décision est justifiée (arrêt Winterwerp).

La judiciarisation des placements n'est pas promue par la Cour. Il est vrai que tel n'est pas son rôle. Cependant, à la lecture de la jurisprudence, le tribunal -même statuant à juge unique- apparaît bien la seule autorité offrant des garanties au patient quant aux respects de ses libertés fondamentales : "si la décision privative de liberté émane d'un organe administratif, l'article 5 § 4 astreint les Etats à ouvrir aux détenus un recours auprès d'un Tribunal" (arrêt Winterwerp) ; "ni le bourgmestre, ni le procureur ne peuvent passer pour représenter les traits distinctifs d'un tribunal" (arrêt de Wilde, Ooms, Wersyps). Dans le même esprit, on peut citer encore : "un système de contrôle judiciaire périodique doit permettre de s'assurer que les éléments médicaux qui avaient fondé la décision initiale, demeurent tout au long de la décision litigieuse" (affaire X contre Royaume Uni).

# Estimation of post-mortem interval based on the changes of phosphorylase activity in skeletal muscles

ZG. LIAO*, G. QUATREHOMME**, A. OLLIER**, JW. WU*

*School of Forensic Medicine, West China University of Medical Sciences, Chengdu 610041, P.R. China
**Laboratory of Forensic Medicine, Institute of Medicine of Nice, 06107 Nice Cédex 2, France

It is well known to establish the time of death, in certain instances, is very important in Forensic practice. In the past, it depended primarily on the early postmortem signs, such as development of livor mortis, the stage of rigor mortis and changes in the body temperature from loss of heats. But there are many factors that affect postmortem changes and the time of death was variously established based on these appearances. The authors, during using an enzyme histochemical process to investigate the enzymes, discovered that the changes of phosphorylase (PPr) activity is more sensible to the postmortem changes than other enzymes such as dehydragenase. In order to clarify the relationship between the changes of the enzyme activity and the time interval after deaths, we devised this experiment.

## MATERIALS AND METHODS

### Materials

1) Thirty-six male mice of the same age were divided into 9 groups at random. Each group included 4 mice. The animals were sacrificed and kept at 20° C. The samples were respectively taken from the quadriceps femoris at 0, 2, 4, 6, 8, 12, 16, 20 and 24 hours after death. Samples of each group were embedded in single block and frozen with liquid nitrogen.

2) Four rabbits were sacrificed and kept at 15°C. Samples were taken from the quadriceps femoris at 0, 2, 4, 6, 8, 12, 16, 20 hours after death and were treated as those above.

3) The left psoas major of human was taken during the autopsy from 7 corpses due to various causes of death and with known postmortem interval. The samples were frozen with liquid nitrogen.

### Methods

The frozen specimens were cut at 8 microns in a cryostat at -12° C. The slices were mounted with cover glass for enzyme histochemistry stain.

# 4. Post Mortem Chemistry

TITLE : THANATOCHEMICAL BLOOD CHANGES IN A FEW BEGGARS AND TRAMPS SOCIAL CASES

AUTHORS : Prof.Dr.Vl.Beliş, Prof.As.Dr.N.Drugescu, Biol.G.Mureşan, Acad.Lect.Dr.M.D.Gangal
National Medico-Legal Institute Bucharest, ROMANIA
9. Vitan Bârzeşti Ave., Tel/Fax: (401).321-0260

Grounds of Forensic Pathology activity in Romania are determined by law. So, it is a legal compulsion to process an autopsy to any :

- violent death (homicide, accident or suicide),
- sudden and/or suspect death,
- suspected medical error,
- death that appears earlier than 24 hours from admission to a hospital,
- person with unknown identity.

These items have determined a large number of autopsies ( about 3500) performed every year at the National Medico-Legal Institute Bucharest.

In fig.1, 10-15 % represent unidentified corps with a positive diagnosis of sudden or suspect death. The number of nameless persons arrays a continuous ascension. Simultaneous, the macroscopic aspect of the corps shows a major physical degradation (cachexy) in a large number of cases. In some of the cases, pathological findings are not able to support a suitable death cause diagnosys. These reasons had determined us to operate laboratory analyses to some unidentified corps wich were autopsied in our unit.

The selection criteria in research lot was the physical aspect, age and gross pathological changes. Physical aspect was almost decisive. Using this criteria we were able to select a number of 32 cases, characterized by physiological misery and often by cachexy. Age of the nameless corps was approximate, and have the following distribution :

| Age Group | 0-10 | 11-20 | 21-30 | 31-40 | 41-50 | 51-60 | over 60 |
|---|---|---|---|---|---|---|---|
| Number | 0 | 0 | 3 | 10 | 14 | 5 | 0 |

Sex distribution of the main group was 6 female and 26 male.

All of the 32 nameless corps were finally identified to be beggars and tramps wich lived in public places (subway and railway stations, markets or parks), with no social assistance usage and a posotive history of chronic alcohol abuse.

Pathological examination was performed (both macroscopic and microscopic) in order to observe any pathological diagnosis. Most of unidentified corps had a positive diagnosis of liver disfunction. In 25 cases fatty liver was confirmed by microscopy. In 5 cases cirrhoses and in 2 cases cardiac liver were found. Fibrondular pulmonary sclerosis (uni/bilateral ) (23) and pleural symfisis (6) were another chronic diseases frequently finded. Miocardofibrosis (minor) and degenerative vascular changes by atherosclerotic process in a variable degree were observed at a majority of cases. (Fig.2) Distribution of pathological changes was :

Hepatic 32 cases (6f/26 m)

Pulmonary 30 cases (5f/25 m)

Heart and vascular 28 cases (3f/25 m)

We have to emphasize that pathological findings are moderate and could not explain by themselfs the zhanatologycal mechanism ; these circumstances suggested the necesity of laboratory analysis.

Accepted laboratory test performed routinely to the mentioned cases were total proteins, total bilirubin, ketonic elements and glucose.

Total proteins were found lower than 6,4 g% in 16 cases. (Fig.3)

Total bilirubin over 1 mg% existed in 14 cases.

Ketonic Elements were discovered in 9 cases, 4 cases were positive to indican.

Glucose under 65 mg% was identified in 12 cases.

In order to observe the implication of these thanathochemical findings in the death cause mechanism, we made a randomly selection of 32 cases having a specific thanatological diagnosis. We selected 6 females and 26 males, covering all major death causes ( Fig.4)

Violent deaths 7 cases

Nonviolent deaths 25 cases

- 11 pulmonary
- 11 heart and vascular
- 2 sepsis
- 1 tumor

Total proteins under 6,4 g% were found in 5 cases, total bilirubin over 1 mg% - 10 cases, ketonic elements were positive in 4 cases and glucose was under 65 mg% in just one cases but was higher than 120 mg% in three cases.

Comparing the two groups it is evident that even common biochemichal findings are able to support a more specific death diagnose in absence of major pathologic symptoms.

Total proteins and glucose level are able to explain that limitation of nutritional input associated with persistent alcohol abuse and chronic degenerative diseases are chained in a process finalized by death.

In order to make these findings most specific, we studied (using datas from NMLI activity) both cachectic and low glucose figure cases from 1991 to 1994. The number of bodies with chemichal and morpho-pathological chained death cause have growth almost exponentialy in this period of time.

## CONCLUSIONS

The investigation study was promoted by the increasing number of social cases which were authopsied in National Medico-Legal Institute Bucharest. ( Fig.5)

The selection criteria were age, morpho-physiologic aspect and pathological findings that could not entirely explain the death mechanism.

Drop of total proteins and glucose associated with a positive reaction of ketonic elements and indican was find in a major number of cases from the main group, relative with witness group.

The laboratory findings (total proteins, glucose and ketonic corps) shows that, in the thanatological chain, ordinary biochemical fluctuations could be more implicated than pathological changes ; these changes authorize a new, correct and exact death mechanism interpretation.

Even if usual biochemical changes might be explained by morphological alterations, their intrication in death mechanism is important and relevant in some questioning cases.

## BIBLIOGRAPHY :


Belis V (1990) Moarte subita. In: Medical Publishing (ed) Indreptar de practica medico-legala, Bucureşti, P 35-43

Irwing J, Cohle SD (1988) Sudden death by diabetic ketoacidoses. Am J of For Med and Path 2

Mitrica KN (1981) Blood - organic substances. In: MedicalPublishing (ed) Clinical laboratory. Biochemistry, Bucharest, P 176-182, 206-214, 241-243

Moraru I (1967) Moarte subita . In: Medical publishing (ed) Forensic Medicine, Bucureşti, P 132-148

Scripcaru Gh, Terbancea M (1983) Sudden death. In: Medical publishing (ed) Forensic Pathology, Bucureşti, P 80-93

Zamfirescu M, Popescu A (1991) Biochimia sângelui. In: Medical publishing (ed) Tratat de Biochimie medicala, vol.2, Bucureşti, P 67-112

**Fig.1** THANATHOCHEMICHAL BLOOD CHANGES
AGE AND SEX DISTRIBUTION - MAIN GROUP

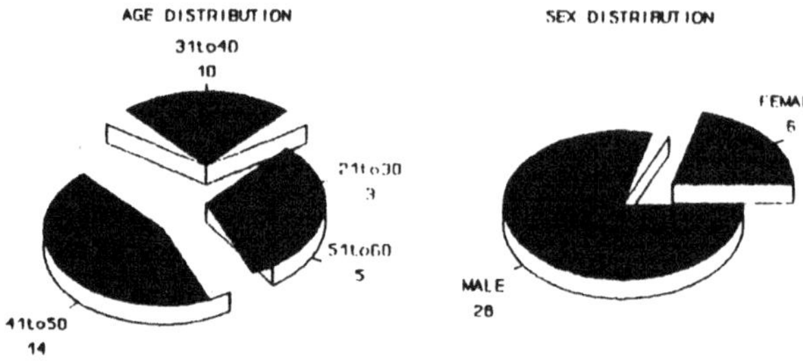


**Fig.2** THANATHOCHEMICHAL BLOOD CHANGES
PATHOLOGY DIAGNOSYS=MODERATE; MAIN GROUP

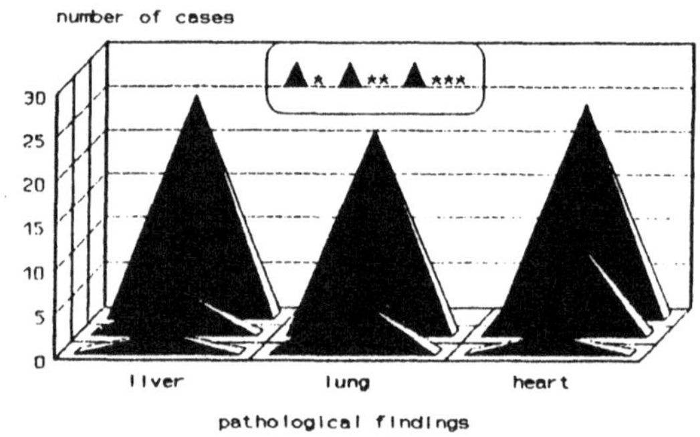


llver: *-cardiac/**-cirrhoses/***-fatty.
lung: *-pleur.symphyzys/**-fibronodular sclerozys
heart: *-complex/**-ASC/***-miocardofibrozys

**Fig. 3**
THANATHOCHEMICHAL BLOOD CHANGES
IDENTIFIED vs UNIDENTIFIED

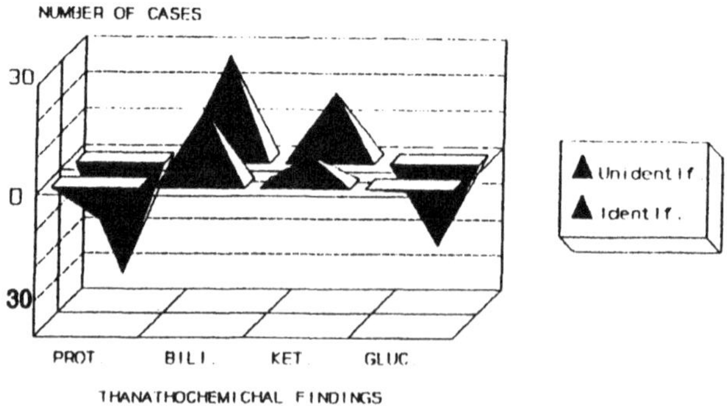


ACCEPTED VALUES: prot.under 8.4g, bilir.over 1mg, ketonic +,glucose under 65mg.

## 4. THANATHOCHEMICAL BLOOD CHANGES THANATHOLOGY-WITNESS GROUP-

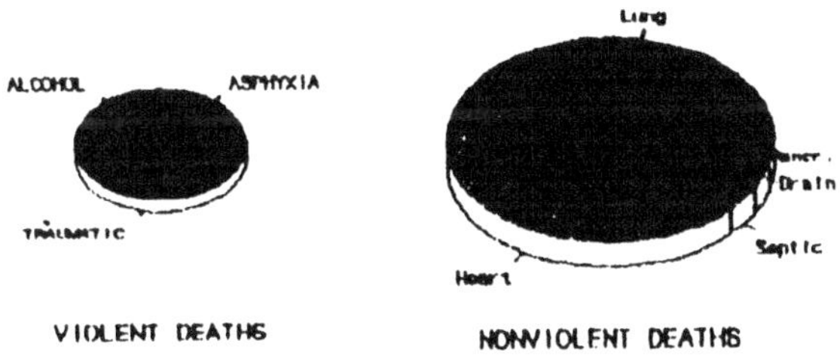


Fig. 5-THANATHOCHEMICHAL BLOOD CHANGES
TIME EVOLUTION: severe weight loss & glucose level

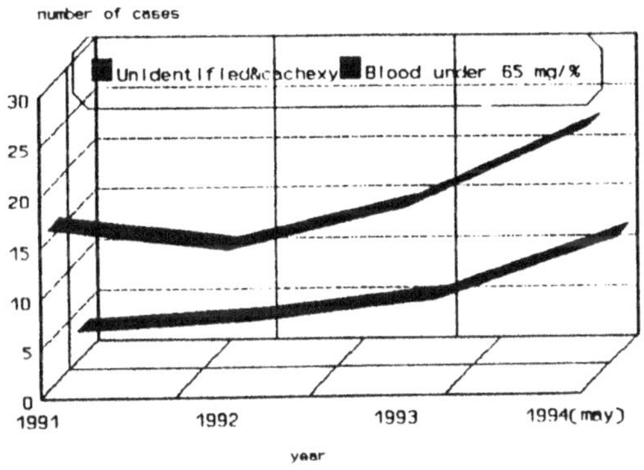

# Estimation of post-mortem interval based on the changes of phosphorylase activity in skeletal muscles

ZG. LIAO*, G. QUATREHOMME**, A. OLLIER**, JW. WU*

*School of Forensic Medicine, West China University of Medical Sciences, Chengdu 610041, P.R. China
**Laboratory of Forensic Medicine, Institute of Medicine of Nice, 06107 Nice Cédex 2, France

It is well known to establish the time of death, in certain instances, is very important in Forensic practice. In the past, it depended primarily on the early postmortem signs, such as development of livor mortis, the stage of rigor mortis and changes in the body temperature from loss of heats. But there are many factors that affect postmortem changes and the time of death was variously established based on these appearances. The authors, during using an enzyme histochemical process to investigate the enzymes, discovered that the changes of phosphorylase (PPr) activity is more sensible to the postmortem changes than other enzymes such as dehydragenase. In order to clarify the relationship between the changes of the enzyme activity and the time interval after deaths, we devised this experiment.

## MATERIALS AND METHODS

### Materials

1) Thirty-six male mice of the same age were divided into 9 groups at random. Each group included 4 mice. The animals were sacrificed and kept at 20° C. The samples were respectively taken from the quadriceps femoris at 0, 2, 4, 6, 8, 12, 16, 20 and 24 hours after death. Samples of each group were embedded in single block and frozen with liquid nitrogen.

2) Four rabbits were sacrificed and kept at 15°C. Samples were taken from the quadriceps femoris at 0, 2, 4, 6, 8, 12, 16, 20 hours after death and were treated as those above.

3) The left psoas major of human was taken during the autopsy from 7 corpses due to various causes of death and with known postmortem interval. The samples were frozen with liquid nitrogen.

### Methods

The frozen specimens were cut at 8 microns in a cryostat at -12° C. The slices were mounted with cover glass for enzyme histochemistry stain.

The cover glasses were put into a stain trough for incubation using the method developed by TAKEUCHI (1962) (1) for demonstration of PPr and observed under the light microscope. The positive results appeared as blue in color and evaluated by a semi-quantitative method.

The evaluation of the results was made as follows : the results of stain were divided into 4 levels according too the stain intensity of two types of muscle fibers and the morphological changes of the sarcoplasmic reticulum. The grading standards were shown in table 1

*Table 1 : Grading standards of PPr in skeletal muscle by enzyme histochemistry stain*

| GRADE* | STANDARDS |
|---|---|
| + + + | Both of two types of muscles were stained in blue. Type I was light blue and type II was dark blue. The sarcoplasmic reticulum was clear and appeared as a network. |
| + + | Color faded in type I. Type II became shallow light and sarcoplasmic reticulum appeared as parallel arranges. |
| + | The color of type I fully disappeared and type II became shallow light blue. The sarcoplasmic reticulum blurred and appeared as in small spots. |
| - | The color in both types disappeared completely or only a little shallow light blue was left. |

* +++ = extremly positive ; ++ = strong positive ; + = positive ; - = negative

RESULTS

The activity of PPr in mice muscles weakened 6 hours after death and gradually decreased as time elapsed. All muscles became negative 20 hours after death.

The activity of PPr in rabbits muscles weakened 6 hours after death and markedly decreased at 16 hours after death. Negative results were found 20 hours after death.

The changes of enzyme activity in the human psoas major were similar to that of mice. The results are shown in table 2.

*Table 2 : the results of enzyme histochemistry stain in skeletal muscles*

| | Postmortem interval (hours) | | | | | | | | | | | | | | | |
|---|---|---|---|---|---|---|---|---|---|---|---|---|---|---|---|---|
| Samples | 0 | 2 | 4 | 6 | 7 | 8 | 12 | 16 | 17 | 18 | 20 | 21 | 24 | 26 | 30 | 34 |
| QF of mice | +++ | +++ | +++ | ++ | | ++ | ++ | + | | + | — | | — | | | |
| QFof rabbits | +++ | +++ | +++ | ++ | | ++ | + | + | | + | — | | | | | |
| PM of human | | | | | ++ | | | | + | | — | — | | — | — | — |

Q.F. = quadriceps femoris ; P.M. = psoas major

## DISCUSSION

Phosphorylase (PPr) falls in catalogue of glycosyltransferases. It locates in endoplasmic reticulum and its activity is most intensive in skeletal muscles. It exists in two forms which are histochemically demonstrated both in animal and human (2-3). The function of PPr is to catalyse both the synthetic and decomposition reactions of amylose and its activity is regulated by the glycogen concentration (4). The direction of the reaction depends on the pH value of media. In normal physiologic condition, it catalyses the decomposition of glycogen which produces glucose-1-phosphate. The method of enzyme histochemistry is based on the principle of the synthetic process, in which amylose is composed. In this process, G-1-p acts a substrate. Glycogen added to the substrate mixture may serve as the primer for polyglucose formation from glucose-1-phosphatase by PPr activity (5). Synthetic glycogens stain with iodine. It made muscle appear in blue at the site of the enzyme. The intensity of color indicates the activity of the enzyme.

As the result of our investigation, the activity of PPr began to decrease in 6 to 8 hours after death either in human or in animal. In 12 to 16 hours it decreased markedly and after 20 hours it completely disappeared as shown in table 2. With the exception of the samples kept at 4° C, the rate of diminishing activity was slow. The enzyme activity of these samples was still 3 plus after 10 hours. It was positive 26 hours after death. It seems that the changes of temperature have certainly an influence on the enzyme activities. But, in general, at room temperature, the enzyme activity changes are relatively stable.

As regards the psoas major of cadaver, according to our experiences, there are 3 advantages to take samples from the left psoas major :

1)The muscle is abundant for repeatedly sampling.

2) The psoas major is free from interference environmental factors except for infections in the posterial peritonum.

3) The samples taken laterally from left are more convenient at autopsy for the operator.

These findings are preliminary results. There are still some problems such as the results must be photographed due to discoloration of stain with the time elapsed. This should be further studied. However, it is suggested that the changes of PPr activity postmortem could be used as one of the indicators to estimate the time of death.

REFERENCES

1. TAKENCHI T (1962) Histochemistry of intracellular polysaccharide synthesis. Ann Histochem 7:61-80

2. BOCEK RM, BEATTY CH (1966) Glycogen synthetase and phophorylase in red and white muscle of rat and rhesus monkey. J Histochem Cytochem 14(7):549

3. TAKENCHI T., KOBAYAKAWA S (1955) Distribution of tissue amylophosphorylase in various tissues of human and mammalian organs. J Histochem Cytochem 3:481-491

4. MUNGER R et al (1993) Correlations of glycogen synthetase and phosphorylase activities with glycogen concentration in human muscle biopsies. Evidence for a double-feedback mechanism regulating glycogen synthesis and break down. Metabolism : clinical and experimental 42(1):36-43

5. TAKENCHI T et al (1978) Histochemical demonstration of total phosphorilase activity for diagnosis of carcimona cells in human stomach and intestines. Stain Technology 53(5):257

# Electrical fatalities - serum myoglobin concentration as a characteristic marker?

K. Püschel [1], Ute Lockemann [1], J. Bartel [2]

[1] Institute of Forensic Medicine, University of Hamburg, Butenfeld 34, 22529 Hamburg, Germany

[2] Laboratory Association Dres. med. Limbach and Colleagues, Im Breitspiel 15, 69129 Heidelberg

## Introduction

Elevated serum myoglobin levels may originate from a variety of triggering mechanisms. Points of special interest concerning fatalities were the site of blood sampling, the postmortem interval, the influence of resuscitation and the cause of death with special reference to electrical current [2, 4, 6, 7, 8].

## Material and methods

The postmortem serum myoglobin levels of 58 fatalities were investigated. Quantitative determination of myoglobin in 100 blood samples from different sites after varying postmortem intervals was performed by particle-enhanced nephelometry (Behringwerke Marburg).

## Findings

In the 100 serum-samples a broad variety of myoglobin amounts with concentrations between 2 and 1310mg/l were found . An increase of the myoglobin values with the passage of postmortem time is obvious (fig. 1).

The topographical sampling site (sinus sagittalis superior, right heart ventricle, vena portae and vena femoralis) plays an important role; the highest concentrations are found adjacent to striated muscles (i.e. in blood from the heart or the femoral vein). In 8 out of 9 cases the lowest myoglobin-concentration was found in the sinus sagittalis.

There was no significant correlation of myoglobin values and death by electric current. The myoglobin values of the fatalities due to electric current (n=8) ranged between 16 mg/l and 896 mg/l. Compared to other causes of death statistical analyses of the myoglobin-concentrations of the electrical fatalities did not give hint to any diagnostic value of this parameter (fig. 2).

According to our data neither resuscitation nor the cause of death seemed to have a striking influence on the level of serum myoglobin. The most important factor was the postmortem interval.

Discussion

Our findings are to a certain extent in accordance with literature: While most authors describe a general postmortem elevation of myoglobin levels in cases of natural death as well as of violent death [3, 6], others deny this phenomenon, at least for the first four days postmortem [2, 8].

The relationship between severe antemortem trauma (polytrauma), survival time and an elevation of myglobin in the serum could not be investigated in detail because there were only very few traumatic cases (n=11) in our material (without longer lasting survival periods). Further investigations are necessary.

Resuscitation procedures had no striking influence on serum myoglobin levels.

Some authors describe a correlation between electric shock and serum myoglobin levels in living patients [1], intensive lesions of striated muscles caused by electricity [5] and elevated myoglobin levels in electrical fatalities [6]. Others deny this [2, 4].

The authors who described or supposed an elevation of serum myoglobin concentration as a consequence of the influence of electric current referred to electron-microscopical findings and radioimmunological investigations [1, 5, 6] to determine the myoglobin concentration.

The groups who did not state a correlation between electrical current and serum myoglobin levels either used the method of histology [2] or radio-immuno-assay [4].

Urban et al. [6, 7] concluded that serum myoglobin might be very worthful and characteristic as a proof of intravital exposition to electrical current. According to these authors defibrillation and even short time exposition to electricity with higher currencies do not lead to an increase of myoglobin concentration similar to that of deaths due to electricity [6]. On the other side investigations of Pankratz et al. [4], who also applied the radioimmunological testing method did not verify any correlation between the myoglobin concentration of electrical fatalities and different causes of natural death.

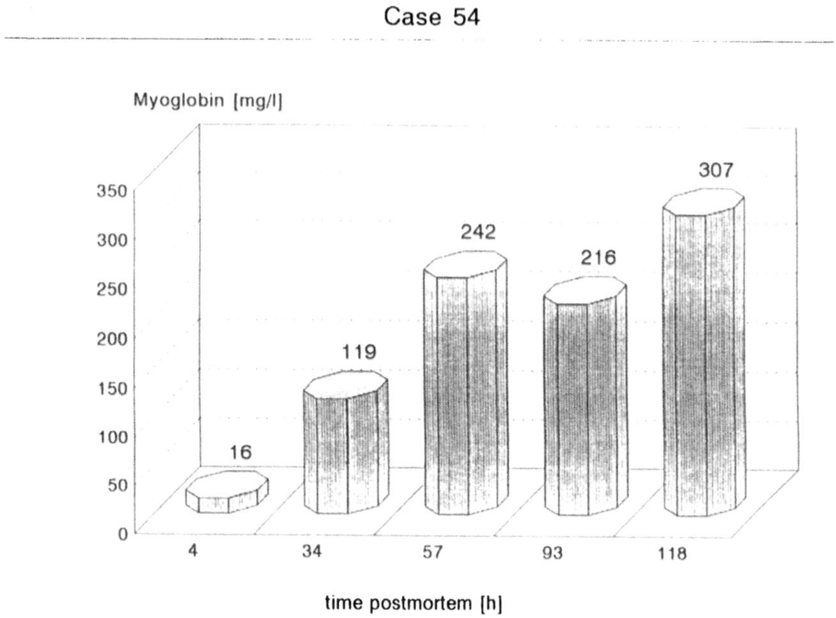


Fig. 1: Increase of serum myoglobin concentration with the passage of time in a 59-year-old male electrical fatality

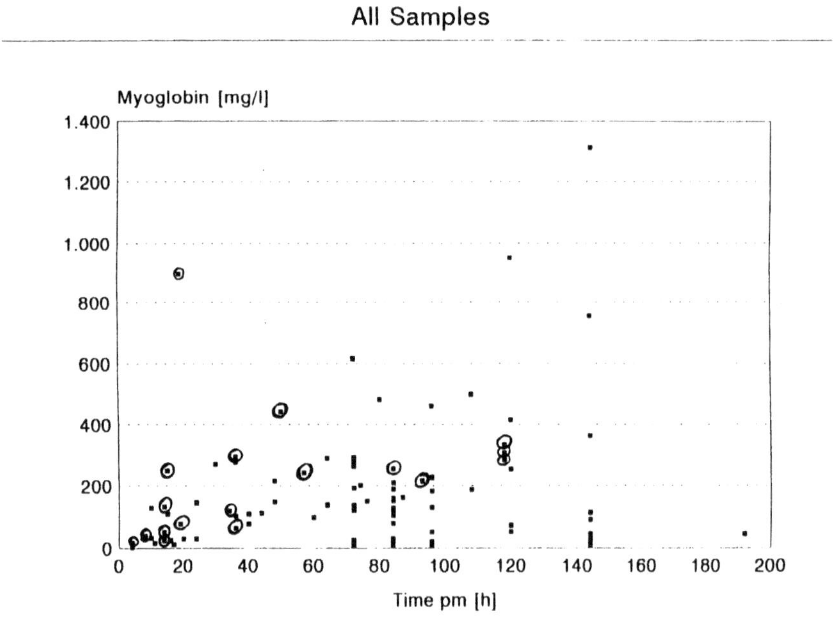


Fig. 2: Distribution of all serum myoglobin values.
⊙ = electrical fatalities

Due to the specifity of the antibody for myoglobin, our method of nephelometry is independent from slight hemolysis. Severe autolysis rendered the nephelometric analysis impossible. However, even in extreme hemolytic samples from healthy individuals we could never detect falsely elevated myoglobin levels. The influence of the applied method concerning postmortem intervals and consecutive hemolysis should be considered when discussing correlations between different causes of death and serum myoglobin levels.

As a consequence of this pilot study further investigations are planned with more homogeneous groups of different causes of death and defined post mortem intervals of blood sampling. Special attention must be paid to the characteristics of electric current. Possibly cases of death in the bath tub with hot water must be differentiated from other cases of electrical fatalities.

## Literature

1. Bhatt DL, Gaylor DC, Lee RC (1990) Rhabdomyolysis due to pulsed electric fields. Plast Reconstr Surg 86:1-11

2. Keil W, Yoshida H, Ishiyama I (1984) Untersuchungen zur Wirkung von Elektrizität auf den Myoglobingehalt humaner Herz- und Skelettmuskulatur. Z Rechtsmed 91:185-193

3. Miyaishi S (1990) An enzyme immunoassay for human myoglobin and its application to forensic medicine. Jpn J Legal Med 45:6-25

4. Pankratz H, Liebhardt E (1990) Myoglobinkonzentrationen des Leichenblutes bei Stromtodesfällen. Beitr gerichtl Med 48:325-327

5. Püschel K, Brinkmann B (1979) Zur Histomorphologie vitaler Muskelreaktionen nach Stromschädigung. Beitr gerichtl Med 37:141-146

6. Urban R, Schröder G, Tröger HD (1988) Myoglobingehalt der Herzmuskulatur nach postmortaler Stromeinwirkung. Beitr gerichtl Med 46:345-349

7. Urban R, Tröger HD (1986) Bestimmung der Myoglobinkonzentration - Diagnose des Stromtodes. Vortrag, Jhrstag Dt Ges Rechtsmed, St. Gallen

8. Volk P, Begemann M (1971) Zur Frage der prä- und postmortalen Einschwemmung von Myoglobin in das Blut. Beitr gerichtl Med 28:115-116

# POST-MORTEM CHEMISTRY : ITS APPLICATIONS TO DIAGNOSIS

Prof. Enrique VILLANUEVA

Department of Legal Medicine, University of Granada, Spain.

Several years of intense research activity in thanatochemistry have gone by and been resourcefully compiled by Prof. Coe in several revisions. (1). We believe the time has now come to incorporate it into daily practice. To do this, we must choose those parameters that are truly useful and that definitely represent an advancement over traditional methods.

In all autopsies, vitreous humour and pericardial fluid should be extracted and electrolytes, glucose, urea, and creatinine be determined. Depending on the pathological syndromes and the autopsy findings, complementary biochemical tests would include other, more specific parameters. Biochemical results from blood and, in particular, from cardiac blood must be interpreted extremely carefully, including in the analysis of toxic substances.

Regarding the diagnosis of cause of death, at least in Latin countries, the pathologist must not only determine the immediate cause of death, but also many other matters such as any con-causes of interest. The contribution of the non-causes in the final outcome are deduced from the sequence of physio-pathological processes that leave a biochemical trace at each step.

It is understandebly difficult to change from a morphological to a biochemical mentality, however, biochemistry is dynamic, functional, the essence of the injury. It is therefore essential in reconstructing the events and is the best method for interrogating the corpse.

Thus understood, thanatochemistry finds its applications in the following situations:

A) the diagnosis of pathologic processes visible only as functional alterations:

- Comas, intoxications, deaths due to acute cardiac crisis.
- Neuro-endocrine and metabolic alterations (dehydration).

B) Complementary diagnosis in deaths due to:

a) Asfixia and hypoxic syndromes; b) myocardial infarction; c) anaphylactic shock; d) disseminated intravascular coagulation syndrome; e) differential diagnosis of vital and post-mortem injuries.

C) Diagnosis of previous non-causes - determination of pathological state:

a) alcoholism; b) artheriosclerosis; c) diabetes; d) acute hepatic and renal failure; e) damage produced by free radicals.

Of all the clinical situations just mentioned, some of them need a more extended discussion.

DIAGNOSIS OF DIABETES

Diabetes can be diagnosed by high glucose levels in vitreous humour. When blood is taken from peripheric vessels, however, false positive results may be obtained. (2). The author, in reviewing more than 6 000 vitreous humour specimens tested by glucose-specific laboratory procedures, never found values of over 200 mg/dl except in diabetics. In our study, (3) we found an average glucose level of 51 mg % in postmortem chemical analyses of vitreous humour taken in the first hour after death. From 15 hours on, postmortem glucose values were undetectable.

There exist accurate methods for the diagnosis of the two different clinical situations that may represent themselves: diabetic status and diabetic coma. Diabetic status can be determined by measuring glycosylated hemoglobin, or even better by the determination of glycosylated protein (fructosamine), which can give us an idea of blood glucose levels during the two weeks prior to death. (4).

Diabetic ketoacidosis is therefore easily identified by the presence of high glucose values greater (>500 mg %) accompanied by ketones in the vitreous humour.

Dehydration may occasionally be present, causing an increase in sodium concentrations in vitreous humour.

Acute renal failure associated with nitrogen retention can be established by an increase of urea and creatinine in vitreous humour.

## COMAS

Postmortem biochemical diagnosis of acute hepatic failure is more complicated, since elevated levels of ammonia and hepatically significant enzymes (GOT, GPT, LDH, etc.) routinely occur after death, making their interpretation valueless.

Wright and Coe found significant elevations of Cerebrospinal fluid glutamine after death in cases of documented hepatic failure. (1).

## DEATH DUE TO ACUTE CARDIAC CRISIS

During the last few years, a team of researchers from the University of Granada (together with some other collaborators) (5) have been trying to solve the problem as where myocardial infarction occurs only a few hours before death, routine macroscopical and microscopical examinations are very reliable, or some other situations, such as where the myocardial anoxia is temporary and produces a reversible injury, conventional techniques are not of use for an exact diagnosis. (6).

The injury in the heart can cause ventricular arrythmia, producing the death of the person. Morphological changes might not be detected, but biochemical changes might have occurred. During the last few weeks, two methodological approaches (with similar bases) have been developed: immunocytochemistry and biochemistry. (7, 8, 9).

From our study (10) we concluded that a combination of various morphological and biochemical analyses are of great value in these cases. We have also proposed a discriminant analysis that gives a formula including the best predictors variables for the postmortem diagnosis of myocardial infarction.

DEATH DUE TO ANAPHYLAXIS

Autopsy findings in cases of death due to anphylactic shock tend to be unspecific. Diagnosis is made by exclusion and from paramedic data.

Brizinski and Kellenberger, MacCormick, and others have discovered that immunoglobulins remain stable post-mortem. Based on this discovery, a vast field, that could be called immunothanatology, has developed, having evident diagnostic applications. (11).

DIFFERENTIAL DIAGNOSIS OF VITAL AND POST-MORTEM INJURIES

In this area, works appearing in the bibliography have primarily been concentrated on enzymatic studies, such as the one by Dachum *et al.* (1992). (12).

In our department, we rejected prostaglandins as they give very contradictory results, and instead studied a new inflammatory marker D-Dimer (13).

REFERENCES

1. COE JI (1993) Postmortem chemistry update. Emphasis on forensic application. The American Journal of Forensic Medicine and Pathology 14(2):91-117
2. COE JI (1975) Postmortem peripheral blood glucose and cardiopulmonary resuscitation. Forensic Sci. Car. 6(4):1-2
3. VILLANUEVA E, CESPEDES F and CASTELLANO M (1978) Estudio de los valores de glucosa, urea y proteinas y pH en humor vítreo en función de la data y de la causa de la muerte. Actas de las II Jornadas Mediterráneas de Medicina Legal 83-94
4. VALENZUELA A (1988) Postmortem diagnosis of diabetes mellitus: quantification of fructosamine and glycated hemoglobin. Forensic Sci. Int. 38:203-208

5. HOUGEN HP, VALENZUELA A, LACHICA E and VILLANUEVA E (1992) Sudden cardiac death: a comparative study of morphological, histochemical and biochemical methods. Forensic Sci. Int. 52:161-169

6. RAMOS V (1994) Estudio postmortem de la peroxidación lipídica, glutación peroxidasa y superóxido dismutasa en tejidos y fluidos humanos. Tesis doctoral. Universidad de Granada.

7. LEADBEATTER S, WAWMAN HM and JASANI B (1990) Further evaluation of immunocytochemical staining in the diagnosis of early myocardial ischaemic hypoxia damage. Forensic Sci. Int. 45:135-141

8. FU CHENZHONG, SONG YIXUAN and ZHU JIAZHEN (1993) Immunocytochemical study with anti-muscle action anti-body (HHF 35) on myocardial ischaemia and reperfusion injury in rats. Forensci Sci. Int. 59:25-34

9. BRINKMANN B., SEPULCHRE MA and FECHNER G (1993) The application of selected histochemical and immunohistochemical markers and procedures to the diagnosis of early myocardial damage. Int. J. Legal Med. 106:135-141

10. VALENZUELA A, HOUGEN HP, VILLANUEVA E, LACHICA E and LUNA JD (1990) Evaluation and comparison of morphological and biochemical techniques for the postmortem diagnosis of myocardial infarction. Acta Medicinae Legalis et Socialis XL:269-273

11. YUNGINGER JW et al. (1991) Laboratory investigation of deaths due to anaphylaxis. Journal of Forensic Sci. 36(3):857-865

12. DACHUN W and JIAZHEN Z (1992) Localization and quantification of the nonspecific esterase in injured skin for timing of wounds. Forensic Sci. Int. 53:203-213

13. HERNANDEZ-CUETO C, VIEIRA DN, GIRELA E, VILLANUEVA E and OLIVEIRA de SA F diagnostic ability of D-Dimer in the establishment of the vitality of wounds. Journal of Forensic Science (in press)

# 5. Toxicology

DETERMINATION OF NICOTINE AND COTININE IN ANCIENT HUMAN BONE SAMPLES:

Balabanova S.[1], and Scherer G.[2]
1. Institute of Legal Medicine, University of Ulm, Germany, and
2. Analytical Biological Laboratory of Prof. Adlkofer, München

## Introduction

Recently, the presence of nicotine and its principal metabolite cotinine, in human material (hair, bone, soft tissues, teeth) obtained from artficial and natural mummified bodies found in Africa, Asien, and Europe, dated from a period spanning from 5000 to 1400 years was demonstrated. Both alkaloids were detemined by radioimmunoassay and gas chromatography/mass spectrometry (1-4). Positive results were found in 60 % approximately, in dependence od regions and periods.

Nicotine is the principal alkaloid of the tobacco plants, but also it is present as secondary alkaloid in several other plants. In the body nicotine is speedy metabolized to cotinine. As a rule its concentrations in the body are significantly highest as these of nicotine.

In order to estiamte the approximately source of nicotine in the prehistorical human bodies, the relation between nicotine and cotinine in samples obtained from Africa and Europe was now investigated.

## Material and Methods

Bone samples, obtained from excavations sites located in Egypt (atrifical mummified bodies, n=4), and in Europe (natural mummified bodies, n=20), dated 3000 to 1400 years, ere investigated for nicotine and cotinine. The material was prepared as described in previous studies (1-4). Brielfy, after careful washing, the bone were pulverized, 1 g. homogenized with NaCl 0.9% and centrifuged.

100 µl supernatant, 100 µl orto-cotinine-solution (100 ng/ml) as interne standard, 300µl 5 ml NaOH, 25 µl 5% anti-foam-solution and phenol red (200 mg/l), and 50 µl dichlormethane were mixed and centrifuged. Aliquot of 2 µl were injected into the gas chromatograph (Hewlett-Packard 5890) for analysis.

In addition, bone samples obtained post mortem at autopsy of smokers and non-smokers (traffic accidents) were investigated for nicotine and cotinine (n=15).

To determine the possible effects of the bone matrices on the nicotine and cotinine measurements, standards were added to samples without nicotine or cotinine. The standards were recoverred quantitatively.

The lower limit of detection was for nicotine 2 ng/ml, and for cotinine 3 ng/ml.

## Results

The results showed the highest nicotine levels in samples obtained from artifical mummified bodies from ancient Egypt. The levels ranged from 248 - 2800 ng/g for nicotine, and from 0 to 82 ng/g for cotinine. In the samples obtained from naturaly mummified bodies nicotine was found in concentrations from 18 to 238 ng nicotine/g, and from traces to 48 ng cotinine/g. The nicotine levels measured in samples obtained at autopsy of smokeres were: traces (1 case) to 170 ng/g. The cotinine levels were in 1 case traces up to 202 ng/g. In the samples from non-smokers both, nicotine and cotinine were not found. The chromatograms of nicotine and cotinine found in the samples were identical with these of the standards.

Discussion and Conclusion

The present results demonstrated the highest nicotine levels in samples obtained from artifical mummified bodies from ancient Egypt. The cotinine levels reached only up to 3 % of the nicotine concentrations. This suggest that, possibly, plants containing nicotine were used post mortem at the embalming procedure. Already in the antiquity, it was known that nicotine posses anti putrefactive and insect and bacteria repulsive effects. It is conceivable that in the first time the nicotine present in the plants, penetrated the body. A metabolic process was not more present, but possibly, nicotine was metabolized to cotinine by a post mortem occuring oxydation.

The nicotine levels determined in samples obtained from naturaly mummified bodies, were significantly lower than these found in the artificial mummified bodies. The cotinine levels were indeed lower than these of nicotine, however reached up to 50%, in some cases up to 90% of the nicotine concentrations.

In bone samples obtained from recent individuals (smokers), the nicotine levels were significantly lower than these of cotinine but in some cases, similar or even highest. This can be explanined by a possible accumulation of the alkaloids in dependence of the duration of smoke, the individual metabolic processes, and also by the time between lest smoke and death.

The degree of influence of environmental factors after death on the substances present in the body, has not yet been clarified. Ambient moisture, decomposition processes, and embalming practice may play a roll. Necrobiochemical, necrochemical or decomposition processes to may lead to synthesis of nicotine are not known. Consequently, the presence of nicotine may be related to the use of plants containing the alkaloid as principal or secondary alkaloid.

In conclusion, the relation between the concentrations of nicotine and cotinine make up possible to clarified the question if plants containing nicotine were used at fumigation or at other order of therapy ante mortem, or post mortem at the embalming procedure. The question if tobacco plants or other plants containing nicotine as secondary alkaloid were used, remained to be clarified.

References:

1. Balabanova S, Parsche F, Pirsig W (1992) First Identification of Drugs in Egyptian Mummies. Naturwissenschaften 79:358
2. Parsche F, Balabanova S, Pirsig W (1993) Drugs in ancient populations. The Lancet 341:503
3. Balabanova S, Teschler-Nicola M, Strouhal E (1994) Nachweis von Nicotin im Kopfhaar von natürlich mumifizierten Körpern aus dem christlichen Sayala. Anthrop. Anz. 2:167-173
4. Balabanova S, Boyuan W, To be published in Homo 1994

# DRUG ABUSE SUBSTANCES IN THE CASE RECORD (1988-1992) OF THE INSTITUTE OF FORENSIC MEDICINE - MILAN UNIVERSITY

M. CALIGARA, F. GIGLI, F. LODI, M. LEVRATTI, R. PAOLETTI, L. SIRONI

Institute of Forensic Medicine, University of Milan, Via L. Mangiagalli, 37 20133 MILAN

INTRODUCTION

The aim of our study was to assess the diffusion of substances of abuse (drugs, psychopharmaceuticals and alcohol) throughout the population of a metropolitan city such as Milan, not only quantifying the phenomenon, but above all focusing on its trend over the years.

MATERIALS AND METHODS

The study regards subjects belonging to all the age brackets who died unexpectedly of exogenous injury causes, without being subjected to any therapeutical treatment and subjected to a post-mortem examination at the Milan Institute of Forensic Medicine over the years 1988-1992.

During the autopsy, samples of blood, urine and bile were collected and subsequently subjected to following chemical and toxicological tests: EMIT Syva and/or RIA Abuscreen Roche and TOXI-LAB for detection of morphine, cocaine, cannabinoid, methadone, barbiturate, benzodiazepines and amphetamine, GLC/HS for the determination of ethanol.

RESULTS

The study comprised 2391 subjects (out of a total of 6927 autopsies carried out), with a prevalence (77.25%) of male subjects. Of these, 1493 subjects (62.44%) were found to be positive to one or more of the substances examined in our research. As far as the male subjects are concerned, the percentage of positive cases remained more or less constant over the five-year period, around 61-66%; as for the female subjects, the percentage of positive cases remained below 50%, with the exception of 1990 where it reached 55.37%.

The most represented age-bracket of our study was the 16-35 one with 1321 subjects (55.25% of all the cases examined), of which 85.31% was made up of male subjects. This age-bracket also registered the highest percentage of positive cases: 78.30% males and 65.50% females. Even the trend registered in the age-bracket immediately after the above-mentioned one (36-50) is of particular importance.

Contrary to the other age-brackets, the number of positive cases was greater for women than for men in the "over 65" age-bracket.

Furthermore, the study was divided according to the years and, depending on the anamnestic and post-mortem examination results, cause of death in homicide, accidental, road-accident, suicide and acute narcotism (AN). The group of accidental deaths comprises accidents at work, domestic accidents and other types of events unrelated to traffic.

The "suicide" group predominates in the first two years of the period examined, while the AN group prevails in the three years that follow.

AN cases aside, the form of injury that registered the highest pecentage of positive cases is the one represented by homicide victims, with values exceeding 50% in the 1990-1992 three-year period.

The increase in positive cases in the accident group is of particular importance, from 31.25% in 1991 to 54.76% in 1992.

A progressive fall in the number of positive cases was registered in the road-accident group, from 45.92% in 1989 to 32.50% in 1992; an even more marked reduction was registered in the suicide group, where the percentage of positive cases fell from 50% in the first three years to slightly over 30% in the subsequent three-year period.

If we consider to what extent the different forms of injury contribute to the overall number of positive cases in our study, we find that AN alone represents over 50% of the positive cases; these are followed, in decreasing order, by suicides, road- accidents, murders and other accidents.

On assessing for each year the number of positive cases for each form of injury compared to the overall positive cases, it must be underlined that the AN group contributed the least in 1988 (46.07%) and the most in 1991 (62.10%) with a 16.40% increase compared to the previous year.

The greatest increases were, however, registered in the homicide and other accidents groups. The positive cases of the former, compared to the overall amount of the year, rose from 4.50% in 1989 to 10.06% in 1990, a 119.17% increase. The positive cases in the other accidents group, still compared to the overall amount of positive cases in the same year, soared from 3.19% in 1991 to 7.64% in 1992, a 138.56% increase. On the other hand, the greatest fall was observed in the suicide group, where the positive cases, compared to the overall positivity of the year, fell from 22.87% in 1990 to 14.33% in 1991, a 37.35% decrease.

The overall assessment of the forms of injury in relation to the age-brackets emphasizes how the 16-35 age-bracket is the most represented in each group, with the exception of the suicide group, where subjects aged over 65 are the most represented (202 out of 726 cases - 27.82%). AN cases aside, the highest percentage of positive cases were registered in the 16-35 age-bracket for homicides (59.69%) and in the 36-50 age-bracket for suicides (56.55%).

The substances detected in the positive cases (1493) were on the whole 2404, for the most part morphine (920 positive cases), followed by benzodiazepines (596 positive cases). The number of times each substance was detected, assessed in relation to the number of positive cases (1493), resulted: morphine 61.6%, cocaine 12.9%, cannabinoid 4.2%, methadone 2.2%, barbiturate 6.4%, benzodiazepines 39.9%, amphetamine 10.7%, ethanol (>0.8 g/L) 23.0%. In each form of injury there is a substance that appears more frequently: cocaine in homicides, benzodiazepines in suicides, alcohol in road-accidents and other accidents, and, naturally morphine in AN.

As for the latter, the fact that it is the group that presents the greatest amount of positive cases must be underlined, not only because it is the group which is most present numerically, but also, and most of all, because an overall amount of 1506 positivity reactions relating to the substances analysed in the study were found in the 808 cases. Thus, apart from a considerable amount of morphine, all the other substances were also present.

The discovery of a value equal to 1.86 (obtained from the ratio between the 1506 positivity reactions and the 808 positive cases) is proof of how in this form of injury the habit of taking one or more substances of abuse simultaneously is particularly significant. Even though to a much lesser extent, this habit was also found in all the other forms of injury, as proof of how widespread this phenomenon is throughout the population of Milan, a tendency which had already been registered in the mid-eighties.

## REFERENCES


Marozzi E, Lodi F, Gambaro V, Saligari E, Mariani R, Caligara M (1985) Rapporto sull'attività della Sezione Autonoma di Tossicologia Forense "C.M. Cattabeni" dell'Istituto di Medicina Legale e delle Assicurazioni dell'Università di Milano "Considerazioni su 1385 indagini operate su materiale cadaverico nel periodo 1957-1983" Riv It Med Leg VII: 1234-1267

Goj C, Saligari E, Caligara M (1986) Incidenti del traffico e dati alcoolimetrici: rilievo casistico nel settorato medico-legale milanese (1979-1893) Riv It Med Leg VIII: 447-463

Grandi M, Caligara M (1988) Diffusione di alcool e benzodiazepine nella popolazione milanese Atti del Convegno di studi su: "L'evoluzione tecnologica e l'assicurazione contro gli infortuni sul lavoro e le malattie professionali" Palermo 2-3 maggio 1986 A. Giuffrè Ed. Milano: 151-155

Lodi F, Marozzi E, Grandi M, Marozzi F, Caligara M, Agosta E (1990) Incidenti del traffico ed intossicazioni voluttuarie: aspetti tossicologici e medico-legali. Nota preventiva Zacchia 63°, VIII, IV: 269-273

Lodi F, Marozzi E, Grandi M, Saligari E, Caligara M, Carucci M, Marozzi F, Paoletti R, Zoja R, Rolandi A (1990) Diffusione di sostanze di interesse tossicologico nella casistica del settorato milanese. Zacchia 63°, VIII, IV: 275-284

**INTEREST OF INCLUDING DEXTROPROPOXYPHENE RESEARCH IN SYSTEMATIC TOXICOLOGICAL SCREENING : POISONINGS AND FORENSIC ASPECTS**

EYSSERIC H., MARKA C.,VINCENT F.*, BESSARD J.*, BESSARD G.*, BARRET L.
Laboratoire de Médecine Légale, Faculté de Médecine, Domaine de la Merci, 38706 La TRONCHE CEDEX
*Laboratoire de Pharmacologie et Analyses Toxicologiques, CHU, BP 217, 38043 GRENOBLE CEDEX 9

Dextropropoxyphene (DP) is a synthetic analgesic drug structurally related to methadone. In France, DP is not liable to narcotic legal control. This explains its wide use as a substitute in the treatment of drug addicts. DP is mainly metabolized in the liver via a N-demethylation into norpropoxyphene (NP), with a plasma half-life ranging from 1.6 to 24 hours, whereas NP half-life is longer, ranging from 11.5 to 50 hours.

DP abuse has been described for many years **(1)(3)(4)** but only very few cases have been recorded in France **(5)**. Because of a sudden increase of DP poisoning in 1992, we decided to include DP analysis in the systematic screening applied to drug abusers autopsies.

Results of a retrospective and prospective study, conducted in the Grenoble Forensic Laboratory, including analytical screening, GC/MS confirmation, and DP and NP dosages are presented.

Results were interpreted according to Clarke **(2)** :

| | |
|---|---|
| Therapeutic plasma concentration of DP : | 0,05 to 0,75 µg/ml |
| Toxic blood concentration of DP : | > 1 µg/ml |
| Potentially lethal blood concentration of DP : | > 2 µg/ml |

## Materials and methods

Over the period of 1990 to 1993, 35 medicolegal fatal poisonings related to narcotic abuse were studied.
DP was systematically included in the screening since November 1992. The other cases were analysed in a retrospective manner.
The screening was achieved in blood with FPIA (TDx and ADx Abbott) and/or EMIT (Syva). It included barbiturates, benzodiazepines, antidepressants, cannabinoids, benzoylecgonine, opiates, amphetamines, acetaminophen, aspirin and propoxyphene.
The qualitative confirmation was conducted by GC/MS and DP and NP dosages were achieved by GC/FID.

## Results

### 1. Role of DP in fatal narcotic poisonings (Grenoble 1990-1993)

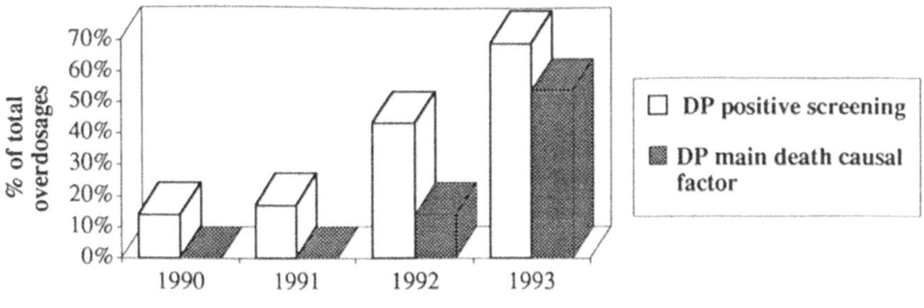

**2. Blood analytical data of 17 DP positive screening cases**

| | Case number | FPIA approximation (µg/ml) | DP (GC/FID) µg/ml | NP (GC/FID) µg/ml | DP + NP (GC/FID) µg/ml | DP/NP | Ethanol (GC/FID) g/l | Other drugs |
|---|---|---|---|---|---|---|---|---|
| DP significantly contributed to death in 6 cases | 1 | 7,73 | 6,7 | 26,5 | 33,2 | 0,25 | 0 | - |
| | 2 | 4,48 | 3,0 | 3,0 | 6,0 | 1,0 | 0 | - |
| | 3 | 14,95 | 15,4 | 8,8 | 24,3 | 1,75 | 0,1 | BZD* |
| | 4 | 11,81 | 12,4 | 18,8 | 31,2 | 0,66 | 0 | BZD* |
| | 5 | 12,12 | 8,0 | 5,0 | 13,0 | 1,6 | 0,72 | - |
| | 6 | 8,19 | nd | nd | nd | nd | 0,92 | BZD*, ADP* |
| | mean ± sem | 10,38 ±1,90 | 9,10 ±2,18 | 12,42 ±4,45 | 21,52 ±5,25 | 1,05 ± 0,28 | | |
| DP significantly contributed to death in 6 cases | 7 | 15,66 | 14,0 | 14,0 | 28,0 | 1,0 | 0 | Opia.**, cannab. |
| | 8 | 9,44 | 8,6 | 11,0 | 19,6 | 0,78 | 0 | Opia.**, BZD* |
| | 9 | 0,92 | 0,7 | 3,0 | 3,7 | 0,21 | 0,62 | Opia.**, BZD* |
| | 10 | 0,89 | 0,7 | 1,8 | 2,4 | 0,36 | 0 | Opia.** |
| | mean ± sem | 6,73 ± 3,59 | 5,97 ± 3,27 | 7,46 ±2,98 | 13,43 ±6,23 | 0,59 ±0,18 | | |
| DP screening was within therapeutic range in 7 cases | mean ± sem | 0,16 ± 0,09 | | | | | | Opia.** |

nd : not determined, BZD* : therapeutic level of benzodiazepine,
ADP* : therapeutic level of tricyclic antidepressant,
Opia.** : toxic level of opiates, cannab. : cannabinoids.

## Discussion

DP use significantly increased among drug abusers around 1992 partly because of restriction in the buprenorphine prescriptions due to new regulations. For example, 30 % of the urines collected among 100 drug abusers were found positive for DP in 1994 in Grenoble.

Our retrospective study confirms this sudden increase as no fatal case was observed before 1992 whereas 10 cases were observed after 1992.

In these cases, DP was mainly responsible for death in 6 cases and was associated with opiates at a toxic level in 4 cases. In 7 other cases DP levels were within therapeutic range. DP was thus found in 17 cases among 35 drug abusers autopsies with a DP/NP ratio rather compatible with a chronic use.

Our study also confirms the interest of DP screening. A positive result must be confirmed at least by a qualitative analysis like GC/MS or better by a specific dosage, because FPIA only allows a semi-quantitative approximation. This is particularly true for NP because of a poor correlation between FPIA and GC results.

## References


**1** - Caplan YH, Thompson BC and Fisher RS (1977) Propoxyphene fatalities : blood and tissue concentrations of Propoxyphene and Norpropoxyphene and a study of 115 medical examiner cases. J Anal Toxicol 1: 27-35

**2** - Clarke EGC (1986) Dextropropoxyphene. In : Clarke's isolation and identification of drugs in pharmaceuticals, body fluids, and post mortem materials. Second edition. London. The Pharmaceutical Press. 522-523

**3** - Cox DE and Pounder DJ (1992) Evaluating suspected Co-proxamol overdose. Forens Sci Int 57: 147-156

**4** - Kaa E and Dalgaard JB (1989) Fatal Dextropropoxyphene poisonings in Jutland (Denmark).Z Rechtsmed 102: 107-115

**5** - Kintz P and Mangin P (1993) Abbott Propoxyphene assay : evaluation and comparison of TDx FPIA and GC/MS methods. J Anal Toxicol 17: 222-224

# HAIR EXTRACTION FOR DRUGS OF ABUSE BY COCA COLA (TM): THE ULTIMATE METHOD

**Pascal KINTZ**

**Institut de Médecine Légale, 11 Rue Humann**
**67000 STRASBOURG**
**FRANCE**

## 1. INTRODUCTION :

Technically, testing hair for drugs of abuse is no more difficult or challenging than testing in many other "alternative" matrices (eg. liver, bone...). In fact, the application of analytical methods and instrumental approaches like immunoassays, chromatographic separations and spectroscopic identifications are in most cases quite similar, regardless of the initial matrix.
Many papers have been published about extraction procedures for drugs in hair of drug addicts. Cocaine, and opiates can be extracted after acid (1), alkaline (2), or enzymatic (3) hydrolyses, or enzymatic disintegration (4), supercritical fluid extraction (5) or directly by methanol (6).
Solubilization of the drugs in the hair must be such that analytes are not altered or lost. Care is necessary to prevent the conversion of cocaine to benzoylecgonine and 6-monoacetylmorphine to morphine.
Only a few papers compare these techniques. Difference of efficiencies between enzymatic and acid hydrolyses are not statistically different (1, 7). Methanolic direct extraction gave lower opiate recoveries when compared to acid (7) or enzymatic hydrolyses (8).
The solubilization procedures of the drugs in hair appear to be well documented. For the analyst it is therefore difficult to determine the most accurate method, as results are dependant on the extraction choice.
In this study, in order to demonstrate that drug solubilization can be achieved under various conditions, hair samples were incubated with Coca Cola (TM), a world known soft drink.

## MATERIALS FOR EXAMINATION

Hair samples were obtained from 7 male and 3 female subjects, aged 22 to 31 years deceased from fatal heroin or cocaine overdose .
Hair samples, weighing at least 30 mg (50 mg is better), were cut as close as possible to the skin from the posterior vertex.
The hair was decontamined by washing the specimen two times in 5 ml dichloromethane for 2 min at room temperature. This procedure was shown enough to remove external contamination, since the GC/MS analysis of a third wash remained negative, although the former was positive.

## SAMPLE EXTRACTION

The strands of hair were pulverized in a ball mill and then incubated at ambiant temperature overnight in 2 ml Classic Coca Cola (TM) in presence of 100 ng of each of the following internal standards, morphine-$d_3$, codeine-$d_3$, cocaine-$d_3$, 6-monoacetylmorphine-$d_3$, cocaethylene-$d_3$ and benzoylecgonine-$d_3$. After incubation, samples were extracted with 10 ml chloroform isopropanol-n-heptane (50 : 17 : 33, v/v), under alkaline conditions (2 ml of phosphate buffer at 1 mol/l and pH 8.4). After agitation and centrifugation, the organic phase was purified by an additional acid extraction (5 ml of 0.2 M HCl) and the aqueous layer was re-extracted with 2 ml phosphate buffer, 1 ml 1M NaOH, and 5 ml chloroform. After agitation and centrifugation, the organic phase was taken off and evaporated to dryness at 45 °C in a Speed Vac Concentror. BSTFA + 1 % TMCS (30 µl) was added to the dry extract, which was sealed and heated at 70°C for 20 min. The derived extract was transfered to an autosampler (HP 7673), and a 1 µl portion was injected into the GC column.

## GC/MS METHOD

The GC system consisted of a Hewlett Packard (5890 Series II) chromatograph with a 5971 mass selective detector, operated at 70 eV with an ion source temperature of 180-190°C. The electron multiplier voltage was set at +400 V above autotune voltage. The 5971 was daily autotuned with PFTBA. The flow of carrier gas (helium, purity grade N55) through the column (HP-5 MS capillary column, 5 % phenyl - 95 % methyl siloxane, 30 m x 0.25 mm i.d.) was 1.0 ml/min.
The column oven temperature was programmed to rise from an initial temperature of 60°C to 290°C at 30°C/min and kept at 290°C for the final 5 min. Splitless injection with a split valve off-time of 1 min was employed. Injector temperature was 270°C.
Analytes were identified and quantified based on comparison of retention times and relative abundance of two confirming ions to the deuterated internal standards.

## 2. RESULTS AND DISCUSSION :

In all the 10 cases, it was possible to extract with Coca Cola (TM) the target compounds from the hair. Chromatograms obtained are clean (Figure 1 and 2). Results are presented Table 1. Concentrations are in the range of previous published papers (1-8). However, when compared with acid hydrolysis, the detected amount of drugs were lower of 30 to 60 %, clearly indicating that all the drug is not solubilized in Coca Cola (TM).

**Table 1 :**

Concentrations (ng/mg) observed after overnight incubation with Coca Cola (TM) and 0.1 N HCl.

| CASE | METHOD | COC | BZE | CE | MOR | COD | 6-MAM |
|---|---|---|---|---|---|---|---|
| 1 | Coca | - | - | - | 0.28 | 0.07 | 1.73 |
| | HCl | - | - | - | 0.47 | 0.21 | 3.44 |
| 2 | Coca | - | - | - | 0.56 | 0.13 | 2.66 |
| | HCl | - | - | - | 1.58 | 0.41 | 4.97 |
| 3 | Coca | - | - | - | 2.47 | 2.29 | 2.99 |
| | HCl | - | - | - | 5.06 | 3.94 | 6.33 |
| 4 | Coca | - | - | - | 2.03 | 1.21 | 4.27 |
| | HCl | - | - | - | 4.00 | 2.31 | 6.67 |
| 5 | Coca | - | - | - | 1.48 | 0.99 | 6.33 |
| | HCl | - | - | - | 2.37 | 1.24 | 10.37 |
| 6 | Coca | - | - | - | 0.77 | 0.18 | 3.51 |
| | HCl | - | - | - | 0.99 | 0.34 | 5.27 |
| 7 | Coca | - | - | - | 3.37 | 1.56 | 11.24 |
| | HCl | - | - | - | 6.41 | 3.27 | 24.03 |
| 8 | Coca | 19.18 | 1.24 | 0.63 | - | - | - |
| | HCl | 37.45 | 4.01 | 1.21 | - | - | - |
| 9 | Coca | 6.37 | 1.51 | - | - | - | - |
| | HCl | 12.44 | 2.03 | - | - | - | - |
| 10 | Coca | 10.66 | 1.09 | 0.33 | - | - | - |
| | HCl | 24.37 | 3.44 | 0.47 | - | - | - |

COC : cocaine, BZE : benzoylecgonine, CE : cocaethylene
MOR : morphine, COD : codeine, 6-MAM : 6-monoacetylmorphine

**References :**

1. Welch MJ, Sniegoski LT, Allgood CC, Habram M (1993) Hair analysis for drugs of abuse: evaluation of analytical methods, environmental issues, and develoment of reference materials. J Anal Toxicol 17:389-398

2. Sachs H, Arnold W (1989) Results of comparative determination of morphine in human hair using RIA and GC/MS. J Clin Chem Clin Biochem 27:873-877

3. Moeller MR, Fey P (1992) Identification and quantification of cocaine and its metabolites, benzoylecgonine and ecgonine methylester, in hair of Bolivian Coca chewers by gas chromatography/mass spectrometry. J Anal Toxicol 16:291-296

4. Offidani C, Strano Rossi S, Chiarotti M (1993) Improved enzymatic hydrolysis of hair. Forensic Sci Int 63:171-174

5. Sachs H, Uhl M (1992) Opiatnachweis in Haarextratten mit Hilfe von GC/MS/MS und Supercritical Fluid Extraction (SFE). Toxichem Krimtech 59:114-120

6. Kauert G, Meyer LV, Herle I (1992) Drogen und Medikamentennachweis im Kopfhaar ohne extraction des Haaraufschlosses mittels GC/MS. Zbl Rechtsmed 38:33

7. Cirimele V, Kintz P, Mangin P (to be published) Comparaison des techniques d'extraction de la cocaine et des opiacés dans les cheveux. Toxicorama

8. Sachs H, Raff I (1993) Comparison of quantitative results of drugs in human hair by GC/MS. Forensic Sci Int 63:207-216

# FATAL CHLOROQUINE POISONING - CLINICAL COURSE AND AUTOPSY FINDINGS

Muhm M[1], Mortinger H[2], Malzer R[1], Binder R[2], Stimpfl T[2], Vycudilik W[2], Laggner AN[1] a. Bauer G[2]

[1] Emergency Department, University of Vienna, Währinger Gürtel 18-20, A-1090 Vienna.
[2] Institute of Forensic Medicine, University of Vienna, Sensengasse 2, A-1090 Vienna.

## INTRODUCTION:

Whereas chloroquine is a widely used medical drug for the treatment of malaria, amebiasis and rheumatic diseases, its intentional overdose is a rare event.

The fatal dose in adults is estimated to be 2-3 g.

Reports of patients with acute chloroquine poisoning have pointed out quick and complete absorption from the gastrointestinal tract followed by sudden collapse with intractable cardiac arrest in most cases.

## CASE REPORT:

A fourteen year old, so far healthy, female was transferred to our Emergency Department after ingestion of 50 tablets Resochine® (12.5 g chloroquine-diphosphate; 7.5 g free base) in a suicidal attempt.

Because of cardiac and respiratory arrest, life support - including catecholamines and mechanical ventilation - was started immediately by the pre hospital emergency care team.

Initial asystolia switched to spontaneous circulation with torsades and broadened QRS-complexes in ECG after one hour of cardiopulmonary resuscitation. At admittance lactate was 13.6 mmol/l, potassium level was low (2.6 mmol/l). Blood chloroquine level was 35 µg/ml - one of the highest levels ever reported in literature.

Dispite gastric and gut lavage, diazepam infusion, adequate substitution of electrolytes and intensive shock treatment including high doses of iv epinephrine, haemodynamics deteriorated and rapidly progressive multi organ failure (ARDS - acute renal failure) in combination with disseminated intravascular coagulation lead to fatal outcome after nine hours.

## POSTMORTEM EXAMINATIONS:

Autopsy showed no significant alterations of the internal organs with exception of multiple cerebral petechiae according to disseminated intravascular coagulation.

The microscopically examination showed a non specific, central lobular hepatic lipoid degeneration.

Extensive postmortem chemical analysis detected highest chloroquine tissue levels in the brain (40 μg/g). In the other organs the tissue levels ranged from 24 μg/g (heart) to 16 μg/g (liver), in blood a postmortem concentration of 3 μg/g was detected (for detail information see tab.1 and lit.1).

Tab.1: distribution of chloroquine (μg/g) in various tissues - postmortem analysis

| | μg/g |
|---|---|
| gastric mucosa | 0 |
| blood | 3 |
| liver | 16 |
| kidney | 24 |
| spleen | 20 |
| anterior wall of heart | 23 |
| inferior wall of heart | 24 |
| medulla | 40 |
| cerebellum | 36 |
| skeletal muscle | 15 |
| skin | 6 |

Measurement of electrolyte contents in the heartmuscle showed no significant changes with exeption of high calcium levels according to catecholamine treatment.

## CONCLUSIONS:

1. The mechanism of chloroquine´s cardiotoxicity remains still unknown.
2. In case of overdose chloroquine is a highly lethal drug with bad prognosis despite intensive care treatment.
3. Adequate therapy includes primary and secondary elimination, early mechanical ventilation, electrolyte substitution, forced diuresis, sympathomimetic drugs and high doses of diazepam (lit.2).

## LITERATURE:

(1) Noirfalise A (1978) Chloroquine intoxication: two case reports. Forens. Sci. 11:177-179

(2) Riou B, Barriot P, Rimailho A, Baud FJ (1988) Treatment of severe chloroquine poisoning. The New England Journal of Medicine 318:1-6

# FOUR HUMAN HYDROGEN SULPHIDE INALATION FATALITIES BY INDUSTRIAL HAZARD

S.PEROTTI*, M.C.RICOSSA*, V.GAMBARO**

*INSTITUTE OF FORENSIC MEDICINE, UNIVERSITY OF BRESCIA - SPEDALI CIVILI- P.LE SPEDALI CIVILI, 1- 25123 BRESCIA- ITALY
** INSTITUTE OF PHARMACEUTICAL CHEMISTRY AND TOXICOLOGY - UNIVERSITY OF MILAN - V.LE ABRUZZI, 42 - 20131 MILAN - ITALY

## INTRODUCTION

Four cases of death from acute hydrogen sulphide poisoning are described, that occurred during work outdoors. Under a shed roof, the sulphur from accumulated material, in contact with free water, started an exothermic reaction, with progressive development, of hydrogen sulphide. Three workers died immediately, and one helper.
Autopsy could only be done three days after the event, but post-mortem changes were limited as the corpses had been refrigerated once 24h had passed.
The clothing and hair smelled of sulphur, which was found in the conjunctival sac of all four victimes, who presented conjunctival hyperemia.
At autopsy al corpses showed visceral congestion, pulmonary edema and fluidity of the blood, togheter with green coloured skin and greenish colouring of the brain, probably evedence of HS poisoning.

## SULPHIDES ANALYSIS

Some of the biological samples to us were analyzed to see if they contained sulphides.
There are reports (1, 2) that is more important to find such compounds, resulting from reaction with H2 S in the organic matrix, than to test for the blood pigment sulphemoglobin, wich may in fact not even form in acute poisoning case.
The international literature proposes various analytical techniques for sulphides in biological matrices.
The most widely employed is certainly that of Baselt, proposed in numerous analytical toxicology tests (3, 4): this method involves separation by microdiffusion and colorimetric detection.
Other techniques achieve quantitative determination by direct potentiometry, using cyanide-selective electrodes (5, 6), or gas (7), or ion chromatography (8) for detection.
To start with qualitative screening in blood and brain was done using Baselt's microdiffusion and colorimetry techniques, slightly modified by us; H2 S is released into a cornway cell using 1N sulpuric acid, and detection is based on methylene blue staining.
The qualitative results of this screening procedure were confirmed by gas chromatography with atomic emission detection (GC-AED).
This combines the selectivity of GC with a hightly specific detector.
The molecules eluted from the chromatographic column are passed through helium plasma where the high energy fragments them into excited atoms, which emit light. The light, characteristic for each chemical species is passed over a series of diodes, positioned at different points in the focal plane, so that the emission of each element can then be measured.

Brian samples were analyzed. Tissue levels were measured with the head-space method; the biological matrix was placed in sealed vials, and acidified to release H2 S from the tissue, bound as a salt, wich passes into the gaseous state.

## RESULTS

The findings are summarized in the table below:

| | Qualitative microdiffusion/colorimetric method | | GC-AED |
|---|---|---|---|
| | Blood | Brain | Brain |
| Case n.1 | + | + | 1,3 ug/g+/-0,2 |
| n.2 | + | + | 1,5 ug/g+/-0,1 |
| n.3 | + | + | 1,1 ug/g+/-0,1 |
| n.4 | + | + | 1,9 ug/g+/-0,5 |

Chemico-toxicological investigations started out on a general level, so as to exclude any other exogenous substances being involved in these four deaths.

We checked initially for the most widely used addictive drugs, for ethanol and organic solvents, and for the gases most frequently encountered in cases of acute poisoning, such as cyanides and carbon monoxide (the latter as the percentage of carboxy-hemoglobin).

All these tests gave negative results.

## CONCLUSION

In conclusion, classical forensic medical criteria were employed to diagnosis poisoning, and served as a basis for conclusive judgement on the cause of death.

These cases were unusual on account of the rarity of this type of poisoning in the medical-legal literature, and since hydrogen sulphide was detected by the analytical method described.

## REFERENCES


1- M.Montagna et al.
Arch.Soc.Lomb.Med.Leg.Ass. 10, 21-27 (1974)

2- R.C.Baselt: Advances in analytical toxicology. Year Book Medical Publishers, Inc.Chicago, London, Boca Raton

3- Clarke's Isolation and Identification of Drugs
London, The Pharmaceutical Press, 1986

4- S.D.Ferrara: Il laboratorio di farmacologia e tossicologia clinica. C.G. Edizioni Medico Scientifiche

5- F.Mc Auley, D.S.Reive
J.of Anal.Toxicology 7, 213 (1983)

6- B.C.Mc Analley, W.T.Lowry, R.D. Oliver, J.C. Garriott
J.of Anal. Toxicology 3, 11-114 (1979)

7- S.Kage, T.Nagata, K.Kimura, K.Kudo
J.Of Forensic Sciences 33, 217-222 (1988)

8- L.R. Godwin, D.Francom, F.P. Dieken, J.D. Taylor, M.W. Warenycia, R.J. Reiffenstein, G.Dowling. J.of Anal.Toxicology 13, 105-109 (1989)

## COMPARATIVE STUDY OF BIOLOGICAL FLUIDS ETHANOL CONCENTRATIONS

*Pinto da Costa J; Rangel R; Carneiro de Sousa MJ*

Medico-legal Institute, Biomedical Sciences Institute "Abel Salazar", Faculty of Medicine of Oporto; Faculty of Law, University Portucalense "Infante D. Henrique";
Jardim Carrilho Videira 4000, Porto, Portugal.

### Introduction

In Forensic Toxicology a suitable blood sample for the determination of blood ethanol concentration (BEC) is not always available. In these cases some alternative biological tissues and fluids have been investigated for their relevance in predicting the BEC. In order to recognize how ethanol concentrations varies among five different biological fluids, we compared the ethanol concentrations in cardiac blood, femoral blood, urine, vitreous humour and synovial fluid. These samples were collected whenever possible from 64 corpses autopsied at the Medico-Legal Institute of Oporto (IMLP).

### Materials

Reagents used were of analytical grade.

Standards and blanks were prepared from biological negative pools at the forensic toxicology laboratory in the IMLP.

Varian 3400 gas chromatograph equiped with Genesis headspace injector, a flame ionization detector and a J&W Scientific capillary column with a DB-1 stationary phase.

### Results

From all cases 77% gave negative values for ethanol with a good correlation over the five samples analised if available. The comparison between the ethanol positive results are presented in the tables and graphics given below:

| ETHANOL FEMORAL BLOOD/OTHER FLUID RATIO | | | | |
|---|---|---|---|---|
| Case | F. B./C. B. | F.B./ V.H. | F.B./S.L. | F.B./Urine |
| 1 | 0,857 | 1,500 | 2,400 | 1,333 |
| 12 | 1,079 | 0,872 | 0,972 | 0,765 |
| 14 | 0,985 | 0,835 | 0,833 | 0,776 |
| 22 | - | 1,022 | - | - |
| 23 | 1,063 | 0,708 | 0,850 | 0,810 |
| 25 | 0,977 | 0,846 | 0,937 | 0,843 |
| 28 | 0,841 | 0,902 | 0,961 | 0,705 |
| 32 | 0,973 | 0,821 | 1,019 | 0,643 |
| 33 | 1,400 | 0,778 | 0,875 | 0,609 |
| 37 | 1,076 | 0,950 | 1,053 | 0,884 |
| 44 | 1,102 | 1,102 | 1,250 | - |
| 49 | 1,722 | 1,069 | 1,069 | - |
| 50 | - | 1,026 | 1,081 | - |
| 51 | 1,625 | 1,444 | 0,963 | - |
| 54 | 1,075 | 1,015 | 1,026 | 0,838 |
| 58 | 1,000 | 0,846 | 1,222 | 0,733 |
| 60 | 1,176 | 0,588 | - | 0,606 |
| 61 | - | 1,031 | - | - |
| 62 | 0,235 | 1,000 | - | - |
| 63 | 0,400 | - | - | 4,000 |
| 64 | 1,045 | 0,886 | 0,940 | 0,826 |
| Mean +/- 1 SD | 1.13 +/- 0.35 | 0.96 +/- 0.22 | 1.10 +/- 0.37 | 0.80 +/- 0.87 |
| Range | 0.235 - 1.722 | 0.588 - 1.500 | 0.833 - 2.400 | 0.606 - 4.000 |

COMPARISON OF ETHANOL'S MEAN VALUES

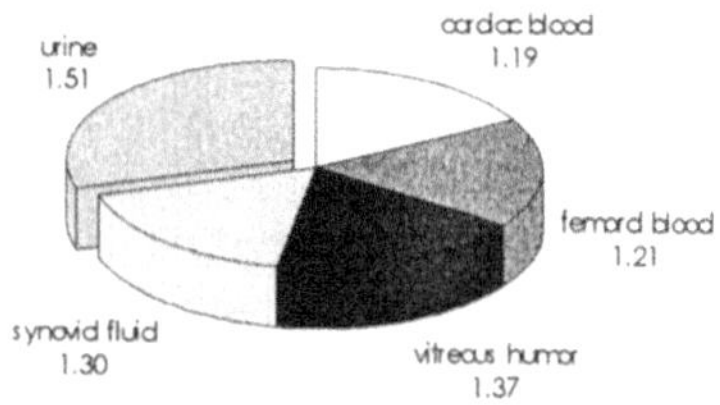

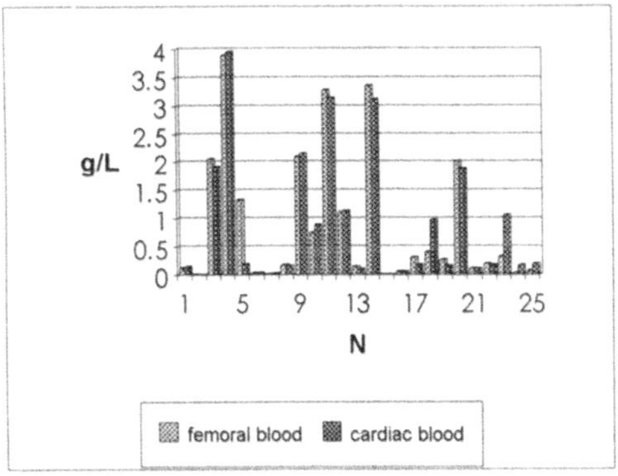


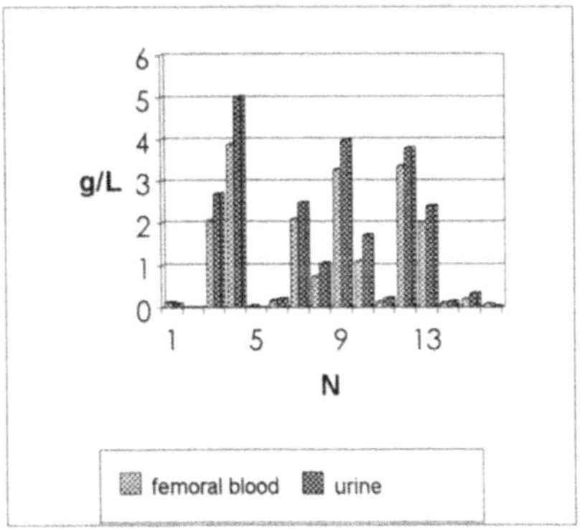


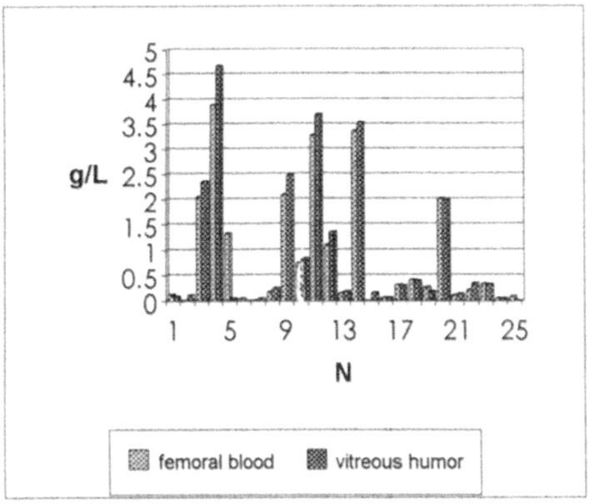


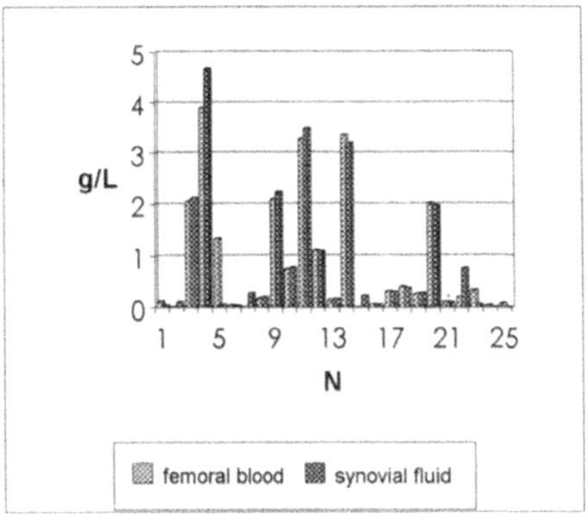


## Discussion and Conclusions

The ethanol analysis of convenient samples demonstrates a good correlation between the concentrations found in femoral blood and the corresponding concentrations in other fluids. Except for urine samples in which 86% showed a higher concentration of ethanol compared with femoral blood and where the evaluation of the femoral blood/urine ratio gave a wider range and a higher standard deviation from the mean. Also it was only possible to collect urine at autopsy in 39% of the 64 cases and not all were in very good conditions for analysis.

Synovial fluid was available in 89% of all cases; however some of the samples showed blood infiltrations and had little sample size (less than 50 uL). The natural high viscosity of the synovial fluid leads to less accurate pipetting measures and, together with the difficulties in the sample collection, demonstrates that it can be a valuable alternative sample, just when blood or other aqueous liquids are unavailable or in poor condition.

The correlation between ethanol concentrations and the corpse's putrefaction condition was inconclusive due to the little amount of data available. We expect to continue these studies in order to accomplish valuable indications about the role of the cadaver's putrefaction and other factors in the ethanol's variations among the fluids collected at the autopsy.

## References


- Budd RD (1982) Ethanol levels in post-mortem body fluids. J Chromatogr 252:315-318
- Leahy M, Farber E, Meadows T (1968) Quantitation of ethyl alcohol in the post-mortem vitreous humour. J Forensic Sci 13:498-502
- Winek C, Bauer J, Wabha W, Collom W (1993) Blood versus synovial fluid ethanol concentrations in humans. J Anal Toxicol 17: 233-235

# DRUG INDUCED AND DRUG RELATED DEATHS IN 1993 AT THE MEDICO--LEGAL INSTITUTE OF LISBON

**ISABEL PINTO RIBEIRO - MD. PhD Forensic Pathologist**
**Faculty of Medicine - University of Lisboa**
**Instituto de Medicina Legal de Lisboa**

**MÁRIO JOÃO DIAS - Forensic Toxicologist**
**Instituto de Medicina Legal de Lisboa**

## INTRODUCTION

Drug abuse has medico-legal implications, namely in Forensic Pathology because it can shorten life as well as lead directly or undirectly to death. **Drug induced deaths** are the direct effect of overdose. **Drug related deaths** refer, on one hand, to death that result from pathological alterations due to long time consume or, on the other hand, to violent deaths in which drugs consume and /or its influence on the victims is a determinant factor in the circumstances of the intervention of the external agent. The purposes of the medico-legal investigation of drug abuser's are, apart from the diagnosis of the direct cause of death, to establish the relation between drug abuse and death in order to assess its mortality.

## MATERIAL AND METHODS

### Autopsy Reports

All reports from 2498 autopsies performed at the Medico-legal Institute of Lisbon were examined and 153 were selected as drug induced or drug related deaths. Data concerning age, sex, toxicology results, autopsy findings, direct cause of death and medico-legal ethiology of death was taken from each report.

### Toxicological Studies

Blood, liver and urine samples were collected during autopsy and screened for drugs of abuse. The extraction procedure used was achieved into isopropanol /chloroform mixture (1:9, v/v) from alkaline solution (pH 9.5) after previous hydrolysis. Analyses of extracts were carried out on gas chromatography / mass spectrometry (GC/MS), after derivatisation with pentafluoropropionic anhydride .The quantitation was based on peak area ratio to internal standard nalorphine.

## RESULTS

From the 153 cases selected, two were excluded refering to foetuses - one intra-uterine death of a toxicodependent mother who died in hospital,13 days after admission by overdose - and one intra-partum death whose mother took heroin 4 to 6 hours before onset of labour (toxicology revealed positive result for heroin in the foetus ).

TABLE 1- Distribution by age and sex.

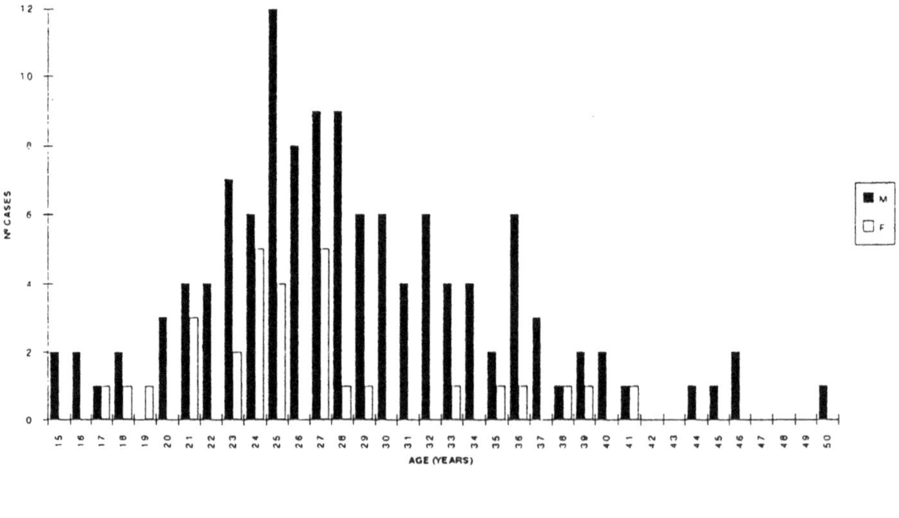

TABLE 2 - Distribution of drugs identified.

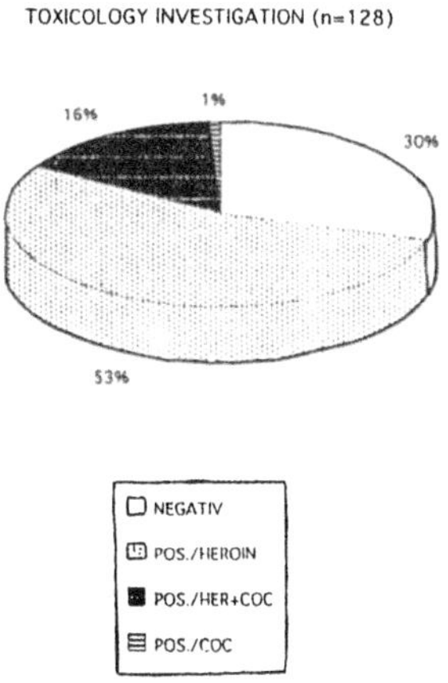


TABLE 3 - Autopsy results in terms of direct cause of death and medico-legal ethiology of death.

| DIRECT CAUSE OF DEATH | Nº OF CASES | MEDICO LEGAL ETHIOLOGY |
|---|---|---|
| Overdose | 67 | Overdose - Drug induced |
| Bronchopneumonia | 1 | Natural - drug related |
| Pulmomonar embolism | 1 | Natural - drug related |
| Pulmonar enphisema | 1 | Natural - drug related |
| Endocarditis | 1 | Natural - drug related |
| Cardiac Hipertrophy | 1 | Natural - drug related |
| Epilepsy | 3 | Natural - drug related |
| Cerebral abcess | 1 | Natural - drug related |
| Hepatitis | 1 | Natural - drug related |
| Sepsis - AIDS | 9 | Natural - drug related |
| Asphyxia-asp.gastr.contents | 4 | 1 Accident / 3 overdose |
| Electrocussion | 1 | Suicide |
| Asphyxia - Hanging | 2 | Suicide |
| Asphyxia - Strangulation | 1 | Homicide |
| Intoxication - Alcohol | 1 | Accident ? |
| Intoxication - Carbon Monoxide | 1 | Accident |
| Intoxication - Carbon Monoxide | 4 | Suicide |
| Intoxication -oral - Pesticides | 4 | Suicide |
| Intoxication - Medicament | 4 | Suicide |
| Traum Injury - Blunt Instrum. | 2 | Accident |
| Traum Injury - Blunt Instrum. | 6 | Road Traffic accident. |
| Traum Injury - Blunt Instrum. | 6 | Suicide |
| Traum Injury - Blunt Instrum. | 2 | Homicide |
| Traum Injury - Blunt Instrum. | 1 | Unascertained |
| Traum Injury - Sharp Instrum | 5 | Homicide |
| Traum Injury - Fire arms | 3 | Homicide |
| Unascertained | 15 | Unascertained - drug rel. |
| Unascertained - Late OD Complicat. | 3 | Natural - Drug related |

TABLE 4- Final results in terms of drug induced and drug related deaths studied in 1993.

| DRUG INDUCED | DRUG RELATED | | |
|---|---|---|---|
| OVERDOSE | VIOLEN DEATH<br>ACCIDENT - 11<br>SUICIDE - 21<br>HOMICIDE - 11<br>UNASCERT.- 1 | DEATH DUE TO PATHOLOGIC COMPLICATIONS | UNASCERTAINED DIRECT CAUSE OF DEATH |
| Total = 70 | Total = 44 | Total = 22 | Total = 15 |
| 46.50% | 29% | 14.50% | 10% |

An analysis of 158 cases of drug induced and drug related deaths from the year 1992 revealed similar results in what concerns to age and sex distribution,percentage of drugs consumed and of unascertained direct cause of death. Comparison of the results between 1992 and 1993 is different,showing a decrease in deaths by overdose and an increase in violent deaths (almost doub le) and pathologic complications (tripled). Victims of drug induced and drug related deaths are mainly males ( 4 to 1 ) among 23 and 36 years of age. Heroin is the drug most commonly identified - 69% respectively 53% alone and 16% in association with cocaine. Drug related deaths either violent or due to pathologic complications of drug abuse represent 53.50% of the total cases studied,i.e,exceed the number of drug induced deaths.

**CONCLUSIONS**

1°-Victims of drug induced and drug related deaths are mainly males ( 4 to 1 ) among 23 and 36 years of age.
2°-Heroin is the drug most commonly identified - 69% respectively - 53% alone and 16% in association with cocaine.
3°- Drug related deaths either violent or due to pathologic complications of drug abuse tend to increase in relation to drug induced.
4°-To assess the true mortality of drug abuse it is unavoidable to detect drug related deaths.

**REFERENCES**

- S.J. Mule, G.A., Casella. Confirmation and Quantitation of Cocaine, Benzoylecgonine, Ecgonine methyl ester in Human Urine by GC/MS. J.Anal Toxicol12: 153 - 155 (1988)
-Wetli C "Investigation of drug-related deaths" Am J Forensic Med Pathol,5(2):111-120,1984
-Knight B Forensic Pathology Ed. Eduard Arnold,London,1991
-Johnston E,Goldbaum L,Whelton R "Investigation of sudden death in addicts - with emphasis on toxicological findings in thirty cases" Medical Annals of the District of Columbia,38(7):375- 380,1969
-Ribeiro I P "Causas de morte de toxicofílicos autopsiados no IMLL no ano de 1992"Boletim de Medicina Legal e Toxicologia Forense,VII(1):75-85,1993

# Development of hepatitis B-, hepatitis C- and HIV-prevalence among drug abuse-related fatalities (Hamburg 1984-1993)

Ute Lockemann[1], K. Püschel[1], F. Fehlauer[1], R. Laufs[2], S. Polywka[2], M. Sanchez-Hanke[1], A. Heinemann[1], W. Schulz-Schaeffer[1]

[1] Institute for Legal Medicine, University of Hamburg, Butenfeld 34, 22529 Hamburg

[2] Institute for Microbiology and Immunology, University-Hospital Eppendorf, Martinistraße 20, 20246 Hamburg

## Introduction

Virus infections are common among drug abusers and the medical complications are severe [1, 2, 3, 4]. Many infections are due to an insterile technique of injection (needle sharing); disease transmission via blood or body fluids may also be associated with sexual intercourse.

## Findings

Since 1984 postmortem serological investigations in drug abuse-related fatalities (899 cases) have been carried out.

At first only **hepatitis B** infections were diagnosed. In 1984 the HBV-prevalence in drug abuse-related fatalities was 88%, during the following years it decreased to 30% in 1989, after that a steady increase up to 55% in 1993 was obvious. 11% of the infections were identified as "active" hepatitis B.

Since 1986 **HIV-1-antibodies** could be shown; the prevalence rate of HIV-1 has decreased since that time from 23% in 1986 and has stabilized on a rather low level of about 5-7%.

**Hepatitis C** can be diagnosed since 1989; it turned out to be a severe medical problem for intravenous drug addicts because of the malignant clinical course. The prevalence rate of HCV antibodies increased from 43% in 1988 to 58% in 1993.

Coinfections are common. 1993 46% of all drug abuse-related fatalities had suffered from at least two virus infections. 80% of this subgroup suffered from HBV and HCV, 7% from HIV, HBV and HCV.

The infection rate of women corresponds to their proportion among drug abuse-related fatalities.

## Conclusions

Hepatitis infections are common among intravenous drug abusers; nearly 50% are positive for hepatitis B and/or hepatitis C; coinfections are frequent. The rate of hepatitis C infections is increasing.
Compared with other big cities the HIV-1-prevalence in Hamburg is comparably low and seems to be stabilizing at a rate of 5 to 7% of HIV-infected drug users.
Although a severe morbidity is associated with drug abuse the fatal course is mostly caused by overdosage of heroin.
Postmortem screening proved to be useful concerning the investigation of the epidemiology of virus diseases among drug addicts. A continuous monitoring of the serological parameters gives a representative impression of the spread of hepatitis B, hepatitis C and HIV infections among this high risk group.

## References

1. Levine DP, Sobel JD (1991) Infections in intravenous drug abusers. Oxford University press, New York-Oxford

2. Pont J, Neuwald CH, Salzner G (1991) Antibody prevalence of parenterally transmitted viruses (HIV-1, HTLV-I, HBV; HCV) in Austrian intravenous drug users. Infection 19:55-58

3. Püschel K, Lockemann U, Schneider V et al. (1992) HIV-prevalence among drug deaths in major cities of central and northern Europe. Forensic Sci Int 57:57-62

4. Trübner K, Polywka S, Püschel K, Laufs R (1991) Hepatitis C in deceased drug addicts. Int J Leg Med 104:251-254

# Influence of Antemortem Medication on the Determination of Brain Death

Takeshi Saito, Sanae Takeichi and Yasuhiro Nakajima
Department of Forensic Medicine, Tokai University School of Medicine
Isehara, Kanagawa 259-11, JAPAN

## Introduction

The short-acting barbiturate widely used as depressant is commonly used in intracranial hypertension. It has been more than twenty years since the first reports by Shapio et al. [6,7] describing the efficiency of high dose barbiturates as depressants of increased intracranial hypertension in neurosurgical patients. Patients who are treated with barbiturate as depressants of cerebrospinal pressure, are given extraordinary high doses of barbiturates. They show the respiratory arrest and suppression of nervous system, therefore they may be misdiagnosed as brain death. Practically, barbiturate coma must be excepted from the state of brain death. Although diagnosis of brain death has to be performed considering the level of brain barbiturate concentration, it is impossible to examine the brain. The barbiturate concentrations are practically examined in the blood only.

This report describes one case examined the pentobarbiturate concentrations of ante- and post-mortem specimen. To our knowledge, this is the first report on barbiturate concentrations in the brain after barbiturate therapy.

## Materials and methods

Barbiturate was measured by gas chromatography/mass spectrometry (GC/MS) with using the method of Barbour [1].

## Case report

A 16-year-old girl sustained a left parieto-occipital head injury when she fell from a height of 18 m. On arrival at the emergency room she was drowsy, with a GCS score 7 of 15. Subcutaneous hematoma on the left parieto-occipital region was found. She was hospitalized in the neurosurgical intensive care unit. She was administered mannitol and pentobarbiturate. On the second day of hospitalization, the craniotomy was done. Pupils showed mydriasis. Then the EEGs and ABR became not responded. These conditions were continued during next day, and she was diagnosed as brain death. She died at fifteenth day of admission. She was given 1 g of pentobarbiturate in total dose during eight hours of the initial stage.

## Results and discussion

Figure 1 shows the plasma concentrations following the intravenous injection of 1g of pentobarbiturate during 8 hours. Pentobarbiturate was detected in plasma untill 10 days after cessation of treatment. Usually, pentobarbiturate is eliminated in a few days [5]. One report has carefully examined the pharmacokinetics of high dose pentobarbiturate in hypothermic, brain-injured children. Schaible et al. [5] reported an average serum half-life of 26 hours, in good agreement with earlier single dose data in adult [2,4]. In our case, administration of vasopressin was started at the fourth day of hospitalization and finished at the ninth day. It is reported that patients given vasopressin decreased diuresis [3]. The elimination-curve of pentobarbiturate was influenced by vasopressin. It is, therefore, evident from this study that the pharmacokinetics of pentobarbiturate are altered in the presence of vasopressin.

The concentrations of pentobarbiturate in autopsy materials are shown in Table 1. Pentobarbiturate concentration in the cerebrum were 5.03 μg/g even 15 days after cessation of the treatment. In the case of brain death a large amount of barbiturate remained in the brain even if blood concentration was not detective, perhaps cerebral blood flow was stagnant in the brain. Barbiturate therapy is continued for several days usually. In such a case, the barbiturate concentration in the brain is more abundant compared to our case. The effect of high dose of lipid-soluble pentobarbiturate is terminated by redistribution into tissues such as muscle and fat these capable of storing large quantities of the drug at equilibrium. It is thought that pentobarbiturate may remain as the high dosed cases fall into brain death. Up to now blood concentration of barbiturate was used determing of brain death, but it is not reliable for diagnosis of brain death. This study indicated that the high level of barbiturate in the brain was maintained for a long period. Such circumstances, may suggest barbiturate coma, even if barbiturate concentration of the blood was not detective after brain death.

The investigation on barbiturate therapy is summarized above and it is evident that further studies from different approaches are necessary. The diagnosis of brain death must be taken carefully in the case treated with barbiturate.

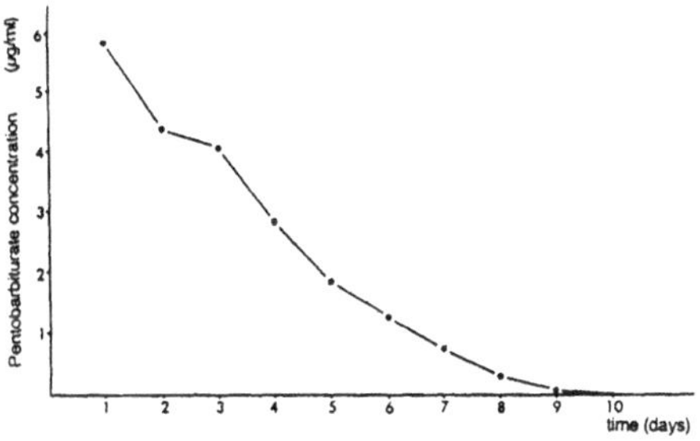


Fig.1. Plasma concentration-time curve of pentobarbiturate after intravenous administration, 1 g of pentobarbiturate during 8 hours.

Table.1. Concentration of pentobarbiturate in the blood and different regions of brain.

| Sample | μg/g, ml |
|---|---|
| cerebrum | 5.03 |
| cerebellum | 5.43 |
| blood | N.D. |

**References**


1. Barbour AD (1991) GC/MS analysis of propylated barbiturate. J Anal Toxicol 15: 214-215.
2. Ehrnebo M (1974) Pharmacokinetics and distribution properties of pentobarbital in humans following oral and intravenous administration. J Pharm Sci 63: 1114-1118.
3. Fjellested-Paulsen A, Höglund P, Lundin S, Paulsen O (1993) Pharmacokinetics of 1-deamino-8-D-arginine vasopressin after various routes of administration in healthy volunteers. Clin Endocrinol 38: 177-182.
4. Reidenberg MM, Lowenthal DT, Briggs W, Gasparo M (1976) Pentobarbital elimination in ptients with poor renal function. Clin Pharmacol Ther 20: 67-71.
5. Schaible DH, Cupit GC, Swedlow DB, Rocci ML Jr (1982) High-dose pentobarbital pharmacokinetics in hypothermic brain-injured children. J Pediatr 100: 655-660.
6. Shapiro HM, Galindo A, Wyte SR, Harris AB (1973) Rapid intraoperative reduction of intracranial pressure with thiopentone. Br J Anaesth 45: 1057-1062.
7. Shapiro HM, Wyte SR, Loeser J (1974) Barbiturate-augmented hypothermia for reduction of persistent intracranial hypertension. J Neurosurg 40: 90-100.

# MEDICO-LEGAL EVALUATION OF DRUG ADDICTION. PROSPECTIVE STUDY

*Silveira Ribeiro C; Magalhães T; Carneiro de Sousa MJ; Pinto da Costa J*

Medico-legal Institute, Faculty of Medicine, Biomedical Sciences Institute "Abel Salazar", University of Oporto; Faculty of Law, University Portucalense "Infante D. Henrique"; Jardim Carrilho Videira 4000, Porto, Portugal

## INTRODUCTION

The new law of consumption and possession of drugs (Decree 15/93 of 22/1), especially mentions the necessity of performing medico-legal examination of the suspects. Two articles assume the examination: art. 43° and 52°.

## MATERIAL AND METHODS

The casuistry of 91 cases studied in 1993 in the Medico-Legal Institute of Oporto is shown. The sex distribution shows a high predominance for the male sex (82 cases) in relation to the female one (9 cases). The great majority of the cases was found for persons between the 20 and 29 years-old (68 cases); 19 cases were between 30 and 39 years-old, 3 between 10 and 19 and 1 between 40 and 49 years-old.

## RESULTS

Most of the examined already had a criminal background (48 cases). In 57 cases the persons were in prison and the exams were requested by the Court of Law. The criminality background was associated with robbery, burglary, consumption and possession of drugs. In 34 cases the examined was waiting the process in liberty.

The drug most used for initiation of the consumption was hashish, but there were other ones involved (Table I).

The means of consumption most used was inhaling (87 cases). The rarest way was the intravenous (7 cases). In 10 cases the aspirated means was also used.

It is important to study the underlying motives and the beginning age of consumption. Most of them began when they were 10-19 years-old (72 cases). Before that age we only registered one case. In the 20-29 years-old we found 18 cases.

The influence of friends is the most point reason for the initiation. So the importance we must pay to the education and relationships of our youngsters in order to try to decrease this problem (Table II).

The actual drug in use was heroin (Table III) and the means most used keep beeing the inhaled one (Table IV).

As the law foresees, we can perform analytical exams in order to help clarifying the exam and decide about the influence of drugs. The analytical results showed mostly negative data. The reason would be the suspension of the use of drugs some time before the examination (Table V).

As a matter of public health and as the majority of the individuals were detained in prison, we studied the serological marks of hepatitis and AIDS (Table VI).

## CONCLUSIONS

As results, we found the following profile for the individuals examined in this context:

Male; arrested; previous charges; initiation from 10 to 19 years-old with hashish; actual age 20 to 29 years-old consuming heroin; positive for hepatitis C; experience detoxification programme ineffective.

| (n=111) | INITIATION DRUG |
|---|---|
| Hashish | 88 |
| Heroin | 13 |
| Cocaine | 4 |
| Other | 6 |

Table I

| (n=91) | INITIATION |
|---|---|
| Friends influence | 45 |
| During militar service | 22 |
| Personal/social problems | 8 |
| Curiosity | 4 |
| Others | 12 |

Table II

| (n=110) | ACTUAL DRUG IN USE |
|---|---|
| Heroin | 49 |
| Cocaine | 35 |
| Hashish | 22 |
| Other | 4 |

Table III

| (n=134) | MEANS |
|---|---|
| Inhaled | 68 |
| Injected | 47 |
| Aspirated | 15 |
| Other | 4 |

Table IV

| TOXICOLOGY | | | n |
|---|---|---|---|
| Negative | Blood | | 89 |
| | Urine | | 68 |
| Positive | Blood | cocaine | 2 |
| | Urine | morphine | 17 |
| | | cocaine | 4 |
| | | codeine | 2 |

Table V

| SEROLOGY | ANTIBODIES | n |
|---|---|---|
| Hepatitis | HBe | 12 |
| | HBs | 11 |
| | HBc | 19 |
| | HCV | 30 |
| AIDS | | 0 |

Table VI

## BIBLIOGRAPHY


•Carneiro de Sousa MJ, et al (1993) Contribuição para o diagnóstico e quantificação de substâncias - Artigo 71°, Dec.Lei 15/93 de 22/1. Bol Med Leg Tox For VII(1):111-120

•Fekjaer HO (1992) Les toxiques ne font pas le bonheur. Forum Mondial de La Santé 13:395-400

•Garcia Marques (1993) Incidência da droga na criminalidade: A imputabilidade do toxicodependente. Bol Med Leg Tox For VII(1):41-60

•Grams AC, Santos A (1993) Inquérito sobre o consumo de droga, Bol Med Leg Tox For VII(1):139-144

•Grams AC, Rangel R (1993) Enquadramento social da toxicodependência. Bol Med Leg Tox For VII(1): 145-148

•Grams AC (1993) Medidas preventivas de toxicodependência. Bol Med Leg Tox For VII(1)133-138

•Lopes Cardoso A (1993) Despenalização da droga. Bol Med Leg Tox For VII(1):19-26

•Magalhães T, Carneiro de Sousa MJ (1993) Avaliação do estado de toxicodependência. A propósito de 20 casos. Bol Med Leg Tox For VII(1):237-242

•Maurer M (1992) Unir les efforts contre l'abus des drogues. Forum Mondial de La Santé 13:349-354

•Pinheiro MF, Pinto da Costa D (1993) Droga em Portugal - 1991/1992. Bol Med Leg Tox For VII(1):209-220

•Pinto da Costa J, et al (1993) Inquérito sobre a droga. Bol Med Leg Tox For VII(1):165-208

•Samarasinghe D (1992) Pas de plaisir dans la drogue. Forum Mondial de La Santé 13:401-405

•Wodak A (1992) Faire face aux toxicomanies: une tâche diverse et multiple. Forum Mondial de La Santé 13:113-124

# Experimental Studies on Concentration-Time Profiles of Ethanol and Acetaldehyde in Various Organs

Sanae Takeichi, Takeshi Saito, Yasuhiro Nakajima and Yoshihisa Seto
Department of Forensic Medicine, Tokai University School of Medicine
Isehara, Kanagawa 259-11, JAPAN

**Introduction**

The present study was designed to measure the ethanol and its toxic metabolite acetaldehyde concentrations in post-mortem tissue specimens of corpse from whom no quantity of the blood could be collected. Another purpose was to discuss the toxic effects of ethanol and/or acetaldehyde on the various organs.

First, ethanol and acetaldehyde concentrations were investigated with the lapse of time in the various tissue specimens of rats ingested ethanol after an overnight fast. Next, rats were administered disulfiram (1) before ethanol ingestion, and these concentrations in the various tissues were measured.

Ethanol and acetaldehyde concentrations were determined by gas chromatography.

**Materials and methods**

Male wistar strain rats weighing about 250 g were divided into two groups. Group I consisted of 25 rats, and group II consisted of 25 rats.

Group I: Ethanol was administered *per os* as an absolute solution at a dose of 4 g/kg of body weight to rats after an overnight fast.

At 0.5, 1, 2, 3 and 4 hours after the administration, they were decapitated and the blood, various tissues were removed.

Group II: Rats were pretreated twice with disulfiram as a 1 % solution in arabic gum at a dose of 10 mg/rat, 16 and 4 hours before ethanol administration.

Various tissue samples were obtained in the same way of group I.

Procedure and conditions of gas chromatography are as follows.

The extraction procedure for headspace capillary gas chromatographic method, minor modification from the method of Mendenhall et al (2), was adapted.

*Reagents*

The extraction mixture was prepared by adding 1.0 g of thiourea and 17 ml of 70 % perchloric acid in 500 ml of distilled water. The internal standard was prepared from an aqueous stock solution containing 10 $\mu$g/ml of dioxane.

*Extraction procedure*

Each 1 g tissue homogenized in a solution containing 2.5 ml of diluted solution and 0.5 ml of internal standard solution and centrifuged at 3000 g for 5 min. The supernatant fluid (0.8 ml) was immediately added to a headspace vial.

The whole blood (0.2 ml) was pipetted directly into the headspace vial containing 0.4 ml of diluted solution, 0.1 ml of internal standard and 0.1 ml of physiological saline solution.

**Results and discussion**

1. The present study showed that ethanol concentrations in the various tissues, that is the brain, liver, myocardium, lung, spleen, kidney etc. of corpse could be detected using gas chromatographical method as described above.
2. The time course of ethanol concentration showed a rapid rise to reach a peak after 2 hours of administration and was followed an elimination curve. The

values were somewhat lower in the liver and myocardium than in the blood, but similar values were detected in the brain and blood. It seems that an amount and/or relativery higher activity of alcohol dehydrogenase participate the lower ethanol levels in the liver and myocardium.

3. In rats pretreated with disulfiram, acetaldehyde concentrations in the blood, and other tissues increased gradually after ethanol administration, and acetaldehyde varied in different tissues. (blood > myocardium = brain > liver). It suggested that in the liver acetaldehyde degradative reaction may occur through other than aldehyde dehydrogenase system, that is, microsomal ethanol oxidizing system (MEOS) and so on.
4. In rats pretreated with disulfiram, ethanol concentrations in the blood and other tissues showed somewhat lower levels than those of untreated rats, and the peak shifted to the right, that is, the peak appeared at the time of 3 hours after ethanol administration. It seems that an amount acetaldehyde in the blood may delay both alcohol absorption and excretion.
5. Pretreatment with disulfilam brought about somewhat higher levels of ethanol in the brain and myocardium than the blood, and relatively higher levels of acetaldehyde in the brain and myocardium than the liver. It may suggest the toxic effect of ethanol and/or acetaldehyde to brain and heart.
6. Further studies on concentrations and isozyme patterns of aldehyde dehydrogenase in various tissues are necessary.

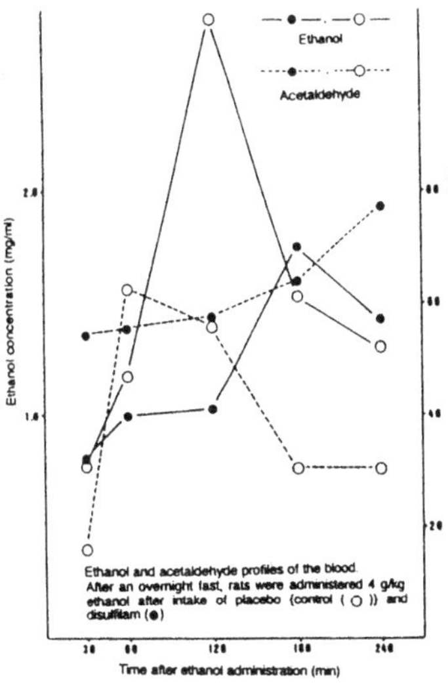


Ethanol and acetaldehyde profiles of the blood.
After an overnight fast, rats were administered 4 g/kg ethanol after intake of placebo {control ( ○ )} and disulfilam (●)

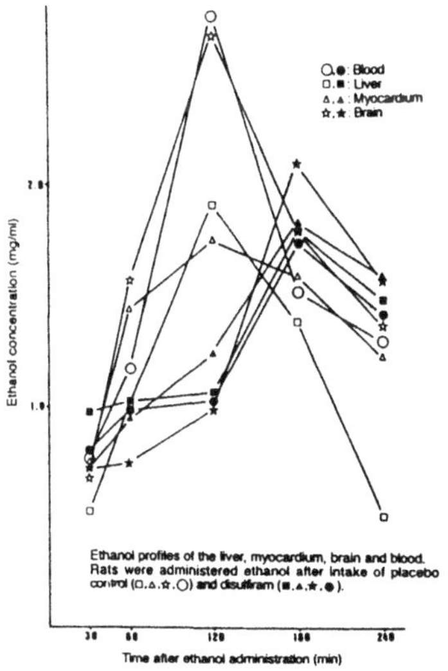


Ethanol profiles of the liver, myocardium, brain and blood.
Rats were administered ethanol after intake of placebo control (□,△,☆,○) and disulfiram (■,▲,★,●).

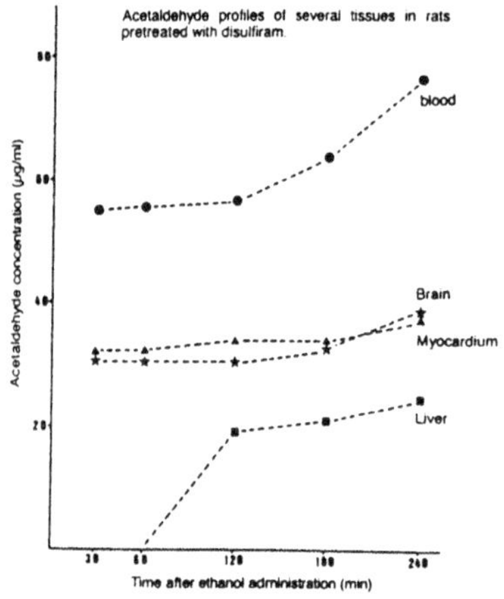


Table.1

| | Ethanol concentration (mg/ml or g) | | Acetaldehyde concentration (μg/ml or g) | |
|---|---|---|---|---|
| | placebo | disulfiram | placebo | disulfiram |
| Blood | 2.74 | 1.75 | 62.6 | 77.1 |
| Liver | 1.90 | 1.74 | (-) | 24.0 |
| Myocardium | 1.76 | 1.82 | (-) | 37.7 |
| Brain | 2.65 | 2.11 | (-) | 38.5 |
| Spleen | 2.25 | 1.76 | (-) | 36.4 |
| Kidney | 2.19 | 2.12 | (-) | 38.9 |
| Lung | 2.08 | 1.78 | (-) | 28.0 |

Table.1
Peak concentrations of ethanol and acetaldehyde in rats that were administered 4 g/kg ethanol, 16 and 4 hours after pretreatment with placebo and disulfiram.

**Footnotes**

(1) Nocbin, that is aldehyde dehydrogenase inhibitor Tanabe pharmaceutical company, Tokyo.

(2) Mendenhall CL, MacGEE J, Green ES (1980) Simple rapid and sensitive method for the simultaneous quantitation of ethanol and acetaldehyde in biological materials using head-space gas chromatography. J Chromatogr 190: 197-200.

# POST-MORTEM DISTRIBUTION AND HISTOLOGIC STUDY ON A FATAL CASE DUE TO ACCIDENTAL INGESTION OF CARBON TETRACHLORIDE.

TOMBOLINI A., CINGOLANI M.
Istituto di Medicina legale e delle Assicurazioni - Universita' degli Studi di Ancona

Key words: carbontetrachloride - acute intoxication - oral ingestion - distribution - gas chromatography - head space.

## INTRODUCTION

Carbon tetrachloride (tetrachloromethane, $CCl_4$) is a well known chemical agent with toxic property. $CCl_4$ is responsible of several cases of acute poisoning subsequent to inhalation of vapour or ingestion of liquid (1). In an adult human, the mean lethal dose by mouth appears to lie between 5 and 10 mL, but as little as 2 mL, has killed on several occasions (2, 3). The principal toxic actions are central nervous system depression and cellular necrosis in the liver and kidneys or both. $CCl_4$ is readily absorbed by the lungs. It is also well absorbed by the intestinal tract. It is metabolized in the liver by the cytochrome P-450-dependent mixed-function oxidase to only a slight extent (4). Excretion of ingested $CCl_4$ is almost entirely by the lungs; this is due to its extreme volatility. However a small amounts is also excreted by urine.
The review of the litterature revealed three works that studies the body distribution of $CCl_4$. Only one of them (5) describes the distribution pattern in a human adult who died 7 days after a single dose inhalation exposure to $CCl_4$. No studies we found about the distribution pattern of $CCl_4$ after ingestion. The aim of the present study is to determine the distribution pattern of $CCl_4$ in the human body in a fatal case due to ingestion of the chemical, highlighting the implication in forensic toxicology.

## MATERIALS AND METHODS

Case history. A 75 years old white male ingested accidentally an unknown quantity of $CCl_4$. After two days of intensive care he died. The external examination and the autopsy allowed to esclude causes of death not related with the intoxication. The histological findings confirm the liver and kidney cellular necrosis.
Sampling and storage. During the autopsy, we collected several biological fluids and tissues listed in table 1. One mL of each biological fluid or one gram of each tissue was sealed immediately in suitable vials. We made several vials for each specimen in order to repeat the analisys at least three times. All the vials were storaged at - 20 °C.
Toxicological analysis. The toxicological analysis was performed on a Carlo Erba Gascromatographer equipped with a Carbopack Carbowax 2 m X 0,8 cm packed column and a flame ionization detector (FID). The head-space tecnic was used. The gaschromatographic analysis of each sample was repeated three times, sampling each time from a new vial. The final value of the peak area was the average of the three peak areas obtained. To calculate the concentration of the $CCl_4$ in the sample, an external standard at a known concentration was prepared and analyzed in the same way of the other samples.

## RESULTS

The results of the toxicological analysis are listed in table 1.

**Table 1. $CCl_4$ concentration in biological fluids and tissues**

| SAMPLE | CCl4 (mcg/l) | SAMPLE | CCl4 (mcg/l) | SAMPLE | CCl4 (mcg/l) |
|---|---|---|---|---|---|
| Urine | 328,5 | Brain (cortex) | 243,2 | Muscle | 71,1 |
| Venous blood | 143,4 | Brain (basal ganglia) | 216,1 | Pancreas | 657,9 |
| Arterious blood | 57,5 | Brain (medulla oblongata) | 243,3 | Spleen | 68,3 |
| Bile | 169,8 | Cerebellum | 175,3 | Liver | 58,6 |
| Umor vitreus | 170,5 | Lung | 127,3 | Kidney | 150,5 |
| Testis | 237,3 | Myocardium | 78,5 | | |

## DISCUSSION

The analytical results listed in Tables 1 describe the distribution pattern of $CCl_4$ in the body after ingestion. Among biological fluids analyzed, the urine shows the highest concentration of $CCl_4$. This is probably related to the fact that the absorption phase is completely ended (the subject survived for two days). It is noteworthy that the concentration in the systemic venous blood is almost two and half times greater than in the arterious one according to the clearence power of the lungs. As the acute narcotic effect of $CCl_4$ is due to the chemical agent itself and not metabolites (6), it is advisable to asses the $CCl_4$ concentration in the systemic venous blood in order to make connection between the deep of narcosis and the $CCl_4$ blood level. The humor vitreus and the bile have an almost equal level of $CCL_4$. As the humor vitreus is less subjected to the bacterial contamination and consequently post-mortem putrefaction than other biological fluids, it could be a suitable sample for toxicological analysis. The presence of $CCl_4$ in the bile indicates the chemical is also excreted by liver not only by lungs and kidneys.

Among tissues analyzed, we found a very high level of $CCl_4$ in the pancreas. Actually we cannot explain the reason why the pancreas shows a so high affinity for the chemical.

Also brain and testis have a high affinity for $CCl_4$. The concentration of the chemical is indipendent from the brain zone of sampling; only the cerebellum is caracterized for a less level of $CCl_4$. Further, as the chemical agent itself is responsible of the acute narcotic effect of $CCl_4$, the deep of the narcosis could be well correlated with the $CCl_4$ concentration in the brain.

The lungs and the kidney show an almost equal concentration of the chemical. Lower level of the chemical are in the muscle, miocardium and spleen.

The liver, a frequently analyzed tissue in forensic toxicology, shows the lowest concentration and consequently is a bad sample in case of $CCl_4$ oral acute intoxication. This is in contrast with the data of Krobenke and Pribilla (5) in which the liver is caracterized by a higher concentration than the kidney and the lungs. This can be explained considering the different way of introduction of the chemical in the body. In case of oral ingestion the liver is the first organ along the blood flow and subjected to a sudden raised in concentration of $CCl_4$ during the absortion phase with a rapid metabolism of the molecule. This causes a decrese in affinity for the massive necrosis of the liver cells due to the fast metabolites accumulation. In case of inhalation the $CCl_4$ distributes itself slowly in the body and in the liver like in other organs so that the cells damage is less severe. This is according to the clinic of $CCl_4$ acute intoxication in which nervous symptoms are said to predominate in inhalation exposures, whereas gastrointestinal and hepatorenal injuries are more prominent after ingestion (7, 8, 9)


1) CLARKE E.G.C. (ed.), Isolation and identification of drugs, Pharmaceutical Press, London 1969, 240

2) PHELPS B.M, HU C.H., Carbon tetrachloride poisoning: report of two fatal cases and a series of fatal animal experiments, JAMA, 82, 1254-1256, 1924

3) LAMSON P.D., MINOT A.S., ROBBINS B.H., The prevention and treatment of carbon tetrachloride intoxication, JAMA, 90, 345-349, 1928

4) ANDREWS L.S., SNYDER R., Toxic effects of solvents and vapours, in ADMUR M.O., DOULL J., KLAASSEN C.D., Casarett & Doull's Toxicology, MacGraw-Hill, New York, 1993, p.683

5) KORENKE H.D., PRIBILLA O., Suicid durch einmalighe Inhalation von tetrachlokolhenstoff ($CCl_4$) mit leuko-encephalopathie, Arch. Tox. 25, 109-126, 1969

6) ANDREWS L.S., SNYDER R., Toxic effects of solvents and vapours, in ADMUR M.O., DOULL J., KLAASSEN C.D., Casarett & Doull's Toxicology, MacGraw-Hill, New York, 1993, p.683

7) ADAMS E.M., SPENCER H.C., ROWE V.K., McCOLLISTER D.D., IRISH D.D., Vapor toxicity of carbon tetrachloride determined by experiments on laboratory animals, Arch. Ind. Hyg. Occup. Med., 6, 50-65, 1952

8) HARDIN B.L,, Carbontetrachloride poisoning - a review, Ind. Med. Surg., 23, 93-105, 1954

9) GUILD W.R., YOUNG J.V., MERRIL J.P., Anuria due to carbon tetrachloride intoxication, Ann. Int. Med., 48, 1221-1227, 1958

# ACUTE METHAMIDOPHOS POISONING

**H.Tsoukali*, V.Antoniou**, N.Zantopoulos**, M.Tsougas***

***Department of Forensic Medicine and Toxicology, Medical Faculty, Aristotle University of Thessaloniki, 54006 Thessaloniki, GREECE**
****Center of Veterinary Institutions of Thessaloniki, 26th Oct. 80, 54627 Thessaloniki, GREECE**

Pesticides, organophosphates and carbamates in particular, are the cause of the 50% of suicidal, homicidal and accidental poisoning in Macedonia, Greece[1]. Methamidophos (O,S-dimethyl-phosphoramidothioate) an organophosphorous insecticide which is widely used in agriculture in spite of its extremely high toxicity, is the commonest pesticide encountered in poisoning cases.

Methamidophos, under the trade names of Tamaron, Monitor, etc.is widely used at cotton, vegetables and potatoes agriculture. In poisoning cases, it is also known as cholinesterase activity inhibitor.

In the present paper, optimum chromatographic conditions (TLC, GC, HPLC)[2,3] for methamidophos identification and quantitation in postmortem materials are presented. Its distribution in tissues from 3 fatal poisoning cases are also, presented.

## Materials and methods

Standard solutions of technical grade methamidophos were prepared in methanol and the starting concentration was 1 mg/ml.

Ten-gram specimen of tissues available was homogenized with water, allowed to stand overnight and filtered. An aliquot of the sample was adjusted to pH:8-9 by ammonium hydroxide solution and extracted twice with a double volume of the mixture ethanol:acetic ethylester:chloroform (1:1:3). The organic layer was evaporated to dryness and the residue was reconstituted and identified.

**Thin layer chromatographic condition**
Plates : Kieselgel G
Developing solvents : Methanol-ammonioum hydroxide (98:2)
Spray solution : Iodoplatinate spray, acidified

**Gas chromatographic conditions**
Chromatograph : HNU systems
Column : OV-17
Temperature : $200^{0}$ C
Detector : NP
Carrier gas : Nitrogen

**High performance liquid chromatographic conditions**
Chromatograph : MERCK-HITACHI 655A
Column : Lichroma RP 18 (p.s.:5u)
Mobile phase : Acetonitrile/water (90:10)
Flow rate : 1 ml/min
Detector : UV 268nm

## Results

Qualitative determination (screening procedure) was performed by TLC while quantitative (with parathion as external standard) by GC and

HPLC (table 1):

**Table 1. Analytical data of methamidophos determination**

| | | | |
|---|---|---|---|
| TLC | $R_f$ of methamidophos | : | 0.75 |
| | $R_f$ of parathion | : | 0.80 |
| GC | $R_t$ of methamidophos | : | 1.17 min |
| | $R_t$ of parathion | : | 6.02 min |
| HPLC | $R_t$ of methamidophos | : | 3.17 min |
| | $R_t$ of parathion | : | 2.92 min |

Methamidophos concentrations in tissues (úg/g or úg/ml for blood) from three fatal cases are presented on table 2.

**Table 2. Methamidophos concentrations in fatal intoxications**

| Case | Sex | Age | Stomach contents | Blood | Liver | Kidney | Lung |
|---|---|---|---|---|---|---|---|
| | | | úg/g | úg/ml | | úg/g | |
| 1 | M | 55 | 1.12 | 0.4 | 0.2 | 0.6 | 0.4 |
| 2 | M | 34 | 25.00 | 1.2 | 0.5 | 0.8 | 0.9 |
| 3 | F | 18 | 52.05 | 1.0 | 0.9 | 1.1 | 1.2 |

## Discussion

Chromatographic determinations were performed with parathion as external standard.The analytical methods described ensure identification and quantitation in human biological fluids and tissues. They require short time for analysis and provide adequate sensitivity.

The concentrations of methamidophos in stomach contents, blood, liver, kidney and lung at three fatal intoxications vary widely but the analytical data can be an indication of a bad prognosis or diagnosis as bibliographic references are poor concerning pesticide fatal poisoning[4,5,6]. In the present cases, stomach contents was the best sample for use in screening tests as the quantity of ingested pesticide in all cases was unknown. Lung sample relatively to other tissues, appear to have higher concentrations of pesticide.

## REFERENCES


1. Tsoukali-Papadopoulos H (1990) Pesticides:Toxicity data. Proceedings of 9th Journees Internationales Mediterraneennes de Medecine Legale, Isola di Capo Rizutto,Italy
2. Tsoukali-Papadopoulos H(1987) Analytical Toxicology. Monograph Thessaloniki-Greece, P 22-25
3. Sharma VK, Jadhav RK, Rao GJ, Saraf AK, Chandra H (1990) HPLC method for the analysis of organophosphorous and carbamate pesticides. Forensic Sci Int 48:21-22
4. Costa JP, Sousa C (1981) Death by organophosphates pesticides. J of Foren Sci Soc 21(2):133-136
5. Gellhaus H, Hausmann E, Wellhoner HH (1989) Fast determination of Demeton-s-methylsulfoxide in blood plasma. J of Anal Toxic. 13:330-332
6. Yashiki M, et al.(1990) Determination of Disulfoton and its metabolites in the body fluids of a Di-syston intoxication case.Forensic Sci Int,48:145-154

# Fatal intoxication of goats by pendimethalin (Stomp) herbicide

H.Tsoukali*, N.Zantopoulos**, V.Antoniou**

*Department of Forensic Medicine and Toxicology, Aristotle University, Thessaloniki, 54006 Greece
**Center of Veterinary Institutions of Thessaloniki, 26th Oct. 80, Thessaloniki, 54627 Greece

Animal intoxication by pesticides is quite often in Macedonia Greece especially during springtime[1,2]. A mildly toxic to mammals herbicide used lately is pendimethaline (Stomp) (N-(1-ethylpropyl)-3,4-dimethyl-2,6-dinitrobenzenamine). The acute oral LD50 values for the technical grade Stomp in male and female albino rats are 1250 and 1050 mg/kg body weight respectively[3]. These values indicate that Stomp is only slightly toxic by ingestion.

Death of 15 out of 100 goats after drinking water probably contaminated by Stomp was the toxicological problem. No bibliographic references dealing with intoxication by this product could be found or any information about methods of identification in biological fluids.

In the present work, fast methods of analysis using thin-layer chromatography (TLC), gas-liquid chromatography (GLC) and high performance liquid chromatography (HPLC) are described. Also, detailed case report and interpretation of results are thoroughly discussed.

## Case report

A group of 100 goats while pasturing, drank water from a water deposit. Fifteen of them died 2-3 hours after that fact. A man confessed later that he had washed out a bottle containing Stomp herbicide which had been used at his field. An autopsy was performed with characteristic finding of hyperaemia.Stomach contents and tissues were sent to the laboratory for toxicological analysis.

## Materials and methods

**Reagents and chemicals:**Authentic Stomp was provided by American Cyanamid Co and all other reagents were of analytical grade provided by Merck. Standard solutions dissolved in methanol were kept cool in a refrigerator prior to use.
**Instrumentation:**Thin layer chromatography was performed by DESAGA AS-30 applicator.The gas chromatograph used was the HNU Systems equipped with a flame ionization detector. The column was packed with OV-25. The temperature of the injection port and the column were set at 225$^{0}$ C.The liquid chromatograph used was the MERCK HITACHI 655A-11 equipped with a variable wave length UV as detector.
**Procedure:**Stomach contents and tissues from 15 goats out of 100, were subjected to toxicological investigation. For the analysis, 20 g of stomach contents and tissues were homogenized. The pH was adjusted to 9 with ammonium hydroxide and extraction was performed by chloroform. Identification was done to the dry residue by thin layer, gas liquid and high performance liquid chromatography.

## Results and discussion

The conditions for chromatographic determination of Stomp herbicide with parathion as external standard, were as follows:

**Thin layer chromatographic conditions**

Plates:Kieselgel G
Developing solvents:n-Hexane/acetone (65/35)
Spray reagent:Palladium chloride solution
$R_f$ of Stomp:0.68
$R_f$ of parathion:0.55

**Gas chromatographic conditions**

Chromatograph:HNU Systems
Column:OV-25
Temperature:225$^0$ C
Detector:FID
$R_t$ of Stomp:10.28 min
$R_t$ of parathion:5.85 min

**High performance liquid chromatographic conditions**

Chromatograph:MERCK-HITACHI 655A-11
Column:Lichrospher RP-8 10úm
Mobile phase:Acetonitrile/water (90/10)
pH:3.5
Detector:268nm
$R_t$ of Stomp:3.74 min
$R_t$ of parathion:2.94 min

Identification of Stomp by TLC was based on the $R_f$ values, while by GLC and HPLC on the retention times $R_t$ of samples vs standard solutions. The only reference available for the identification of Stomp was that of the technical and formulated material[4,5]. Parathion was used as external standard. The analytical methods described ensures Stomp identification in biological samples and require little time, while they provide adequate reliability.

The stomach contents and tissue are very important samples for use in toxicological analysis particularly in cases of pesticides poisoning, even after one day postingestion. Unfortunately, no other tissues were brought for analysis in order to evaluate tissue distribution. Also, because of lack of knowledge of any bibliographical references, it was not possible to compare the present results with results found by other investigators.

## REFERENCES

1. Antoniou V, Tsoukali-Papadopoulou H, Epivatianos P (1988)Veterinary toxicological analysis in northern Greece during 1986.Bull of Greek Veterinary Society 39:3
2. Antoniou V, Tsoukali-Papadopoulou H, Epivatianos P (1993)Pesticides In:Applied Veterinary Toxicology, University Studio Press(ed),Thessaloniki,Greece, P 65
3. American Cyanamid Company informations : Stomp, Toxicology
4. American Cyanamid Company(1976) Recommended method of Stomp analysis
5. American Cyanamid Company(1972) Method of Stomp analysis

# 6. Jurismedicine

# ON THE DOCTOR'S DUTY TO INFORM THE PATIENT IN AUSTRIA

Georg Bauer
Head of the Institute of Forensic Medicine, University Vienna
A-1090 Vienna, Sensengasse 2.

## Preface

As members of the medicolegal profession we closely watch the jurisdiction regarding the doctor's duty to inform the patient. We have taken the trouble to compile and analyze the relevant precedents from former years. Also, one of the most important tasks of medicolegal instruction and post-graduate education is to acquaint the students and the doctors with the latest state and trends of the judicature.

## The judicature and their statistical evaluation

Table 1 gives a survey of a total of 20 judgments rendered by the Austrian Supreme Court; virtually all are decisions in civil law cases. The period covered is from 1904 to 1981. Of course it is only a rough survey to give a brief outline. On the left, in a few words, the intervention at issue and the injury caused, then next to this, the year of the relevant Supreme Court judgment, and, in the right column, whether the Supreme Court confirmed or dismissed a duty of the doctor to inform the patient.

From the statistics, a few highlights as a matter of interest, such as for example regarding the third judgment in Table 1, in 1915, in a case of orthopedic surgery, in which the court went on to elaborate its finding by saying that the patient, trusting in the skill of Viennese surgeons, had shed all misgivings and, therefore had undergone the surgery, that furthermore there was no need to inform the patient for the simple reason that, anyway, the patient could not understand and assess the information given by the physician.

Nowadays such a judgment would be unthinkable; the judgment dates from 1915, in this connection, therefore, from times long past.

Summing up. From 1904 to 1981, thus in a period of 77 years, there were only 20 cases of Supreme Court judgments dealing with the doctor's duty to inform the patient was practically no subject in judicature, at least not in the first decades of the period covered by our report.

Making the sum of judgments according to positive or negative outcome for the doctor, we see that altogether only five times was the doctor's duty to inform the patient confirmed, whereas in the overwhelming number of cases, namely 13 times, the duty to inform the patient was dismissed. In other words, only in five times was judgment entered for the patient, and 13 times against the patient. In the remaining two judgments no position of consequence was taken up.

For comparison, as it is representative of modern times, Table 2 shows the period from 1982 to 1993. By chance again 20 Supreme Court judgments. At first glance we see that now the court has found for the patient far more often, the right column showing far more frequent confirmations of the duty to inform the patient.

In this time of only 12 years, from 1982 to 1993, in comparatively few years, the Supreme Court has also again had to deal 20 times with this contentious matter between patient and doctor regarding information. I would direct your attention to these figures: in the first 77 years 20 judgments, in the last 10 years also 20 judgments!

When counting the actions in which the court found for or against the physician, or for or against the patient, we see that now in 16 cases the court found for the patient, and in only three cases the doctor's duty to inform the patient and thereby a liability of the physician was dismissed.

In the intermediary result, when assessing the overall period of 90 years, we see that the number of convictions of a doctor for omitted or insufficient information of the patient has considerably increased.

To round off the statistical evaluation, we determined the number of convictions of the doctor per year, namely for the period from 1904 to 1981, on the one hand, and then for the period of 1982 to 1993, on the other hand.

Table 3 shows that, as from 1992, the Supreme Court has pronounced against the doctor 22 times more frequently than in the period from 1981 back to the turn of the century.

**Causes and landmarks of this development**

The causes for this development are obvious, although each may rank an order of importance differently, possibly in relation to regional specifications. But it is a fact that far-reaching changes have occurred in the medical services with an exploding development of medical science and possibilities, fundamental changes in society, and, accordingly, both - doctor and patient - are radically different from what they were in former times.

In interaction with these aforesaid changes the development is reflected in the jurisdiction, mainly in judgments drawn upon again and again as legal precedents.

Such judgments creating a legal precedent therefore often contain guide lines for the next years and decades.

The 1982 divide is not arbitrary. In 1982 the Supreme Court passed a judgment that - as I see - has indeed put the relevant jurisdiction on a new basis (Table 4).

It is absolutely decisive whether the question of the duty of the doctor to inform the patient is treated as a point of fact or a point of law. In 1941, the Reichsgericht decisively qualified as point of fact whether and to what extent in the individual case the information of the patient by the doctor is required. Subsequently, the doctor's duty to inform the patient was again and again qualified as a point of fact. Up to this judgment of the 23rd of June 1982, again a case of paralysis of the vocal cords following strumectomy, in which the Supreme Court now declared the issue of adequate information to be a point of law.

Since this judgment, therefore, the extent to which in the individual case the doctor must inform the patient is subject to appeal on the point of law.

Let me explain: point of fact, in this connection, means that in the last resort the question of whether or not the patient has been informed will be judged from the medical, that is to say, the medical expert's side. As a point of law, on the other hand, the decision lies within the competence of the legal experts, that is to say of the court. Of course this is somewhat simplified.

The beautiful formula "salus aegroti suprema lex" with which in the last resort the information of the patient can be ranked in second place is well known. The catchword is still being used in Austria today, but in view of the aforementioned judgment of 1982 and the legal precedent it has created, it is very much relativized in its meaning.

Close study of the individual judgments together with the grounds on which these are based - a very arduous matter, I assure you clearly reveals a dogmatic and verbal approximation to foreign jurisdiction; of late, Austrian Supreme Court judgments almost regularly cite from commentaries on the German penal code. Also Austria has come to adopt the line that increasingly puts first emphasis on the personal right of the patient.

The last "quantum jump" occurred in 1992 (Table 5).

In Germany the burden of the proof that the patient had agreed to the treatment and had been adequately informed has always lain with the physician.

In Austria, as opposed to this, the legal profession has never seen unanimity as to the legal rating of a doctor's medical, surgical or therapeutic intervention in his treatment of the patient, the Supreme Court having more often than not taken the view that the burden of proof that the doctor had failed to adequately inform the patient lay with the plaintiff.

With the judgment of the 12th November 1992 this has also become past history, as with this judgment, again in conformity with German judicature, the burden of the proof of adequate information now lies with the doctor also in Austria.

**Conclusion**

In this short paper I have tried to give a brief survey of Austrian jurisdiction regarding the doctor's duty to inform the patient, the external and internal causes and their interrelation. A close study of the judgments rendered reveals that the decisive dogma on which the issue hinges would be whether the question of the doctor's duty to inform the patient is a point of fact or a point of law. The more frequent convictions since the judgment of the year 1982 seem to speak for this hypothesis.

Let me conclude with what could be seen as a gratuitous remark: speaking as a doctor, as a patient, as a medicolegal expert and as an Austrian: regarding the doctor's information of the patient, we are fit and ready for Europe.

**TABLE 1**

**JUDGMENTS RENDERED BY THE SUPREME COURT REGARDING THE DOCTOR'S DUTY TO INFORM THE PATIENT IN AUSTRIA (1904 - 1981).**

| TREATMENT-DAMAGE | YEAR | DUTY TO INFORM CONFIRMED OR DISMISSED |
|---|---|---|
| Cosmet.X-radiation-deterioration | 1904 | confirmed |
| Cosmet. eye-operation-shrinking bulb. | 1906 | confirmed |
| Orthopedic op. - disfigurement | 1915 | dismissed |
| Vasoligature-sterility | 1934 | without statem |
| Varicotomy - abscess | 1955 | confirmed |
| eye-operation - blindness | 1954 | rejected |
| strumectomy - recurrent paresis | 1955 | dismissed |
| strumectomy - vocal damage | 1956 | dismissed |
| strumectomy - tetany | 1956 | dismissed |
| electric shock - vertebral fracture | 1957 | dismissed |
| X-radiation - burns | 1959 | dismissed |
| strumectomy - vocal damage | 1959 | dismissed |
| operation ext.-total resect.of stomach | 1959 | dismissed |
| diathermy-burns | 1960 | dismissed |
| X-rad. naevus - soft part damage | 1964 | confirmed |
| nasoplastic surgery - blindness | 1964 | confirmed |
| radicular blocking - cauda damage | 1969 | dismissed |
| broken needle in the lever | 1969 | dismissed |
| cystotatic therapy | 1973 | dismissed |
| transfer - transport damage | 1981 | dismissed |

**TABLE 2**

**JUDGMENTS RENDERED BY THE SUPREME COURT REGARDING THE DOCTOR'S DUTY TO INFORM THE PATIENT IN AUSTRIA (1982 - 1993).**

| TREATMENT-DAMAGE | YEAR | DUTY TO INFORM CONFIRMED OR DISMISSED |
|---|---|---|
| strumectomy - vocal cord damage | 1982 | dismissed |
| mediastinuscopy-vocal cord damage | 1982 | dismissed |
| stone removal - lesion of ureter | 1983 | confirmed |
| operation on the head - cerebral damage | 1984 | confirmed |
| scientific experimentation | 1984 | confirmed* |
| lumbar puncture - cauda damage | 1986 | confirmed |
| premature birth - cerebral damage | 1986 | confirmed |
| tympanoplastiy - facialis paresis | 1987 | confirmed |
| vagotomy - no success | 1987 | rejected |
| infiltration-pneumothorax | 1988 | confirmed |
| strumectomy-tetany | 1989 | confirmed |
| infiltration-pneumothorax | 1990 | confirmed |
| sterilisation-tubar gravidity | 1990 | confirmed |
| corticoid therapy - gravidity | 1990 | dismissed |
| keloplasty - disfigurement | 1990 | confirmed |
| bronchoscopy-dental defect | 1991 | rejected |
| cosmet. chin reduction - no success | 1991 | confirmed |
| prostatectomy - urinary incontinence | 1992 | confirmed |
| hospitalisation - hospitalism/sepsis | 1992 | confirmed* |
| knee operation - infection | 1993 | confirmed |

* with reservation

## TABLE 3

FINDINGS FROM THE STATISTICS OF JUDGMENTS RENDERED BY THE SUPREME COURT REGARDING THE DOCTOR'S DUTY TO INFORM THE PATIENT IN AUSTRIA

FREQUENCY OF THE CONVICTION OF A DOCTOR FOR INSUFFICIENT INFORMATION OF THE PATIENT

| PERIOD 1904 - 1981 | PERIOD 1982 - 1993 |
| --- | --- |

PROPORTION 1 : 22

## TABLE 4

DECISIVE MARKER IN THE JURISDICTION REGARDING INFORMATION OF THE PATIENT IN AUSTRIA

JUDGMENT BY THE AUSTRIAN SUPREME COURT OF 23. 6. 1982

IT IS A POINT OF LAW

TO WHAT EXTENT IN THE ACTUAL CASE THE DOCTOR MUST INFORM THE PATIENT

## TABLE 5

APPROXIMATION LASTLY IN THE JUDGMENT BY THE AUSTRIAN SUPREME COURT OF 12.11.92

THE BURDEN OF PROOF
FOR THE SUFFICIENT INFORMATION OF THE PATIENT
LIES WITH THE DOCTOR

# ADVERSE DRUG REACTIONS AND MEDICAL MALPRACTICE

Burkhard Madea

Institut für Rechtsmedizin der Universität zu Köln, Melatengürtel 60-62, D - 50823 Köln
Fax 0221 - 4784261

## 1. Introduction

The Western countries, for instance America and Germany, are drug-consuming societies. More than 1.6 billion prescriptions for more than 30.000 different drugs are written each year in the United States (4). In the Federal Republic of Germany in 1991 more than 750 million drug packages were prescribed for which the health insurance had to pay more than 21.8 billion DM (3, 6).
However although drug therapy is the most prevalent form of all therapy, the discussions on medical malpractice focus on injuries incurred by invasive diagnostic and therapeutic procedures.
Nevertheless Adverse Drug Reactions (ADR) are comparatively frequent and ADR can of course form the basis of the physicians' liability.
Although ADR are mainly defined as noxious and unintentional and occur at doses used in man for prophylaxis, diagnosis or therapy, the iatrogenic factor in the genesis of ADR should not be overlooked, since such a factor can be regarded as malpractice and violation of the duty of care.
According to Burnum, out of 1.000 patients, 42 ADR were observed which were qualified in 45% as unpredictable and unavoidable, in 55% as unnecessary and potentially preventable.
According to a review by Gross on the frequency of ADR in 1.000 patients, 20 to 200 ADR, among them 2 to 20 fatal cases, are to be expected. For the Federal Republic of Germany 50.000 life-threatening ADR, 150.000 severe and 1 million mild ADR are reported each year. Compared to these epidemiologic data on the frequency of ADR, malpractice actions due to wrong drug therapy are astonishingly rare.

## 2. Our own cases

In the last years, we had to deal with 19 cases where the physicians were charged with manslaughter by the prosecution, due to wrong drug therapy. The following disciplines were concerned: Internal Medicine 8x, Psychiatry 4x, Surgery 3x, Anesthesiology 1x, Urology 1x, Dental Surgery 1x, Pharmacy 1x. It seems interesting that Psychiatry and Surgery are concerned relatively frequently. The following drugs were in question as releasing the ADR: Psychopharmacologic drugs 5x, Infusions/Transfusions 4x, Chemotherapy 2x, Antibiotics 3x, Azulfidine 1x, Atropin 1 x, Disoprivan 1x, Adrenaline 1x, Antirheumatics 1x. Corresponding to the high frequency of Psychiatry as an involved discipline, psychopharmacologic drugs are leading here.
In most cases the prosecution was informed by the deceased's relatives who in some cases definitely claimed wrong drug therapy, especially in cases with new or rare indications for drug therapy (for instance chemotherapy of sigma cancer; chemotherapy of chronic polyarthritis in a case of renal insufficiency) or in cases where death occurred unexpectedly although the clinical state of the patient was quite good.
Medical negligence and malpractice in drug therapy should be classified according to the real mistakes which occur in practice (wrong drug, mixing up of drugs; wrong dosis, mainly overdosages; wrong application; individual contraindication not considered; drug-interaction not considered; side effects/complications of drug therapy/not noticed in time; information about risks and side effects of drug therapy omitted). Drug actions as well as ADR can be classified as being within or without the pharmacodynamic profile of the drug.
In the majority of our cases the ADR was within the pharmacodynamic profile (n = 1; toxic reactions, which does not necessarily mean that plasma concentrations are in a toxic range). In 4 cases the ADR was without the pharmacodynamic profile (Lyell-Syndrome; anaphylactic shock), in other cases the classification remained unclear.

In 11 cases, the causal connection between drug therapy and death was affirmed, in 8 of these cases medical negligence as well, in 4 cases the physicians were condemned for manslaughter (table 1). The condemnations comprise the classic malpractice constellations like mixing up of drugs, wrong application, overdosage. The expert evidence on negligence and on the causality between drug therapy and death could be given quite easily in these cases.
Giving expert evidence on negligence and causality is much more difficult in cases of drug interaction or synergistic action of drugs when therapeutic doses were administered and the plasma concentrations were in therapeutic range.
In 8 cases the causal connection between drug therapy and fatal outcome could not be proved, mainly due to concurrent causes of death or while there was no clear anatomical or toxicological cause of death (table 2).
Among these are also cases with phenothiazine therapy and, in 2 cases, sudden death was probably due to cardiac arrhythmias. Sudden death in phenothiazine therapy is already long known and discussed.
However in 1 case, severe cardiac diseases with mitral valve replacement and absolute arrhythmia were known and it can be questioned whether a "slumber" therapy with thioridazine to treat a trigeminal neuralgia is really indicated.

## 3. Discussion

From our own cases it becomes at first evident that ADR may be of forensic significance. When giving an expert opinion on drug-associated deaths the literature on ADR should be considered: For instance if the ADR is within or without the pharmacodynamic profile of the drug. ADR outside the pharmacodynamic profile (allergy, pseudoallergy, idiosyncrasy) can also form the basis for the assumption of medical malpractice; for instance when from the history known allergies were not taken into consideration or contraindicated drugs were prescribed. However the majority of our cases "outside the pharmacodynamic profile" were not predictable and unavoidable (3x Lyell-Syndrome).
Concerning the cases with ADR within the pharmacodynamic profile (toxic reactions) 2 groups have to be distinguished: Plasma concentrations outside the therapeutic level (overdosage): In these cases the causality between drug therapy and death can be proved quite easily, if other causes of death are absent and secondly the group with therapeutic plasma concentrations, where a causal connection between drug therapy and death is probable but cannot be proved without doubt.
Especially when ADR are reported in severely ill patients, the causality may often not be clear. Therefore, in our own material, in some cases the causality between drug therapy and death remained unclear, although without doubt the therapy was incorrectly applied.
A collection of only 19 cases of ADR which raised the suspicion of medical malpractice is of course too small for overall general conclusions, but the following final remarks are possible: High risk patients for ADR, as they were identified in clinical epidemiologic studies on ADR, are patients with renal insufficiency, malignant haematologic-oncologic diseases, and such patients are found also in my material: 3 patients (3 from the group Internal Medicine, n = 7)) suffered from renal insufficiency which caused an ADR through relative overdosage.
The most prevalent group of drugs are the psychopharmacologic agents and in some of my cases the question arises whether a sufficient individual benefit-risk estimation was made. In some cases this can be doubted, even in cases where the causality between drug therapy and death could not be proved. In studies on the clinical epidemiology of ADR the prevalent drug groups were: Antibiotics, cytostatic drugs, glucocorticosteroids, anticoagulants. However in the own cases other drug groups were prevalent and, regarding the clinical status in the major group, no acute life-threatening diseases were present. According to Stephany et al. (1976) fatal ADR were observed only in severely ill patients, so that the risk of therapy was justified. Therefore a sudden unexpected death under drug therapy may raise suspicion of medical negligence, especially when further determinants of ADR like old age, malignant diseases, long duration of hospitalisation, many drugs prescribed are missing. The expert evidence on causal connection between drug therapy and death is however much more difficult than in other malpractice cases with invasive therapy since

- the connection between drug and death is not "apparent",
- drugs may "copy" symptoms of diseases,
- to state a causality is difficult for the reasons discussed,
- evidence and proof of causality cannot always be derived from concentrations and doses.

**References**


1. Burnum JF (1976) Preventability of Adverse Drug Reactions. Ann Internat Med 85:80-81
2. Gross R (1989) Güterabwägungen in der klinischen Medizin. Zentrum für medizinische Ethik Bochum. Medizinethische Materialien 25
3. Madea B, Henßge C, Lignitz E (1994) Fahrlässige Tötung durch medikamentöse Therapie. Rechtsmed 4:123-131
4. Rosenow III EC, Rosenow SE (1989) Legal Implications of Adverse Drug Reactions. In: Vevaina JR, Bonde RC, Kassoff E, (eds) Legal Aspects of Medicine. Springer, New York, Berlin, Heidelberg, pp 112-118
5. Schönhöfer PS, Wessly-Stickel B, Schulte-Sasse H, Werner W (1989) Flächendeckende Erfassung schwerer, potentiell lebensbedrohlicher unerwünschter Arzneimittelwirkungen. Verh Dtsch Ges Innere Med 95:687-690
6. Schwabe U, Paffrath D (1992) Arzneiverordnungs-Report '92 - Aktuelle Daten, Kosten, Trends und Kommentare. G Fischer, Stuttgart, Jena
7. Stephany W, Gierlichs HW, Planz G, Rahn KH, Heintz R (1976) Zahl und Art von Arzneimittelnebenwirkungen in einer Medizinischen Klinik. Dtsch Med. Wschr 101:9-13


**Causality between drug therapy and death affirmed**

| | |
|---|---|
| • *mixing up of drugs*<br>KCl instead of NaCl<br>Adrenaline instead of xylocitin | 2x |
| • *mistake in manufacturing*<br>overdosage of electrolytes in infusion | 1x |
| • *administration of contraindicated drug*<br>Sorbit in a case of fructose- intolerance<br>Disoprivan in a case of allergic asthma<br>malignant neuroleptic syndrome in a case with simultaneous administration of latrosom and Anafranil | 3x |
| • *wrong application of drug*<br>intravenous instead of i.m. injection of crystalline penicillin with resultant crystal embolism) | 1x |
| • *rare side effect or adverse drug reaction*<br>Lyell- Syndrome after ingestion of Azulfidine in Crohn's disease<br>Lyell- Syndrome after ingestion of Doxy-Wolff in tonsillitis<br>Lyell- Syndrome after ingestion of Diclofenac, Volon A and Bupivacain in a case of pain in the shoulder | 3x |
| • *relative overdosage*<br>overdosage of penicilline G in a case of renal insufficiency<br>→ epileptic fit | 1x |

Table 1

## Causality between drug therapy and cause of death not affirmed

| | |
|---|---|
| • intravenous infusion of bile instead of blood | Competetive cause of death |
| • 500 mg Atropine (!) i.v. | Competetive cause of death |
| • too fast infusion of clomethiazole | Competetive cause of death |
| • Leponex therapy of schizophrenia | no obvious cause of death |
| • Melleril therapy of trigeminal neuralgia | no obvious cause of death |
| • adjuvant chemotherapy of sigma cancer | cause of postoperative complications (perforation of small intestine) unclear |
| • chemotherapy of polyarthritis with Methotrexat | competetive cause of death |
| • Diazepam, Dolantin, Neurocil in relative overdosage in a case of intravenous heroin addict | competetive cause of death |

**Table 2**

# TRANSSEXUALITY. SOCIO-PROFESSIONAL HANDICAP IN PORTUGAL

*Magalhães T; Carneiro de Sousa MJ; Pinto da Costa J; Almeida F*

Medico-legal Institute, Faculty of Medicine, Biomedical Sciences Institute "Abel Salazar", University of Oporto; Faculty of Law, University Portucalense "Infante D. Henrique", Hospital Magalhães Lemos; Jardim Carrilho Videira 4000, Porto, Portugal

## OBJECTIF

The authors wish to call attention to the social and professional difficulties that the transsexuals have in their integration and to the role that legal medicine has in this subject in relation to the diagnosis, evaluation and contribution to the integration of these patients.

## MATERIAL AND METHODES

The number of transsexuals in Portugal, as everywhere else, is not known. The authors contacted 8 cases through a judicial office who accepted voluntarily to answer an inquiry which was done under the supervision of a psychiatrist. There were other cases contacted but who did not authorise their publication. Two of these cases were studied at the Medico-legal Institute of Oporto (cases 7 and 8) and 2 others at the Medico-legal Institute of Lisbon (cases 1 and 5). The type of transsexuality was predominantly female/male (6 cases) instead of the most common referred to in the literature. The authors paid special attention to the age of the first manifestations (4.8 years-old - average), the age of the begining of the idea of sex change (15.3 years-old - average) and to the age at which they decided to change sex (26.5 years-old - average).

## RESULTS

**Case 1**: Female/male, 45 years-old, single, licentiate in philology, lives with his father. Operated in Spain: mastectomy and hysterectomy; the Portuguese Medical College authorised the phalloplasty (not yet done). Legal process in course; Medico-legal examination done. Archivist; considered as homosexual by his co-workers (motive for jokes); retired due to his transsexuality. Economic problems due to his lack of professional integration. Main social problem: lack of identity card.
**Case 2**: Female/male, 46 years-old, single, holds a degree in philology and literature; lives with his mother. Operated in Belgium: mastectomy and hysterectomy; phalloplasty not yet done (economic problems). Solved judicially without medico-legal examination. Problems of professional and social integration while he had no identity card (he worked as a cleaner in a restaurant). At present, he is a teacher in a private college and also a student in a superior course. Refers to economic difficulties but no serious social problems of reintegration.
**Case 3**: Male/female, 35 years-old, single, primary grade, lives alone, has a partner who kept her (also had the help of her mother); drug addict (heroin) under treatment. Operated in several countries, mostly in Morocco: excision of penis and testicles; had some plastic operations. Did not iniciate the judicial process due to lack of money; never examined in a Medico-legal Institute. Unenployed; she was a stripteaser abroad; difficulties in social integration. Main problem: lack of identity card.
**Case 4**: Female/male, 27 years-old, single, University graduate, lives with his parents, who initially accepted very badly. Operated in Spain: mastectomy and hysterectomy. He is going to

initiate the judicial procedure this year; not yet examined in a Medico-legal Institute. Lawyer (works as a liberal professional), asked permission at the Lawyer College to change his professional name (accepted); professional problems, everybody knows the case and jokes about it. Economic difficulties and problems of social integration.

Case 5: Female/male, 31 years-old, single, University graduate, lives alone. Operated in Spain: mastectomy and hysterectomy. Judicial procedure under way (initiated in 1994); examined in the Medico-Legal Institute. Engineer (works as a liberal professional); good professional integration. No economic problems. Good social and family integration. Main problem: lack of identity card with professional consequences.

Case 6: Female/male, 45 years-old, University graduate, married with two children. The husband accepts the situation, but the divorce procedure is under way. Lives with the husband and children. Late diagnosis. Under hormonal treatment; he is going to have surgery. Professor of elementary education. No economic and social problems, because his transsexuality is not yet known socially.

Case 7: Female/male, 31 years-old, single, primary grade, lives with a girl-friend (intends to marry her and adopt a child); emigrant. Operated in Switzerland (initiated in 1984). Because of social difficulties in Portugal, emigrated and sufferd economic and health problems initially (worked as fruit picker); had no identity documents and due to this has been judged and condemned. Gave up legal process; medico-legal examination was done. Actually waiter; good socio-professional integration.

Case 8: Male/female, 34 years-old, single, primary grade, lives with a boy-friend who intends to marry her; emigrant. Operated in Germany. Judicial process concluded for the sexual change; medico-legal examination was done. Considered as homosexual, worked as prostitute before emigration; the family accepted the situation. Is a dancer at present but has some economic problems. The social and professional integration is good.

## CONCLUSIONS

1. Portugal has not yet any legislation on this subject;
2. The judicial procedure took too much time;
3. The Portuguese Courts has authorised the legal sexual change in a great majority of the cases;
4. The costs of these clinical treatments are too high;
5. The Social Assistance do not compensate for the surgery nor the treatments;
6. These surgical operations are not allowed by the Deontological Medical Code, but the Medical College is beginning to accept this problem;
7. Not all the cases were examined at the Medico-Legal Institutes;
8. The lack of identity cards is the main problem for transsexuals;
9. Usually these patients do not want other people to know about them.

## BIBLIOGRAPHY


- Acordão Supremo Tribunal Justiça (16.11.1988). Boletim Ministério Justiça 381:579-591
- Calanca A (1991) The transsexual after sex change. Evolution and prognosis. Helv Chir Acta 58(3):257-60
- Código Deontológico (1985). Rev Ordem Médicos 3:1-28
- Decisões de 1ª Instância, sentença (10.12.1991). Colectânea Jurisprudência I:301-307
- Documento A2-163/89 e A3-0016/86, Parlamento Europeu (1.9.1989). Documentos de Sessão, Série A
- Dragomirescu VT (1986) Causal interpretation of the medico-legal reaction in the behavior. Acta Med Leg Soc 36(2): 225-35
- Elchardus JM et al (1986) Ethics and expert testimony: a specific example case of transssexualisme. Acta Med Leg Soc, 36(2):28-34
- Pinto da Costa J (4.1.1994) Sexo Dúbio. Jornal de Notícias, Última Página
- Transsexualidade (1992). Questões de Bioética, Assembleia da República, Coleção Temas 3(II-1)

# DIPLOPIE IATROGENIQUE: POSSIBLE RESPONSABILITE PROFESSIONELLE

S.PEROTTI*, F.SEMERARO**

*INSTITUT DE MEDECINE LEGALE DE L'UNIVERSITE DE BRESCIA
**CLINIQUE OPHTALMOLOGIQUE DE L'UNIVERSITE DE BRESCIA

Le travail a pour but analyser, sous le double point de vue de la faute professionelle et du dédommagement, un cas de paralysie oculaire survenue suite à une intervention de polypectomie avec évidement ethmoidal. Une diploplie persistante de l'oil gauche a en effect déterminé le début d'un contentieux judiciaire au cours duquel fut plaidée la responsabilité du chirurgien dans l'apparition de la paralysie oculaire.

## DESCRIPTION DU CAS

S.V.souffrait depuis longtemps d'épisodes récurrents de bronchite asthmatique accompagnée de difficultés respiratoires dues à une polypose nasale gauche. Il devenait donc nécessaire de pratiquer une intervention chirurgicale consistant en une polypectomie avec évidement ethmoidal. Avant l'opération, il fut procédé à un examen radiologique normal des cavités paranasales qui a montré une opacification des sinus maxillaire et frontal gauches.

Tout de suite aprés l'opération apparut une hématome périorbitaire gauche associé à une hémorragie sous-conjonctivale homolatérale, qui fut traitée par une thérapie médicale. Environ 10 jours aprés la sortie de l'hôpital, S.V. remarqua l'apparition d' une diplopie dans la vision latérale gauche. Lors d'une premièr examen ophtalmologique, le trouble fut attribué à une parésie du muscle droit interne de l'oil gauche. Par la suite, une examen par résonance magnétique nucléaire montra un épaississement du troisième médian du muscle droit interne de l'orbite gauche avec des limites floues par rapport au profil osseus médian de l'orbite, lequel était à peine représente. Un examen ophtalmologique approfondi au cours d'une consultation permit de constater un déficit de motricité extrinsèque de l'oil gauche provoqué par une bride cicatricielle adhérente du muscle droit interne qui empêche l'élongation au cours de l'abduction mais qui conserve quand même sa capacité de contraction et donc d'abduction.

# DISCUSSION ET CONCLUSIONS

La sphénoethmoidectomie intranasale est une opération qui a été décrite dès 1930 (Yankauer).

Cette opéeration a ensuite été modifiée et ameliorée jusqu'à devenir une procédure sure, efficace et utile dand le cas de patients atteints de rhinosinusite hypoplasique chronique, même si Maniglia (1989) prétend que, malgré les récents progrès de la technique chirurgicale, on reincontre encore aujourd'hui les complications secondaires de la chirurgie nasale des sinus. Bien que son emploi soit controversé par des spécialistes oto-rhino-laryngologistes, comme le montrent les programmes d'enseignement assez rare, ceus qui continuent a utilisér cette technique ont obtenu des résultats satisfaisants avec très peu de complications (Friedman et Katsantonis, 1990).

L'approche transnasale a l'avantage d'être facile à réaliser, avec une souffrance minime pour le patient et une bonne visualisation du labyrinthe ethmoidal, du sphénoide, de la lame criblée et de la fosse ethmoidale. La réussite de l'intervention est liéee à la connaissance précise de l'anatomie chirgicale de la zone (Pech et coll.,1982). Les sinus paranasaux sont en effect entourés par des structures importantes. Même les différences anthropologiques peuvent être importantes.

Friedman et Kern (1979) ont consignée les résultats de 1000 ethmoidectomies intranasales dans les quelles l'incidence des complications était de 2,8%: les complications les plus sérieuses étaient constituées de ménengites suite a une rhinorrhée.

Maniglia e coll. (1984) signalèrent ensemble les graves complications au cours d'opérations d'ethmoidectomies: cécité, déficit de motricité oculaire du à des traumatismes extrinsèques des nerfs, rhinorrhée avec méningite, dommages aux artères carotidiennes et lésions cérébrales qui ont provoqué le décès des patients.

Plus récemment (1989), le même Auteur a décrit, sur 40 cas de graves complications secoindaires de la chirurgie nasale des sinus, 8 cas qui montraient un dommage aux muscles extraoculaires et aux nerfs.

En particulier, dans deux cas, la cécité s'ajoutait à la paralysie des muscles droit, médian et oblique supérieur. Dans les deux cas la procédure chirurgicale consistait en une ethmoidectomie intranasale.

Parmi les cas décrits par Maniglia et coll. (1981), deux cas concernaient des complications de la motricité oculaire èxtrinsèque. Dans un cas, l'exploration chirurgicale de la paroi mediane de l'orbite et du muscle droit médian de droite montrait quelque temps après une cicatrice tissulaire près de l'insertion du muscle droit médian qui apparaissait prive du nerf. Après l'opération chirugicale corrective des restrictions marquées de la motricité concernaient les visions médianes, latéerales et obliques, tandis qu'en position primaire les images n'étaient pas doubles. Ce cas présente beaucoup de similitudes avec celui que nous devions examiner, comme ce la fut constaté lors de la visite ophtalmologique effectuée lors de l'expertise. Malheureusement, il n'y avait pas, dans le cas que nous mentionnons, de description détaillée de l'opération ni l'indication raisonnée de l'utilité d'une nouvelle intervention corrective; par conséquent, après avoir établi la responsabilité du chirurgien, on pouvait immédiatement quantifier le dommage permanent. L'absence de rapport clinique détaillé, tant pour l'évolution que pour l'opération, ne permet pas d'identifier avec certitude les éventuels vices de consentement, comme souligné par Malcontenti et Mora (1989), mais permet seulement de supposer qu'il n'y a pas eu d'information préalable du patient concernant les complications possibles puisqu'il n'existe pas de documentation appropriée pour la prouver. Le résultat de l'examen par réssonance magnétique nucléaire effectué tout de suite après l'opération ainsi que le suivant concernant la diplopie due a une bride adhérente du muscle droit médian permettent de supposer légitimement qu'il y a lesion, au cours de l'évidement ethmoidal, de la paroi médiane de l'orbite en l'absence de conditions d'accèss chirurgical particulièrement difficiles. Par conséquent, l'opération devait après être considerée comme une intervention routinière normale pour un spécialist oto-rhino-laryngologist et la fracture de la paroi médiane de l'orbite, dans ces circostances, concrétise un comportement pour le moins imprudent du chirurgien. Le déficit d'abduction du muscle droit médian de gauche et la diplopie consécutive ont été en outre évalués, pour la responsabilité civile, à 4-5% pour le dommage biologique.

## BIBLIOGRAPHIE

FREEDMAN H.M. et KERN E.B. (1979)
Complication of intranasal ethmoidectomy: a review of 1000 consecutive operations
Laryngoscope, 89, 421

FRIEDMAN W.H., KATSANTONIS G.P. (1990)
Intranasal and transantral ethmoidectomy: a 20 years experience.
Laryngoscope, 100, 343

MALCONTENTI R., MORA E.(1989)
Sulla responsabilita' professionale dello specialista O.R.L. in casi di interventi chirurgici endonasali e sui seni paranasali.

Aspetti casistici e considerazioni medico-legali. In Atti del Convegno su "La responsabilita' medica in ambito civile. Attualita' e prospettive", Siena 22-24 settembre 1988. Giuffre' edit. Milano

MANIGLIA A.J., CHANDLER J.R., GOODWIN W.J., FLYNN J. (1981)
Rare complications following ethmoidectomies: a report of eleven cases.
Laryngoscope, 91, 1234

MANIGLIA A.J (1984)
Visual loss associated with orbital and sinus diseases
Laryngoscope, 94, 1050

MANIGLIA A.J. (1989)
Fatal and major complications secondary to nasal and sinus surgery
Laryngoscope, 99, 276

PECH A., GOUBERT J.L., BESSON J. (1982)
La polypose du nez et des sinus
Encycl.Med.Chir., 395, A10

YANKAUER S., (1930)
Demonstration of intranasal surgery on wet specimen
Laryngoscope, 40, 642

# 7. Pathology

# EXPERIMENTAL STUDIES ON POSTMORTEM INTERVAL, USING A DEEP THERMOMETER

Hitsunori AIHARA* and Mariko AIHARA**
* Department of Legal Medicine, Yokohama City University School of Medicine, 3-9 Fukuura, Kanazawa-ku, Yokohama-shi, Kanagawa 236, Japan
** Shonan Junior College, 82 Inaoka-cho, Yokosuka-shi, Kanagawa 238, Japan

## 1. Introduction

The experiments concerned the decline in the intracephalic temperature, the muscle temperature, the forehead temperature, and the abdominal temperature (liver temperature), etc. of a dead body under thermal environments. Using experimental dogs that died of different causes, conditions were created such as cooled body or covered, and experiment were run concerning the rate of decline in body temperature under these various conditions. This is a report on this research.

## 2. Experimental method and materials

A. Constant-temperature constant-humidity chamber

It is 20.7 m³ large and can be regulated to any temperature from -10°C to 50°C+1°C, and a constant temperature can be maintained. It is a room whose humidity is normally set to 50-65%.

B. Equipment used, method of measurement, experimental method, and experimental conditions

a. Clinical thermometer: Deep temperature monitor DDT-1, CTM-201, CTM-205, and monitor 203 for the cardiac muscle were used, and each monitor was equipped with a deep temperature probe, catheter probe, and needle probe.

b. Recorder: Six-point intermittent recorder TFR-101 and twelve-point intermittent recorder TFR-201, with the chart speed set to 60 mn/hr.

c. Method of measurement: The PD-5 deep temperature probe was used for measuring the abdominal temperature, the PD-12 for the forehead temperature and room temperature, the PD-K04 catheter probe for the rectal temperature, the needle probe (length 80 mm) for the intracephalic temperature, and the needle probe (length 50 mm) for the muscle temperature.

## 3. Results of the experiments

A. Experiments under outside air

a. The case of death by cyanide poisoning (Fig. 1)

Concerning the declining curves for organ temperatures at five locations after death, the intracephalic temperature goes down 2-3°C at 1 hr, 1-4°C at 2 hr, 2°C at 3 hr, 1°C per hour at 4-5 hr, and there after 0.8°C at a time. Regarding the forehead temperature and muscle temperature, the rate of decline in forehead temperature is somewhat larger, being 2.2-2.3°C in the first hour, 1.4-1.8°C in the second hour, and 1.2-1.3°C in the third hour, and with no great difference in the fourth hour and thereafter, declining by 0.8-0.4°C each hour. The abdominal temperature and rectal temperature both decline slowly, 0.5-0.7°C in the first hour, 0.6-1.0°C in the second hour, 0.9-1.0°C in the third hour, and 0.9-1.0°C per hour thereafter.

B. Experiments with covered corpses

After the entire body or just the trunk and head were covered with a blanket or moistened blanket in 20-23°C constant temperature and constant humidity, death was caused by blood loss, brain damage, and a asphyxiation, and for comparison it was done without covering the body. Three dogs were used for each cause of death.

a. Entire body covered with blanket (cause of death: blood loss)

The fall in the intracephalic temperature was delayed, especially in the initial stage, for both the blanket-covered group and the control group. The rate of decline in the intracephalic temperature is 2.1°C in the first hour and 2.0-3.0°C in the second hour, being slower and reaching room temperature in 17 hours in the covered group, as compared with the control group, which was 4.3°C and 3.2°C and reached room temperature in 12 hours. The forehead temperature fell 1.7°C in the first hour and 2.6°C in the second hour, as compared with 2.3°C and 2.8°C in the control group, and thereafter the rate of decline showed no great difference. The rectal temperature falls more slowly than in the control group, though not to the extent of the intracephalic temperature and forehead temperature. Specifically, whereas in the covered group the rectal temperature fell by 1.9°C in the first hour following death and by 1.0°C in the third hour, in the control group it was 2.1°C and 1.3°C, taking 19 hours to reach room temperature, but the not reaching room temperature in covered group even after 24 hours. The muscle temperature showed about the same decline as the rectal temperature.

C. Estimation of time since death from Fiddes cooling rate table

If the rectal temperature is measured twice without moving the body and there are no fluctuations in the outside air temperature, the essential cooing time is calculated from this, so Fiddes has tried to estimate the time since death from the ratio between this and the originally measured decline in the rectal temperature. Thus, applying Fiddes's cooling rate table, a cooling rate table for dogs corresponding to Fiddes's calculation method was devised based on the decline in rectal temperature, forehead temperature, and intracephalic temperature of dogs that died from asphyxiation at 22°C. (Fig. 2)

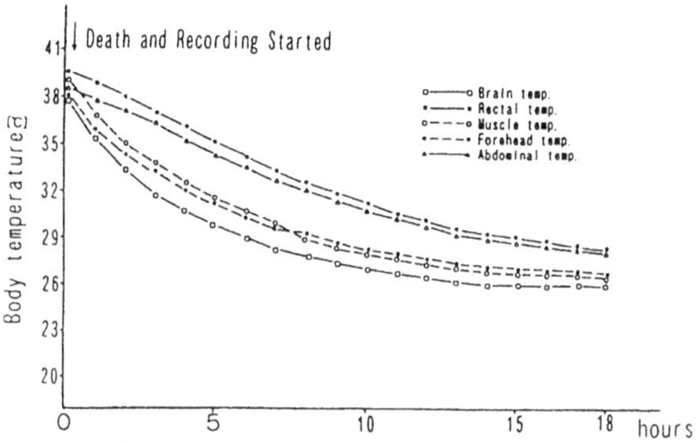


Fig.1 Death by hydrocyanism

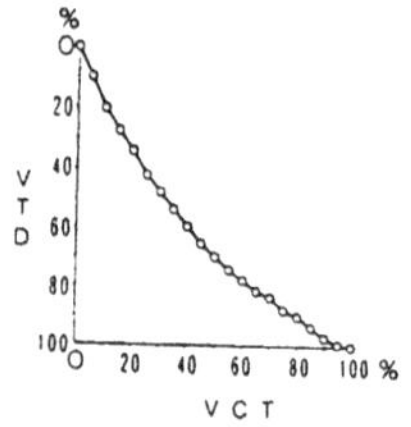


t=Postmortem Interval (t<V.C.T)

Rectal temperature = θ ℃

| Rectal temperature * V.T.D | ** V.C.T |
|---|---|
| 10.1 | 5.0 |
| 20.3 | 10.0 |
| 27.5 | 15.0 |
| 34.1 | 20.0 |
| 42.0 | 25.0 |
| 47.8 | 30.0 |
| 53.6 | 35.0 |
| 59.4 | 40.0 |
| 65.2 | 45.0 |
| 69.6 | 50.0 |
| 73.9 | 55.0 |
| 77.5 | 60.0 |
| 81.2 | 65.0 |
| 83.3 | 70.0 |
| 87.7 | 75.0 |
| 89.9 | 80.0 |
| 93.5 | 85.0 |
| 97.1 | 90.0 |
| 99.3 | 95.0 |
| 100.0 | 100.0 |
| % | % |

Percentage fall in Virtural Temperature Difference (V.T.D)

$$\frac{38.2-\theta}{V.T.D} \times 100$$

Percentage of Virtural cooling Time (V.C.T)

$$\frac{t}{V.C.T} \times 100$$

※Percentage fall in Virtural Temperature Difference (V.T.D)

※※Percentage of virtural cooling Time (V.C.T)

Fig.2 Cooling rates death by strangulation (animals covered entirely with blanket)

4. Discussion

The rate of cooling of a corpse is important as an index for the time since death, so more advanced judgment methods must be considered. With this purpose in mind, the authors have applied deep thermometers to the intracephalic temperature and forehead temperature, etc. in addition to the long-used rectal temperature and has estimated the time elapsed since death using dog cooling rate tables prepared based on the Fiddes cooling rate table. As a result, it was found that it is possible to make an estimate regardless of the cause of death, length of time since death, size of the body, or whether the body is covered or exposed. Moreover, as shown by the dog cooling rate tables obtained from experiments under various air temperatures, although there are large variations in the actual rate of cooling of a corpse and the time required until it is completely cooled, it was learned that the relationship between the ratio of the time elapsed since death to the effective cooling time and the cooling percentage, that is, the ratio with respect to the effective temperature difference of the falling temperature at that time, agrees very closely regardless of differences in the corpse's body build, nutrition, whether it is clothed, and the air temperature. The percentage cooling curve is used for estimating the time elapsed since death, and if body temperatures are taken at least twice at intervals of several hours and the air temperature at that time is also measured, then by comparison with this curve the effective cooling time is estimated, and in turn the time elapsed since death is estimated with an error of plus or minus one hour.

postmortem interval, rectal temperature, brain temperature, environmental temperature

# SUDDEN DEATH IN PREGNANCY CAUSED BY BLEEDING FROM ARTERIOVENOUS MALFORMATION IN BRAIN STEM

**Uzelac-Belovski Zorica†, Skender Milica‡, Alempijevic Djordje†, Jecmenica Dragan†**

†Institute of Forensic Medicine, Medical Faculty, 31a Deligradska Street, YU-11000 Belgrade, Yugoslavia.
‡Institute of Pathology, Medical Faculty, 1 Dr Subotica Street, YU-11000 Belgrade, Yugoslavia.

Sudden death is defined as unexpected dying of apparently health persons during short interval of time. Many of such cases might have forensic significance (8).

Arterio-venous malformations (AVM), as well as cavernous and venous angiomas and capillary telangiectasia represent vascular malformations (12). About 6 % of arterio-venous malformations (AVM) are located in posterior cranial fossa (10). AVMs are composed of abnormal vascular channels (arterial, venous or mixed type) separated by bridges of brain tissue which is usually altered, with signs of marked gliosis as result of AVMs compressing. AVMs are predominant cause of brain hemorrhages especially in young normotensive adults(11). Prior to hemorrhage, there are often repeated microhaemorrhages in AVM surrounding tissue. Brain hemorrhage seldom occurs in pregnancy (7) and its major cause is ruptured AVM(11).

There is an interesting case report on 28-year old female who died suddenly in the 6th month of pregnancy. She was regularly controlled by her physician during pregnancy. No disturbances of health were recorded. She never had neurological signs or symptoms before. She died suddenly during sleep. The medicolegal autopsy was carried out in the Institute of Forensic Medicine in Belgrade. Massive subarachnoid hemorrhage was found, especially around the brain stem, with blood in ventricular system. Also, smaller intracerebral haematoma in brain stem (junction of pons and medulla oblongata) was recorded.

Routine H&E and van Gieson elastica stained sections revealed an AVM in the triangular zone between the olivary nuclei. The AVM was composed of abundance of dilated vascular canals. Some of them have had fragmented inner elastic membrane, and some of them had hyaline deposits and nodular thickening of intima with intraluminal protrusion. Surrounding brain tissue was edematous, and there were signs of nerve cells necrosis.

AVMs are represented by network of abnormal vascular channels which are not "true type" arteries neither veins(9). In about 64% diagnosis of AVM is established before the age of 40, more often in males than females (5,9). About 90% of AVM are located in brain hemispheres, and only 10 % in brain stem and cerebellum. Usual localization of AVM is subarachnoidal space from where the, usually conically shaped AVM, spreads through the underlying brain tissue. AVM in the brain stem are located deeply in the brain tissue(9). Brain tissue around AVM frequently manifest necrotic changes as well as thrombosis and calcifications. Presence of AVM induce atrophic and gliotic changes in surrounding brain tissue due to chronic compression and/or ishaemia. Sometimes an epileptic focus may arise in that tissue. Haemorrhages from ruptured AVMs might be localized, massive and fatal. Massive AVMs are more often accompanied by focal neurological signs and/or epileptic seizures weather smaller AVMs are frequently source of fatal subarachnoidal bleeding. AVM represents developmental abnormality of blood vessels characterized by tendency of enlargement. Thus, symptoms of AVM may arise during second decade of life, or even later (5).

Several studies deal with problem of sudden death. In forensic study on 2030 autopsies was in about 5% subarachnoidal heamorrhage were found (2). It was pointed out that vascular malformation might cause spontaneous brain stem bleeding in the young normotensive adults (4). Intracranial haemorrhages during pregnancy seldom occur, but they have poor prognosis (7). In most cases intracranial haemorrhage during pregnancy is result of bleeding from AVM or ruptured aneurysm (6). Vascular malformations are most frequent cause of intracranial bleeding during pregnancy. Risk rate for rebleeding during pregnancy is about 27% (11). Pregnancy is not a risk factor of bleeding from AVMs in woman who had not previous bleeding (3). Intracranial heamorrhage from ruptured cerebral aneurysm or AVM represent heavy complication in pregnancy which, in about 5 to 12 % have lethal outcome. AVMs are documented in intracranial haemorrhage during pregnancy in about 23 % of cases, and bleeding was found before delivery in about 92 % (1).

In case we report forensic significance is that young pregnant female, although in the 3rd decade of life, has never had any neurological symptoms or signs before the fatal subarachnoid hemorrhage. Our attempts to prove histologically previous bleeding from AVM were unsuccessful. Concerning this fact we conclude that pregnancy might be a risk for bleeding from AVM even in cases without previous attacks of subarachnoid hemorrhage.

LITERATURE:

1. Dias MS, Sekhar LN (1990) Intracranial hemorrhage from aneurysms and arteriovenous malformations during pregnancy and the puerperium. Neurosurgery 27:855-65, discussion 8

2. Helpern M, Rabson SM (1945) Sudden and unexpected natural death: General considarations and statistics. N Y State J Med 45:1197-1201

3. Horton JC, Chambers WA, Lyons SL, Adams RD, Kjellberg RN (1990) Pregnancy and the risk of hemorrhage from cerebral arteriovenous malformations. Neurosurgery 27:867-71, discussion 8

4. Kashiwagi S, van Loveren HR, Tew JM Jr, Wiot JG, Weil SM, Lukin RA (1990) Diagnosis and treatment of vascular brain-stem malformations. J Neurosurg 72(1):27-34

5. Leestma EJ (1988): Forensic aspects of neuropathology. In: Leestma EJ (ed) Forensic Neuropathology, 1st ed. Raven Press, New York, P 41

6. Lin TK, Chang CN, Wai YY (1992) Spontaneous intracerebral hematoma from occult carotid-cavernous fistula during pregnancy and puerperium. Case report. J Neurosurg 76(4):714-7

7. Maymon R, Fejgin M (1990) Intracranial hemorrhage during pregnancy and puerperium. Obst Gynecol Surv 45(3):157-9

8. Milovanovic M. (1981) Naprasna smrt. In: Milovanovic M (ed) Sudska medicina, Medicinska knjiga, Beograd-Zagreb, P 22

9. Okazaki H (1989) Cerebrovascular disease. In Okazaki H (ed) Fundamentals of neuropathology: morphologic basis of neurologic disorders, Igaku-Shoin Medical Publishers Inc., New York, P 76

10. Perret G, Nishioka H (1966) Report on the cooperative study of intracranial aneurysms and subarachnoid hemorrhages. J. Neurosurg 25:467-490

11. Sadasivan B, Malik GM, Lee C, Ausman JI (1990) Vascular malformations and pregnancy. SurgNeurol 33(5):305-313

12. Stein MB, Wolpert MS (1980) Arteriovenous Malformations of the Brain. I: Current Concepts and Treatment. Arch Neurol 37:1-5

# CIVILIAN MASSACRE IN UZDOL, BOSNIA AND HERZEGOVINA

Anđelinović Š, Ivanović J, Definis-Gojanović M, Drmić I

Department of Pathology and Forensic Medicine, Clinical Hospital Split

58 000 Split, Croatia

## DESCRIPTION OF THE EVENT

On September 14, 1993, forces of the Army of Bosnia and Herzegovina attacked the small mountain village of Uzdol in the Rama region. The attack happened early in the morning, surprising numerous inhabitans in their sleep.
According to the official report, the village was burnt and 42 Croats killed, thirty of them civilians and twelve members of the Croatian Defence Council. There are indication that this number does not represent the total number of the dead because the territory was not completely examined, and it is possible that more victims were burnt in the hauses (1).
The bodies of 27 killed civilians, members of 8 families from the village, were transported to the our department, on September 17, 1993, and forensic expertise was performed.

## RESULTS

All the cadavers showed initial postmortal changes. Eighteen were women and the age of victims ranged from 10 to 87 years. Twenty-two persons were of older age, while three under 15. One family lost eight of its members. In the 26 victims, one to seven gunshot wounds in the area of the head, trunk or the extremities were found. In six victims close-range gunshot wounds were found on the head and chest. In case of a man shot in the back of his head the muzzle was placed directly against his head. All the other victims had long-range gunshot wounds. The localization of the long-range wounds was most found in the occipital region, the temporal region, the cheek and the back of the head. Five persons were killed by shots to the chest and abdomen, whereas six died of wounds to the back of the trunk. Two women had cuts on the head. The blows by heavy and sharp objects were so severe that they resulted in multiple fractures of the head bones and conquassation of the brain. One man had his ears cut off. One body was almost completely carbonized.
Brutality of this massacre is confirmed by the fact that one old woman, bed-ridden for years, was killed in her bed.

Our report of this crime, only one in series, will not be finished by a conlusion. It serves only to present the facts which reveal the truth and enforce our search for the end of aggression, hate and human suffering.

## REFERENCES

1. V2 Gornji Vakuf tasked by RC Zenica. Special report 15 September 1993. Investigate alleged massacre at Uzdol (YJ 1856)

# Medico-legal connexions of ruptured cerebral vascular abnormalities

AUTHORS : Prof. Belis V. (MD), Dragoteanu C. (MD), Curca C. (MD), Dermengiu D (MD), Computer Ann. Anghel A.
*National Institute of Legal Medicine "Mina Minovici" - 75669, Sos. Vitan-Bârzesti 9, Bucharest-4, Romania*

Gross pathology aknowledges several abnormal cerebral vascular structures:"berry aneuryams involving the Circle of Willis, cerebral angioma ( showing histopathological displasia of both arterial and venous vessels), polyvascular and disembryogenetical expressed abnormalities.Sometimes connected with cerebral atherosclerosis, the "microaneurysms" (Charcot-Bouchard 1968) or the "cryptic angioma (Richardson, 1972 ) are found to be death-related.
All these predisposing vascular abnormalities, some of them genetically determined, can in certain circumstances be the cause of sudden unexpected death by intracranial bleeding ( intracerebral haemorrhage or haematoma, bleeding in the epi / subdural / subarachnoid spaces, or both ).
These predisposing factors, connected with age and sex, must also be kept in mind when establishing the medico-legal causality in lethal head injury cases.

## METHODS

We have selected 49 cases with intracranial haemorrhages due to ruptured aneurysms, from over 8300 autopsies performed in the National Institute of Legal Medicine in Bucharest, between 1990-1992 . We studied different triggering factors that might be involved in determining sudden death: food and alcohol intake, physical exertion -related or not to sexual intercourse -, temperature and barometric variations, excessive tiredness, pregnancy, associate diseases - diabetes mellitus, hypertension, atherosclerosis -, etc. When available, pathology data, the clinical expression and the onset form of the disease, along with antemortem laboratory examinations (angiography,computed tomography, cerebro spinal fluid exams ) were taken into account. All the cases were completed with histopathological examination and toxicological determination of the alcohol blood levels.

## RESULTS

We found intrahaemorrhages due to ruptured aneurysms being 0.58 % of all autopsies (Fig.1), 1.63 % of non-violent deaths, and 3,75 % when referring to the total number of intracranial haemorrhages (1308 cases).

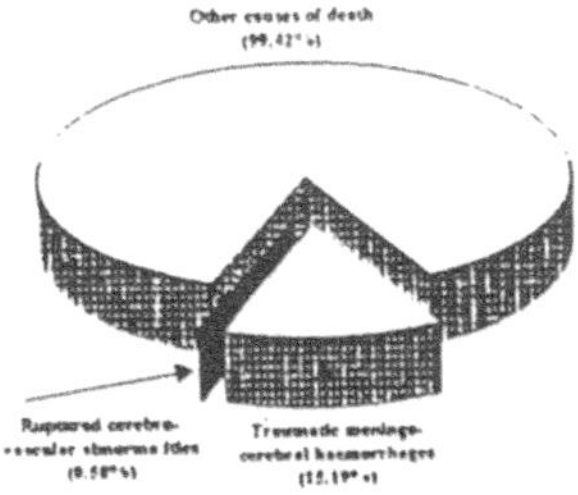


Fig. 1 Sudden death due to ruptured cerebral aneurysms

Our study reveals that aneurysms or other vascular defects are more frequently found in men (61 %). It seems obvious that the third decade of age is mostly involved (Fig.2) especially in unmarried people.

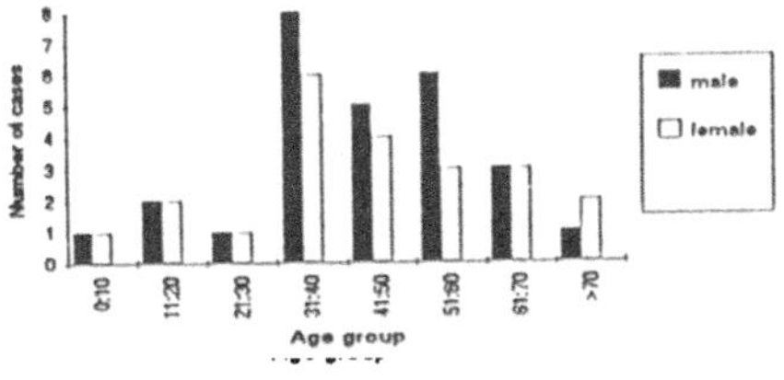


Fig.2 Sex and age distribution of the ruptured cerebrovascular abnormalities

It seems obvious that the third decade of age is mostly involved, especially in unmarried people (Fig.3).

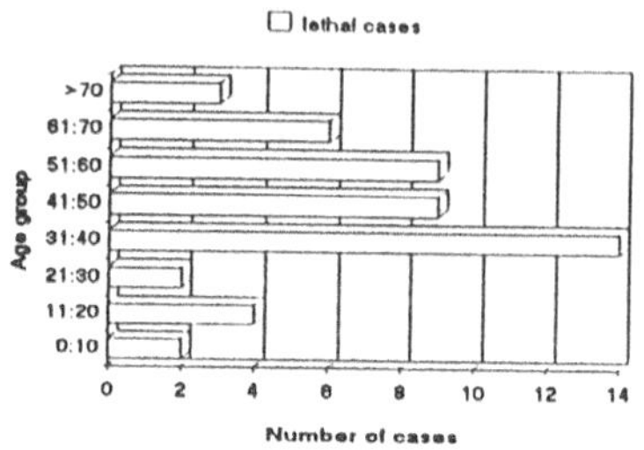


Fig.3 Age related morbidity

We tried to determine the seasonal incidence: it apears that ruptured cerebral aneurysms has two peaks of morbidity in January-March and August-September (Fig.4). It is already known that Japanese studies emphasize the part played by seasonal factors in triggering cerebrovascular bleeding (Owada,1973).

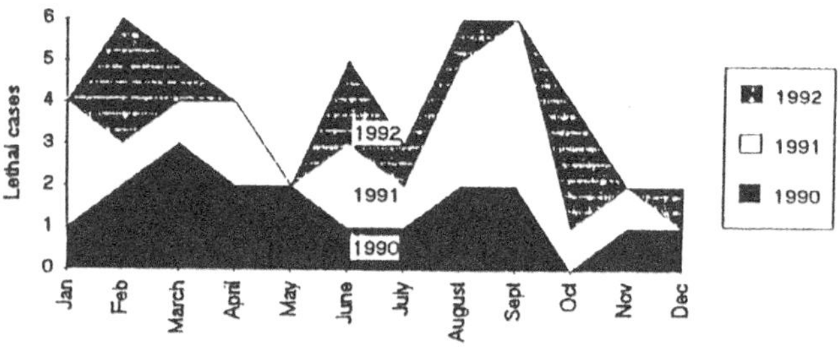


Fig. 4 Seasonal correlations

Death can occur very rapidly after massive intracranial bleeding ( sometimes almost instantaneous - induced by bulbar inhibition) but more frequently, a profound comatous interval delays death for hours / days. In consequence, the majority of such cases are reported by hospitals (Fig.4) .

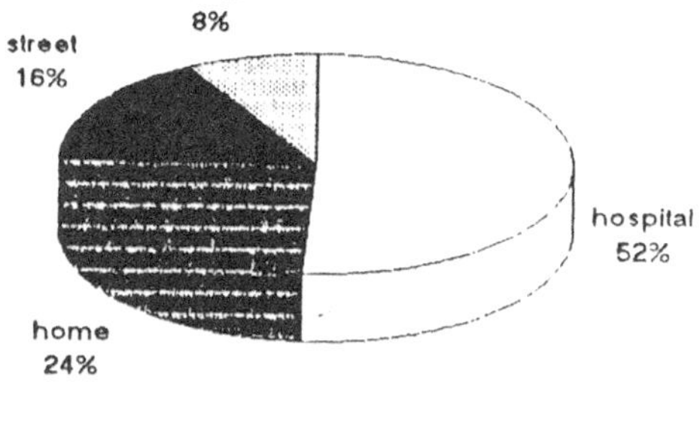


Fig.4 Origin of reported deaths

In only 16,8% cases could a prodromal syndrome be recorded ( violent headache, dizziness, emesis ). We found 15 cases in which a head injury was recorded and confirmed during the autopsy ( 40 % light head trauma - conccusion, head bruises -, 60 % moderate to severe head trauma - cerebral contusions - ), whereas 34 cases (69,38% ) were "pure" intracranial bleeding as a direct complication of the cerebrovascular abnormality. However it is very interesting to observe that we found a plurality of intracranial haemorrhagic types ( Table 1 ).

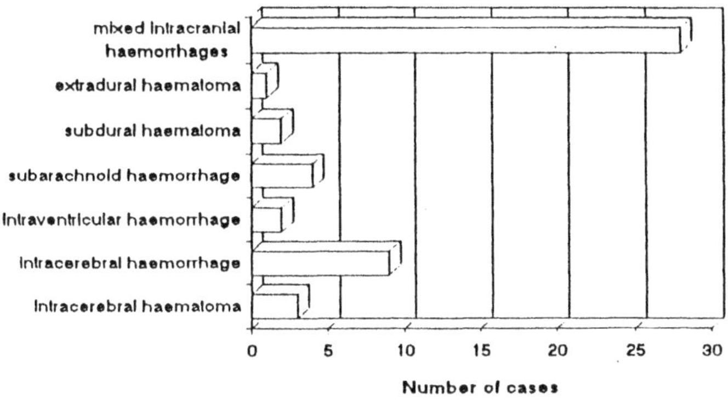


Table 1 Intracranial haemorrhages in sudden death; pathological findings in 49 cases

## DISCUSSION

Some of the results of our study are similar to Western statistics, but others are quite different: for instance we found that sudden death (sometimes reported as suspect death), as a complication of abnormal cerebral vascular bleeding is only 0.58%.

The subarachnoid haemorrhage is considered to be one of the most frequent complications of cerebral vascular abnormalities ( 3, 4 ). Our study reveals an interesting variety of intracranial haemorrhagic types ( Table 1 ), the"pure" subarachnoid haemorrhage being a very rare occurrence ( 1.32% ). More frequently the autopsies revealed differently located haemorrhages: intracerebral haemorrhage, intraventricular haeemorrhage, associated types or similar located haematoma. The precipital factors most frequently related to the rupture of abnormal cerebral vessels have been: physical exertion, alcohol intake, hypertension and atherosclerosis. From the series of 15 head trauma cases associating the already mentioned vascular pathology, we could determine in 6 cases ( listed in Table 2 ) that the head injury took place prior to the vascular accident, being in fact, a precipital factor of the intracranial haemorrhage; the head trauma could not "per se" have caused death, but was acting on the vascular pathological condition.

In our experience, the third decade of age was mostly involved suggesting that geografic or etnic factors might be involved.

The most frequent site of ruptured arterial abnormalities was found to be the middle cerebral artery.

The short interval between the onset of symptoms and death explains why many cases are initially labeled as "suspicious deaths".

Table2

| No. | Sex/age | Diagnostic | Clinics | CSF exam. | Angyography | External examination |
|---|---|---|---|---|---|---|
| 1. | Female, 45 | Subdural haemat., intraventricular hg. | Deep coma | Yellow | "Cold" temporal area | Head bruises |
| 2. | Male, 39 | Intracerebral and meningeal hg. | " | Blood | Intracavernal carotic aneurysm | Multiple lacerations on vertex |
| 3. | Female, 55 | Intracerebral hg., advanced atheroscl. | " | Pink | Middle cerebral arterial angioma | Frontal wound, vertex lacerations |
| 4. | Male, 61 | Intracerebral and meningeal hg. | " | Blood | " | Cranium base "hinge fracture" |
| 5. | Female, 31 | Intracerebral hg., intraventricular hg. | Sudden death | Blood | Middle cerebral arterial aneurysm | Frontal,zygomatic, and mandibular bruises |
| 6. | Female, 40 | Subarachnoid hg. | Sudden death | Blood | " | Left zygomatic and palpebral bruises |

## CONCLUSIONS

1. Our study reveals that the aneurysms or other vascular defects are more frequently found in men , in the age interval 31-40 years.

2. This pathology seems to be season - related, having two peaks of high incidence between January-March and August-September.

3. Ruptured abnormal cerebral vessels result not only in subarachnoid haemorrhages but also in extra/subdural haemorrhages, intracerebral and intraventricular haemorrhages.

## REFERENCES


1.Belis Vladimir. Patologie medicolegala .Traumatismul craniocerebral , p.23-29., Ed. Teora (1990.)

2.Di Maio, DJ and Di Maio, VJM: Forensic pathology, pp 159-162, Elsevier, New York * Amsterdam * Oxford (1989).

3.Knight B. The coroner autopsy, Arnold (1985).

4.Knight B. Forensic pathology, Arnold (1990)

5.Lindenberg R. Mechanical injuries of brain and meninges. In Medicolegal investigation of death (Eds. Spitz, WU and Fisher, RS), pp 447-456, Charles C Thomas, Splingfield Illinois (1973).

6.Mason J.K. The pathology of violent injury, Arnold, Edinburgh (1978)

7.Stehbens W.E. Pathology of the cerebral blood vessels, C.V.Mosby Co, Saint Louis, (1972).

# AN ACID BATH MURDER

S.M. Claydon, M.R.C.Path., D.M.J. (Path)
Senior Lecturer in Forensic Pathology
Wales Institute of Forensic Medicine
University Hospital of Wales College of Medicine
CARDIFF CF4 4XN

**KEY WORDS**

Acid bath; homicide

## CASE REPORT

On Monday 25th 1991 at 15.00 hours passers-by heard cries for help coming from a locked, rented garage in East London. They called the police and the fire brigade, who forced entry at 15.15 hours. A young woman was found lying, still conscious, behind the garage door, and a black industrial bath, filled with fuming hydrochloric acid, was discovered at the rear of the fume-filled garage. The young woman was taken to the local hospital where she died at 18.10 hours with severe acid burns.

## POST MORTEM FINDINGS

70% of the skin surface showed thick grey acid burns. The pattern of burning suggested that the woman had been placed in the acid bottom first, with her face, hands and lower legs above the surface of the liquid. Drips had then apparently run down onto the tops of her feet when she climbed out of the bath. Her clothing had offered some protection against the acid.

Internal examination showed bruising over the front of the strap muscles of the neck covering an area 10 cms vertically by 6 cms horizontally. Under the jaw on the right side were three circular bruises, each one centimetre wide, involving the salivary glands. The cricoid cartilage was broken five millimetres left of the midline and the mucosal lining of the larynx contained petechiae. The lungs were dark red, distended and heavy, being filled with blood stained frothy fluid. Histology confirmed these findings and also showed the burning of the respiratory mucosa, which showed occasional dark grey patches on macroscopic examination. The cause of death was given as "Inhalation of toxic fumes with burns".

## THE TRIAL

The husband of the deceased woman was tried and convicted of murder at the Central Criminal Court, Old Bailey, in June 1993. He had rented the garage and purchased the acid and the bath, saying that these were for the restoration of old ceramic bathroom furniture. Sales people recalled he had climbed into the bath and sat in it while still in the shop.

## DISCUSSION

Contact with hydrochloric acid produces the typical grey discolouration of the skin seen in this case. The effect is more one of tanning rather than corrosion although corrosion would occur slowly (over a period of weeks). A comparison of the effects of corrosive substances is shown in Table 1.

Injury by corrosive agents is uncommon in Western Countries and is usually due to accidental exposure. In other parts of the world, mineral acids may be used for homicide, assault and suicide. In Malaya, formic and acetic acids have been ingested by young female rubber-workers as a means of suicide.

Disposal of a body by placing it in corrosive liquid has only been described previously during the investigation of the Haigh murders in Britain in the 1940s. More usual methods for illegal disposal of a corpse include burial (with or without dismemberment), submerging in water, or setting on fire. The most unusual aspect in this particular death is that this young woman "came back to life" following manual strangulation which fractured the cricoid cartilage. Fracture of the cricoid cartilage due to other causes such as accidental injury usually results in death due to laryngeal oedema if the victim survives the initial impact. In this case the acid fumes appear to have acted as a very severe form of "smelling salts", stimulating the brain and causing the unfortunate woman to resume breathing. If anything can be said in defence of her husband it is that he genuinely believed she was dead before placing her in the acid and making his escape.

## TABLE 1

## ACTION OF CORROSIVE SUBSTANCES ON HUMAN TISSUES

| SUBSTANCE | EFFECT |
|---|---|
| Hydrochloric acid | Less corrosive than sulphuric or nitric acid; produces grey burns. |

| | |
|---|---|
| Sulphuric acid | Highly corrosive; produces grey/black burns. |
| Nitric acid | Highly corrosive; produces yellow/brown burns. |
| Sodium hydroxide | Corrosive; produces white/grey burns with a soapy residue. |
| Carbolic acid (phenol) | Stiffens tissues and bleaches them white. |
| Lysol (phenol and cresol) | Stiffens tissues and turns them brownish purple. |

## REFERENCES

Glaister J. Medical Jurisprudence and Toxicology. 7th Edn. 1942 pp. 189; 457-62. Livingstone: Edinburgh

Groves J., Gray R.F. A Synopsis of Otolaryngology. 4th Edn. 1985. p. 374 Wright: Bristol.

Knight B. Forensic Pathology 1991 pp. 528-9. Edward Arnold: London.

Simpson K. Forensic Medicine, 8th Edn. 1979 pp 35, 40. Edward Arnold: London

# TRAUMATIC THROMBOSIS OF THE INTERNAL CAROTID ARTERY: TWO CASES BY DIFFERENT PATHOGENESIS

*Francesco De Ferrari, Mariagrazia Birbes, Mario Restori*
*Institute of Forensic Medicine - University of Brescia, Spedali Civili - Brescia (Italy)*

The thrombosis of the carotid artery resulting from non-penetrating trauma is a not frequent, but well known event and it has been reported in the literature since a long time (Clarke et al. 1955, Yamada et al. 1967, Fleming et al. 1968, Gurdjian et al. 1971). Crissey and Bernstein (1974) described four pathogenetic mechanisms of the thrombosis: 1) a direct blow to the neck, 2) a blow to the side of the head resulting in hyperextension and rotation of the head with stretching of the carotid artery and consequent rupture of the intima, 3) an intraoral blunt trauma, 4) basal or other skull fractures that can damage the intrapetrous portion of the internal carotid artery.
Afterwards other authors have reported cases of traumatic carotid artery injuries (Dragon et al. 1981, Moar 1987). Some of the common findings reported are the following: the lack in half of the subjects of external signs of neck trauma, the presence of a lucid interval from one or more hours, according to some authors, up to some days, according to other authors (only 10% of subjects develop neurological symptoms during the first hour). After the lucid interval neurological symptoms arise consisting of transient ischemic attacks or a major stroke. The most common pathology finding is an intimal tear. Other lesions or pathogenetic mechanisms reported are: intramural hematoma, pseudoaneurysm and vascular spasm; in all cases however the carotid lesion is followed by thrombosis. The site of the thrombosis is usually in the area of the carotid bifurcation or just above in the first 3 cm of the internal carotid artery. Complete common carotid artery occlusion is rare. Embolism of the thrombotic material from the site of injury is believed to be a common mechanism of cerebral ischemia. Delayed embolism may explain the lucid interval.
We recently observed two necroscopy cases of carotid thrombosis which developed after blows to the face.

Case 1

A 50-year-old man was punched in the face during a quarrel. Just after the fight he was visited by a doctor and he didn't report any trouble. After about 4 hours hemiplegia with drowsiness and aphasia suddenly arose. The next day the patient died. At the necropsy excoriations of the face (left orbit and zygomatic regions) were observed; the cadaveric section indicates encephalomalacia of the left hemisphere; the left middle cerebral artery was completely occlused by an embolus of thrombotic material and two intimal tears with dissection of the media and thrombosis of the internal carotid artery were found.

Case 2

A 65-year-old man suffering from hypertension was struck with fists to the face during a quarrel. After about half an hour the man showed functional impotence at his left upper limb and after 15 minutes he fell in to a coma state. Three days later he died in a coma depasse'state. The autopsy indicated ecchymosis at the left eye and left zygomatic region; at the section a broad infarction of the right cerebral hemisphere and a thrombosis of the whole internal carotid artery with occlusion at the beginning of middle cerebral artery were found. At the initial tract of the internal carotid an atherosclerotic plaque with concentric stenosis of the lumen of about 70% was noticed.

## HISTOLOGICAL FINDINGS

Histological preparations had been prepared according to the usual techniques of fixation and inclusion and stained with hematoxylin/eosin and Azan modified according to the Heidenheim and Alcion's technique. The histological findings confirmed the macroscopic reports. In the first case the dissection of the media with a recent thrombus in the lumen was observed; the examination of the Azan stained sections of the media showed a very moderate fibromuscular dysplasia without atheromasic lesions. In the second case an atherosclerotic lesion of the vessel wall with myointimal fibrosis and cholesterol clefts was observed; the vessel lumen was occluded by a recent thrombus and the media was fairly conserved.

## DISCUSSION

The cases presented show some characteristics that are frequently noticed in post-traumatic thrombosis of the carotid artery. These are: the absence of signs of neck trauma that suggests an indirect pathogenetic mechanism determining a lesion distant from the injury site; the presence of a lucid interval that is the rule in this kind of lesion and finally a symptomatology of cerebral hemispheric ischemia.

Nevertheless the pathogenetic mechanism is different in these two cases. In the first one the pathogenesis is the Crissey and Bernstein's second type. As a matter of fact in this case intimal lacerations had been found. On the contrary in our second case no intimal tears had been found, but an atherosclerotic plaque producing stenosis of the lumen was present. In this case none of the other Crissey and Bernstein's pathogenetic mechanisms took place. We therefore suggest a further pathogenetic hypothesis: the vasospasm, which has already been reported by other authors.

Vasospasm, in our case, should result from systemic vasoconstriction with hormonal-adrenergic action determined by the emotional stress resulting from the quarrel and the fight. At the stenosis site (the beginning of the internal carotid artery) the spasm caused a serious slowing or even the arrest of the blood flow with consequent thrombosis afterwards propagated to the whole internal carotid up to the middle cerebral artery. This mechanism explains the relatively short period of time (about half an hour) of the lucid interval, shorter than the one reported in literature. This is different to the first case, in which the cerebral ischemia resulted from embolization, the lucid interval lasted about four hours. Finally it is interesting to remark that in these two cases the different pathogenetic mechanisms implicate different consequences from the forensic and legal point of view also. In the first case the trauma caused the death. In fact the moderate fibromuscular dysplasia can explain the dissection of the media, but the intimal tears are a result of the traumatic stretching of the carotid artery. On the contrary in the second case the pre-existing atherosclerotic lesion has been a prevalent contributory factor to the thrombosis.

# REFERENCES

- Clarke PRR, Dickson J, Smith BJ (1955) Traumatic thrombosis of the internal carotid artery following a non-penetrating injury and leading to infarction of the brain. Br J Surg 43: 215-216.
- Crissey MM, Bernstein EF (1974) Delayed presentation of carotid intimal tear following blunt craniocervical trauma. Surgery 75: 543-549.
- Dragon R, Saranchak H, Lakin P, Strauch G (1981) Blunt injuries to the carotid and vertebral arteries. Am J Surg 141: 497-500.
- Fleming JFR, Petric D (1968) Traumatic thrombosis of the internal carotid artery with delayed hemiplegia. Can J Surg 11: 166-172.
- Gurdjian ES, Blaise A, Renato WS, Thomas LM (1971) Spasm of the extracranial internal carotid artery resulting from blunt trauma demonstrated by angiography. J Neurosurg 35:742-747.
- Moar JJ (1987) Traumatic rupture of the cervical carotid arteries: an autopsy and histopathological study of 200 cases. For Sci Intern 34:227-244.
- Yamada S, Kindt GW, Youmans JR (1967) Carotid artery occlusion due to non-penetrating injury. J Trauma 7:333-342.

# SUICIDAL FIREARM WOUNDS OF THE HEAD BY A 5,56 mm BULLET - - REPORT OF TWO CASES

Definis Gojanović M, Anđelinović Š, Ivanović J, Drmić I

Department of Pathology and Forensic Medicine, Clinical Hospital Split

58 000 Split, Croatia

## INTRODUCTION

Wounds in the mouth are not uncommon, most of these wounds being suicidal. If a person shoots himself through the mouth, the entrace gunshot wound is usually in the posterior third of the palate.In such a way self inflicted gunshot wounds with high velocity projectiles, such as caliber 5,56x45 mm (Vo > 900 m/s, Eo > 1700 J), will result in an exit wound where half of the head and face is dispersed and brain blown out. In addition to the kinetic energy of the missile, the effect of the pressure of the powder gases (above 1500 bars) is important too because of the closed oral cavity (1).

The effect high velocity projectiles shows many vagaries and the most unexpected injuries may be found. In decomposed bodies gunshot wounds are greatly modified. In those cases, the examination of the scene is essential, specially to determine whether the death was accidental, suicidal or homicidal (2,3).

Here we present two cases of suicidal gunshot wounds to the head by 5,56 mm bullets, assault rifle CETME, committed by two Spanish soldiers, who where members of the UN peace forces placed in Bosnia and Herzegovina.

## CASE REPORT A

In July 1993, a 19-year-old soldier was found dead on his work place. There were no suspicious circumstances regarding his death. It was obviously a suicide with a rifle CETME LC, ammunition 5,56 mm, by placing the muzzle of the fun deep into the mouth. The main autopsy finding was an exit wound like a big skin laceration of the scalp with underlying multiple bone fractures and some missing fragments of bones in the parietal region. The greater part of the cerebrum was missing, the rest was conquassated and the cerebellum was contused. The entrance gunshot wound was hidden deep in the oral cavity.

At the time of death the soldier was drunk.

## CASE REPORT B

Some days after, a second Spanish soldier, a 23-year-old man, was found dead in a small clearing surrounded by thorn bushes and a stone wall, approximately 15 km from Spabat., six days after he went missing. The body was starting to decompose. The forensic expertise was performed with no other information.

At the postmortem examination we found the skull in many fractured fragments, with putrefactive changes to the skin and with no brain. After reconstruction of the skull some fragments were missing from the right parieto occipital region. As one possibility, we supposed that the cause of death was a gunshot wound of the head with the exit wound in the posterior part of the head. Due the lack of an entrance point of the bullet, it was presumed that, in this case too, the muzzle was put deep in the mouth.

Later, we received the police report of scene investigation with more precise details concerning the case itself but with some wrong conclusions.
At the end, on the basis of the autopsy findings, subsequent analyses (positive "paraffin test" on the soldier's hands, the large concentration of antimony on the later discovered fragments of head bones which were missing), traces found at the scene and statements of witnesses, the case was closed as a self-inflicted gunshot wound of the head (through the mouth).
This man had maritial problems and he had been depressed in recent times. At the time of death, he too was drunk.

## CONCLUSION

The properties of a lighter and faster projectile would cause greatly increased tissue destruction. In the case of putrefactive changes and practically non-existent entrance gunshot wounds, it is difficult to conclude on the cause and mechanism of death, because differential diagnostic of the other types of wounds or injuries have to be taken into consideration (for example, contusion wounds after blunt force injuries of the head). Special difficulties exist in those cases when any information about the circumstances of death is unknown or the investigation of the scene is poorly conducted.
So, we underline the interest of a forensic scientist to have a good knowledge of gunshot wounds inflicted by high velocity projectiles as well as the necessity for more cooperation between the police and other investigators with the medical examiner.

## REFERENCES


1. Hogg IV (1987) Rifles. In: Modern small arms. Bison Books, London,P 90
2. Fackler ML, Bellamy RF, Malinovski JA (1988) The wound profile: illustration of the missile - tissue interaction. J Trauma 28:21-29
3. Oliver JD, Whitty GF (1988) Wound-dynamic studies in Australia. J Trauma 28:57-67

# HEPATIC STEATOSIS: EFFECT&CAUSE. FORENSIC AND SOCIAL MEDICINE SIGNIFICATIONS

Dragoi S. Gheorghe, MD, PhD, DSc- University of Craiova, Romania, Dpt. of Human Anatomy and Forensic Medicine; Academic Hospital No.2, Dpt. of Pathology, Cytodiagnosis and the Center of Experimental Haematopathology and Haematologic Diagnosis

## Introduction. Objectives

Lipides storing into the hepatic functional structures elements, well-known under the name of "Hepatic steatosis" is frequently remarked along the histopathologic practice. It is multifactorial determined but in the case of irreversibility it becomes an appearing and developing causal factor of the hepatic fibrosis. The main cause of the hepatic steatosis is the alcoholism (*Addison T.*, 1836). A deficiency in proteins and cholines was charged concerning the pathogenesis of the alcoholic hepatitis (*Best Ch., Hartroft W.S., Lucas S.S., Ridout J.H.*, 1949). Later on, strong proves have been brought to the relationship between the pathogenesis of the hepatic lesions dealt to the alcoholism and the direct toxicity of the ethanol and/or its metabolism advantage (*Lieber C.S.*, 1962, 1983, 1985, 1988; *Salaspuro M., Lindros K.*, 1985; *French S.W.*, 1989). The following questions to know the morphopathogenesis of the hepatic steatosis are still unclarified: a) the mechanisms responsible of the triglycerides hepatic increasing into the postalcoholic hepatic steatosis; b) the basis mechanism by means of which the chronic consumption of alcohol stimulates the mesenchimatous cells to produce collagen and the induction of their proliferation; c) why do only a part of the drinkers or just a part of the alcoholics present hepatic touching? d) what is the mechanism of the "cells' death" by alcohol? In this paper we suggest to achieve a classification of the stages of the evolution of the hepatic stasis and the criteria of morphogenetic variability of the phenotypes of these lesions, using my own observation data.

## Material and Study Methods

Microanatomic investigations have been achieved using a group of 800 cases registred along a period of 11 years (1983- 1994) into the hystopatology laboratory of the Academic Hospital No. 2 Craiova and the Forensic Medicine Institute of Craiova. The subjects are aged between 25- 65, 650 of them being males and the rest females. Parallel we studied the hepatic structures from a group of 43 complete cases of primary and/or secondary hepatic lesions; 6 foetuses (2-8 months), 8 newborns (0-30 days), 7 infants (11-12 months), 4 teenagers (16-20 years), 6 mature persons (25-60 years) and 8 old persons (60-80 years). The fragments of hepatic tissues were fixed in 10% formaldehyde neutralized by calcium carbonicum and 10% formaldehyde Baker (to fix lipides). A part of the fixed fragments followed the classic techniques of wax embedded and the other part have been preserved to be used for achieving iced microtome sections to get general and special reactions for lipides. The seriated sections achieved after wax embedded were differentially colored: Popper- fluorescence, Herxheimer- Sudan III or IV, Sudan Black B, polarized light, Gain Blue Nil sulfate- for working out the lipides general characteristics. Then, *Adams et al., Laulier et al.*, Gold- hydroxamat (*Adams et al.*), plasmate reaction Cain, PAS *Adams et al., Hirsh- Peiffer* with violet of Cresyl) to work out the lipides varieties.

## Results

The relating of the microanatomic changes induced within the lipide storing is made referring to the territory supporting the important changes in ontogenetic and morphogenetic dynamic. The main element describing is still the hepatic cell that presents different variable degrees of lipide storing along the genesis and evolution of steatosis: 1) microvascular steatosis with an appearance of a "foamy degenerescence" and without nucleus dislocation from its central place; 2) macrovascular divided steatosis and lipide vacuoles forming that pushes away the nucleus to the cytoplasma periphery of the hepatic cell; it also keeps a marginal area of cytoplasma between the lipide vacuole and the cell membrana. The acinus topography of the hepatic cells with macrovascular lipide storing is variable with age and the fundamental disease where this lesion has been differentiated: as concerning the malnourished or perfused newborn there are panacinar macrovascular lesions; a minimum, diced steatosis can be considered as normal for those patients of an average or old age; to get the hepatocytes of the periportal acinar zone number one it can be frequently met into the severe anemia cachexy (*Mac Sween R.N.M.*, 1987) , proteinoenergetic denutrition (*Chaudhuri*, 1972), phosphor intoxication (*Dias- Rivera*, 1950), along the corticoids therapy (*Zimmerman H.J.*, 1978; *Zimmerman H.J., Isaak K.G.*, 1987); to get hepatocytes from the 3rd acinar zone (central perivenular) with extension to the second and the first zone appears into steatosis from the alcoholic hepatocytes but in fatness and intestinal short- circuit diseases; 3) the kystic steatosis was found to be frequently associated to hotbeds of necrobiosis of the hepatic cells and of the differentiation of an acinar collagen reaction. Important changes have been observed at the level of the stromal elements that take place into the genesis of the hepatic fibrosis by perisinusoidal and central perivenular collagenizing and by phenomena of sinusoidal capillarisation. These changes have been remarked on the colored sections using special methods: van Gieson, Gomori, PAS, Hale. We identified type I and III collagen and also a positive material PAS diastasic resistant around a central vein into the perisinusoidal space and around some hepatic cells presenting the phenomena of cariorexis and cariolisis (obvious sign of apoptosis). The central perivenular sclerosis has been described at alcoholics and it was considered as a factor of prognosis into the evolution to cirrhosis (*Nahano*, 1982). Into the unleashed cirrhosis, the Disse space is thickened by modifying the matrix and it appears to be a basal vascular membrana. This phenomenon is called "the capillarisation of the sinusoids" (*Schaffner*, 1963). As a consequence of the fibrosis process, the sinusoidal sanguine flow is changed and therefore, the phenomena of malnutrition of the hepatic cells appears. A semiquantitative assession of the hepatic fibrosis has been tried (*Morselt*, 1978) and a quantitative one, by a coloringmetric method based on the selective capacity of two colorings: Red Sirius and Green Fast, the first one dealing to the collagen and the second to the noncollagen proteins (*Jiemenez W.*, 1985). Finally there exist specific antibodies led against different types of collagen and other proteins of the matrix that allow to estimate the relative quantities and the distributions of these compounds into the normal and pathologic liver. Studies made by means of specific antibodies have shown that type I collagen is present into the portal space and type III is found into the lobules.

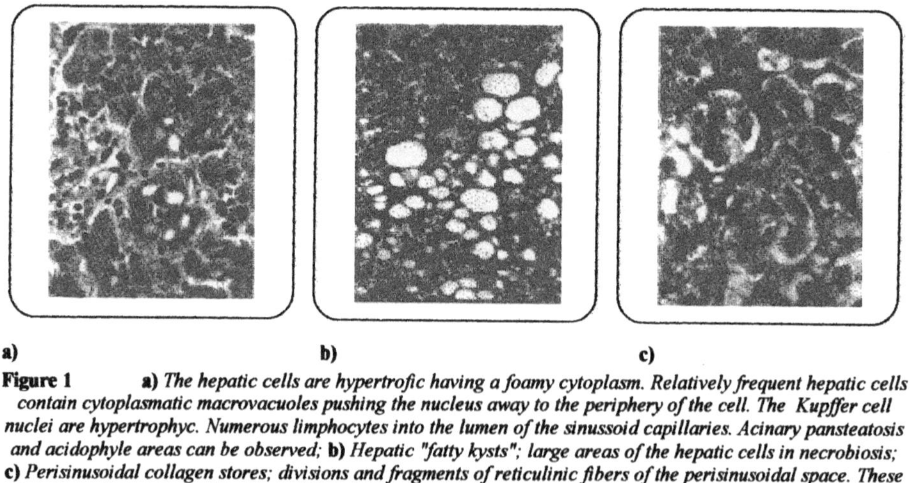

**a)** **b)** **c)**

**Figure 1** **a)** *The hepatic cells are hypertrofic having a foamy cytoplasm. Relatively frequent hepatic cells contain cytoplasmatic macrovacuoles pushing the nucleus away to the periphery of the cell. The Kupffer cell nuclei are hypertrophyc. Numerous limphocytes into the lumen of the sinussoid capillaries. Acinary pansteatosis and acidophyle areas can be observed;* **b)** *Hepatic "fatty kysts"; large areas of the hepatic cells in necrobiosis;* **c)** *Perisinusoidal collagen stores; divisions and fragments of reticulinic fibers of the perisinusoidal space. These elementary lesions contribute to establish the microanatomic diagnosis of "central hyaline sclerosis" frequently growing to cirrhosis. (Haematoxyline-Eosin coloring technique).*

**Conclusions**

The hepatic steatosis an elementary, reversible, plurifactorial, determined lesion. It can become a cause of the hepatic fibrosis genesis and evolution closed by necrosis and swell induced alcohol, There have been remarked a morphologic variability of the hepatic steatosis: 1) microvascular hepatic steatosis; 2) macrovascular hepatic steatosis: divided periportal, zonal periportal (zone 1 acinar) and the pericentral zone (zone 2, 3 acinar); 3) kystic hepatic steatosis. The topography of the hepatic steatosis has a predictive character: 1) microvascular hepatic steatosis with triglycerides is met into the gravidic chronic steatosis in prolonged therapies with tetracyclin and Reye Syndrome (at the young people after a pseudoinfluenza syndrome); 2) macrovesicular hepatic steatosis with triglycerides is frequently observed in alcoholism, denutrition and protidic deficiency, cardiac liver. Elementary lesions taking part into the getting of the hepatic fibrosis are the result of the interaction between the parenchimatous cells (hepatic cells), mesenchimal cells (endothelial, sinusoidal cells, lipocytes-ito, miofibroblasts) and the hepatic matrix (collagen, glycoproteins and proteoglycans). The persons having steatosis or perivenular fibrosis present a greater risk of an evolution to an irreversible hepatic disease than those having a simple steatosis. The diagnosis of steatosis must cover three stages: 1) a macroscopic stage, based on the chromatic and on the changes of the shape of the liver; 2) a microscopic stage, establishing of the steatosis phenotype; the degree of the hepatic fibrosis; the content of the steatosic vacuoles; 3) molecular stage, using the markers of keratin (antibodies CAM 5, 2) and lymphocytes T (CD8). As concerning the social plane- the medical education has a major part and the limit of the alcohol consumption as a factor of the genesis but of the involution of the hepatic steatosis process, too.

**References**

01. Benhamou JP (1992) Foie. In: Godeau P (ed) Traite de Medicine, Tom1- Foie Flammarion, Paris

02. Burt DA, Mac Sween MNR (1993) In: Benhamou JP (ed) Hepatologie Clinique, Flammarion, Paris, P 810-815

03. Cook GC, Hutt MSR (1967) The liver after Kwashiorkor. British Medical Journal 3:454-457

04. Desmet VJ (1984) Alcoholic liver disease. Histological features and evolution. Acta Medica Scandinavica Supplementum 703:111-126

05. French SW (1981) The Mallory body: structure, composition and pathogenesis. Hapathology 1:76-83

06. Hall P (1985) Pathology and pathogenesis of alcoholic liver disease. In: Hall P (ed) Alcoholic Liver Disease: Pathobiology, Epidemiology and Clinical Aspects, Edward Arnold, London, P 41-68

07. Lieber CS (1984) Alcohol and the liver. Hepatology 4:1243-1260

08. Scheur PJ (1988) Liver disease in the alcoholic. In: Scheur PJ (ed) Liver Biopsy Interpretation, Bailliere Tindal, London P 83-98

09. Van Waes, Lieber CS (1977) Early perivenular sclerosis in alcoholic fatty liver: an index of progressive liver injury. Gastroenterology 84:684-650

10. Wakil SJ, Stoops JK, Joshi VC (1983) Fatty acid synthesis and its regulation. Annual Review of Biochemistry 52:537-579

# THE GLIAL ALTERATION IN SOME CASES OF SUDDEN DEATH AN ETIOPATHOGENICAL ASSESSMENT

M.L. Dressler[1], T. Adelmann[2], I. Talos[2], Dorina Lungu[2], Octavia-Irina Dressler[1]

[1] University of Medicine and Pharmacy Timisoara;
[2] Institute of Forensic Midicine Timisoara;
str. Balantei 3, 1900 Timisoara, Romania

The progresses achieved in the research concerning the glial cell system determined us to emphasize some data that were at the very basis of our studies. Therefore the glial cell plays a well-defined role in the nervous cells' homeostasis: it facilitates the nervous impulse transmission and has a symbiotic action, similar to the reticulo-endothelial system. We appreciate as of great importance the processes of glial hyperplasia that might induce neuronal depolarization or effects similar to a bioelectric isolation. For the first hypothesis we considered essential the role of the neurointerstitial duality: neuronal alteration induces glial modifications and viceversa.
As a first step we made a retrospective study in our collection of histologic samples.

## MATERIAL AND METHOD

We have been selecting from a number of 2913 sudden deaths that occurred among 1973-1974 (a time span of 12 years) 686 cases that interested persons aged from 0 to 40. Among these we reconsidered in 141 cases the gliosis phenomenon; this 4,8% from all sudden deaths and 20,5% from those occurred to the cases among 0 and 40 years. In these 141 cases we found sucklings, children and young adults that had significant glial alterations. At that time, in spite of the significant high incidence of these alterations at younger age (2,5 percent), we did not regard them as having possible interference with the thanato-generating syndrome.

## RESULTS

Early observations emphasized that in many cases the death was considered functionally caused or due to incipient diseases; nowadays, considering the morpho-physio-pathologic aspects we could not sustain the same opinion. Anyway such alterations could not satisfactory explain the cause of the death. In 20 cases we found the SIDS and the Pokkuri syndrome markers. Our retrospective study developed in a period in which these two syndromes were still debatable, has been encouraging. Further, following the WHO methodology we observed systematically the cases of SIDS, Pokkuri syndrome, and other deaths that occurred at youth and that had no relevant cause. The case of a 13 year old girl allowed us to unravel a thanato-generating syndrome due to a cardio-respiratory arrest through the disfunction of the CNS's vital centers and consecutive to a pericapillar and perincuronal gliosis mainly located in the cerebral trunk. Similar findings occurred recently in the case of a 20 year old female.

B.C., aged 13, while at school passes a trip of paper to a class mate, she is seen by the teacher, lays her head on the desk and dies. Her medical record from the Chidren's Neuropsychiatric Center reveals a blackout that has occurred two years before and yet another two ones on a few months after the first; On this last occasion she felt sick, dizzy and was consequently admitted to hospital. She was 11 years and 8 months old at that time and the results of the investigation went against the diagnosis of epilepsy. An EEG with high incidences of the delta and the tetha rhythm, by comparison to the age of the patient, hyperactive through hyperpnea on a diffuse irritative background; the same aspect after being activated with Ahypnon. Her psychological profile shows her as being sensitive structured, with emotional liability and socially isolated. QI = 77. EEG control after one month was normal, so the patient's parents felt reassured and they did not see the doctor again. After two years, interval during which no other fits occurred, the instant death befalls her. The final diagnosis was:

1. Conversion type of neurotic reaction
2. Instrumental disorders.
3. Poor to normal intellect.

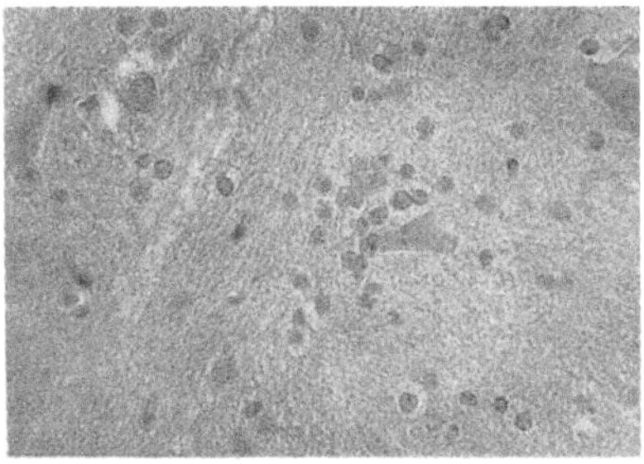

Pict. 1

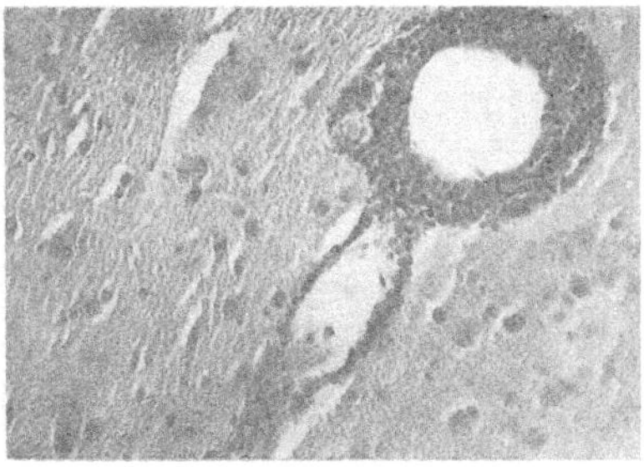

Pict. 2

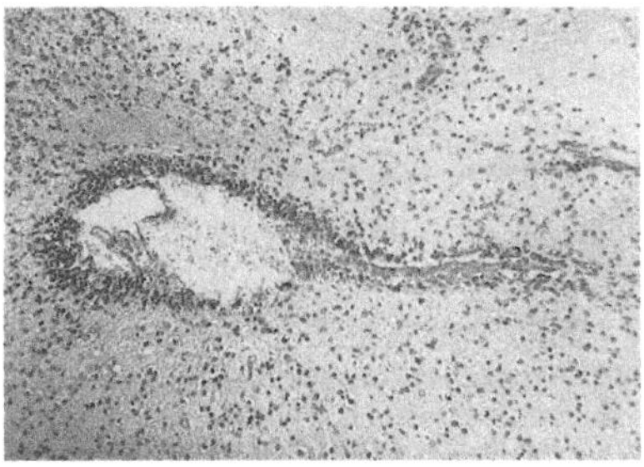

Pict. 3

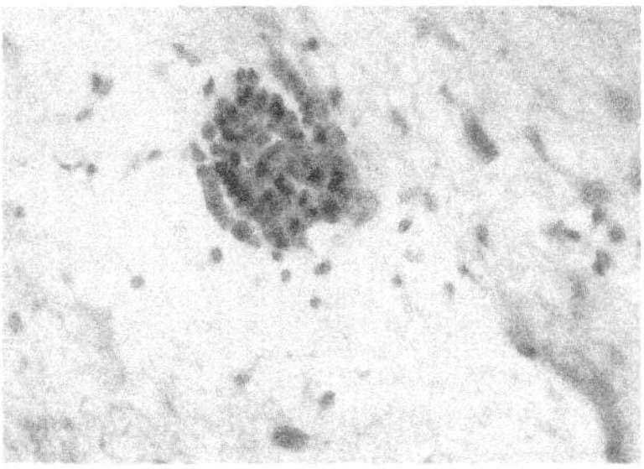

Pict. 4

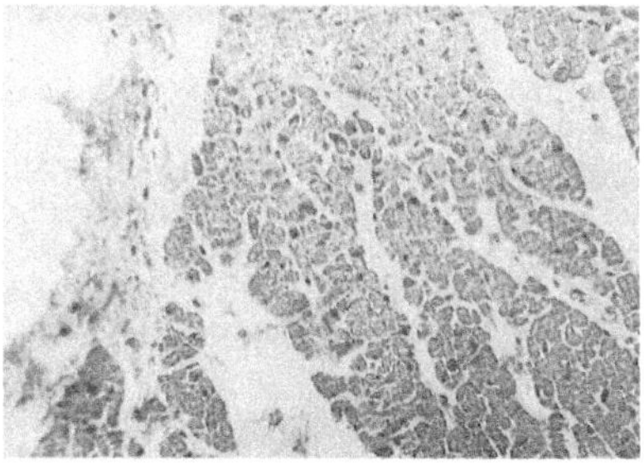

Pict. 5

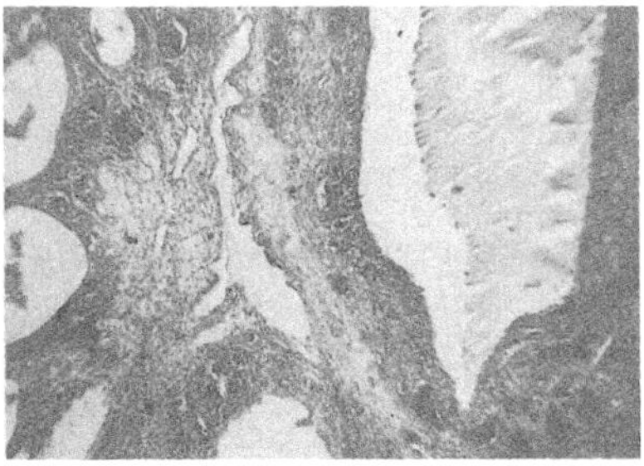

Pict. 6

The medico-legal report supplies the following highly significant macroscopically data: soft areas scarcely evident, longiline type, cerebral stasis and edema, moderate thymus hypertrophy, the hypertrophy of the lymphatic ganglion system, the hearth slightly diminished "in drop-pattern", with a moderate decrease of the transparentness of the mitral valve, splenic hypertrophy, a very clear ovarian polychistosis. The thorough toxicological investigation rules out intoxication. The seriated microscopically analysis of the neuroendocrine system and of all the internal organs makes evident the following: pericapillary, perineuronal, glial hyperplasia in a few areas with a "mufle" configuration of the perivasculatory glial, lesions which are diffusely present in the cerebral hemispheres'white matter, the basis nuclei, quadrigemenal tubercles, the cerebral trunk. (see pictures 1-4) We may also notice the hemorrhage micro-foci in the neurohypophisis, edema and pulmonary

hyperemia, diffuse bands of sub-endocardiac (pict. 5), lymphatic foliate configurations with moderate hypertrophy of the germinative centers, polychistic ovarian degeneration. (see picture 6)
L.M., age 20, collapses (April 1994) in obscure conditions and looses consciousness; she survives 9 days in deep coma with major respiratory disorders compilated to bronchopneumonia. Her pathologic antecedents are still unknown. The suspicioned cerebral contusion was infirmed by the autopsy. The microscopic investigation of the CNS reveals similar alteration of the nervous tissue as those mentioned above. (see picture 7, 8).

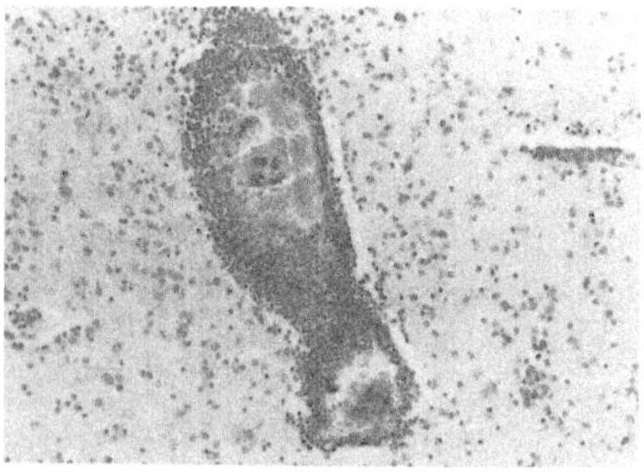

Pict. 7

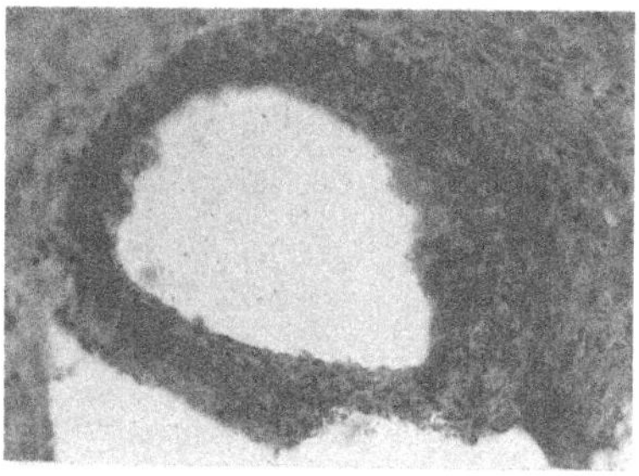

Pict. 8

DISCUSSION OF THE CASE

The most relevant finding in the studied case was the diffuse glial hyperplasia. As it is mentioned in the literature, the diffuse gliosis in CNS might be due to various factors, including *in utero* suffering, infectious diseases, chronic hypoxia, etc. The "functionally caused" instantaneous death of the child, adolescent or young adult may present a similitude and/or a "continuity" with the SIDS of the sucklings, and/or the Pokkuri Syndrome that also has some similar morphological markers.
A certain ethiologic factor was not clearly established in the discussed cases; thus we could not exclude an antecedent silent postvaccinal and parainfectious encephalomyelitis, due to an autoimune allergic mechanism, as it was demonstrated on animals.
No matter how close we were or not to a morbid entity, these cases allowed us to unravel a death-generating syndrome. The polychistic ovarian degeneration that occurred at a 13 year old girl was owing to the gliosis that interested the cyclic commanding center in the hypothalamus (Goldzicher &Axebrod, 1962). This is an argument for the presumed glial affectation of the vital centers from the cerebral trunk. The intimate death-causing mechanism might be the hypoxidosis generated by the diffuse general glyosis which results in severe malfunction of the electrogenesis, of conveying the information among the neurons, as well as the dissociation of the functional interrelations in the central nervous system, that frenates the rhythmic distribution of the nervous influx at the level of the vital centers. We estimate that, in certain releasing conditions (stress, physical effort) or/and -even minor- itercurrent diseases this death-generating mechanism might appear through limitation of the vital nervous centers' homeostasis. This limitation is favorised by the functional dissociation induced by the gliosis that are electric isolating and depolarizing. The "functionally caused" instantaneous death of the child, adolescent or young adult may present a similitude and/or a "continuity" with the SIDS and/or the Pokkuri syndrome.
As we persevered in our attempt to emphasize the ethiological factors of the diffuse gliosis we developed an experiment on 40 white mice. They were divided in 4 categories and were exposed weekly, on three rounds to acute intermittent hypoxia in an atmosphere containing CO about 1/200 - 1/230 or O2 about 4,8-5,8/100 and to citotoxic hypoxia (dibutox injected in dose of 20 mg/kg). Actually we tried to simulate the conditions of transport, suppleness and useless hipoxia. At the moment convulsions appeared the mice were reanimated. After the third round of exposure, 10 mice were sacrificed in about three weeks, and their CNS was microscopically studied. But unsteady glial cell agglomeration other significant alterations were not detected. The category injected with dibutox (2-

izobutyl 4,6 dinytrophenol) showed neurofibrilar fragmentation. To mention that the females in this group became aggresive and had devoured their whelps. At the moment we cannot take the final conclusions of this experiment.

BIBLIOGRAPHY


1. ANDERSON (1985) Pathology - Nervous system, The C. V. Mosby Company, pg. 1873-1874
2. BRISON A. M. (1970) Sudden unexpected death in infancy, Med. J. Australia, pg. 292
3. DAVIDES M. J. (1992) Unexplained death in fit young people, British Medical Journal Nr. 6853, volume 305, pg. 538-539
4. DEMOULIN J. C., TASTREZ M. (1994) La mort subite d'origine cardiaque, aspects anatomopathologiques, Revue Médicale de Liège, vol. XXXIX, nr. 11:489-493
5. DRESSLER M. L. & colab. (1987) Aspecte privind moartea subita la copil, adolescent si adultul tinar, Timisoara Medicala nr. 3, Tom. XXXII:19-24
6. GEORMANEANU M. (1981) Moartea subita si sindromul "aproape pierdut" la sugar, Pediatria, vol. XXX, nr.:213-218
7. GUILLEMINAULT CH. Le syndrome de la "mort subite du nourrison" et des enfants dits "réchappés du syndrome de la mort subite" - quelques résultats expérimentaux. Monographies - Le syndrome de la mort subite et inexpliquée du nourrison, Editées par H-L-VIS, pg. 23-37
8. HUGELIN A. (1989) Etat actuel des connaissances sur les centres repiratoires, Monographies pédiatriques, Editées par H-L-VIS, pg. 13-21
9. IONESCU B., DUMITRACHE C., PLESA E. (1984) Ovarul polichistic virilizant, Ed. Medicala, Bucuresti, pg. 135-138
10. LINDENBERG R. (1982) Anoxia does not produce brain damage, The Japanese Journal of Legal Medicine, volume 36, nr. 1:38-57
11. MARESCH, SPANN (1987) Angewandte Gerichts-Medizin 2 Auflage, Ed. Urban Schwarzenberg, pg. 22
12. MASAHIKO M. (1990) Studies on asphyxia, on the changes of the alveolar walls of rats in the hypoxia, III. The hypoxic state by carbon monoxide Gas. Japanese Journal of Legal Medicine, vol. 44 (3):218-222
13. NAEYE R.L. (1974) Hypoxemia and the sudden infant death syndrome, Science, 1974, pg. 186-837
14. NAITOW MICHIOKI (1981) A consideration on the true nature of sudden infant death, The Japanese Journal of Legal Medicine, vol. 35, nr. 3:151
15. NAVARRO C., DIEMER N.H. (1991) Selective vulnerability in brain hypoxia, Neurobiology, vol. 6, Issue 3:149-182, by CRC Press, Inc
16. POETS F.C., DAVID S.P. (1993) Prone sleeping position and dudden infant death, the New England Journal of Medicine, vol. 329, nr. 6:425-426
17. PONSONBY A.L. (1993) Factors potentiating the risk of sudden infant death syndrome associated with the prone position, The New England Journal of Medicine, vol. 329, nr. 6:377-382
18. PONSONBY A.L. & colab. Thermal environment and sudden infant death syndrome: case - control study, British Medical Journal, vol. 304, nr. 6822, pg. 277-282
19. SOUTHHALL D., SAMUELS M.P. Reducing risks in the sudden infant death syndrome, British Medical Journal, nr. 6822, pg. 265-266
20. TASHIRO KITA, TOHRU O. (1991) Histopathological study on the changes of pulmonary arteries of Guinea-pigs strangulation, Japanese Journal of Legal Medicine, 45 (506), pg. 404-410
21. WHYTE R.K. (1992) First day neonatal mortality since 1935: reexamination of the cross hypothesis, British Medical Journal, nr. 6823, vol. 304:343-348

# NEONATICIDE IN PARIS 1987-1992

Authors: Pierre FOURET[1] and Dominique LECOMTE [2]

1. Service d'Anatomie Pathologique, 4, rue de la Chine, 75970 Paris Cedex 20 and Faculté de Médecine Saint-Antoine (Paris). 2. Institut Médico-légal de Paris and Faculté de Médecine Cochin-Port-Royal (Paris).

There are still cases of neonaticide[1-3]. The aim of this study was to summarize the autopsy findings and to examine circumstances of births in a recent series observed in Paris from 1987 through 1992.

**Methods**

Cases of neonaticide were retrieved from the files of the Institut médico-légal de Paris during the period 1987 through 1992. We then selected cases with an identified perpetrator. The deaths were examined with respect to the following parameters: sex, age, race, height and weight, autopsy and microscopic findings, method of homicide. Data from the investigative reports recorded for law-enforcement purposes were used to evaluate characteristics of the mother. We also studied maternal behavior during pregnancy and delivery.

**Results and comments**

A total of 19 cases were retrieved during the 5-year period. We were able to review the investigative reports in 11 cases.

There were 5 male and 6 female fetuses. The body length (average 50 centimeters, range 45- 56) and weight (average 3 kilograms, range 3.46- 2.46) were consistent with full term pregnancies. Evidence of live birth (respiration or swallowing at autopsy or microscopic examination) was found. There were no major pathological diseases. The autopsy findings were severe multiple injury in 3 cases, asphyxia in 4 cases, and both asphyxia and multiple injuries in 2 cases. One additional case showed severe burns on a large dorsal area. There was no lesions in 1 case.

From the autopsy findings alone, the death could be considered as intentional in 9 cases (strangulation and/or severe multiple injury, burns). The multiple injuries involved ribs, long bones and head and resulted from throwing the baby out of the window or dumping it from a high floor. In 1 of these cases, however, the umbilical cord was around the neck, the baby had been put under a blanket and finally thrown away. It was not clear when the death exactly occurred , although the mother claimed that the baby was dead from asphyxia due to neglect before she dumped the body. There were strangulation marks of in 4 cases. Strangulation was done by hand or by ligature. In 1 case , there was also toilet paper forced into the mouth. In 1 case with marks around the neck and major inconsistencies in the history, however, the evidence of strangulation was finally estimated to be unconvincing. Amniotic liquid inhalation was observed in 1 death due to strangulation. In 1 other case of asphyxia , amniotic liquid inhalation was at first the only identified cause of death until the mother admitted to smothering. In the case with no lesions, the cause of death was deliberate neglect (the baby was left in the cold in January). Finally, the burns were judged to be unintentional in 1 case (the delivery was done in a bidet accidentally filled with hot water). This stresses that the autopsy findings must be related to the circumstances collected at the scene and during the following investigation.

In all but 2 cases, the pregnancy was concealed or denied, although the mother had consulted a general practitioner or an obstetrician in 6 cases. Three offenders had an obstetrical past: 1 had an illegitimate 8-year- old son left to his grandmother in Portugal, 1 had an abortion, 1 had a son with her and had already perpetrated a double neonaticide, which was only discovered at the time of the current killing. All mothers were informed about contraception and abortion. Three of them had used contraceptives: pill, condoms or intra-uterine device. Abortion was not performed because it was too late (beyond the legal deadline in France) in 4 cases, although 1 was informed she could have an abortion in a foreign country. In 1 case, the mother said she could not be away from home for 2 days. Anonymous legal delivery was planned in 3 cases, but the delivery occurred a few days earlier, so that the mother was surprised and had no time to go to hospital. This suggests that women denied an abortion or planning to have an anonymous legal delivery are at risk to commit neonaticide. It is likely that awareness of physicians or family-planning staff and a better education of the mothers could had prevented the killing in such cases.

Usually, the mother was alone during delivery and did not seek help, which is in contrast to the expected attitude of searching for medical attention from a normal mother. In 1 case, the mother was attended by her sister who was also present when the baby was thrown through the window. In 2 cases, the "boy-friend" (actually a pimp) or the offender's mother and sister were considered aware and unhelpful. They were also prosecuted and convicted (1 year imprisonment for the boy-friend). The delivery usually occurred in a bedroom, a bathroom or into toilets at home, at the workplace and in 1 case at an airport. After the delivery, the body was usually concealed in a dustbin, in a plastic bag , a cupboard or behind a wall. It was found by parents, a friend, or persons not related to the offender ( a doorkeeper, a passer-by, a housemaid, a neighbor). In some cases, the body was lying on the sidewalk near the residence, but responsibility for the fetus was denied by the mother sometimes with parents as accomplices. In 1 case, the mother went to the hospital for vaginal hemorrhage, where the pregnancy was finally diagnosed. All these circumstances were highly suspect. At least, there was lack of attention at birth usually presented as the result of maternal inexperience and fear.

The average age of the mother was 21 years (range 15 -26). Nine were unmarried, 1 was married without the knowledge of her parents, and 1 was divorced. All but 2 were French, 1 was from Spain and 1 other was from Portugal. Two were Arabs, 2 were black (Caribbean) and the remaining was white. There were 2 Muslims, 3 Christians and 1 Jewish. One had a record (she had stolen a credit card) and was engaged in prostitution. None had a history of alcohol abuse or illicit drug use, and none was considered insane by the psychiatric evaluation. However, the intelligence level was estimated as less than average in 7 cases. Five women were living with mother and father, and 2 with mother and stepfather. Seven had at least 1 brother or 1 sister (1 had 7 sisters or brothers). The household standard of living was low or very low in 8 cases. Strikingly, 7 mothers had no income at all, being unemployed or at school. Moreover, the remaining 4 had very low income (30,000 french francs per year) or were forced to give their money to parents or their boy-friend. The ambiance prevailing at home was bad in 7 cases with a violent family history in 4 cases. In summary, two types of women could be described: 1) 5 women were teenagers, not very clever, attending school, of modest background, primipare, who had no trust in the parents and panicked at the time of delivery; 2) 6 were older women, with obstetrical past, often a victim under the power of relatives.

Finally, out of the 11 cases 3 were not yet put on trial at the time of our study. Four offenders received a jail sentence (4 months, 6 months, 6 years, and 12 years for the mother who had perpetrated 2 consecutive neonaticides). Except for the 6 and 12 years imprisonment, the sentences were thus relatively light with 2 additional cases receiving only probation orders. This may be due to the circumstances of pregnancy, family context, young age of the offenders, and probably because the jury was more satisfied with counselling the mother than condemning her, even though an offence had been committed. In 2 cases, the defendant was not convicted, because the killing could not be proven.

**Acknowledgements:**

We are indebted to the Judges and staff of the Juvenile Courts of Bobigny, Créteil and Paris for helping us in reviewing the investigative reports of these cases.

**References:**

1. Mitchell EK, Davis JH (1984) Spontaneous births into toilets. Journal of Forensic Sciences 29: 591-6.

2. Funayama M, Sagisaka K (1988) Consecutive infanticides in Japan. The American Journal of Forensic Medicine and Pathology 9: 9-11.

3. Kellet RJ (1992) Infanticide and child destruction - The historical, legal and pathological aspects. Forensic Science International 53: 1-28.

# MANNER OF DEATH - DIFFICULTIES IN DETERMINATION AND IMPORTANCE OF AUTOPSY

Hans Petter Hougen
University Institute of Forensic Medicine, Copenhagen
and Dade County Medical Examiner Department, Miami, Florida.

## INTRODUCTION

The manner of death is usually of greater importance for the judicial system than the cause of death although the two are of course closely linked. It is therefore of great importance that all possible information is taken into consideration before the final determination of not only the cause of death, but also the manner. This is illustrated with three case histories and the importance of autopsy is stressed based on analysis of death certificates and autopsy reports.

## MATERIALS AND METHODS

Case stories from Copenhagen Institute of Forensic Medicine 1993 and Dade County Medical Examiner Department, Miami, 1991 and 1992.

Four hundred consecutive autopsy reports from the Institute of Forensic Medicine, Copenhagen, were studied as follows:

Copies of the death certificates, which were all filled in and signed before the autopsy, were checked for the manner of death (natural, accident, suicide, homicide or unknown). The final autopsy report with the results of different further information, like microscopy, toxicology, neuropathology and microbiology results were checked for the same information and the results compared case by case.

## CASE HISTORIES

<u>Case No. 1:</u>

A 35-year-old male, known to be an alcoholic, was found dead lying prone on the pavement. A considerable amount of blood surrounded his face and upper part of the body. Blood was in his mouth and nose, but no injuries could be found neither to the head nor to other parts of the body. External examination in the autopsy room disclosed a bruise in the back of the head, which was not visible until the head was shaved. The bruise was horizontal 5 x 4 centimetres with a sharp lower edge. The skull had several fractures, both on the top and base and the brain had a traumatic subarachnoid haemorrhage as well as small lacerations and contusions in the right occipital parietal and posterior temporal lobes. The liver was fatty, but without schirrosis and there were no gastric ulcers or varicose veins of the oesophagus. A blood stained board was found near the victim, and typing of the blood showed that it was his.

Case No. 2:
Burned remains of a male were found in a forest. The grass surrounding the body in an area of about 5 $m^2$ was also burnt, but the surrounding trees were unharmed. A pair of shoes (later identified as the deceased's) were nicely arranged side by side and a match box was lying close to the shoes. No fuel container was found. The autopsy showed soot in the respiratory tract indicating that he had been alive at the time, and the toxicological examination showed that his carbon monoxide haemoglobin was only 10% and traces of gasoline were found in the lung tissue. He was identified by means of dental records.

Case No. 3:
A car exceeding the speed limit in a populated area was spotted by the police and by refusal to stop the situation developed into a chase through the city. Suddenly the driver seemed to lose control and crashed into a tree at a speed of approx. 150 kms/h. The driver was killed instantly. The autopsy showed multiple severe trauma to all parts of the body. The alcohol and drug screening was negative. The case was initially classified as an accident, but at the deceased's domicile a note was found, which was interpreted as a suicide note.

RESULTS OF THE PROTOCOL STUDY
A total change in manner of death due to the autopsy results was observed in 53% of the cases (Table 1). This was mainly due to the fact that unknown manner of death is one the major criteria for performing forensic autopsies in Denmark. When the group of unknown manner of death was examined, 80% was determined after the autopsy (Table 1). The autopsy also proved to be of importance in some of the cases where the manner of death was thought to be known before autopsy. In 7% of the cases, where the manner of death had been determined as either normal, accident, suicide or homicide, it had to be changed after the autopsy. This was mainly in cases where presumably natural death among alcoholics turned out to be accidents.

**Table 1. Manner of death before and after autopsy.**

| Manner of death | % |
|---|---|
| Altered after autopsy | 53 |
| Unknown - changed to Known after autopsy | 80 |
| Known Altered after autopsy | 7 |

## DISCUSSION

In case No. 1 natural death was one of the tentative diagnoses at the crime scene investigation. The autopsy results combined with the results of the technical examination of the board, however, clearly indicated that this was a homicide.

The autopsy results and toxicology in case No. 2 were also important to classify the case as suicide, but here the scene investigation also was of great value, especially the position of the shoes, which was indicative of suicide.

Suicides disguised as road traffic accidents is a known phenomenon (1), but case No. 3 would not have been classified as a suicide, if the decedent's domicile had not been searched. Neither the scene examination nor the autopsy could disclose the manner of death in this case.

The final determination of the manner of death and also the cause of death are based on several factors, where both the victim identification including all possible personal information, scene investigation and victim examination are of great importance. However, the protocol study and also two of the three case studies show that victim examination should not be limited to only external examination. The autopsy is of great importance where the manner and cause of death are unknown, but the present results also show that in several cases where the manner of death is thought to be obvious after an external examination, the autopsy gives further information, which can alter the determination of manner of death. The autopsy can also give additional valuable and interesting results regarding the pathology of the deceased. It is therefore **not** recommended to reduce the number of medico-legal autopsies (2), on the contrary high autopsy frequency is a must if we want to give qualified opinions on the cause an manner of death (3).

## REFERENCES

1. Cooper PN, Milroy CM (1994) Violent suicide in South York, England. J Forensic Sci 39: 657-667

2. Reyes Martin A, Gómez Alcalde MS (1994) Autopsy: how much analysis and how much judgement? XVI Congress of the International Academy of Legal Medicine and Social Medicine. Programme p 80

3. Asnæs S, Paaske F (1980) Uncertainty of determining mode of death in medicolegal material without autopsy - A systematic autopsy study. Forensic Sci Int 15: 3-17

# DEATHS RELATED TO IATROGENIC COMPLICATIONS: FIVE YEARS' EXPERIENCE AMONG CORONER'S AUTOPSIES IN A GENERAL HOSPITAL

K.Y.Lam, A.C.L.Chan, P.Dickens. Department of Pathology,
University of Hong Kong,
Queen Mary Hospital, Hong Kong.

The records and request forms of 1,455 consecutive coroner's autopsies performed in Queen Mary Hospital from 1987 to 1991 were reviewed to give a comprehensive view of the deaths related to iatrogenic complications in a large general hospital. 'A history of recent operation or therapeutic/diagnostic procedure' was the indication for requesting coroner's autopsies in 13.1% (191 cases) of all the cases. Among these 191 cases, in only 36(19%) was the cause of death directly related to the medical intervention (rather than natural course of the disease). In addition, there were 6 other deaths related to iatrogenic complications in which the clinicians failed to suspect medical intervention as the cause of death. Thus, a total of 42 deaths related to medical intervention were identified, accounting for 2.9% of coroner's autopsies and 0.3% of all deaths in the hospital. In these 42 cases, the cause of death was related to minor therapeutic/diagnostic procedures in 23 cases (55%), major surgery in 13 cases (31%) and therapeutic drugs (including vaccination) in 6 cases (14%) [Table]. The two commonest encountered medical interventions causing death were insertion of central venous lines (4 cases) and endoscopic retrograde cholangiopancreatography (4 cases). Deaths directly related to iatrogenic complications therefore accounted for only a small proportion of coroner's cases in which the indication for requesting such autopsies was 'a history of recent operation or therapeutic/diagnostic procedure'. These deaths resulted from both simple and complicated diagnostic/therapeutic procedures, and represented known complications of the procedures. The relatively high frequency of deaths related to minor therapeutic/diagnostic procedures (55% of the cases) might reflect their common usage in hospital. It highlights the need for awareness of the risks associated with these relatively simple procedures so that such deaths can be prevented in the future.

## TABLE: DEATHS RELATED TO IATROGENIC COMPLICATIONS

### 1. MINOR THERAPEUTIC/DIAGNOSTIC PROCEDURES

| PROCEDURE | CAUSE OF DEATH |
| --- | --- |
| 1. Sentagen tube for oesophageal varices | ruptured oesophagus |
| 2. sclerotherapy for oesophageal varices | ruptured oesophagus |
| 3. insertion of chest drain | haemothorax |
| 4. ERCP | ruptured duodenum |
| 5. ERCP | ruptured duodenum |
| 6. ERCP | lacerated oesophagus |
| 7. ERCP | peri-pancreatic abscess |
| 8. Percutaneous transhepatic bile duct drainage | haemoperitoneum |
| 9. angioplasty | blocked bypass graft & myocardial infarction |
| 10 angioplasty | failed procedure & myocardial infarction |
| 11. radiofrequency ablation | ruptured right ventricle |
| 12. central venous line insertion | haemothorax |
| 13. central venous line insertion | pneumothorax |
| 14. central venous line insertion | mediastinal haemorrhage |
| 15. central venous line insertion | pneumothorax |
| 16. intravenous line infusion | infection |
| 17. liver biopsy | ruptured liver with haemorrhage |
| 18. fine needle aspiration of liver | ruptured liver with haemorrhage |
| 19. bronchoscopy | laceration of bronchi and fungi infection |
| 20. upper endoscopy | perforation of stomach |
| 21. colonoscopy | perforation of colon |
| 22. peritoneoscopy | ruptured liver with haemorrhage |
| 23. barium swallow | aspiration of contrast medium |

### 2. MAJOR OPERATIONS

| PROCEDURE | CAUSE OF DEATH |
| --- | --- |
| 1. oesophagectomy | anastomosis leakage |
| 2. oesophagectomy | lacerated aorta |
| 3. oesophagectomy | uncontrolled bleeding |
| 4. gastrectomy | stump leakage |
| 5. valve replacement | lacerated aorta |
| 6. valve replacement | lacerated artery |
| 7. ligation of patent ductus arteriosus | ligation of aorta |
| 8. operation for peripheral vascular disease | bleeding from the graft |
| 9. operation for peripheral vascular disease | bleeding from the graft |
| 10. inappropriate laparotomy for abdominal pain | bronchopneumonia |
| 11. laparotomy in a case of acute pancreatitis | perforated duodenum |
| 12. operation for the lumbar spine | spinal cord injury |
| 13. release of contracture | wound infection |

### 3. DRUG-RELATED

| DRUG | CAUSE OF DEATH |
| --- | --- |
| 1. anti-fugal agents | anaphylactic shock |
| 2. anti-anginal drugs | anaphylactic shock |
| 3. corticosteroid | exacerbation of tuberculosis |
| 4. corticosteroid | multiple infection |
| 5. chemotherapy | liver failure |
| 6. vaccination | encephalopathy |

# PLACE OF THE SCANNING ELECTRON MICROSCOPE IN THE TAXONOMIC IDENTIFICATION OF DIATOMS IN THE DIAGNOSIS OF DROWNING

B. LUDES[1], S. QUANTIN[1], N. MESSADDEQ[2], M. COSTE[3], N. NORTH[1], R. BURY[2], M. FABRE[2], P. MANGIN[1].

1 : Institut de Médecine Légale, 11 Rue Humann 67085 STRASBOURG CEDEX, FRANCE
2 : Service Central de Microscopie Electronique, 11 Rue Humann 67085 STRASBOURG CEDEX, FRANCE
3 : CEMAGREF, 50 Avenue de Verdun, BP 3, 33611 GAZINET CEDEX, FRANCE

## INTRODUCTION

Since the diagnosis of drowning is one of the most difficult diagnoses in forensic pathology, a number of tests changes in body fluids such as blood, vitreous humour, cerebrospinal fluid, histological changes have been proposed to confirm this diagnosis.
Most of these tests are considered inconstant and could occur irrespective of drowning and, the only one considered reliable by Auer and Mottonen (1) and Peabody (2) is the diatom test. However, the use of this last method as an indicator of drowning is very controversial, and its reliability is still disputed.
The reliability and validity of the diatom test depend upon the proper techniques used, the exclusion of contamination and the correct interpretation of the results. The diatom test involves a complete taxonomic analysis of the diatoms recovered from water samples and from the organs of the victims.
The scanning electron microscope (SEM) is described by Pachar and Cameron (3), as a simple and rapid method for processing organ and water samples for identification and classification of diatoms.
We describe the method of processing the samples and discuss its accurateness as routine laboratory test.

## MATERIAL AND METHOD

*** Water samples :**
Samples of water from the site where the body was found or where the immersion probably occurred are collected in clean containers as well as stones, found in the water in order to collect attached diatoms by scraping. After a overnight sedimentation, the gross volume is decanted, the remainder is centrifuged and cleaned by incubation in hydrogen peroxide (130 vol %) at 80°C for 12 h. After three rinsings with diatom free distilled water a finalspin at 3000 rpm produces a pellet. This pellet is air dried and examined under dark field microscope to determine if diatoms are present. If there are diatoms, 100 µl of the pellet is transferred onto a coverglass, air dried, and coated with a conductive gold layer and examined under S.E.M.

*** Organ sample :**
During autopsy, blocks of 10 g of lung, liver, kidney and brain tissues were removed without contamination and minced with scissors.The tissue strips were then dropped into Becher flasks (50 ml) and boiled in twice the volume of concentrated analytic nitric acid under a fume hood during 40h. After 5 to 6 rinsings with diatom free distilled water a final centrifugation (3000 rpm for 15 min) produces a pellet. The precipitate (100 µl/slide) is transferred to round coverglasses (0.8 cm diameter) using a disposable micropipette, air dried for a few minutes. Then the coverglasses are coated with a conductive gold layer and examined under the SEM.

## RESULTS

Examples of centric diatoms recovered from organ samples of immersion cases are shown in fig. A and B. Details of the frustules are very important for the identification and could only be recorded by S.E.M.

**Legend of the figures :**

**A:** *Melosira granulata* (S.E.M)

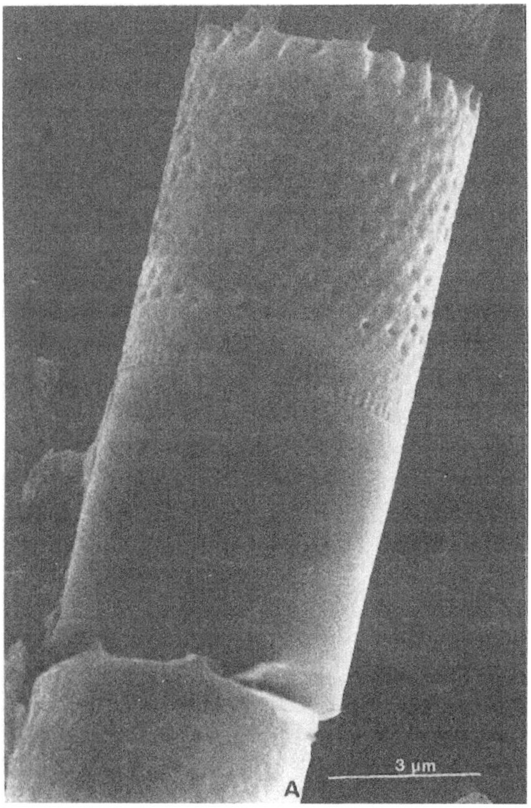

**B:** *Melosira granulata* (light microscope)

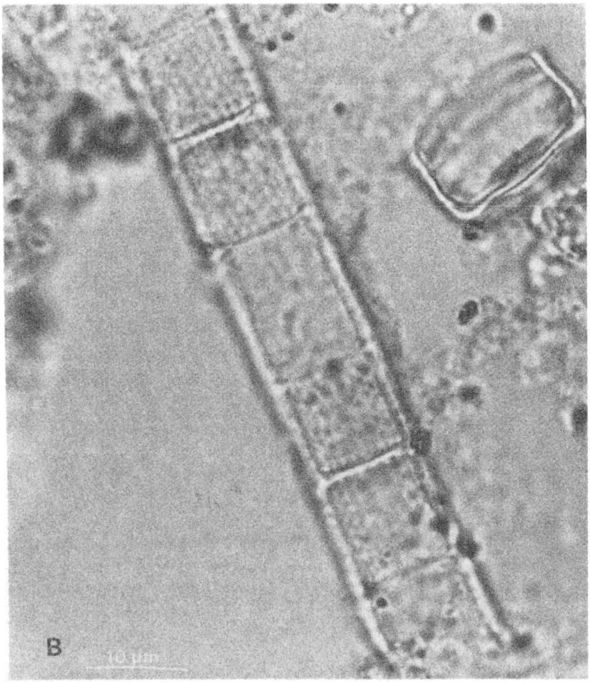


## DISCUSSION AND CONCLUSION

The described extraction method could sometimes alter the morphology of noncentric diatoms and allow the study of both water and organ samples. Light microscope examination seems in our hands accurate enough to give a quantitative analysis of the diatoms and in most cases for taxonomic diagnosis in the case of noncentric diatoms. This examination is also easier and less time consuming.

For centric and small diatoms which are extremely difficult to find with the light microscope, the examination of diatoms under SEM is probably the most effective technique to facilitate their identification, the photographic record and the taxonomic analysis. In fact the details of the frustules which are very important for the identification can only be recorded by SEM. However, qualitative diatom analysis is more an exercise for the expert diatomologist rather than a routine laboratory test.

## REFERENCES

1. AUER A, MOTTONEN M (1988) Diatoms and drowning. Z Rechtsmed 101:87-98
2. PEABODY AJ (1980) Diatoms and drowning : a review. Med Sci Law 20:254-261
3. PACHAR JV, CAMERON JM (1992) Submersion cases : a retrospective study 1988-1990. Med Sci Law 32:15-17

# CEREBRAL EMBOLISM AFTER AN ABDOMINAL TRAUMA. CASE REPORT

*Magalhães T; Carneiro de Sousa MJ; Pinto da Costa J; Hamonet Cl*

Medico-legal Institute, Faculty of Medicine, Biomedical Sciences Institute "Abel Salazar", University of Oporto; Faculty of Law, University Portucalense "Infante D. Henrique"; Faculty of Medicine, University of Paris XII;Henri Mondor Hospital, Creteil; Jardim Carrilho Videira 4000, Porto, Portugal

## INTRODUCTION

The complexity of the medico-legal evaluations can become worse if questions of causality and medico-liability are raised together. The authors present one of these cases.

## CLINICAL HISTORY

A 52-year-old man was the victim of a road traffic accident (15 May 1991), resulting in a splenic and diaphragmatic laceration.
There was a previous history of hypocoagulation with warfarin (INR 3.5)(*) because of a mechanical mitral prothesis ("Maqui") since 1990.
Due to the trauma he underwent a total splenectomy and repair of the diaphragmatic laceration. So, the warfarin had to be suspended and treatment with heparin (5000 U SQ q12 h) was initiated.
Five days after the surgery, the heparin treatment was interrupted and warfarine resumed. On the seventh day he developed a cerebral embolism with motor aphasia and right hemiparesis. The embolic origin was confirmed and the heparin therapy (full dose) was resumed.
This case had a Civil Legal process and the question was the traditional evaluation of the damages (temporary and permanent disability). The victim's damage was also evaluated in a three-dimensional perspective (lesion, function and handicap) as we use at the Medico-legal Institute of Oporto:
1.Lesions - Loss of the spleen and cerebral left infarctus.
2.Functions - Slight/medium difficulties (slowness and discomfort / medicinal and/or technical help) concerning manipulation and prehension with the right hand, control of the urine, sleep, vigilance, temporal and space orientation; important difficulties (human assistance in treatment or complement) for oral communication, writing, memory and emotional behaviour; sexual incapacity.
3.Handicaps - Total dependence on a third party to perform a great number of normal activities. Aid of a psychiatrist in order to help in his emotional and social life; permanent total work disability.

## RESULTS

1.Medico-legal conclusions:
a)Causality between the road traffic accident and the loss of the spleen;
b)Causality (although indirect) between the road traffic accident and the cerebral embolism;

---

(*) $INR = \left(\frac{\text{Patient PT}}{\text{Normal PT}}\right)^{ISI}$

IRN - International Ratio
ISI - International Sensitivity Index
PT - Prothrombin time

c)Prejudices:

1.Permanent total work disability;

2.Permanent incomplete disability (80%) for the daily life;

3.Pain and suffering: degree 6 (ascendent scale of 7 degrees);

4.Cosmetic injury: degree 2 (ascendent scale of 7 degrees);

5.Loss of amenity: degree 3 (ascendent scale of 5 degrees);

6.Dependency on a third party for the great majority of normal activities, social and emotional life (woman, medical doctor, psychologist and physiotherapist);

d)Medical liability.

2.Judicial resolution (sentence):

a)The accused should give 1/10 of the expenses and corresponding compensation due to the absence of work capacity, mental injuries and the expenses for treatments and transportation (concerning the loss of the spleen);

b)The accused should also give half of 9/10 of the compensation costs, corresponding to the lack of work capacity, mental injuries and expenses due to the treatment and transportation (concerning the cerebral embolism);

c)The expenses for the third party should be paid in 55% by the accused;

d)The insurance company pays for the accused in relation to these two previous points;

e)The accused was convicted, for the crime of corporal offense by negligence, to 60 days in prison or a fine;

f)The accused lost his driving licence for a period of 60 days.

## DISCUSSION

1.**Causality between the road traffic accident and the cerebral embolism:**

a)The cerebral embolism is not of traumatic origin, but the spleen excision increases the risks of thromboembolism[1,3,4,9];

b)The previous state could explain the appearance of the cerebral embolism (we know that 10% of embolisms appear in patients with heart valvular prothesis[2]). However, the hypocoagulation with warfarin, decreases the risk of embolism among the patients with mitral valvular prothesis, around 0.5%/year[4], so, the probability for this occurrence was only of 0.5%/year, if the traumatism did not happen;

c)An incorrect hypocoagulant therapy can lead to embolism. When a patient with warfarin is operated, it is necessary to change this medication for heparin in a prophylatic dose. After the surgery it is necessary to begin the anticoagulant therapy again, which means to continue with the heparin until the warfarin is efficient. In this case this did not happen and the patient stayed for 3 to 4 days without protection of the anticoagulants.

2.**Medical liability**

There was a case of medical liability. However, the legal representative of the victim, his wife, who is a nurse, declared that the situation was of medical malpractice, but she did not want to accuse the medical doctors involved in the case.

The absolute medical secret is an utopia, because life in society has his obligations and puts a conflit between the interest of the patients and the Justice of the State[8]. As medico-legal experts the doctors have the obligation to inform the Public Prosecutor of the fact.

3.**Judicial resolution**

The experts, according to the Common Law (article 601° Civil Procedure Code)[5], should answer to the different questions asked by the parties involved. However, these questions are not enough to describe the totality of the damage[7]. The task usually gives priority to the numbers, having as main points four elements: temporary disability, consolidation, permanent disability and mental injuries.

The type of examination that we follow at the Medico-Legal Institute of Oporto is much more like the modern task, giving priority to the proof. We consider the following points:
a)to establish the victim's previous state;
b)to analyse the full documentation of the victim;
c)to report all the medical acts performed after the accidents as well the surgery and medical care;
d)to establish the causality between the consequences and the accident;
e)to indicate the normal period of time of inactivity due to the lesions;
f)to indicate the pain and suffering of the victim;
g)to examine the victim and describe the consequences (lesions, function and handicap);
h)to describe other relevant facts.
However, in Common Law the judge evaluates freely the medico-legal report and establishes his conclusions but he is limited by the task (article 661° Civil Procedure Code)(5). As in this task, the problem of the previous state and also the medical liability, were not in discussion, the judge did not value all the information given by the medico-legal report and made his own conclusions that have prejudiced the victim.

## CONCLUSIONS

1.The integral compensation of the damage in Common Law demands a complete and personalized medico-legal examination and report;
2.However, the same law (by the type of tasks and limits imposed on the Judges), creates difficulties in the practical application of this norm, as happened in the present case.

## REFERENCES

1.Andreas AE, Albert S (1993) Current Problems in Surgery Mitral Valve Replacement, XXX(6):575-577
2.Aronow WS (1991) Etiology and pathogenesis of thromboembolism. Herz 16(6):395-404
3.Brito R, Esteves A Bastos J (1982) Afecções cardiovasculares e doentes esplenectomizados. Jornal do Médico 109:433-435
4.Cardoso V (1980) Cirurgia conservadora das lesões esplénicas. Jornal do Médico 104:977-979
5.Código do Processo Civil (1986) , Livraria Almedina, Coimbra
6.Hadengue A (1980) Séquelles des splénectomies. In: Dérobert L. La Réparation Juridique du Dommage Corporel. Flammarion Médecine - Sciences, Paris, Chapitre 44:718-793
7.Oliveira Sá F (1992) Do Panorama em Portugal. In: Clínica Médico-Legal da Reparação do Dano Corporal em Direito Civil, APADAC, Coimbra, P 69-70
8.Pinto da Costa J (12.1.1994) Deontologia e Sigilo Profissional, Comunicação, Maternidade Júlio Diniz
9.Taveira Gomes, Magalhães T (1992) Avaliação do dano corporal em traumatizados do baço. Boletim Medicina Legal Toxicologia Forense VI(1):73-78

# ABOUT FORENSIC PROBLEMS OF POST-MORTEM EXAMINATIONS IN SEINE-SAINT DENIS (PARIS NORTHEASTERN SUBURB)

B.Marc, J. Varnier, P. Zillhardt, M. Soutoul, B.Richard, F. Boubrit, N.Richard, M.Dubaele, C.Padonou et M.Garnier

**Urgences médico-judiciaires, Hôpital Jean Verdier, AP-HP, avenue du 14 juillet, 93143 Bondy Cedex , FRANCE**

French Civil and Penal Procedure Codes require a police officer or a public prosecutor to investigate deaths if the police are aware of violent, criminal, suspect or unknown causes of a death or if a retrieved body needs to be identified. The police officers need to inspect the scene of the death helped by a medical doctor to explain appearances of the body and the circumstances of death. For that purpose, a medical doctor may be required by the police or the justice authorities to assist , using penal procedure facilities.Commonly in those circumstances, the required practician is the nearest and is often poorly experienced in the matter of death examination and certification.

In order to offer what is required by the justice in these cases, the Emergency Forensic Unit (EFU) of the Jean Verdier hospital in the Paris suburb has extended its activity to death examination. This emergency forensic unit is based at an university hospital centre to the north-east of Paris. The population concerned is more than one million, half the inhabitants have heavy socio-economic problems and large immigrant population (North Africans, West Africans, Yugoslavians mostly ) and a high deliquency level including drug addiction especially amongs young people .

During 1993, our unit has realized 6622 forensic clinical examinations of living persons for the whole Seine-Saint Denis department population and 436 forensic examinations of death either at the death or crime scene, either at hospital or in one of the department district morgues.

Death examination compared to the global activity has increased from 208/2363 in year 1991 and 306/4475 in year 1992 to 436/7058 in year 1993.These examinations were made at any time of day or night and any day of the year by a team of forensic practicians trained in forensic medical examination at a university medical unit.

The 436 forensic examinations of death realized included investigations of deaths, examinations of scenes of death, external examinations of homicide victims and scene of crime examinations, examinations of traffic accidents victims (drivers, passengers, pedestrians,...), forensic examination of death at work place, a.s.o.

## DEATH EXAMINATION PROCEEDINGS

Our death examination procedures include the scene of the death examination, the analysis of all the findings at the scene regarding the body and the research of a detailed history of the circumstances surrounding the death and as much medical information as possible.

As death examination of sudden natural deaths is often done on people for whom emergency care has been realized by medical mobile units, a large and accurate medical information can be used.

The forensic practicioner requires all the information he can get relative to a death in order to determine as correctly as possible the two main points :

- the complete circumstances surrounding the death
- the direct cause of the death.

The information obtained can be very different for each type of death and range from natural death of the elderly so electrical death at work, violent homicide or drug overdose of an opiate addict.

A standardized examination of the body, first with his clothes and surroundings, then completely naked is always realized, even on putrefied bodies.Then, every abnormality of the skin surface or general strucure of the body is described e.g.wounds, contusions, abrasions, lacerations, incisions, fractures, combination of wounds such as abrasion and contusion often seen in pedestrian deaths, gunshot wounds, venous punctures, neck lesions and general signs such as cyanosis, petechiae and external hemorrhages.

Photographic documentation of the cases and injuries is often realized using an autofocus reflex camera to obtain fine color pictures that may be questioned for a second time.Some objects can be retained for further analysis such as syringes, bottles, liquid in a glass or in a venous infusion, ammunition etc.

The examination describes the characteristics of death (rigidity, hypostasis, rectal temperature, putrefaction, etc.) and helps to appreciate the delay from death to examination.

After the complete external examination, **body fluids** are sampled for toxicological analysis on blood, urine and vitreous humor if possible. Further sampling can be done ( vaginal sample, gunshot residues, liquid in suspect bottle or syringe, etc.).

Blood,urine and vitreous humor are sampled in sterile containers, some with lithium heparin for blood alcohol samples and the analysis is realised shortly after the sampling.

Centrifugation is required for blood samples and vitreous humor and samples can be freezed afterwards to allow further controls or quantitative toxicology.

After physical examination and laboratory tests, most of the causes of death are known and the death certificate can be given to the judicial authorities .

The medico-legal autopsy was prescibed (i) for homicidal cases to provide a complete pathological examination to the judge, (ii) for undetermined causes of death (no medical element, putritied bodies, ...), (iii) when sample collection was impossible to certify a suspected toxic or drug abuse death.

For example, the screening for drugs of abuse in urine, realised with the Roche Abuscreen® ONTRAK™ assays, was possible in 12/17 cases.Post-mortem delays were under 24 hours for 12/17 cases and over 24 hours for the remaining five cases.Cocaine was retrieved by means of the Roche Abuscreen® ONTRAK™ assays in 6/12 cases in the sampled urine, cannabis in 7/12 cases and morphine in all the cases.

Furthermore, blood and urine toxicological analysis which were done in the drug, alcohol and toxic related deaths (n=49) showed the following results : alcohol 19/49 cases, benzodiazepines 19/49 cases, barbiturates 10/49 cases, tricyclics 8/49 cases, morphine 4/49 cases, carbamates 3/49 cases, chloroquine 1/49 case.

## DISCUSSION

We have presented the results of a one year survey ( year 1993) of the death examination activity of the Emergency Forensic Unit from Jean Verdier Paris suburb hospital.

Our method, including a rapid toxicological screening (i.e.Roche Abuscreen® ONTRAK™ assays) seems efficient in most of the cases.Its limits are those of the doubt or the impossibility to obtain samples or to realize a good external examination (body remains, putrefaction).

The indications of that method must be observed to always use the same criteriae to demand a forensic autopsy.

The means required for an adequate medical examination system (personnel, staffing, technical and laboratory facilities, instrumentation) can be easily provided , using hospital equipment and Emergency Forensic Unit organization.

That type of organization permits us to offer, in a whole department with a large population, a fonctional and accurate service to the justice in cases of initial death investigations.

We also believe that to these advantages may be added the very low cost, the ability to help police officers and public prosecutors at any time with a short delay and the fact that non-invasive procedures are used which never hinder a complete autopsy if a doubt remains.

The following **guidelines** are followed :

**no medico-legal autopsy is required** and the certification of the death is done
if 1) simple post-mortem examination and correct medical information collection
and 2) clear forensic hypothesis
and 3) accurate toxicological screening (good and sufficient samples, positive detection)

or **a medico-legal autopsy is required** to permit the certification of the death and to give the cause of death
if either 1') difficult post-mortem examination and poor medical information collection
or 2') no clear forensic hypothesis
or 3') no accurate toxicological screening (poor samples or none, negative detection).

Analysis of blood samples is done by common methods. The screening for drugs and drugs of abuse in urine is realised with the Roche Abuscreen® ONTRAK™ assays.
This is a manual and qualitative method using a latex agglutination inhibition method which permits a search for amphetamines, barbiturates, benzodiazepines, cocaine, cannabis, morphine and phencyclidine . The cutoff values of drug concentrations are as follows :
barbiturates 200 ng/ml, benzodiazepines 100 ng/ml, cocaine 300 ng/ml,cannabis 50 ng/ml and morphine 300 ng/ml.

## RESULTS

The **various types of deaths** observed were classified as follows after a death scene examination, a complete external examination of the body and toxicological and other analysis of sampled body fluids: illicit drug abuse related deaths 17,CO intoxications 7, road and vehicular fatalities 39, accidental deaths 2, accidental deaths at work 3, gunshot related deaths (suicidal and criminal ) 46, drug, alcohol and toxic related deaths 49, hangings 42, drownings (suicidal and accidental) 10, train accident related deaths 5, knife wounds reed deaths 5, self stabbing related deaths 2, violence reed deaths 7, fairs from height 24, natural deaths 90, undetermined causes of death 40. For all of these deaths, a toxicological screening was realized including alcohol , suspected drugs or toxic substances used for a suicide and suspected drugs or toxic substances in accidental cases (drugs of abuse, CO, cyanide,...) if necessary.
For homicidal deaths the toxicological screening always included drugs of abuse and alcohol to give some elements on the circumstances of death.

# SOME MEDICOLEGAL CHARACTERISTICS OF HOMICIDES WITH FEMALE VICTIMS

Obradović M., Baralić I., Čukić D., Pražić A., Savić S.

Institute of Forensic Medicine, Medical Faculty, University of Belgrade, Yugoslavia

## INTRODUCTION

Growth of aggression and violence is an important characteristic of life in modern time. Aggression is directed towards self or other people. Recent researches of our population confirm these observations; numbers of suicides and homicides rise progressively, contrary to previous opinions of inverse proportionate relationship between suicide and homicide rates. There is not much information about female victims of homicide in literature. This is why we tried to give our medicolegal contribution to observations of this phenomenon, assuring that results can improve prevention.

Some characteristics of female victims of homicide will be described: age, occupation, marital status, places of origin and living, methods, objects with which homicide is completed and role of alcohol.

## MATERIAL AND METHODS

Records of autopsies of the Institute of Forensic Medicine in Belgrade were examined, with respect to a ten-year-period, 1980-1989. Anamnesis and autopsy were the mainstays of analysis in each case of homicide.

## RESULTS AND DISCUSSION

There were 336 victims of homicide in the ten-year-period, of which 102 (30.4%) were of female sex.

Age analysis shows that majority of victims belong to the fourth decade of life (24.5%), which is followed by the third (22.5%), sixth and second decade, the latter two decades having similar percentages (table 1). There is a large fall in frequencies of occurrence of female victims with ages in the seventh, eighth or ninth decade. Domination of the third and fourth decades of life in age structure of female victims of homicide is associated with reproductive and generative activities with jealousy, emotional problems, disagreements and confrontations between spouses etc.

There was no significant statistical difference between numbers of victims from urban and rural areas.

As far as occupation of victims is concerned, a great majority of them were housewives, followed by manual workers, clerks etc., indicating that housewives were with the highest risk.

The married women had the highest proportion (52.9%) and were followed by the singles, divorced, widows and engaged (table 2). The high proportion of the married indicated importance of impaired relations between spouses as a motive for homicide.

Significantly positive blood alcohol level was detected in 12.7% of female victims and 7.8% of victims were alcoholics. It is well known that alcoholism and drunken state have an important role in genesis of a homicidal act. However, this is more obvious in consideration of murderers.

Spiky and sharp mechanical objects were most frequently used in the analyzed cases and were followed by firearms, blunt objects etc. (table 3).

## FINAL NOTES

Obtained results help to describe a female victim of homicides in our population.They may also help social services in planning prevention.

Table 1. Age of female victims of homicide (1980-1989)

| Age | urban N | urban % | rural N | rural % | total N | total % | rate |
|---|---|---|---|---|---|---|---|
| 11-20 | 9 | 17.3 | 1 | 3.8 | 13 | 12.7 | 1.5 |
| 21-30 | 11 | 21.1 | 6 | 23.1 | 23 | 22.5 | 1.8 |
| 31-40 | 12 | 23.1 | 8 | 30.8 | 25 | 24.5 | 2.1 |
| 41-50 | 7 | 13.5 | 5 | 19.2 | 15 | 14.7 | 1.3 |
| 51-60 | 9 | 17.3 | 2 | 7.7 | 14 | 13.7 | 1.3 |
| 61-70 | 3 | 5.8 | 3 | 11.5 | 8 | 7.7 | 1.7 |
| 71-80 | 1 | 1.9 | - | - | 2 | 2.0 | 0.9 |
| 81-90 | - | - | 1 | 3.9 | 2 | 2.0 | 0.9 |
| Total | 52 | 100 | 26 | 100 | 102 | 100 | 1.4 |

Table 2. Marital status of female victims of homicide (1980-1989)

| Marital status | Percentage |
|---|---|
| married | 52.9 |
| not married | 16.7 |
| divorced | 15.7 |
| widows | 7.8 |
| unknown | 5.9 |
| engaged | 1.0 |
| Total | 100 |

Table 3. Methods of committing homicides with female victims (1980-1989)

| Methods of homicide | Number of cases | Percentage |
|---|---|---|
| stab wounds and incisions | 51 | 50.0 |
| gunshot wounds | 21 | 20.5 |
| blunt objects | 15 | 14.7 |
| manual strangulation | 11 | 10.8 |
| funal strangulation | 2 | 2.0 |
| burns | 2 | 2.0 |
| Total | 102 | 100 |

# PERSONAL IDENTIFICATION OF PLICAE PALATINE IN EVOLUTIVE AGE

C.PAGANELLI*, M.FORNACIARI**, L.VISCONTI*, F.DE FERRARI**

*DENTAL CLINIC UNIVERSITY OF BRESCIA-ITALY
**INSTITUTE OF FORENSIC MEDICINE UNIVERSITY OF BRESCIA-ITALY

## INTRODUCTION

Rugoscopy, the study of palatal rugae, represent a method of individual identification and, like finger prints, has a subjective specificity, usefull with person victims of big trumas with extended fragmentation or high temperature action. In these cases, the hard tissues standing near and the umidity of the oral cavity give big resistance to the palatine mucosa and its plicae. So it is possible to proceed to the identification with comparison, even of partial zone of rugoscopic system.

## MATERIALS AND METHOD

The group of subjects studied was selected between the patients treated in the Orthodontic Department of the Dental Clinic (University of Brescia). We extracted patients that were submitted to a recall program for orthodontic reason. We chose gypsum models of 100 patients (53 female and 47 males) aged 10-16 years before wearing an orthodontic appliance. The same patients were investigated after minimum 3 years of orthodontic treatment. From an alginate inpression we obtained extra hard gypsum model to evaluate the rugoscopic formula according to the Santos classification and the Carrea graphical representation. In particular we distinguished the plicae on the basis of morphological aspects in simple and composite ones, dividing both as indicated in the following prospect.

## SANTOS FORMULAE

Simple lines:

| | |
|---|---|
| 1) straight line | 6) forked line |
| 2) curved line | 7) trifurkated line |
| 3) broken line | 8) branched line |
| 4) undulating line | 9) "U" line |
| 5) corner line | 10) anomalous line |

Composite lines:
Two or more combinationes of simple lines.

## RESULTS

No modification of rugoscopic formula was observed even in patients undergone to orthodontic treatment. Particularly the retroincisal papilla, a very characteristic profile, remained unvaried. Absolute individuality of the drawing of the palatal rugae was found.

## CONCLUSION

Our study demostrates, according to the literature, the elevated individual specificity of the plicae drawing and its stability even if the technical inaccuracy of the plicae palatine in an orthodontic model could be considerable; these models are the only disponible data to compare with a cadaver. We can conclude that rugoscopy offers a god opportunity, not to be neglected, between technical aids for personal identification and should be recommended to provide sistematically survey of palatal conformation and to keep these models in appropriate store to permit comparative study.

## BIBLIOGRAPHY

1) ENGLISH, S.F. ROBINSON, J.B. SUMMITT, et AL.: Individuality of human palatal rugae J.of Forensic Sciences, vol.24, n.4, 718-726, 1984.

2) J.U.CARREA : La identification humane por las rugositades palatines. Rev.Ortodoncia, 2, 1937.

3) G.LOMENZO, N.RIZZO, S. SCIABICA :Lo studio delle rughe del palato ai fini identificativi in medicina legale - Atti XXVIII Congresso Nazionale Soc.It.di Medicina Legale e delle Assicurazioni. Parma, 3-7 ott.1983

4) C.BUCCELLI, G. QUAREMBA, C. MATARASSO et Al.: Sull'analisi computerizzata delle impronte palatine per l'identificazione - Atti XXVIII Congresso Nazionale Soc.It.di Medicina Legale e delle Assicurazioni. Parma 3-7 ott.1983.

5) G.M.MARINO, F. NOTTURNI, C.SFERRA:Studio sulle pliche palatine sui gemelli Atti XXVIII Congresso Nazionale Soc.It. di Medicina Legale e delle Assicurazioni. Parma 3-7 ott.1983.

# A CHILD ABUSE BY ANORECTAL PENETRATION - A CASE REPORT

F. Paysant[1], B. Ludes[1], F. Becmeur[2], A. Tracqui[1], S. Fink[3], P. Mangin[1]

1. Institut de Médecine Légale, 11 rue Humann, Strasbourg, France
2. Service de Chirurgie Infantile, Hôpitaux Universitaires de Strasbourg, France
3. Service de Pédiatrie Grands Enfants, Centre Hospitalier Général, Haguenau, France

Child abuse is a non rare situation. The reasons why anal abuse is frequent are not difficult to understand. In fact, the anus and the rectum are distensible muscular organs which permit containment of the penis even in small children.
At all ages there is surprisingly little disturbance of function following anal abuse ; constipation, diarrhea, or incontinence are unusual. In the series of Hobbs (3), physical injury resulting from anal penetration was commonly found when routine examination of respected abused children was undertaken.
The medical examination of every child where symptoms, signs, or situation raise the possibility of abuse or neglect must include anal inspection (4,2).
In these cases, there are no absolute criteria for diagnosis of sexual abuse, the cases included a spectrum of certainty ranging from complete proof ( statement by child, admission by abuser with corroborative physical and forensic evidence) to lesser degrees of certainty for example genital wart infection, with evidence of disturbed family relationships or behaviour disorders in child.

## CASE REPORT

A two years and four months old little girl was brought by her mother to the pediatrics department.
The child was complaining about anal pain, and the mother explained that her daughter had been looked after by the man living with her the day before .
After the examination, a few wounds and bruises at the legs were noticed. On the head some lice were found, and the ears were dirty.
The skin of the perianal area was painted with eosine masking some very important anal wounds. It was impossible to make a serious examination in good conditions, therefore it was decided to make a protoscopic examination under general anaethesia in order to visualize the overall lesions.
It allowed us to notice :

- a very important skin thickening, with permanent skin changes of the anal margin
- an eversion of the anal canal
- a large opening of the anus, with healing lesions at 2 and 9 hours
- tears and wounds of the anal mucosa measuring 5 cm long
- some haemorrhages of the anal mucosa, located on the back wall.

The testing of the anal sphincter showed an atony.
The genitalia examination found some bruises on the vulva.
Anal swabs were taken during the examination.

During the hospitalization, the girl was examined by a pedopsychiatrist, who noticed: " Child, sad, passive, very attentive to her close environment which could attest repetitive sexual assaults". The psychiatrist's examination is in accordance with our clinical findings.
During the examination of the forensic samples, spermatozoa were found on the nappies worn by the child the day of the examination.
The assailant questioned by the police confessed the rape by anal penetration.
The interest of this case is the concordance of the clinical findings, the psychiatric examination, the forensic sample examination and the police inquiries. Futhermore, the circumstances are in accordance with those described by other authors (3).

In preverbal children, statement of the child cannot be obtained and therefore, the diagnosis has to rest on physical evidence such as signs of genital or anal damage are of great importance.
The anal examination must be a routine part of overall pediatric assessment of the child suspected of abuse (1,3).
For some authors (3) the anus is inspected with the child lying on the left side on a couch with hips and knees flexed and with a pillow under the head ; when the child is very young, on his mother's knees. The child must be relaxed in order to achieve a satisfactory examination. In this position, the buttocks are gently separed with both hands, without exerting traction on the anus. During this time the examiner may become aware in some children of external venous engagement. Also localized gentle traction on the anus allows clear visualization for fissures and an assessment of the tone of the anus.
If there are some typical signs of abuse, we do not recommend digital rectal examination to assess the grip of the anal sphincter which is said to reduce following abusive penetration. We have avoided this technique, not wishing to violate the child further and certainty not recommend routine instrumental examination. These investigations should be performed under general anaesthesia. Appropriate forensic and bacteriological swabs as well as photographs should be taken.
As some of the physical signs are dynamic, photographs must also be interpreted along side the examining doctor's report.

The differential diagnosis includes accidental injury (penetration extremely uncommon), laxity due to neurological disease (sipa bifida), rectal tumor, chronic severe constipation, post mortem anal dilatation.
Accordingly to the follow-up work of Hobbs and Wynne (1989), it is possible to reassure in every case of anal abuse that the child's anus will return to normal and that there will be no permanent damage. The follow-up examination to check an healing is a futher reassurance to the children.

A) Lichenification
B) Anal margin tears
C) Rectal mucosa tears

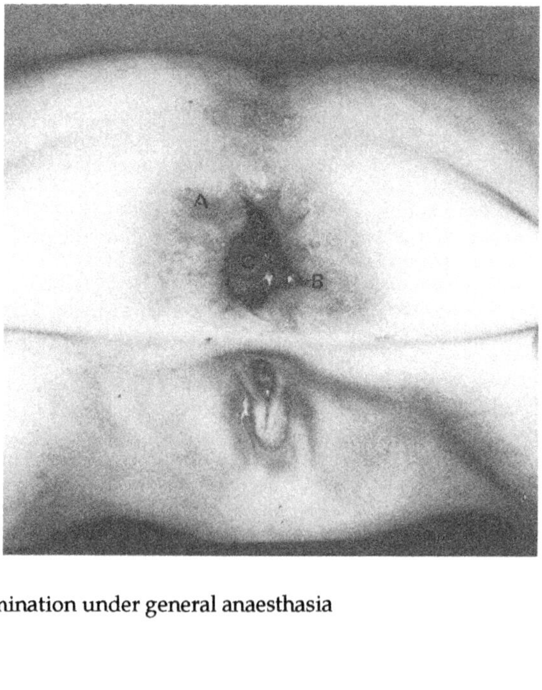


Examination under general anaesthasia

HOW TO DEAL WITH ANAL SEXUAL ABUSES:

1) It is necessary to decide an early hospitalization. A multidisciplinary team (pediatrics, surgeons, psychiatrists and forensic pathologists) is very important to deal with such cases.

2) A general examination is essential to search wounds and bruises, and to estimate the body and the clothing hygiene. It is necessary to estimate the growth development. The physician must proceed to an Xray and an ocular examination of the child.

3) A very early and detailed examination of the anorectal area must be carried out. Sometimes a protoscopic examination under general anaethesia is necessary to show all the lesions.

3) Sexually transmitted diseases (S.I.D.) must be searched (H.I.V., hepatitis B and C, syphilis, gonococcus, chlamydiae).

5) A collection of the forensic samples :

- to seize the clothes, the underclothes and the baby's nappies ;
- to swab the anus, the rectum and the vagina.

6) A examination by the pedopsychiatrist is very important to estimate the psychologic shock of the abuse and to help the child face this shock.

7) Notification of the assault should be addressed to the local authorities (social workers or public prosecutor). In France, child abuse is a derogation from the medical secrecy law.

8) After magistrate instructions, it is necessary to collect blood from the suspect(s) and to carry out DNA fingerprints to identify the author of the assault(s).

CONCLUSIONS

Anal abuse of boys and girls of all ages, from babies to teenagers is one part of the whole spectrum of sexually abusive behavior toward children. A greater awareness and willingness of physicians to examine and evaluate physical findings of anal examination would be a major step forward in the detection and presentation of this major form of child abuse.

BIBLIOGRAPHY:

1. Bras PM, Alengrin D, Rougé D, Arbus L (1985) Les sévices sexuels à enfants. Etude médico-légale et criminologie. Le Concours Médical 107(40):3777-3784

2. Eckert WG, Katchis S, Donovan W (1991) The pathology and medicolegal aspects of sexual activity. The American Journal of Forensic Medicine and Pathology 12(1):3-15

3. Hobbs CJ, Wynne JM (1989) Sexual abuse of english boys and girls : the importance of anal examination. Child Abuse & Neglect 13:195-210

4. Manser TI (1992) The result of examination of serious sexual offences : a review. Journal of the Royal Society of Medicine 85:467-468

# A POSSIBLE MISTAKE BETWEEN AN ENTRANCE HOLE AND A FISTULE ORIFICE

***AM Perez-Cao*, JV Montañana**, EA Gutierrez*, E Smith** and C Valero****

* Instituto Nacional de Toxicología. Madrid. SPAIN
** Instituto Anatómico Forense. Valencia. SPAIN

## CASE REPORT

In 1993, a 36 years old man was killed inside a room where several shots were fired. The victim showed two entrance and two exit holes. Furthermore, there was a fifth wound, but it didn\`t follow a clear track inside the body and no bullet was recovered. This wound was located on a swelling place in the right iliac fossa and it had a purulent aspect. It consisted on a round hole of 5 mm diameter with a concentric abrasion around it, 3 mm width (fig. 1). For all these reasons the pathologist thought that it was not a gunshot wound, however he sent it to the laboratory to be examined.

When the wound was examined with the stereoscopic microscope, powder particles, powder soot and metallic particles close to the edges of the hole were detected (fig. 2). Nevertheless, inside the wound the track had no residues. Then, the atomic absorption spectrophotometry analysis was carried out in order to detect the soot metals. Samples around the hole were cut, introduced into propylene tubes, weighted and leached in 10% Suprapure grade nitric acid solution. Lead, antimonium and barium were analyzed in a Perkin-Elmer spectrophotometer mod. Zeeman 3030. Thirty seven ppm of lead and less than one ppm of antimonium were detected, but there was no barium in the sample. We thought of the posibility of the wound being an entrance hole when both, the optic examination and the metallic concentrations were considered.

This discrepancy lead us to contact again with the pathologist who decided to perform an X ray examen. It showed a bullet lodged and embedded inside the forth lumbar vertebral body (fig. 3).

When this sample was cut a full metal jacketed bullet appeared (fig. 4). A neoformation of the bone structure filled the cavity that the bullet had destroyed at the moment of the shooting. With the stereoscopic microscope, this bone neoformation showed a different structure than the undamaged vertebral body, their trabecules were perfectly arranged and were slightly thicker than the normal ones. All this neoformed tissue was completely calcifed and in the adjancent area to the bullet, the bone had a greenish colour, due to the oxide of the bullet. External surface of the vertebra was perfectly remodelated above the neoformation and no callus had been developed.

The bullet was covered by a greenish coat that looked like a salt deposit. Around the bullet was a cavity that contained a blackish and soft material (fig. 5). Starting from this area multiple fistulous tracks ran to the external surface of the vertebra. Excrescences produced by bone neoformation were seen on this surface (fig. 6).

All these phenomena made evident that the bone cicatrization had ended. In this case, it is clear that both, the consolidation and the restoration of the bone, had been completed, therefore the time elapsed from the shot should have been very long, in no case less than six months.

Once this man\`s clinical report was studied, we were able to see that in 1981 he was shot on the right side of his abdomen, causing him a liver fissure and perforations both in the lower cava and in the transverse colom. At the hospital the doctors practiced him a laparotomy and during the postoperative process some important complications came out, consisting in a massive infection and intestinal obstructions.

In 1989 the man presented a fistule on the right iliac fossa, the same that we observed in the body after his death.

## CONCLUSIONS

In order to easily understand the results obtained at the laboratory, it is necessary to know all the precedings and circunstances that surrounded the case. That is why it is essential the communication between the pathologist and police with the laboratory\`s examiner. In this case, the excised wound, in spite of being anomalous, was compatible with a gunshot entrance hole, as for its aspect as for the presence of gunshot residues. However, the pathologist found the wound located over a swelling area but he couldn\`t find a clear track inside the body.

After checking the victim\`s clinical record, there were evidences of an old fistule placed in the same spot. This is how we could conclude that the wound was not an entrance hole but the cutaneous end of the fistule. The presence of residues in its surroundings can be explained by the contamination of the shot that took place in the crime scene.

Therefore, as it can be seen, this was a very estrange happening.

## LEGENDS OF FIGURES

(1) - The wound located on a swelling area. The hole has a diameter of 5 mm and a concentric abrassion of 3 mm wide. It presents an excentric deposit of gunshot residues. (2) - Powder particles, soot and metallic particles surrounding the edges of the hole. The arrows point to powder particles. (3) - Radiography after the victim`s death in wich a full metal jacketed bullet lodged inside the forth lumbar vertebra can be seen. (4) - Lateral view of parasagital section of the vertebral body in wich the full metal jacketed bullet was embedded. (5) - The bullet shows a greenish colour coat on its surface due to the oxide (white arrow). The bone is embedding a greenish substance (blak arrow) and a blackish and soft material filling the cavity between the bone and the bullet is present (6) - Lateral view of lumbar vertebra in which it can be seen a number of fistulous tracks and bone escrescences. A-Anterior. B- Transverse apophysis.

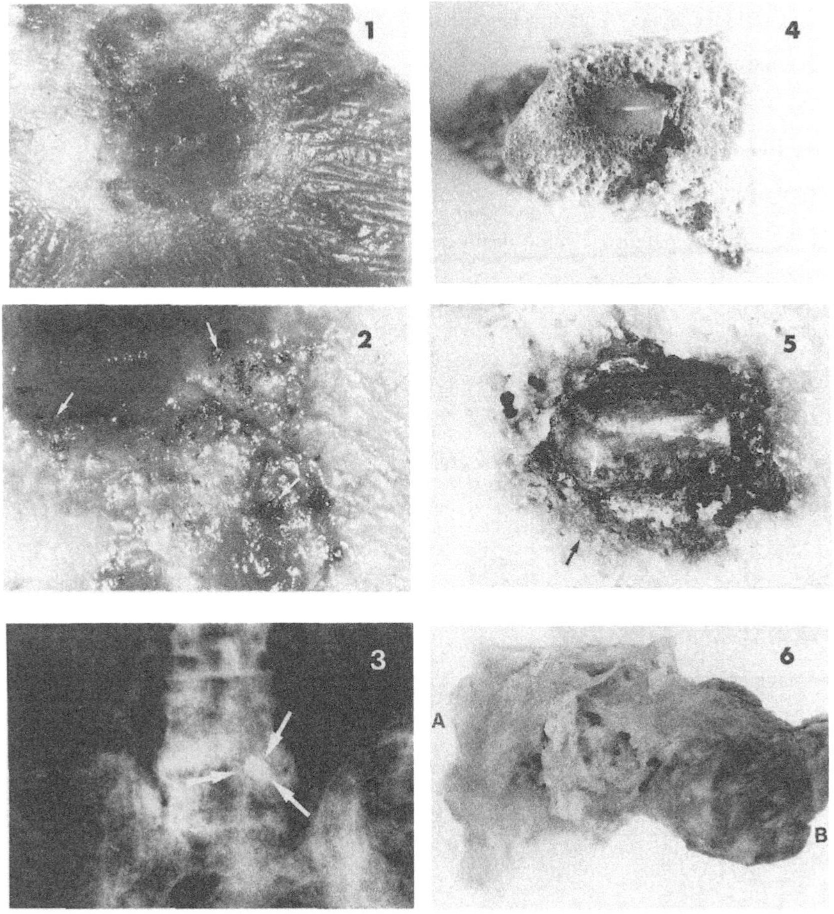

## STUDY OF NATURAL DEATH IN A RURAL AREA OF CATALONIA, ( 1980-89)

PEREZ PEREZ, ROSA MARIA; CAMPS SURROCA, MANEL.
MEDICINA LEGAL Y TOXICOLOGIA. FACULTAD DE MEDICINA.
AVDA. ROVIRA ROURE, 44. 25006 LLEIDA. SPAIN.

The material used for the analysis consisted of the documents of autopsies performed in a rural area of Catalonia (Spain). This area has about 40.000 inhabitants.

There were 37 cases of natural death, accounting for 13,02% of total mortality.

The natural death rate during the 1980-89 period was higher for males than females (3:1), and the commonest causes of death were cardiac and cerebral pathology.

### INTRODUCTION.

In the forensic practise, natural death quite often has to be investigated, since the death certificate could not be signedso they became of judicial interest. After a proper evaluation of the case, by studying antecedents , autopsy findings and complementary investigations their natural character is established.

There are 3 main causes of these deaths:

*Deaths that happen without medical assistance.

*Deaths of patients under medical care whose pathology shows an atypical evolution or whose main cause of death is still unknown by the doctor.

* Sudden death.

### MATERIAL AND METHODS.

We have collected and studied all the natural death cases which occurred in a rural area of Catalonia over a ten year period (1980-89).

Each case gives us interesting epidemiological data : sex, age, marital status, profession, month, year and season when death took place and finally we studied the autopsy document, defining the cause of the death.

### RESULT.

During the 10 year period (1980-89) studied in this rural area in Catalonia a total of 284 cases were registered of which, 37 were considered natural death, 13.2% of the mortalities registered. The average annual incidence of these deaths is 9.25/100.000 in our studied area.

Evaluating all of the epidemiological data we found out that males were overrepresented

(75.67%) compared to females, which means a proportion between the sexes of 3:1.

Regarding the age 30% natural deaths take place during the sixth deacade of life but most deaths occur between the age of 40 to 80, 28, a total of (70%). There were three cases in childhood age, I mean under ten, and a single case in each one of the remaining decades of life.

The average age was 57, the standard derivation 23.37 .

There was a predominance of married people in a little more than a half of the deaths(51.35%) folllowed by the single persons (29.73%), and the rest were vidows.

Regarding professions most had primary activities or belonged to the world of commerce, although the most frequent situation, rating almost 40%, were retired people.

These deaths took place mostly during October. The last term of the year in coincidence with Autumn carried a 35.13% of the deaths. The same number of cases took place during the period between springtime and summer with a little increase in summer.

Among the 10 years studied we have found that the two years 1986-87 cover more cases of natural death (35.1% of de total).

When we looked at the CAUSE OF DEATH in the autopsy document we observed four case where it was not stated. There were only indications of a natural death which eliminates the judicial intervention. From a medical point of view it was not clear in three of the cases since the corpse was found in a skeletal state dating more than three months old, which invalidated a propoer autopsy study. The fourth case was initially considered as natural and then sudden infant death syndrome was established.

The rest of the autopsies show the main pathology that has caused death: 45.9% were caused by cardiac failure, that is acute myocardial infarction, which is the cause of half of the cardiac deaths. Regarding frequency, they are followed by aortic valvular cardiopathy and acute cardiac insufficiency (3 cases each). Two of the cases were considered cardiac collapse and one death was due to papillary muscle rupture of the left ventricle and another one to aortic rupture.

After cardiac death the most frequent deaths were those located at the SNC level, where cerebral haemorrage (70%) was often found, including subarachnoideas. There were also some cases of cerebral thrombosi and we observed a death caused by sudden rupture of a cerebral aneurism.

Referring to the respiratory pathology implied in this report there were three groups with equal frequency, thromboembolism of the lungs, acute edema and acute bronchopneumonia.

Finally when the cause had a gastrointestinal origin there were only three cases: a gastric perforation, mesenteric necrosis and one pancreatic haemorrage.

**DISCUSION.**

In our study the autopsies of natural deaths occurred in 13% of our forensic practice, compared to other studies which point out that these autopsies represent, according to forensic centres, 67% of the practise realized over 30 years, or even the 80% in places like England or Wales.

The epidemiological data of these type of death vary very little in other studies and the proportion of 3:1men:woman remains constant. Also regarding the age the sixth and seventh decades of life one still predominant, an event that coincides with our experience. All the ages of life, even in three cases in pediatric age and one of these cases was confirmed as a sudden death syndrom. The data of the profession also coincided since the primary activities workers predominate.

Deaths were more common in the coldest months of the year.

From the forensic point of view the cause of death is the most important and it is documented in the extensive literature that cardiac causes are the most frequent and among them coronary atherosclerosis is the most common. Acute myocardial infarction comprised 50% of the deaths, in our study, although it can be the 90% of these causes.

Another cause of cardiac origin is the aortic valve pathology, which although it follows ischemic pathology in frequency it is usually regardedas a relatively influential.

When the cause of death is located in the SNC haemorrages are noted both cerebral and subarachnoidal the last one being the most frequent.

In the respiratory pathology any process is noted, although the thromboembolism is the one that appears more often.

In the gastrointestinal pathology there are processes that do not really produce sudden death but they are medical emergencies, and with a proper assistance are not necessarily fatal.

In one only cases was death due to a mesenteric necrosis and it appeared in a child before he was one year old. This way should evaluate other circumstances.

Only one death was labeled as sudden death syndrome (2.7%) of the total natural mortalities).

To periodically check these kinds of deaths carries a great forensic and of course medical-clinical trascendency in order to evaluate the causes of deaths. Although being natural ones, these deaths contribute an important part of the daily thanatological practise, taking into account there is a chance that the growing number of less common causes of sudden death will increase in the following years.

# COMPARISON OF TWO EXTRACTION METHODS OF DIATOMS EXTRACTIONS FROM ORGAN SAMPLES IN THE DIAGNOSIS OF DROWNING

S. QUANTIN[1], B. LUDES[1], N. NORTH[1], M. COSTE[2], P. MANGIN[1].

1 : INSTITUT DE MEDECINE LEGALE, 11 Rue Humann 67085 STRASBOURG CEDEX, FRANCE
2 : CEMAGREF, 50 Avenue de Verdun, BP 3, 33611 GAZINET CEDEX, FRANCE

## INTRODUCTION

The diatom test has been proposed by several authors to provide supportive evidence of drowning but the relationship between diatoms and a diagnosis of death by drowning is very controversial.
The reliability of this test is still disputed. Gylseth and Mowé (3), Schellmann and Sperl (8) and Foged (2) are of the opinion that since diatoms can be found at autopsy in other subjects, they cannot be used as evidence of drowning. On the other hand, Auer and Mottonen(1), consider that accurate diatom counts can, in most cases, discriminate between drowning and non drowning cases especially when post-mortem mutilation or decomposition occurred or following resuscitation attempts. Peabody (7) stressed that the diatom method is supportive evidence of the diagnosis of drowning only when performed by an experienced examiner and following rigorous criteria.
The diatom investigations are performed using proper techniques including exclusion of contamination of both glass containers and reagents and the correct interpretation of the results. They involve a complete taxonomic analysis of the diatoms recovered from water samples and from the organs of the deceased.
We present our experience in comparing quantitative and qualitative diatom analysis using light microscopy of both water taken at the site of drowning and post-mortem tissues samples recovered during the autopsies of **27 bodies** died by drowning.

## MATERIAL AND METHODS

The analyses were conducted on material collected during autopsies of bodies recovered from water (river Ill and canals) in the Strasbourg area. For 27 bodies, the cause of death was the drowning and the post mortem period ranged from 1 to 60 days. We include the tissues of 5 corpses for which drowning was not the cause of death as control samples. Organ samples of both immersion and control samples were divided in two sets : the first was enzymatically digested by the proteinase K and the second underwent chemical digestion with concentrated nitric acid.

### 1) Organ samples

a) Chemical digestion method

Blocks of 10 g of lung, liver, kidney and brain tissues were removed during autopsy without contamination and minced with scissors. The tissue strips were then dropped into Becher flasks (50 ml) and boiled in twice the volume of concentrated analytic nitric acid under a fume hood during 40 h. After 5 to 6 rinsings with diatom free distilled water a final centrifugation (3000

rpm for 15 min) produces a pellet. The precipitate was transfered onto a coverglass using a disposable micropipette.
Under the light microscope, the diatoms were evaluated both quantitatively and qualitatively and the results were compared with those obtained from the known or suspected site of drowning.

b) Enzymatic digestion method
The tissue blocks (10g) were minced and mixed with 500 µl of 10 mg/ml proteinase K (Boehringer-Mannheim) and 100 ml of 0.01 M Tris-Hcl buffer (pM 7.5) containing 2 % SDS. The mixture was incubated at 50°C overnight, a futher 500 µl of proteinase K was added and the solution was incubated for 8 h. After complete digestion of the tissues, the solution was diluted with 100 ml of distilled water and centrifuged at 3000 rpm for 15 min. The upper layer was then removed. The sediment is transferred onto a coverglass and examined under the light microscope.

**2) Water samples**

Two samples of water (100 ml per sample) from the site where the body was found or where the immersion probably occured, were collected in clean containers as well as stones found in the water, in order to collect attached diatoms by scraping. The samples were centrifuged at 2500 rpm for 15 min. and diatoms were cleaned by incubation in hydrogen peroxide (130 vol %) at 80°C for 12 h. After 5 to 6 rinsings with diatom free distilled water a final centrifugation (3000 rpm for 15 min.) produces a pellet. After removing the supernatant the sediment is air dried and examined under the light microscope.

## RESULTS

In all the bodies examined, the chest cavity was closed and there was no direct contact between the immersion water and the lung due to total decomposition of the thorax.
Diatoms were found in 16 lung samples, 9 kidney samples, 7 liver samples and 5 brain samples.
All cases in where diatoms were recovered from the major circulatory organs, diatoms were also present in the lungs and vice versa. In 41 % of the positive lung samples more than 5 different genera and more than 60 diatoms/10 g of tissue were found in 66 % of the samples. The 2 digestion methods gave approximately the same yields of diatoms. The maximum diatom content of samples from closed organs involved 3 different genera and was approximately 15 diatoms/10 g of tissue with both methods.
In the organs of immersed bodies recovered from the river Ill and the canals of the area of Strasbourg, the most common genera identified were *Cocconeis* v. *placentula, Navicula, Frustulia, Cyclotella* v. *dubia, Nitzschia, Melosira, Fragilaria*. These genera were also identified as dominant genera in the water samples.
Similar morphological characteristics were found in the diatoms recovered from water, lung and other organ samples in 10 cases. These cases were considered as positive cases, indicating death by aspiration of water into the lungs.
No control samples showed the presence of diatoms. No diatoms were recovered in samples of distilled water or concentrated nitric acid.

## DISCUSSION

In our case work for which the drowning was the cause of death, we made a positive diagnosis of aspiration of water using the diatom analysis only when the number of diatoms of similar genera was above a minimal established limit in the lungs (20 diatoms per microscope slide) and

inclosed organ samples (5 complete diatoms, with exclusion of fragments). Those findings allowed a sufficient margin for exclusion of sources of contamination.
The chemical digestion procedure used in all the cases showed fragmented frustules which did not allow identification of those diatoms. So, the proteinase K digestion method is the most adapted method in our hands for the extraction of diatoms in organs.
In 10 cases, quantitative analysis showed a large number of diatoms in the lungs and in other organs tested. The diagnosis of drowning by the diatom analysis was not made unless similar genera were identified in both organ and water samples. This drowning group represented 37 % of our small series, which was higher than the 20 % reported by Neidhart and Greedyke(5), and less than the 57.9 % reported by Auer and Mottonen(1) in a larger series.
In 16 cases numerous diatoms were present in water and in lung sample but not in other organs. Since the number of diatoms in the lungs was above the established limit, death by drowning could be assumed but no definitive conclusion could be reached, since diatoms could have entered the lungs passively when the body remained immersed in water under increased hydrostatic pressure.

## CONCLUSION

According to Pachar and Cameron(6), the extraction with concentrated nitric acid could result in significant loss of diatoms during the process. We performed routinely an enzymatic digestion procedure with the proteinase K.
This method is suitable in terms of rapidity and efficiency and less hazardous and pollutive since the number of diatoms found is similar to that with acid digestion.
Thus, in our experience the proteinase K digestion procedure seemed to be the most suitable for extracting diatoms from human tissues and did not require strong acids which are dangerous to deal with and problematic in view of environmental pollution.

## REFERENCES

1. AUER A, MOTTONEN M (1988) Diatoms and drowning. Z Rechtsmed 101:87-98

2. FOGED N (1983) Diatoms and drowning. Once more. Forensic Sci Int 21:153-159

3. GYLSETH B, MOWE G (1979) Diatoms in lung tissue. Lancet 29:1375

4. KOBAYASHI M, YAMADA Y, ZHANG WD, ITAKURA Y, NAGAO M, TAKATORI T (1993) Novel detection of Plankton from lung tissue by enzymatic digestion method. Forensic Sci Int 60:81-90

5. NEIDHART DA, GREEDYKE RM (1967) The significance of diatom demonstration in the diagnosis of death by drowning. Am J Clin Pathol 48(4):377-382

6. PACHAR JV, CAMERON JM (1992) Submersion cases : a retrospective study 1988-1990. Med Sci Law 32:15-17

7. PEABODY AJ (1980) Diatoms and drowning : a review. Med Sci Law 20:254-261

8. SCHELLMANN B, SPERL W (1979) Nachweis im knochen Mark (Femur) Nichtertrunkener. Z Rechtsmed 83:319-324

# NAIL-GUN SUICIDE

N. ROMAIN, B. LUDES, A. GERAUT, A. TRACQUI, P. MANGIN
Institut de Médecine Légale, 11 rue Humann, 67085 STRASBOURG Cedex

Nail-guns are tools frequently used in the industry, particularly in building construction. If they sometimes cause accidents, they're exceptionnaly used to commit suicide. We are going to report such a recent case and compare it with the other cases of the literature.

## CASE REPORT

In february 1993, on a building site, a physician of the emergency service was called to take in charge an injured man. The patient, a 46-year-old man, was unconscious and presented a round right frontal wound with cerebral and blood issue. As soon as he was admitted at the Hautepierre's Hospital, a C.T. scan was realised and showed a right frontal depressed fracture, an intra-ventricular bleeding and the presence of a metallic foreign body in the pineal gland. Despite a surgical intervention, he died a few hours later.
The autopsy, we have performed, revealed :
- two surgical wounds, one hiding the entry site, with a large ecchymosis of the scalp ;
- a subarachnoidal haemorrhage ;
- an attrition of the right frontal and the left temporal lobes ;
- an intra-ventricular bleeding ;
- the presence in the left temporal lobe of a metallic strait nail.

Except the cranio-cerebral lesions no other significant finding was done.
The search of alcohol and drugs in blood and urine was negative.

According to the police investigation, the man was found by his collegues,on his knees, the muzzle of a nail-gun (Hilti TX 36M), whose the grip layed on the ground, pressed against his front. According to his relatives, he did not show any symptoms of depression and no suicide note was found. Nevertheless, his wife declared that he had ingested, the same morning, 8 tablets of Doliprane (paracetamol) and 10 tablets of Aspro (aspirine) although he did not complain.
We think that the hypothesis of a nail-gun suicide is the most convincing. In fact, several arguments plead in this favor :
- the position, in which the man was found, allowed him to neutralise the security system and in this way to fire ;
- the absence, except the cranio-cerebral injuries, of other signs of violence ;
- the preservation of the nail's form while is usually bent during accident by ricochet.

The ingestion, the same morning, of an important quantity of analgesic without any pain may be explained by the premeditation of the act and the fear of suffering.

## DISCUSSION : ACCIDENT, HOMICIDE, SUICIDE

We will exclude of this discussion :
- the injuries due to nails without nail-gun ;
- the injuries by cattle-gun whose functionning is not entirely similar.

I Nail-gun functionning

This tool appeared in the 1950's. It is used for driving nails into rigid materials such as wood, concrete or steel and so is mainly used for construction. Most of them function with powder cartridge. In principle, it is impossible to fire if the muzzle is not firmely applied against the surface to nail or if the angle between the muzzle and this surface exceeds some degrees.

II Accidents

Quite numerous nail-gun accidents have been described. The victims are :
- either the operator himself, usually after a misshandling. All the part of the body can be affected, particularly the limbs.
- or a co-worker or a bystander, usually after the overpenetration of the work-surface or after the ricochet of the nail on this surface. Any part of the body can be affected.
According to S.J. Mc Corkell, after its ricochet the nail is bent except if it is very rigid. To appreciate exactly the nail's form, standard radiographs made in two views at 90° to one another should systematically be performed.

III Homicide

To our knowledge, no case of nail-gun homicide has been reported in literature. However, we can't exclude its use as a weapon for example by firing through a thin wall. V.J.M. DiMaio tell that workers fired tin cans or even rabbits.

IV Suicide

Only seven cases of suicide or attempts of suicide have been reported in literature. The comparative study of these seven cases and our case gives prominence to some similarities.
1°) Sex
In all cases they are men.
2°) Age
All are adults, 26 to 50 year old.
3°) The trade
By their profession, known in 6 cases, these men commonly used this tool. The functionning of this machine to attempt suicide requires a good knowledge of its. In fact one has to press fermely and perpendicularly the muzzle to his body to neutralise the security system in order to fire.
4°) Localisation of the lesions
- cranio-cerebral lesions in 5 cases out of 8
- chest lesions in 3 cases out of 8
All, except one, were fatal.
5°) Nail's form
In the five cases where the nail's form was precised, it was strait, what is, according to S.J. Mc Corkell, against an accident by ricochet.

## CONCLUSION

Using a nail-gun to attempt suicide is exceptionnal but usually fatal. The distinction between suicide and accidental death is sometimes difficult and is based on several arguments. Nevertheless, it is essential because of the medico-legal consequences.

**REFERENCES**

DiMaio VJM, Spitz WU (1972) Variations in Wounding Due to Unusual Firearms and Recently Available Ammunition. J Forensic Sci, 17, 3 : 377-386.

Fekete JF (1981) Suicide by Self-Inflicted Head Injury with Nail (Stud) Gun. A Case Report. J. - Can Soc of Forensic Sci 14, 4 : 188-191.

Goonetilleke UKDA (1976) A Stud (Cartridge) Gun Suicide (A Case Report). Med Sci Law 16, 3, : 181-184.

Mc Corkell S, Harley JD, Cummings D (1986) Accident, Homicide, or Suicide. Am J Forensic Med Pathol 7, 3 : 192-195.

Opeskin K, Cordner S (1990) Nail-Gun Suicide. Am J Forensic Med Pathol 11, 4 : 282-284.

Stanbridge R (1982) Self-inflicted nail-gun injury of the heart and lung : a short report. Injury 14, 3 : 285-286.

Weedn VW, Mittleman RE (1984) Stud Guns Revesited : Report of a Suicide and Literature Review. J Forensic Sci 29, 2 : 670-678.

# Death cases due to gas weapons
## - Autopsy findings and experiments -

**Rothschild MA and Schneider V**

**Institute of Forensic Medicine, Freie Universität Berlin**
**Hittorfstr. 18, D-14195 Berlin, Fax: +49-30-8383684**

In Germany a large variety of gas and warning firearms is available on the free market. You only have to be 18 years old to purchase them. These gas and warning weapons - like starter pistols - are mostly imitations of real weapons, but are produced with less solid materials. All models - and there are about 500 different types on the German market - have a barrier inside the barrel, so that no real bullets can be fired out of these weapons. The ammunition is blank cartridges or tear-gas cartridges, mainly of calibres 8 or 9 mm. As propelling charge black powder or nitrocellulose is used, causing gas pressures between 300 and 500 bar [8].

These gas and warning firearms are usually bought by people who like to collect them as models or for self-protection, and are then loaded with tear-gas cartridges. Since some years gas and warning firearms have been "discovered" by some people as a useful instrument for harming others or themselves.

For this reason some of the gas weapons have been modified: in a suicide case [2] a 63-year-old man connected a steel pipe to the muzzle of a gas pistol and loaded it like a muzzle-loader with two steel bullets. An 8 mm blank cartridge was used as propelling charge. He committed suicide by shooting himself through the mouth. The two steel bullets penetrated the base of the skull and caused lethal injuries of the brain. In another case a 50-year-old man replaced the barrel and the cylinder of a gas revolver with a steel pipe and loaded it with a real calibre .22lfr cartridge. With this weapon he commited suicide by shooting himself in the head, where the missile was found in the brain.

But in most cases gas and warning firearms have not been altered at all and were used with blank cartridges only. Shots with blank cartridges can cause severe and lethal injuries when fired at close range or as contact shots [e.g. 1,2,4-7]. Even without any alteration of the gas weapons, the expanding propellent powder gas of the blank cartridges can cause a penetration of skin and thin bones and result in extensive soft tissue damage when the muzzle of the gas weapon is in contact with the body.

For example in an accident case [4], a 57-year-old man used to carry his gas pistol in the waist between his trousers and his pants. Unfortunately this pistol was in some way triggered while he was riding his bicycle. The man was found dead about ten minutes after the shot was heard. There was a contact shot wound in the right inguinal region and underneath an extensive wound cavity, in which the femoral vein was ruptured totally. The man had died due to loss of blood. In another case a 58-year-old man committed suicide by shooting himself with a gas weapon in the back of the neck [3]. Above the contact shot wound the skin was ruptured laterally for 9 cm. The neck muscles were ruptured and there were haemorrhages in the dura and the cerebellum. In this case the cause of death was due to an air/gas embolism in the right ventricle of the heart.

In a case of homicide with a gas weapon [2] a man pressed the muzzle of a gas revolver to the neck of his 19-year-old wife and fired. By hospitalization there was a small ruptured skin wound on the left side of the neck, which was bleeding severely. Underneath was an extensive wound cavity, which reached to the hypopharynx. After postoperative care under antibiotic treatment, the woman left the hospital against medical advise on the 7th day, and 5 days later she was found dead, due to a massive blood aspiration, which was caused by an abcess displaying the external carotid artery. The arterial wall was destroyed by an inflammation, which was caused by powder particles.

To examine how powerful gas weapons loaded with blank cartridges are, we made various shooting experiments. Using different types of gas weapons and blank cartridges we fired at parts of bodies from different ranges. These parts were heavily injured remains of people whose bodies were dismembered by railway accidents.

Nearly all gas weapons penetrated the skin and resulted in extensive wound cavities with injuries of major blood vessels when the muzzle of the weapon was in contact with the body. At a distance of 1 to 2 cm from the body about half of the gas weapons tested were still able to produce such injuries. At a distance of 6 cm none of the gas weapons tested were able to penetrate the skin.

Most of the gas weapons caused severe injuries when fired at contact through a T-shirt, but were not able to cause a penetration of the skin when fired through jeans. And also soft but thick materials like sweatshirts could protect the skin, because most of the propellent powder gas was lost within the layers of the textile material.

The shooting experiments showed the power of the gas weapons, when fired close to the body. If the victim is unclothed or only wearing thin clothes like a T-shirt, a contact shot from such a weapon will cause severe injuries. We hope, if there will be one common European weapon law, that these gas and warning firearms will be more restricted.

## References

[1] Levine RA, Stahl CJ (1968) Eye injury caused by tear-gas weapons. Am J Ophtalmol 65: 497-508

[2] Maxeiner H, Schneider V (1989) Verletzungen und Todesfälle durch Gas/Schreckschußwaffen. Arch Kriminol 184: 84-92

[3] Rothschild MA, Maxeiner H (1994) Unusual findings in a case of suicide with a gas weapons. Int J Leg Med 106: 274-276

[4] Rothschild MA (to be published) Tödliche Gaspistolenverletzung als "Arbeitsunfall". Rechtsmedizin

[5] Sattler W, Wagner HJ (1986) Tödliche Verletzungen durch projektillose Patronen. Kriminalistik 40: 485-486

[6] Stahl CJ, Young BC, Brown RJ, Ainsworth CA (1968) Forensic aspects of tear-gas pen guns. J Forensic Sci 13: 442-469

[7] Tausch D, Sattler W, Wehrfritz K, Wehrfritz G, Wagner HJ (1974) Tödliche Schußverletzungen mit "unbedenklichen" Gas- und Schreckschußfaustfeuerwaffen. Z Rechtsmed 75: 71-77

[8] Tausch D, Wagner HJ (1978) Über zwei tödliche Verletzungen mit Gas- und Schreckschußwaffen. Kriminalistik 32: 451-452

# The value of ultrastructural study of the lungs in diagnosing asphyxiated deaths in mice

Saadia R.*, Karima M.**, Sawsan A.**, Afaf M.** and Nahed A.**

Departments of Histology* and Forensic Medicine and Toxicology**,

Faculty of Medicine, El-Minia* and Assiut** Universities, Egypt

## INTRODUCTION

The causes of rapid hypoxic deaths and rapid anoxic deaths are due to defective or total failure in blood oxygenation; reduced oxygen-carrying capacity of the blood; impaired circulation resulting in a reduction of oxygen delivery per unit of time or depression of the oxidative processes in the tissues (Gorden et al., 1988).

The present study was concerned with deaths initiated by defective oxygenation of the blood in lungs or by failure in oxygenation using three methods in mice. The morphological findings obtained by electron microscope of the lungs were studied.

## MATERIAL AND METHODS

Twenty healthy male albino mice of average 28 gm weight were divided into four groups, five animals each. The first group was put into a box to inhale butane gas. The second group was injected intramuscularly with 26 mg morphine sulphate / kg body weight (Dreisbach, 1983 and Paget and Barnes, 1964). The third group was asphyxiated by strangulation. The last group was sacrificed by decapitation (control group).

Small specimens from the lung tissues were fixed immediately according to Sabatini et al. (1963) then post fixed in osmium tetraoxide and embedded in epon. Ultrathin sections were stained with urany acetate and lead citrate and examined by transmission electron microscope.

# RESULTS

Gross appearance: The lungs of all animals in the first group were atelectatic and red in color. In the second group, the lungs were markedly atelectatic. In the third group, the lungs were enlarged and congested.

Electron microscopic appearance:

Control group: As shown in Fig. (1), type I (arrow), type II pneumocytes, surfactant (double arrows), mitochondria (M) and lamellar bodies (L). (x 4.000).

Butane gas group: Fig. (2): The surface of the alveoli is corrugated and wavy (arrow). The alveolar spaces are filled with debris (d). The amount of surfactant is reduced with interstitial edema in some places (x 5,000).

Morphine injected group: Fig. (3): There is marked narrowing of the alveoli. The alveolar surface is greatly corrugated and the amount of surfactant is markedly decreased. Type II pneumocytes shows dense irregular nuclei (N) and mitochondria (M) and swollen lamellar bodies (x 5,000).

Strangulation: Fig. 4): There is widening of the alveolar surface, increase in the amount of surfactant (arrows), destruction of cells (double arrows) and marked decrease of lamellar bodies (x 4,000).

# DISCUSSION

The present study revealed that electron microscope examination is capable of making certain diagnosis of different hypoxic states. In cases of butane gas inhalation and morphine injection the examined lungs seem to be similar (decreased surfactant coats and interstitial edema) but distinct differences were found. In cases of morphine injection, the alveolar surface was more corrugated. The lamellar bodies were swollen and increased in amount due to failure of type II cells to discharge the contents of these bodies. The cellular changes were evident and event degeneration of cells especially type II pneumocytes . In contrary to previous groups, the lungs of strangulated animals had wide alveoli thinned walls, and marked increase of surfactant.

# REFERENCES


- Dreisbach RH (1983): Handbook of poisoning, 11th edition, Librairie du liban, P.O. Box 945 Beirut, Lebanon, P. 356.
- Gorden I, Shapiro HA, Berson SD (1988): Forensic Medicine, 3rd edition. In: Churchill Livingstone (ed.), Edinburgh, London, Melbourne and New York, P. 80.
- Paget, Barnes (1964): Evaluation of drug activities: pharmacometrics. In: Laurence and Bacharach (ed.), Vol. 1, Academic Press, New York.
- Sabatini Dd, Densch K, Barrnett RJ (1963): Cytochemistry and electron microscopy, the preservation of ultrastructure and enzymatic activity by aldehyde fixation. J. Cell Biol. 17:58.


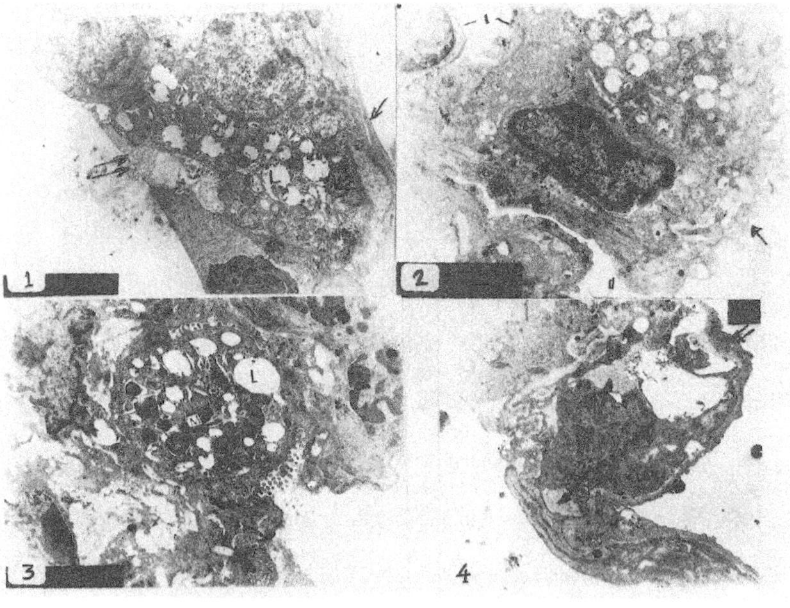

# CHANGING PROFILE OF THE MANNER OF DEATHS IN ADANA

SALAÇIN S.[1,2], ÇEKIN N.[1], GÜLMEN M.K.[1], SEN F.[2], ALPER B.[1]

1. The Department of Forensic Medicine, Medical School of Çukurova University, Adana, Turkey.
2. Adana Morque Department of The Branch of The Council of Forensic Medicine of Turkey.

## INTRODUCTION:

As it was mentioned before, the Morgue department of Adana is the only authorized department to conduct medicolegal autopsies and the official expert unit of the medico-legal investigations in this city. During the last couple of years in daily practice the prominent changes in the incidence of the manner of deaths was noticed. This study was planned to evaluate the exact changes in the profile of medicolegal deaths. It is well known that the medical examiner's records provide information for justice. But it is also invaluable epidemiologic data for local governers, education planners and puplic health officers.

## MATERIALS AND METHODS

The data of medical examiner's office were reviewed for the year 1992-1993. The data of 1969 cases were analyzed to find out the changing profile of cause and manner of deaths, and characteristics of medicolegal deaths in Adana. The age and sex distributions of total cases were studied statistically. The results were compared and discussed with the statistics of 1992-1993 and the previous studies performed on the medicolegal autopsies in this city and also with the others.

## RESULTS AND DISCUSSION

In the year 1993, medicolegal deaths, regarding the total deaths in Adana City, had increased about 1.5%. It was 939 in 1992 but 1030 in 1993. The manner of death in 1969 medicolegally investigated deaths in the years 1992-1993 were summarised separately for each year in table 1. Our data revealed a peak of frequency related to the homicides. As it is shown in table 1; homicides had increased 3.53% in all medicolegal deaths in the year 1993 compared to the year 1992. It was also astonishing to find out that deaths due to firearm injuries were the leading cause of deaths in homicide cases in 1992 and 1993(Table-2). On the other hand, our previous reports showed that stabbing was the leading cause of death in homicide cases, and firearm related deaths in previous 6 years were very low with only 90 cases(1,2). Contrary to this there was an obvious increase; 86 to 108 respectively in 1992 and 1993 with a total of 194(Table-3). Prominent increasing in firearm may be attributable to easy availability of guns because of the related law changes(3,4). On the other hand, deaths due to stabbing, increased 3.03% in all homicide cases. Stabbing related deaths had also showed an increase(58.06%) compared to 1992. In one of our previous report, stabbing related deaths in 9 years were totaly 186 cases(2). There was an increase each year since 1983, but last two years, it was obvious in the period of 1992-1993. It was 31 cases in 1992, 49 cases in 1993. Suicides had increased 0.95% in all medicolegal deaths in the year 1993 considering the year 1992. Suicidal deaths due to hanging, had increased 2.52% regarding the all suicide cases(Table-4). Intoxication related deaths due to agrochemicals had not shown any differences from the previous findings(1,3,5,6). It was a reflection of the local life style. A slight decrease was noticed in ingestion agrochemicals which might be related to the Cutdown project of these chemicals(6). Deaths due to accidents had decreased 4.53% in all medicolegal deaths in the year 1993 comparing 1992(Table-5). Blunt trauma related deaths due to accidents had increased 6.39%, traffic accidents which also was the major component of blunt trauma cases had increased 8.89%.

| | 1992 n % | 1993 n % |
|---|---|---|
| ACIDENTS | 688(73.27%) | 708(68.74%) |
| HOMICIDES | 110(11.71%) | 157(15.24%) |
| SUICIDES | 43( 4.58%) | 57( 5.53%) |
| NATURAL | 77( 8.20%) | 92( 8.93%) |
| UNDETERMINED | 21( 2.23%) | 16( 1.55%) |
| TOTAL | 939(100%) | 1030(100%) |

TABLE-1:THE FREQUENCIES OF THE MANNER OF DEATHS "1992-1993"

| CAUSE OF DEATHS | 1992 | 1993 |
|---|---|---|
| FIREARM INJURIES | 72 | 92 |
| STABBING | 31 | 49 |
| BLUNT TRAUMA | 5 | 9 |
| MISCELLANEOUS | 2 | 7 |
| TOTAL | 110 | 157 |

TABLE-2: HOMICIDES CASES in 1992-1993

| | |
|---|---|
| 1983-1988 | 9.00% |
| 1992 | 28.89% |
| 1993 | 36.08% |

TABLE-3: THE FREQUENCIES OF THE FIREARM DEATHS THROUGH THE YEARS.

| CAUSE OF DEATHS | 1992 | 1993 |
|---|---|---|
| INTOXICATION | 13 | 22 |
| HANGING | 14 | 20 |
| FIREARM INJURIES | 6 | 6 |
| BLUNT TRAUMA | 5 | 5 |
| BURNING | 4 | 1 |
| MISCELLANEOUS | 1 | 3 |
| TOTAL | 43 | 57 |

TABLE-4: SUICIDE CASES in 1992-1993

| CAUSE OF DEATHS | 1992 | 1993 |
|---|---|---|
| BLUNT TRAUMA | 473 | 532 |
| DROWNING | 87 | 72 |
| BURNING | 70 | 56 |
| ELECTROCUTION | 27 | 19 |
| INTOXICATION | 26 | 18 |
| MISCELLANEOUS | 5 | 11 |
| TOTAL | 688 | 708 |

TABLE-4:ACCIDENTAL DEATHS in 1992-1993

REFERENCES:

1. Salaçin S. An analysis of the medicolegal autopsies performed in Adana, Turkey in 1983-1988. Am J Forensic Med Pathol, 12:191-193, 1991.

2. Salaçin S, Kasar H, Alper B, Çekin N, Sen F. Demography of fatal stabbing: A nine year experience. Oral presentation of XII.Meeting of the International Academy of Legal Medicine and Social Medicine. Genoa, Italy, 1992.

3. Salaçin S, Çekin N, Gülmen MK, Sen F, Alper B. Incidence of autopsies and the rates of the manner of death in 939 medicolegal deaths in Adana city,Turkey. Oral presentation of the 13th Meeting of IAFS. Düsseldorf, Germany. 1993.

4. Salaçin S, Çekin N, Gülmen MK, Sen F, Alper B. Epidemiology of 939 medicolegal deaths in Adana city, Turkey. Oral presentation of the 13th Meeting of IAFS. Düsseldorf, Germany. 1993.

5. Salaçin S, Sen F, Alper B. The spectrum of fatal poisonings in Adana City(1983-1989), Turkey. Poster presentation of the Research Conference on Mechanism in Toxicity: Elucidation and Application. Il Ciocco, Italy. 1990.

6. Salaçin S, Alper B, Sen F. The spectrum of acute fatal pesticide poisoning in the city of Adana. Journal of Forensic Medicine, 9:37-43, 1993.

Correspondent: Serpil Salaçin M.D. Çukurova University, Medical School, Dept.of Forensic Medicine, 01330, Balcalì, Adana Turkey

# MULTIPLE SUICIDAL GUNSHOT WOUNDS

SAVIC S., PRAZIC A., CUKIC D., DUNJIC D. and KOVACEVIC S.

Institute of Forensic Medicine, Medical Faculty, University of Belgrade, Yugoslavia

## INTRODUCTION

There are several parameters which are to be established and considered prior to diagnosis of suicidal origin of death from gunshot wounds: distance between the muzzle and the surface of the body, site of the entrance wound, direction of its penetration through the body, number of wounds, etc. In practice, cases of suicides by firearms with only one gunshot wound are most often encountered. However, there are cases in literature where two or more suicidal gunshot wounds have been found. Intentions of authors of this work were to find a proportion of cases with multiple gunshot wounds in the total number of suicides by firearms; to observe some characteristics of this kind of wound (number, localization, distribution, severity, etc.); to observe certain problems of diagnosis and differential diagnosis of origin of such wounds.

## MATERIAL AND METHOD

There were 728 autopsies in cases of suicides of male persons in Belgrade in a ten-year-period (1980-1989). Records of these cases were the principal material of this work. Suicides by firearms were extracted and cases with two or more gunshot wounds per person were specially analyzed.

## RESULTS AND DISCUSSION

One hundred and forty of 728 suicides of male persons were committed by firearms. Of these, the majority were with a single gunshot wound each (135 or 96.4%). There were 5 (3.6%) suicides with two or more gunshot wounds. In the research of suicidal gunshot wounds in Victoria (Australia) in 1988 Selway found 2.1% of them to be multiple /5/, Thomsen and Albreksten in Denmark 0.8% /6/ and Jacob et al. in Dusseldorf 1.5% /3/.

All the suicides by firearms in our study were completed by one weapon only. There are rare case reports of two different weapons used for committing suicide /4/. Of five suicides with multiple gunshot wounds, four were committed with pistol and one with hunting rifle.

Number of wounds per person was from two to five. A peculiar curiosity is a case described in literature with nine suicidal gunshot wounds in the precordial region /1/. In our autopsy material 3 persons were with 2 wounds each, one person had 3 and one had 5 wounds. Localization of wounds were: head in 2 cases, chest in one case, both head and chest in 2 cases.

It is not easy to explain the multiplicity of suicidal gunshot wounds in a case. The explanation is certainly specific in each particular case. There are opinions that this method of suicide suggests a mental impairment of a victim. However, in our material no mental diseases were confirmed in 3 of 5 cases. In some cases the multiplicity of suicidal gunshot injuries may be due to clumsiness in handing firearms. In our opinion, certain of the wounds of our cases can be regarded as tentative injuries (wounds that penetrate only subcutaneous tissue), analogous to known and described suicidal tentative incisions and stab wounds.

FINAL NOTES

Suicides with two or more gunshot wounds are particularly interesting and important from medicolegal point of view. In such cases homicide is always suspected and investigation requires special attention. In establishing suicidal origin of death from multiple suicidal gunshot wounds in a single case, it is important to exclude existence of two or more wounds which would cause immediate inability of the injured person to move and act (if person uses only one weapon) /2/.

LITERATURE

1. Habbe D, Thomas GE, Gould J (1989) Nine-gunshot suicide. Am J Forens Med Pathol 10:335-337

2. Introna F, Smialek JE (1989) Suicide from multiple gunshot wounds. Am J Forens Med Pathol 10:275-284

3. Jacob B, Barz J, Haarhoff K, Sprick C, Wörz D, Bonte W (1989) Multiple suicidal gunshots to the head. Am J Forens Med Pathol 10:289-294

4. Rogers DR (1989) Simultaneous temporal and frontal suicidal gunshots. Am J Forens Med Pathol 10:338-339

5. Selway R (1991) Gunshot suicides in Victoria, Australia. Med Sci Law 31:76-80

6. Thomsen JL, Albreksten SB (1991) An investigation of the pattern of firearms fatalities before and after the introduction of new legislation in Denmark. Med Sci Law 31:162-166

## Studies on Examples of Drowning with Fresh Water Inhalation
## - Cerebral Blood Flow and Blood Electrolyte Levels -

Akiko SAWAGUCHI [1], Jun-ichi KOTANI [2], Nobuko NAKADA[1] and Toshiko SAWGUCHI[1]
Tokyo Women's Medical College, Tokyo 162[1] and
Kitasato University, School of Medicine, Kanagawa 228[2], Japan

### Introduction

The cerebrovascular flow (CBF) dynamics and other features have already been reported in a rabbit model for rapid and prolonged death by drowning (drowning in artificial sea water)(Kotani et al. 1992, 1993). In the present study, an attempt was made at prolonging the time required for drowning in fresh water (tap water) and a comparative study was conducted on the CBF dynamics at the surface and deep layers of the cerebrum and changes in the blood electrolyte level.

### Material and methods

I ) CBF determination

Using a semiconductor laser-type tissue flow meter ( LBF-220 by Biomedical), 0.55mm needle-type sensors were implanted in a shallow layer of the right hemisphere (depth, 5mm) and in a deep layer (depth, 12mm) of the left hemisphere of the cerebrum for hemodynamic determination.

II) The water to be inhaled

As in the previous test , 230 ml (6cm $H_2O$ at 24.6q 1.0 OxC) of tap water was stored in a tank (Sawaguchi et al. 1990, 1991).

III) Determination of NazkzCl

The blood sample that was used for blood gas analysis was also analyzed for the electrolytes using the Fuji Dry Chem. 800(R).

IV) Determination of $SaO_2$

A 4 Fr Opticatheter (R) was inserted into the femoral artery and left at the aortic arch. SaO2 was continuously determined using an Oximetric 3(R) (a product of Abbott Laboratories, analytical range from 100 to 10% in clinical use).

V) Methods and others

The method was the same as before: following the positioning of CBF and $Pto_2$ sensors, implanting deep electroencephalographic electrodes, and other preliminary procedures were performed (Sawaguchi et al. 1991, Kotani et al. 1992). Those that exhibited constant states in several physiological parameters after a certain time interval were used as test animals. They were forced to inhale fresh water for a certain duration by switching the air circuit that is directly connected to the airway to the drowning tank circuit.

All procedures were carried out in compliance with "The Guideline for Animal Experimentation in Tokyo Women's Medical College"

### RESULTS

1) The relationship between the duration of inhalation of drowning water (corresponding to the drowning time) and death by drowning

Among the animals that inhaled the fresh water for 10 to 60 seconds [ 10", 15", 20", 25" and 30" (number of animals that succumbed = 0/number of animals = 1 each), 45" (1/2), 50"(1/3), 55"(1/2), and 60" (3/4)], 10 escaped drowning. After 2 house, each parameter generally returned to the pre-test level in these animals.

2) A model in which the time period for the drowning process is prolonged

Inhalation of drowning water for 25 seconds opening the air circuit for 10 seconds second water inhalation for 25 seconds (n= 9).

3) Time lag from inhalation of drowning water to irreversible respiratory arrest and a loss of blood pressure

Time to respiratory arrest: 417 ± 133 seconds (max. 610, min. 218). Time to a loss of blood pressure: 487 ± 157 seconds (max. 676, min. 165).

4) Inhalation and draining of drowning water

The water that was inhaled for a total of 50 seconds amounted to 94.2 ± 9.0 ml (max. 108, min. 78). The amount of fluid expelled into the air circuit before respiratory arrest was 16.6 ± 5.6ml (max. 26.3, min. 7.6).

There was no linear correlation between the time required for respiratory arrest and elimination of the blood pressure.

5) Changes in the blood Na K Cl level

Na (arterial) immediately before the test, 141.0 ± 2.4 mEq / l: one minute later 103.6 ± 14.0; 3 minutes later, 126.5 ± 6.1; 5 minutes later, 126.4 ± 7.5; and 7 minutes later, 129.2 ± 11.2 K (arterial) immediately before the test, 3.39 ± 0.80; 1 minute later, 6.36 ± 2.00; 3 minutes later, 6.27 ± 0.92; 5 minutes later 7.00 ± 0.84; and 7 minutes, 7.40 ± 1.08. Cl (arterial) immediately before the test, 104.3 ± 4.9; 1 minute later, 77.1 ± 13.4; 3 minutes later, 93.5 ± 8.3; 5 minutes later, 92.6 ± 7.0; and 7 minutes later, 95.2 ± 9.8. Na Cl level of the venous blood, on the other hand, were slightly lower until 3 minutes later but generally approximated the base line. The venous K content was slightly lower than that of the arterial blood but exhibited a generally similar fluctuation pattern. Even in the examples of the development of VF, no particular rise in the K level was noted .

6) SaO2 fluctuations

It was 98.1 ± 1.2% immediately before the test and 24.4 ± 8.6% 1 minute later, requiring 184.0 ± 122.0 seconds to reach a level below 10%, which corresponded to the level approximately 4 minutes before the mean time required for respiratory arrest.

7) CBF fluctuation

As in the test using sea water, the overall patterns of the CBF dynamics were variable, generally showing a pattern that primarily reflected changes in the blood pressure. At the level near the surface, CBF fluctuated, corresponding to the violently changing blood pressure pattern at the initial stage of drowning. The CBF at the deep level of the cerebrum, however, showed no parallel changes. Some even exhibited a phenomenon to buffer the extreme changes in blood pressure. In the letter half of the drowning process, on the other hand, the near-surface layer did not reflect the blood pressure changes directly, Instead it gradually formed a plateau level or remained at a certain level with little fluctuation before reaching the final stage of drowning(Fig. 1., 2.).

## Discussion

Among the animals that inhaled the fresh water for 10 to 60 seconds, 10 escaped drowning. When brine was inhaled, almost all (12/13) succumbed after inhalation of 46 ± 7 ml for 10 seconds. After inhalation lasting for 15 to 30 seconds, all (8/8) died from drowning (Kotani et al. 1993). It is interesting to note that in a complete drowning state from inhalation of fresh water, death occurs 1 to 2 minutes (mean) sooner than inhalation of brine (Kotani et al. 1992).

When compared with death by drowning (n=54) from complete drowning in fresh water (Kotani et al. 1992), the time lag was approximately doubled, and the amount of water that was inhaled was generally equal to the volume (96.1 ± 23.2ml) of water recorded for the complete drowning model .

We could not find a direct correlation and were not certain whether these phenomena, changes in CBF and blood electrolyte levels were specific to drowning in fresh water and caused by hematological changes. However, these are worthy of consideration as general trend.

Even when a sufficient volume of CBF is proven in the later half of the drowning process, the blood SaO2 level is below 10%, which is ineffective for oxygen consumption by the brain tissue. In view of the example of resuscitation, however, maintenance of the blood flow (although the blood itself may contain little oxygen) is a more advantageous phenomenon for the brain, in contrast to the anoxic state also due to asphyxia but caused by processes such as cervical compression (Nakada and Kotani 1994).

## References

Kotani J, Sawaguchi A, Funao T, Nakayama S, Nakada N (1993) Re - evaluation of death by asphyxia based on cerebral blood flow (VIII) - A study on examples of drowning with short duration to water inhalation. Jpn J Legal Med 47 : 91

Kotani J, Sawaguchi A, Funao T, Nakada N, Koshizawa A (1992) Re- evaluation of death by asphyxia based on cerebral blood flow (VII) - On the information on electric potentials obtained from deep electroencephalographic electrodes - Jpn J Legal Med 46 : 393-399

Nakada N, Kotani J (1994) The role of haptoglobin in asphyxia mechanism (II) -Acute drowning and hanging - Jpn J Legal Med 48 : 26-32

Sawaguchi A, Kotani J, Funao T, Nakada N, Nakamura S,Sawaguchi T (1990) Cerebral blood flow and serum haptoglobin in the diagnosis of death by rapid drowning. Acta Medicine legalis et Socialis XL: 129-138

Sawaguchi A, Kotani J, Funao T, Nakada N (1991) Death from rapid drowning: Findings of Cerebral blood flow and serum haptoglobin. In : Nagano T. (ed) Proceeding of the first international symposium ADVANCES IN LEGAL MEDICINE. Tanaka Shobundo Graphic Art Co. Ltd, Kanazawa, pp170-172

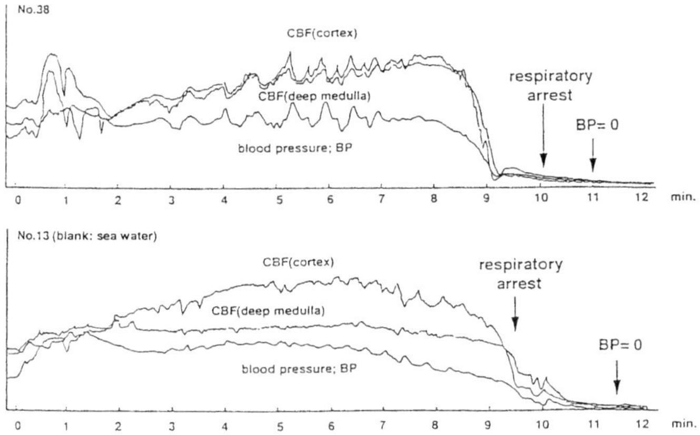


Fig. 1. Changes in the CBF and BP in a model stimulating a slow process of death by drowning in fresh water - A typical type -

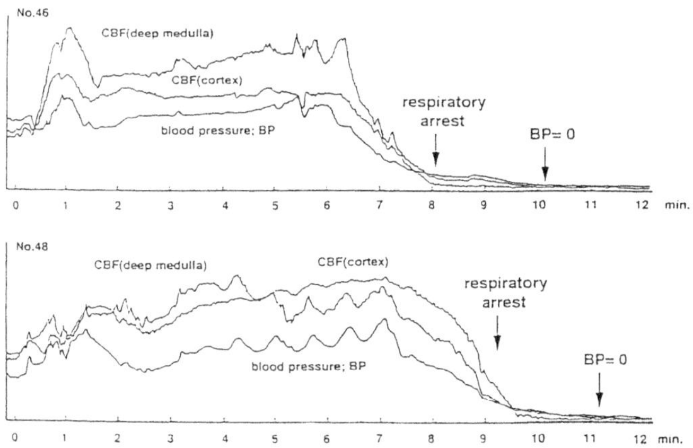


Fig. 2. Changes in the CBF and BP in a model stimulating a slow process of death by drowning in fresh water

# Statistical Estimation of Diagnostic Accuracy of Sudden Infant Death Syndrome (SIDS) in Japan

Toshiko Sawaguchi, Akiko Sawaguchi, Toshiharu Fujita*, Makio Kobayashi**

Dept. of Legal Medicine, Tokyo Women's Medical College

*Dept.of Epidemiology, Institute of Public Health

**Dept.of Pathology, Tokyo Women's Medical College

## Introduction

Sudden infant death syndrome(SIDS) is the most frequent cause of death in infants in developed countries where mortality due to infections and malnutritions has been dramatically reduced[1)2)]. In Japan also, the syndrome is a significant cause of death among infants but data concerning the precise insidence are insufficient[2)]. In the present survey, data concerning the accuracy of diagnoses of SIDS were collected from the Japanese Pathology and Autopsy Reports and analysed to arrive at an accurate figure for the incidence of this syndrome.

At the Second National Institute of Child Health and Human Development (NICHHD) Conference held at Seatle in 1969, SIDS was defined as follows:"the sudden death of an infant under one year of age which remains unexplained after a thorough case investigation, including performance of a complete autopsy, examination of death scene, and review of the clinical history.". In view of this definition, an autopsy is mandatory for the diagnosis of SIDS. The definition by the Ministry of Heallth and Welfare of the Japanese Government has dual standards (broad and narrow definitions) and an autopsy is required only according to the narrow definition .This can be explained by the fact that autopsies are conducted much more infrequently in Japan in comparison with other countries; but this fact makes an accurate determination of the incidence of SIDS in Japan difficult. We suspect that the clinical diagnosis of SIDS is currently based on the broad definition. Facing the current status of SIDS diagnosis based on this double standard, we attempted to find percentage accuracy of correct diagnoses as well as a possible trend for over-or under-diagnosis, by comparing the results of clinical and pathological diagnosis. The results are reported herein, together with trends in clinical diagnosis(pre-autopsy diagnosis), and erroneous diagnosis.

## Methods

Records of sudden deaths among those under 1 year were extracted from the Japanese Pathology and Autopsy Reports for a 5-year period(from 1987 to 1991) and their clinical diagnosis and diagnoses of the major and associated lesions were evaluated.Special attention was focused on those with a clinical diagnosis of SIDS that had been confirmed at autopsy;those with a diagnosis of SIDS given only after autopsy (the so-called underdiagnosis ); and those with a diagnosis of SIDS given before autopsy but negated at autopsy(the so-called overdiagnosis,).The results were computed as follows:

The following designations were given: the total number of cases subjected to autopsy, A;clinical diagnosis of SIDS, E;pathological diagnosis of SIDS, F;SIDS not listed in the clinical diagnosis, E;SIDS not included in the pathological diagnosis, F. Accurate diagnosis confirmed at autopsy, erroneous diagnosis, and diagnostic oversight, were designated as a, b, and c, respectively. The percentage overdiagnosis P(F/E) was computed by b/a+b; underdiagnosis P(F/E) by c/A-(a+b)[3]; and percentage accurate diagnosis P(F E/E) by a/a+b. Data were obtained for each year and a mean was computed for the successive 5 years(Figure 1). Significant differences were determined by a $x^2$ test and cochren-amitage test for annual fluctations of each index.

## Results

1.Basic data

The total number of cases of sudden death in infants under 1 year that were extracted from Japanese Pathology and Autopsy Reports for a 5-year period (from 1987 to 1991) was 162 with the following breakdown:17 in 1987, 35 in 1988, 28 in 1989,35 in 1990, and 47 in 1991.

2.Percentage overdiagnosis(percentage errors)

No statistically significant trend in the rate of overdiagnosis(percentage errors) was noted in the annual changes for the 5-year period(from 1987 to 1991).The mean percentage overdiagnosis was 21.98% in these 5 years.

3.Percentage underdiagnosis(percentage oversight)

No statistically significant trend in the percentage under diagnosis of SIDS was noted in the annual fluctations for these 5 years(from 1987 to 1991).The mean percentage underdiagnosis was 18.14 x 10 -7 in these 5 years.

4.Percentage correct diagnosis

There was no statistically significant trend in annual changes of the correct diagnoses of SIDS in the 5 year period (from 1987 to 1991). The mean percentage for correct diagnosis was 78.12% in these 5 years.

5.Trends in diagnosis before autopsy(clinical diagnosis)

Among the cases with a diagnosis of SIDS at autopsy, a clinical diagnosis of SIDS had been given to 58.7%, while 20.2% had been classified as sudden death according to clinical diagnosis. The cases with a clinical diagnosis of SIDS include some for whom an appropriate pathological diagnosis was not available and the clinical diagnosis had to be used as the final diagnosis.

6.Trends in overdiagnosis of SIDS in clinical diagnoses

Among the cases with a clinical diagnosis of SIDS, 57.69% were reclassified as sudden death and 15.4% as sudden death and the neonatal state at autopsy.

## Discussion

In examining the incidence of sudden death among infants under 1 year of age, extracted from the Japanese Pathology and Autopsy Reports as basic data, we note that the occurrence for 1991 was 2.4 times that for 1987, indicating increases in the incidence of sudden deaths (if we do not question the causes) for this age group. Compared with the overseas figures, the percentage of autopsies conducted in Japan is very low. Even so, it would be safe to state that the incidence of SIDS is on the rise in Japan, if one considers the fact that the number of cases with a pathological diagnosis of SIDS has been increasing although the total number of autopsies remains unchanged, the accuracy of a clinical diagnosis of SIDS(judged by referring to the comparison with the pathological diagnosis of SIDS) has been the same (computed to be near 80%).

We feel that now it is necessary to establish the basis for distinguishing SIDS from mere sudden death at autopsy diagnosis.

The diagnosis of SIDS is essentially determined by a process of exclusion. As it was exemplified by the existence of ventriicullar septal defect(VSD) in the incidental findings at autopsy, complete exclusion may be difficult in some instances.

The accuracy of clinical diagnoses of SIDS was compared against diagnoses of other diseases, using the same computation method. In an example of diabetes mellitus, the percentage diagnosis error was 0.517 for men and 0.436 for women(o.143 for men and 0.242 for women when diabetes alone was listed ); and the percentage oversight was 0.0032 for men and 0.0031 for women. Compared with these figures, the diagnostic accuracy for SIDS does not appear to be particularly low..

References

1)Knight B (1992) Sudden Infant Death Syndrome. In : Legal Aspects of Medical Practice. Churchill Livingstone, London , 285-290

2)Nishida H (1992) Study for Sudden Infant Death Syndrome. In: Katou Y (ed) Report for Study Comission of Infantile Psychosomatic Disorder by Ministry of Health and Welfare in1992 in Japan, Tokyo, P221-224

3)Katabami J, Honda Y (1989) Comparative Study between Clinical Diagnosis and Pathological Diagnosis for Diabetes Mellitus by the Japanese Pathology and Autopsy Reports. Indication of Health and Welfare 36:10-17

Figure 1. figure for calculation of diagnostic accuracy

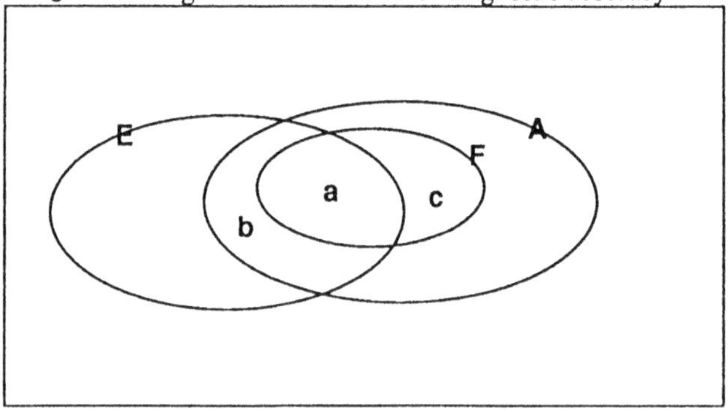


A: total number of cases subjected autopsy
E: clinical diagnosis of SIDS
F: pathological diagnosis of SIDS
b/a+b: percentage overdiagnosis
c/A-(a+b): percentage underdiagnosis
a/a+b: percentage accurate diagnosis

# HOMICIDE IN THE BATHTUB

Schmidt P, Madea B

Institute of Forensic Medicine, University of Cologne, Melatengürtel 60-62, 50823 Cologne, Germany

## Introduction

Homicide in the bathtub or homicide with subsequent submersion of the corpse are rare events. In a retrospective survey of 36 fatalities in the bathtub in Ghent from 1934 to 1983 Devos et al. (1985) reported 2 homicides. In a series of 42 deaths in the bath in Copenhagen and Gothenburg from 1961 to 1969 Geertinger and Voigt (1970) encountered 1 homicide. Among 245 fatalities in the bathtub in Hamburg from 1971 to 1988 Trübner and Püschel (1991) found 13 homicides and claimed that the pattern of injury had been quite indicative of the manner of death. On the other hand, in a case of manual strangulation with subsequent submersion of the corpse in a bathtub described by Spitz (1993) initial examination of the body at the scene had only revealed two small whitish areas on the side of the neck whilst the autopsy of the dried body showed unequivocal nail marks.
We report on 2 homicides illustrating the variety of different scenes in cases of death in the bathtub and elucidating possible pitfalls.

## Case reports

In case 1 a 32-year-old woman was found dead in the bathtub lieing undressed, face down, with her mouth and nose beneath the surface of water. The electrical cord of a vibrator was wrapped around her neck. On the floor of the living room a pool of blood was encountered with a trace of dragging leading in the direction of the bathroom. The autopsy revealed a ligature mark of the neck, corresponding paleness of the mucous membrane of the gullet and multiple petechiae of the conjunctivae. In addition a deep incised wound of the throat was found, but there were no signs of blood aspiration, air embolism or marked anemia of the internal organs due to hemorrhage. Findings indicating drowning were not encountered. Defensive injuries were not found, nor were findings of electrocution. In court the perpetrator confessed that in the course of a fight with sexual background he had first strangled the woman with the electric cord, inflicted the incised wound of the neck and then submerged the corpse in the bathtub.

In case 2 a 55-year-old woman was found by her son submerged face down in her bathtub, with mouth and nose beneath the water. Faint hemorrhages and scratches of the skin of the neck recognized on external examination at the scene were assumed to be related to a necklace. The bathroom showed no signs indicating that a struggle had taken place. The autopsy revealed multiple hemorrhages in the muscles of the neck, fractures of the superior horns of the thyroid cartilage surrounded by hemorrhage, hemorrhages of the mucous membrane of the larynx, numerous petechiae of the skin of the face, the conjunctivae and the pleural surfaces of the lungs, in addition signs of agonal swallowing of water. Defensive injuries were not encountered.

## Discussion

In case 1 the autopsy findings were in good agreement with the later confession of the perpetrator. There is no doubt that referring to Trübner and Püschel (1991) the scenario and autopsy findings of this fatality were highly indicative of the manner and cause of death. According to the classification of Krüger et al. (1987) the corpse had merely been deposited in the bathtub and this was of no importance for the occurrence of death. The motive for this behavior could not be elucidated. In comparison Devos et al. (1985) reported a homosexual being strangled and then put into the bathtub to make the fatality appear non-homicidal. In another case the perpetrator had explained that he had stabbed his wife and then had given her a shower to remove the traces (Krüger et al., 1987). In a further case of our material the perpetrators described that after stabbing they had submerged their victim in the bathtub to control whether it still breathed or was actually dead.

In case 2 the lethal strangulation was not discovered at the scene. Particularly in cases of ligature or manual strangulation the police forces and the forensic pathologist may be confronted with serious difficulties in establishing the cause of death. The observation of Spitz (1993) has been mentioned above. Mueller (1975) had already emphasized that abrasions of the skin due to manual strangulation or other causes may barely be visible at wet skin, but become quite obvious some hours later. Madea et al. (1987) demonstrated in a series of postmortem experiments that the intensity of ligature marks is markedly diminished by exposure to water. In particular the surface pattern reflecting the nature of the ligature may disappear. Bode and Kampmann (1981) succeeded in making an experimentally produced strangulation furrow completely disappear by combined treatment with ointments and exposure to water. Recently Betz and al. (1993) showed in an experimental model that petechial bleedings of the conjunctivae may diaappear after 4 hours in fresh water probably due to haemolysis caused by the hypo-osmolaric medium. These observations and experimental results underline that a thorough autopsy should be carried out on every suspicious fatality in the bathtub.

## References

Betz P, Penning R, Keil W (1994) The detection of petechial hemorrhages of the conjunctivae in dependency on the postmortem interval. Forensic Sci Int 64:61-67

Bode G, Kampmann H (1981) Die Bedeutung postmortaler Einflüsse auf die Erkennbarkeit von Strangmarken. Arch Kriminol 168:156-160

Devos Ch, Timperman J, Piette M (1985) Deaths in the bath. Med Sci Law 25:189-200

Geertinger P, Voigt J (1970) Death in the bath. J For Med 17/4:136-147

Krüger U, Schuster D, Wegener R (1987) Zum Problem "Badewannentod". Kriminalistik forens. Wiss. 65/66:62-65

Madea B, Henßge C, Oehmichen M (1987) Der Einfluß der Wasserexposition auf die Erkennbarkeit von Strangmarken. Arch Kriminol 180:114-122

Mueller B (1975) Ertrinken. In: Mueller B (ed) Gerichtliche Medizin, vol 1. Springer, Berlin, Heidelberg, New York, pp 477-493

Spitz WU (1993) Asphyxia. In: Spitz WU (ed) Medicolegal Investigation of Death. 3rd ed. Charles C. Thomas, Springfield, Illinois, pp 444-497

Trübner K, Püschel K (1991) Todesfälle in der Badewanne. Arch Kriminol 188:35-46

# Détermination de la distance de tir par analyse d'images: radiographie des residus de tir au calibre .22 lr.

**Christian SCHYMA**

Institut für Rechtsmedizin , Stiftsplatz 12, D - 53111 BONN (RFA)
(Directeur Prof. Dr. med. U. HEIFER)

## Introduction

Lorsqu'il y a usage d'armes à feu il importe de répondre aux cinq questions suivantes: 1. Qui a tiré ? 2. Quelle arme a servi ? 3. Quelle munition a été employée ? 4. Quelle était la direction de tir ? 5. Quelle était la distance de tir? Cette dernière est l'une des questions les plus importantes pour la reconstitution des faits.
Le principe de la technique ici présentée n'est pas nouveau. Il y a vingt cinq ans BÖHM et al. (1969) avaient déjà essayé la radiographie pour déterminer la distance de tir. Mais aujourd'hui nous disposons d'un matériel technique plus sophistiqué. Ainsi il est projeté de numériser les radiographies et de les examiner à l'ordinateur (publication de l'auteur qui paraîtra prochainement).

## Méthode

Trois armes de calibre .22 long rifle - le calibre le plus répandu en Allemagne - ont été choisies: un pistolet Walther (longueur du canon 97 mm), un revolver Taurus (canon de 152 mm) et une carabine Krico (longueur du canon 60 cm). Pour la grande série d'expérimentations nous avons employé la ".22 standard" (long rifle) de Dynamit Nobel. Il s'agit de cartouches à balle de plomb pesant 2,6 grammes et à percussion annulaire; soit la cartouche "petit calibre" typique. Au stand de tir, des chiffons de coton ont été étendus de 20 cm sur 20 cm et fixés devant le pare-balle. Ensuite nous avons effectué des séries de tirs en commençant à zéro, c'est-à-dire en pressant la bouche du canon sur l'étoffe. La distance de tir a été augmentée de 5 cm en 5 cm jusqu'à 50 cm. A partir de 50 cm nous avons modifié la distance du pas de 10 cm en 10 cm jusqu'à 5 mètres. Afin d'éviter une contamination des spécimens, les chiffons ont été mis dans des couvertures plastiques. Dans d'autres essais le coton a été remplacé par des morceaux de peau prélevés lors des autopsies.
Les radiographies ont été effectuées à l'aide d'un appareil Philips. Après les expérimentations préliminaires on pouvait constater que les résidus de tir formaient des traces visibles avec des tensions de tube entre 28 et 59 kV. La durée d'exposition devait être adaptée à la tension et à la sensibilité des films radiographiques employés. Elle variait entre 200 millisecondes et 5 secondes. Les films radiographiques jouaient un des rôles les plus importants: les meilleures images ont été réalisées avec des films industriels. Cependant le film Kodak XOmat offre quelques avantages: il est prêt à l'usage, enveloppé de papier, il existe des formats pratiques et les coûts ne sont pas trop élevés. Aussi les films de radiographie dentaire ont donné des résultats très satisfaisants. Nous n'avons employé ni amplificateurs ni cassettes ni filtres. Les échantillons ont été mis directement sur le film. La distance entre film et foyer était de 60 cm. Après une période de 15 minutes de développement à la main les radiographies séchées sont photographiées sur des pellicules de petit format (24 x 36 mm).

**Résultats et discussion**

Les radiographies montrent toutes des traces annulaires à l'orifice d'entrée de la balle. L'intensité de cet anneau de nettoyage diminue un peu avec la distance croissante, mais elle dépend beaucoup plus de la tension de l'étoffe. Plus le chiffon est tendu mieux est le nettoyage de la balle. KIJEWSKI et LANGE (1974) décrivirent des expériences analogues. Même à la distance de 5 m on observe un anneau bien identifiable (figure 1: 2 m).

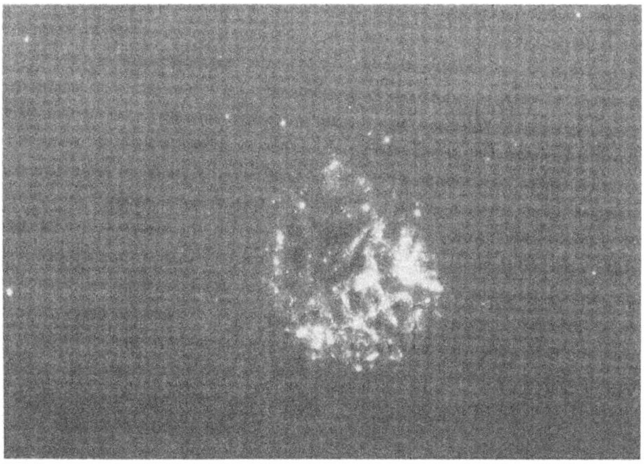

Figure 1:
distance de tir 2 m (révolver). "Anneau de nettoyage" net au centre

Les traces métalliques se composent de particules de dimensions bien différentes (exemple figure 2): il y a une poussière de petites sphères de 20 µm et moins. Ce sont les résidus de l'amorce (antimoine, plomb et baryum). Les plus grandes particules (plomb) mesurent presque 1 mm et proviennent de la surface du projectile, limées dans le canon. Ces phénomènes sont documentés par SELLIER (1982).

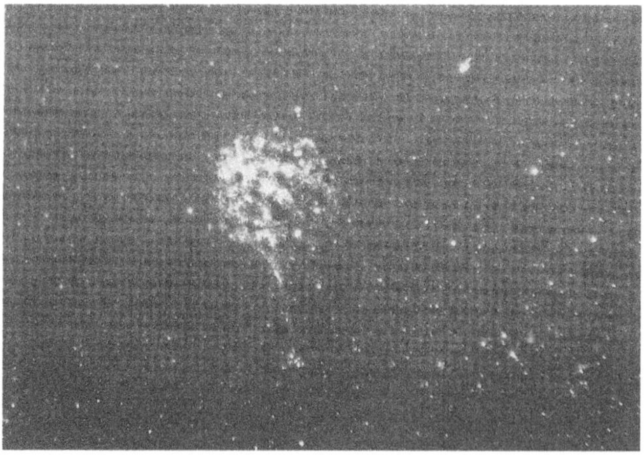

Figure 2: distance de tir 50 cm (révolver). Expansion de la "poussière" sur tout le champ d'observation

Pour les distances de 0 à 15/20 cm (figure 3) il y a des zones autour de l'entrée de la balle de très grande densité métallique dans lesquelles on ne distingue plus les particules singulières. Entre 20 et 50 cm de distance le nombre de particules par champ d'observation ne change guère mais la distribution est de plus en plus expansive. Au-delà de 50 cm de distance le nombre de particules diminue de façon sensible, mais il reste à peu près constant jusqu'à 90 / 100 cm. A partir d'un mètre les distances ne peuvent être classées par intervalles de 50 cm. Mais jusqu'à 3 m (voir figure 1) il y a encore des particules à trouver qui distinguent les distances au-dessous et au-dessus de 3 m.

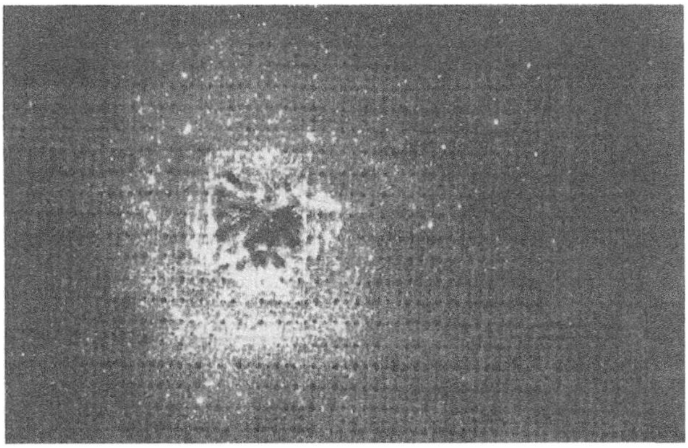

Figure 3: distance de tir 10 cm (révolver). Grande densité concentrée autour de l'entrée de la balle

Pour déterminer la distance de tir il faut comparer la radiographie du vêtement avec celles de la série de tir. Aux distances jusqu'à 1 m une précision de plus ou moins 5 cm est réalisable et une comparaison directe des photographies suffit. Au-delà d'un mètre il faut une évaluation approfondie: connaissance de la distribution des particules dans un système de coordonnées, séparation des particules infimes des fragments plus grands et analyse de leurs dimensions. Actuellement nous sommes en train de développer un logiciel pour rendre la détermination de la distance de tir jusqu'à 2 m plus précise.

La comparaison de différentes sortes de munitions et des types d'armes montre des différences qui distinguent les munitions et les longueurs de canon. C'est pourquoi il faut exiger de connaître l'arme et la munition employées pour éviter des erreurs graves en déterminant la distance de tir, telles sont les différences observées.

Les radiographies de la peau montrent la même distribution de particules si l'on compare les mêmes distances de tir.

La méthode présentée a le grand avantage de ne pas détruire la pièce à conviction.

**Littérature**

1. BÖHM E, SCHREIBER HP, SUCHENWIRTH, H (1969) Röntgenologische Untersuchungen zur Schußentfernungsbestimmung. Dtsch. Z. ges. gerichtl. Med. 65: 112-121

2. KIJEWSKI H, LANGE J (1974) Möglichkeiten und Grenzen einer Schußentfernungsbestimmung aus dem Schmutzring. Arch. f. Kriminol. 154: 179-183

3. SELLIER K (1988) Schußentfernungsbestimmung. Schmidt-Römhild, Lübeck

# An Autopsy Case of Traumatic Sinus Thrombosis

Yoshihisa Seto, Sanae Takeichi and Takeshi Saito
Department of Forensic Medicine, Tokai University School of Medicine.
Isehara, Kanagawa 259-11, JAPAN

**Introduction**

An autopsy case of traumatic superior sagittal sinus thrombosis is reported.

**Case Report**

A 38-year-old male slipped accidentally and fell from a height of 4.6 m onto a concrete floor. He was brought to an adjacent hospital, but immediately transferred to our university-hospital. He complained headache, but consciousness was clear. After admission to the hospital (2 hours after the accident), his consciousness level showed 20 in the Japan Coma Scale (JCS), that is 12 of 15 in Glasgow Coma Scale (GCS) score, without palsy.

**Clinical findings:**

Some radiograms showed a transverse linear fracture of the parietal bone across the sagittal suture, and fractures of the 11th and 12th thoracic vertebrae. A computed tomography (CT) scan of the head indicated acute subdural hematoma, and cerebral contusion on both sides of the frontal lobe.

He became unconscious five hours later, therefore an operation was performed to remove the hematoma. His consciousness level increased (JCS30) after the operation, but three hours later it gradually decreased, and then five hours after the operation became finally unconscious. A computed tomogram revealed cerebral swelling, and a medication to reduce intracranial pressure was began, but the critical condition was not improved. A cerebral angiogram revealed filling defect in the superior sagital sinus suspecting sinus thrombosis. In a short time, the electroencephalogram became flat, and six days later he died.

**Autopsy findings:**

Subcutaneous hemorrhage on the right parietal region (6 x 5 cm) and a small excoriation on the left occipital and parietal regions were seen. An operative wound was seen on the frontal region. As internal views, one linear fracture crossed obliquely the sagittal suture from the frontal to the occipital bones, still more it extended to the base of the skull. The dura matter showed red brown, and a small lacerated wound was seen at the point where the fracture crossed over the sagittal suture. The sinus was occluded with thrombus consisting of red cells from the near of superior sagittal sinus to the right and left transverse sinus. The brain weighed 1360 g. The brain was slightly reddish, and the gyri were completely flat showing cerebral swelling and softening, especially in the brain stem and cerebellum. Although the right frontal pole had been already removed by operation, both the frontal poles were crushed extensively, and both temporal poles were contused slightly with slight subdural hematoma.

**Conclusions and discussion**

Both clinical symptoms and autopsy findings indicated that he died from acute cerebral swelling due to traumatic thorombosis of the superior sagittal sinus. In this case, a small intimal wound of the superior sagittal sinus that triggered the thrombus might be induced by the linear fracture of the skull.

Although there are some reports[1] of superior sagittal sinus thrombosis due to various causes such as various infections, pregnancy, and trauma and so on, it seems seldom in the case of head injury[2]. Arita et. al.[3] investigated 33 cases of traumatic sinus thrombosis. They indicated that thrombosis was seen in the superior sagittal sinus (52%), and transverse sinus (45%), and the fracture of the skull across the sinus was found in 45% of the cases. On the other hand , it is noteworthy that no fracture cases were observed in the half. It is thought that there are three factors to induce sinus thrombosis. 1. Pressure on sinus with bone fragment and/or hematoma, causing constriction of the sinus, 2. Lesion of intima of the sinus, 3. Hyperactivity of blood coagulation system. In our case, it seems that the cause is 2.

It is necessary to investigate carefully the sinus thrombosis in the case with head injury, especially skull fracture.

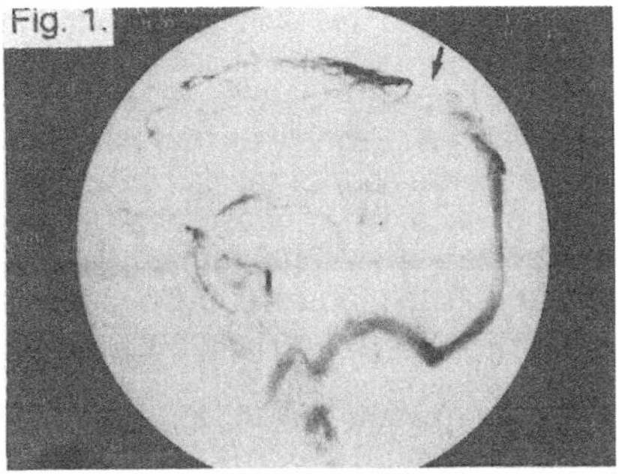


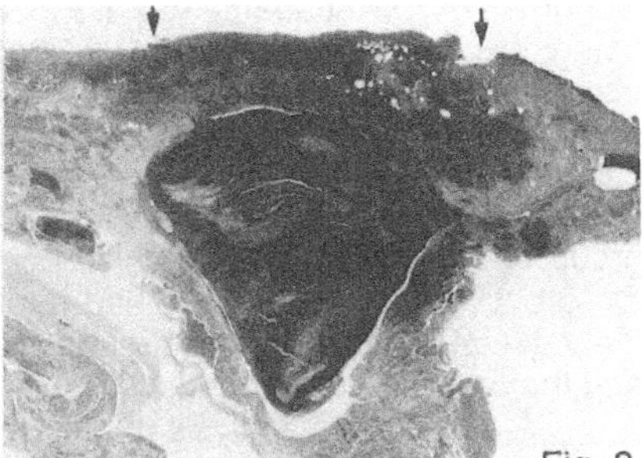

Fig. 2.

Fig. 3.

Fig. 1. Angiography: the superior sagittal sinus was completely occluded just under the fracture, 22 hours after the accident.
Fig. 2. Thrombus in the superior sagittal sinus and lacerated region of duramater ( ↓ ).
Fig. 3. Lesions of the adventitia and intima of the sinus.

## References


1. Gettelfinger DM, Kokmen E (1977) Superior sagittal sinus thrombosis. Arch Neurol 34: 2-6.
2. Krayenbühl HA (1966) Cerebral venous and sinus thrombosis. Clin Neurosurg 14: 1-24.
3. Arita K, Uozumi T, Sakoda K, Ohta M, Mishima H, Gocho M, Ohshima H (1990) A 2case of post-traumatic superior sagittal sinus thrombosis developing chronic intracranial hypertension. J Hiroshima Med Ass 43: 1170-1176.

MEDICO-LEGAL STUDY ON THE SKIN COLOR OF CADAVERS EXPOSED TO EXHAUST FUMES

( ETUDE DE MEDECO-LEGALE SUR LA COULEUR DE LA PEAU DE SOURIS MORTES EXPOSEES AU GAZ D'ECHAPPEMENT )

Takaaki SHINOMIYA, Kaoru SHINOMIYA and Chitoshi ORIMOTO
Department of Legal Medicine, School of Medicine, Ehime University
( Chaire de Médecine Légale, Faculté de médecine, Université d'Ehime )
Shitsukawa, Shigenobu-cho, Onsen-gun, Ehime-ken,791-02, Japan

Summary:

In previous experiments done on nude mice, postmortem exposure to exhaust fumes caused a marked change in skin colour. The skin of the mice exposed to exhaust fumes after death visibly reddened in comparison with the skin of the control group mice which did not receive postmortem exposure. At the 15th Congress of the Academy in Zaragoza in 1991, we showed this skin colour change using the CHROMAMETER CR-200, which objectively determines colour value using a system of three dimensional colour space CIELAB (*L*a*b** CIE 1976).

In supposing that carbon monoxide (CO) in the exhaust fumes had been the cause of the skin colour change, we compared the skin colour of the mice with the content of the CO in the tissues of the three groups of mice; the control group (A), the group of dead mice who received postmortem exposure to exhaust fumes (B), and the group of living mice who had been exposed to exhaust fumes (C). Concerning the value of $a^*$ of the three groups (A,B,C), there is a positive significant difference, and the order of the value of $a^*$ is C > B > A.

A quantitative analysis of the content of CO ( µl / g) in the tissues follows;

| Group | A | B | C |
|---|---|---|---|
| Liver | $0.90 \pm 0.164$ | $4.04 \pm 1.629$ | $50.77 \pm 6.447$ |
| Auricle | ND | $2.87 \pm 0.739$ | $2.80 \pm 1.340$ |
| Skin | ND | $1.63 \pm 0.503$ | $2.64 \pm 0.814$ |

In conclusion, the CO in the exhaust fumes entered the body through the skin thereby causing the skin to redden. The degree of skin colour change corresponded to the change in the value of $a^*$.

key words : forensic medicine, carbon monoxide, color, skin, nude mice, exhaust fumes.

Nous émettons une hypothèse que l'oxyde de carbone dans les gaz d'échappement traverse la peau des souris nues, entre dans leur corps après la mort, puis se joint à l'hémoglobine et à la myoglobine dans les tissus cutanés, les tissus sous-cutanés et éventuellement les tissus musculaires. Au cours de cette expérimentation, nous avons vérifié l'existence d'oxyde de carbone dans la peau des souris nues qu'on avait exposées au gaz d'échappement.

1° Matériels expérimentaux :

1) Souris nues, mâles, Jcl:AF-nu. Poids moyen : 25,2g.

2) CHROMAMETER CR-200, fabriqué par Minolta Camera S.A. Japon.

3) Air dosé à 0,2% d'oxyde de carbone.

4) Une petite voiture, 4 places, 4 portières, Mitsubishi Mirage E-A152A, fabriquée par Mitsubishi Motor Corp., Japon.

2° Méthodes expérimentales:

1) Exposition à du gaz d'échappement ou à de l'air dosé à 0,2% d'oxyde de carbone[1,2,3]

Nous avons exposé deux familles de souris pendant une période de quatre heures à deux sortes de gaz: du gaz d'échappement pour la famille 1, et de l'air dosé à 0,2% d'oxyde de carbone pour la famille 2. Chaque famille consistait en trois groupes de cinq souris: deux groupes de cinq souris asphyxiées à l'azote et un groupe de cinq souris vivantes. Cinq souris mortes de chaque famille ont servi de groupe témoin; elles ont été laissées à l'air naturel pendant une période de quatre heures.

On a exposé cinq souris mortes et cinq souris vivantes de la famille 1 à du gaz d'échappement dans une petite voiture pendant une durée de quatre heures. La concentration en oxyde de carbone dans la voiture s'est rapidement élevée à peu près 4 % et s'est ensuite maintenue environ à ce niveau de 10 à 50 minutes après la mise en marche du moteur; puis a baissé petit à petit pendant les 4 heures suivantes.

On a exposé cinq souris mortes et cinq souris vivantes de la famille 2 à de l'air dosé à 0,2% d'oxyde de carbone dans une chambre à gaz pendant une durée de quatre heures.

2) Détermination de la couleur[1,4,5]

Immédiatement après avoir exposé les souris nues au gaz, on a déterminé la couleur de la peau de la région iliaque des souris. Pour ce faire, on a utilisé le CHROMAMETER CR-200.

3) Détermination de l'oxyde de carbone dans la peau, les pavillons de l'oreille et le foie des souris.

On a déterminé la teneur (en µl par g) en oxyde de carbone contenu dans les tissus des souris, soit par la chromatographie en phase gazeuse[6,7], soit par l'ECOLYZER CR-200[2,8].

3° Résultats et réflexions tirés de notre expérimentation sur la famille 1:

À l'œil nu, la peau des souris exposées au gaz d'échappement après la mort a plus rougi que celle du groupe témoin. De plus, la peau des souris mortes intoxiquées par le gaz d'échappement est la plus rouge, comparée à la peau des deux autres groupes de souris (les groupes A et B).

Voici les résultats de la couleur de peau des souris, déterminés d'après le CHROMAMETER CR-200 (Fig. 1).

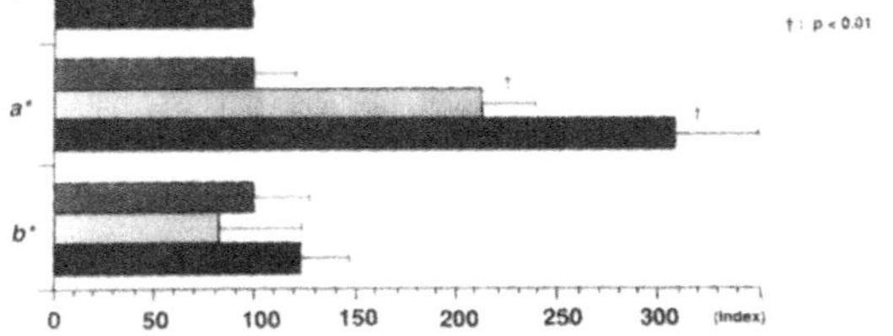


Fig.1: Skin color of nude mice, as determined by the CHROMAMETER CR-200.

Le *L**, le *a** et le *b** du groupe A, le groupe-témoin, sont tous posés comme indices 100. Le groupe B et le groupe C sont exprimés en pourcentages par rapport au groupe A.

En ce qui concerne le *a**, l' indice du groupe C est le plus élevé sur l'échelle; le groupe A est, lui, le plus bas sur l'échelle. Il y a aussi une différence significative ($p<0,01$) entre les indices des groupes A et B. Il y a également une différence significative (p<0,01) entre le groupe B et le groupe C. En ce qui concerne le $L^*$ et $b^*$, il n'y a pas de différence significative entre les indices des trois groupes.

En ce qui concerne les teneurs en oxyde de carbone dans les tissus des souris, voici le diagramme de la chromatographie en phase gazeuse (Fig. 2).

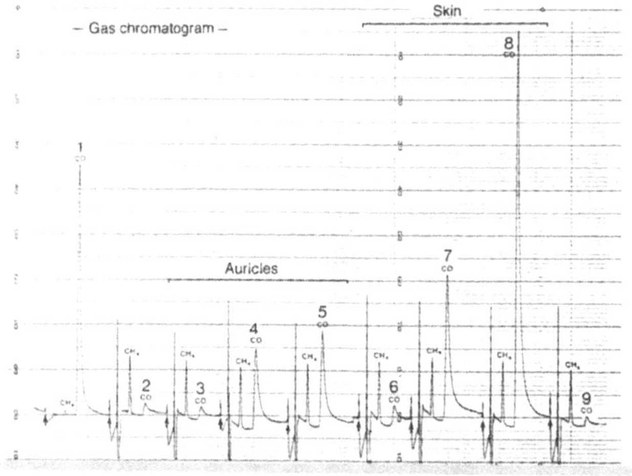


Fig. 2 : Experimental exposure of mice to exhaust fumes: -Gaschromatogram

La courbe numéro 1 est le niveau standard en oxyde de carbone à 46,4 ppm. Les courbes numéro 2 et numéro 9 représentent les teneurs en oxyde de carbone dans l'air naturel du laboratoire. Les courbes numéro 3, numéro 4 et numéro 5 représentent les teneurs en oxyde de carbone dans les pavillons des oreilles des souris de chaque groupe.

Les courbes numéro 6, numéro 7 et numéro 8 représentent les teneurs en oxyde de carbone dans la peau des souris. Les courbes numéro 3 et numéro 6 sont du groupe A, le groupe témoin. Les courbes numéro 4 et numéro 7 sont du groupe B, les souris mortes exposées au gaz d'échappement. Les courbes numéro 5 et numéro 8 sont du groupe C, les souris exposées vivantes au gaz d'échappement.

Voici la teneur en oxyde de carbone dans chaque tissu organique sur les trois groupes de souris (Fig. 3).

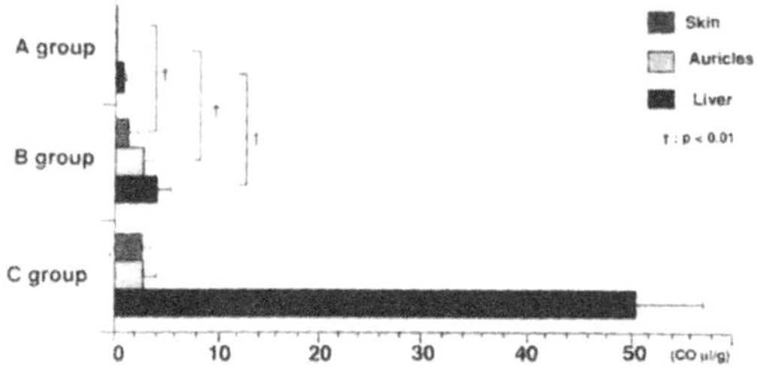


Fig. 3 : Content of CO in the skin, in the auricles and in the liver.

En ce qui concerne le groupe A, le groupe témoin, on n'a trouvé pas d'oxyde de carbone dans les pavillons des oreilles, ni dans la peau des souris. On n'en a trouvé que dans le foie.

Au sujet du groupe B, les souris exposées au gaz d'échappement après leur mort, on a trouvé de l'oxyde de carbone dans les tissus.

Pour ce qui est du groupe C, les souris exposées vivantes au gaz d'échappement, on a bien sûr trouvé de l'oxyde de carbone dans les tissus, et les teneurs en oxyde de carbone y sont plus élevées que dans les groupes A et B.

Quand le groupe de souris a été exposé au gaz d'échappement après leur mort, nous pouvons certifier que la couleur de peau était devenue plus rouge que celle du groupe témoin, et aussi qu'il y avait de l'oxyde de carbone dans leur peau et leur pavillons d'oreilles.

L'oxyde de carbone a pénétré dans la peau des souris par diffusion simple, et s'est joint à l'hémoglobine et à la myoglobine dans les tissus cutanés, les tissus sous-cutanés et éventuellement les tissus musculaires.

Dans l'avenir, il nous reste à prouver l'existence de carboxyhémoglobine et de carboxymyoglobine dans les tissus mentionnés ci-dessus.

Dans le cas de la famille 2, où les souris ont été exposées à de l'air dosé à 0,2% d'oxyde de carbone, les changements sont les mêmes en ce qui concerne les résultats de la couleur de peau et des teneurs en oxyde de carbone dans les tissus pour les 3 groupes de souris, mais la variation est très faible.

## 4° Conclusion

Quand le groupe de souris a été exposé au gas d'échappement après leur mort, nous pouvons certifier que la couleur de peau était devenue plus rouge que celle du groupe témoin, et aussi qu'il y avait de l'oxyde de carbone dans leur peau et leurs pavillons d'oreilles.

Remerciments:

Les auteurs voudraient remercier la Fondation Médicale de la Préfecture d'Ehime pour avoir bien voulu les subventionner dans la poursuite de leurs recherches.

## BIBLIOGRAPHIE

1. Shnomiya T, Shinomiya K(1992) Essai d'identification d'échantillons médico-légaux à partir du CHROMAMETER. Acta Medicinae Legalis et Socialis XLII: 339-346
2. Shinomiya T, Shinomiya K(1989) Variation de dégagement de l'oxyde de carbone dans la tache de sang et dans les tissus viscéraux. Acta Medicinae Legalis et Socialis XXX IX:131-143.
3. Shinomiya K, Orimoto C, Shinomiya T(1994) Experimental exposure to carbon monoxide in rats(I) - Relation between the degree of carboxyhemoglobin saturation and the amount of carbon monoxide in the organ tissues of rats -. Jpn J Legal Med 48:19-25.
4. Serup J, Agner T(1990) Colorimetric quantification of erythema -- a comparison of two colorimeters (Lange Micro Color and Minolta Chroma Meter CR-200) with a clinical scoring scheme and laser-Doppler flowmetry. Clin Exp Dermatol 15: 267-272.
5. Rosenstiel SF, Johnston WM(1988) The effects of manipulative variables on the color of ceramic metal restorations. J Prosthet Dent 60:297-303.
6. Poter K, Volman DH(1962) Flame ionization detection of carbon monoxide for gas chromatographic analysis. Anal Chem 34:748-749.
7. Mizutani K, Shinomiya K, Shinomiya T(1988) Hepatotoxicity of dichloromethane. Forensic Science International 38:113-128.
8. Orimoto C, Shinomiya K, Shinomiya T(1985) A method for the determination of carboxyhemoglobin saturation in blood by using the Ecolyzer Model 2600. Jpn J Legal Med 39:331-338.

# RETROSPECTIVE POST-MORTEM STUDY OF 118 PEDESTRIANS

*Silveira Ribeiro C; Santos A; Carneiro de Sousa MJ; Pinto da Costa J*

Medico-legal Institute, Faculty of Medicine, Biomedical Sciences Institute "Abel Salazar", University of Oporto; Faculty of Law, University Portucalense "Infante D. Henrique"; Jardim Carrilho Videira 4000, Porto, Portugal

## I - Introduction

Deaths of pedestrians have been considered one of the most common cause of death in road fatalities. The kind of vehicle, the speed, its design and the characteristics of the victims (child or adult) makes a difference to the dynamics of the impact (location of impact, severity of injuries and body distribution). The aim of this study is to get an overview of pedestrian deaths in the North of Portugal and try to characterize the dynamics of the accident.

## II - Material and methods

The authors studied all the corpses of pedestrians involved in traffic accidents and examined in the Medicolegal Institute of Oporto during 1993 (n = 118). Each case was studied with regards to the accident reconstruction, medical and autopsy data analysis. Blood alcohol concentration was analysed except when there was survival over 24 hours and/or surgery. Finally the authors performed a map of the topographic distribution of the injuries both on the external and internal examination of the corpse.

## III - Results

From the total of 118 victims studied, 63 were males and 55 females. The age average of the victims was 51.8 years old and the group most affected was in the seventh decade of life (22.8%). The age distribution is given in Table I. The majority of the accidents involved four wheel cars (57.6%) (Table II) and occurred when the victim was crossing a road (41.5 %) (Table III).

| AGE OF THE VICTIM | % |
|---|---|
| 0-9 | 12.7 |
| 10-19 | 5.9 |
| 20-29 | 6.8 |
| 30-39 | 6.8 |
| 40-49 | 5.9 |
| 50-59 | 11.9 |
| 60-69 | 14.5 |
| 70-79 | 22.8 |
| 80-89 | 12.7 |

**Table I**

| VEHICLE INVOLVED | % |
|---|---|
| MOTORCYCLE | 16.1 |
| FOUR WHEEL | 57.6 |
| VAN | 13.6 |
| BUS | 4.3 |
| TRUCK | 7.6 |
| UNKNOWN | 0.8 |

**Table II**

| PLACE | % |
|---|---|
| CROSSING A ROAD | 41.5 |
| ROAD SIDE | 28.8 |
| CITY STREET | 29.7 |

**Table III**

| WEATHER CONDITIONS | % |
|---|---|
| DRY | 72.9 |
| WET | 5.9 |
| RAIN | 10.2 |
| UNKNOWN | 11.0 |

**Table IV**

| ALCOHOL BLOOD LEVEL | % | |
|---|---|---|
| NOT REQUESTED | 55.1 | |
| REQUESTED | 44.9 | ⇒ 28.8% ( NEGATIVE)<br>16.1% (POSITIVE) |

**Table V**

No important predominance of lateral external injuries was found in spite of the study of side impact. The study of the weather conditions showed that 72.9% of accidents happened in dry weather (Table IV). The blood alcohol concentration was studied in 44.9 % of cases. Of these

16.1% were positive (minimum - 0.15 g/l and maximum - 3.61 g/l) (Table V). The majority of the accidents occurred in the afternoon and early evening. The weekly distribution showed a predominance on saturday (30 cases). In 54.2 % of the cases the survival was less than 24 hours (4.85 hours average) and in 45.8 % was over 24 hours (12.75 days average). Almost 60% of victims passed through two hospitals. The cause of death was most often associated with head injuries (48.4%) (TableVI), the majority of them connected with soft tissue injuries being 51 % related with brain damage ( Fig.1).

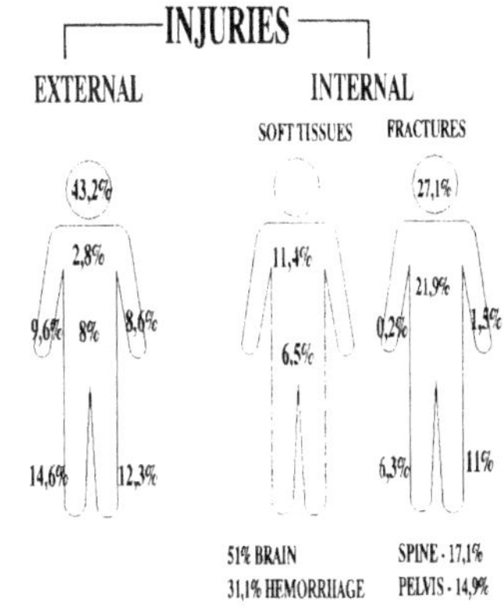


Fig.1

FATAL INJURIES

| LOCALIZATION | % | INFECTIOUS COMPLICATIONS |
|---|---|---|
| HEAD | 48,4 % | 26,3 % |
| POLITRAUMA | 44,9 % | 11,3 % |
| ABDOMEN | 3,3 % | 50 % |
| CHEST | 2,6 % | 0 % |
| SPINE | 0,8 % | 100 % |

**Table VI**

## IV - Discussion

In this study the most affected victims belong to the age group 70 - 79 years old. This indicates the greater risk of old people being involved in a traffic accident such as running over. The decrease of sight, hearing and physical ability may be an important factor. With the population´s effect of aging this establishes an important public health problem. Concerning the blood alcohol concentration 16.1% of victims were under the influence of alcohol (maximum level 3.61 g/l and minimum 0.15 g/l) and the drunken state might have contributed to decreased awareness of the pedestrian.

## V - Conclusion

The forensic autopsy of victims of traffic accidents was 11.5 % of the total number of autopsies performed in the Medico-Legal Institute of Oporto in 1993. This gives evidence to the problem of " pedestrians traffic" versus " vehicle traffic". Emphasis must be given to this problem in the scope of public health as it constitutes an important cause of death in elderly people (over 65). The quartet of vehicle / driver / state of road / pedestrian should be better studied for, as running over motif were appointed : vehicle over speed, bad road signaling, driving and / or pedestrian inattention. The most frequent cause of death was associated with head injuries, resulting either from throwing forward or direct impact whit, 51 % related to brain damages, followed by the politrauma (44.9 %) complicated in both cases with infection in 26.3% and 11.3% respectively.

## BIBLIOGRAPHY


•Ashton SJ, Mackay GM (1978) Pedestrian injuries and death. In : Mason JK, ed. Pathology of Violent Injury London, Edward Arnold.

•Inge Morild (1994) Traffic deaths in Western Norway. A study from the country of Hordaland 1986-1990. Forensic Sci.Int., 64: 9-20.

•Phyllis, Agran F (1994) Acidentes em crianças por atropelamento. Diferenças em função da sua localização. Pediatrics (ed.port.), 2- 2: 113-119

•Pinto da Costa J (1979) Estudo sistemático de lesões traumáticas em casos mortais de acidentes de tráfego. O Médico, 93-1472: 307-319

•Samuel, Ciricillo F (1992) Severity and outcome of intracranial lesions in pedestrians injured by motor vehicles. J.of Trauma , 6: 899-903.

•Simpson K (1960) The interpretation of the surface pattern of vehicular injuries. Med.Sci. Law,1: 420-428.

# APPLICATION OF RIGID ENDOSCOPES FOR FORENSIC EXAMINATION OF STAB WOUNDS

**Karol Śliwka[1], Jarosław A. Berent[1], Danuta Miścicka-Śliwka[1], Elżbieta Bloch-Bogusławska[1], Ferdynand Tyloch[2]**

**Forensic Medicine Institute[1] and Department of Urology[2], The Ludwik Rydygier's University School of Medical Sciences in Bydgoszcz, ul. Skłodowskiej-Curie 9 85-094 Bydgoszcz, Poland, tel/fax ++48 52 41 12 49**

**Key words**
post mortem endoscopy, stab wound, canal

**Introduction**

Most methods of clinical diagnostics, such as different radiological, ultrasonographic or finally endoscopic examinations have very limited use in forensic medicine. It is the result of the fact, that a pathologist can evaluate almost everything directly, with no application of any device. There are only a few published papers concerning the forensic autopsies assisted with such methods [1-7].

The above mentioned ways like the forensic endoscopy can sometimes be useful, when it is necessary to examine regions which are difficult to reach during typical autopsy, e.g. the fundus of the eye or external auditory canal or the nose with the throat [1,2,4]. Some trials have been made to x-ray the canal of experimental stab wounds in parenchymatous organs [6]. The very specialized postmortal radiological surveys have also been used in purely scientific goals [3,5].

We have not found any paper concerning the other use of endoscopy, stab wounds examination with the rigid endoscope before the opening of the body cavities to evaluate the primary anatomical contexts.

Exact evaluation of the canal of the stab wound and its appearance is of essential value for criminological purposes. A very important question is the angle of inserting the knife or the other sharp tool into the body. Conventional method of examination by preparation in layers can unsettle the initial anatomical relationship and that is why it was worth checking any other way as a means for examining the canal of the wound before the opening of the body. Such possibilities were born with the rapid development of endoscopy. The only paper dealing with this topic we found was our preliminary report [7].

**Aim of the paper**

The aim of investigation was endoscopic evaluation of the stab wounds prior to opening of the body cavities with regard to internal appearance of the wound canal and direction of its course and, generally, checking the usefulness of endoscoping of the stab wounds in forensic post mortem diagnostics.

**Material and methods**

Human bodies with stab wound of the chest or abdomen directed to our institute by the public prosecutor's office have been investigated. The rigid front-viewing endoscope made by Storz (length 250 mm, diameter 5 mm, 0° type) connected by the flexible wave-guide (length of 1.5 m) to the cold light source with halogen bulb (12 V, 150 W) has been used. The observations were provided directly by endoscope or using the Olympus colour TV camera and monitor. Some of them were also recorded with VHS video recorder. The small vacuum aspirating device has been using to remove the blood and other body fluids. The angle of inserting the endoscope was measured on the external surface of the body using a simple protractor.

**Results**

We have managed to introduce the endoscope in all cases. Extravasated blood made the observations impossible. It was necessary to remove it first using the vacuum aspirating device. The appearance of the angles and edges of the wound on the external surface of the chest organs (phot. 1-3 and fig.1) allows us to find the position of the sharp edge of the knife in relation to the anatomical surfaces of the body.

**Phot 1.** Sharp end of the wound

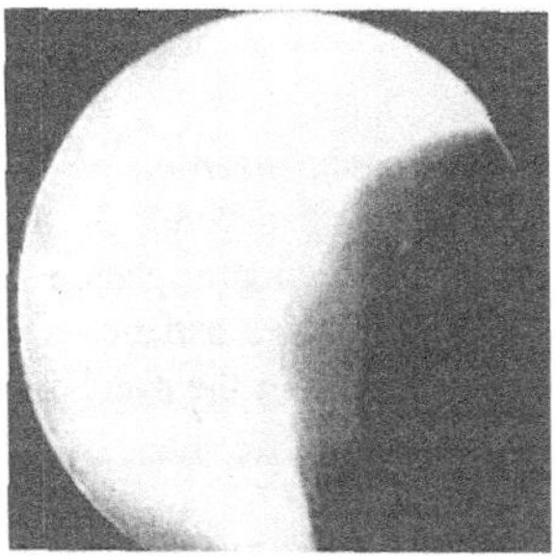

**Phot 2.** Edge of the wound

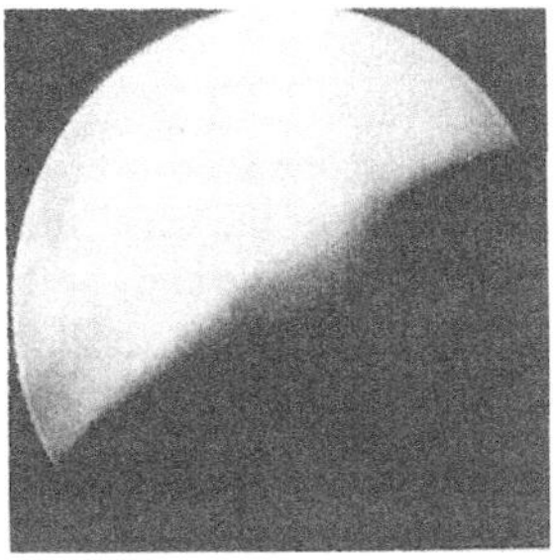

**Phot 3.** Non-sharp end of the wound

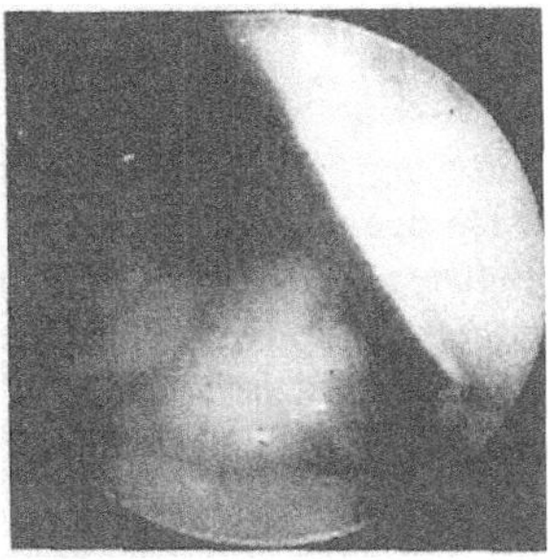

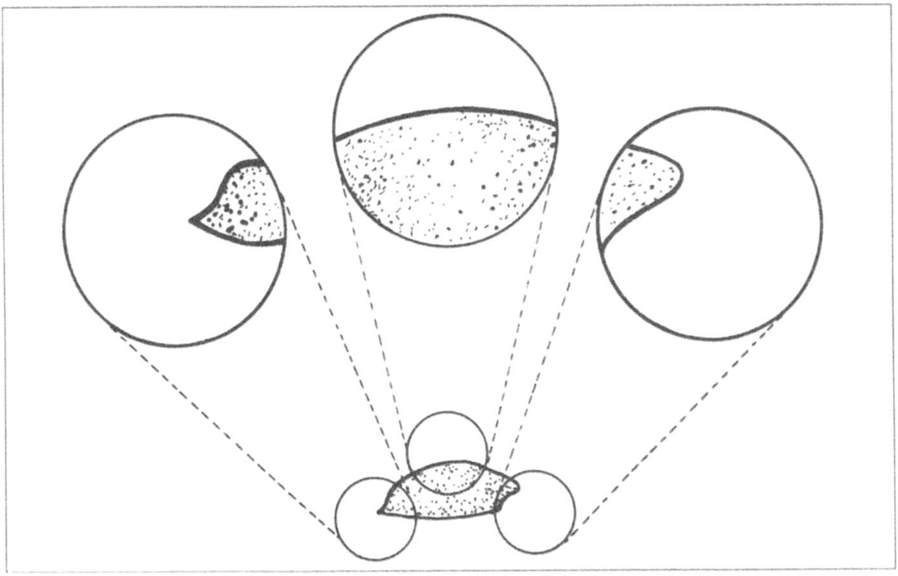

**Fig. 1** Schema of the wound on the pericardium. The circles shows areas visible on the photographs: left - phot. 1, the middle - phot. 2, right - phot. 3.

The canal of the wound, according to the wound of the heart, can be traced up to the heart wall. The deeper observation is very difficult because of presence of the fluid and clotted blood. The trials to aspirate the blood from the heart ventricles have failed. Similar difficulties were observed in the cases of heart tamponade. That is why, the accurate finding of the angle of the canal is possible after inserting the end of the endoscope in the pericardium. It should also be pointed that the wounds on the heart usually were moved even a few centimeters in relation to pericardium wound. It can make a big differencies to the so found striking angle. In our opinion the most proper measurement of the angle is based on the position of the pericardium wound. The position of the endoscope was measured in relation to frontal and sagittal plane of the body. The total depth of the wound was not always possible to establish, because of the impossibility of establishing the bottom of the wound. Nevertheless the precise evaluating of the part of the canal visible in endoscope was possible in all the cases.

The endoscopy has an advantage over the conventional methods because the result is found directly after insertion of the endoscope and it is very accurate.

We have found a big difficulties within the abdomen. It was nearly impossible to find the wound of the bowels.

**Discussion**

Probing of the wounds with the endoscope is a difficult method. Proper insertion of the endoscope is complicated when the course of the canal is not regular, which depends on the relative movements of the appropriate layers of the body at the moment of striking in relation to the time of autopsy. Nevertheless the finding of the canal is possible with some patience and experience within the range of the chest. In the case of the abdomen the finding of the distal part of the canal is almost impossible.

**Fig. 2** Schema of measurement of the angle of impact. Left - conventional, right - using endoscope.

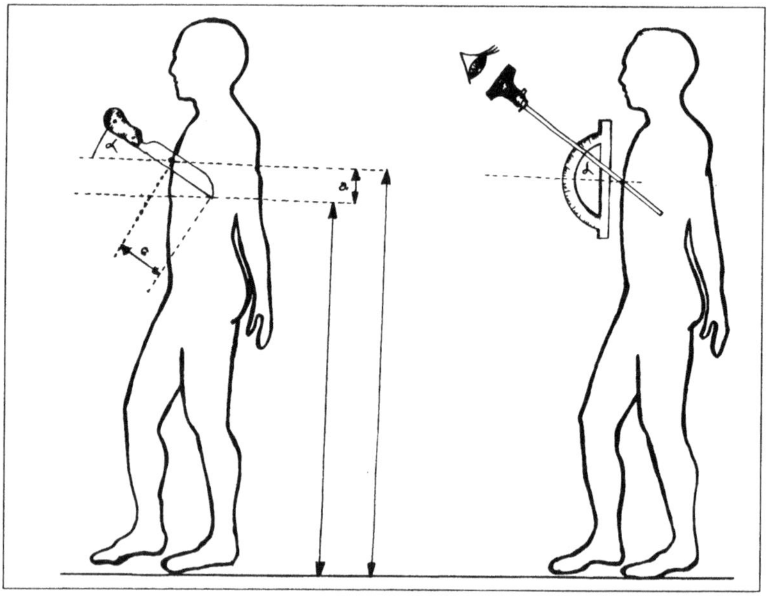

The end position of endoscope shows directly the tool position - which is easy to measure using a simple protractor (fig. 2).

Using the TV camera simplifies the observation for more than one person at the same time and allows us to video record it for scientific and didactic purposes.

## Conclusions

**1. Endoscopy of the stab wounds allows us to discard the old rule that the stab wounds should not be probed anyway.**

**2. Anatomical structures without physiological mobility are the best for establishing the canal course.**

**3. Endoscopy of the stab wounds of the thorax usually allows us directly to find and measure the striking angle.**

## References

1. Amberg R, Lemmen KD, Pollak S et al (1992) Postmortale endoskopische Diagnostik. Beitr Gerichtl Med 50:241-250

2. Amberg R, Lemmen KD, Unsold R et al (1993) The use of postmortem endoscopic examinations in forensic autopsies. IAFS 13th International Meeting, oral presentation no. 24/9/50/3A, Dusseldorf

3. Falkenstein DB, Riccobono C, Sidhu G et al (1975) The endoscopic intrahepatic cholangiogram. Clinicopathologic correlation with postmortem cholangiogram. Invest Radiol 10:358-365

4. Saternus KS (1988) Einsatzmoglichkeiten fur Rhinoskopie und Otoskopie bei der forensichen Autopsie. Beitr Gerichtl Med 46:497-502

5. Schmitz-Moormann P, Riedel R and Ihm P (1981) Morphometrische Untersuchung der Kaliberschwankungen am normalen Ductus pancreaticus major. Z Gastroenterol 19:299-306

6. Varro A, Hertel V and Bajanowski T (1990) Rontgendarstellung von Stichkanalen in parenchymatosen Organen. Arch Kriminol 186:98-106

7. Śliwka K, Bloch-Bogusławska E and Berent JA (1993) Próba zastosowania endoskopów sztywnych w ocenie przebiegów kanałów ran kłutych. III Łódzkie Sympozjum "Przestępstwa przeciwko życiu", oral presentation no.7, Cesarka k/Łodzi, Poland

# POSITIVE FINDINGS IN THE HEART CONDUCTION SYSTEM (HCS) IN CASES OF SUDDEN DEATH

Suárez-Peñaranda, JM and Concheiro-Carro, L
Institute of Legal Medicine. University of Santiago de Compostela. Spain.

There is no doubt that arrhythmia plays the major role in most cases of sudden cardiac death. Nevertheless, not many studies of the HCS have been performed, which have focused on the underlying mechanism of sudden death, because the methodology of its study is considered expensive and time consuming.

The HCS was investigated in twenty-seven cases of sudden cardiac death. A complete post-mortem examination was done in every case to rule out non-cardiac death, including toxicological investigation when drugs of abuse were suspected. Sudden death was defined when occurring in the first six hours from the onset of the symptoms.

The study of the HCS was done using a simplified method, based upon the description of Charlton and Williams.

Five of the twenty-seven cases investigated showed pathological changes in the HCS, which were considered responsible for the death of the individuals. These cases are described in detail below.

Case 1: A 32-year-old healthy man, who suddenly felt bad during the night. In the morning, he was found dead by his wife.

The atrioventricular junction showed a low insertion of the septal tricuspid leaflet, and the atrio-ventricular node (AVN) was elongated. A wide gap in the CFB allowed an aberrant communication between the AVN and the ventricular septal myocardium. The bundle of His was subendocardially located, on the left side of the CFB, and showed mild fibrosis.

Case 2: A 21-year-old woman was found dead in her bedroom by her family. The most outstanding finding in the sino-atrial node (SAN) was luminal obstruction of its artery. It showed important medial fibromuscular hyperplasia, with focal distribution. The AVN showed fibre disarray with persistent fetal dispersion, characterised by islands of conduction tissue separated from AVN, embedded in the CFB. Small arterial vessels in the summit of the inter ventricular septum showed similar findings to those described in the SAN artery.

Case 3: A 45-year-old man, alcoholic abuser, was found dead in his bedroom.

The AVN was slightly elongated, but the most outstanding feature was the fibrosis with isolation of specific conduction tissue. This finding was also indentified in the bundle of His, which was eccentrically placed to the right side of the CFB. The fibrosis was not homogeneous, and in some areas was not well established and fibroblastic cells were seen.

The left bundle branch was a slender tract crossing across the CFB, and the right bundle branch was surrounded by a fibrous sheath.

Case 4: A 31-year-old, healthy, man died suddenly while watching TV.

In the AV junction, a septal tricuspid leaflet with a low insertion was seen. A wide gap in the central fibrous body, which was partially replaced by fatty tissue, allowed an abnormal communication between the AVN and the atrial muscle, and the septal ventricular myocardium.

Case 5: A 40-year-old, healthy, man was found dead at home by his family.

The bundle of His could not be identified. A marked fibrosis of the summit of the interventricular septum and the central fibrous body caused obliteration of this structure. Nevertheless, terminal bundle brunches showed no abnormalities except for focal fibrosis of the left bundle brunch.

We found that the simplified method for the study of the HCS we have attempted in this paper is reliable and provides valuable histological information about the major elements of the HCS: SA, AV, bundle of His and bundle brunches. It is not excessively time-consuming for the technician and is suitable for routine use in a general pathology laboratory.

Our positive findings in the investigation of the HCS in cases of sudden cardiac death support the opinion, previously expressed by Bharati, that abnormalities of the conducting system may be the only pathological finding in cases of sudden death, thus encouraging the performance of HCS studies in such cases.

# DELAYED SUBDURAL HEMATOMA DUE TO MINOR HEAD INJURY

Tsuneo SUZUKI, Kiyoshi YOSHIKAWA and Kazuo UMETSU

Department of Forensic Medicine, Yamagata University School of Medicine, Yamagata, 990-23, Japan

## Introduction

In subdural hemorrhage, there may be a latent interval before clinical signs and symptoms appear. When there is a lucid interval, this may be longer than the average four hours, and there is no upper limit to this interval, because the acute subdural hemorrhage merges into a chronic condition. In severe acute lethal subdural bleeding, however, associated brain damage causes uninterrupted coma from the time of injury, although in cases without brain damage, lucid intervals tend to be short or nonexistent[1]. The present case, however, suggests that the lethal subdural hematoma may develop rapidly several days after the time of minor head injury.

## Case

A woman aged 80 was found dead in the face-down position in her living room in the morning. She fell to the floor and had an abrasion and some minor bruises on the forehead several days before. However, she had not shown any symptoms before her death, and she went to bed at 9.00 p.m. on the night before as usual.

## Autopsy findings

Externally, there was no injury around the head except a small scab in the left corner of the forehead (Fig.1). There were several minor hemorrhages in the frontal portion of the scalp (Fig.2). There was no fracture of the skull. Opening the skull, a fresh subdural hematoma, approximately 70g, was found on the right frontal and temporal lobes (Fig.3). No brain damage was found. The histological studies of the scalp showed marked cell infiltration in the areas of hemorrhaging (Fig.4). Some histocytes around the area of hemorrhaging had brownish small pigments. They were proved to be hemosiderin pigments by the hemosiderin staining (Fig.5). The histological findings showed that all of the bruises had occurred several days before her death, and she had no injuries on the head immediately before her death.

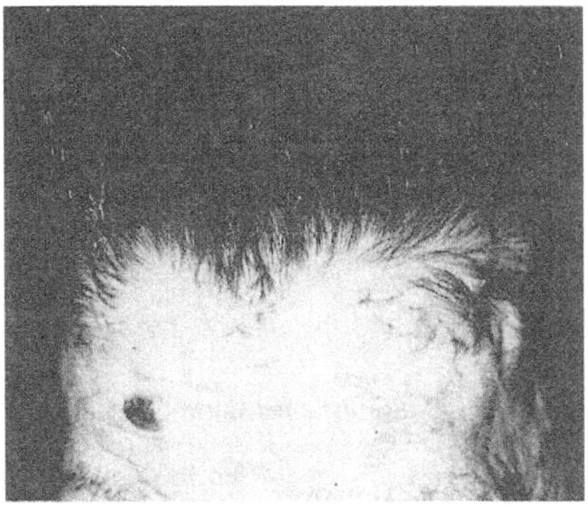

Fig.1 A small scab at the left corner of the forehead(↑).

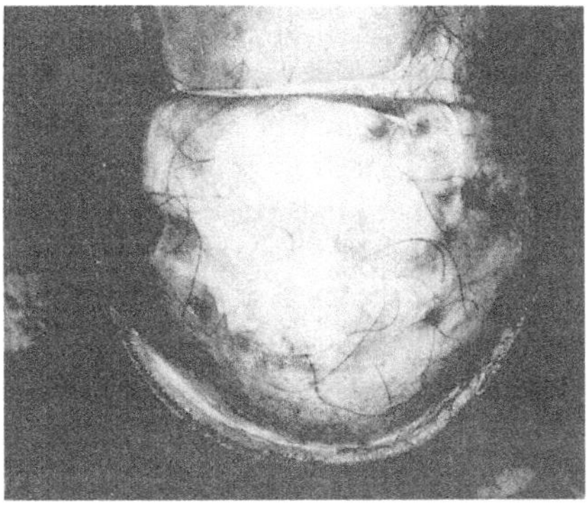

Fig.2 Several areas of hemorrhage in the frontal portion of the scalp.

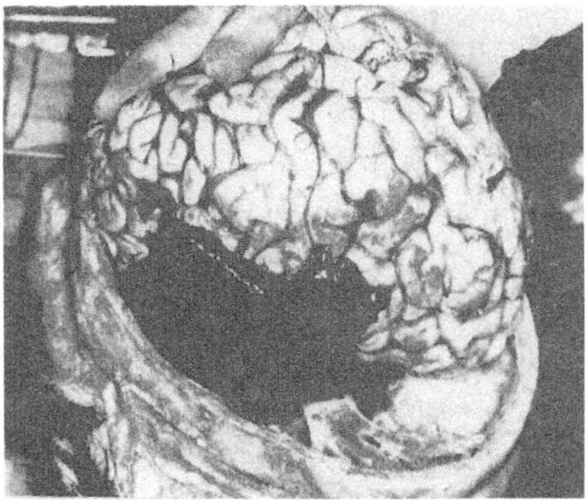

Fig.3 A fresh subdural hematoma approximately 70g on the right flontal and temporal lobes.

## Discussions

It is known that in elderly individuals, subdural hematomas may occur without apparent head injury or with very minor injury, and symptoms may develop over days[2]. The lesions, however, are frequently seen as an incidental finding at autopsy where death was caused by some unrelated condition[1]. In the present case, the histological findings proved that she had very minor head injuries on the frontal area and the life threatening subdural hematoma developed suddenly several days after the time of injury. It is easy to understand that the minor head injuries caused the subdural hematoma because of her old age. However, it was noteworthy that the subdural hematoma was life threatening and also there was a lucid interval of several days between the time of injury and the onset of the fatal subdural hematoma. The present case suggested that there may be the lethal subdural hematoma with lucid interval of several days in elderly individuals.

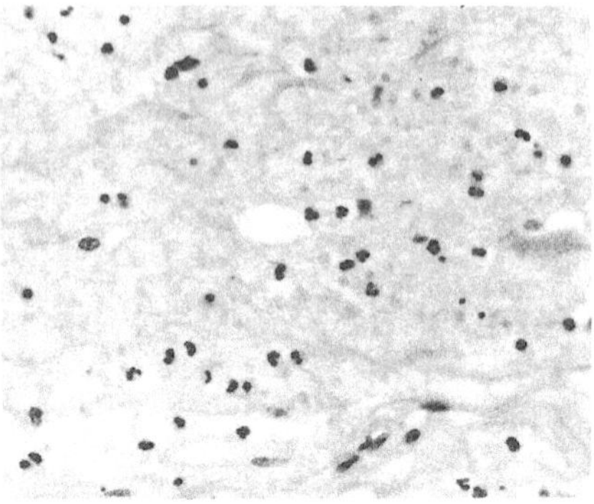

Fig.4 Cell infiltration in the areas of hemorrhage in the scalp.

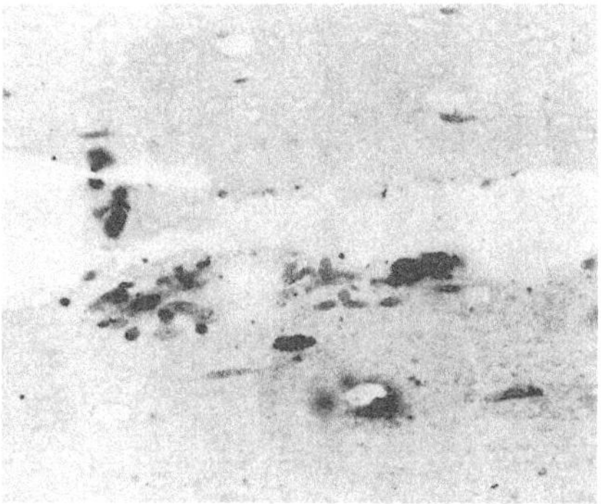

Fig.5 Hemosiderin staining of the areas of hemorrhage.

**Reference**

1) Knight B (1991) Forensic Pathology. Edward Arnold, London–Melbourne–Auckland, pp173–175

2) DiMaio D, DiMaio V (1989) Forensic Pathology. Elsevier, New York–Amsterdam–Oxford, pp156–159

# Dynamics of Subcellular Localization of Leukotoxin (9:10-epoxy-12-octadecenoic acid) in Lungs of Rats as Revealed by Immunoelectron Microscopy

Takehiko TAKATORI[1)], Wei-dong ZHANG[1)], Shigeru IWASAKA[2)], Masataka NAGAO[1)], Yoshihiro YAMADA[1)] and Kimiharu IWADATE[1)]

[1)]Department of Forensic Medicine, Faculty of Medicine, University of Tokyo, Tokyo 113, Japan

[2)]Department of Pathology, Faculty of Medicine, University of Tokyo, Tokyo 113, Japan

## Introduction

9:10-Epoxy-12-octadecenoic acid (Leukotoxin: LTx, Fig. 1) has been reported to exist in polymorphonuclear leukocytes (PMNs) and is of interest because of the important anti-inflammatory role played by PMNs in response to tissue inflammation and injury. Moreover, LTx has been found in burned skin and has been shown to exert an uncoupling effect on mitochondrial respiration as a shock factor (Suzuki *et al.* 1981; Yokoo *et al.* 1986; Hayakawa *et al.* 1991). These findings indicate that LTx is an important substance in living organisms and thus worthy of attention.

We have already reported the immunohistochemical dynamics of LTx in lungs of rats exposed to pure oxygen. Positive reactions with anti-LTx serum were observed not only in neutrophils but also in alveolar macrophages. The present study examined the intercellular localization of LTx in neutrophils and alveolar macrophages of rats exposed to pure oxygen using the pre-embedding method with anti-LTx IgG(Fab) purified and immunoelectron microscopy.

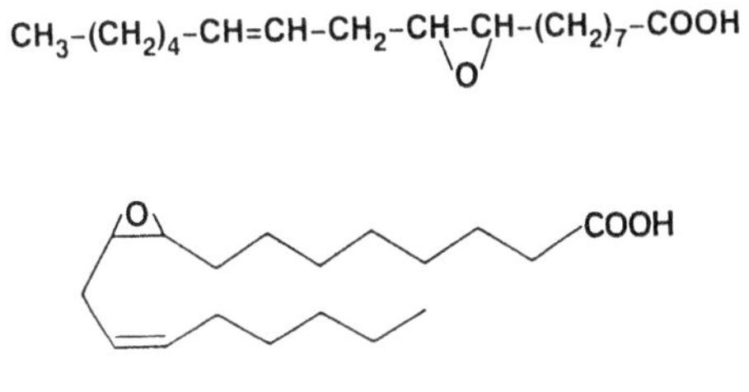


Fig. 1. Structure of leukotoxin (9,10-epoxy-12-octadecenoic acid).

## Materials and Methods

### *Animal treatment*

Male Sprague-Dawley rats (n=4), weighing 210±10 g, were used for all experiments. The control rats (n=2) were exposed to ambient air until sacrifice. The experimental rats (n=2) were continuously exposed to pure oxygen for 72 h. The atmosphere in the glass inhalation chamber was maintained at more than 95% $O_2$ during all experiments, and the temperature at 22±2°C. All rats were provided food and water *ad libitum*, and sacrificed under light diethyl ether anesthesia.

### *Sample treatment*

After a given period of exposure, the lungs of the rats were perfused intratracheally with 4% paraformaldehyde (PFA) dissolved in 0.1 M phosphate buffer (PB, pH 7.6) for 10 min and removed from the thoracic cavity under light diethyl ether anesthesia. The samples were cut into pieces measuring 3×3×2 mm, refixed in 2% periodate-lysineparaformaldehyde (PLP) for 12 h at 4°C, and then washed with 5 ~ 20% sucrose dissolved in 0.01 M phosphate-buffered saline (PBS, pH 7.4) at 4°C. They were then cut into sections 6 ~ 10 μm thick with a cryostat.

*Preparation of TEM samples*

A polyclonal antibody against LTx reported previously was used (Akabane *et al.* 1993). Anti-LTx IgG was purified by a protein-A column from anti-LTx serum and digested into Fab fragments with papain for immunocytochemical staining. The concentration of protein was measured by spectrophotometry (Nippon-Bunko Ubest-55).

We employed the pre-embedding method for anti-LTx IgG(Fab) immunocytochemical staining.

## Results and Discussion

Positive reactions with the anti-LTx IgG(Fab) were observed in neutrophils and alveolar macrophages of the rats exposed to pure oxygen for 72 h, whereas no reaction was seen in the control rat lungs (Fig. 2). As seen in Fig. 3, positive reactions with the anti-LTx IgG(Fab) were strong in the rough endoplasmic reticulum (rER) and cell membranes, and weak in mitochondrial membranes of alveolar macrophages and neutrophils.

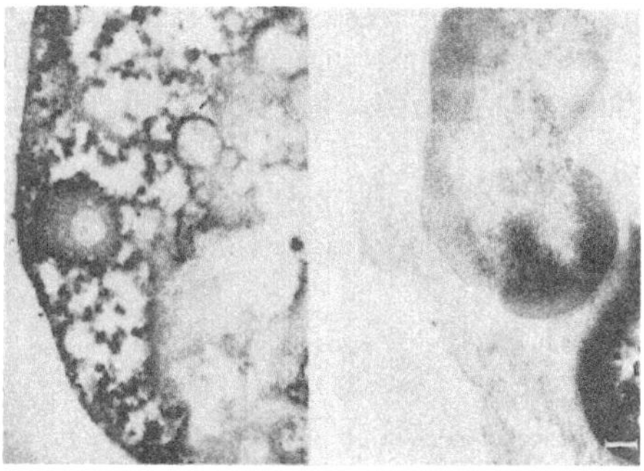

Fig. 2. Positive reaction with anti-LTx IgG (Fab) in neutrophils of the lung of a rat treated with hyperoxia for 72 h (left) compared with a control (right). Pre-embedding method. Bar=370 nm.

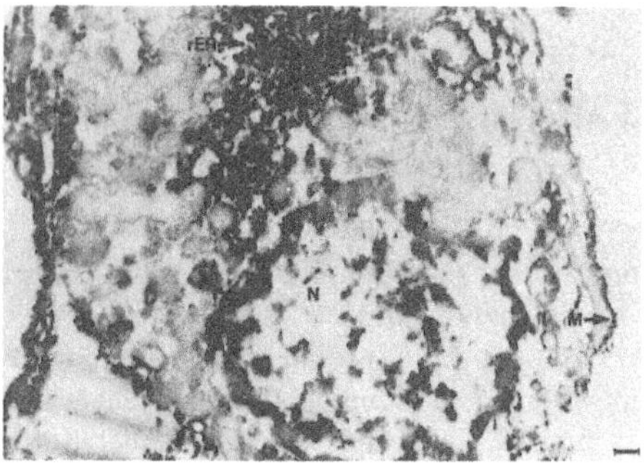


Fig. 3. Positive reaction with anti-LTx IgG(Fab) evident in the rough-endoplasmic reticulum (rER) and cell membrane (M) of an alveolar macrophage of a rat treated with hyperoxia for 72 h. Pre-embedding method. Bar=460 nm.

Under hyperoxic conditions, radicals such as superoxide and/or hydrogen peroxide are increased 15 ~ 20-fold in mitochondria of the lung and the production of oxidant from the lung is increased by 25% or more (Halliwell 1979; Turrens and Boveris 1980; Halliwell 1982). Many unsaturated fatty acids in cell membranes, moreover, react with these radicals to produce cell damage (Cross *et al.* 1987). Linoleic acid exists in the phospholipids of biomembranes, similarly to arachidonic acid, and is oxidized by epoxygenase and converted to LTx. The LTx produced via the linoleate cascade is of considerable interest, since leukotriene produced from the arachidonate cascade is closely related to lung damage and/or remodeling.

Although biochemical and physiological studies on LTx has progressed over the last decade, the localization of LTx in cells is still unclear. This is believed to be the first demonstration of the ultrastructural localization of LTx in neutrophils and alveolar macrophages of rats exposed to hyperoxia by TEM together with immunocytochemical staining. The findings indicate that LTx is produced in biomembrane-rich organelles of alveolar macrophages as well as neutrophils and is dependent on the duration of hyperoxic treatment. It is suggested that LTx is closely related to biological reactions and appears to be an important chemical mediator in pulmonary diseases.

## References

Yokoo K, Hayakawa M, Sugiyama S, Ozawa T, Aoyama H, Izawa Y, Kondo T, Hayakawa Y (1986) A novel uncoupler of mitochondrial respiration, 9,10-epoxy-12-octadecenoate, exists in human burned skin. J Clin Biochem Nutr 1: 121-127

Suzuki K, Aoyama H, Izawa Y, Kobayashi M, Ozawa T (1981) Isolation of a substance toxic to mitochondrial function from the burned skin of rats. Burns 8: 110-117

Hayakawa M, Kosaka, K, Sugiyama, S, Yokoo, K, Aoyama, H, Izawa, Y, Ozawa, T (1991) Proposal of leukotoxin, 9,10-epoxy-12-octadecenoate, as a burn toxin. Bio Chem Int 21: 573-579

Akabane H, Nagao M, Zhang W-D, Yamada Y, Oono T, Takatori T (1993) Production and characterization of antibodies reactive with leukotoxin. Jpn J Legal Med 47: 93-97

Turrens JF, Boveris A (1980) Generation of superoxide anion by NADH dehydrogenase of bovine heart mitochondria. Biochem J 191: 421-427

Halliwell B (1979) Oxygen-free radicals in living systems: Dangerous but useful? In: Shilo M (ed) Strategies of Microbial Life in Extreme Environments. Dahlem Konferenzen, Berlin, P 159

Halliwell B (1982) Superoxide and superoxide-dependent formation of hydroxyl radical are important in oxygen toxicity. Trends Biochem Sci 7: 270-275

Cross CE, Halliwell B, Borish ET, Pryor WA, Ames BN, Saul RL, McCord JM, Harman D. (1987) Oxygen radicals and human disease. An Int Med 107: 526-545

# Sex Determination with a Discriminate Function Analysis of Deciduous Teeth Size in Plaster Models

H. TSUTSUMI, T. KOMURO and T. TAKEI
Department of Legal Medicine, Nihon University School of Dentistry, Tokyo, JAPAN

## 【 INTRODUCTION 】

There have been many reports on sex determination using permanent teeth. However, there have been only a few reports on sex determination using deciduous teeth. Plaster models of the teeth of 3-year-old Japanese children (96 males, 98 females) were used to record the crown length, crown width and crown thickness of 5 maxillary and 5 mandibular deciduous teeth (30 measurement values). Furthermore, a number of practical formulae were derived from only the crown width and crown thickness values because the were of deciduous teeth in children 4 years and older progresses rapidly, making the crown length measurement unreliable. These formulae were calculated for the maxillary teeth alone and mandibular teeth alone. The formulae based on only the crown width or thickness were also calculated for both maxillary and mandibular teeth . A step-wise discriminate analysis was then used to ascertain the most reliable measurements and a practical formula subsequently devised.

## 【 MATERIALS AND METHODS 】

1. Materials

96 Males , 98 Females . Plaster model of the teeth of 3-year-old Japanese children.

2. Measurement dimensions and standards

On 20 deciduous teeth of the maxillary and mandibular left and right sides on plaster models, clinical crown length, width, and thickness were measured using slide calipers with digital scale (1/100 in accuracy). Measurement of 20 teeth in each plaster model was conducted twice. Each mean measured value was obtained from identical teeth in the identical arch quadrant. The measured values of 30 items were used as factors for sex determination(Fig.1).

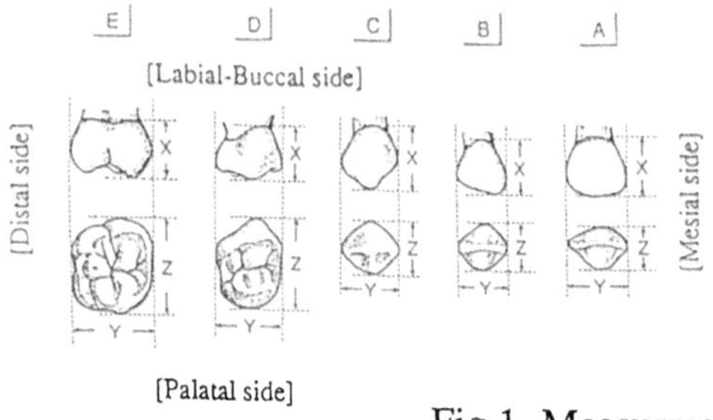


X: Crown length
Y: Crown width
Z: Crown thickness

A| : Maxillary right deciduous central incisor
B| : Maxillary right deciduous lateral incisor
C| : Maxillary right deciduous canine
D| : Maxillary right first deciduous molar
E| : Maxillary right second deciduous molar

Fig.1. Measurment Items

## 【 RESULTS 】

1. Sex difference of measured values

The mean value for each measurement was greater in males than in females.

Significant differences in the values recorded were seen in 28 out of the 30 measurements taken. The measurement items not exhibiting these significant differences were the crown width of the maxillary lateral incisor and the crown thickness of the mandibular second molar(Table 1).

2. Sex determination by discriminate analysis

In case of sex determination using 30 measurement values(Table 2) .

Determinant analysis for judgment of sex with all measured levels as factors was conducted and coefficients ($L_1$- $L_{30}$) and constants for determination with each measured dimension were shown.

3. Sex determination by stepwise analysis

Calculation of a formula for sex determination under various conditions(Table 3).

4. Table 4 shows the results obtained by this study and by Black, T.K..

The accuracy ranges were obtained using stepwise determinant formulaus for sex determination under various conditions. Black, T.K. conducted sex determination by stepwise analysis using American Caucasian deciduous teeth (plaster models).The accuracy ranges in this study were higher under all conditions than Black's study.

## 【DISCUSSION】

The eruption order of deciduous teeth was central incisor→ lateral incisor → first molar → canine → second molar, and the completion time was almost 2 years after birth. With respect to results of maxillary teeth, the second deciduous molar was not selected as a factor in both Black's study and our study. Moreover, since the deciduous canine was not selected in this study, these teeth are not considered as factors for sex determination(Table 5). Therefore, when eruption of the first deciduous molar is complete (about 1 year after birth), this method is applicable. With respect to the mandible

### Sex difference of measured values

Table 1. Mean and S.D. for 30 measurements items

| | | Item | Male Mean | Male S.D. | Female Mean | Female S.D. | Significanse |
|---|---|---|---|---|---|---|---|
| Maxillary | A | Cl | 5.23 | 0.47 | 4.97 | 0.43 | ** |
| | | Cw | 6.50 | 0.35 | 6.36 | 0.36 | * |
| | | Ct | 5.20 | 0.32 | 4.97 | 0.29 | ** |
| | B | Cl | 4.79 | 0.44 | 4.49 | 0.39 | ** |
| | | Cw | 5.32 | 0.37 | 5.25 | 0.37 | |
| | | Ct | 5.02 | 0.40 | 4.82 | 0.35 | ** |
| | C | Cl | 5.46 | 0.44 | 5.22 | 0.44 | ** |
| | | Cw | 6.54 | 0.36 | 6.37 | 0.29 | ** |
| | | Ct | 6.02 | 0.40 | 5.81 | 0.41 | ** |
| | D | Cl | 4.94 | 0.40 | 4.65 | 0.36 | ** |
| | | Cw | 7.21 | 0.40 | 6.96 | 0.34 | ** |
| | | Ct | 8.97 | 0.44 | 8.72 | 0.41 | ** |
| | E | Cl | 4.71 | 0.39 | 4.39 | 0.43 | ** |
| | | Cw | 9.18 | 0.44 | 8.98 | 0.39 | * |
| | | Ct | 10.24 | 0.44 | 10.03 | 0.40 | ** |
| Mandibular | A | Cl | 4.63 | 0.46 | 4.37 | 0.43 | ** |
| | | Cw | 4.13 | 0.25 | 3.97 | 0.28 | ** |
| | | Ct | 4.05 | 0.32 | 3.86 | 0.23 | ** |
| | B | Cl | 5.05 | 0.52 | 4.77 | 0.46 | ** |
| | | Cw | 4.63 | 0.27 | 4.52 | 0.25 | * |
| | | Ct | 4.44 | 0.30 | 4.32 | 0.25 | * |
| | C | Cl | 5.89 | 0.44 | 5.68 | 0.50 | * |
| | | Cw | 5.65 | 0.32 | 5.53 | 0.31 | * |
| | | Ct | 5.62 | 0.37 | 5.48 | 0.35 | * |
| | D | Cl | 5.39 | 0.38 | 5.09 | 0.39 | ** |
| | | Cw | 8.18 | 0.44 | 7.95 | 0.37 | ** |
| | | Ct | 7.72 | 0.48 | 7.41 | 0.36 | ** |
| | E | Cl | 4.79 | 0.38 | 4.53 | 0.46 | ** |
| | | Cw | 10.28 | 0.45 | 9.99 | 0.42 | ** |
| | | Ct | 9.38 | 0.42 | 9.27 | 0.37 | |

(mm)

Cl;Crown length
Cw: Crown width
Ct: Crown thickness

** : $P < 0.001$
* : $P < 0.01$

### In case of sex determination

using 30 measurement values

Table 2. Coefficient and constant

| | | Item | Coefficient(Ln) | |
|---|---|---|---|---|
| Maxillary | A | Cl | L1 | -0.680 |
| | | Cw | L2 | -0.580 |
| | | Ct | L3 | 0.323 |
| | B | Cl | L4 | 1.751 |
| | | Cw | L5 | -2.538 |
| | | Ct | L6 | 0.772 |
| | C | Cl | L7 | -0.462 |
| | | Cw | L8 | 0.471 |
| | | Ct | L9 | -0.331 |
| | D | Cl | L10 | 0.076 |
| | | Cw | L11 | 2.131 |
| | | Ct | L12 | 0.906 |
| | E | Cl | L13 | 1.704 |
| | | Cw | L14 | -0.335 |
| | | Ct | L15 | -0.662 |
| Mandibular | A | Cl | L16 | 0.049 |
| | | Cw | L17 | 1.815 |
| | | Ct | L18 | 2.687 |
| | B | Cl | L19 | 0.889 |
| | | Cw | L20 | -0.358 |
| | | Ct | L21 | -2.506 |
| | C | Cl | L22 | -1.251 |
| | | Cw | L23 | -0.657 |
| | | Ct | L24 | 0.357 |
| | D | Cl | L25 | 1.243 |
| | | Cw | L26 | 0.799 |
| | | Ct | L27 | 1.550 |
| | E | Cl | L28 | -0.728 |
| | | Cw | L29 | 1.095 |
| | | Ct | L30 | -3.144 |
| Constant | | | L0 | -17.147 |

teeth, the values for the deciduous molars are especially necessary, as Black demonstrated. In the case of the deciduous canine teeth, the crown width and thickness were selected once each, but the selection order was later. Even if there are materials which cannot be measured, it is considered that the mean value of deciduous canine teeth shown in Table 1 can be inserted in to the formula for sex determination.

Since the accuracy for sex determination obtained from infant bones to date has been around 50%, the accuracy obtained by this method is considered to be sufficiently applicable for infant sex determination.

Reference: Thomas K. Black, Sexual Dimorphism in the Tooth-Crown Diameters of the Deciduous Teeth, Am. J. Phys. Anthrop., 48, 77-82 (1978).

Table 3 Discriminant function for sexing the deciduous dentition ( by Stepwise analytical method )

| Function | Percent Correctly classified Male | Female | Total |
|---|---|---|---|
| 1 Function using the 30 measurements | | | |
| - 20.861 + 1.257 ($\overline{D}$ Cw) + 1.232 ($\underline{E}$ Cl) + 2.042 ($\overline{A}$ Ct) - 2.568 ($\overline{E}$ Ct) + 1.271 ($\overline{D}$ Ct) - 2.533 ($\underline{B}$ Cw) + 1.322 ($\underline{B}$ Cl) + 1.622 ($\underline{D}$ Cw) + 1.771 ($\overline{A}$ Cw) | 71.8% | 79.6% | 75.7% |
| 2 Function using the 20 measurements | | | |
| - 20.841 + 1.563 ($\overline{A}$ Ct) + 2.902 ($\underline{D}$ Cw) - 3.079 ($\underline{B}$ Cw) + 2.502 ($\overline{A}$ Cw) - 4.079 ($\overline{E}$ Ct) + 2.172 ($\overline{D}$ Ct) + 1.853 ($\overline{E}$ Cw) + 1.650 ($\underline{B}$ Ct) - 1.220 ($\overline{C}$ Cw) | 72.9% | 80.6% | 76.8% |
| 3 Function using the maxillary teeth alone | | | |
| - 20.745 + 2.601 (A Ct) - 1.536 (D Cw) + 2.205 (B Cw) | 74.0% | 74.5% | 74.2% |
| 4 Function using the mandibular teeth alone | | | |
| - 20.489 + 2.296 (D Ct) + 1.519 (D Cw) - 2.500 (A Ct) + 2.937 (E Ct) + 0.821 (E Cw) - 1.517 (D Ct) | 68.8% | 78.6% | 73.7% |
| 5 Function using the crown width alone | | | |
| - 19.365 + 1.555 ($\underline{D}$ Cw) + 0.758 ($\overline{E}$ Cw) + 2.050 ($\overline{A}$ Cw) - 1.444 ($\underline{B}$ Cw) | 64.6% | 74.5% | 69.6% |
| 6 Function using the crown thickness alone | | | |
| - 12.811 + 1.631 ($\underline{A}$ Ct) + 2.017 ($\overline{D}$ Ct) - 1.196 ($\overline{E}$ Ct) + 2.537 ($\overline{A}$ Ct) - 2.238 ($\overline{B}$ Ct) | 66.7% | 67.3% | 67.0% |

Table 4
Stepwise discriminate functions for sexing the deciduous dentition

| | Nunber of variables selected | | Percent correctly classified | | | | | |
|---|---|---|---|---|---|---|---|---|
| | | | male | | female | | total | |
| | Black | This study | Black | This study | Black | This study | Black | This study |
| 1) | 4 | 9 | 72.5 | 72.9 | 62.5 | 80.6 | 67.7 | 76.8 |
| 2) | 2 | 3 | 69.6 | 74.0 | 57.8 | 74.5 | 63.9 | 74.2 |
| 3) | 2 | 6 | 69.6 | 68.6 | 62.5 | 78.6 | 66.2 | 73.7 |
| 4) | 3 | 4 | 68.1 | 64.6 | 68.8 | 74.5 | 68.4 | 69.6 |
| 5) | 4 | 5 | 66.7 | 66.7 | 62.5 | 67.3 | 64.7 | 67.0 |

1) Function using crown width and thickness measurements of the maxillary and mandibular teeth.
2) Function using the maxillary teeth alone.
3) Function using the mandibular teeth alone.
4) Function using crown width measurements alone.
5) Function using crown thickness measurements alone.

Table 5. Number of measurement items selected by Stepwise analytical method

| | | Black | This study | | | Black | This study |
|---|---|---|---|---|---|---|---|
| Maxillary | | | | Mandibular | | | |
| A | Cw | 3 | | A | Cw | | 2 |
| | Ct | 1 | 2 | | Ct | | 2 |
| B | Cw | | 2 | B | Cw | 1 | 1 |
| | Ct | | 1 | | Ct | | 2 |
| C | Cw | 1 | | C | Cw | | 1 |
| | Ct | | | | Ct | | 1 |
| D | Cw | | 3 | D | Cw | | 1 |
| | Ct | 3 | | | Ct | 2 | 3 |
| E | Cw | | | E | Cw | 1 | 3 |
| | Ct | | | | Ct | 3 | 3 |
| Total | | 8 | 8 | Total | | 7 | 19 |
| | Cw | 4 | 5 | | Cw | 2 | 8 |
| | Ct | 3 | 4 | | Ct | 5 | 11 |

Cw:Crown width
Ct:Crown thickness

# IDENTIFICATION OF CALVARIUM THANKS TO THE AFTER-EFFECTS OF A MASTOIDECTOMY

J.N. VIGNAL, F. CRISPINO.(1)

(1) INSTITUT DE RECHERCHE CRIMINELLE DE LA GENDARMERIE NATIONALE, département ANTHROPOLOGIE (Institute of Forensic Sciences of the French Gendarmerie, forensic anthropology department),

Key-Words : Anthropology, identification, calvarium, mastoidectomy, pathology after-effects.

Traditionally, the anthropological techniques make it possible to determine the race, the sex, the age and the height of a person. But if these elements are sufficient within the frame of classical anthropology, they are not complementary within the frame of forensic anthropology. In our study, we had to determine the identity of a skeleton for juridical reasons (death duties, remarriage, etc...), and for psychological reasons (acceptance of the death of a next-of-kin). The positive identification is very often established through an odontological comparison. But when that comparison cannot be achieved, we can subtitute an anatomo-pathological study.

At the end of 1992, a calvarium (skull with no mandible) was discovered in a forest by hunters.

No clothes nor object could be found nearby.

The dentition was almost completely destroyed and no other part of the skeleton could be found.

It seemed to be impossible to make a positive identification of the body. However, the anatomo-pathological study made it possible to establish the identity of the skull.

The skull was sent to the forensic anthropology department of Institut de Recherche Criminelle de la Gendarmerie (Institute of Forensic Sciences of the French Gendarmerie).

The study of the skull at the anthropological level allowed us to establish the following elements :

- Racial root : subject of type occidental leucodermis of the Mediterranean group.
- Sex : male (established by the ASCADI and NEMESKERI method).
- Subject's age : between 50 et 57 (this approximation was determined through the MEINDL-LOVEJOY and MARTIN methods).

We could not precisely date the death, but according to the state of preservation of the skull and to the lack of putrid smell, we could assess that the death was prior to 1992.

At the anatomo-pathological level, we could objectivize :

- A bone crack on a big part of the inferior and middle levels. This destruction was apparently due to the penetration of an object, probably a firearm projectile, by the left tympanal bone and through the sphenoid and exiting by the right wing of the sphenoid.

- The presence of an osteoid on the left parietal. It appeared as a compact lens with a smooth, whitish, and sessile surface which is characteristic. It could evoke whether an ossified haematoma is caused by a localized traumat or a benign tumour.

- The after-effects of a right mastoidectomy. The latter was objectivized by a right mastoid which was high, concave and fistulous and showed a bony reorganization. That mastoidectomy conveyed a common surgical operation following infections of the middle ear complicated by some mastoiditis that usually takes place in during childhood.

As the dentition was not exploitable, we could not establish a positive identification by an odontological study.

On the other hand, the after-effects of the mastoidectomy was a remarkable objective identification criterion.

All the information given above were passed on to the Gendarmerie authorities concerned.

It appeared that the anthropological form sent to the Gendarmerie authorities of the district where the skull was found was compatible with that of a caucasian male in his early fifties missing since 1990 who had suicidal tendencies. The Gendarmerie contacted the wife of this missing person who could correspond to the victim. She declared that her husband had undergone an operation of the right ear when he was about 6 years old.

Thus, this calvarium could be identified by way of the anthropometrical and anatomo-pathological conclusions.

The identification of a person could be achieved thanks to the existence of a compatible anthropometrical profile and the confirmation by the family of a surgical operation which was suspected during the anatomo-pathological study.

This case shows :

- The importance of acquiring and comparing antemortem and postmortem information for the positive identification of a victim.

- The relevance of "paleopathological" methods in the field of judiciary identification.

# 8. Forensic Odonto-Anthropology

TEETH PRESENT, TEETH MISSING AND PROBABILITY: USEFULNESS IN COMPARATIVE IDENTIFICATION

FRONTY P*, GEORGET C, SAPANET M.

* Chirurgien Dentiste Expert, Chargé de cours à la Faculté de Médecine et de Pharmacie de Poitiers; 3 bis rue des Ecossais 86000 POITIERS (FRANCE)

During a comparative identification, the forensic dental surgeon has to find the various similitudes between the ante and post-mortem elements on the one hand. One the other hand, he has to define the convincing value of each similitude. He must thus determine the degree of certainty according to which the examined skull does indeed belong to the missing individual. Only one characteristic feature is analysed in this article: the dental formula, that is to say the number and the layout of the missing teeth.

## NUMERICAL ANALYSIS

A human being has got 32 teeth when his denture is complete. His dental formula varies according to his ethnic background, his heredity, his age and his oral hygiene and health. The following mathematical reasoning starts from the postulate according to which the distribution of the missing teeth would be equiprobable.

Let 'n' be the number of missing teeth: 'n' varies from 0 to 32. Let 'C' be the number of dental configurations. The number of possible configurations is indeed given by the following formula:

$$C_{32}^{n} = \frac{32!}{n!(32-n)!} = \frac{32 \times 31 \times 30 \times \ldots \times (32 - n + 1)}{n!}$$

There are 32 possible configurations over a number of individuals with 1 missing tooth each: for n=1, C=32 (fig.1).
There are 496 possible configurations over a number of individuals with 2 missing teeth each: for n=2, C=496 etc.

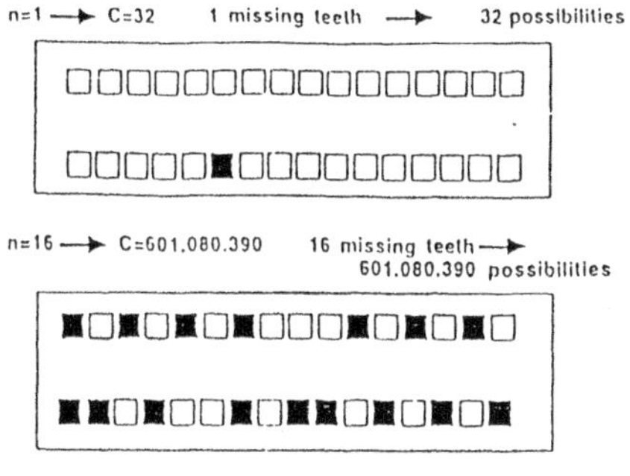


Fig. n°1: Distribution of missing teeth.

The results are shown on the following chart (fig.2). Their graphic representation (fig.3) shows a symmetry of histograms, very high values of C when n is included between 5 and 27, with a top number of C with 16 missing teeth.

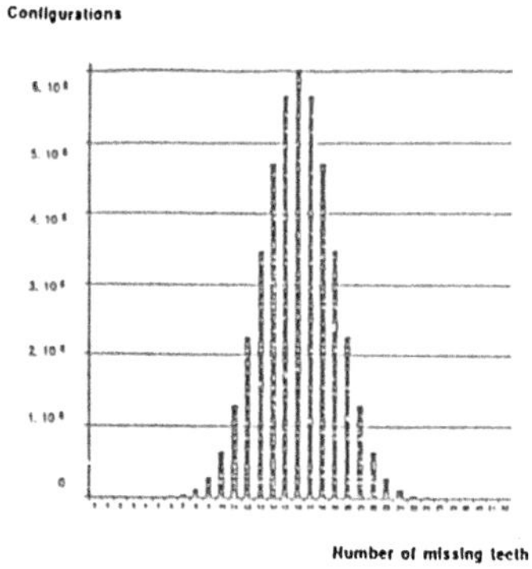


Fig. n°3: Number of equiprobable configurations according to missing teeth.

| n | P | n | P | n | P |
|---|---|---|---|---|---|
| 0 | 1 | 11 | $10^{-7}$ | 22 | $10^{-7}$ |
| 1 | 1/32 | 12 | $10^{-8}$ | 23 | $10^{-7}$ |
| 2 | 1/500 | 13 | $10^{-8}$ | 24 | $10^{-6}$ |
| 3 | 1/5000 | 14 | $10^{-8}$ | 25 | $10^{-6}$ |
| 4 | $10^{-4}$ | 15 | $10^{-8}$ | 26 | $10^{-5}$ |
| 5 | $10^{-5}$ | 16 | $10^{-8}$ | 27 | $10^{-5}$ |
| 6 | $10^{-5}$ | 17 | $10^{-8}$ | 28 | $10^{-4}$ |
| 7 | $10^{-6}$ | 18 | $10^{-8}$ | 29 | 1/5000 |
| 8 | $10^{-6}$ | 19 | $10^{-8}$ | 30 | 1/500 |
| 9 | $10^{-7}$ | 20 | $10^{-8}$ | 31 | 1/32 |
| 10 | $10^{-7}$ | 21 | $10^{-7}$ | 32 | 1 |

Fig. n°2: Probability and dental formula

## CLINICAL ANALYSIS

Actually there is no equiprobability because some cases happen more often: these are called recurrent configurations. For instance, in a western european population, when each individual lacks four teeth (n=4), one will frequently find symmetrical dental formulae where the following elements are missing:

- either the wisdom teeth: due to extractions or agenesis
- either the first premolars: due to orthodontic treatment
- either the first molars: due to early caries and extractions.

It would be necessary to undertake some statistic studies in order to determine the percentage of recurrent cases according to the various studied populations, the age, the sex etc. The rarer the configuration, the better the probability to identify.

## STUDY OF A CONCRETE EXAMPLE (fig.4)

For a skull with three missing teeth, the forensic dental surgeon would proceed as follows:
- in the first place, he brings to the fore the various similitudes between ante and post mortem elements. He particularly gathers the individual's dental track in order to determine his dental formula and to compare it with that of the skull. The presence of incoherent elements marks the end of his work. The absence of such elements enables him to look for the probability of identification.
- in the second place, he determines the probability P1 to have an individual with three missing teeth whatever their place (for instance P1=2/100) according to his human group and his age.
- then he determines the degree of rarety of the examined configuration. If he is not dealing with a recurrent case, the probability P2 to have an identical dental formula among this sample of individuals with three missing teeth is about 1/5000 (fig.2).
- he afterwards looks for the chances of appearance of each similitude between ante and post mortem, in this population: P3 for a crown on tooth number 16, for instance 5/100; P4 for a Richmond on tooth number 22, for instance 1/200.

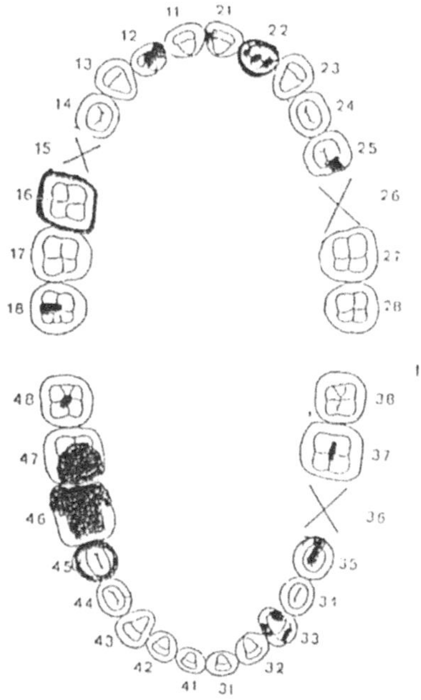


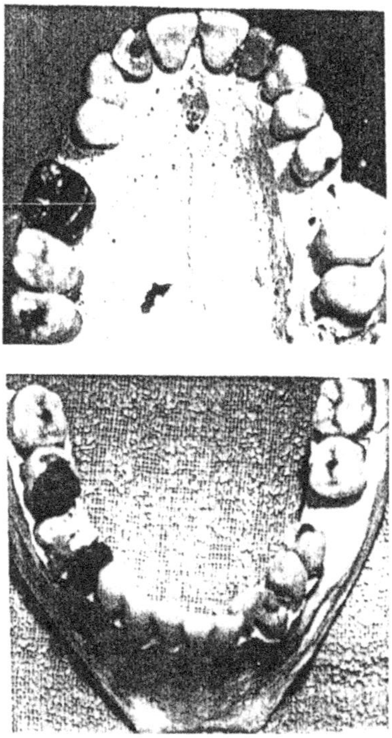

Fig.4: ante-mortem odontogram victim's jaws

- Finally, he calculates the probability P according to which the examined skull does belong to the missing individual. Indeed, <u>**if all the analysed events are independent**</u>, and only in that case, this probability P is equal to the product of each probability:

$$P = P1xP2xP3xP4 = 2/100x1/5000x5/100x1/200.$$

The probability to find another case with the same four characteristics is about $10^{-10}$

## CONCLUSION

Establishing a similarity between ante and post mortem dental formulae is a very good mean of identification, particulary:

- when the number of missing teeth is included between 5 and 27 (the top number being 16), and
- when the layout of the missing teeth corresponds to a rare distribution.

In practice this analysis is complementary of all the characteristic features observed on the denture and on the skull. The opinion of the forensic odontologist, even his certainty, will be formed only after these thought processes which associate the knowledge of the specialist and a bio-statistical approach.

KEYWORDS: Forensic odontology, comparative identification, probability, dental formula

# DETERMINATION OF THE LEGAL AGE IN THE ADULT BY EXAMINATION OF THE TEETH : GRAPHS AND PATHOLOGICAL VARIATIONS

GEORGET C.*, FRONTY P., SAPANET M.

* Chirurgien dentiste expert, Chargé de cours à la Faculté de Chirurgie Dentaire de Nancy, Président de l'Association Française d'Identification en Odontologie médico-légale - 5 rue Voltaire 35400 AMBOISE (FRANCE)

**KEYWORDS:** Forensic odontology, age assessment, charts, abacuses, pathological variations

## INTRODUCTION

Several authors (Gustafson, Miles, Shiro-Ito, Lamendin, Dalitz, Johanson, Bang et Tramm...) have perfected methods which allow the age of an individual to be assessed by examination of the teeth. [3,4,5]

Two methods are used :

Gustafson's method

Based on examination of microscopical sections, this method takes a large number of factors into account (wear and tear, periodontal recession, deposition of secondary dentine, deposition of cement, root reabsorption and root transparency). The changes observed are noted down as indices which are added together [5]. From the final index obtained, the age is read off from a linear regression curve.

Lamendin's method

This non-destructive method analyses two criteria (periodontal recession and transparency of the dentine) [3,4].The length of the periodontal disease (P) and of the transparency of the root (T) are measured in relation to the length of the root. The age is estimated by using the formula :

$$A = 0,18P + 0,42T + 25,5$$

For these methods, single root teeth must be used which have not have endodontal treatment, have no pathological resorption of the apex, have very little caries in the neck of the tooth and do not have any periodontal pathology.

If the tooth examined has each of these criteria, an unfavourable environment may exist which may alter the results. Certain criteria are particulary sensitive to the environment (wear and tear, deposition of cement and periodontal disease). Others are sensitive to dental pathology (secondary dentine or root reabsorption).

## STUDY OF THE CRITERIA : PHYSIOLOGICAL AND PATHOLOGICAL AGING OF THE TEETH :

### 1- Enamel and wear and tear

The enamel with its avascular, acellular, highly mineralized structure, undergoes physiological wearing down which occurs particulary on certain surfaces :

- the occlusal surfaces in contact with the opposing teeth
- the proximal surfaces in contact with the adjacent teeth.

Pathology, parafunction or dental treatment can cause premature or late wearing down of the enamel (tooth position, occlusion, removal of teeth, bruxism, polishing or the state of the opposing teeth) [2].

The criteria of "abrasion" in Gustafson's method should therefore be considered after taking the dental environment into account, as this can greatly alter the true values.

## 2- Dentine pulp complex and deposition of secondary dentine

Dentinogenesis continues throughout the life of the pulp. The normal aging process causes a permanent deposit of dentine on the walls of the pulp chamber which causes a reduction in the volume of the pulp cavity [1].

Dental pathology often causes dystrophic calcification. Even if this criterion can be estimated visually in Gustafson's method, the small differences seen make it difficult to quantify.

## 3- Cement and deposition of cement

The normal aging process for cement is shown by continuous cementogenesis throughout the life of the tooth on the arch (tooth with or without the pulp). This process slows down in older people. Occlusal stimuli and physiological migration occuring at the apical end of the root, cause abnormal reabsorption and deposition which produce heterogeneity of the tooth surface. Apical deposition of cement compensates for passive eruption due to friction on the teeth.

Pathology (periodontal disease, frictional stress , vitamin deficiency or osteoporosis...) cause a considerable increase in the thickness of the cement.
This hypercementosis then disturbs the linear relationship which there is normally between the thickness of the cement and the person's age. Estimation of the age is therefore altered [2].

## 4- Root reabsorption

Although Gustafson stated that this reabsorption was "very characteristic and showed well demarcated grooves", this criterion should be used with caution because it is linked more to pathology than to normal physiological aging.

## 5- Periodontal tissues and periodontal disease

Progressive atrophy of the periodontal tissues is manifest by migration of the epithelial attachment towards the apex. This recession of the tissues is nowadays delayed more and more by the effect of periodontal treatment and improved dental hygiene. It is not unusual to see people over 50 years old with healthy periodontal tissues, or periodontal disease that is just beginning.

Pathology, however, speeds up migration of the epithelial attachment. A example which shows the difficulty in assessing this problem, is that of periodontitis in an adult, which begins between 30 and 40 years old with the periodontal tissues being affected from the beginning more and more frequently with horizontal bone loss. A functional cause (malocclusion, grinding the teeth...) should always be looked for.

## 6- Dentine and root transparency

Aging of the dentine is shown by peritubular dentine deposition on the internal surfaces of the canaliculi. This deposition can even obliterate the canaliculus altogether. It is called "sclerosis" of the dentine. This causes an increase in mineralization which makes the dentine translucent. It is particulary seen in the root. This process which begins at the apex, worsens with age, invading the dental root, little by little, in the direction of the crown [2,3].

Transparency of the root is a fairly reliable factor, because it is affected very little by dental pathology, apart from very severe caries.

## CONCLUSION

Criteria affected by parafunction, pathology or treatment can affect the results noticeably. Experts should readjust the value they place on criteria by taking any dental pathology or the environment of the teeth into consideration.

Out of the methods in use, the following protocol emerges :

- -Lamendin's method (non-destructive) is used to begin with
- -Gustafson's method (microscopic section) is used later on
- - The results obtained from the two methods are compared
- - the experimenter checks for coherence between the two results
- - if there is a large difference, the causes are looked for.

Research currently taking place should allow the subjective factors in certain methods to be eliminated. This research is particularly focused on transparency of the root. Only through statistical analysis will it become clear if the new method gives a better estimation of age.

## REFERENCES

1) Badillo F., Brouillet JL. (1991) Modifications de la pulpe en fonction de l'âge : incidences thérapeutiques. Réalités cliniques, 2:193-200

2) Clergeau-Guerithault S (1991) Vieillissement physiologique et cavité buccale, Réalités cliniques 2:171-177

3) Lamendin H. (1981) Critères dentinaires pour appréciation d'âge ; études de la translucidité et des canicules : Intérêts en odonto-stomatologie légale. Rev. Odont.Stom.Lég.,2:111-119

4) Lamendin H., Humbert JF., Tavernier JC., BRUNET G., Nossintchouc R. (1990). Estimation de l'âge par une méthode à deux critères dentaires, Chir Dent France 539:93-96

5) Gustafson G (1969) Odonto-stomatologie médico-légale, SC Edition et imprimerie, Bruxelles

# Identifying a bank robber

H. Kritscher+), J. Szilvássy*) & G. Bauer*)

+) Dr.Herbert Kritscher: Anthropologische Abteilung des Naturhistorischen Museums Wien, Burgring 7, A - 1014 Wien
*) Univ.Prof.Dr.Johann Szilvássy and Univ.Prof.Dr.Georg Bauer: Institut für Gerichtliche Medizin der Universität Wien, Sensengasse 2, A - 1090 Wien

The surveillance camera (fig. 1) shows a man of medium height, wearing a grey wadded quilted jacket, blue peak-cap and black leather gloves. He had a red-white chequered shawl wrapped around his head to hide his identity. The man had entered the bank, stepped up from behind to the customer standing in front of the cashier's counter, and pressed a weapon against the left side of her back, reached over the customer's shoulder with his right hand holding a small white plastic bag and told the cashier to put the money inside the bag. To the cashier he said: "This is a raid, give me all your five-thousand Schilling notes; I am holding your customer hostage, no alarm, no prepared alarm package". Altogether 173.500,-- Austrian Schillings were handed over.

Fig. 1

After this, he went out towards the left with the hostage, still pressing the weapon against the left side of her back, and left the bank together with the hostage.
First shot made by the surveillance camera caught the right profile of the muffled robber. Despite the heavily muffled head, the right ear was clearly discernible and could be used for identification purposes by means of comparisons, as a suspect

had been arrested (Knussmann 1988; Bauer, Kritscher & Szilvássy 1994, 1994a; Bauer, Kritscher, Szilvássy & Unterdorfer 1994).

This suspect was submitted to forensic-anthropological examination, according to morphological and metric points of view, and the results were subsequently photogrammetrically evaluated.

The customary head and body measurements were taken, in order to make true to scale pictures, in particular with regard to the ear characteristics and body proportions.

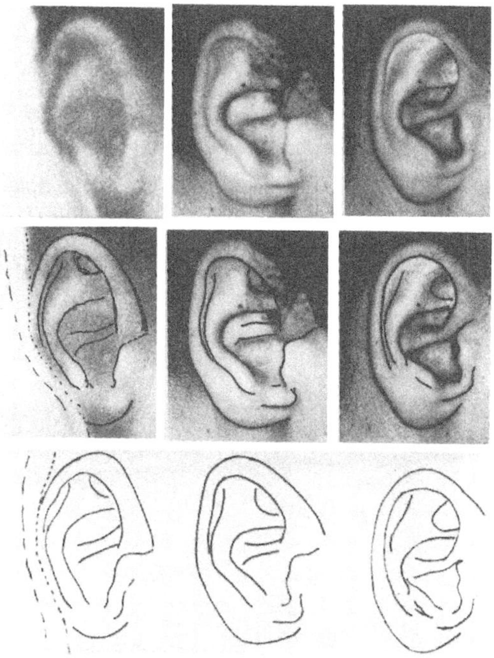

Fig.2

In the course of the medicolegal examination of the suspect (fig. 2), the right ear was measured and then documented from the front - in the standard view - in the scale 1:1. In the middle, the suspect's right ear in semiprofile position corresponding to the surveillance camera shot, and on the left, the surveillance camera's shot of the robber's ear, also brought to a 65-mm ear length.

In the second row, the characteristics of the external ear (conch) drawn into the picture and thereby made clearly vicible, and in the third row, the graphic representation of these essential morphological characteristics, to that now the morphology of the external ear of the robber and that of the suspect can be compared accurately and quickly.

The next step was to bring these graphic representations into a system of coordinates, and to compare one by one a defined segment of the bank robber's external ear with a defined segment of the suspect's external ear.

The compared details were: the crus helicis, the anterior, upper and posterior section of the helix, the fossa triangularis, the incisura intertragica, the sulcus and antihelix, the antitragus and tragus respectively, and finally the incisura intertragica, and the ear lobe.

Summarizing it can be said that the bank robber's right ear as caught by the surveillance camera, and the suspect's right ear proved identical in virtually all segments.

With the aid of the photographs we also tried to bring the body proportions into relation with each other in 3 surveillance shots. Fig. 3 shows another surveillance shot on the left, in the middle the suspect in a posture corresponding to the surveillance photograph, and, on the right, a graphic superprojection.

The same methodology and sequence were applied to the other surveillance photographs.

The procedure for this superprojections was as follows: a photograph of the suspect, each time in a comparable posture, was brought to a certain lower arm length, marked in the pictures or sketches respectively with small arrows to illustrate the distance chosen for the further comparison. Now the surveillance

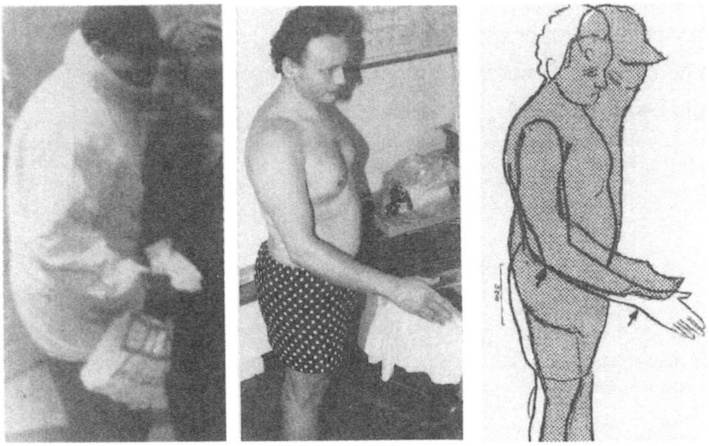

Fig.3

camera shot of the bank robber was equally zoomed, namely to a same lower arm length so that the bank robber's lower arm length and the suspect's lower arm length coincided.

The superimposition or superprojection of the graphic representations then showed that also the other body proportions coincided.

We see this as further, not unimportant indication, that the bank robber shown by the camera and the examined suspect are one and the same.

To summarize, we think we can say that by means of our morphologic-anthropometric examinations it was possible to ascertain the identity of the bank robber to a large degree, in particular as the coinciding morphology of the auricles can be rated as strong a proof as are identical fingerprints.

Literatur:

Bauer G, Kritscher H, Szilvássy J (1994) Analysis of Identity by Superimposition. Proc. IV. Int. Meeting on Forensic Med., Alpe - Adria - Pannonia, Personal Identification, Italy, Grado, 12.-14.5.1994, 23f.

Bauer G, Kritscher H, Szilvássy J (1994) Identification of a bankrobber. Programme XVIth Congr. Int. Acad. Legal Med. and Soc. Med., Strasbourg, France, 31.5.-2.6.1994, 163.

Bauer G, Kritscher H, Szilvássy J, Unterdorfer H (1994) Ein Fall aus der forensischen Anthropologie: Die Identifizierung eines Scheckbetrügers. Abstracts der 3. Frühjahrstagung, Region Süd der Deutschen Ges. f. Rechtsmed. 3.u.4.6.1994, Innsbruck, Vortrag 46.

Knussmann R (1988) Methoden des morphologischen Vergleichs in der forensischen Anthropologie. In: Knussmann R, Hrsg (1988) Anthropologie. Handbuch der vergleichenden Biologie des Menschen, Band I, 1. Teil, G. Fischer, Stuttgart-New York, 368ff.

# INDEX FOR RECORDING TOOTH ABRASION MICROFAILURES;

T A M index for determination of Puech Number[1].

PUECH Pierre-François, LEONETTI Georges, CIANFARANI François and ALBERTINI Henri: Forensic Anthropology and Odontology, University of Marseille La Timone; BP 191, 30012 Nimes, France.

A methodology for the scanning microscopic evaluation of surface abrasion deterioration of tooth enamel is developed and illustrated by comparison of damages caused by repetition of a specific abrasive test on different qualities of enamel.

## 1. Scope

1.1. This standard contains the record into groups (Puech Number) based on similar morphological characteristics, of the microfailures resulting from abrasive wear.

## 2. Terminology

2.1. Abrasion is a wear damage due to hard particles or hard protuberances forced against and moving along a solid surface.

2.2. Wear damage to a solid surface generally involve progressive loss of material in the form of chipping, pitting or scratching.

2.3. Spalling is the separation of macroscopic particles from a surface in the form of flakes or chips, usually associated with rolling element bearings and gear teeth, but also resulting from impact events.

2.4. Pitting is a form of microfailure characterized by the presence of surface cavities the formation of which is attributed to processes such as fatigue, local adhesion, cavitation, erosion or abrasion.

2.5. Scratching is the mechanical removal or displacement, or both, of material from a surface by the action of abrasive particles or protuberances sliding accross the surfaces.

2.6. Damage may include loss of material, surface deformation and any other changes in microstructure, properties or appearance.

2.7. Surface topography is the geometrical detail of a solid surface.

(1) Original description of the TAM index is from PUECH P.-F.

## 3. Significance and use

3.1. The TAM index provides a qualitative guide for tooth enamel surface resistance appreciation.

3.2. The rating is based initially on the results of the following standard abrasion test.

3.3. The numerical rating is not suitable for direct use in quantitative models.

3.4. The value of the TAM index practice lies in the examination and identification of surface and subsurface microfailures and in the evaluation of abrasive wear to weight the relative resistance order of tooth enamel in a generally comparable abrasive environment.

## 4. Basis of classification

4.1. A visual examination with the use of a low-power magnifying glass determines the extent of abrasive wear and the location of striae and pits. A more detailed examination through a scanning microscope is made using magnifications from 20x to 5000x.

4.2. Tooth enamel characteristics of hardness and wear resistance are associated with disadvantages like poor chemical resistivity and brittleness.

4.3. Pits and striae have various sizes and shapes. Small imperfections can be easily detected in striae, due to the space repetition of the damages.

4.4. To record microfailures in tooth enamel, we provide experimental data in Sabra rats maintened on a standard diet until the age of 40 days. Half of them had received 25 ppm of fluoride in the drinking water "ad libitum".

4.5. Young human adult teeth from a non-fluoridated population and from an endemic fluorosis area with a tooth surface index of fluorosis (TSIF) value of 4, were also tested.

4.6. Each lingual surface of the teeth was scratched from the occlusal surface towards cementum enamel junction, and from the mesial border to the distal one using a tungsten calibred burr loaded with 250gr at a speed of 15 cm/sec. The surfaces were cleaned of soft tissue by successive washing with 0.1M ammonium carbonate.

4.7. Part of the teeth, fluorosed and not, were first etched with 30% phosphoric acid for 60 seconds, then rinsed thoroughly with tap water.

4.8. The specimens were prepared for SEM examination and micrographs of surface topography were examined.

CLASS 1

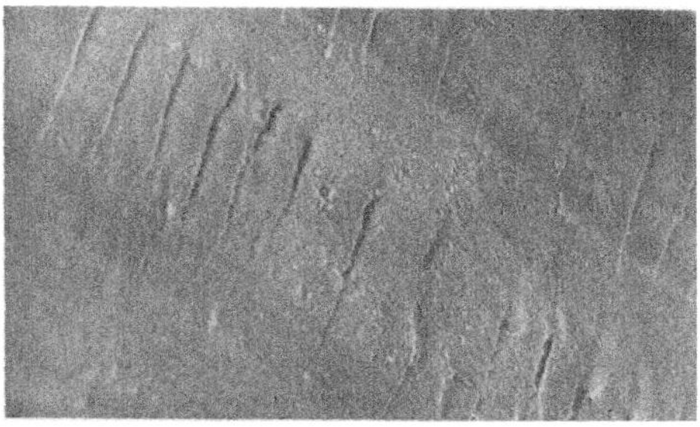

CLASS 2

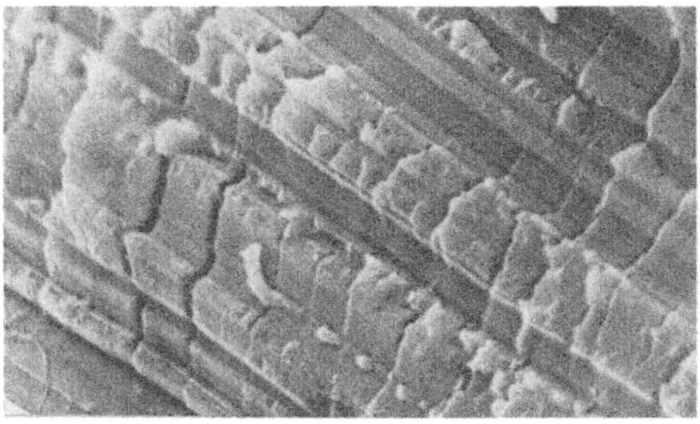

CLASS 3

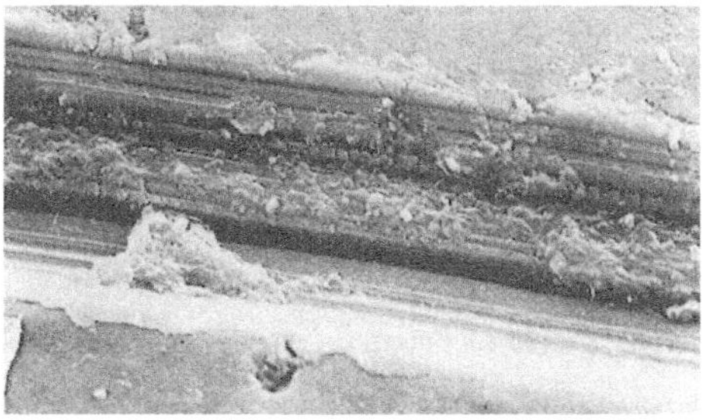

CLASS 4

CLASS 5

micrographs 5000x

4.9. In rats, the SEM photographic analysis failed to distinguish between the experimental grooves cut in normal enamel and the fluoride-enriched enamel. Fluoridated water had only a topical effect.

4.10. The fluorosed human teeth underwent a higher rate of abrasion and frequent breaks along the tops margins of the groove walls occured. The scars were oriented opposite the direction of movement of the burr and resembled 'chevrons'.

4.11. The human fluorotic teeth pretreated with acid displayed an even higher rate of abrasion. The 'chevron' formation were larger and the groove presented a granular surface.

## 5. Tooth abrasion microfailures (TAM) index

5.1. The following Puech Number rating and classifications shall be used when reporting the microfailures:

| rating | classification |
|---|---|
| 1 | smooth indented surfaces |
| 2 | parallel cracks areas |
| 3 | rough aspects with fissures |
| 4 | cracks at the opening junctions |
| 5 | broken junction and porous floor |

5.2. The various visual appearances illustrated in Figs. 1 through 5 are magnificated 5000x and further evaluation criteria for alterations are as follow:

5.2.1: a ductile action is inferred from smooth furrows. A plastic deformation occurs by the movement of lattice dislocations and / or diffusional creep: CLASS 1.

5.2.2: tensive cracks by cleaving occurs in some indented areas in parallel fractures: CLASS 2.

5.2.3: tensive cracks are accompagned by splits giving a general rough aspect to the depression: CLASS 3.

5.2.4: scars and chips cause 'chevron' formations by brittle fracture of the enamel surface at the junction of the striation. This process is common in fluorotic enamel: CLASS 4.

5.2.5: the etched fluorotic enamel appears to be more friable in the subsurface layer and a porous aspect is present in the groove floor. Zones of altered resistivity have been induced by fluoridation: CLASS 5.

Key terms: TOOTH SURFACE, WEAR RESISTANCE, ABRASION INDEX.

# An attempt of scientific evaluation in facial reconstruction : preliminary results

**Quatrehomme G*., Garidel Y.**, Liao Z.G.*, Grevin G.***, and Ollier A.***

* Laboratoire de Médecine Légale, Faculté de Médecine, Avenue de Vallombrose, 06107 NICE CEDEX 2 (France).

** Laboratoire d'Ethnologie, Faculté des Lettres, 98 Bd E. Herriot, BP 209 NICE CEDEX 3 (France).

*** Laboratoire d'Anthropologie Physique, 19 Rue Frédéric Mireur, 83300 DRAGUIGNAN (France).

We developped an attempt of scientific evaluation of three-dimensional facial reconstruction, by comparison of the face of a person after death and the face after reconstruction.
This is a prospective study.

## METHODOLOGY

Three stages were used as following : *First stage :* photographs of the face, taken within 24 hours after death ; autopsy and preparation of the skull. *Second stage :* a second working party, after anthropological and cephalometric study, achieves three-dimensional facial reconstruction, and takes photographs of the work. It has to be pointed out that the second gang worked independantly and have not seen the face of the deceased before performing the reconstruction of the face. *The third stage* is the comparison of photographs.

Three-dimensional reconstruction was performed through a quite known technique. Small cylindrical markers are applied at specific points. The length corresponds to values derived from measuring males and females facial tissue thickness. We used data which are published for Black, European, and Japanese males and females, by RHINE and CAMPBELL (1). We have to notice that 3 ranges of body build are possible : emaciated, normal, and obese (RHINE and al., cited by UBELAKER (2) ).
In this work, we used facial tissue thickness values for normal body build.

## RESULTS

This is a prospective study and these results deal with two premilinary cases : a 75 year old man and a 78 year-old man.

In the case number 1, reconstruction was considered to bear a resemblance with the deceased. In contrast the case number 2 was judged to be not really satisfactory by the first gang. Then a second reconstruction was performed by the second team, with a new advice : to use obese facial tissue thickness values.
The result was judged as a better result.

## DISCUSSION

The results are quite satisfactory But several boundaries have been established. Anthropological and cephalometric study are helpful for giving clues to perform face reconstruction. But in spite of the precise study of the craniofacial skeleton, there are important mistakes of reconstruction, especially for the nose and the topography of the eyes. A few aleatory data are unknown (such as the colour of the eyes, the shape and colour of the hair...), which limits the quality of reconstruction.

Three approaches are described in the literature : (i) sketching a likeness, using information provided by a forensic anthropologist ; (ii) rebuilding the face directly over the cranium ; (iii) using a computer.
These technics begin with an attempt to estimate the amount of muscle and other soft tissue.
The thickness employed in reconstruction should match the sex, race, and body build of the unidentified individual.
These approaches to facial reconstruction have merit. Rebuilding probably provides more accurate proportions, but requires much more time and effort than sketching and does not produce as life-like an appearance. Computer-assisted facial reproduction produces rapid, economical, and realistic facial images. It allows components to be added directly to cranial features (3).

Positive identifications have been described in the literature. For example SADLER (reported by UBELAKER (2)), used a cranium accompanied by a mold of the face made immediately after death, although SADLER was not aware of its existence when he made his reconstruction. The cast made from the death mask incorporates postmortem changes in the soft tissue ; even so, it strikingly resembles the modeled face. GATLIFF (4) reported on that, in 12 years (after 1967), 70 % of their 33 reproductions led to successful identifications. They observed that accuracy ranged from "rather poor" to a startlingly faithful likeness". In an interessant prospective study, HELMER in 1989 (5), reported a double-blind trial where two examiners reconstructed the soft tissue on lifelike casts of 12 skulls. They worked independently after having been given information about age, sex, and constitution of the person. The authors concludes that the reconstruction of soft tissue on the skull proved to be a relatively useful method of identifying unknown skulls, provided information on the colour and length of the hair, and possibly on the hairstyle as well, is at the examiner's disposal.

## CONCLUSIONS

In recent years, facial reproduction has emerged as an increasingly important tool within forensic anthropology.

The technique can be useful in presenting an image to the public in a search of missing person, especially when other avenues of investigation have not been successul. We hold little hope of producing a completely accurate reproduction, correctly noting that some aspects of the facial anatomy cannot be absolutely correlated with underlying bony tissue.

Nevertheless the goal in forensic medicine is not to get perfect accuracy, but to bear enough resemblance to the missing person.

## BIBLIOGRAPHY

1. Rhine JS, Campbell HR (1980) Thickness of facial tissues in American Blacks. Journal of Forensic Sciences 25 : 847-858.

2. Ubelaker DH (1991) Human skeletal remains. Excavation, analysis, interpretation. Manuals of Archeology-2. Taraxacum Washington, second edition, p 124-125

3. Ubelaker DH, O'Donnel G (1992) Computer-assisted facial reproduction. Jounal of Forensic Sciences 37 : 155-162.

4. Gatliff BP, Snow CC (1979) From skull to visage. Journal of Biocommunication 6 : 27-30.

5. Helmer R, Rohricht S, Petersen D. and Moer F (1989) Plastic face reconstruction as a possibility for identifying unknown skulls. An evaluation of the reliability of the reconstruction technic by a double-blind trial. (German, English abstract). Archiv für Kriminologie 184 : 142-160.

# DETERMINING THE LEGAL AGE BETWEEN 12 AND 14 YEARS OLD : CONTRIBUTION FROM RADIOGRAPHIC EXAMINATION OF DENTAL MINERALIZATION

SAPANET M.*, LETIENT A., GEORGET C., FRONTY P.

Médecine Légale, CHU BP 577, 86021 POITIERS (FRANCE)

In France, children under 13 years old cannot be punished by the law. This fact is well known to young delinquents, who make full use of it. When the age of a young delinquent is unknown, the magistrate asks an expert to examine the child. The expert may use various methods for this. The aim of this study is to check if examining the dental age is a precise enough method between the ages of 12 and 14 years old.

## MATERIALS

We used panoramic dental X-rays of patients who consulted in the department of Dentisty and Maxillofacial Surgery in the Poitiers University Hospital. The selection criteria were either sex, age between 10 and 14 years old and white Caucasian race. The exclusion criteria were malformation syndromes, dental dysplasia, multiple dental agenesis and an history of orthodontic treatment.

Mineralization of the teeth was examined for each patient and the stage of dental development was classified according to the criteria described by MOOREES (2), there being twelve stages in all. The two classifications have a number of similarities. We did not however take the criteria for the length of the dental roots into account.

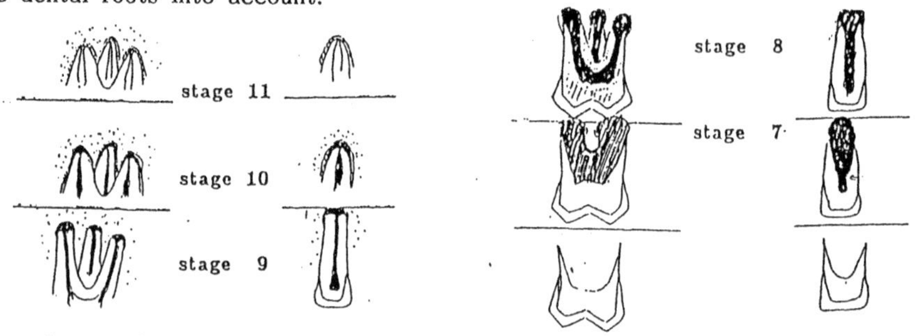


stage 0 : no alterations in the bony matrix
stage 1 : uncalcified space in the bony matrix
stage 2 : start of calcification
stage 3 : occlusive plate or incisor edge totally calcified
stage 4 : dentine visible, pulp not visible
stage 5 : junction of enamel and dentine visible
stage 6 : start of formation of the root, pulp cavity not visible
stage 7 : radicular bifurcation and pulp cavity visible, wide conical shaped canals
stage 8 : parallel-sided canals, apex mostly open and blunderbuss shaped
stage 9 : narrowing of the canals, apex has lost its blunderbuss shape, still open
stage 10 : apex closed, periapical area still wide or non-uniform
stage 11 : apical region has an homogeneous bony matrix

The teeth are named according to the international nomenclature of the FID. The age is expressed in months.

## Sample description

number : 169 patients

Sex distribution : male 78, female : 91, sex ratio 0,462

Age distribution : mean 143,01 months, min. 120 months, max. 168 months.

Age distribution according to sex :
male mean age 143,231 ; SD 14,379
female : mean age 142,824 ; SD 16,348
Fisher-Snedecor's F = 0,029
p = 0,85
In the sample, there was no significant difference between the two groups.

Distribution of the stages according to sex :

| stage | male | female | sum |
|---|---|---|---|
| 0 | 42 | 39 | 81 |
| 1 | 11 | 13 | 24 |
| 2 | 24 | 35 | 59 |
| 3 | 28 | 42 | 70 |
| 4 | 109 | 98 | 207 |
| 5 | 49 | 54 | 103 |
| 6 | 63 | 97 | 160 |
| 7 | 141 | 135 | 276 |
| 8 | 442 | 394 | 836 |
| 9 | 369 | 389 | 758 |
| 10 | 356 | 382 | 738 |
| 11 | 708 | 1058 | 1766 |
| sum | 2342 | 2736 | 5078 |

Khi= 56.65
p < 0.000001

There was a significant difference between the two groups. The rest of the study shows a difference between the sexes.

## METHOD

### Choice of teeth :

In the whole of the sample, only the age group from 12-14 years old was studied. In this group, not all of the teeth are as useful as each other for determining the age. Some of them have already finished the mineralization process, others are too variable to be of any use. For each tooth, the stage of mineralization was correlated to the actual age by using two groups : a group of those under 13 years old and one for those over 13 years old. The Khi2 test was employed to show how useful the tooth was for the study. The tooth was included in the study if the Khi2 result was suitable and p<0,05.

tooth '11', sex '2'

| stage | =>13 | <13 | sum |
|---|---|---|---|
| 9 | 0 | 7 | 7 |
| 10 | 2 | 12 | 14 |
| 11 | 19 | 46 | 65 |
| sum | 21 | 65 | 86 |

Khi = 3.86
p = 0.145 ++=>excluded

example: tooth '35', sex '2'

| stage | =>13 | <13 | sum |
|---|---|---|---|
| 5 | 0 | 1 | 1 |
| 6 | 0 | 6 | 6 |
| 7 | 0 | 11 | 11 |
| 8 | 1 | 24 | 25 |
| 9 | 4 | 14 | 18 |
| 10 | 8 | 3 | 11 |
| 11 | 9 | 5 | 14 |
| sum | 22 | 64 | 86 |

Khi = 36.27
p = 0.0000003 ++=>included

On the panoramic dental X-rays, assessment of the stage of mineralization for the maxillary teeth was made difficult by superimposition of the teeth. To avoid any error, only the mandibular teeth were analysed.
For the rest of the study, only four pairs of mandibular teeth were looked at : the canines, premolars and second molars.

## Assessment of the age

For each sex and for each pair of teeth, a rule was drawn up to estimate the age according to the stage of mineralization : "if the stage is below the value 'S', the age is estimated to be below 13 years old'.

compare actual age/age assessment

| actual age \ assessment | =>13 | <13 | sum |
|---|---|---|---|
| =>13 | true | untrue | |
| <13 | untrue | true | |
| sum | | | N |

Khi, p

% error 'Er'= (sum untrue)/N

example: teeth '37,47' sex '1' , 'S' = 9

| actual age \ assessment | =>13 | <13 | sum |
|---|---|---|---|
| =>13 | 29 | 7 | 36 |
| <13 | 12 | 36 | 48 |
| sum | 41 | 43 | 84 |

Khi (Yates) = 23.24 p = 0.00000143

'Er' = 7+12/84 = 22.61 %

The estimated age and the actual age are compared in table 5. The rule holds if the actual age and the estimated age are the same. The risk of error 'Er' is calculated by the total number of incorrect assessments divided by the total number of assessments 'N'.

## RESULTS

Depending on the sex the tooth number and the stage 'S', these tables show the risk 'Er' of making a mistake in estimating the age with respect to the legal age of 13 years old, for individuals between 12 and 14 years old. The best results are those where 'Er' is low.

MALE

| tooth num | N | Stage 'S' | p | 'Er' % |
|---|---|---|---|---|
| 33, 43 | 81 | 9 | 0.002 | 30.8 |
| 34, 44 | 83 | 9 | 0.000001 | 21.6 |
| 35, 45 | 79 | 8 | 0.00015 | 27.8 |
| 37, 47 | 84 | 8 | 0.0000015 | 22,6 |

FEMALE

| tooth num | N | Stage 'S' | p | 'Er' % |
|---|---|---|---|---|
| 33, 43 | 87 | 9 | 0.15 | ---- |
| 34, 44 | 92 | 9 | 0.004 | 34.7 |
| 35, 45 | 89 | 8 | 0.0002 | 32.5 |
| 37, 47 | 90 | 8 | 0.00001 | 28,8 |

## DISCUSSION

Normally, the expert's job is to determine the age of the individual. His answer is an estimated mean age with maximum and minimum values (2 standard deviations for $p<0,05$).

The dental age may be evaluted by cutting new teeth or mineralization of the teeth. Several authors have attempted to obtain more precise ages : MOOREES (2), ANDERSON (1), CIAPPARELLI, by using different mineralization criteria.

tooth 37, 47

'M'= stages of Moorees
'S'= stages in our study

| | Anderson | | Moorees | | Clappar. | | | Study | |
|---|---|---|---|---|---|---|---|---|---|
| 'M' | ms | sd | ms | sd | ms | sd | 'S' | ms | sd |
| 8 | 8.5 | 0.9 | 7.8 | 0.8 | 9.1 | 0.9 | 7 | 8.5 | 0.7 |
| 9 | 9.5 | 0.9 | 9.1 | 1.0 | 9.7 | 0.9 | | | |
| 10 | 10.6 | 1.0 | 9.9 | 1.1 | 10.4 | 1.6 | 8 | 11.8 | 0.9 |
| 11 | 11.5 | 1.1 | 10.6 | 1.3 | 11.7 | 1.0 | | | |
| 12 | 12.4 | 1.2 | 11.3 | 1.1 | 12 | 1.1 | 9 | 12.8 | 0.7 |

tooth 37,47

'S'/age

| 'S' | Nb | Means | SD |
|---|---|---|---|
| 7 | 28 | 124.60 | 7.62 |
| 8 | 67 | 139.85 | 10.57 |
| 9 | 61 | 156.26 | 9.36 |

ANOVA
Kruskall-Wallis H = 113.905
p = 0.000000

In this table, we compared these author's results with those of our study. We note that for the second mandibular molar (pair 37 and 47) and our stage 9, which is completely comparable with Moorees' stage 12, there are slight differences in the mean values. This confirms the importance of having a homogeneous reference population. The standard deviations are different : this may be due to the difference in the sample sizes or to the criteria used to define the stages of mineralization. Choosing criteria which include an assessment of the length of the dental roots does not necessarily improve precision.

In all of the cases, use of these reference tables produces a result expressed as the mean age with the standard deviation. For teeth 37 or 47, male patients, MOORES' stage 12 or our stage 9, the result would be a mean age of 12,8 ± 14 months.

In our opinion, this result is of no pratical use, contrary to an age assessment for identification of a corpse, because the range is too wide and it does not inform the magistrate of the risk of error. The question should therefore be asked in a different way. Instead of asking "what is the child's age ?", it would be better to ask "is this child over 13 years old" ?. The answer (YES/NO) could be given together with the risk of error.

## CONCLUSION

This study shows that the rate of error remains high, because for children between 12 and 14 years old, it is at least 20 %. The other methods for assessing the age (bony age...) should be studied using the same technique , in order to find the most reliable method. At any rate, these figures put into perspective the confidence that an expert can have in determining the dental age.

## REFERENCES

(1) ANDERSON D.L., THOMPSON G.W., POPOVICH F.(1976).Age attainment of mineralization stages of the permanent dentition. J.Forensic Sci.,21,191-200
(2) MOOREES C.F.A.,FANNING E.A.,HUNT E.E.(1963). Age variation of formation stages for ten permanent teeth. J. Dental Res.,42,264-273.

## KEYWORDS

Forensic odontology, age assessment, dental radiograph, dental development

# 9. Clinical Legal Medicine

# CLINICAL LEGAL MEDICINE

BRAHY G., EUGENE-DAHIN B., RAVACHE-QUIRINY J., BOXHO Ph.
Institut de Médecine Légale de l'Université de Liège, 39 rue Dos Fanchon, B - 4020 Liège (Belgique).

Forensic Medicine has known deep changes in the past twenty years.
In most countries of romanic culture, Institutes of Legal Medicine have progressively passed from thanatological Legal Medicine or Medico-Legal pathology to Clinical Legal Medicine.
Magistrates were increasingly faced with problems such as aggressions, sexual assaults, drugs, medical liability, that needed a doctor who could give them medical information while understanding judicial requirements.
Whether one agreed or not, it was no longer possible to run Institutes of Legal Medicine and to meet financial expenses with only accidental, criminal or suicidal deaths.
In Belgium we have no real organisation of the Forensic Medicine or Pathology. Legal Medicine is not recognized as a speciality in Belgium. Therefore, through the intermediary of the European Council of Legal Medicine or by directly contacting the national authorities, the Royal Society of Legal Medicine in Belgium and appointed active professors are endeavouring to have this discipline recognised as a separate speciality. We have already obtained from judicial authorities a modification of an article in the code of criminal instruction. The King's Attorney is now accompanied by one or two forensic doctors instead of one or two physicians.

In a parallel way, we have obtained in each Court of Appeal, the appointment of a commission to recognize the qualification of expert doctors whose names will appear on official lists.

Thus we may hope that, in future, there will be a real medico-legal organisation in Belgium, an acknowledgment of the speciality in Legal Medicine and in expertise medicine for bodily damage. The organisation would function under the aegis of the Ministry of Justice and of the Society of Legal Medicine. The result should be a real academic formation, identical in all universities.
Reverting to Clinical Legal Medicine, there exist 6 fields in which forensic doctors are actually concerned:
1. agressions and wounds
2. sexual assaults and rape
3. maltreatment of children
4. internments
5. medical liability from a penal point of view
6. drugs.

Agressions and wounds.
Assault is any violent contact between the human body and another physical object.
Wounds cover all bodily lesions.
Wound has a wider significance than a lesion.
Illness covers all internal bodily lesions, alteration of organic and functional health.
The degree of punishment is determined by the intensity or the intrinsic seriousness of the wounds, and the intensity is measured according to the more or less long incapacity of the victim to exert physical work.
Incapacity for usual professional work cannot be taken as a criterion.
The law considers physical work in general.

Sexual assaults and rape.
Before 89 the material element for rapes was the illicit conjunction of the sexes with a non-consenting woman. The author, therefore could only be a man.

In July 89, the new law widened the definition of rape. Article 1 stated that rape is any act of sexual penetration by any means, committed on a non-consenting person, rape being considered as a crime.
If consent exists, it is only considered valid under three conditions:

- having been given in advance or at least during the act, by a person who acts freely and by someone who is mentally able of measuring the consequences.
- Age has been arbitrarily set at sixteen.

Traditional aggravating circumstances remain unchanged.

Other aggravating circumstances:
Bodily torture or sequestration.
Particularly vulnerable person.
During the medical examination, the victim can be assisted by a doctor of her own choice; his fees are paid by the Justice.

The sexual agression kit evolved in the framework of the new law, is part of all the initiatives taken in recent years to improve assistance, reception and information for the victims of physical and sexual violence.
Booklets are at the disposal of the victims; various recommendations have been made to doctors.
It is of primary importance to protect children under age. Article 61 of the code of ethics expressively takes this occurrence into account.
When the attending doctor or the gynaecologist see a victim of sexual assault, he must inform her on what will happen if a complaint is lodged, in that the legal procedure involves the requisition of a Medical Expert appointed by a judge.

Establishment of facts and samples to be taken:
- First of all, traces of assault, traces of non-consent, traces of active violence.
- opinion as to the apparent age of the patient, mentally handicapped or under influence of drugs.
- the bodily examination involves:
  . detailed case history, social, familial as well as personal concerning the facts.
  . general and gynaecological examination with the S.A.S. Sexual agression kit.

There are two kinds of kits, one for the suspect and the other for the victim.
A kit contains a set of phials for samples, paper bags for clothes, explanations, and a guide for the doctor. This guide describes the various steps of the medical examination, as follows: collecting the clothes, the evidence of general lesions, putting the samples together, then the gynaecological examination.
If appropriately used, the kit is the best method for collecting samples for possible later use.
I speak of "possible further use" since according to our experience, if it is classical to look for sperm, its identification is seldom attempted, unless the author is known or becomes known later on.

MALTREATMENT OF CHILDREN

The field of maltreatment of children is one of the most difficult and delicate in Legal Medicine.
If a diagnosis of characterised ill treatment is not established, the child will be exposed to major risks.
On the other hand, a wrong diagnosis of maltreatment may entail serious consequences for the family.
The diagnosis of maltreatment must not rest solely on the plain and simple description of lesions.
This would imply unawareness of the whole problem of characterised ill treatment on one hand and, on the other, unawareness of a far more subtle form of maltreatment, that is to say passive ill treatment.
The diagnosis of passive maltreatment is sometimes very difficult to arrive at. Very often, our conviction only rests on convergent elements based on a mesologic case history.
The medical examination is important, but it cannot and must not be an isolated fact.
The present policy in cases of maltreatment has progressively slipped from a criminal and repressive policy to a psychomedical-social policy, from the notion of someone to punish to the notion of someone to treat, or rather that of a family cell to be taken care of.
Multidisciplinary teams have been appointed in each province of the French community.

THE ADVANTAGES OF SUCH TEAMS ARE REAL:

- multidisciplinary character.
- diagnostic means are often implanted in a hospital centre.
- receiving the parents: without adequate reception, no dialogue is possible and no therapy can be considered.
- the possibility, when facing the parents, of asserting that there has been maltreatment and to seek with them the deep causes of it.

The multidisciplinary teams, however, are limited: they are not allowed any power of constraint on the parents.
The teams are not compulsory intermediaries.
They do not geographically cover all the territory.
We also have the emergency cases.
In this framework the forensic doctor can play a useful part if he takes the trouble of giving a wider meaning to the usual mission he is entrusted with, and does not stop at a description of the lesions.
He must give an extensive meaning to the notion of origin of maltreatment, by seeking three-dimensional causes of family : dysfunction that involves the child, the parents and the environment, and also by giving an extensive meaning to the consequences, and by voicing a detailed opinion on the prognosis and on the treatment to be undertaken.

## INTERNMENT AND PSYCHIATRIC HOSPITALISATION

Since the new law of June 90, there has been no talk of "internment" but instead, of "admittance for psychiatric observation". This change in the law not only involves a different terminology, it also means a change of mentality.
The new law is markedly in accordance with the European Convention on Human Rights. It involves:
- a written request from any person concerned.
- a first medical certificate.

These documents are sent to the Justice of the Peace or to the King's Attorney if the situation is urgent.

### PROCEDURES

The urgent procedure alone is of interest to the forensic doctor.
Following a complaint or ex officio, the King's Attorney, asks the forensic doctor for a detailed medical certificate. Then he may decide on inmediate internment of a dangerous mentally sick person. Within 24 hours, he has to inform the Justice of the Peace.
The Justice of the Peace proceeds to the psychiatric establishment and hears the patient. The judgement is given out in the Council Chamber.
The Justice of the Peace may decide to confirm the psychiatric observation. He may also decide to end the observation period.
An appeal to the First Court can be presented within 15 days after notification.

### THE MEDICAL CERTIFICATE

The following facts must be stated:
- The doctor must specify from which serious mental illness the patient is suffering from, even if it is temporary;
- A serious peril to his health and to his safety, entailing a serious menace to others or to himself;
- It must be an emergency case;
- The patient refuses all treatment and even hospitalisation.

These four conditions must absolutely be fulfilled.

THE EXPERIENCE OF THE INSTITUTE OF LEGAL MEDICINE IN LIEGE

From January 93 to April 94, we have been requested 49 times with 24 positive results : observation.
In more than 80% of the cases, the complaint was made by a member of the family.
In 15% of the cases, there were individuals arrested for disturbance of public order, sexual assaults, violent behaviour and assaults.

After a two years' experience with this law, it appears that:
- the Justices of the Peace strongly tend to waive complaints by first of all directing the claimants to the King's Attorney so as to control the urgency of the situation.
- some doctors are too quick and show little scrupule when filling in certificates.
The doctor may be submitted to pressure exerted by the family, or by fear they feel in such situations, and also by incomplete knowledge and a certain apprehension of psychiatry.
Many medical certificates are also too laconic or do not fulfil the conditions stipulated by the law.
The word "illness" does not necessarily mean "chronic". The episode may be acute and temporary.
A frequent problem is that of drug addicts and alcoholics. According to the law, the fact of drinking or taking drugs is not sufficient.
However, hospitalisation in a psychiatric unit is accepted.
If the state of addiction justifies an important alteration of the mental state by extension of the term of "illness".

It would be possible to speak now about drugs and Medical liability. But I think that we have all the same problems with these two topics.

So, as we have not a lot of time for the other lectures, I'll stop here and thank you for your attention.

Institut de Médecine Légale de l'Université de Liège,
Directeur : Professeur BRAHY,
Docteur B. EUGENE-DAHIN, Première Asssistante,
Docteur J. RAVACHE-QUIRINY, Première Assistante,
Docteur Ph. BOXHO, Attaché.

# KINETIC VISUAL ACUITY AND ALCOHOL INGESTION

*Irina Dressler, Svetlana Dressler, M.L. Dressler*

University of Medicine and Pharmacy Timisoara
1900 Timisoara, str. Balantei, Romania

The visual acuity for moving objects named "kinetic visual acuity" (KVA) represents a dynamic pattern of the morphoscopic perception. Usually, KVA is determined with special instruments presenting on a windscreen the optotyp marks (commonly used for the determination of the *static visual acuity*) but in moving.

We used for this study a self-conception instrument that projected the marks on a circular move with the radius of 16.2 cm. and with a speed -continuous adjustable- among 0 and 200 rotations per minute.

The examination takes place in the obscure room. First, the biggest mark (corresponding to a visual acuity -VA- of 0.1) is projected at maximum speed. The rotation speed is gradually diminished and the value at which the subject perceives correctly the mark's orientation is noted/put down. We have proceeded in the same way for all VA's treads (11 altogether). Finally a curve is drawn, with the VA's treads marked on the "Y" axis and the rotation speed on the "X"'s. (Fig. 1)

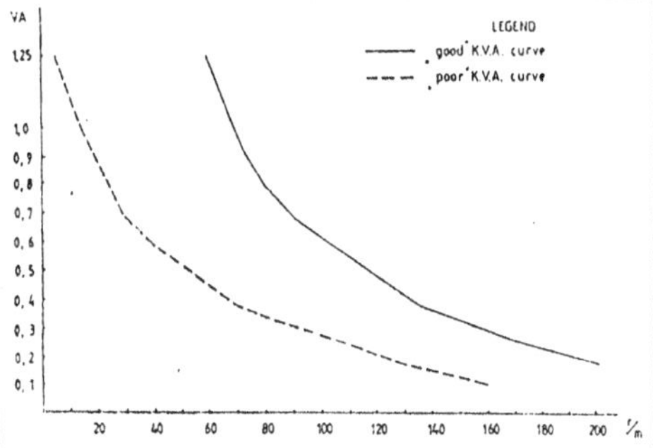


Fig. 1 K.V.A. GRAPHIC REPRESENTATION

This curve is considered to be as better as it is placed upper right (in the area corresponding to high speed and good VA).

KVA depends to a certain extend on the static visual acuity and, mostly, on the proper coordination of the volitive eye movements, especially those needed for firm and rapid decisions as driving.

MATERIAL AND METHOD

We studied the effect of alcohol ingestion concerning KVA in a group of 20 youth (age among 24 and 30), 15 males and 5 women; they had all a VA of 1.25 at both eyes and no ocular disease.

Each subject was ophtalmologically examined before and after the alcohol ingestion for two hours. The alcohol was administered as spirit/liquor in quantity to obtain a blood concentration of 0.5/1000. According to Widmarck [13] the proposed level of alcoholemia should be reached in 45-50 min., and the maximum of elimination in about 2.5-3 hours from the ingestion. That is the reason for we have limited the follow up time to two hours.

UNFOLDING OF THE EXPERIMENT

Each subject was ophtalmologically examined after a time, needed for adaptation in dark (around 30 min.); a preliminary KVA curve was drawn and used as reference.

After that, a certain amount of alcohol (see above) was offered to be consumed in 5 min. and KVA's curve was drawn every 30 minutes, for two hours. A single person (female) in the group asked for a reduced dose of alcohol; in this case the experiment was continued with half of dose. The average of the curves we obtained was drawn as follows (Fig. 2).

RESULTS AND DEBATES

As can be seen in Fig. 2 the alcohol ingestion had an obvious negative influence on the reference curve;

after an hour the curve's profile begins to ameliorate. After two hours the curves were at least as good as initial. In some peculiar cases there were interesting findings. We present them beyond because that shows great differences in the way that the same quantity of alcohol may influence KVA. This influence depends on many factors but mostly on the individual resistance.

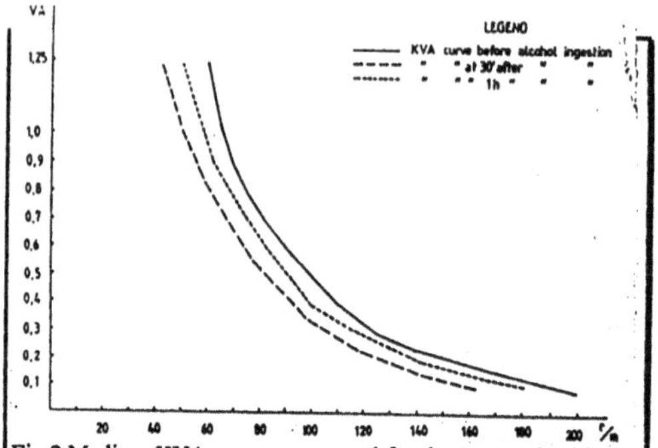


Fig. 2 Medium KVA curves computed for the 20 tested subjects

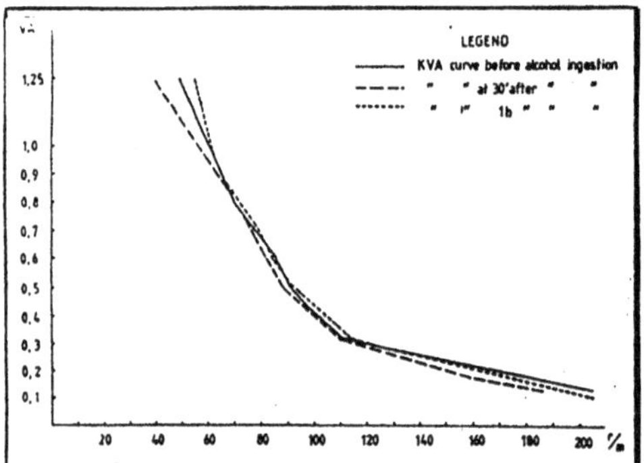


Fig. 3 CASE H.V., AGE 24, 82 Kg WEIGHT, ALCOHOLEMIA 0,5 ‰

*Case 1 (Fig. 3):* male, age 24, 82 kg. weight; At 30 minutes the curve is easily influenced and at one hour it is close to the initial.

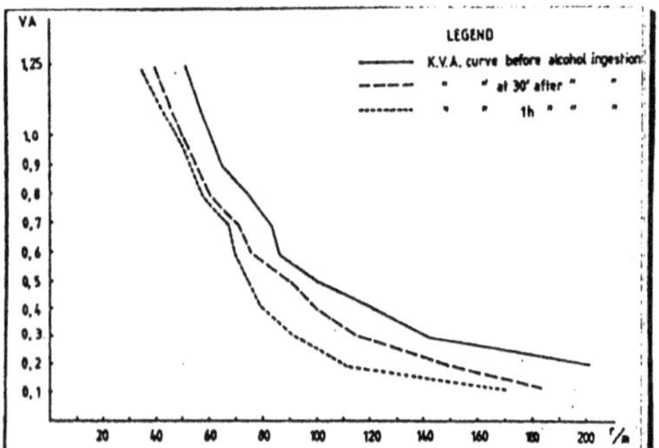


Fig. 4 CASE C.S., MALE, AGE 25, 75 Kg WEIGHT, ALCOHOLEMIA 0,5 ‰

*Case 2 (Fig. 4):* male, age 25, 72 kg. weight; At 30 minutes the curve is obviously deformed, but after one hour it is deeply influenced. Amelioration is detected only after two hours.

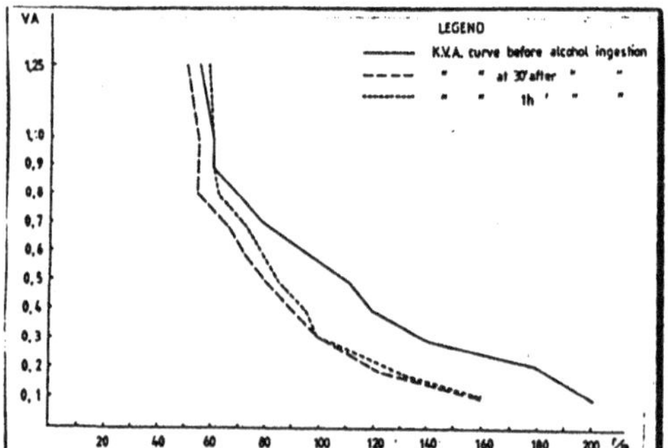


Fig. 5 CASE K.B FEMALE, AGE 27, 63 WEIGHT, ALCOHOLEMIA 0,25 ‰

*Case 3 (Fig. 5):* female, age 27, 63 kg. weight. This is the one who claimed for under-dose; the first curve was deformed in spite of an alcoholemia of 0.25‰. After an hour the same aspect was noted for high speed, becoming better for slow rotation.

This important role of the individual resistance emphasizes that to settle an unchanging limit of alcoholemy (1 g/1000 in our legislation) to mark a border between contravention and penalty is nearly impossible. Two persons of same age and with close alcoholemias might react in different modes, according to their own physiology. Low blood concentrations of alcohol, "accepted" by the law may induce important alterations of coordination, generating traffic accidents. In our opinion "legal accepted limit" has to be decreased to zero.
In some cases, to the end of the experiment, better results were detected, comparing with the reference. We ascribe that to a better accommodation to the dark, that has increased the **retina's sensibility of perception** and to the "training" subjects were submitted by repetition of the examination.

CONCLUSIONS

1. The alcohol influences negatively the AVK, especially in the period on which alcoholemia increases.
2. KVA is affected by alcohol ingestion depending on an individual resistance factor.
3. "Legal accepted limit" that marks a border between contravention and penalty for car drivers doesn't have a very solid physiological basis as long as even lower levels of alcoholemia may induce troubles of oculomotor coordination that makes traffic accidents more easily to occur.
4. Improvement of KVA during examination may be due to the training achieved by repeating the same probe and to a well adaptation to the dark.

BIBLIOGRAPHY

1. CERNEA P. (1986) Fiziologie oculara, Ed. Med. Bucuresti, pg. 198-199
2. DRESSLER S. (1977) Teza de doctorat, Timisoara
3. DRESSLER S. (1979) Oftalmologia, 3:201-202
4. DRESSLER S. (1986) Oftalmologia, 3:191-196
5. DRESSLER S. (1987) Oftalmologia, 4:261-264
6. DRESSLER S., CIUMAGEANU D. (1986) Oftalmologia, 1:21-24
7. HONEGGER H., SCHAFFER W.D., JAEGER W. (1969) Albrecht von Graefes Arch. 178/1969, pg. 132-146
8. KENNARD C., CLIFFORD R.F. (1988) Physiological Aspects of Clinical Neuro-Ophtalmology, Year Book Medical Publisher, Inc. Chicago, Illinois, pg. 249-60; 321-339
9. LEGRAND J. (1968) La revue de l'alcoolisme, Tome XIV, 4:257-262
10. LEGRAND J. (1968) Ann. d'occ., Tome 201, 11:1081-1096
11. MORARU I. (1967) Medicina Legala, Ed. Medicala Bucuresti.
12. MORTON-GRANT W. (1986) Toxicology of the eye, Charles C. Thomas Publisher, Springfield, Illinois.
13. WIDMARCK I. quoted by Moraru I. [11]

# CLINICAL LEGAL MEDICINE

Professor D. MALICIER
Professor of Legal Medicine at the University of Lyon,
Director of the Institute of Forensic Medicine in Lyons,
Chief of the Emergency Section at E. Herriot Hospital in Lyons.

Legal Medicine is the discipline that provides a link between medicine and the law. This link works in two ways : medicine applied to law, the law applied to medicine. Legal Medicine, therefore, plays a double role :

## I. IT ENLIGHTENS THE MAGISTRATE WHO MUST APPLY THE LAW

The forensic doctor provides the magistrate with the medico-technical elements that will enable him to take a decision with regard to medical affairs.

The expert is asked to give extensive information such as : determination of the cause of death entailing a medico-legal problem ; assessment of post traumatic sequelae after a road accident and evaluation of the various forms of prejudice (evaluation of partial permanent invalidity) ; and assessment of the mental state of a person at the time of the facts he is charged with.

In France, the forensic doctor also plays an important part in the handling of contentious business between the insured persons and the social security organisms. He does social security expertises and acts in the settlement of strictly medical litigations. However, these expertises have a considerable socio-economic importance since, for example, they help to determine if payment of daily compensations (illness or work accident) is justified by the person's state of health.

The experts who do these expertises in the framwork of social legislation are forensic doctors ; their conclusion is imposed on the parties, whether they are pesons socially insured or social security doctors. The teaching of social legislation is given by professors of legal medicine.

## II. LEGAL MEDICINE IS ALSO THE LAW APPLIED TO MEDICINE

Medical activities and hospital or liberal functions are régulated by laws that all doctors must be acquainted with. In fact, they must know 1) the code of deontology applicable to all doctors. Disregard of the code entails disciplinary sanctions ; 2) the contract of care, which is the basis of medical liability since the MERCIER decree of 1936 ; 3) the relations between doctors and administrations and all state organisations.

They are also bound to respect : a) former Art. 378 of the Penal Code concerning medical discretion ; b) medical ethics ; c) the legislation on taking of organs and d) the legislation concerning experimentation on a healthy individual for non-therapeutic purposes.

## III. HOSPITAL INTEGRATION OF LEGAL MEDICINE

Legal Medicine has been practiced in France for decades in medical faculties and in institutes of Legal Medicine.

In 1958, the DEBRE law was voted for the integration of all academic disciplines in hospitals. In Lyons, Professor ROCHE created a multivalent emergency unit in the Edouard Herriot Hospital. Legal Medicine is sometimes integrated in the toxicology laboratory of some universities, such as in Strasbourg where medico-legal tradition is still very strong.

The Emergency Unit is the integration site most adapted to legal medicine, since one is faced with the highest number of medico-legal problems (blows and wounds, alcoholemia, rape, drug addiction ...).

Hospital integration enables the forensic doctor to acquire solid technical knowledge in the field of expertises concerning living individuals. It is highly beneficient for him, since he can appreciate inconcreto the events resulting in damage due to a medical error and also obtain the advice for his colleagues in all specialities.

In Lyons, integration exists in four hospitals :

1. Hospital Edouard Herriot : Pavillon "N" is the most important emergency unit in Lyons, with 28 000 patients, of whom 2 000 return for post-emergency care. There is a psychiatric unit in Pavillon "N" and two hospitalisation units.

The activity of the reception service, which is a medico-legal service and a medical emergency one, covers : intensive care, psychiatry including suicide attempts : 25% ; malaise : 20% ; non-suicidal intoxications : 5% ; medico-legal consultations : 10% ; cardiology : 10% ; pneumology : 10% ; digestive tract : 10% ; miscellaneous : 5%.

Moreover, in the emergency unit, there exist other consultations for drug addiction, deep mental patients, intentional blows and wounds, rape cases, assaults against modesty, battered women, voluntary interruption of pregnancy and therapeutical interruption of pregnancy, toxicology, internal medicine and post-emergency care. In all, 4 000 cases per annum.

2. Hospital Centre Lyons South : The activities are the same as those of Pavillon "N" ; however, the hospital is smaller. The originality of this hospital centre lies in the fact that there is a penitentiary medical unit, where all delinquent patients come from the lyonese region, suffering from an acute pathology.

**3 and 4.** Croix Rousse Hospital and Hôtel Dieu : There is an orthogenic centre directed by a forensic doctor.

## IV. DUTIES AND ROLE OF THE FORENSIC DOCTOR

1. In the hospital : Integration varies widely in France. It is compulsorily clinical, viological or anatomo-pathological.

Such integration leads to the fact that some forensic doctors, sometimes, have exclusively clinical activity at the university hospital in the morning. This concerns some of our colleagues who are surgeons : neuro-surgeons, orthopaedic surgeons, stomatologists. Other colleagues are integrated in the hospital in psychiatric units or in units of penitentiary medicine. Some integrations are made in the field of toxicology and even in the field of anatomo-pathology or of electroencephalography.

Integration is very varied in the hospital ; however, we are at present observing the development of real units of legal medicine, with consultations for wilful blows and wounds, alcohology, drug-addiction and also consultations for battered women. The consultations are created in all centers where there is a professor of legal medicine, but this is not the case for all university hospitals.

2. The Institute of Legal Medicine : It is needless to say that post mortem examinations are done in the Institutes of Legal Medicine. In Paris, we have Professor LECOMTE, in Lille, Professor GOSSET, in Marseilles, Professor CIANFARANI, in Strasbourg, our colleague MANGIN, and we should not forget Professor COUDANE at the University Hospital Centre of Nancy. In some towns with a university hospital, there is no Institute of Legal Medicine and the thanatological unit is integrated in the hospital, as is the case of towns such as Grenoble, Brest, Rennes, Toulouse, Nice, Angers and Nantes. Personally, we prefer doing post mortem examinations in the university institution, since there is no coercive and ocasionally perverse weight of the hospital administrative authorities when death involves medical liability.

Finally, due to financial problems in many hospitals, a confusion may occur between the anatomo-pathological unit and the legal medicine unit. Most French pathologists are not competent in the field of legal Medicine, and to have the same place with two responsible persons is likely to raise problems of authority with regard to the staff and to the attribution of credits.

3. Wards of Legal Medicine : Legal Medicine wards concern forensic doctors. In some French toxns, the bodies are examined by a civil status doctor ; in others they are seen by general practitioners ; therefore, many medico-legal deaths are reported as natural ones : hangings, medicamentous suicides, accidental intoxications or death due to road accidents. In Lyons, the medico-legal ward examines 700 bodies a year.

4. Laboratories of Scientific Police : There are five in France. Two of them are directed by personalities in Legal Medicine : Paris and Lyons witch, by the way, is the seat of Interpol. In the three other French towns where there are such laboratories, the directors are not forensic doctors in the usual sense.

5. Expertises in Penal, Civil, Administrative Social Security Affairs and in Military Pensions for Professional Respiratory Diseases.

6. Teaching activities : In Lyons, 1 500 hours of teaching are given by university hospital forensic doctors. There are also ten educational programmes that depend on lyonese legal medicine (but wich are also to be found in other faculty towns). The teaching of Legal Medicine in the four medical faculties of Lyons : certificates of thanatology and criminalistics, of medical law, of compensation for bodily damage, of aptitude for expertises, of toxicology, of philosophy and of medical ethics, of medical economics, of social security, criminalistics and drug addiction.

7. Research activities : a) Thanatology : at present, research is being done on sudden cardiac death through dysplasia of the right ventricle, and on suicidal behaviour ; b) Toxicology : presence of drugs in hair and nails ; c) Medico-Legal psychiatry: research on deviant behaviour, intra-family pathologies, overall cost of drug addicts during detoxication cures.

8. Publications of the medico-legal group : In France, we have a "Collection of Legal Medicine and of Medical Toxicology", created by Professor ROCHE and containing 200 volumes on the medico-legal speciality, that are taken as reference in French-speaking countries. It is a pleasant duty to congratulate Professor ROCHE, who is an international personality in French legal medicine : his publications ensure the development of legal medicine in a country where it has not always had its patent letters of nobility.

## V. THE FUTURE OF LEGAL MEDICINE

Legal Medicine is a discipline of yesterday, and also a discipline of today and especially of the future. Scientific disciplines have often criticized legal medicine since the latter has replaced them in some functions at university hospital levels. However, legal medicine is progressing in France and new specialities exist, such as poison control, drug control and medical ethics.

Progress in medicine has brought about an increase in medical accidents : problems of medical liability and of ethics are more and more numerous. Not a week passes without newspapers publishing a case of medical liability. In France, the forensic doctor has to state whether an error is medical or not, and in most cases, there is a college of specialists in which the forensic scientist plays a coordination role between different specialities.

Legal Medicine has greatly progressed in the last fifteen years, especially with the advent of genetic printing and the considerable development of research in toxicology, particularly concerning hair.

Scientific legal medicine plays an increasingly important part in providing scientific proof, a capital element for informing Justice. Most fortunately, in France, human testimony, so questionable, is decreasing. In French-speaking countries the great advocates of legal medicine are on one hand magistrates who know the value of the work done by members of this discipline, and lawyers on the other.

## VI. CONCLUSION

Clinical legal medicine in France is now in full development. The forensic scientist is, in the beginning, a specialist in thanatology, but he is above all a member of a human social discipline in which listening and dialoguing with a patient under expertise is essential.

# LES VIOLENCES SUR MINEURS EN SEINE SAINT DENIS

B. Marc, J.Varnier, P.Zillhardt, M.Soutoul, B.Richard, F. Boubrit, M.Dubaele et M.Garnier

**Urgences medico-judiciaires, hôpital Jean Verdier, AP-HP Avenue du 14 juillet 93143 Bondy Cedex France.**

Depuis quelques années, notre société s'est rendue compte que les actes de violence physique ne concernaient pas seulement les adultes mais que les enfants pouvaient en devenir les victimes. Il est apparu que ces violences étaient certainement plus fréquentes qu'il n'y paraissait au premier abord et qu'elles etaient souvent recouvertes par un voile de silence surtout lorsqu'elles avaient lieu dans le milieu familial. Des campagnes d'information ont été déclenchées pour inviter les témoins de ces violences à se porter dénonciateurs, mais les statistiques sont encore trop parcellaires pour avoir une idée précise de l'importance du phénomène.
Les urgences médico-judiciaires de l'Assistance Publique de Paris représentent un lieu privilégié pour connaître l'importance et la nature des différents actes de violence puisqu'en principe , les dépôts de plaintes pour coups et blessures ou sévices à enfants doivent faire l'objet d'un constat médico-légal initial rédigé par un spécialiste de ces unités.
En ce qui concerne la Seine Saint Denis, les urgences médico-judiciaires de l'hôpital Jean Verdier fonctionnent depuis 1989 et il est donc devenu possible d'établir un bilan des violences exercées sur les mineurs pour le début de la décennie 1990 puisque la quasi totalité des victimes signalées aux brigades des mineurs ont été examinées dans le service.

## RESULTATS

La violence envers les mineurs peut être arbitrairement classée en deux grande catégories
- les sévices à mineurs qui correspondent à des coups, à des blessures (articles 222-7 à 222-14 du Code pénal en vigueur traitant des violences), à des manques de soins ou d'alimentation (articles 222-3 et 222-4 du Code pénal en vigueur traitant du délaissement d'une personne hors d'état de se protéger et article 222-6 du Code pénal traitant de l'omission de porter secours)

- les violences sexuelles qui correspondent à des viols donc des pénétrations sexuelles (articles 222-23 à 222-26 du Code pénal) ou aux agressions sexuelles autres que le viol (articles 222-27 à 222-32 du Code pénal).

## INTERPRETATION DES RESULTATS

### 1- LES SEVICES SUR MINEURS

Les chiffres rapportés dans le tableau 1 montrent qu'entre 1990 et 1993, en valeur absolue, **779** enfants victimes de sévices ont été examinés aux urgences médico judiciaires.

Tableau 1: Nombre d'enfants mineurs examinés aux urgences médico-judiciaires de l'hôpital Jean Verdier entre 1990 et 1993

| ANNEES | 1990 | 1991 | 1992 | 1993 |
|---|---|---|---|---|
| VIOLENCES SUR MINEURS | 42 | 124 | 235 | 378 |
| VIOLENCES SUR ADULTES | 838 | 1020 | 2257 | 2960 |
| VIOLENCES SEXUELLES SUR MINEURS | 135 | 143 | 181 | 236 |
| VIOLENCES SEXUELLES SUR ADULTES | 148 | 123 | 110 | 127 |

Le nombre de mineurs victimes de sévices examinés dans le service a augmenté régulièrement depuis 1990 (+195% entre 1990 et 1991, + 89% entre 1991 et 1992, + 60% entre 1992 et 1993).
Il ne faut pas en conclure que cette progression représente seulement la progression de la violence sur les mineurs dans le département car il faut tenir compte que cette progression est aussi la conséquence de la meilleure connaissance de l'existence du service par les utilisateurs.

Les violences exercées sur les mineurs augmentent d'une année à l'autre ce qu'on voit en comparant ces chiffres à ceux de la violence exercée sur les adultes, objet des graphiques d'activité ci-dessous.

**Activité détaillée des U.M.J. Jean Verdier AP-HP**
**Année 1993**

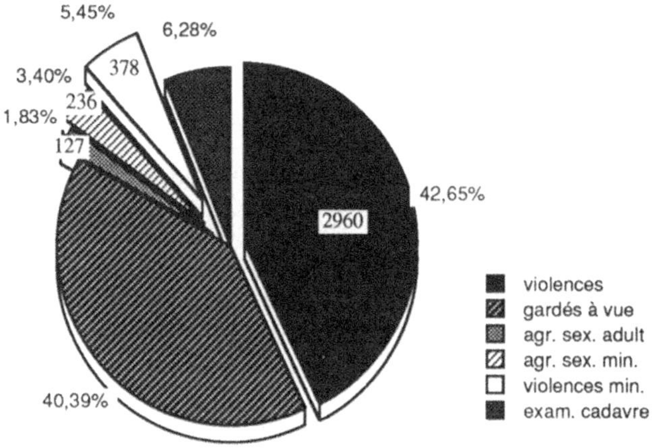


**Violences sur adultes et sur mineurs. Années 1990-1993**
**Urgences médico-judiciaires Jean Verdier, AP-HP**

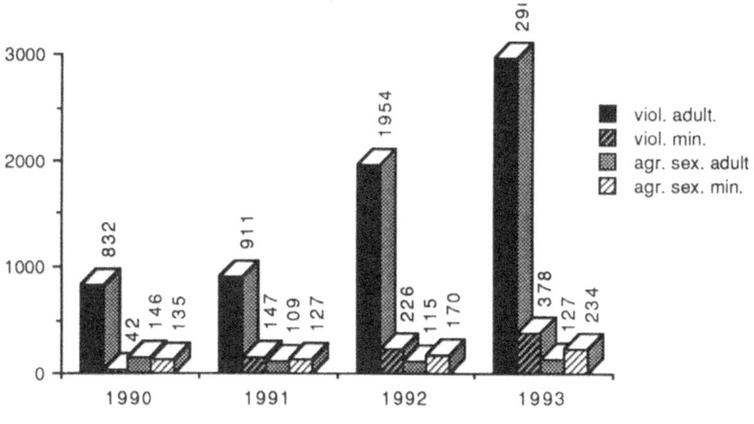


Au cours de la même période de 4 ans, 7075 victimes adultes de coups et blessures volontaires ont été examinées auc UMJ.

Les sévices sur mineurs représentent donc 11% de la violence générale.

Au plan de la progression annuelle les constats médicaux des victimes de coups et blessures volontaires ont évolué de la façon suivante :

+21% entre 90 et 91, +121% entre 91 et 92, +31% entre 92 et 93.
On peut donc estimer que sur une durée de 3 ans, la progression du nombre d'examens de victimes adultes a été de +173%.

Dans le même temps , toutes choses égales par ailleurs , la progression des examens d'enfants adressés pour sévices a été de +344%.

## 2- LES VIOLENCES SEXUELLES

Entre 1990 et 1993, 508 patients adultes victimes de violences sexuelles ont été examinées aux UMJ. Pendant la même période **695** mineurs victimes de sévices sexuels ont été examinés.
On peut donc dire que globalement les violences sexuelles perpétrées sur les mineurs sont supérieures de 36% à celles exercées sur les adultes.
La progression annuelle de ce type de violence est très inquiétante.
En effet, si en 1990 le nombre de victimes mineures était sensiblement identique à celui des adultes ( 135 versus 148), en 1993, le nombre de victimes mineures d'agression sexuelle a pratiquement doublé : 127 cas en 1990 versus 236 cas en 1993.
La prise en charge de ces enfants victimes de violences physiques ou sexuelles mobilise un important personnel spécialisé au niveau du département . En ce qui concerne les mesures d'urgence en 1993, 614 mineurs ont été examinés aux UMJ , pour 30 d'entre eux une hospitalisation a été demandée à la suite de l'examen réalisé.

## CONCLUSION

On peut donc conclure qu'en Seine Saint Denis, la progression du nombre d'examens d'enfants victimes de sévices ou de violences sexuelle a été plus importante que celle des adultes victime d'actes de violence volontaire ou de viols.
Cette différence très significative en faveur des examens d'enfants est certainement due en grande partie aux diverses campagnes d'information qui ont été programmées tant auprès du grand public qu'auprès du personnel spécialisé que sont les enseignants, les assistantes sociales ou le personnel des services de PMI. Elles ont certainement entraîné un nombre plus élevé de signalements auprès des autorités judiciaires.

# Les violences faites aux femmes en Algérie : du social au judiciaire

A. OUSSADIT

Centre Hospitalier Universitaire de Tlemcen - 13000 TLEMCEN (Algérie)

Jamais le problème de la femme en Algérie n'a été posé avec tant d'acuité et d'importance qu'il ne l'est aujourd'hui. Jamais il n'est apparu plus clairement que les transformations politiques et sociales étaient étroitement liées au changement du statut de la femme. A travers une étude médico-légale réalisée dans deux villes de l'ouest algérien, nous avons tenté de faire le point sur la question en prenant comme repère un point particulier de la condition féminine : l'intégrité physique. Nous en avons tiré quelques enseignements.

Il faut rappeler que pendant des siècles la famille algérienne est restée immuable parce qu'ayant adopté une structure défensive, elle se trouvait à l'écart des causes susceptibles de provoquer son évolution. Elle portait en elle les éléments statiques absorbant ou neutralisant les influences du cadre politico-social.

Face au colonisateur, la société algérienne s'est refermée sur elle-même pour préserver et maintenir les valeurs constitutives de sa personnalité collective. Elle a réagit en maintenant les femmes à l'écart. L'homme dérouté par le mode de vie occidental retrouvait auprès de la femme le sentiment sécurisant de la pérennité de ses origines et aussi l'exercice de son autorité?

Le destin de la femme semble fixé irrémédiablement dès la naissance. Celle-ci n'est d'ailleurs pas fêtée de la même façon selon le sexe du nouveau-né. L'arrivée d'une fille se fait dans le silence! Pendant toute la grossesse, la future mère a espéré porter un garçon et redouté la naissance d'une fille.
Les garçons constituent une force de travail et de combat ; ils restent dans la famille dont ils assurent la richesse et la puissance tandis que les filles quittent le foyer paternel pour celui du mari. Dans la petite enfance se constituent des systèmes d'habitudes acquises par l'éducation ; ils sont transmis au jeune enfant par son entourage et son environnement dans les discours, les paroles, les gestes et les comportements.
Là où elle est arrivée par naissance, ses droits sont très réduits ; elle n'est qu'une simple passagère bénéficiant du gîte et du couvert. Sa vraie vie sera ailleurs où il lui faudra s'adapter au prix d'une soumission totale. Ses vertus de bonne conduite, de bonne ménagère puis de bonne mère de garçon seront son seul recours et sa seule raison d'être.

Les contraintes sociales s'accentuent au fur et à mesure que le moment du mariage approche. La virginité fait alors l'objet d'une attention particulière. La virginité de la jeune fille symbolise sa pureté et celle de sa famille. C'est son bien le plus précieux! Aussi est-elle institutionnalisée ; elle est une valeur culturelle et un fait social. La jeune fille est dépossédée de son propre corps dans ce qu'il y a de plus

intime puisque la sauvegarde de l'intégrité de l'hymen est l'affaire de toute la famille. Comme la sexualité, la virginité est placée sous contrôle social ; elle ne saurait être laissée à la gestion des individus ou liée à l'affectivité. En contrepartie, la vierge se trouve extrêmement valorisée.
L'âge pubertaire et la période prénuptiale constituent donc une époque où les interdits se multiplient, la jeune fille doit redoubler de discrétion dans ses mouvements, ses gestes, ses paroles. Dans un tel climat de défiance elle est plus enfermée que jamais.

Le mariage sera la finalité pour la femme qui se verra désormais confier deux tâches fondamentales :
- assurer la reproduction
- prendre en charge les travaux domestiques et gérer l'intérieur du foyer.

Le mariage ne saurait être la consécration d'un couple ; il s'agit pour l'homme comme pour la femme d'une étape qui permettra d'accroître la famille.

En Algérie où l'Islam est la religion de l'Etat, le Code de la Famille qui s'inspire du Droit Musulman prend en charge le domaine social et le statut personnel. D'après ce code, le but proclamé du mariage est de "fonder une famille basée sur l'affection, la mansuétude et l'entraide". Il est précisé deux autres finalités :
- "protéger moralement les deux conjoints"
- "préserver les liens de famille".

Il est par ailleurs prescrit aux conjoints de "sauvegarder des liens de parenté et les bonnes relations avec les parents et les proches".
"La femme est placée sous l'autorité du mari à qui elle doit obéissance et égards en sa qualité de chef de famille. L'épouse est tenue d'allaiter sa progéniture si elle est en mesure de le faire et de l'élever". Ainsi donc se trouve reconnue et fixée la vocation maternelle de la femme. Nous avons donc brièvement tracé le cadre dans lequel évolue la femme en Algérie.

Quels sont les résultats de nos statistiques? Le portrait de la femme victime de violence qui ressort de notre étude confirme cette situation de minorité qui la caractérise : minorité économique et minorité sociale.

La colonisation, le contact avec le monde occidental, sa participation active à la guerre de libération ainsi que les trente années d'indépendance ne lui ont pas donné la possibilité d'une émancipation durable. Les traditions et les coutumes continuent de l'emprisonner dans une condition difficile. La primauté de l'homme sur la femme est quasi-absolue. La dépendance économique de la femme semble la cause primordiale de son maintien dans un perpétuel état d'asservissement sur fond d'analphabétisme. la famille traditionnelle encore très vivante semble à peine ébranlée par les changements survenus depuis une trentaine d'années. Force est de constater que des résistances s'opposent de façon très profonde à une évolution du statut de la femme.

# THE MEDICO-LEGAL SYSTEM IN TURKEY, UNDERGRADUATE AND POSTGRADUATE CURRICULUM OF THE FORENSIC SCIENCES

SALAÇIN S, ALPER B, ÇEKIN N, GÜLMEN MK

The Department of Forensic Medicine, Medical School of Çukurova University, Adana, Turkey.

Surveys of the medico-legal system in Europe and other continents were presented at the International Meetings held in the last years. The medicolegal system and the education and training model of Turkey were not appeared at none of these meetings. A brief presentation of the topic was written by one of the authors and published years before[1]. In this paper a review of the evolution of the medicolegal system in Turkey is presented.

## HISTORY

Some historical milestones must be mentioned before presenting the current status of the medico-legal system in Turkey. Before the begining of the 19th century, the absolute authority on legal problems and Islamic religous laws rested with the Archiatre, who was appointed by the ruler of the Ottoman Empire. During the reigns of Sultan Mahmut II and Sultan Abdul Mecit the first Criminal Code and its second and third revisions were puplished. During this time, the economic and political relations, mainly with France and the other European countries, influenced the creation and modelling the legal system. The first Legal Medicine lecture was created at the Military Medical School in 1839, and the first medicolegal autopy was performed at the same school in 1841. In 1869 a Civilian Health Council was created, and had the responsibility of the health and welfare problems. This Council had offered the advices to the courts and to the Ministry of Health and Welfare, also had the responsibility to prepare the preliminary reports related with the health and welfare laws. The Council is still existing with additional responsibilities, basically similar of those in the past. Two important regulations concerning phycians' responsibilities in legal medicine were accepted in 1915 and 1917 respectively. At the same time Forensic Medicine had became a speciality in the medical sciences in 1917. Following the foundation of Turkish Republic in 1923, the laws relating to the Organization of Forensic Sciences and Medicine rewritten. Subsequent revisions of these laws were done in 1953, 1967 and 1982 respectively.

## PRESENT STATUS OF THE MEDICO-LEGAL SYSTEM

The republic of Turkey covers over 300.000 square miles and population of 60 million people, in 76 cities. At present, the medicolegal services are mainly provided by two separate bodies, Forensic Science Organization (FSO) and Universities. There are also criminal investigation departments and narcotics laboratories operated by the Ministry of Interior or the Police Departments and Military staff. All medicolegal services, education, training and researches are provided by these bodies.

A body known as the Forensic Science Organization (FSO) had been created directly under the jurisdiction of the Ministry of Justice. It had been centered in Istanbul University. FSO works as an official expert Institute with a composition six departments in the center. Those are Morque Department (Forensic Pathology Lab.), Chemical Analysis Department, Biology Department, Physical Analysis Department, Phychiatry and Behavioral Science Department, Traffic Department. Some of those departments has own special subunit laboratories such as; Chemical Department has Toxicology, Drug Analysis and Clinical Toxicology laboratories, Biology Department has Paternity testing laboratory and Stain Analysis laboratory, Physical Analysis Department has Firearms and Questioned Documents subunits.

Turkey is divided in seven Forensic Provinces. Each province has a Branch of FSO. The FSO has six local branches, are established in six cities as two departments, The Morque Dept. and The Chemical Analysis Dept., some of the Branches situated within or adjecent to the medical schools of universities. The directores of the branches are also the directores of Forensic Medicine Dept. of medical schools. Specialist such as forensic medicine, pathologists, toxicologists, pharmacists, biochemists and biologists work as staff in each Branch. These Branches are responsible for all routine medicolegal services, have full autopsy facilities and laboratories for forensic pathology and toxicology. Clinical forensic medicine services, including the examination of live persons for assaults, sexsual offences, drunkenness etc., also provided by the staff of these branches. The FSO has also the Clinical Expert Units, created in 13 cities.

## EDUCATION AND TRAINING

The academic duties of Forensic Sciences, such as undergraduate and postgraduate teaching in forensic sciences and resarch are mainly conducted by the universities. The deparments of Forensic Medicine are founded in 17 Medical Schools, and The Institutes of Forensic Sciences are built up in Ankara and Istanbul Universities. Medical education lasts six years in Turkey. All medical practitioner are qualified to be an expert witness in the court and also to perform medicolegal autopsies. Forensic Medicine lectures are compulsory in Medical Schools. Most of the lectures are held by the forensic medicine professors for the students of 8, 9., 10. semesters, as 50 hours lecture and 10 hours practice exercises. Some of them held this training program as full time 3 weeks attendence to the department for 9. and 10. semesters students. Undergraduate curriculum composed of Forensic Thanatology, Forensic Traumatology and Causalty, Forensic Pathology, Clinical Forensic Medicine, Medical Ethics, Medical Legislation and Forensic Professional Laws, etc.. Forensic Medicine lectures are also compulsory for the School of Dentistry, Law Schools, Police Academies and Military Schools. Those lectures for these schools are held by the Forensic Medicine professors of Medical Schools. The curriculum for these schools are prepared to consider their necessities.

In Turkey, to have a postgraduate student status in a Medical School, candidates must take the National Board Examination and have at least good marks. The topics related to the Forensic Medicine are included in this examination. Postgraduate training in Forensic Medicine regulated by the law of the medical practitioners, as other specialities. According to this law postgraduate training lasts two years, but the Forensic Medicine specialist diploma is given by the most of departments as early as three or even more years. The recent effort to change the official period of the training will influence the continious improvement.

The programs for MS and PhD degree in forensic sciences are running in the forensic medicine institutes and some of the forensic medicine departments. Medical practitioners, chemists, biologists, pharmacists, lawyers etc.. can apply for this programs as full time or extern position.

## CONTIUNING EDUCATION

Contiuning educative activities provided by the seminars, workshops, conferences and also some lectures on spesific topics, held in the departments. On the national platform, Annual Forensic Medicine Days have been organized and sponsored by the FSO since 1984. The aim of these meetings are to arrange close relationships between the forensic scientists and the judges, and also to get the oportunities to discuss the common legal problems. The first National Forensic Sciences Meeting was held in Adana, in 12-15 April 1994.

The Forensic Medicine Society founded in 1992 and published and circulated newsletter monthly to the colleaques. Forensic Medicine Journal has been published quarterly since 1983 by the FSO. There is also Legal Journal has been published by the Ministry of Justice for more than 20 years.

## REFERENCE:

1. Salaçin S. Forensic Medicine in Turkey. The American Journal of Forensic Medicine and Pathology 1982, 3:179-180.

Correspondent: Salaçin Serpil M.D. Çukurova University, Medical School,
Dept. of Forensic Medicine, 01330, Balcalı, Adana-TURKEY.

## PURSE SNATCHING : THE AGED AS TRIPLE VICTIMS

N. TELMON[*/**], D.ROUGE[*], B.VELLAS[**], J.L.ALBAREDE[**], L.ARBUS[*]

[*] Service Médico-Judiciaire - CHU Toulouse-Rangueil (Pr L.ARBUS)
1 avenue Jean Poulhes F-31054 Toulouse Cedex

[**] Service de Médecine Interne et Gérontologie Clinique (Pr J.L. ALBAREDE)
170 avenue de Casselardit F-31300 Toulouse

From the angle of both geriatrics and legal medicine, the elderly person who is attacked in the street is a victim in three ways. Purse snatching is an assault to which an elderly person is typically exposed in an urban environment. In this kind of attack, the age of the victim is a factor before, during and after the aggression.

1 - before the assault :

Age is a factor of "victimisation" in several respects ; that is to say that the situation of the victim facilitates the task of the aggressor. In the first place, the elderly person is considered as an easy, defenceless victim, who often carries money in their purse. In the second place, because of age there are physical or psychological difficulties in warding off attack, even if it is only impaired sight or hearing, which make it more difficult to foresee the possibility of assault.

2 - at the time of assault

The attacker, either running or on a scooter or similar two-wheeler, violently snatches at the victim's purse or bag. This causes the victim to lose his or her balance, and the elderly person will generally fall. In addition, other injuries are possible, which are rarely isolated and are generally related to the fall : pulled brachial plexus, skin lacerated by the handbag strap. This type of aggression generally involves elderly, able-bodied women. Several age-linked factors will either make a fall more likely or aggravate its consequences.

a - the factors making a fall more likely are numerous. They are mostly related to the difficulty of the elderly person in keeping his or her balance, but are also due to slower reaction times and decreased muscular strength. The weight of the subject intervenes to a lesser degree.

b - the consequences of the fall will be aggravated by osteoporosis, especially as the victims are in majority female. Reduced bone mass, making for fragility, in association with intrinsic and extrinsic factors (the assault in this case) lead to lack of protection or cushioning when falling and a fracture will result. Three main types of injury are observed :

- fracture of the femoral neck, due to impact on the hip
- fracture of the upper part of the humeral neck, due to impact on the base of the shoulder
- Colles fracture, due to a fall on the wrist in a movement of self-protection.

The first two injuries are all the more common because the elderly person may not always have the reflex of trying to cushion the fall by protecting themselves with their hands.

3 - after the assault

The physical and psychological trauma are increased by age. The consequences of the fall may be considerably aggravated in the elderly person by various possible infraclinical pathologies and the victim will decompensate following the attack. The typical example is fracture of the femoral neck. Here, the consequences are of three kinds :

1 - the vital prognosis of fracture of the femoral neck is severe, both in the short term (11% of deaths) and in the long term (over 30% of deaths at one year),

2 - there is considerable loss of autonomy ; less than half the patients regain the same degree of autonomy that they had before.

3 - lastly, the social consequences should not be neglected, since loss of autonomy often leads to entry into an institution. One-third of victims with fracture of the femoral neck cannot continue to live in their former home.

The prognosis is better for fractures of the upper limbs, but however short the period spent in hospital, it remains a danger for the elderly person. An example is the case of an elderly woman aged 76, who during an attack fell on her left shoulder. This resulted in a three-piece fracture below the left humeral tuberosity which was treated by immobilisation of Dujarrier type for six weeks. She spent two days in the emergency department, then two months in a rehabilitation centre. Functionally, limited range of movement persisted in the upper arm, particularly in external rotation and backward movement of the shoulder.

Before the assault she lived alone, but because of the functional limitations, together with the onset of psychological and physical dependence, she has had to go into a home for the aged.

Lastly, psychological repercussions (anxiety, feelings of insecurity, tendency to withdrawal) are frequent in the elderly person after assault, whatever the objective gravity of the consequences. An example is the case of an elderly woman aged 74, who had her handbag snatched but did not suffer serious physical harm ; the only injuries were bruises and grazes. Nevertheless, it was more than six months before she felt psychologically able to go out of her home, do her shopping and take part in the social activities of her home area.

The picture need not always be so sombre. One patient, an elderly woman aged 79 presented after assault a true cervical fracture of the left femur of Garden IV type, treated by an intermediate prosthesis. She lived alone at home. After two weeks in a surgery department and five weeks in a department of rehabilitation, she still has a limp, but she can walk with one stick and was able to return home.

In conclusion, purse snatching, which mainly affects the aged, has physical and/or psychological consequences which extend far beyond the theft itself. The elderly person is a victim of his or her age at all moments of the assault : beforehand, as he or she is an easy victim; during, because a fall is very probable ; and afterwards, because a fall often has serious consequences in the elderly person.

References :


Creditor M.C.(1993) Hazards of hospitalisation of the Elderly, *Annals of Internal Medecine.* ; 118 : 219-223

Cummings S.R., Kelsey J.L., Nevitt M.C., O'Dowd K. (1985) Epidemiology of osteoporosis and osteoporotic fracture. *Epidemiolo. Rev.* ; 7 : 178:208

Harper C.M., Lyles Y.M.(1988) Physiology and complications of bed rest. J. Am. Geriatr. Soc.; 36:1047-1054

Hirsch C.H., Sommers L., Olsen A., Mullen L., Winograd C.H. (1990) The natural history of functionnal morbidity in hospitalized older patients. *J. Am. Geriatr. Soc.* 38:1296-1303

Holmberg S., Conradi P., Kalen R., Thongren K.G.(1986) Mortality after cervical hip fracture. *Acta Orthop. Scand.*, 57, 8-11

Overstall P.M., Exton-Smith A.N., Imms F.J., Jonhson F.(1977) Fall in the elderly related to postural imbalance. *Br. Med. J.* , 1, 261-264

# 10. Bodily Damage Evaluation in Europe

# LE MANDAT D'EXPERTISE POUR L'EVALUATION DU DOMMAGE CORPOREL
# PROJET D'UN MODELE EUROPEEN UNIFIE

GIACOMO CANEPA

Professeur à l'Institut de Médecine Légale
Via de Toni 12, Université de Gènes, Italie

La diversification des systèmes juridiques dans les différents pays de la Communauté Européenne représente un obstacle sérieux à l'émanation d'une seule législation, valable pour tous les pays. Mais une série de nouvelles acquisitions dans le domaine de l'évaluation du dommage corporel consent de pouvoir envisager, au moins, une uniformisation du mandat d'expertise, qui se base sur les orientations suivantes :

1) En Italie une nouvelle méthodologie a été envisagée par GERIN (1952), qui a souligné que le dommage corporel en droit commun doit être considéré comme une ménomation de la validité biologique qui représente, en soi-même, une valeur patrimoniale : un "dommage biologique" qui exige une réparation, en soi-même, sans considérer si cette "validité" ou intégrité biologique de l'être humain est employée, ou non, dans une activité productrice de biens économiques. Cette orientation a été suivie par l'Ecole médico-légale de Gênes (FRANCHINI, CANEPA, CANALE) et de Pise (BARGAGNA). Au Tribunal Civil de Gênes, et ensuite de Pise, se sont vérifiées les premières applications judiciaires de la nouvelle méthodologie.

2) Aux Etats-Unis, à partir de 1980, a été suivie une méthodologie biologique analogue ("medical impairment") par l'élaboration d'un Guide pour l'évaluation de dommage permanent suivant une critériologie purement biologique, adoptée par l'A.M.A. ("American Medical Association") en 1984.

3) En France, une méthodologie analogue a été illustrée en 1982 par l'élaboration d'un "Barème Fonctionnel" (Concours Médical) et ensuite, par un barème très

détaillé, pour l'évaluation des "déficits fonctionnels séquellaires" ("Evaluation médico-légale des incapacités permanentes en droit commun"), proposé et adopté par la "Société de Médecine Légale et de Criminologie de France", en 1991.

4) Enfin ce même sujet a été l'objet d'une discussion, au niveau européen, à l'occasion du "XII Symposium de l'Académie Internationale de Médecine Légale" que j'ai organisé à Gênes en 1992 dont les actes ont été publiés sur la revue de l'Académie en 1993 ("Acta Medicinae Legalis et Socialis"). Sur la base de ces prémices je pense qu'un modèle utile pour le mandat d'expertise, en ce domaine, est représenté par les questions suivantes, qui sont posées aux experts par le Tribunal de Gênes depuis 1972 :

"L'expert, après avoir examiné le blessé, les actes judiciaires et la documentation médicale, doit
1) décrire les lésions subies au moment de l'accident, leur évolution, les traitements pratiqués et l'état actuel de l'expertisé ;
2) décrire les précédents morbides éventuels, présents au moment de l'accident ("état antérieur") ;
3) évaluer la durée de l'invalidité temporaire (total et partielle), en spécifiant de cette dernière la mesure (en pourcentage) ;
4) évaluer, si l'expertisé est engagé dans une activité de travail, l'incidence éventuelle (totale ou partielle) de l'invalidité temporaire sur l'activité de travail, en spécifiant la durée de cette incidence (totale ou partielle) sur l'activité de travail;
5) évaluer si actuellement existent des séquelles permanentes des lésions subies, en spécifiant s'il est possible de prévoir des possibilités d'aggravation ou d'amélioration. Dans le cas d'une réponse positive à cette dernière question, l'expert donnera toute information utile sur l'évolution future, son degré de probabilité et, s'il pense qu'un nouvel examen est nécessaire, l'époque de ce nouvel examen sera précisée ;
6) s'il y a des séquelles permanentes, l'expert précisera si telles séquelles auront une influence négative sur la validité (biologique) de l'expertisé, en spécifiant cette influence en pourcentage ;
7) l'expert précisera si l'invalidité permanente est telle d'exercer une influence négative sur l'activité professionnelle de l'expertisé, en spécifiant s'il y a une incompatibilité entre l'invalidité permanente et l'exercice de l'activité ou bien seulement une limitation, dont il donnera la description (pas une évaluation en pourcentage) ;
8) dans le cas d'incompatibilité, l'expert indiquera d'autres activités qui soient, totalement ou partiellement, compatibles, compte tenu de la personnalité du sujet;
9) l'expert enfin donnera des renseignements sur le montant des dépenses médicales et de soins, en spécifiant aussi si des dépenses de ce type sont prévisibles pour l'avenir".

Je pense, enfin, qu'une discussion sur ce type de mandat d'expertise sera utile et pourra contribuer à l'élaboration d'un mandat d'expertise unifié au niveau européen.

## Références bibliographiques

**American Medical Association** (1984) Guides to the evaluation of permanent impairment. 2nd Edition, A.M.A., Chicago

**Bargagna M. et Busnelli F.D.** (1988) (textes réunis par) La valutazione del danno alla salute, CEDAM (ed), Padova

**Canale M. et Gianelli Castiglione A.** (1990) (textes réunis par) La valutazione del danno alla persona da invalidità permanente, Giuffrè (ed), Milano

**Canepa G., Filauro F., Giaretti R., Lomi A.** (1986) La valutazione tabellare dell'invalidità in responsabilità civile. Il "barème fonctionnel" dal 1982, Giuffrè (ed), Milano

**Canepa G.** (1990) la contribution italienne à l'élaboration d'un barème des invalidités en droit commun. Journal de Médecine Légale - Droit Médical 33:125-131

**Diamant-Berger O., Fournier C., Loeb R., Muller P., Nicourt B., Roche L., Rousseau C.** (1982) Barème fonctionnel indicatif des incapacités en droit commun. Avant propos. Le concours Médical, n. 25 (suppl.)

**Franchini A.** (1959) La valutazione medico-legale del danno biologico di rilevanza patrimoniale. Responsabilità Civile e Previdenza 24:19

**Gerin C.** (1953) La valutazione medico-legale del danno alla persona in responsabilità Civile. (Rapport aux Journées de Trieste en 1952). Rivista degli Infortuni e delle malattie professionali 40:371

**Piganiol G.** (1992) La méthodologie de l'expertise du dommage corporel dans les pays de la CEE. Imprimerie Soulisse et Cassegrain, Niort

**Société de Médecine Légale et de Criminologie de France** (1991) Evaluation médico-légale des incapacités permanentes en droit commun. Alexandre Lacassagne (ed), Le Concours Médical (ed), Lyon-Paris

# L'EVALUATION DES SOUFFRANCES ENDURÉES CHEZ LE SUJET EN ETAT VEGETATIF PERSISTANT

**P.A. DELPLA[2], D. ROUGE[1], G. GERAUD[2], M.C. ARNE-BES[3], J. LAGARRIGUE[4], L. ARBUS[1-3]**

**1. Unité Médico-Judiciaire 2. Service de Neurologie 3. Service d'Explorations Fonctionnelles Neurologiques 4. Service de Neurochirurgie**

**CHU Rangueil, 1, avenue Jean Poulhès 31054 Toulouse**

Les "souffrances endurées" sont à la fois **physiques ou corporelles** (la douleur proprement dite) **et morales**, atteignant et compromettant le psychisme et la qualité de vie du blessé. Il appartient à l'expert de les apprécier **"in abstracto",** d'essayer de les quantifier (d'où l'expression classique de "quantum doloris"), ce qui suppose, d'abord, qu'il qualifie le préjudice en lui assignant un adjectif ou un adverbe (ou encore mieux un chiffre) en référence à des échelles d'appréciation, ensuite, qu'il procède à une description minutieuse et si possible exhaustive de **"toutes les douleurs physiques et morales, les désagréments et les gênes qui dans un premier temps ont émaillé la période évolutive et qui dans un second temps ne constituent pas les éléments d'un déficit fonctionnel durable"** (NICOURT). Une telle mission, où la subjectivité de l'expert se mêle à celle du malade, sera particulièrement délicate à mener **chez le sujet qui est ou a été privé de sa conscience**, c'est-à-dire de sa "capacité de percevoir et d'intégrer les stimuli et d'y répondre de façon psychologiquement adaptée".

Ainsi, chez l'individu en état végétatif, défini comme un "appauvrissement massif des fonctions supérieures avec conservation des fonctions végétatives de l'encéphale" (JENNETT et PLUM 1972), la difficulté est bien d'**appréhender le niveau de perception et d'intégration des stimuli "nociceptifs"** au sens large du terme, qu'ils soient physiques ou psychiques, externes ou internes. Autrement dit, quelle est à côté de la douleur vécue ou observée (objectivée), la **souffrance présumée** d'un tel sujet ? Et comment, si cela est possible, la quantifier ?

**Le coma et l'état végétatif**, "états frontières entre la vie et la mort" (VIGOUROUX et coll. 1965), constituent une perte de l'expression consciente usuelle. C'est à l'évidence une pathologie déroutante pour le malade qui ne communique pas et ne retrouve plus son univers habituel mais aussi pour l'entourage qui n'a pas accès d'emblée au contenu de la vie psychique du patient, à ses émotions, et qui se pose alors la question de la "présence ou non" du sujet.

Dans l'état végétatif, le maintien de la vigilance contraste avec l'absence d'activité consciente, autrement dit avec la perte globale (plus ou moins complète) des fonctions des centres supérieurs ou corticaux, celles du tronc cérébral (dans leur ensemble) étant à l'opposé conservées. Ces patients, encore dits en état de "vie végétative" ou qualifiés de "grabataires arelationnels" (VIGOUROUX et coll. 1965, 1972) permettent d'appréhender, par opposition au coma -cet état de non réponse dans lequel le sujet repose les yeux fermés et ne peut être éveillé-, les notions de **vigilance** ou niveau de conscience et de conscience au sens du contenu ou de l'expérience perceptivo-cognitive. La première repose sur le fonctionnement d'un **système réticulé activateur ascendant** (SRAA) contenu dans la substance réticulée de la moitié supérieure du tronc cérébral (substance réticulée ponto-mésencéphalique). Cependant, pour que cet état d'éveil, assimilable à un niveau de réactivité globale de l'organisme, acquière une signification "psychologique", il faut encore que les effets activateurs du SRAA, lui-même stimulé par les diverses afférences sensorielles (et également corticales), puissent s'exercer sur un cortex cérébral au moins en partie intact : c'est donc le **néocortex** qui **donne à la conscience son contenu**, qui permet la perception et l'intégration au plus haut niveau des divers stimuli. C'est bien ce contenu cortical de la conscience qui va intéresser l'expert dans l'évaluation des souffrances endurées car c'est lui qui intègre l'expérience perceptivo-cognitive de la douleur, la transforme en vécu affectif douloureux et conditionne d'une façon plus générale la vie psychique et émotionnelle de l'individu.

**L'état végétatif persistant ou chronique (EVP)** est une des évolutions possibles à long terme du coma, évolution dont la fréquence va croissant avec les progrès de la réanimation neurologique et que l'on peut considérer comme le degré extrême des séquelles observées, en particulier après un traumatisme crânien.

**Le diagnostic en est clinique, devant un blessé "grabataire arelationnel stabilisé" :** les messages qui lui sont transmis n'entrainent de sa part aucune réponse reconnaissable (il n'y a notamment aucune réponse aux ordres simples et la douleur n'est pas en apparence localisée) et, de la même façon, son comportement spontané ne fournit aucun renseignement sur l'état de sa vie intra-psychique. Cliniquement, la posture est constamment hypertonique avec des formules diverses, le plus souvent proches d'un état de décortication plus ou moins symétrique ou d'une triple flexion ; des stimulations variées entrainent un renforcement de cette rigidité. S'il existe une gamme assez étendue d'activités motrices spontanées telles que mouvements oculaires horizontaux conjugués lents, quelquefois brusques, sans fixation ou poursuite volontaire, mouvements de la bouche et de la face (mâchonnements, grincements de dents, baillements, grimaces, sourires ...), mouvements plus rares du cou et des membres, celles-ci sont considérées comme sans but, sans contenu identifiable, sans intention. C'est cette absence d'activités conscientes qui contraste avec le maintien de la vigilance (dont témoignent l'ouverture des yeux et l'identification de cycles veille-sommeil) qui caractérise l'état végétatif. Les données complémentaires de l'électrophysiologie ou des études métaboliques confirment cette conclusion : l'électroencéphalogramme montre des activités lentes peu ou pas réactives, irrégulières dans le temps, dans la bande delta ou thêta ; les potentiels évoqués corticaux sont altérés ou abolis alors que les potentiels du tronc cérébral sont normaux ; les études au PET-scan révèlent une activité métabolique cérébrale très ralentie d'un niveau comparable à celui d'une anesthésie profonde. L'on peut malgré tout s'interroger sur la véritable signification "fonctionnelle" de l'EVP : certes, c'est par définition l'absence de quelque chose que contient précisément la vie non végétative : absence de relation, absence de conscience, absence de vie mentale ? Mais, pas plus que la clinique, ni les données électrophysiologiques, quelquefois contradictoires et manquant de spécificité, ni les données métaboliques, trop peu nombreuses encore, ne permettent de répondre à la question suivante : la persistance d'une lésion ou même l'absence d'activité dans une structure, traduite par exemple par un métabolisme effondré, permet-elle de conclure à l'abolition d'une fonction ? Autrement dit, les sujets dits "végétatifs" n'ont-ils ni conscience ni activité cognitive parce qu'ils ont perdu l'organe qui les sous-tend ? Qui en effet est capable de dire quelle(s) structure (s) doit (doivent) être détruite(s) ou muette (s) pour conclure que la conscience a disparu ? Dans ce domaine, le seul couplage structure-fonctions est certainement trop simpliste.

Il faut ensuite établir la chronicité du trouble clinique, autrement dit le caractère persistant, sinon définitif de l'état végétatif. Ce diagnostic d'irréversibilité peut raisonnablement être posé après un an d'évolution : passé ce délai, les chances de retour à la conscience, bien que non absolument impossibles, sont exceptionnelles. C'est dire en tous cas que pendant cette première année, et même au-delà, chaque manifestation neuro-végétative et comportementale, même fruste ou considérée comme sans but, doit être soigneusement notée, analysée et critiquée en fonction notamment des circonstances de survenue : spontanée, lors des soins ou pendant les tentatives de stimulation de l'éveil, réactions comportementales du malade en présence de son entourage proche qui ne manque pas de signaler des gestes ou des attitudes survenus, dans leur opinion, de manière adaptée en réponse à des stimulations précises . S'il n'est pas toujours possible de faire la part de l'objectif et de l'affectif, le praticien doit tout faire pour valider la reproductibilité de ces ébauches de réponses qui peuvent à la limite faire sortir le patient du cadre végétatif dans celui du patient sévèrement handicapé mais susceptible de communiquer : réactions à des stimulations externes généralement nociceptives, telles que modifications du rythme respiratoire et/ou cardiaque, vasodilatation locale avec phénomène de dermographisme, hypersudation, modifications du diamètre pupillaire... Certains auteurs comme BARAT et MAZAUX ont pu rapporter chez un enfant dans le coma, un ralentissement significatif du rythme cardiaque à la stimulation spécifique de la voix maternelle et ce à l'exclusion de toute modification lors d'autres stimulations auditives non signifiantes. N'est-ce pas là une manifestation neuro-psychologique particulière, située à un premier niveau de communication, certes élémentaire, mais qui témoigne peut-être de la réalité de phénomènes de perception, de mémoire, de reconnaissance, voire même d'un certain langage ?

De ce fait , **le vocabulaire utilisé doit faire l'objet de la plus grande rigueur.** Ainsi, de même qu'on ne peut parler de coma devant un malade qui manifeste des signes d'éveil (pour cette raison, le terme de "coma chronique" fréquemment employé, est à proscrire), les termes de "mort corticale" ("neocortical death"), proposé par BRIERLEY en 1971, de "mort cognitive" (BERESFORD 1978) ou encore ceux de "mort mentale" ou "mort subjective" (FREER 1984) sont inacceptables à la fois sur la forme et sur le fond : sur la forme, parce que le terme de mort est impropre et ambigü, créant une confusion avec l'expression française de "mort cérébrale", synonyme du "coma dépassé" décrit en 1959 par MOLLARET et GOULON qui correspond à la destruction irréversible de l'ensemble du contenu de la boîte crânienne ("whole brain death" des anglo-saxons) : ici, le sujet est bien cliniquement mort, dépourvu de toute activité encéphalique et également privé des fonctions du tronc cérébral qui sont complètement abolies ;sur le fond, car comme on a assimilé la mort cérébrale à la mort tout court, il n'y aurait peut-être qu'un pas pour assimiler la mort du néocortex à la mort du cerveau en ce qu'il a de noble, donc par proximité, à la mort du cerveau tout entier et ainsi à la mort elle-même. Mais, si l'état végétatif est caractérisé par une incommunicabilité et une dépendance extrême avec conservation des fonctions du tronc cérébral, les connaissances médicales actuelles ne permettent pas pour autant de répondre à certaines questions fondamentales : persiste-t-il une activité intra-psychique qui ne peut s'exprimer ? Qu'en est-il de la souffrance du patient ? Ressent-il la douleur, la faim, la soif ? Quelle est la signification des pleurs que l'on observe parfois ou de certaines mimiques laissant l'obervateur, même le plus averti, perplexe ? De telles incertitudes incitent à une grande prudence dans l'approche médicale -y compris en situation d'expertise- de tels malades ayant perdu apparemment toute capacité d'expression et d'action et dont la condition n'est ni celle d'un mort ni celle d'un mourant mais, comme l'a rappelé le Comité Consultatif National d'Ethique -dans un avis rendu en 1986 à l'occasion d'expérimentations pratiquées chez un malade en état végétatif par un médecin-, celle d'"un être humain à part entière et qui a d'autant plus besoin d'être protégé qu'il est en état de grande fragilité" ... Il ne saurait donc être question de mort, quand bien même l'individu aurait perdu une fonction essentielle à la vie, un attribut déterminant de la personne humaine. Certes, la "**personne de fait**", telle que définie en 1987, dans le rapport du Comité Consultatif National d'Ethique consacré à la Recherche Biomédicale, comme "l'être conscient de chair et de sang, de regard et de parole, de sensibilité et de vouloir, de raison et de liberté..." semble bien être perdue. Mais la "**personne de droit**" , cette "unité vécue de sujet vivace en nous et de ses prérogatives attitrées par l'égard d'autrui, la disposition juridique, le statut civique, la règle morale" semble au contraire demeurer, conserver son statut, quelles que soient les péripéties, les avatars de la "personne de fait". Peut-être parce qu'elle est cette réalité qui relève moins de l'être que du rapport à l'autre, car s'il est une personne, c'est nécessairement qu'il y a une autre personne pour le reconnaître et s'affirmer elle-même comme personne dans cette reconnaissance".

**Bibliographie**

- MATHE J.F., JOSEPH P.A., VERCELLETTO M., RICHARD-CREMIEUX I. (1991) Approche neuropsychologique de l'éveil des comas traumatiques. Neuro-Psy. 6, n° 8 : 416-427

- TASSEAU F., BOUCAND M.H. (1991) Coma, état végétatif chronique et éthique. Le point de vue du praticien. Commentaires juridiques. Neuro-Psy. 6, n° 9 : 464-470 et 473-476

- COHADON F., RICHER E. (1993) Etats végétatifs post-traumatiques. Neurochir. 39 : 269-280

# INTEREST OF EVOKED POTENTIALS IN THE MEDICO-LEGAL ASSESSMENT IN PROFESSIONAL HEARING LOSS

I. François*, H.J. Smolik**, J.C. Petiot**, M.T. Petiot**, A. Marin*, A. Gisselman*.

** Laboratoire d'Ergonomie et de Psychophysiopathologie du Travail, Faculté des Sciences, 6 Bd Gabriel, F-21000 Dijon, France.
* Laboratoire de Médecine Légale, Faculté de Médecine, 7 Bd Jeanne d'Arc, F-21000 Dijon, France.

In France, hearing-loss may be considered as an occupational disease, and, in this event, compensated, only if the profession is listed in the 42nd table of professional compensation drawn by the general and social security systems.
The present standards are lacking. So, it is the occasion to look for other diagnostic means to assess the compensation. With this purpose in mind, we have at present and experiment in progress.

## 1. Present standards of compensation, for professional hearing loss.

They are governed by the 42nd table of professional compensation drawn by the general and social security systems, published on April 20th, 1963, modified on November 3rd, 1981.
As for all occupational diseases circumstances of
- the length and kind of noise exposure
- standards of diagnosis and severity are demanded.

The hearing loss is calculated by addition of the deficit on frequence 500, 1000, 2000, and 4000 Hertz with respective coefficients of 2, 4, 3 and 1. The total will be divised by 10 to obtain the D.A.L. (Déficit Audiométrique Légal), the legal audiometric deficit. A minimal loss of 35 dB for the best ear is required.

## 2. Difficulties due to requirements

The are mainly due to subjectivity of both the measured deficiency and of the method of measurement.

### 2.1. The measured deficiency
Hearing is the tool of communication, of relationships with others and environment. Each person has his own level of hearing, depending on his past education, environment, habits and so on.
With the same hearing loss, the inconvenience will be very different from one person to another. Furthermore, for a given deficiency, the tolerance and problems cannot be predicted. And neither can the distribution of frequences determine the consequences.

### 2.2. The method of measurement
At the moment, the Social Security considers as valid only the tonal and vocal audiometry. This is assuming that the examiner is very well trained, and also that there a good participation of the patient, so that the test is reliable. We must not forget that we are in a particular situation, the compensation of a disease which originates from work.

A lot of grudges and frustrations express themselves in this kind of situation, reflecting all the suffering felt during the job. The patient is anxious not to be considered as handicapped as he feels, and the increase, perhaps the simulation of the disorders is frequent, and some experts think that it is systematic.

### 2.3. An exposure-free period is necessary

The 42nd table requires that the measurements be made after a period of 3 weeks to one year without any exposure to the professional noise.
So :

- What about the situation of the employee during this period ? sick leave ? unemployed pay ? other ? but what ?
- There is no possibility to certify that during this period the employee will not be exposed to another noise, which could injure his auditory nerve.

All these arguments induce us to look for another method, non aggressive, more objective, giving a diagnosis with only one test, in order to evaluate a professional hearing loss and to determine the basis of the compensation.
The Auditory Brainstem Responses, studying the auditory nerve directly, affirms the central origin of the deafness, therefore, that it is not reversible. At the same time the severity is known, with only one test. Our idea of research comes from these findings.

## 3. Material and methods

The study, now in progress, included 80 subjects, all men, aged from 35 to 65.
Forty of them are suffering from a professional deafness (or hearing loss). The others were voluntary witnesses, who were not exposed to a professional noise. They were all classified in age groups.

All the tests were passed in the same experimental conditions, after a period of holiday (in order to avoid a temporary lowering of the auditory threshold due to fatigue).
Each subject benefited from first a manual tonal and vocal audiometry, then a computerized audiometry (of the Bekesy type) with the determination of bone conduction. Then each subject benefited from evoked potentials.

## 4. Analysis of the results

The results, measured after analysis of variance of the D.A.L. will be compared group to group : average, standard-deviation, by plans with two factors : age and group.
The air and bone conductions, with manual and computerized audiometry will be compared to each another, before being compared to the perturbations of evoked potentials, especially peakwave I, III, V and the latency peak interval I-III and I-V, so as to look for a correlation, given in D.A.L., between audiometric results and Auditory Brainstem Responses.

## 5. Discussion

Although we do not have all the results, we have some questions :
- Acceptability if Auditory Brainstem Responses compared to the audiometry. It appears to be excellent, particularly with our instruments, with pasted electrodes, without needles, absolutely without injury.
- Validity of Brainstem Responses versus audiometry. It will be determined by the results, for the material and technical aspects.

For us, the question is the relationship between an evoked potential graph and a daily hearing inconvenience. Trying to resolve the technical aspect ot the compensation of this professional disease, introducing a more objective test in order to evaluate a deficiency which is the expression of social life, we do not solve the human problem hidden beyond the demand of compensation.

## 6. Conclusion

The present standards of the medico-legal compensation of professional hearing loss are not satisfactory. We propose here a protocol in order to evaluate the substitution of the Auditory Brainstem Responses for audiometry as basis of the compensation, but we are very concerned about the human aspects of this proposition.

Nevertheless, this technique could avoid litigations due to the revelation of a deafness of another kind (transmission, or both transmission and perception).

# EVALUATION OF NEUROPSYCHOLOGICAL SEQUELAE IN ELECTRICAL INJURIES

A. GERAUT*, B. LUDES*, A. TRACQUI, J. REIS**, N. CREMEL**, J.M. WARTER** and P. MANGIN*

* Institut de Médecine Légale, 11 rue Humann, 67085 Strasbourg, France.
** Service de Neurologie et de Neuropsychologie, Hôpitaux Universitaires de Strasbourg, 67000 Strasbourg, France.

## Introduction

The disorders that are considered in the evaluation of bodily damage after an electrical injury generally concern cutaneous, neurological (1,2,5,7), cardiovascular, renal, ocular or hearing sequelae. The neuropsychological sequelae are underestimated or unknown, however, they seem to be frequent and lead to alterations in the social and the professional behaviors (3).

## Material and method

We have seen 5 male patients during a medical appraisal. The electrical injuries occurred at work and the age range was from 24 to 36 years old. The path of current was from arm to leg in three cases and from arm to arm in two cases.

First, a comprehensive anamnestic questioning and a meticulous semiological investigation carried out. Second, a checkup was performed by a neuropsychiatrist including : an interview with the patient and his family, followed by a complete series of tests with, in particular, a thematic aperception test and different clinical scales for depression, intelligence, attention and memory.

## Results

We noticed that all patients presented sensory disorders of upper extremities : four with weakness, numbness and tingling (two of them with sensory deficit). Four developed difficulties to move their fingers and to grip, and a bilateral carpal tunnel syndrome was noticed in three cases. As for lower extremities, four cases of peripheral sensitivomotor neuropathies were found. Three patients presented a diffuse polyalgia syndrome.

All patients developed a depression that was severe in two cases and very severe in three cases. From the questioning, it appears that no latent period was observed between injuries and psychological impairments. For all the patients, the affects were reduced with investments only focused on survival, and death was continuously present in the content of thought. Moreover, we noticed a reduction of the normal motivation, as well as of the initiative capacity with disturbances of their daily behavior : irritability, instability and important sexual desorders. Anxiety and asthenia were pronounced and associated with sleep difficulties.

The neuropsychological disorders included alteration of memory that was very disturbed in one case, below average in two cases and average in two cases. A slackening of attention was found for all the patients and an alteration of occupational memory was noticed for two of them. Intellectual performances according to the IQ were highly deteriorated for two cases, below average for one case and subnormal for two cases. At the same time, the capacity of learning functions according to verbal learning was very altered for two patients and below average for three of them.

## Discussion

In order to evaluate bodily damage the more correctly as possible, we tried to compare this symptomatology to the three following syndromes : subjective post-traumatic syndrome, post-traumatic neurosis and post-traumatic stress disorder. It is apparent from this comparison that one can exclude the first one because no dizziness or cephalalgia were noticed in our patients. However, psychological reorganisation including behavioral disorders, reduction of performances, alteration of cognitive functions, sleep disturbances that are present in the three previous syndromes are also noticed in our observations. But, unlike post-traumatic neurosis, we did not find a latent period.

Moreover, no repetitive reminder syndrome (intrusive images of the event that interfere with normal functioning) occurred whereas it is a major symptom of post-traumatic neurosis and post-traumatic stress disorder. In our observations, we also noticed sensory subjective symptoms such as diffuse polyalgia syndrome, severe depression that lead to isolation, and severe anxiety. It seems to our neuropsychiatrist that the efficiency of the treatment depends especially on the educational background (4). This leads us to wonder whether we can talk about a more specific post-electric syndrome.

## Conclusion

The small number of subjects limits both the generalizability and validity of the observations. However, it is necessary to insist on the neuropsychological sequelae in evaluation of bodily damage after an electrical injury (6). It would also seem that current intensity does not influence appearance of neurological sequelae.

## Bibliography

1. Farrell DF, Starr A (1968) Delayed neurological sequelae of electrical injuries. Neurology 18:601-606
2. Goasguen J, Martini L (1984) Les séquelles neurologiques de l'électrisation. Médecine et Armée 12 (4):327-332
3. Hooshmand H, Radfar F, Beckner E (1989) The neurophysiological aspects of electrical injuries. Clinical electoencephalography 20 (2):111-120
4. Mancusi-Ungaro AR, Tarbox AR, Wainwright DJ (1986) Post traumatic stress disorder in electric burn patients. JBCR 7 (6):521-525
5. Rosenberg DB, (1989) Neurologic sequelae of minor electric burns. Arch Phys Med Rehabil 70:914-915
6. Steinbach G, (1970) Evaluation des séquelles neuro-psychiatriques en réparation du dommage corporel. Rev franç dommage corp 16 (3):515-519
7. Grube BJ, Heimbach D, Engrau LH, Copass MK (1990) Neurologic consequences of electrical burns. The Journal of Trauma 30 (3):254-258

# *REFLEXIONS SUR L'AGGRAVATION ET L'ETAT ANTERIEUR DANS LA REPARATION DU DOMMAGE CORPOREL*

M. LARCHE-MOCHEL (1 et 2), C. DALM (2) et J. DOIGNON (1)

(1) Laboratoire de Médecine Légale, Université de Bordeaux II (Bordeaux - France)
(2) Inspection médicale du travail d'Aquitaine (Bordeaux - France)

## I. DEFINITION DE L'AGGRAVATION

L'aggravation peut être, définie en Médecine Légale, comme l'état physique ou mental consolidé ou guéri, qui, dans un temps plus ou moins précoce ou tardif, va subir une dégradation.

Rappelons que la consolidation est le moment où la lésion est fixée et prend un caractère permanent sinon définitif tel qu'un traitement n'est plus en principe nécessaire sauf pour éviter une aggravation. On parle alors de traitement d'entretien.

La guérison se caractérise par l'absence de séquelles.

## II. LA NOTION D'ETAT ANTERIEUR

Cette notion d'état antérieur peut s'entendre comme un état pathologique existant avant l'accident en cause, parfois ; ou, d'autres fois, comme un état pathologique existant avant l'aggravation.

### 1. ETAT PATHOLOGIQUE EXISTANT AVANT L'ACCIDENT EN CAUSE :

On entend alors par état antérieur "toute prédisposition, tare ou affection pathologique quelle qu'elle soit, connue ou non, congénitale ou acquise, consécutive à une maladie ou à un accident, que présente un individu au moment où survient la fait litigieux".

Cet état antérieur pathologique peut interférer avec l'accident de plusieurs manières :

. L'état antérieur pathologique **peut être la cause de l'accident** : un sujet épileptique présente une crise comitiale alors qu'il conduit un véhicule et perd la contrôle de celui-ci,

. L'état antérieur pathologique, **inconnu et cliniquement silencieux,** peut avoir été **révélé** par l'accident. Sans celui-ci rien ne dit qu'une évolution de la pathologie se serait produite. Elle aurait peut être toujours gardé une expression silencieuse.

L'accident peut entraîner une décompensation passagère de l'état antérieur qui était silencieux et justifier une ITT et un quantum doloris ou donner lieu à une décompensation durable ce qui justifiera en outre l'attribution d'une IPP.
Il faut bien distinguer la révélation de l'état antérieur par l'accident, de la révélation d'un état antérieur par l'examen complémentaire réalisé à l'occasion de l'accident (découverte d'un cancer du poumon à l'occasion d'une radiographie thoracique pour contrôler l'intégrité du gril costal) par exemple ; dans ce cas, il n'y a alors aucune relation entre les deux faits.

. Aggravation par l'accident d'un état antérieur pathologique connu : un état antérieur connu et parfois traité, existe, et l'accident va aggraver cet état antérieur.

. Ainsi : M.B. est un diabétique connu, insulinodépendant et bien équilibré. A la suite d'un accident, avec traumatisme abdominal, survenu en avril 1989, son diabète devient plus important qu'il n'était et instable. On réussit cependant à le rééquilibrer avec une glycémie moins favorable qu'elle n'était autrefois, et avec des doses d'insuline plus importantes. L'accident de 1989 a aggravé de façon durable un état antérieur qui jusque là paraissait stabilisé.

. Aggravation des séquelles de l'accident par l'état antérieur : les conséquences d'une plaie de jambe peuvent être aggravées tant au niveau de l'évolution que des séquelles par des antécédents variqueux ou par un terrain diabétique. Peut également être évoquée ici l'aggravation des séquelles d'un accident par un état psychiatrique antérieur à l'accident, cadre dans lequel nous plaçons les pathomimies.

**2. L'ETAT PATHOLOGIQUE ANTERIEUR A L'AGGRAVATION :**

Cet état peut être représenté par des séquelles constatées le jour de la première expertise après la consolidation et ayant donné lieu à l'appréciation du dommage.

L'aggravation, et ce sera le sens le plus fréquent de la demande d'expertise en droit commun, s'appréciera en comparant l'état constaté lors de l'expertise statuant sur la demande d'aggravation, à l'état constaté à la consolidation. Cette aggravation peut d'ailleurs être prévisible et mentionnée comme telle dans le rapport de la première expertise.

## III. CONSOLIDATION, STABILISATION, AGGRAVATION CERTAINE INELUCTABLE :

Il arrive parfois, et cela n'est plus exceptionnel, que lors de l'expertise, du fait de la gravité des lésions initiales et de l'importance des séquelles, une aggravation des lésions dans un laps de temps plus ou moins court soit certaine.

Le terme de consolidation peut paraître alors mal adapté car la pathologie continue à évoluer et certains experts préférent parler de stabilisation. C'est le cas par exemple d'une victime porteuse d'une séropositivité HIV post-transfusionnelle en relation avec un accident.

## IV. EVALUATION DES PREJUDICES

L'aggravation d'un préjudice suppose que précédemment évalué, il vienne à augmenter.

L'évaluation de l'aggravation nécessite une appréciation précédente correctement effectuée avec des mesures objectives (amplitude des mouvements, mensurations, dosages etc...) pour qu'une analyse comparative puisse être réalisée.

L'aggravation du préjudice peut être une aggravation de l'état de la victime, transitoire ou définitive ou, et c'est une notion relativement récente, se traduire par le remboursement de "prestations nouvelles". Deux notions que l'expert doit bien connaître pour ne pas les confondre.

A. Le remboursement des prestations nouvelles à l'organisme de sécurité sociale ; que celles-ci aient été prévisibles ou imprévisibles lors de la décision initiale, par exemple : demande par la sécurité sociale de remboursement de nouveaux débours (traitement médicamenteux, changement ou mise en place de prothèses, etc...).

*B. L'aggravation de l'état de la victime :*

. Cette aggravation peut être simplement représentée par la nécessité de reprise des soins, de nouveaux traitements, d'interventions chirurgicales sans que les séquelles fonctionnelles soient modifiées. Toutefois, ces soins nouveaux pourront donner lieu à une nouvelle ITT, à un nouveau quantum doloris et éventuellement à un nouveau préjudice esthétique. Une nouvelle date de consolidation devra être fixée. L'expert pourra conclure qu'il existe "des données péjoratives sur les autres chefs de préjudices" que l'IPP, s'il ne souhaite pas employer le terme d'aggravation lorsque celle-ci n'est pas modifiée.

. L' aggravation pourra d'autre part entraîner, comme nous l'avons constaté dans les observations précédentes, des séquelles durables nécessitant une nouvelle évaluation de l'IPP dans le sens d'une augmentation. Outre l'IPP, tous les éléments du préjudice précédemment évoqués devront être appréciés.

. Sans doute, faudrait-il traiter aussi des frais futurs, et des soins après consolidation. Cette question délicate fera l'objet d'une autre étude.

EN CONCLUSION, la notion d'aggravation qui paraît simple à définir sur un plan strictement médical est sur le plan médico-légal une notion complexe. L'expert doit avoir en mémoire que l'aggravation, pour être prise en considération, doit avoir pour cause directe et déterminante des infirmités pour lesquelles l'imputabilité à l'accident est admise.

# *UN CAS DE BLESSURE MORTELLE PAR PROJECTILE DE PISTOLET DE SCELLEMENT*

M. LARCHE-MOCHEL (1 et 2), C. DALM (2) et J. DOIGNON (1)

(1) Laboratoire de Médecine Légale, Université de Bordeaux II, Inspection Médicale du travail d'Aquitaine (Bordeaux - France)
(2) Inspection Médicale du travail d'Aquitaine (Bordeaux - France)

## *DE L'ACCIDENT DE TRAVAIL AU SUICIDE*

Un jeune homme de 20 ans posait des goujons permettant la fixation de consoles au moyen d'un pistolet de scellement à tir direct dans une poutre de béton armé. Après différents essais, plusieurs goujons avaient été posés, mais avaient provoqué un léger cratère dans le béton. Le dernier goujon que l'ouvrier voulut placer ricocha et l'atteignit à la tête entraînant son décès.

l'autopsie médico-légale montrait un orifice de pénétration ovalaire de 15 mm X 5 mm, situé à 1 cm au dessus et en avant de l'attache supérieure de l'oreille gauche.Les bords de cet orifice étaient ecchymotiques et avaient un aspect contus. Des suffusions hémorragiques et des ecchymoses étaient retrouvées à la face profonde du cuir chevelu, au niveau du muscle temporal gauche et plus discrètement au niveau du muscle temporal droit. Au niveau de l'écaille temporale gauche, un orifice à l'emporte pièce correspondait exactement dans sa forme, ses dimensions et sa situation à l'orifice cutané précédemment décrit. L'ouverture du crâne mettait en évidence une intense hémorragie méningée et une dilacération du parenchyme cérébral.

Le projectile, retrouvé dans la région occipitale droite, partie postérieure, se présentait sous la forme d'une pièce métallique d'environ 55 mm de long et 5 mm de diamètre. Une extrémité était très aigûe, l'autre filetée sur 23 mm. La pièce était recourbée presque à angle droit à la jonction de la partie filetée et de la partie lisse.

Ce décès fut pris en charge sans contestation au titre des accidents du travail.

Six ans plus tard, Monsieur B, âgé de 46 ans était retrouvé à son domicile, dans son lit, un pistolet de scellement de même type que lors de la première observation, entre ses cuisses. Un contrôle radiographique montrait l'absence de projectile à l'intérieur du corps.L'autopsie médico-légale permettait de noter qu'un projectile, entré par un orifice en étoile dans la région fronto-pariétale paramédiane droite, avait dilacéré la région fronto-temporale droite, traversé la base du crâne, cheminé de haut en bas à travers le cou en labourant le larynx, pénétré dans la cage thoracique droite en créant un hémothorax et en blessant le poumon droit pour sortir par la région thoracique postérieure droite.Des débris plastiques de couleur verte ont été prélevés au niveau de la face profonde de la plaie d'entrée.

Le projectile sera retrouvé à proximité du corps. Il s'agissait d'un clou d'acier de scellement, aigu d'un côté et ayant un embout plastique amovible de l'autre. L'enquête confirmera le suicide.

Ces deux observations ont en commun l'utilisation du même type de pistolet à scellement : le pistolet à scellement à tir direct. De plus, entre ces observations, la réglementation avait changé interdisant l'utilisation de ce type d'outil.

## ***UN APPAREIL COMPLEXE***

### Utilisation

Le pistolet de scellement est utilisé pour fixer des tampons, des clous, des crochets, des équerres, des pattes d'huisserie ou d'isolant, des nattes de drainage dans les tunnels (métro, routiers, ferroviaires), dans des matériaux divers : béton, pierre, briques, acier, poutrelles métalliques, etc...

C'est un appareil qui utilise, pour fixer une pièce dans un matériau approprié, l'énergie d'une petite charge d'explosif. Il ne faut pas le confondre avec les pistolets à clouer pneumatiques qui utilisent comme source d'énergie l'air comprimé.

### Composition

Le pistolet de scellement est constitué d'un canon, d'un dispositif de percussion, d'une détente et d'une crosse.

Deux grandes catégories d'appareils doivent être distinguées. Ceux où les gaz de la charge agissent directement sur la pièce de fixation ; il s'agit des pistolets à tir direct ; ceux dans lesquels l'énergie est transmise indirectement à la pièce de fixation au moyen d'une pièce intermédiaire appelée masselotte, qui ne quitte pas l'appareil : il s'agit des pistolets de scellement à tir indirect.

Les pistolets à tir direct se sont révélés beaucoup plus dangereux que ceux à tir indirect en raison d'une vitesse de projection du goujon ou clou considérable (pouvant atteindre 700 mètres par seconde).

Les projectiles sont très variés : clous, goujons, boulons filetés de formes et de dimensions diverses suivant l'usage désiré.

## ***UNE LEGISLATION A CONNAITRE***

### En ce qui concerne la prévention

Des circulaires de 1954 et 1956 conseillaient des mesures de prévention lors de l'utilisation de ces pistolets et déconseillaient leur utilisation par des jeunes ouvriers de moins de 18 ans. Il faudra attendre un arrêté de 1977 pour voir interdire l'usage des pistolets de scellement à tir direct, pistolet incriminé dans nos deux observations.

Actuellement, l'Article R 234.21 du Code du travail interdit d'occuper les jeunes travailleurs de moins de 18 ans aux travaux de scellement à l'aide de pistolets à explosion, sauf dérogations pour l'apprentissage et les élèves fréquentant les établissements d'enseignement technique.

### En ce qui concerne la pathologie professionnelle

Les accidents en relation avec les pistolets de scellement sont actuellement exceptionnels en raison, très vraisemblablement, des règles d'utilisation et des perfectionnements intervenus dans la conception de ces outils.

Cependant, ils continuent à provoquer une pathologie, non plus prise en charge au titre des accidents de travail, mais une pathologie entrant dans le cadre des maladies professionnelles.

Les déficits audiomètriques bilatéraux par lésion cochléaire irréversible, supérieurs à 35 DB sur la meilleure oreille peuvent être pris en charge au titre du tableau n° 42 du régime général et n°46 du régime agricole chez les sujets utilisant de façon habituelle des pistolets de scellement.

ils provoquent également des affections ostéoarticulaires confirmées par des examens radiologiques à type d'arthrose du coude, d'ostéonécrose du semi-lunaire (maladie de Kienbôch) et d'ostéonécrose du scaphoïde carpien (maladie de Kôlher). Tableau n° 69 du régime général et n°29 du régime agricole.

***CONCLUSION***

Nos observations montrent que le pistolet de scellement à tir direct, outil industriel, pouvait se comporter comme une vraie arme à feu susceptible d'entraîner la mort de façon accidentelle ou volontaire, ressemblant dans cette deuxième hypothèse au pistolet d'alarme par un détournement de son usage. L'interdiction de ces outils à tir direct et l'évolution de la technique ont permis de limiter ce type d'accidents. Cependant, ils persistent à faire parler d'eux non plus en salle d'autopsie, mais à l'occasion de rapport d'expertise en maladie professionnelle.

# PROFESSIONAL HANDICAP IN VICTIMS OF LOWER LIMB TRAUMATISMES. PRELIMINARY STUDY

*Magalhães T; Carneiro de Sousa MJ; Pinto da Costa J; Matos E; Hamonet Cl*

Medico-legal Institute, Faculty of Medicine, Biomedical Sciences Institute "Abel Salazar", University of Oporto; Faculty of Law, University Portucalense "Infante D. Henrique"; Faculty of Medicine, University of Paris XII;Henri Mondor Hospital, Creteil; Jardim Carrilho Videira 4000, Porto, Portugal

## OBJECTIF

The authors compare the evaluation by the rate of permanent disability (PD) with a three-dimentional evaluation of the damage (lesion, function and handicap), from a professional point of view.

## MATERIAL AND METHODES

A total of 60 victims of lower limb injuries, due to road traffic accidents, examined at the Medico-Legal Institute of Oporto, were studied. The great majority of the victims were men with an average of 35.5 years-old. The distribution of the lesions showed a predominance for the legs (Table I). The stiffness was the most important and common consequence (Table II). For the statistical analysis the Spearman Rank Order Correlation Test was utilised. For the evaluation of the PD the Scale of Disability for Occupational Accidents and Diseases was used[3], which considers values from zero to hundred percent (lesional criteria). To the three-dimensional evaluation the "Handicapomètre DAC"[1] adapted to a medico-legal evaluation was used; through it we analysed some **functions** of carriage and displacement, including the usual modalities of displacement (to remain in a lying position, to turn in a recumbent position, to sit straight, to stand straight, to change from a sitting to a standing position, to walk or to displace in a wheel chair, run or displace rapidly in a wheelchair and to pick up from the ground) and the **situations of professional handicap** considering the possibility of doing his common work: in fulltime, or part-time, or after adaptation of occupational post, or possibility of work after professional replacement. For this three-dimensional evaluation five degrees of severity were established (Table III).

## RESULTS AND DISCUSSION

A high correlation was found between the **PD** and the **lesional sequels** (R=0.88), **functional sequels** (R=0.46) and **professional handicap to the ordinary work** (R=0.70). However, in 21 cases (Table IV) with permanent total disability (to the ordinary work in fulltime), the PD was between 0% and 70%. In the other cases (degree 0, 1 and 2) the PD was between 0% and 75%. In the 13 cases which the capacity to work was preserved for the usual job in fulltime (degree 0), 2 people lost their job and 2 others continued in "stopping work" although healted. In the 24 cases degree 1, the PD given was in one case 20% and in two cases 35%, 2 people became unemployed and two others continued in "stopping work" by doctor's goog willness. In the two cases degree 2, one person got an PD of 50% and the other of 75%. In the group of 20 people with capacity to resume their job although at part-time, after adaptation of the poste or after professional replacement, 3 became unemployed and 1 continued in "stopping work" by doctor's good willness. So, although the accordance between the two types of evaluation (in a global point of view), there are some exceptions wich question the validity of an assessment based only in lesional criteria in view of the integral compensation of the damage[2].

## CONCLUSIONS

1.Both methods of evaluation gave similar results, but sometimes, the evaluation considering only the lesion (percentage of disability), did not show the real consequences of the damage;
2.The medico-legal examination in Common Law should also consider the function and situations of handicapped;
3.The three-dimensional evaluation renders it possible, informing the judge in order to guide him to a compensation according to the real needs of the victim, considering his professional and social reintegration.

| LESIONS (n=60) | % |
|---|---|
| Leg fractures | 33.3 |
| Multiple fractures | 30.0 |
| Femur fracture | 13.3 |
| Hip fracture | 6.6 |
| Rotula fracture | 6.6 |
| Foot fracture | 6.6 |
| Ligament lesions of the knee | 1.8 |
| Hip desarticulation | 1.8 |

Table I

| SEQUELS (n=77) | % |
|---|---|
| Stiffness | 43.2 |
| Athrophy | 12.4 |
| Axial deviation | 8.2 |
| Amputation | 6.2 |
| Pain syndrome | 6.2 |
| Ankylosis | 4.1 |
| Misaligned callus | 4.1 |
| Osteomielity | 3.1 |
| Trophique problems | 3.1 |
| Clubfoot | 2.0 |
| Ligamentar instability of the knee | 2.0 |
| Shortning | 2.0 |
| Lenthning | 1.1 |
| Dislocation of synphysis pubis | 1.1 |
| Lost of rotula | 1.1 |

Table II

Table III

| Degree | LESIONS | FUNCTION AND SITUATION |
|---|---|---|
| 0 | No lesion | "Normal" |
| 1 | Minimal | Difficulties, slowness or disconfort |
| 2 | Average | Utilization of either medicinal or technical aid or both |
| 3 | Important | Human assistance in incitement or complement |
| 4 | Very important | Impossible (human substitution) |

Table IV

| DAC | 0 | 1 | 2 | 3 | 4 | | | | | | | | | | | | | | | Total |
|---|---|---|---|---|---|---|---|---|---|---|---|---|---|---|---|---|---|---|---|---|
| | | | | | PART-TIME | | | | | AFTER ADAPTATION | | | | | AFTER REPLACEMENT | | | | | |
| IPP(%) | | | | | 0 | 1 | 2 | 3 | 4 | 0 | 1 | 2 | 3 | 4 | 0 | 1 | 2 | 3 | 4 | |
| 00-05 | 11 | 12 | - | - | - | - | - | - | - | - | - | - | - | - | - | 1 | - | - | - | 24 |
| 06-15 | 2 | 10 | - | - | - | 3 | - | 1 | - | - | 2 | - | - | - | 2 | 1 | - | - | - | 21 |
| 16-40 | - | 2 | - | - | - | 2 | 2 | - | - | - | 1 | 1 | - | - | - | - | - | - | - | 8 |
| 41-70 | - | - | 1 | - | - | - | - | - | - | - | - | 1 | - | - | - | 1 | 2 | - | 1 | 6 |
| 71-75 | - | - | 1 | - | - | - | - | - | - | - | - | - | - | - | - | - | - | - | - | 1 |
| TOTAL | 13 | 24 | 2 | 0 | 21 | | | | | | | | | | | | | | | 60 |

## REFERENCES


1.Hamonet Cl, Brugere J-M, Margeat H (1991) Étude comparée des résultats obtenus avec une nouvelle méthode tridimensionelle d'évaluation et le barème du concours médical dans 124 cas d'expertises judiciaires. Gazette du Palais, 25 Juillet, 15-23

2.Neto A, Martins H (1990) Artº 562, in: Código Civil Anotado (7ªed). Livraria Petrony Lda., Lisboa

3.Tabela Nacional de Incapacidades para Acidentes de Trabalho e Doenças Profissionais (1993). Decreto-Lei 341/93 de 30/9

# HANDICAPPED PEOPLE IN PORTUGAL

*Magalhães T; Carneiro de Sousa MJ; Pinto da Costa J; Hamonet Cl*

Medico-legal Institute, Faculty of Medicine, Biomedical Sciences Institute "Abel Salazar", University of Oporto; Faculty of Law, University Portucalense "Infante D. Henrique"; Faculty of Medicine, University of Paris XII;Henri Mondor Hospital, Creteil; Jardim Carrilho Videira 4000, Porto, Portugal

## INTRODUCTION

The actual number of handicapped people in Portugal is unknown but we calculate that there should be about 800.000 to 900.000 for a total population of 9.800.000 inhabitants. The evaluation of each case and the support they receive depends on the origin of the handicap.

## MATERIAL AND METHODS

The authors analysed the problem of the handicap in Portugal (the responsible entity, the type of disability evaluation, the type of support conceded and the number of cases that are known), according to origin (natural disease or age, occupational disease, industrial accident, road traffic accident, war injuries and assault) using official statistics.

## RESULTS

### 1.Natural disease and age

The social security takes care of these patients. The medical doctors belonging to this service are charged with evaluating the disability, which should be referred in a percentage of permanent disability (PD). There are many types of annuities of invalidity: complementary (≤ 24 years-old), of invalidity (> 24 years-old), special education and a supplement of permanent assistance of a third party. In 1993 there were 2.627/100.000 inhabitant/year beneficiaries from these annuities (496 from age and 2.131 from natural disease)[3,7].

### 2.Occupational disease

The National Insurance and Occupational Diseases Institution deals with this problem concerning the responsibility for the compensation. It is up to the experts in the courts or in the medico-legal Institutes to do the evaluation and fix the PD. The compensation is done in an annuity. The total beneficiaries were of 162/100.000 inhabitants/year in 1993. In 51.4% of the cases there was a PD between 10% and 40%, 25.4% under 10%, 12.6% of 100% and 10.6% between 50% and 99%[8].

### 3.Work accident

The insurance companies are responsible in these kinds of accidents. The evaluation (PD determination) is up to the experts (court or medico-legal Institutes). The compensation can also be done in capital (PD < 20%), in a fixed annuity (PD 20-30%) and in a bring up to date annuity (PD > 30%). The total of beneficiary handicapped people was of 672/100.000 inhabitants/year in 1993. In 59.4% of the cases there was a PD between 15% and 59%, 31.8% under 15%, 5.7% between 60% and 99% and 3.1% of 100%[10].

### 4.Road traffic accident

The insurance companies take the responsibility in these events. They have their own experts who solve the great majority of the cases. If a legal process is necessary to solve the problem, then the experts from the medico-legal Institutes are charged with doing the evaluation (patrimonial and mental injuries are considered)[4]. The compensation is done in capital. There is a limit for the compensation in case of responsibility for the risk. The number of non-mortal victims during 1993 was 684/100.000 inhabitants/year[9].

**5.War injuries**

These victims depend on the Ministry of Defence. The evaluation of the handicapped people is done by the medical doctors of the medical service who fix a PD. The calculation of an annuity, which is the form of compensation, is done based on the salary at the moment of the accident, and they add a supplement based on the minimum salary. In 1993 there were about 254/100.000 inhabitants/year of beneficiaries[1].

**6.Assaults**

The aggressor is responsible for the compensation of the prejudices caused (patrimonial and mental injuries), but if that is not possible and if the damages are very serious, the State can assume the compensation.

**Rehabilitation and professional training:**

The National Secretary of Rehabilitation and the Institute for the Employment and Professional Formation are the responsible entities for this matter. In 1993 only 10.9/100.000 inhabitants/year of handicapped people were in professional training[5,6].

## DISCUSSION AND CONCLUSIONS

**1.**The different kinds of evaluation, compensation and reintegration according the origin of the handicap causes situations of injustice and disparity;

**2.**The examination always considers the evaluation of the PD (lesion criteria) and does not pay attention to the function and situation of handicap;

**3.**A great number of these evaluations are done by medical doctors without specific training in this field;

**4.**These three items mentioned previously are not the best if the goal is the complete rehabilitation and socio-professional reintegration of these individuals as consigned in the law[2,4];

**5.**A three-dimensional evaluation (lesion, function and handicap) should be considered so that compensation, may be more than economic support and become a group of measures capable of providing the correct reintegration of the handicapped in his familial, social and professional environment;

**6.**The type of evaluation and compensation should be the same for everybody.

## REFERENCES

1.Associação de Deficientes das Forças Armadas e Secção de Pensões da Repartição Geral do Pessoal do Exército

2.Constituição da República Portuguesa (1982), 1ª Revisão, Imprensa Nacional-Casa da Moeda, Lisboa

3.Estatísticas de Protecção Social, Associações Sindicais e Patronais (1990) Instituto Nacional de Estatística

4.Neto A, Martins H (1990) Código Civil Anotado (7ª ed). Livraria Petrony Lda., Liboa

5.Programa de Apoios à Contratação de Pessoas Deficientes no Mercado Normal de Trabalho, Instituto do Emprego e Formação Profissional, Ministério do Emprego e da Segurança Social

6.Programa de Instalação por Conta Própria de Pessoas Deficientes, Instituto do Emprego e Formação Profissional, Ministério do Emprego e da Segurança Social

7.Secretariado Nacional de Reabilitação, Divisão de Estudos e Projectos, Núcleo de Estatística (1993) - Valores estimados para 1993, tendo por base as taxas da OMS; Estatísticas Demográficas Instituto Nacional de Estatística e Anuário estatístico da Segurança Social - IGFSS

8.Secretariado Nacional de Reabilitação, Divisão de Estudos e Projectos, Núcleo de Estatística (valores corrigidos referentes a 1991). Caixa Nacional de Seguros e Doenças Profissionais

9.Secretariado Nacional de Reabilitação, Divisão de Estudos e Projectos, Núcleo de Estatística (valores projectados até Out. 93). Direcção Geral de Viação

10.Secretariado Nacional de Reabilitação, Divisão de Estudos e Projectos, Núcleo de Estatística (valores corrigidos referentes a 1991). Instituto de Seguros de Portugal; A Actividade Seguradora em Portugal, vol.II; Caixa Nacional da Previdência - Funcionários e Agentes da Função Pública

# LA REPARATION DU DOMMAGE CORPOREL EN EUROPE : TENTATIVE D'HARMONISATION

par André MARIN, Professeur de Médecine Légale à la Faculté de Médecine de DIJON

## I - JUSTIFICATION DE CETTE TENTATIVE

Tout ce qui concerne l'Europe devient à la mode. Néanmoins, ce n'est pas par souci de conformisme que nous proposons une tentative d'harmonisation de l'indemnisation du dommage corporel dans les différents pays de l'Europe. Il s'agit, en fait, d'une nécessité, et ce pour deux raisons :

1 - L'accroissement actuel et futur des accidents entre les citoyens de pays étrangers : le brassage des populations devient de plus en plus important, notamment pour des raisons de travail ; c'est en particulier le cas des frontaliers. Par ailleurs, le tourisme se développe entre les pays voisins ; et l'ouverture prochaine du tunnel sous la Manche va encore accentuer ce phénomène.

2 - Il s'agit d'une question de justice : il y a, en effet, des pays où les cotisations d'assurance sont élevées, et donc les modalités de réparation sont plus généreuses. Il y a, à l'inverse, des pays où les cotisations d'assurance sont plus faibles, avec des modalités de réparation moins importantes.

Or, la convention de La Haye (4 Mai 1971) a prévu que la règle générale consiste à appliquer la législation du pays où a eu lieu l'accident.

Certains blessés auront donc versé leurs cotisations dans un pays, et obtiendront ensuite réparation dans un autre pays, avant de revenir dans leur propre pays d'origine où ils devront enfin vivre avec leur handicap.

D'où la nécessité, sinon d'une règlementation commune unique, impossible à mettre en place aujourd'hui, mais au moins d'un essai de rapprochement et d'harmonisation.

## II - LES DIFFICULTES A PREVOIR

Ces difficultés sont de deux ordres : légales et médico-légales.

### 1 - Difficultés légales et réglementaires :

a) la notion de faute :

- dans de nombreux pays, le conducteur n'est responsable que s'il est fautif. C'est le fameux article 1382 du Code Civil de la Législation Française. Pour demander réparation, il faut donc prouver la culpabilité : c'est le CARE-LESS de la Grande-Bretagne. Il en est de même au Portugal et en Grèce, où la faute doit être prouvée. Certains pays, par contre, acceptent un partage de responsabilité (la Belgique, par exemple).

- en France, la loi BADINTER du 5 Juillet 1985 a modifié cette règlementation : cette loi prévoit, en effet, une responsabilité forfaitaire automatique dans certains cas : notamment, la situation de l'automobiliste face au piéton.

- dans certains pays, il existe une présomption de responsabilité ; c'est le cas, par exemple, de l'Espagne et du Luxembourg, où il faut apporter la preuve contraire.

- enfin, on relève dans certains pays la possibilité d'une responsabilité sans faute, mais souvent avec un plafonnement de l'indemnisation. Ainsi, en Allemagne, dans les cas de responsabilité sans faute, seul le dommage matériel est réparé intégralement ; le dommage corporel est plafonné ; quant aux préjudices personnels, il ne sont pas indemnisés.

Le même plafonnement de l'indemnisation se retrouve au Danemark et aux Pays-Bas.

b) <u>Le contenu de la réparation</u> :

Dans tous les pays du Marché Commun on retient la notion d'une "<u>réparation intégrale</u>" du préjudice. En fait, cette réparation, même intégrale, se fait avec des niveaux et des appréciations très variables.

Schématiquement, on doit distinguer le préjudice économique et le préjudice humain. Selon les pays, on accorde plus ou moins d'importance à l'un ou à l'autre de ces deux préjudices. On peut ainsi opposer trois grandes catégories de nationalités :

- il y a les pays où l'aspect économique est primordial : c'est le cas de l'Allemagne, de la Grande-Bretagne, du Danemark, des Pays-Bas, de l'Irlande. Le Professeur Guy PIGANIOL disait que ces pays privilégiaient "l'homo economicus"

- d'autres pays sont surtout sensibles à la qualité de la vie, aux désagréments dans la vie quotidienne. Il s'agit du Danno biologico" des Italiens, encore appelé "danno alla salute". C'est le dommage à la personne, qui est réparé essentiellement en Espagne, en Grèce, en Italie, au Portugal. Ces pays privilégient donc "l'homo estheticus"

- enfin, certains pays s'efforcent de trouver une solution mixte, tenant compte de tous les aspects de la vie. C'est le cas, en particulier, de la France, de la Belgique et du Luxembourg.

En fait ces distinctions demeurent très schématiques.

c) <u>les modalités de la réparation</u> :

1) L'aspect financier : la réparation financière qui est accordée en fonction du taux d'I.P.P. est très variable selon les pays. Le Président DESSERTINE expliquait ainsi que pour 100 Fr d'indemnisation en France, on obtenait à l'étranger les indemnisations suivantes :

* 149 Fr en Belgique
* 29 Fr en Grèce et au Portugal
* 30 Fr au Danemark

2) Limites de la réparation :
- certains pays accordent la possibilité de soins futurs, éventuellement toute la vie. D'autres rejettent cette possibilité

- les révisions et délais de prescription sont variables selon les nations. C'est ainsi qu'en Grande-Bretagne il n'y a pas de révision possible. En Grèce et aux Pays-Bas, la révision est possible si elle a été prévue. En France, le délai de prescription est de 30 ans (10 ans selon la loi BADINTER)

- il en est de même pour les recours des organismes sociaux : en France ce recours est possible mais uniquement sur les préjudices patrimoniaux. En Grande-Bretagne, ce recours est possible mais avec un plafonnement.

**2) Difficultés d'ordre médico-légal**

a) le rôle de l'expert :

En France et dans beaucoup d'autres pays, l'expertise comprend deux temps : d'une part la description des lésions médicales et de leurs conséquences, d'autre part une interprétation médico-légale de ces séquelles.

Au Danemark, l'expertise est réalisée par le chirurgien traitant.

En Grande-Bretagne, l'expert fait seulement un rapport descriptif. Il n'est pas un arbitre et il n' apporte aucune conclusion médico-légale. Il est donc, en quelque sorte, un témoin oral à l'audience.

A l'inverse, dans d'autres pays l'expert calcule totalement la réparation. C'est ainsi qu'au Luxembourg il y a deux experts, auxquels est associé un avocat calculateur. Ce collège propose une réparation financière globale, comprenant à la fois les dommages corporels et les dommages matériels.

b) les difficultés sémantiques :

Lorsqu'on étudie les diverses missions d'expertise qui sont proposées dans le cadre du marché commun, on s'aperçoit que les mêmes réalités sont parfois décrites sous des mots différents. C'est ainsi que le préjudice moral belge concerne l'impact psychologique du traitement et de ses séquelles. On est là tout proche du quantum doloris français.

Le préjudice physiologique français, encore appelé préjudice fonctionnel ou préjudice biologique, est tout proche de la "danno alla salute" des experts italiens.

c) le problème des barêmes :

Dans aucun pays européen, le barème n'est obligatoire. Souvent il existe, mais il n'a qu'un caractère indicatif. Mais tous ces barêmes ont une valeur et un poids très variables :

- au Portugal, c'est le barême des accidents du travail qui est adopté (tabella national des incapacitades)

- en Belgique est utilisé le BOBI (barême officiel belge d'invalidité). En fait, ce barême n'est qu'indicatif. Il ne s'impose que pour des victimes de guerre, ou encore pour les accidents du travail du secteur public

- en France, les barêmes se sont multipliés. Rappelons en particulier, le barême MELENEC, et aussi le barême du Concours Médical de 1982. Enfin, actuellement, est de plus en plus utilisé le barême de la Société de Médecine Légale et de Criminologie de France ; il s'agit d'un barême essentiellement de caractère fonctionnel, qui a été défini en 1991.

- en Grèce, il existe un barême unique pour les accidents du travail et les accidents de droit commun.

- en Espagne, le premier barême en droit commun date du 16 Juin 1989. Il prévoyait 4 catégories d'invalidité et 7 catégories d'incapacité permanente. Par la suite, au Journal Officiel du 11 Mars 1991, ont été prévues des modalités d'application de ce barême. Ces modalités sont extrêmement complexes, avec une valeur du point qui augmente avec le pourcentage et avec l'âge, avec en outre des facteurs de correction

- enfin, certains pays n'ont pas de barême. C'est le cas de la Hollande, qui utilise surtout le barême américain (AMA), avec en outre une publication des arrêts de jurisprudence tous les deux ans.

- en Grande-Bretagne, de la même façon, il n'y a pas de barême chiffré. Il s'agit seulement d'une comparaison de jurisprudences.

## III - LES POINTS D'ACCORD POSSIBLES

**1 - L'unicité de la médecine** : Il faut d'abord rappeler que la clinique médicale est une. Elle est la même pour le médecin traitant, pour le médecin expert, pour le médecin-conseil d'assurance, pour le médecin de recours. Elle est également la même dans tous les pays. On s'aperçoit d'ailleurs que toutes les expertises prévoient les mêmes chapitres avec :

- les antécédents (en partriculier l'état antérieur)
- les lésions traumatiques
- les traitements et leur évolution
- les séquelles fonctionnelles
- les conséquences sur les activités de la vie personnelle et de la vie sociale.

**2 - Dans l'ensemble des séquelles**, l'évolution se fait de plus en plus vers la distinction de trois domaines différents :

a) la vie quotidienne :

Il s'agit de la gêne rencontrée dans les activités courantes. Cette gêne définit ce que les Français appellent le préjudice fonctionnel, encore appelé le "general damage" des Anglo-Saxons, ou encore le dommage à la santé, ou dommage biologique en Italie.

Ce dommage comprend tous les aspects de la vie quotidienne, vie de relation, vie sexuelle. Il comprend même les pertes d'agrément dans les loisirs, et même la diminution possible de la capacité de gain (mais sans tenir compte de la perte réelle de ressources)

b) l'aspect économique :

C'est le préjudice patrimonial. Celui-ci doit être prouvé. Il correspond à la perte de revenus après la consolidation médico-légale. Il s'agit donc d'un calcul in concreto, qui apprécie la diminution des ressources par rapport à ce qu'elles étaient avant l'accident.

En fait, l'expert n'a qu'un rôle indicatif dans ce domaine. Il apporte au régleur des notions médicales sur les possibilités du blessé de poursuivre son travail comme avant l'accident ou avec des modifiations. En aucun cas il ne doit quantifier le préjudice économique par un taux. C'est le régleur qui calculera dans le concret la réalité de la perte financière. C'est ce que les Anglo-Saxons appellent le "special damage".

c) les préjudices annexes :

C'est probablement ce que les Italiens appellent le préjudice moral. Ce préjudice concerne tout ce qui n'a pas d'aspect patrimonial. En France, ces préjudices comprennent essentiellement :

- le quantum doloris : compensation aux douleurs subies avant et parfois après la consolidation médico-légale. La conception est la même en Belgique, mais avec souvent un taux dégressif, alors qu'en France on utilise presque toujours un taux unique

- le préjudice esthétique, qui est défini qualitativement

**3 - Si on se met d'accord sur ces définitions**, on peut alors proposer une mission commune. Celle que nous avons rédigée après le congrès de DUSSELDORF est la suivante :

*"Examiner M. Mme X et consulter tous documents médicaux utiles en vue de décrire les lésions traumatiques provoquées par l'accident dont il a été victime le ... et d'en évaluer les conséquences médico-légales.*

*1 - Décrire les lésions traumatiques en relation directe et certaine avec l'accident, les traitements qu'elles ont nécessités, leur évolution. Noter les doléances de la victime. Décrire les constatations faites à l'examen, en précisant les lésions séquellaires en relation directe et certaine avec l'événement dommageable et, le cas échéant, celles qui seraient la conséquence d'un état antérieur*

*2 - Déterminer la durée de l'incapacité temporaire fonctionnelle, totale ou partielle (arrêt ou réduction des activités de la vie quotidienne) en relation avec les blessures et les soins reçus. En cas de perte temporaire de l'autonomie, préciser les aides et modalités de compensation qui ont été nécessaires. Le cas échéant, indiquer les conséquences de cette incapacité temporaire sur l'activité professionnelle (durée de l'arrêt de travail, total ou partiel)*

*3 - Fixer la date de consolidation, correspondant à la stabilisation des lésions et à l'arrêt des soins curatifs*

*4 - Décrire les souffrances endurées, physiques et psychiques, du fait des blessures, des traitements et des restrictions d'activité et d'agrément pendant la période de soins (avant consolidation). Evaluer l'importance du quantun doloris qui en résulte sur une échelle de 0 à 7*

*5 - Décrire les restrictions d'activité et d'agrément qui résultent des séquelles traumatiques :*

** dans la vie quotidienne, en exposant les difficultés dans les gestes et activités de la vie courante, les efforts accrus, les désagréments et diminution des plaisirs de la vie, les handicaps dans certaines situations particulières de la vie personnelle*

* *dans les activités spécifiques de loisir*

* *dans les activités professionnelles ou assimilées*

* *dans tout domaine susceptible de réduire la durée ou la qualité de la vie du blessé (domaine sexuel parfois)*

*Evaluer quantitativement l'importance de cette diminution de la capacité fonctionnelle physiologique en proposant un taux de déficit fonctionnel séquellaire par référence à un barème fonctionnel (en précisant le barême utilisé). Le taux de cette incapacité correspond à la différence entre la capacité physiologique antérieure et la capacité actuelle.*

*6 - Lorsque les séquelles traumatiques sont susceptibles de modifier les conditions d'emploi, et donc d'avoir une incidence économique, décrire les conséquences particulières de ces séquelles dans la vie professionnelle ; préciser les gestes devenus difficiles ou impossibles, les efforts accrus, la nécessité éventuelle d'un aménagement des conditions de travail ou d'une réorientation professionnelle, impliquant ou non un séjour en centre de rééducation.*

*7 - Décrire les conséquences à caractère permanent des lésions séquellaires dans le domaine esthétique et évaluer l'importance de ce dommage sur une échelle de 0 à 7*

*8 - Fournir toutes informations utiles sur la nécessité éventuelle de soins après consolidation (y compris le renouvellement de prothèses) en vue de l'évaluation des frais futurs à prévoir*

*9 - En cas de handicap grave, indiquer la nécessité de l'assistance d'une tierce personne, en précisant sa qualification (infirmière, aide soignante, aide ménagère, surveillance...) et la durée de présence effective ou d'intervention.*

*Indiquer si les conditions d'existence du blessé peuvent être améliorées par des aménagements des locaux d'habitation et des équipements spécifiques compensateurs du handicap.*

*10 - Indiquer le cas échéant si des réserves d'ordre médical doivent être émises concernant l'évolution lointaine des séquelles".*

Cette mission est donc extrêmement complète. Chaque nation accordera plus ou moins d'importance à tel ou tel chef de préjudice.

## IV - CONCLUSION

1 - Comme nous l'avons dit, ce travail d'harmonisation nous paraît absolument indispensable.

2 - Il s'agit d'une tâche difficile, qui se heurte à de multiples problèmes.

3 - Par contre, il s'agit d'un travail qui, à notre avis, est possible, à la condition de respecter les législations. Il n'est pas souhaitable, tout au moins aujourd'hui, d'établir une réglementation commune et de mettre en place un véritable droit européen. Par contre, notre

ambition a été de définir une nouvelle mission d'expertise qui puisse s'insérer dans les diverses législations actuellement existantes.

4 - Reste la question de savoir s'il faut créer un corps d'experts internationaux. Cette question demeure ouverte.

# 11. Time of Death Estimation

# COMPUTER SIMULATION OF THE EFFECT OF THERMAL INSULATION ON THE POST MORTEM BODY TEMPERATURE

**Jarosław A. Berent[1], Andrzej Piotrowicz[2], Karol Śliwka[1] and Danuta Miścicka-Śliwka[1]**

**Forensic Medicine Institute[1], The Ludwik Rydygier's University School of Medical Sciences in Bydgoszcz, ul. Skłodowskiej-Curie 9, 85-094 Bydgoszcz, Poland tel/fax ++48 52 41 12 49 and OBR Gastromasz Bydgoszcz[2]**

**Key words**
computer, thermal insulation, post mortem temperature

## Introduction

Using post mortem temperature for estimating the time since death began in last century. The first really comprehensive paper is dated 1863 [1]. Since then, over one hundred papers on this topic have been published. Many possible measurement points were investigated in detail [2, 3]. Several algorithms are known, based either on purely practical measurements or on theoretical considerations tested by experiment. Some of them are just rules of thumb, easy to memorize and use, whereas others require a bit more advanced mathematics [4-6], even involving computer data processing in some cases [9-12].

In the end, the problem is that all of the above mentioned papers are without final solution to the question of ambient temperature changeability and exact influence of body clothes as thermal insulation. The insulation case could have been closed by the multi-measurement approach [13-16]. The other way, is by using the corrective factor, which contains not only the insulation, but also body weight and air circulation around the body. The latter was introduced by Henssge in the one-measurement nomogram method [17, 18], derived directly from the double exponential model by Marshall and Hoare [19-21].

It seems to be, that the sentence prefacing this paper, though almost thirty years old, has not lost any of its value, and shows that the question is still far from final solution.

The aim of this paper is the theoretical calculation of the effect of thermophysical parameters of stratified body insulation on post mortem temperature. Our earlier described analytical formula, which is derived from heat flow theory, was used for such a purpose [22]. It allows us to calculate post mortem temperature or interval with optional changes in ambient temperature and for optional, and even many-layered body insulation of known humidity, and others thermophysical features.

## Assumptions of the method and numerical figures

One of the assumptions of the considered method is the infinite thermal conductivity of the body. In one case (for constant ambient temperature) it follows the newtonian (exponential) type of body cooling curve. This is self-evident disadvantage, because thermal conduction is finite and relatively small. It allows us, however, to analyze the influence of insulation in detail, and this is the aim of this paper.

When one changes the assumption of infinite conduction into finite, the formulas will follow the cooling model by Marshall and Hoare. Because of the frame of this paper, full detailed considerations will not be given. They are contained in the source article [22]. Only the final formula (in simplified form for one-layered insulation type) will be given here.

Data:

$F_c$ body surface area, $F_c$=2.0 $m^2$
$F_z$ external surface of the insulation area, $F_z$=2.2 $m^2$
$a_z$ heat penetration coefficient, $a_z$=4.4 W/$m^2$K
$R_a$ heat penetration resistance, $R_a=F_c/F_z a_z$
$d_u$ insulation thickness, $d_u$=0.005 m
$w_i$ insulation humidity, defined as wet clothes weight devided by dry weight
$\lambda_u$ thermal conductivity of the insulation
$\lambda_w$ thermal conductivity of the water, $\lambda_w$=0.6 W/m K
$R_\lambda$ heat transfer resistance, $R_\lambda = (d_u(1+w_i)F_c) / (F_z(\lambda_u+w_i\lambda_w))$
$m_u$ dry insulation weight (mass)
$c_{us}$ specific heat of the dry insulation
$c_w$ specific heat of the water, $c_w$=4.19 J/kg K
$C_u$ thermal capacity of the insulation, $C_u = m_u(c_{us}+w_i c_w)$
$m_c$ body weight (mass), $m_c$=70 kg
$c_c$ specific heat of the body, $c_c$=2,850 J/kg K
A,B,C constants, $A = m_c c_c(R_a+R_\lambda) + C_u(R_a+0.5R_\lambda)$); $B = 0.5C_uR_\lambda$; $C = F_c/A$

For naked body the following data should be taken: $C_u$=0; $R_l$=0; $F_z = F_c$ =2 $m^2$
Insulated body temperature with optional changes in ambient temperature can be extracted from the formula:

$$\Theta(\tau) = t(\tau) + (\Theta_o - t_o)\,e^{-C\tau} - (1 - B/A)\,e^{-C\tau}\int_0^\tau e^{C\tau}\,dt/d\tau\;d\tau$$

where: $\Theta(\tau)$ body temperature as a function of time,
$\tau$ time,
$t(\tau)$ ambient temperature as a function of time
$\Theta_o$ initial body temperature.

For constant ambient temperature, the formula can be simplified to:

$$\Theta(\tau) = t_o + (\Theta_o - t_o)\,e^{-C\tau} \quad \text{where } t_o=20.0\ ^\circ\text{C and } \Theta_o=37.0\ ^\circ\text{C}$$

The influence of C constant will be shown in the following examples, achieved using a computer simulation.

**Results**

Using the above given formulas and data from the upper part of table 1, the C coefficient was calculated, and then, appropriate temperatures for naked body and four kinds of clothes (dry cotton, dry wool, wet cotton and wet wool) were considered. The results are shown in the lower part of table 1, and on the graph (fig. 1).

**Discussion of results**

As one can see from the graph of temperature against post mortem interval (fig. 1), the differencies between cooling curves are prominent, especially in the central part of the graph, representing a post mortem interval from 4 to 8 hours. For a better example, the cooling time for a body to achieve 23.0 °C is less than 11 hours for the naked body, versus over 15 hours for the body insulated with dry wool.

The humidity of the clothes levels the insulation attributes partially, although it does not cancel them entirely.

The heat penetration coefficient, which has been used as a constant in this paper, in reality, depends on air circulation around the body. These changes cause changes in the C coefficient, meaning that they influence a cooling rate.

**Table 1.** Thermophysical features of the clothes and calculated temperatures and intervals for naked and insulated body.

| Type of insulation | naked body | wet cotton | wet wool | dry cotton | dry wool |
|---|---|---|---|---|---|
| $c_{us}$ J/kg K | --- | 1300 | 1880 | 1300 | 1880 |
| $\lambda_{us}$ W/m K | --- | 0.070 | 0.045 | 0.070 | 0.070 |
| d kg/m$^3$ | --- | 330 | 350 | 330 | 350 |
| $m_u$ kg | --- | 3.63 | 3.95 | 3.63 | 3.95 |
| $w_i$ | --- | 0.5 | 0,5 | --- | --- |
| C x 10$^{-5}$ | 4.411 | 4.356 | 4.276 | 3.616 | 3.167 |
| Θ ( 5h) | 27.685 | 27.761 | 27.873 | 28.866 | 29.624 |
| Θ (10h) | 23.764 | 23.543 | 23.647 | 24.624 | 25.449 |
| Θ (20h) | 20.710 | 20.739 | 20.782 | 21.258 | 21.746 |
| time for Θ=23°C | 10h 55' | 11h 04' | 11h 16' | 13h 19' | 15h 12' |

**Figure 1.** Graphs of the body temperature against the time for naked body and insulated one in four kinds of clothes.

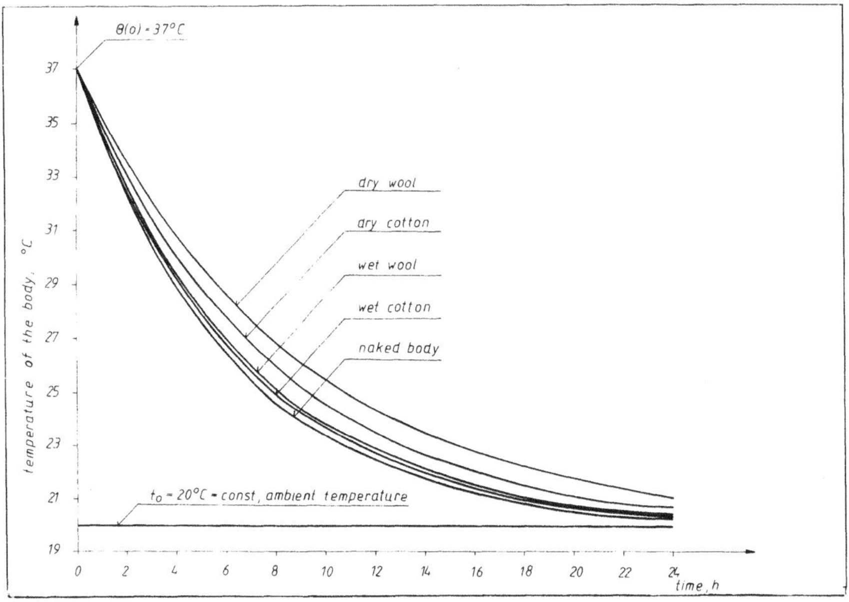


Henssge [17,18] suggests using a so called corrective factor. This is a formal change of body weight to include the insulation, its humidity, and air movements around the body. As a matter of fact, this is a change in the heat penetration coefficient $a_z$. For this purpose, he gives special tables based on practical observations. Such a manoeuvre in a paper of this type is identical to the correction of the C coefficient, and is absolutely admissible. There is only one question: how far one can rely on the tables? Because we have proved that even a change in the type of insulation can generate big alterations of the cooling curve, the authors of this paper are inclined towards multi-measurement methods, because they allow one to find the cooling rate more precisely.

## Conclusions

1. Using purely mathematical methods, the formula for calculation of post mortem body temperature with optional changes in ambient temperature and body clothes/insulation can be derived.
2. Types of clothing and their humidity have essential and calculable influences on post mortem body cooling curves.

## References

1.Taylor AS and Wilkes D (1863) On the cooling of the human body after death. Guy's Hosp Rep October:1809-2211

2.Śliwka K and Miscicka-Śliwka D (1985) Badania nad przydatnością wybranych punktów pomiarowych temperatury zwłok, dla określenia czasu śmierci, na podstawie ciągłej rejestracji temperatury. Arch Med Sąd i Krym 35/2:85-92

3.Henssge C, Madea B and Joachim H (1988) Metoden zur bestimmung der Todeszeit an Leichen. Schmidt Romhild, Lubeck, P 133

4.Marshall TK (1988) Temperature methods of estimating the time of death. Med Sci Law, 5:224-232

5.Knight B (1988) The evolution of methods for estimating the time of death from body temperature. Forensic Sci Int 36:47-55

6.Nokes LDM, Flint T, Williams JH and Knight BH (1992) The application of eight reported temperature-based algorithms to calculate the postmortem interval. Forensic Sci Int 54:109-125

7.Hiraiwa K, Ohno Y, Kuroda Fet al (1980,1981,1982,1983) Estimation of postmortem interval from rectal temperature by use of computer (I-IV). Med Sci Law 20/2:115-125, 21/1:4-9, 22/4:285-289, 23/2:125-130

8.Green MA and Wright JC (1984) Computerstudie zur Todeszeitbestimmung durch Korpertemperatur-messungen. Kriminal Forens Wiss 55.56:111-126

9.Shved EF, Novikov PI and Vlasov AIu (1989) Microcomputer realisation of adaptive technique of modelling the process of death body temperature variability. Sud Med Ekspert 2:4-6

10.Shved EF, Novikov PI and Vlasov AIu (1989) Diagnostical programme for estimation of post mortem interval using microcalculators MK-61 and B3-34. Sud Med Ekspert 1:15-17

11.Lynnerup N (1993) A computerprogram for the estimation of time of death. J Forensic Sci 38/4: 816-820

12.Kitazawa M, Inoue M, Fushimy Y et al (1993) Simple and rapid estimation of postmortem interval from rectal temperature by use of personal computer. IAFS 13th International Meeting, poster no. 10/0607A, Dusseldorf

13.Nokes LDM, Brown A and Knight B (1985) A Self-contained method for determining time since death from temperature measurements. Med Sci Law 23/3:166-171

14.Brown A, Hicks B, Knight B and Nokes LDM (1985) Determination of the time since death using the double exponential cooling model. Med Sci Law 25/3:223-227

15.Green MA and Wright JC (1985) Postmortem interval estimation from body temperature data only. Forensic Sci Int 28:35-46

16.Green MA and Wright JC (1985) The theoretical aspects of the time dependent Z equation as a means of postmortem interval estimation using body temperature data only. Forensic Sci Int 28:53-62

17.Henssge C (1988) Death time estimation in case work. I. The rectal temperature time of death nomogram. Forensic Sci Int 38:209-236

18.Henssge C (1992) Rectal temperature time of death nomogram: dependence of corrective factors on the body weight under stronger thermic insulations conditions. Forensic Sci Int 54:51-66

19.Marshall TK and Hoare FE (1962) Estimating the time of death - the rectal cooling after death and its mathematical expression. J Forensic Sci 7:56-81

20.Marshall TK (1962) Estimating the time of death - the use of the cooling formula in the study of postmortem body cooling. J Forensic Sci 7:189-210

21.Marshall TK (1962) Estimating the time of death - the use of body temperature in estimating the time of death. J Forensic Sci 7:211-221

22.Piotrowicz A, Śliwka K and Berent JA (1994) Analityczna ocena zmienności temperatury ciała post mortem przy uwzględnieniu zmiennej temperatury otoczenia. Arch Med Sąd i Krym 44/1:3-12

# HIGH BLOOD ALCOHOL LEVELS IN CADAVEROUS BLOOD

F. GIGLI, G. LAGIOIA, O. MORINI, R. PAOLETTI, L. SIRONI

Institute of Forensic Medicine, University of Milan Via L. Mangiagalli 37 20133 MILAN

Death caused by acute ethanol intoxication was rarely observed, although it was not unusual, in a retrospective study concerning the post-mortem cases of the Milan Institute of Forensic Medicine.

The study was carried out on post-mortem examinations performed in the 1986-1992 period, taking into account 3094 cases of unnatural death out of an overall number of 9289 autopsies.

As regards the former cases, alcohol levels that were high enough to justify death, in the absence of other forms of injury, were found only in 9 cases.

Existing literature considers the values fatal if they are equal to or greater than 4 g/l, although with reservations due to the rapidity of ingestion and absorption of alcohol, individual tolerance, tolerance phenomena, as well as individual capacity to metabolize alcohol, all factors that might explain fatal poisoning even with lower blood ethanol concentrations or, viceversa, non-letal cases with alcohol concentrations higher than 5 g/l.

Another thing that must be kept in mind is that death due to acute ethanol poisoning may also come after a long coma stage during which alcohol catabolism phenomena are possible, with the subsequent observation of much lower blood alcohol levels compared to to the peak blood concentration. In fact, the blood concentration value decreases by 15-25 mg/h when alcohol is catabolized.

Amongst other things, in a recent study Heatly et al. (1990) observed an average blood alcohol concentration of 3.55 g/l in 175 cases of death due to acute alcohol poisoning: moreover, the Authors also reported numerous cases in which, on the basis of circumstantial and anatomical-pathological data, acute alcohol poisonong was identified as the cause of death even if the alcohol values were clearly lower, indicating the possibility of a partial metabolization of the toxic substance during a more or less prolonged agonal phase.

Considering the above observations, the opposite eventuality deserves to be underlined, i.e. the possibility of finding high blood alcohol levels (even higher than 3 g/l) in subjects who surely died of different causes and whose blood alcohol values deserve being discussed for their possible concomitant role in determining death, due to their influence on the subjects' behaviour just before death.

Out of 3094 subjects examined, 831 cases were "positive": of these, 395 (47.53%) presented blood alcohol levels between 0.2 and 0.8 g/l, 192 (23.10%) had levels between 0.8 and 1.5 g/l, 196 (23.58%) had levels between 1.5 and 3 g/l and 48 (5.77%) had levels higher than 3 g/l.

The toxicological results relating to the alcoholemia determined by the gas chromatography using the Head Space technique showed that out of 3094 cases examined, the femoral blood of 831 subjects (26.85%) showed positivity to ethanol in concentrations greater or equal to 0.2g/l.

The sex-division of the positive cases showed that 85.67% of the subjects were male (712 cases) and only 14.32% (119 cases) were female. In the age-division, the maximum percentage was registered by the 16-35 age-bracket, with 473 cases, 56.92% of the total cases.

In our cases, we observed blood ethanol concentrations greater or equal to 3 g/l in 48 cases, 5.77% of the positive cases and 1.55% of the all the cases examined.

Apart from the 9 subjects who died of acute ethanol poisoning, of these 48 cases, 33 cases relating to accidental events, suicides and homicides showed peremptorily demonstrative evidence of death caused by different exogenous forms of injury; in

1 case the effects of the traumatic-contusion form of injury were believed to have been amplified by a co-existent state of alcohol poisoning which did not allow a timely first-aid intervention; in the remaining 5 cases, alcohol was considered a concomitant cause along with other toxic substances, more precisely morphine and cocaine.

The diagnosis of death due to the exclusive action of alcohol was drawn up on the basis of the overall data collected: anamnestic, anatomical-pathological and chemical-toxicological data.

As far as the anamnestic data is concerned, all the 9 cases had been found dead; alcohol-abuse had been reported in 4 (associated with drug-abuse in 2), exclusively drug-abuse in one case, while the anamneses collected in the remaining cases were negative.

As far as the anatomical-pathological aspect is concerned, no results that justify death were found: only the presence of "general asphyxial notes" (cerebral and pulmonary edema, subpleural petechiae, polyvisceral congestion and fluid blood), in some cases, associated with natural chronic-degenerative pathologies, moreover of moderate entity; four subjects were found to be affected by hepatic steatosis and one had clearly suffered from hepatic cirrhosis.

The chemical and toxicological examinations revealed blood alcohol levels between 3.4 g/l and 3.97 g/l in 7 cases; greater than 4 g/l in the remaining two; 4.47 g/l in the case of a 32-year-old drug-addict, who also had hematic traces of cocaine; and as much as 6.32 g/l in a 28-year-old woman.

Blood alcohol concentrations between 3.00 and 4.25 g/l were found in the blood of 33 subjects who died of different forms of injury: in most cases, the form of injury was of the contusion kind and, more precisely, thirteen traffic accidents, four falls, one fall from a ground-floor and one fall from a horse: in two cases, such events occurred at work. Nine subjects died of mechanical asphyxia and more precisely: four cases of internal suffocation caused by a food bolus, three drownings, one hanging and one choking. The other observations concerned two household accidents caused by fire, two suicides caused by fire-arm shots and one combined injury caused by a fire-arm and a cutting and thrusting weapon.

Apart from three cases considered suicides, amongst the falls the fourth case concerned an accident at work of a tinsmith who, before falling from a scaffolding, had clearly given evidence of being drunk with an euphoric and unusual behaviour. Even the death caused by the fall from the horse was an accident at work regarding a pioneer, known a being a cirrhotic alcoholic with records of numerous falls coinciding with episodes of acute alcoholism.

Even the accidental fall from the ground-floor concerned an alcoholic: the subject, 55 years old, died of rachi-medullar lesions and the post-mortem examination also revealed the presence of a hepatic steatosis.

As far as the car accidents were concerned, six of the subjects who died were driving, one was a passenger, while the remaining six cases concerned subjects who had been run down while walking.

Post-mortem examination of these subjects revealed - besides the typical results related to contusions - the presence of a hepatic steatosis in five cases only, suggesting alcohol abuse.

It is interesting to note that in two cases only, the behaviour of the subjects just before death was manifestly influenced by a state of acute alcoholism, later on confirmed by toxicological examinations: one case concerned a a motorcyclist who had run off the road without any apparent reason, and the other concerned a subject who died after a car accident while driving on the wrong lane of the motorway.

The correlation between acute alcoholism and death in the cases of suffocation caused by a food bolus, was even more evident due to the well-known, acute and chronic, effects favouring alterations in the swallowing and coughing reflexes and the subsequent wedging of the bolus in the lumen of the larynx. A fact to be noted is that all the subjects were still young (in their forties) and three of these were found to have been affected by hepatic steatosis, denoting a parenchymal ailment, probably connected to the effects of a chronic ingestion of alcohol; the latter may

in turn determine the neuro-toxic alterations that could favour an altered and less precise synergy in swallowing.
As for the three cases of drowning, in at least two, the circumstances of the event (one found in an artificial lake and the other in an artificial canal, both during the cold season) made us presume a fall favoured by a state of acute alcoholism to the point of inhibiting any kind of reaction. Instead, the third case was a woman who had drowned while bathing in an artificial lake with her friends: it is not known if a state of acute alcoholism subsisted, for lack of anamnestic data supplied when the body was identified.
The choking case concerned a 38-year-old woman who had been assaulted by her father, exasperated by the fact that his daughter could not find a job and would get drunk.
Even one of the two household-accident cases caused by fire concerned a subject who was known to be an alcoholic.
As for the two suicide cases caused by fire-arms and the homicide caused by the fire-arm/cutting and thrusting weapon combination, in the post-mortem examination all three cases revealed to have been affected by hepatic steatosis, while alcohol-abuse was, anamnestically, known of in one of the subjects only.
The results we are most anxious to underline are the high number of subjects who died of different forms of injury and had blood alcohol levels greater than 3 g/l; the latter value is indicated by the medico-legal and chemical-toxicological literature as being sufficient in determining serious behaviourial alterations.
In fact, all the Authors advanced a series of important alterations for such high blood alcohol concentrations: motorial incoordination, difficulty in articulating words, visual disorders, atonicity, stuporous state and even coma, with the possibility of death for values above 4 g/l.
Such assertions have already been discussed by various Authors (*), who underlined, on the basis of ample case studies, the extreme variability of the lethal concentrations, making the standardisation of rigid patterns regarding the toxic effects of alcohol substantially unapplicable on the medico-legal plane.
Our cases are a further confirmation of the above and result in similar conclusions, even as far as the effects of alcohol on individual behaviour are concerned; in fact, just before death many subjects presented an apparantly normal behaviour, without any recognizable correlation between the confirmed state of alcohol poisoning and the dynamics of the injurious event that caused death.
This confirms how the variability of individual response towards alcohol may allow, taking into account even very high blood alcohol levels, to maintain an apparently unaltered behaviour.
These conclusions lead us to recommend extreme prudence when answering judicial queries regarding the relationship between certain behaviours and a confirmed state of alcoholism and blood alcohol concentrations found in the victim or in the accused; furthermore, one must be extremely prudent when coming concluding that death was caused by acute alcohol poisoning only on the basis of blood alcohol levels greater than the "classic" 4 g/l.

## REFERENCES

1) Adamo M, Bargagna M, Barni M, Dell'Erba A, Fabroni F, Fornari A, Querci V (1989) Manuale di Medicina Legale e delle Assicurazioni. Ed Monduzzi.
2) Agren S, Jakobsson S.W. (1987) Validation of diagnoses on death certificates for male alcoholics in Stockholm. For Scie Int 33: 231-241.
3) Bertol E, Lodi F, Mari F, Marozzi E (1994) Trattato di Tossicologia Forense. Ed. CEDAM.
4) Brandt-Casadevall C, Krompecher T, Gujer H.R. (1990) An unusual case of sudden death in an alcohol addict. Int J Leg Med 104: 55-57
5) Canuto G, Tovo S (1992) Medicina Legale e delle Assicurazioni. Ed. Piccin
6) Cazzaniga A, Cattabeni C.M, Luvoni R (1991) Medicina Legale e delle Assicurazioni. Ed.UTET

7) Falzi G, Morini O (1987) Steatosi epatica e morte "inattesa". Arch. Med. Leg. Ass. 9: 147-155
8) Gerin C, Antoniotti F, Merli S (1986) Medicina Legale e delle Assicurazioni. Ed. SEU.
9) Hammond I.C.B, Rumack B.H and Rodgerson P.O (1973) Blood ethanol: a report of unusually high levels in a living patient. J Am Med Ass 226: 63-4
10) Hansen AU, Simonsen J (1991) The manner and cause of death in a forensic series of chronic alcholics. For Scie Int 49: 171-178
11) Heatley MK, Crane J (1990) The blood alcohol concentration at post-mortem in 175 fatal cases of alcohol intoxication. Med Sci Law 30, 2: 101-105
12) Johnston HRM (1985) At what level does alcohol kill? Med Sci Law 25: 127-30
13) Kubo SI, Dankwarth G, Puschel K (1991) Blood alcohol concentrations of sudden unexpected deaths and non natural deaths. For Scie Int 52: 77-84
14) Lindblad B, Olsson R (1976) Unusually high levels of alcohol. J Am Med Ass 236: 1600-1602
15) Lodi F, Mangili F (1969) Aspetti della diagnosi medico-legale di morte per intossicazione acuta ad alcool etilico. Arc Soc Lom Med Leg Ass 5: 341-358
16) Lodi F, Marozzi E, Grandi M, Caligara M, Marozzi F, Agosta E (1990) Incidenti del traffico ed intossicazioni voluttuarie. Aspetti tossicologici e medico-legali. Atti del V Convegno Nazionale del Gruppo dei Tossicologi Forensi SIMLA. Zacchia Vol VIII Serie 4: 267-273
17) Lujan CC (1992) Alcohol-related deaths of American Indians. Stereotypes and Strategies. JAMA Vol 267 n° 10: 1384-1392.
18) Luvoni R, Marozzi E (1968) Ethyl alcohol distribution in the various fluids of cadavers. J For Med 15: 67-70
19) Marcinkowski T, Przybylski Z (1974) Evaluation of the cause of death in cases of acute alcohol poisoning. J For Scie 4: 233-238
20) Marozzi E, Ronchi E, Marozzi F, Zoja R (1990) Confronto fra i livelli di morfina riscontrati in soggetti deceduti per "acute narcotism" e soggetti morti per altre cause: considerazioni tossicologiche e medico-legali. Arch Soc Lom Med Leg Ass 12: 66-80.
21) Marozzi F, Zoja R (1987) Su un caso di sospetto avvelenamento acuto da alcool etilico: considerazioni medico-legali. Arch Soc Lom Med Leg Ass 9: 286-293.
22) Odesanmi WO (1983) The fatal blood alcohol level in acute alcohol poisoning. Med Sci Law 23: 25-30
23) O'Neill S, Tepton KF, Prichard JS and Quintan A (1984) Survival after high blood alcohol levels. Arc Int Med 144: 641-642
24) Penttila A, Karhunen PJ, Vuori E (1989) Blood alcohol in sudden and unexpected deaths. For Scie Int 43: 95-102.
25) Simpson CK, Knight B (1985) Forensic Medicine. London Edward Arnold.
26) Sullivan J.B, Hauptman M, Bronstein A (1987) Lack of observable intoxication in humans with high plasma alcohol concentrations. J For Scie 1660-1665
27) Tedeschi GC, Eckert WG, Tedeschi LG (1977) Forensic Medicine WB Saunders Company.
28) Zangani P, Sciaudone G, Palmieri VM, Durante Mangoni E, Palmieri L, Baldi F, Canfora A, Cittadini A, De Pietro O, Grieco B, Parisi G, Picciocchi P, Ricci P, Trojsi E (1990) Medicina Legale e delle Assicurazioni Ed. Morano.

## "NORMAL" VALUES IN VITREOUS HUMOR - Reflections and Refutations

Burkhard Madea

Institut für Rechtsmedizin der Universität zu Köln, Melatengürtel 60-62, D - 50823 Köln
Fax 0221 - 4784261

### 1. Introduction

Vitreous humor is used widely in Forensic Pathology as an aid in determining the cause of death due to the fact that postmortem diffusion processes after loss of selective membrane permeability are too fast and erratic in the other body fluids and serum abnormalities of living individuals are thought to be reflected in the vitreous.

I don't want to repeat the known facts on vitreous chemistry, but to remind of some unsolved general problems concerning vitreous chemistry in Forensic Medicine which should be kept in mind in practical casework to avoid a too schematic and simplified application of published "normal values", "reference intervals" or "combined values".

### 2. General considerations and short review of the literature

In Clinical Chemistry most determinations are carried out on blood or serum. Laboratory and methodology specific normal values or reference values exist for most parameters and chemical abnormalities can be diagnosed quite easy. When these chemical abnormalities should be diagnosed postmortem on another fluid compartment than blood or serum several questions arise:

- How are the "normal values" in vitreous humor compared to blood and serum ? Frequency distributions of antemortem serum and postmortem vitreous values in normal individuals must be calculated and compared.
  Correlations between antemortem serum and postmortem vitreous values must be calculated.
- Are chemical abnormalities of serum values reflected in vitreous humor and how fast are abnormal serum values (elevations and depressions) equilibrated in vitreous humor ?
- Are these values stable postmortem in vitreous humor ?

These questions are difficult to answer for methodical problems:

1.) Normal values on human vitreous humor during life are not and will not be available. We have to establish our normal vitreous humor values from postmortem studies on "normal individuals" and compare them to vital normal serum values. Antemortem vitreous values are known from animal experiments and quite large normal ranges were observed, for instance for sodium (15).

2.) The question if and how fast serum abnormalities are equilibrated in vitreous humor can't be answered on living humans as well.

There are only very few animal experimental studies on the equilibration of artificial raised serum values (urea) in the vitreous humor regarding time (14). An apparently slow rate at which serum urea equilibrated in the vitreous humor of dogs was found, more than one hour being required for levels in vitreous humor to reach half those in serum (14).

Studies on vitreous humor with the aim to establish normal values for several parameters began with a paper by Naumann (11), followed by Leahy and Farber (8) especially Coe (3), Swift et al. (13), Blumenfeld et al. (1), Wilkie, Bellamy (14) and several others (for review see 5, 9, 10). These investigations were carried out on differing reference samples regarding age, sex, cause of death, postmortem interval, previous health status, antemortem serum values.

Naumann represents in his results the range of observed values; Leahy/Farber the lower and upper second standard deviation, Coe the observed range, mean value and first standard deviation (fig. 1). What is now the normal range ?

"Normal values" calculated as mean value $\pm 2^{nd}$ standard deviation must fulfill three suppositions which are normally not given:

- Gaussean frequency distribution of values,
- extensive investigations on healthy people or normal individuals,
- extensive investigations on random samples with deviations and disturbances of the investigated parameter.

Especially investigations on random samples with deviations (elevations and depressions) of the investigated parameter are necessary to distinguish certainly normal from certainly abnormal values.

And another point: Vitreous values are used as a mirror of serum values, since due to fast autolysis serum values postmortem do not reflect the serum values at the moment of death. But do in any case the vitreous values reflect the serum values at the moment of death ?

This seems to be true at least for values in normal range and highly elevated values but not with low values. Coe states already 1969: "Although abnormal vitreous values reflect abnormal serum electrolytes, the converse was frequently not true. Many hospital cases with terminal low serum sodium values were found to have vitreous sodium levels within normal limits" (3).

From these and similar observations it becomes evident that the equilibration of serum values - elevated and especially depressed - with vitreous values is slow and vitreous values in normal range may reflect pathological serum values, especially lowered values. Correlations between antemortem serum and postmortem vitreous values are nearly completely missing in the literature. The only study in which correlations are reported is that of Choo-Kang et al. (2). The postmortem vitreous values were however from a pm interval from 23 to 277 hours. The best correlation was found for creatinine and urea with correlation coefficients of $r = 0.98$ and $0.96$. The correlations for sodium and chloride were with $r = 0.59$ and $0.43$ comparatively poor.

Furthermore vitreous humor values of sodium, chloride, potassium, glucose and urea nitrogen vary due to different analytical procedures and instruments used (4).

This all together is of course a reason why we shouldn't speak of "normal vitreous values". But there are additional important reasons. The concept of "normal values" is left in Clinical Chemistry for several reasons (6, 7, 12). According to Murphy "normalcy is a vestigial concept left in medicine from its unscientific era".

Dykbaer and Gräsbeck have concluded that normality is hopeless to define in a useful way and they have suggested that the term "normal values" should be abolished (cit. according 12). Normal values in vitreous humor in dead bodies is in another sense of course nonsense: What shall be normal values in dead persons ? Instead the concept of reference values has been introduced to avoid many of these difficulties surrounding the term "normal values".

Reference values for a diagnostic test in Clinical Chemistry or in Forensic Medicine should include five major categories of specifications:

1.) the reference population, and the way it was chosen,
2.) the environmental and physiological conditions under which the specimens were obtained,
3.) the technique and timing of specimen collection, transport, preparation and storage,
4.) the analytical method that was used, with data regarding its accuracy, precision, and quality control,
5.) the data set that was observed and the reference intervals that were derived.

No study in the literature on reference values in vitreous humor fulfills all these requirements.

## 3. Reference values published in the literature

In spite of the conceptual problems in obtaining reference values in vitreous humor in normal individuals discussed above, the fact that stable normal and stable elevated serum values are reflected in vitreous humor and that vitreous humor values are stable postmortem seem to be proven.

The pm stability of electrolytes and urea is guaranteed for the first 30 hpm, for urea up to 100 hpm. There is enough evidence that vitreous sodium and chloride values are stable over a much longer period than only 30 h (probably 80-100 hpm).

Own reference values (fig. 2) were obtained and calculated from individuals with normal serum values prior to death or from individuals dying suddenly, when autopsy revealed no cause for any chemical abnormality. The range of observed values in our study was greater than in Coe's; the mean values for sodium, chloride, calcium corresponded quite good to

Coe's values. The discrepancies may be due to different methodologies used and differing composition of the reference sample (age, pmi etc.).
However it should be kept in mind that for instance the observed range of antemortem vitreous sodium values in "normal, healthy" dogs was much greater too than postmortem vitreous sodium values in normal individuals given by Coe (15).

**4. Conclusions**
When vitreous chemistry is used for postmortem diagnosis and as mirror of serum chemistry at the moment of death we should be aware of the scientific gaps:
The correlation of serum and vitreous values was only investigated for a range of normal serum values and some values with moderate elevations or depressions but not with severe disturbances of homoiostasis.
As far as I see we have no reference material on cases with lethal serum values comparing these to vitreous values.
We know little on the duration which is needed for depressed or elevated serum levels to equilibrate within the vitreous.
And lastly valid and reliable "discrimination values" which discriminate between certainly normal and certainly abnormal or lethal in vitreous are missing. These conceptual problems are more or less inherent in all studies on vitreous humor chemistry. Mainly markedly elevated values are of diagnostic significance concerning determining the cause of death.
Some of the scientific gaps I mentioned will continue for methodical problems. When vitreous humor chemistry is applied in casework the pathologist should strictly adhere to reference values and methodologies which are comparable to his observed values in an individual case.
He should always ascertain that the individual case matches the criteria of the reference sample group.
For practical purposes an orientation on the values of Coe (3) can be recommended, although his "normal ranges" seem to be too narrow.

**Literature**

1. Blumenfeld TA, Mantell CH, Catherman RL, Blanc WA (1979) Postmortem vitreous humor chemistry in sudden infant death syndrome and in other causes of death in childhood. Am J Clin Path 71:219-223
2. Choo-Kang E, McKoy C, Escoffrey C (1983) Vitreous humor analytes in assessing the postmortem interval and the antemortem clinical status. WJ Med J 32:23-26
3. Coe JI (1969) Postmortem Chemistries on vitreous humor. Am J Path 51/6:741-750
4. Coe JI, Apple FS (1985) Variations in vitreous humor chemical values as a result of instrumentation. J For Sci 30/3:828-835
5. Coe JI (1993) Postmortem Chemistry Update. Emphasis on Forensic Application. Am J For Med Pathol 14/2:91-117
6. Dykbaer R (1982) The Theory of Reference Values. Part 6: Presentation of Observed Values Related to Reference Values. J Clin Chem Clin Biochem 20:889-893
7. Gräsbeck R, Siest G, Wilding P, Williams GZ, Whitehead TP (1978) Provisional Recommendation on the Theory of Reference Values. Part 1: The Concept of Reference Values. J Clin Chem Clin Biochem 17:337-339
8. Leahy MS, Farber R (1967) Postmortem chemistry of human vitreous humor. J For Sci 12:214-222
9. Madea B, Henßge C (1992) Electrolyte Concentrations in Vitreous Humor and Cerebrospinal Fluid. In: Henßge C, Knight B, Madea B (eds) Determination of the Time since Death. Edward Arnold, London, in print
10. Madea B, Herrmann N (1994) Normal values in vitreous humor and on dysregulations which can be diagnosed postmortem. Proceedings of the 13th Congress International Association of Forensic Sciences, Düsseldorf, in print
11. Naumann HN (1959) Postmortem chemistry of the vitreous body in man. AMA Arch Ophthal 62:356-363
12. Sundermann jr FW (1975) Current Concepts of "Normal Values", and "Discrimination Values" in Clinical Chemistry. Clin Chem 21/3:1873-1877
13. Swift PGF, Worthy E, Emery JL (1974) Biochemical state of the vitreous humor of infants at necropsy. Arch Dis Child 49:680-685

14. Wilkie IW, Bellamy JEC (1981) Estimation of Antemortem Serum Electrolytes and Urea Concentrations from Vitreous Humor Collected Postmortem. Can J Comp Med 46:146-149

15. Schoning P, Strafuss AC (1980) Postmortem biochemical changes in canine vitreous humor. J For Sci 25:53-59

| | VUN | | | | | CREATININE | | | | | CALCIUM | | | | |
|---|---|---|---|---|---|---|---|---|---|---|---|---|---|---|---|
| | n | x | range | 1SD | 2SD | n | x | range | 1SD | 2SD | n | x | range | 1SD | 2SD |
| Naumann 1959 | 211 | 79 | 24-172 | | | 211 | 1.2 | 0.3-3.0 | | | 211 | 3.6 | 2.8-5.2mg/dl | | |
| Leahy / Faber 1967 | 30 | | | | 5-29 | 29 | | | | 0.31-1.05 | | | | | |
| Coe 1969* | 60<br>50<br>35 | 17<br>17<br>18 | 6-40<br>4-33<br>3-30 | 7.6<br>6.3<br>7.5 | | | | | | | | 6.7<br>1.67 | 6-8mg/dl<br>1.5-2.0mmol/l | | |

| | Na | | | | | Cl | | | | | Glucose | | | | |
|---|---|---|---|---|---|---|---|---|---|---|---|---|---|---|---|
| | n | x | range | 1SD | 2SD | n | x | range | 1SD | 2SD | n | x | range | 1SD | 2SD |
| Naumann 1959 | 211 | 144 | 118-154 | | | 211 | 144 | 89-145 | | | 211 | 62 | 17-105 | | |
| Leahy / Farber 1967 | 37 | | | | 128-158 | 39 | | | | 108-142 | 43 | | | | 28-89 |
| Coe 1969 * | 60<br>50<br>35 | 143<br>143<br>141 | 135-151<br>131-151<br>131-150 | 4.0<br>4.7<br>4.4 | | 60<br>50<br>35 | 121<br>119<br>118 | 108-132<br>105-132<br>104-130 | 5.9<br>6.1<br>6.8 | | 60<br>50<br>35 | 84<br>66<br>51 | 37-180<br>27-180<br>18-106 | 40<br>36<br>28 | |

* mean pm interval of sample acquisition:
1.75 h (0.5-2.5)
5.75 h (3-10)
17.25 h (10.5-29)

B:\MA-VO-89.TAB

**Fig. 1:** Standard deviations and observed ranges of different parameters in vitreous humor published as normal values in the literature.

| | CHLORIDE | SODIUM | CALCIUM | CREATININE |
|---|---|---|---|---|
| Serum reference values | 98-112 | 135-150 | 2.15-2.75 | 0.5-1.1 |
| Naumann 1959 | 89-145 | 118-154 | 0.7-1.3 | 0.31-1.05 |
| Leahy/Farber 1967 | 108-142 | 128-158 | | |
| Coe 1969 | 104-132 | 131-151 | 1.5-2 | |
| Lower-Upper Quartile | 117-130 | 144.3-155.5 | 1.53-1.85 | 0.38-0.66 |
| Med -s to Med +s | 112-135 | 138-158 | 1.35-2.01 | 0.18-0.79 |
| Med -2s to Med +2s | 100-147 | 128-168 | 1.03-2.33 | - 1.10 |

**Fig.2:** Own reference values (preliminary communication) in comparison to the literature. Presented are lower to upper quartile, which contain 50% of observed values and median ± first and second standard deviation.

# VITREOUS POTASSIUM DETERMINATION AS AN INDICATOR OF POST-MORTEM INTERVAL

## About six simultaneous deaths

F. Paraire*, F. Guillon*, C. Padonou*, M. Durigon

*Department of Pathology, and forensic pathology - Hospital R. Poincaré - 92380 Garches - France.

The autopsy of six subjects who instantaneously died in a plane crash was considered as an interesting model for studying the sensitivity of the method of determination of the post-mortem delay (PMD) by the measurement of the vitreous potassium (K) concentration.

## PATIENTS AND METHODS

Five adults, passengers of the plane, and one child hit by the plane, were the victims. All these six cadavers were transferred in our department in the same conditions, and were all preserved at 4° C until autopsy.

Two or three ml of vitreous humour were collected before the autopsy, and potassium concentration was determined by flame photometry.

## RESULTS

The PDM was calculated from a formula established in a previous study concerning 500 cases, performed in our department unpublished data :

$$\text{PMD (hours)} = (\text{K concentration in mM} \times 3.23) - 8.2$$

In this previous study the standard deviation was 9 h.

The results obtained in our present study are detailed on the following table ; the mean value ± SD was 21.4 h ± 4.4

| CASES | SEX | AGE | (K) mM/l | PMD (hours) |
|---|---|---|---|---|
| 1 | M | 32 | 9.8 | 23.45 ± 9 |
| 2 | M | 48 | 9.8 | 23.45 ± 9 |
| 3 | F | 33 | 8.8 | 20.22 ± 9 |
| 4 | M | 51 | 11.1 | 27.65 ± 9 |
| 5 | M | 36 | 7.2 | 15.05 ± 9 |
| 6 | M | 12 | 8.3 | 18.60 ± 9 |

## DISCUSSION

The right PMD existing from death to the vitreous humour collection was 19 hours. Thus our estimated PMD was not statistically different. However, even in this particular model. The standard deviation remains quite important.

Thus, the present results confirm the validity of our reference but underlines the law sensitivity of this method.

## REFERENCES

COE JJ (1973) Further thoughts and observations on post-mortem chemistry. Forensic Sci Gazette 5(5):2-6

MADEA B, HENSSGE C, HONIG W, GERBRACHT A (1989) References for determining the time of death by potassium in the vitreous humor. Forensic Sci Int 40:231-243

ESTIMATING THE POST-MORTEM INTERVAL IN IMMERSED CADAVERS : THE EXAMPLE OF AN ANIMAL MODEL

N.TELMON, D.ROUGE, J.F.BRUGNE, O.DELMAS, D.ALENGRIN, P.M.BRAS L.ARBUS

Service Médico-Judiciaire - CHU Toulouse-Rangueil (Pr L.ARBUS)
1 avenue Jean Poulhes F-31054 Toulouse Cedex

Many methods have been proposed to estimate the postmortem interval, based in particular on the heat loss of the cadaver. These methods have the advantage of being simple to use and giving a rapid result. However, they raise real problems when the cadaver has been immersed, either totally, partially or temporarily.

This study compares post-mortem heat loss in an animal model in two different situations: a cadaver in a normal environment or immersed in water.

## MATERIAL AND METHODS

Post-mortem heat loss was studied in 20 dead Wistar rats under different conditions. The temperature of each animal was measured using thermistors placed in the abdominal cavity after incision followed by watertight suture. The temperature was taken every 15 minutes, and the degree of accuracy approached 0.1°C.

The animals were divided into four groups and subjected to different conditions (air : 22.8°C and 2.9°C, water : 22.8°C and 3.5 °C). The volume of air or water was sufficient for the environmental temperature to remain stable during the study. The stability of environmental temperature was checked during the experimentation .

## RESULTS

Heat transfer between the cadaver and the external environment takes place by convection depending on the nature and area of the surface by which exchange takes place and on the nature of the environment. The body surface areas of the animals in the different groups were comparable, given that body surface area is proportional to the weight of the animal. (Table 1)

Table 1

| | weight |
|---|---|
| air | 290.5 g (± 59 g) |
| water | 290,6 g (± 45 g) |

The experimental conditions (animals from a laboratory of experimental surgery) did not permit study of heat loss immediately after death. Mean interval after death was one hour. However, the initial temperature of the animals in the different groups was comparable (Table 2). This delay in the initial measurement of temperature and the small size of the animals certainly account for the fact that we found no plateau of heat loss after death.

Table 2

| | initial temperature |
|---|---|
| air | 29.8°C (± 3.1°C) |
| water | 30.4°C (± 2.8°C) |

Influence of the environment and of temperature
on the kinetics of heat loss :

The progression of the heat loss curve during the first two hours is influenced by the nature of the environment, whatever the temperature of the latter.

In air, the temperature decreases in a logarithmic fashion. In water, heat is lost more rapidly and follows a type 2 polynomial curve (Fig.1)

Fig.1

(air) t°C = 34,244 - 0,11337time + 3,7027e-4time^2 R^2 = 0,997

(water) t°C = 33,200 + -4,8787*LOG(time) R^2 = 0,976

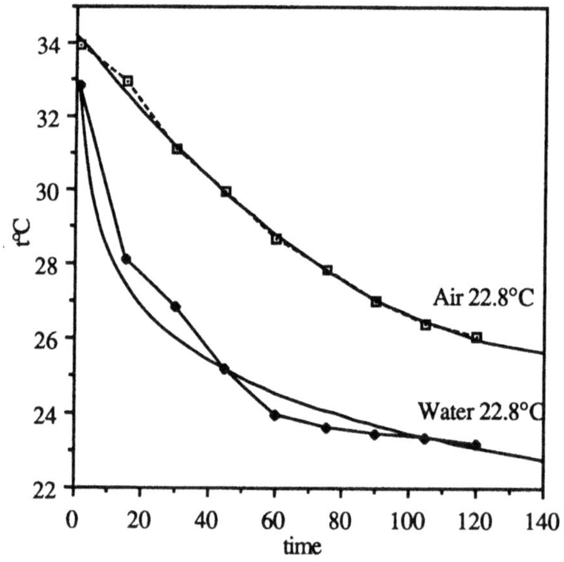


At 22.8°C, after one hour, immersed rat cadavers had lost 7.3°C, where as those in a normal air environment had only lost 4.7°C. The same phenomenon was observed in the two

different environments at a lower external temperature: - 21°C in water and - 16.8° in air.

This acceleration of heat loss in water as compared to air decreases as the post-mortem interval increases. For small animals, heat-loss curves after two hours are almost iinear. The initial decrease of these curves is greater for animals in air because there is a greater difference between the temperature of the cadaver and that of the external environment.

On a mean, equilibrium between the temperature of the cadaver and that of the environment is reached : in air at 22.8° C, in 300 min
in water at 22.8°C, in 240 min
in air at 2.9°C, in 360 min
in water at 3.5°C, in 180 min. (Fig.2)

Fig.2

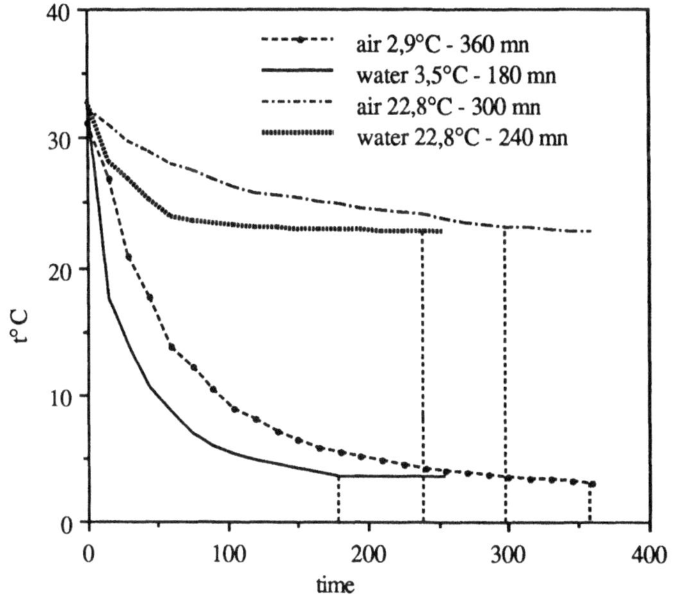


Secondary immersion: a cadaver has first been left in air and then immersed later: the curve of post-mortem heat loss shows three slopes (Fig.3). The first corresponds to heat loss in air, then a second slope represents accelerated heat loss during immersion and then there is a third slope during which the temperature of the cadaver approaches that of the environment. Heat loss therefore depends not only on the various temperatures, but also on the moment at which the cadaver was immersed and on the duration of immersion. Determination of post-mortem interval based on cadaver temperature is not possible in the case of a corpse found in a bath, which may have been filled at any time.

Fig.3

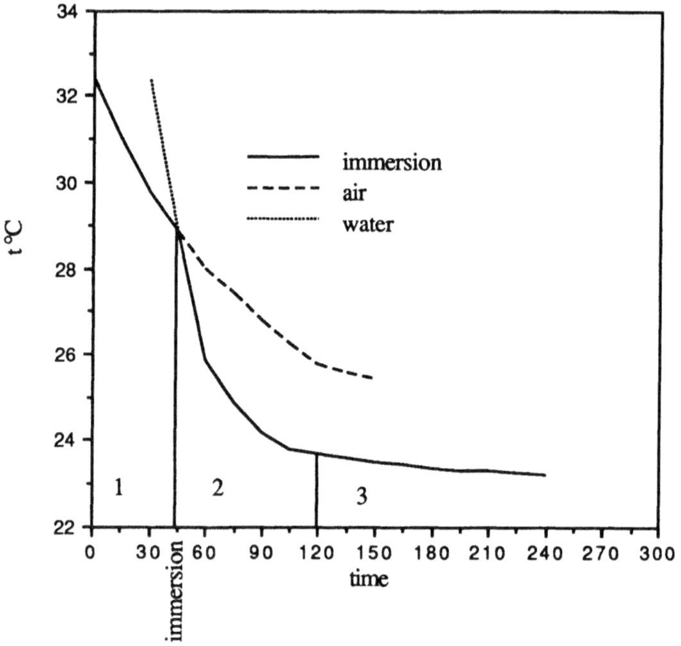


Immersion of a corpse in water accelerates heat loss, the more so if there is a considerable difference of temperature between the corpse and the environment. Therefore, in the case of immersion, all methods of estimation of the post-mortem interval based on temperature overestimate the time elapsed since death. Empirical correction factors exist but do not allow precise estimation. in the event of secondary immersion, estimation of the post-mortem interval by a temperature-based method appears hazardous because of the multiple factors involved: temperatures of the corpse and of the two environments, time spent in air and in water, sequence air-water or water-air.

References :


Henssge C., Death time estimation in case work. The rectal temperature of death nomogram. *Forensic Science International*, 1988, Vol.38, pp. 209-236

Henssge C., Madea B., Gallenkemper E., Death time estimation in case work. Integration of different methods. *Forensic Science International*, 1988, Vol.39, pp. 77-87

Knight, B.H., Estimation of the time since death by body cooling, in *Forensic Pathology*, pp. 72-82

Knight, B.H., The evolution of methods for estimating the time of death from body temperature, *Forensic Science International*, 1988, Vol.36, pp. 47-55

Lynnerup, N., A computer program for the estimation of time of death, *Journal of Forensic Sciences*, JFSCA, Vol 38, N°4, July 1993, pp. 816-820

# 12. Interpretation of Post Mortem Toxicological Data

## COMPARISON BETWEEN MORPHINE LEVELS IN SUBJECTS WHO DIED OF ACUTE NARCOTISM AND SUBJECTS WHO DIED OF OTHER CAUSES

Marina CALIGARA, Fausto GIGLI, Franco LODI, Franco MAROZZI,
Claudio MECACCI, Enzo RONCHI, Riccardo ZOJA
*Institute of Forensic Medicine, University of Milan, Via Mangiagalli, 37 20133 MILAN*

Between 1978 and 1992 1435 autopsies were performed at the Milan University Institute of Forensic Medicine; samples of biological fluids and viscera were collected during the post-mortem examination and chemical and toxicological tests were carried out; once the presence of morphine was determined, it was then dosed via the radioimmunoassay (RIA). None of the cases had been subjected to any pharmacological therapy.

In 1248 subjects (AN), the cause of death was identified as "acute narcotism", that is, besides the presence of morphine during the post-mortem examination, no other factor that might have linked the death to any pathological form, be it natural or due to an exogenous injury, was found.

On the other hand, in 187 cases (NOAN), the cause of death was ascribed to other lethal mechanisms, despite the presence of morphine detected during the chemical tests.

The characteristics of the two samples are illustrated in Table 1, which does not show, as can be noted, any differences between the two classes.

Table 1

| | *AN* | *NOAN* |
|---|---|---|
| n | 1248 | 187 |
| average age | 27 years | 27,6 years |
| male | 1080 | 163 |
| female | 168 | 24 |

In Table 2, the NOANs have been divided according to type of exogenous injury and according to cause of death.

Table 2

| | | Murders | Suicides | Accidents | Road accid. | TOTAL |
|---|---|---|---|---|---|---|
| Hanging | | | 17 | | | 17 |
| Struggling | | 1 | | | | 1 |
| Strangulation | | 1 | | | | 1 |
| Drowning | | 1 | 2 | | | 3 |
| Fire-arm shot | | 29 | 3 | 2 | | 34 |
| Injury thrust and cut | | 6 | 1 | | | 7 |
| Fall | | 1 | 14 | 1 | 46 | 50 |
| CO poisoning | | | 18 | 2 | | 20 |
| Organophosphoric ester poisoning | | | 1 | | | 1 |
| Barbiturate poisoning | | | 1 | | | 1 |
| Burns | | 2 | 1 | 4 | | 7 |
| Natural deaths | 17 | | | | | |

The average values and corresponding standard deviations (SD) of the quantitative levels (mcg/ml) of morphine present in biological fluids (blood, urine, bile) collected were then calculated and the ANs and the NOANs were compared giving rise to the following results (Table 3).

Table 3

AN

| | Blood | Urine | Bile |
|---|---|---|---|
| Mean | 1,272 | 25,097 | 52,617 |
| n | 1208 | 1118 | 1127 |
| SD | 1,084 | 46,511 | 78,066 |

NOAN

| | Blood | Urine | Bile |
|---|---|---|---|
| Mean | 0,455 | 35,963 | 45,304 |
| n | 180 | 157 | 151 |
| SD | 0,634 | 67,534 | 83,496 |

Note: these concentrations are determined with radiommunoassay technique (Abuscreen Roche for morphine)

The two samples were compared using Student's T-test and a statistically significant difference was found as far as the urinary and, above all, hematic, values were concerned.
Still amongst the examined cases, in the NOANs the average blood morphine level was equal to or greater than the one observed in the ANs.
The NOAN cases were then divided, as far as average morphine concentrations both in biological fluids and (where possible) in viscera, into three samples as indicated in Table 4.

Table 4

| Groups | | Blood mcg/ml | Urine mcg/ml | Bile mcg/ml | Liver mcg/g | Kidney mcg/g | Brain mcg/g | Lung mcg/g |
|---|---|---|---|---|---|---|---|---|
| | Mean | 0,455 | 35,963 | 45,304 | 0,593 | 0,873 | 0,265 | 0,556 |
| A | n | 180 | 157 | 151 | 53 | 52 | 52 | 53 |
| | SD | 0,634 | 67,534 | 83,496 | 0,824 | 1,758 | 0,420 | 0,816 |
| | Mean | 0,264 | 31,391 | 36,592 | 0,434 | 0,767 | 0,213 | 0,461 |
| B | n | 159 | 138 | 135 | 45 | 45 | 45 | 45 |
| | SD | 0,313 | 62,179 | 71,645 | 0,676 | 1,823 | 0,307 | 0,758 |
| | Mean | 1,898 | 69,175 | 118,807 | 1,482 | 1,551 | 0,597 | 1,089 |
| C | n | 21 | 19 | 16 | 8 | 7 | 7 | 8 |
| | SD | 0,586 | 93,683 | 131,964 | 1,049 | 1,125 | 0,811 | 0,978 |

NOTE Group A = all cases
Group B = cases with blood concentration of morphine < 1,27 mcg/ml
Group C = cases with blood concentration of morphine >= 1,27 mcg/ml

The results show that the hematic, encephalic and hepatic values of group C are clearly higher than those of groups A and B and that both in group A and in group B the renal values are clearly higher than the hepatic ones, while in group C the values are more or less the same. In terms of pharmacokinetic analysis it can be stated that the data concerning group C are consistent with a morphine distribution and absorption phase (relatively high blood value, hepatic and renal levels below the hematic level with a greater hepatic value or, at least, similar to the renal one). On the contrary, in the other two groups the data found seem to indicate, for symmetrically opposite reasons, a classical elimination phase of the compound.

Having said this, it must be stated that the cases examined in group C can be correlated with death that occurred soon after the intake of the drug, and also presented levels which are similar to the ones observed, on average, in cases relating to deaths ascribed to "acute intravenous narcotism"; the morphine levels in the remaining NOAN cases can instead be correlated with an intake which took place much before death and this result, even though the dose is not known, derives from data obtained on the distribution of the toxic substance dependent upon the morphine levels detected in organic fluids and tissues.

However, the most important data that emerges from the analysis of the above results concerns the fact that in a significant number of cases (21, i.e. 11.6% of the NOAN group) the values of the morphine compound were equal or even much higher than the average values found in deaths caused by "acute narcotism" and despite these levels, usually considered "lethal", the cause of death was completely different.

All this might, perhaps, be explained with the fact that the high morphine levels found can be ascribed to two different pharmacological modalities: in one case the morphine had already exceeded its maximum activity and death occurred when this activity was diminishing; in the second case the morphine had not yet reached its peak activity so in these subjects the heroin might have determined soon after, and on its own, the death of the subject if, so to say, it had not been "overtaken" by another completely different pathological mechanism before having its lethal effect. Perhaps this hypothesis could be confirmed by a few concrete elements in cases of road-accidents or suicide, but it could hardly be applied to murder cases, especially if one considers the consequences involved during criminal proceedings.

On the other hand, due to the high average biliary concentration of morphine found in group C (118.8 mcg/ml) compared to the much lower one found in groups A (45.3 mcg/ml) and B (36.5 mcg/ml), the hypothesis that in group C, since bile is the organic compound where morphine deposits itself for the longest period and a high biliary morphine concentration usually corresponds to the habit of assuming considerable amounts, the subjects were, in any case, more "tolerant" towards the drug's administration and, subsequently, less sensitive to its depressive effects on the central nervous system.

Apart from the above considerations, and although the results found amongst the NOANs of group C were surprising, the most significant data is that the average blood morphine level is clearly and statistically lower than the one found amongst the ANs, considering the above cases both globally (A) and, above all, separately (B that results from class A from which the cases of group C have been removed).

Having said this, it is clear that the cases of group C represent an exception that proves the rule according to which the lethal mechanism of "acute narcotism" usually occurs when the hematic values of morphine reach approximately 1 mcg/ml; however, this is generally the case, but exceptions of considerable importance are possible.

Therefore, data acquired scientifically by using a statistical method, as in the case of death from "acute narcotism", cannot be considered absolute proof in the medico-legal field but, it certainly should not be underestimated since it represents significant "useful reference".

In conclusion, we can therefore assert that the diagnosis of death due to "acute narcotism" must be the result of a "complete" medico-legal approach that enhances the results of toxicological examinations after having deeply analysed any other possible causes of death that could, even alone, be proof of the outcome.

REFERENCES


Bastos ML, Galante L (1976) Toxicological findings in victims of traumatic deaths. J For Sci 21, 1: 176-185

Caligara M, Gigli F, Lodi F, Marozzi E, Marozzi F, Zoja R (1990) Mortalità da droga in Milano nel decennio 1978-1987.Nota I: dati demoscopici. Riv It Med Leg XII : 139-161

Caligara M, Gigli F, Lodi F, Marozzi E, Marozzi F, Zoja R (1991) Mortalità da droga in Milano nel decennio 1978-1987.Nota II: i dati tossicologici. Riv It Med Leg XIII: 839-854

Cimbura G, Lucas DM, Bennet RC, Warren RA, Simpson HM (1982) Incidence and toxicological aspects of drugs detected in 484 fatally injured drivers and pedestrian in Ontario. J For Sci 27, 4: 855-867

Falzi G, Goj C, Lodi F, Marozzi E, Zoja R (1989) "Acute narcotism": rilievi su una casistica di morti ravvicinati. Arch Med Leg Ass 11, 1:

Garriot JC, Sturner M (1973) Morphine concentrations and survival periods in acute heroin fatalities. New England J Med, 289, 24

Garriot JC, Latman N (1976) Drug detection in cases of driving under the influence. J For Sci 21, 2: 398-415

Garriot JC, Di Maio WJ, Zumwalt R, Petty CS (1977) Incidence of Drugs and alcohol in fatally injured motor vehicle drivers. J For Sci 22, 2: 383-389

Grandi M, Lodi F, Marozzi E (1985) Rilievi su di una serie ravvicinata di decessi per "acute intravenous narcotism". Arch Med Leg Ass 7: 158-163

Hine CH, Wright JA, Allison DJ, Stephens BG, Pasi A (1982) Analysis of fatalities from acute narcotism in a major urban area. J For Sci 27, 2: 372-284

Kintz P, Mangin P, Lugnier A, Chaumont AJ (1989) Toxicological data after Heroin Overdose. Human Tox 8: 487-489

Mari F, Bertol E (1983) Morphine plasma levels during opiate overdoses: an year report. Arch Med Leg Ass 3-4: 185-191

Marozzi E, Ronchi E, Marozzi F, Zoja R (1990) Confronto fra i livelli di morfina riscontrati in soggetti deceduti per "acute narcotism" e soggetti morti per altre cause: considerazioni tossicologiche e medico-legali. Arch Med Leg Ass 12: 66-80

Monforte JR, Spitz UW (1975) Narcotic abuse among homicide victims in Detroit. J For Sci 20, 1: 186-190

Norton LE, Garriot JC, Di Maio WJ (1981) Drug detection on autopsy: a prospective study of 247 cases. J For Sci 26, 1: 66

Owens SM, Mc Bay AJ, Cook CA (1983) The use of marijuana, ethanol and other drugs among drivers killed oin single vehicle crashes. J For Sci 28, 2: 372-379

Zimney EL, Luke JL (1981) Narcotic related deaths in the district of Columbia 1971-1979. J For Sci 26, 3: 462-469

# Carbon Monoxide Suicide by Car Exhaust Gas

Marc DEVEAUX (Ph.D.), Eric LAURIER (M.D.), Valery HEDOUIN (M.D.), Eric REVUELTA (M.D.), and Didier GOSSET (Ph.D.).

Institut de Médecine Légale, place Théo Varlet F-59000 Lille, France.

## Introduction

Most of the deaths as a result of carbon monoxide are accidental or behavioral. Inhalation of carbon monoxide as a method of suicide is actually rare, since lighting gas and water gas do no more exist in France. So in case of suicide, the most common source of carbon monoxide is automobile exhaust gas. We describe here a case of suicide in a car by carbon monoxide.

## Case report

In december 1993, at 9.00 a.m., the body of a 30-year-old north-african male was found in a car. He was sat on the driver's side and the back of the seat was sloped, so he was looking sleeping.

Examination of the body showed muscular rigidity, pale pink livor on the back, paradoxal livor around the navel and the anterior face of the legs. The body was quite tepid and there was no trace of fight.

Examination of the car showed an external rubber pipe connected between the exhaust stoke and the binnacle, running through the rear lights and the luggage compartment. Finally the rear loud-speakers were removed, allowing the diffusion of exhaust gas in the passenger compartment. The car was locked and the petrol tank was empty. A knife was found in the gully, probably used for cutting the rubber pipe. This rubber pipe was a part of a vacuum trainer

A complete autopsy was performed. General immunochemical analyses for opiates, cocaine, amphetamines, barbiturates, benzodiazepines, tricyclic antidepressants and cannabinoids in blood and urine remained negative. Blood alcohol concentration and urine alcohol concentration were equal to zero. Determination of carboxyhemoglobin was performed by visible spectrometry and revealed a concentration of 80%.

The victim had an history of suicide tendencies by phlebotomy. We returned a verdict of suicide by carbon monoxide from the exhaust gas of the car.

## Discussion

Death resulting from inhalation of carbon monoxide from exhaust fumes of automobiles may occur in different ways :

1/ accidental or behavioral

a - in a close structure like mechanic garage or multistorey car park [1],

b - in the car itself, due to faulty exhaust system with abnormal communication between the passenger compartment and the outside world [2].

2/ suicide

a - indoors in an hermetically closed garage [3, 4],

b - outdoors : victims are also severly burnt on head or arm [5],

c - in the car itself.

Suicides by exhaust gas in the car itself are discribed since many years : we found two well documented references by Ollivier in 1958 [6] and 1961 [7]. Victims are always inventive to connect the exhaust pipe to the passenger compartment [8]. Carboxyhemoglobin levels in these case are often as great as those of fire victims [5,9]. Exhaust of gasoline engine have amounts of carbon monoxide ranging from 4.5% (moving car) to 12% (idling car).

The unusual nature of our case lies in the way that the car was parked in a busy street since 10.00 p.m.the evening before and no passer-by was astonished before 9.00 a.m. In a second hand, the rubber pipe must have been fixed on site, because the police knew that this car was parked here from many days and that a tyre was flat.

## References


1 Schirmacher P, Zander R (1988) CO-Belastungen bei Personal und Benutzern von Tiefgaragen. Arbeitsmed Sozialmed Präventivmed 24:5-8

2 Caplan YH, Thompson BC, Levine B, Masemore W (1986) Accidental poisonings involving carbon monoxide, heating systems and confined spaces. J Forensic Sci 31:117-121

3 Bowen DAL, Duffy P, Callear A,Fitton J (1989) Carbon monoxide poisoning. Forens Sci Int 41:163-168

4 Pounder DJ (1991) Changing patterns of male suicide in Scotland. Forens Sci Int 51:79-87

5 DiMaio VJM, Dana SE (1987) Deaths caused by carbon monoxide poisoning in an open environment (outdoors). J Forensic Sci 32:1794-1795

6 Ollivier H, Robert F, Desideri D 1958) Un procédé original de suicide oxycarboné. Ann Méd Lég 38:30-31

7 Ollivier H, Vuillet F, Quicke J (1961) Suicide oxycarboné par gaz d'échappement d'automobile. Ann Méd Lég 41:589-592

8 Turletti M, Lubinu F, Sini MG, Testoni S (1979) Suicido da ossido di carbonio mediante gas di scarico di un utoveicolo. Minerva Medicoleg Arch Anthropol Crim 99:121-126

9 Jardé O, Buteux P, Kremp O, Deveaux M, Lenoir L, Doutrellot C (1994) Problèmes médico-légaux posés par la mort au cours des incendies: à propos de 33 observations. J Med Leg Droit Med 37: 3-6

# TOXICOLOGICAL FINDINGS AFTER SEVERAL YEARS OF BURIAL

**H. Käferstein[1], B. Madea[1], G. Sticht[1], H. Sachs[2]**

1. Institute of Legal Medicine, Melatengürtel 60, D-50823 Köln
2. Institute of Legal Medicine, Prittwitzstr. 6, D-89070 Ulm

## INTRODUCTION

Weinig wrote in 1966 a review on toxicological findings after exhumation that the number of papers on the identification of drugs after exhumation is surprisingly small. Although the analytical methods have been improved considerably in the last nearly 30 years, only very few reports in the literature on identification of drugs in exhumated bodies where published (2 - 6). In some cases e.g. Sticht et al. (1981) the identification of drugs was only possible in the stomach or body tissue in the area where the stomach has normally its topographical localisation.

We had the task to perform toxicological analyses in 6 cases - one male and 5 females - after exhumation in order to clear the cause of death. A visiting nurse was under suspicion to have poisoned some of her patients 81 to 92 years of age. The results are presented and discussed.

## CASES AND METHODOLOGY

The lay-time of the exhumated bodies varied between 2.3 and 7.5 years. The bodies were mainly buried in the cold season. In spite of the long lay-times in most cases the gastrointestinal tract was preserved in whole length and continuity, the organs could be identified macroscopically.

For toxicological analysis the organs were prepared according to the well known method of Alha and Lindfors (1959).

The extraction was performed in acidic milieu with hexane, then in alcalic milieu with chloroform. For the identification of basic substances the residue was analyzed using HPLC/DAD and GC/MS. Hair was washed and extracted according to the methodology of Sachs and Raff (1993). The analysis was performed after derivatisation with MSTFA by GC/MS.

## RESULTS

In case 1 - 4 with lay-times up to 5.5 years via the UV-spectra and retention time chlorprothixene could be identified in all organs still avaibable e.g. brain, liver, lung hilus, muscle of the thigth or of the upperarm. But it was not possible to detect chlorprothixene in the hair of these cases.

In case 3 besides chlorprothixene only very small amounts of norchlorprothixene, diazepam as well as small amounts of nordiazepam could be identified.

In case 4 the organs of the abdomen could no longer be identified, therefore liver was not analyzed. It was particularly interesting that various drugs could be identified. These were besides chlorprothixene and diazepam methaqualone, guaifenesin, amitriptyline, diphenhydramine, doxylamine and desalkylflurazepam which could be identified in abdominal tissue, brain and muscles of the thigh. In this case in the hair methaqualone was identified, chlorprothixene was not detectable. The case history showed, that the woman had a chronic misuse of several sedatives exspecially methaqualone.

In case 5 exclusively diazepam and nordiazepam could be identified in the organs. Chlorprothixene and its metabolites however could not be determined. In case 6 with 7.5 years of lay-time only furosemide could be identified.

Table 1: Concentration in Brain (B) and Liver (L) in 5 exhumated bodies
Chlorprothixene (CPT), Diazepam (D), Nordiazepam (N)

| Case | postmortem interval (years) | organ g | water content % | CPT mg/kg | D mg/kg | N mg/kg |
|---|---|---|---|---|---|---|
| 1 | 2.3 | B 490 | 78 | 13 | - | - |
| | | L 720 | 71 | 12 | - | - |
| 2 | 3.5 | B 480 | 73 | 4 | - | - |
| | | L 330 | 71 | 21 | - | - |
| 3 | 4.9 | B 308 | 75 | 4 | 1.7 | - |
| | | L 147 | 65 | 179 | 43 | 1.4 |
| 4 | 5.5 | B 145 | 70 | 18 | 1.0 | - |
| | | L --- | -- | - | - | - |
| 5 | 7.5 | B 365 | 73 | - | 1.4 | 0.33 |
| | | L 350 | 65 | - | 8.0 | 0.35 |

In table 1 the results of the cases 1 - 5 for brain and liver are shown.

While the water content of these organs is comparable to those of fresh bodies, the organ weights are due to postmortem changes decreased widely.

Case 2 shall be briefly addressed some more detailled: The woman was found helpless in her home. The emergency doctor diagnosed a drug intoxication. However in hospital the doctors formulated the differential diagnoses cardiogenic shock due to coronary artery disease or left hemispheric apoplexy together with apoplexy of the brain stem. 3 days later the woman died in cardiogenic shock. The body was buried without further investigations and exhumed only 3 1/2 years later. In the liver then a Chlorprothixene concentration of 21 mg/kg was measured.

Additionally we could identify in this case after separation with HPLC substances with similar UV-spectra using GC-MS, norchlorprothixene, hydroxychlorprothixene as well as 2 different hydroxy-norchlorprothixenes. Another metabolite with corresponding UV-spectrum could not be identified. Sulphoxides of chlorprothixene with different UV-spectra were also found.

The chlorprothixene metabolites in the liver amount to 40 % and in the brain to 10 % of the chlorprothixene amount which corresponds very well to a survival time of a few days.

**DISCUSSION**

The postmortem duration of detection of significant morphological findings which declare the cause of death after exhumation is reported to vary between some weeks and months - depending on the cause of death and other factors (Althoff, 1974). Compared to this organic poisons can be detected over a much longer postmortem interval after burial even in tissues aside the gastrointestinal tract. For the preparation of putrefied tissue the method of Alha and Lindfors can be recommended. By this method pure extracts are achieved which allow an identification via UV-spectra after separation with HPLC. The HPLC can be further recommended for fractionating and sucessive GC/MS-analysis as shown by Daldrup (1992) in cases with very low clonidine-levels in human bodies with lay-times up to 29 months.

Besides the qualitative and quantitative detection of drugs the metabolites can be identified as well. During life oxydative reactions are predominant, but after burial reductive circumstances. Even after several years of burial a basis for the judgement on the time course of an intoxication may be found. In our opinion the detection and identification of many organic drugs which are in use today and may cause death should be possible as long as some identifiable rest of body tissue is present - besides gastrointestinal tract, muscles and brain. This will depend on the state of putrefaction at burial and the circumstances in the earth grave, but a successfull detection of organic poisons should be expected up to 7 - 10 years if there are similar conditions in the grave as in Cologne. In our area we have to assume that the temperature in a grave is between 4°C and 10°C (Weinig 1957).

If we are asked if an exhumation in order to clear a suspicious intoxication does make sense we recommend it always in the interval up to 7 - 10 years postmortem.

The main question is at any rate how positive investigation results are to be valued after such long lay-times and which organs are best suitable for interpretation of the results. Brain is very important for an judgement since a postmortem diffusion from the gastrointestinal tract into the brain cannot take place. On the other hand liver tissue gives according to Christensen (1974) in fresh bodies the best results to form an opinion.

But after long lay-times of bodies each investigation result of material out of the gastrointestinal tract may be falsified by postmortem diffusion. It's our opinion that investigation of brain can deliver the most reliable results. Investigation of hair should be included in the investigation sheme especially after exhumation. After chronic intake of therapeutical doses of chlorprothixene concentatration between 1 to 5 ng per mg hair are probably to be expected. But in haires of our exhumed bodies no chlorprothixene could be detected although high concentrations were found in the organs. However in the case 4 of a known methaqualone abuse this drug was detected not only in brain and muscle but also in the hair. This confirms from our point of view the assumption that the cases 1 to 4 are acute intoxications without preceding chronic chlorprothixene intake.

A correction of the measured values in the tissues using water content is hardly practicable because the water content of brain has not altered significantly even after lay-times of several years whereas the loss of organic substance is remarkable. The question if a correction to the mass of brain in the life time is practicable is to be proved. Assumption for this would be that the brain substance is consumed or extracted postmortem but not the drug. This might be the case for the highly lipophilic chlorprothixene but perhaps not in the same way for some of the metabolites.

In our opinion estimation of drug concentration in brain tissue is essential in every case of intoxication. By this a basis is formed for a valuation of intoxications even after lay-taimes of several years.

**LITERATURE**


1. Weinig E (1966) Gift und Vergiftung. In: R. Sivert's Handwörterbuch der Kriminologie. W. de Gruyter und Co Berlin 333-350

2. Katte W (1967) Strychnin-Nachweis in Kindesleiche nach 5 Jahren Erdbestattung. Arch Kriminol 139:28-31

3. Pöhlmann E, Schwerd W (1976) Zum Nachweis von E 605 in einer nach 21-monatiger Liegezeit exhumierten Leiche. Z.Rechtsmed 77:233-236

4. Käferstein H (1981) Schwer flüchtige organische Gifte in Fäulnisleichen - Nachweisbarkeit und Beurteilungsmöglichkeiten. Beitr Gerichtl Med 39:119-124

5. Sticht G, Ramme H, Dotzauer G (1981) Morphologische und toxikologische Befunde nach 17jähriger Liegezeit einer Leiche. Beitr Gerichtl Med 39:177-193

6. Daldrup T (1992) pers. communication

7. Alha AR, Lindfors RO (1959) Use of Acetone in the isolation of organic poisons from biological material. Ann Med Exp Biol Fennae 37:149-156

8. Sachs H, Raff I (1993) Comparison of quantitative results of drugs in human hair by GC.MS. Forens Sci Int 63:207-216

9. Althoff H (1974) Bei welchen Fragestellungen kann man aussagefähige pathomorphologische Befunde nach Exhumierung erwarten? Z.Rechtsmed 75:1-20

10. Weinig E (1957) In Ponsold A: Lehrbuch der gerichtlichen Medizin. 2. ed. P 509

11. Christensen H (1974) Chlorprothixene and its metabolites in blood, liver and urine from fatal poisoning. Acta pharmacol toxicol 34:16-26

# COMPARISON BETWEEN MORPHINE LEVELS IN THE BLOOD AND IN THE MUSCULO-SKELETAL SYSTEM OF SUBJECTS WHO DIED OF ACUTE INTRAVENOUS NARCOTISM

Marozzi E, Caligara M, Mecacci C, Genovese U

*Institute of Forensic Medicine, University of Milan, Via Mangiagalli, 37 20100 Milan*

This study starts from the difficulties found when establishing the cause of death in subjects who died of probable acute narcotism and found in an advanced state of decomposition, where the only tissue specimen that can be collected is muscle.

Even though the other authors (3, 4, 9, 10) have already dealt with this subject before us, we thought it would be useful to commence a comparative study between morphine concentrations in blood and in the muscle tissue of subjects examined between 24 and 72 hours after death at the Milan Institute of Forensic Medicine.

To do this, we selected 24 cases where there was an history of drug addiction and where no evidence or hint of the cause of death had been found during the post-mortem examination, and where no other suitable data existed that could supply a different cause of death other than death caused by acute narcotism.

Apart from the habitual collection of viscera and biological fluids, during the autopsy, muscle tissue fragments (sternocleidomastoid and iliopsas) were collected.

*Material and Methods*

1 ml of femoral and thoracic blood, 1 g of both muscles (sternocleidomastoideus and iliopsas), 9 ml of distilled water were added. There were agitated using the vortex and preserved at 4 C° for five days and agitated daily. On the sixth day each specimen was agitated once again in the vortex and centrifugated at 5.000 rpm for 15 minutes; 25 mcl of the floating contents were collected and tested with the Radioimmunoassay procedure, using the Abuscreen kit for morphine of the Roche Diagnostic Division.

**Table number 1**

MORPHINE CONCENTRATIONS IN BLOOD AND MUSCLES (mcg/ml or /g)

| Case N° | Age (Years) | Sex | Femoral Blood | Toracic Blood | IP Muscle | SCM Muscle | Blood Alcohol (g/L) | Other drugs found |
|---|---|---|---|---|---|---|---|---|
| 1 | 28 | M | 0,56 | 2,46 | 0,44 | 0,66 | 0,00 | None |
| 2 | 32 | M | 11,25 | 2,49 | 1,51 | 1,71 | 0,49 | None |
| 3 | 30 | M | 0,85 | 2,58 | 0,58 | 0,31 | 0,88 | BDZ |
| 4 | 27 | M | 0,39 | 1,80 | 0,33 | 0,84 | 0,00 | None |
| 5 | 20 | F | 0,79 | 0,53 | 0,00 | 0,00 | 0,00 | None |
| 6 | 40 | M | 0,55 | 1,13 | 0,32 | 0,20 | 0,19 | None |
| 7 | 30 | M | 0,60 | 0,36 | 0,45 | 0,10 | 0,19 | Cannabinoid |
| 8 | 25 | M | 1,01 | 1,39 | 1,82 | 0,77 | 0,00 | BDZ |
| 9 | 35 | M | 0,10 | 0,25 | 0,05 | 0,00 | 1,89 | None |
| 10 | 25 | M | 0,65 | 0,66 | 0,10 | 0,00 | 0,00 | Cannabinoid |
| 11 | 29 | M | 0,84 | 1,18 | 0,06 | 0,61 | 0,00 | None |
| 12 | 22 | M | 0,69 | 0,16 | 0,39 | 0,00 | 0,00 | None |
| 13 | 20 | M | 0,76 | 1,40 | 0,27 | 0,35 | 0,67 | BDZ |
| 14 | 32 | M | 0,52 | 0,30 | 0,00 | 0,00 | 0,79 | None |
| 15 | 27 | M | 0,05 | 0,54 | 0,00 | 0,08 | 1,34 | None |
| 16 | 20 | M | 0,83 | 1,22 | 0,39 | 0,08 | 0,10 | None |
| 17 | 36 | M | 0,06 | 0,56 | 0,00 | 0,05 | 1,30 | Cocaine |
| 18 | 19 | M | 0,80 | 0,68 | 0,20 | 0,06 | 0,00 | None |
| 19 | 28 | M | 0,57 | 1,29 | 0,39 | 0,63 | 0,65 | None |
| 20 | 28 | M | 0,64 | 0,92 | 0,06 | 0,07 | 0,00 | BDZ |
| 21 | 24 | M | 0,51 | 1,32 | 0,33 | 0,10 | 0,00 | BDZ |
| 22 | 34 | M | 0,60 | 0,49 | 0,08 | 0,00 | 1,98 | None |
| 23 | 30 | M | 3,26 | 0,58 | 0,08 | 0,10 | 0,00 | Cocaine |
| 24 | 27 | M | 0,34 | 2,15 | 0,34 | 0,69 | 0,00 | Barbiturates |

Legend: IP = Iliopsoas Muscle SCM = Sternocleidomastoideus Muscle BDZ = Benzodiazepines

Table number 2

MORPHINE CONCENTRATIONS IN BLOOD AND MUSCLE (MCG/ML or G): EVALUATION OF ANALYTICAL RESULTS

| | Femoral Blood | Toracic Blood | IP Muscle | SCM Muscle |
|---|---|---|---|---|
| Observations | 24 | 24 | 24 | 24 |
| Mean | 1,134 | 1,102 | 0,341 | 0,309 |
| Range | 0,050-11,250 | 0,160-2,420 | 0,000-1,820 | 0,000-1,710 |
| Median | 0,620 | 1,025 | 0,295 | 0,100 |
| Standard Error | 0,457 | 0,151 | 0,091 | 0,084 |
| Variance | 5,003 | 0,548 | 0,199 | 0,171 |
| Standard Deviation | 2,237 | 0,741 | 0,446 | 0,413 |

Due to problems mainly relating to lack of time, the brain, lung, kidney liver, urine and bile morphine concentrations were determined only in six of the above cases (Table 3).

Table number 3

MORPHINE CONCENTRATIONS (mcg/ml or /g) IN BODY FLUIDS, TISSUES AND MUSCLES IN 6 STUDIED CASES

| Case N° | Femoral Blood | Toracic Blood | Urine | Bile | Liver | Kidney | Brain | Lung | IP Muscle | SCM Muscle | Blood Alcohol g/L | Other drugs found |
|---|---|---|---|---|---|---|---|---|---|---|---|---|
| 2 | 11,25 | 2,49 | 68,90 | 25,69 | 3,68 | 4,63 | 0,80 | 5,10 | 1,51 | 1,71 | 0,49 | None |
| 6 | 0,55 | 1,13 | 57,64 | 120,93 | 1,35 | 0,91 | 0,50 | 0,62 | 0,32 | 0,20 | 0,19 | None |
| 8 | 1,01 | 1,39 | 0,52 | 6,19 | 1,60 | 1,33 | 0,43 | 1,71 | 1,82 | 0,77 | 0,00 | BDZ |
| 9 | 0,10 | 0,25 | nd | 5,03 | 0,67 | 0,33 | 0,00 | 0,43 | 0,05 | 0,00 | 1,89 | None |
| 16 | 0,83 | 1,22 | 27,60 | 115,61 | 1,26 | 1,95 | 0,18 | 2,50 | 0,39 | 0,08 | 0,10 | BDZ |
| 18 | 0,80 | 0,68 | 26,38 | 49,49 | 1,40 | 0,68 | 0,21 | 0,55 | 0,20 | 0,06 | 0,00 | BDZ |

Legend: IP = Iliopsoas Muscle; BDZ = Benzodiazepines; SCM = Sternocleidomastoideus Muscle; nd = not determined

In particular, we intend to verify whether muscle tissue can be considered a valid alternative specimen to biological fluids and viscera, especially in advanced decomposition cases (where the only tissue available is muscle).

As we already said, it is known that the putrefactive process influences the blood morphine or alcohol concentrations to the point of rendering the results obtained questionable.

Furthermore, the laws in force in Italy often delay the autopsy's execution by a few days, thus making the post-mortem transformation process advance, with the inevitable consequence that the hematic and visceral concentrations found in specimens collected during the post-mortem examination do not correspond to those present in the subject at the time of death.

Recent studies show that heart blood is not always a reliable source since there may be a xenobiotic release from the heart muscle to blood (as, for instance, in the case of digitalin poisoning).

Generally this holds true for most of the xenobiotics, which may be released in the post-mortem phase from the viscera to blood in a different way and this depending on chemical and physical factors related to both the type of substance and the matrix analysed.

Add to this the time interval between the moment of death and the collection of the specimen, as well as the conditions in which the corpse has been preserved.

All this considered, the reliability of hematic values, which are of great importance in the medico-legal toxicology analysis, may be questionable and an alternative biological specimen less affected by post-mortem decomposition, such as muscle tissue, could be useful.

For all these reasons, as already suggested by Garriott et al., alternative specimens must sometimes be used for analysis and evaluation of drug concentrations. Warm and Colleagues (9, 10) and Garriott (4) had already indicated muscle tissue as being the most suited in cases of badly preserved corpses, since its water content remains relatively constant (around 75%) and thus is less affected by putrefactive phenomena.

Data relating to blood and muscle tissue was compared statistically using the line equation Y = a + bx and respectively y = β x.

| Series of values compared | Equation y = bx | | | Equation y = a+bx | | |
|---|---|---|---|---|---|---|
| | β | t | r | b | t | r |
| FB - IP | 2,998 | 4,271 | 0,554 | 2,799 | 3,150 | 0,558 |
| FB - SCM | 3,710 | 5,583 | 0,689 | 3,732 | 4,464 | 0,689 |
| TB - IP | 1,765 | 5,183 | = | 0,870 | 2,884 | 0,524 |
| TB - SCM | 2,171 | 7,199 | 0,117 | 1,358 | 5,443 | 0,758 |

Legend: FB =femoral blood; SCM =sternocleidomastoideus muscle; IP =iliopsoas muscle; TB =toracic blood

The results of the statistical processing are illustrated in table n. 4 and it shows that for peripheral blood the correlation is significantly different from 0 (r values) and 1 (t values).

The results obtained emphasizes a relatively well-defined proportional ratio between blood concentrations (peripheral blood) and muscle tissue concentrations, by virtue of which it is possible to obtain -although not very accurately- the blood concentration from the muscle concentration and vice-versa. This data is in line with what was observed by the other authors interested in the subject in question.

This study has allowed us to observe a difference between the hematic values obtained for peripheral blood compared to the hematic values obtained for thoracic blood, as well as between the morphine concentrations in the two examined muscles. As far as the difference between the blood values, post-mortem diffusion phenomena must be taken into account, as underlined in previous studies and verified in the studies carried out by us and which are still under way at our Institute. For the time being, the meaning of slight differences between morphine concentrations in the two above muscles are not yet clear to us.

In brief, the results of our study show, first of all, that blood positivity to morphine has always been detected in the muscle tissue as well and confirm the validity of muscle tissue as an alternative specimen in cases of "suspected acute narcotism" confirmed and supported by the satisfactory correlation between concentrations in muscle and in blood.

The blood/muscle concentration ratios of morphine could also be used (as suggested by Garriott) to carry out evaluations of the lapse of time between ingestion of morphine and death, since blood and muscle tissue require a given lag time to equilibrate. The results obtained show that, in each case, the muscle /blood ratio is greater than unity.

The results of our research confirm the usefulness of muscle tissue in the case of corpse in advanced state of decomposition where the post-mortem transformation phenomena may determine considerable variations in the tissue and heamatic distribution of the xenobiotics. Furthermore, as already mentioned above, different concentration values of the substance may be found at a hematic level depending on the area of collection. The possibility of disposing of an alternative specimen which is less affected by post-mortem transformation phenomena is of great importance in Italy, where the laws in force often delay the autopsy's execution by a few days in certain cases. The minor influence of putrefactive transformation on muscle tissue makes the data of reference easier to reproduce.

REFERENCES

1) Aderjan R, Buhr M, Schmidt G (1979) Investigation of cardiac glycoside levels in human postmortem blood and tissues determined by RIA procedure. Arch Toxicol 2:107-114

2) Fallani M (1961) Contributo allo studio della circolazione ematica post-mortale. Min Med Leg 81:1084-1115

3) Felby S, Christensen H, Lund A (1974) Morphine concentrations in blood and organs in cases of fatal poisoning. J For Sci 3:77-81

4) Garriott J C (1991) Skeletal muscle as an alternative specimen for alcohol and drug analysis. J For Sci 36:60-69

5) Horncastle D C J (1977) Toxicology: quantitative aspects. Med Sci Laws 17:37-53

6) Jones G R (1985) Post-mortem increases in drug levels. A major challenge for forensic toxicologists. Abstract J Com Soc For Sci 18:167

7) Rouziouse J M, Badinard A, Roche L (1974) Etude de la valeur médico-légale des taux à toxiques obtenus par prélèvement post-mortem. Med Leg Dommage Corp 7:33-36

8) Rouziouse J M, Asmand J (1972) Valeur d'un prélèvement intracardiaque réalisé à l'autopsie pour estimer l'importance d'une intoxication. Bull Med Leg Toxicol 15:82-85

9) Steentoft A, Warm K, Christensen H (1988) Morphine concentration in autopsy material from fatal cases after intake of morphine and for heroin. For Sci Soc 28:87-94

10) Warm K, Steentoft A, Christensen H (1983) Experiences in interpretation with exhumed material illustrated by single case of morphine intoxication. For Sci Soc 23:209-212

# ARTEFACTUAL CYANIDE FORMATION FROM RANITIDINE (ZANTAC™) IN A POSTMORTEM GASTRIC CONTENT

Fredric Rieders, Vincent F. Cordova and Nancy Ruiz-Garcia
National Medical Services, Inc., Willow Grove, PA, USA 19090

The classic paper by Gettler and Baine (7) and the recent comprehensive book on cyanide toxicology by Ballantyne and Mars (2) documents many ways in which cyanide can appear in and disappear from postmortem biologic specimens and the forensic pitfalls this represents. A new source for postmortem cyanide formation from the histamine $H_2$ inhibiting antiulcer drug Ranitidine (Zantac™) by the gastric contents of a woman is here reported.

A 46 year old housewife on Zantac™ tablets, 150 mg q.i.d., arose one morning around 6:00 AM, had breakfast and left with her son to go whale watching. As they started to enter their car around 9:00 AM, she collapsed with pallor, nausea, dyspnea and abdominal pain, but did not lose consciousness, She was helped into the house, where she vomited, rested and started feeling better. However, around 11:00 AM while in the bathroom, she collapsed again. This time she lost consciousness and suffered cardiac arrest, Emergency medical assistance at the scene and CPR procedures at the hospital to which she was taken were unsuccessful and she was pronounced dead by noon. A blood specimen drawn during the CPR around 11:30 AM showed a severe metabolic acidotic picture.

At autopsy, her body was 163 cm long, weighed 57 kg and showed normal dependent lividity. A "bleach-like" aroma of gastric contents (600 cc of greenish-black semisolid mucoid material) was recorded, as was an erosion at her gastroduodenal junction and some autolysis of her gastric mucosa. Greenish-black mucoid aspirate was noted in the tracheal bifurcation. No anatomical cause of death, no other odors, including "cyanide odor"(which the prosector <u>was</u> known to be able to detect) and no suspicious bright or cyanotic colors of skin, muscle, spleen, lung or of gastric mucosa were noted.

Vitreous eye fluid analyses for clinical parameters revealed very high concentrations of LDH, SGOT and CPK enzymes and a very low $CO_2$ content. Unremarkably within normal postmortem limits were bilirubin, urea nitrogen, creatinine, uric acid, alkaline phosphatase- and SGPT- enzymes, as well as calcium, chloride, sodium, potassium and phosphate. For toxicology, 260 g of the gastric contents, the urinary bladder (no urine was present at autopsy), about 200 mL blood as well as portions of liver and brain were furnished to the Coroner's laboratory.

The toxicologic analyses performed during the next four to five weeks were as follows: <u>1.</u> Headspace gas chromatography on blood for alcohol and other common organovolatiles. <u>2.</u> RIA on blood for barbiturates, cocaine, opiates, phencyclidine and related compounds ( RIA cross-reactives?). <u>3.</u> Color test screen on blood (5 mL) extract for strongly acidic drugs. <u>4.</u> Ultraviolet spectrophotometry and thin layer chromatography of base/neutral extract of 25 g liver and of acid/neutral and base extract of gastric contents.

The findings were calculated and reported as 40 mg salicylate and 10 mg ranitidine in the total (260 g) gastric contents received by the laboratory. The gastric contents were described as having a chlorine odor and a pH of 6 to 7. No other positive test results were noted, nor any other abnormal odors or any abnormal colorations of the specimens.

The first tests for cyanide appear to have been made 6 1/2 months after death. Detection by Schönbein-Pagenstecher copper-guaiac test (2), quantitation by Feldstein and Klenshoj's microdiffusate colorimetry (4,5,6) and qualitative confirmation by the Prussian blue test (8) was reported as giving the following results.

> Gastric contents: 4.4 mg Total Cyanide (presumably at a concentration of 16.9 mcg/g of the 260 g gastric contents logged in at Coroner's laboratory)
> Blood: 0.2 micrograms (mcg)/mL
> Liver & Brain: No cyanide was detected.

Twenty months later (i.e. 2 1/4 years after the death), another analysis of gastric contents by the Coroner's laboratory found the cyanide content to have fallen (from 4.4 mg total) to 2.4 mg total - i.e. from 16.9 mcg/g to 9.2 mcg/g.

A cyanide-murder indictment and trial resulted. In the course of trial (4 3/4 years after death), our laboratory (NMS) was asked to give forensic toxicologic expert assistance to the defense, including analyses of the blood and gastric contents and evaluation of the above results.

Quantitative analyses by NMS for Cyanide by Guilbault and Kramer colorimetry (9) and ion selective electrode (1) after microdiffusion (10,11) with qualitative confirmation by copper-guaiac (2) and Prussian blue (8) tests revealed 12.3 mcg Cyanide/mL gastric contents (ph 7) but gave negative results for the blood with a detection/exclusion limit of 0.05 to 0.15 mcg/mL.

In a search for possible sources of the cyanide in the gastric contents, salting out and hydrolysis followed by headspace gas chromatography did not detect any nitriles or benzaldehyde (from e.g. amygdalin). No other volatile residua of potential cyanide sources and no increase in volatizable cyanide was found.

Atomic and ICP spectrometry of the gastric contents did not reveal any "elevated" concentrations of potassium, sodium, copper, lithium, mercury and cobalt or iron - as possible cations of relatively common salts or complexes of cyanide. No cyanide was produced by "incubating" 0.5 mL gastric contents with 5 mL "normal" blood at 5°C or 37°C overnight which mitigated against cyanide-forming microorganisms as a cyanide source.

HPLC at NMS - about 5 years after the death - had revealed that only 1.4 mcg ranitidine/mL was still in the gastric contents, in which the Coroner's lab had found approximately 40 mcg/mL a few weeks after the death. This "loss" prompted us to set up an additional "control" experiment to rule out that the "loss" of ranitidine had produced the cyanide found.

The "control" was arbitrarily a mixture of 0.25 g gastric contents and 25 mg ranitidine, heated at 55°C for an hour - as was 0.25 g gastric content without ranitidine and 25 mg ranitidine without the gastric contents. At the end of the hour, each mixture was microdiffused and tested for cyanide.

The experiment resulted - repeatedly - in additional cyanide formation, based on Guilbault-Kramer colorimetry of cellosolve extracts and of microdiffusates of the reaction mixtures as well as ion selective measurements of the microdiffusate, Schönbein and Prussian blue testing (1,2,9,10,11).

An average of 20 mcg cyanide was generated by incubating 25 mg ranitidine with 250 mg of the gastric contents from the case for 1 hour at 55°C or 17 hours at 37°C and then acidifying and microdiffusing the mixture.

Similar results - formation of low ppm cyanide by the action of 250 mg gastric contents on 25 mg ranitidine - were obtained with three of ten other, randomly selected (but initially cyanide-free and ranitidine-free) postmortem gastric content specimens.

A series of reactions with ranitidine without the gastric contents gave mixed results. Trace amounts of cyanide appeared in a reaction with alkaline sodium borohydride solution and substantial amounts in reaction with sodium dichromate solution. The largest amount was formed by a disodium hydrogen phosphate buffered solution of ascorbic acid and ferrous sulfate, used by Bernard/Brodie and Julius Axelrod as an "in vitro" free radical drug metabolizing model some 50 years ago, similar to the Fenton reaction (12). These results point to an oxidative- and/or free radical dismutative reaction leading to the observed cyanide formation.

Reagents which did not produce cyanide from ranitidine were individual 1% solutions of $H_2SO_4$, NaOH, $Na_2HPO_4$, acidified borohydride or dichromate, $FeSO_4$, ascorbic acid, $CuSO_4$ or $H_2O_2$.

The blood from the case also did not form cyanide from ranitidine in experiments similar to those with the gastric contents. Its ranitidine content when analyzed by HPLC at NMS was no more than 0.02 mcg/mL.

Neither the gastric content from the case, nor the "reagents" above formed cyanide from Cimetidine (Tagamet®) under the conditions described. This is of special interest since cimetidine has a N'-cyano group in its active center, while ranitidine does not - it has instead a c-nitro group in about the same relative position.

Famotidine and nazatadine were then also tested and no cyanide formation was detected.

It is important to realize that the percent "conversion" of ranitidine to cyanide is so small that it does not come even close to any potentially acute or chronic effect - either as cyanide or as its thiocyanate metabolite - in any therapeutic ranitidine dosage schedule. It might be interesting to test for cyanide and thiocyanate in cases of grossly excessive use (overdose) of ranitidine.

The main effect of the phenomenon observed is likely to be a raising of suspicion of poisoning on the basis of the "elevated" gastric cyanide - as do other "unexplained" elevated cyanides. Such "suspicion" can usually be delineated by analysis of other tissues - if done rather promptly after death. Otherwise the tissue analyses may also become a "red herring", as may have happened in the present case.

The mechanism of the cyanide formation in this case needs to be elucidated, since it is likely to be translatable to other potentially misleading sources of cyanide in gastric contents.

The forensic lessons from this case are several:

A new lesson is that ranitidine can give rise to cyanide in gastric contents - but without a body burden it is not a poison - "caveat interpretor" and "sola dosis fucet venum" are very apropos!

Old lessons are (1) "presence" in gastric contents is not synonymous with poisoning, and (2) it is worth to again consider ruling out cyanide right at the autopsy table by means of waving a Schönbein (Macherei Nageli) Cyantesmo™ test paper over the open body and especially over the opened stomach in just about every case - later, it may be more confusing than helpful.

**BIBLIOGRAPHY**


1. McAnalley BH, Lowry WT, Oliver RD, Garriott JC (1979) Determination of inorganic sulfide and cyanide in blood using specific ion electrodes. J Anal Toxicol 3:111-114

2. Autenrieth W, Warren WH (1928) Schönbein-Pagenstecher test for cyanide. In: Laboratory Manual for the Detection of Poisons and Powerful Drugs. P. Blakistone's Son & Co., Philadelphia, pp. 28-29

3. Ballantyne B, Mars TC, eds (1987) In: Clinical and Experimental Toxicology of Cyanides. IOP Publishing Ltd., Bristol, UK

4. Boxer GE, Richards JC (1951) Chemical determination of Vitamin $B_{12}$ II. The quantitative isolation and colorimetric determination of millimicrogram quantities of cyanide. Arch Biochem 30:372-281

5. Epstein J (1947) Estimation of microquantities of cyanide. Anal Chem 19:272-274

6. Feldstein M, Klendshoj NC (1954) J Lab Clin Med 44:166-170

7. Gettler AO, Baine JO (1933) The toxicology of Cyanide. J Med Sci 195: 182-198

8. Gettler AO, Goldbaum L (1947) Anal Chem 19:270-271

9. Guilbault GG, Kramer DN (1966) Ultrasensitive, specific method for cyanide using p-nitrobenzaldehyde and o-dinitrobenzene. Anal Chem 38:834

10. Rieders F (1975) In: Sunshine I (ed) Methodology for Analytical Toxicology, vol I. CRC Press, Boca Raton, FL, pp. 113-115

11. Siek TJ, Dunn AD (1990) A rapid, sensitive and specific screening technique for the determination of cyanide. J Anal Toxicol 14:256

12. Fenton (1933) Industrial and Engineering Chemistry, Analytical Edition (now Anal Chem) 5:19, Cited in: Meites L (ed) Handbook of Analytical Chemistry. McGraw-Hill, pp. 6-45

# 13. Mass Disasters

**RADIOLOGICAL INVESTIGATION IN A MAJOR DISASTER - THE LOCKERBIE PANAM PLANE CRASH**

A. BUSUTTIL - Edinburgh, Scotland

The LOCKERBIE INVESTIGATION differed from other major disaster investigations on a number of matters in particular its size, timing, venue, causation, multi-nationality and the multi-facetted legal requirements related to the multiple international investigations that followed in its aftermath. The incident involved 270 victims, partly from the aircraft and partly from the town; the debris from the plane spread over an area progressively extended to 1352 $km^2$ ( 845 square miles) requiring the participation of thousands of search and investigation personnel recruited from different parts of the Great Britain. The incident took place on the December 21 st. 1988, at 7.05 p.m. at the height of the Christmas vacation period and in bleak wintry conditions with prevalent high westerly winds. This family re-union time resulted in the plane transporting large numbers of young families who were returning to the United States and many armed forces personnel stationed in Britain and students returning to the United States from Britain and other parts of Europe.

Lockerbie is a small unobtrusive market town with a population of 4000 lying close to the A 74, a main route between Scotland and England. When the crash took place there was only one policeman on duty. Because of the presence of light industry in the area a major disaster plan had been prepared by the emergency services for the town. This 'DisPlan' had never been tested in mock exercises and was associated with a less than ideal temporary mortuary site on the upper storey of the local Town Hall, in the initial part of the investigation.

From very early on it had been conclusively shown that the plane had come down due to the presence on board of an explosive device planted there as a consequence of international terrorist activity. The environmental pressure sensitive detonator which had been packaged into a suit case set off the explosion and caused disintegration of the plane at (31,000 feet) 9,300 meters; at which site the oxygen content of the atmosphere is quite low and the environmental air temperature of minus 35 ° C. When the debris hit the gourd, fires were initiated and houses were destroyed both by the falling plane fragments and by conflagration thereby resulting in fatalities among the inhabitants of the town.

Because of the numerous nationals involved in the crash the media coverage was extensive from the very beginning with numerous journalists and camera crews flocking to the area. The bereaved relatives had to travel long distances to come and obtain first hand information from the investigators and give the details which were required by the police-run identification bureau. This multiethnic provenance of the fatalities raised the matter of having to deal in an appropriate and helpful manner with the sensitivities of different religious denominations.

The instructions from the legal officials was that the deaths had to be treated as homicide cases and the scene of the crash, as a ' scene of crime '. In overall charge of the investigation was the local Procurator Fiscal who in accordance with Scottish law required that there was a corroboration by two persons of all the evidence which would eventually have to be presented in a court of law. A full autopsy was instructed in each case to assist with determining personal identity, cause of death and to collect samples for toxicological, histological and other investigations. Requirements of international law and of the multiple simultaneous investigations being carried out by the civilian police on behalf of the P F, national security investigators, security forces from other countries whose nationals had been involved, by air accident investigators, by the aircraft manufacturers and by the carrier (PanAM), all had to be catered for.

RADIOLOGY therefore had a very prominent role to play in this investigation and was therefore carried out on a massive scale. The principal rationale for this was the EXCLUSION OF AN EXPLOSIVE DEVICE & its IDENTIFICATION from any of its component FRAGMENTS that could be retrieved i. e. particularly any of these which had found their way into the bodies and became embedded therein.

This raised various logistic problems. In the first instance an area had to be found within the temporary mortuary sites which could be converted into a safe radiological site. This meant that this site had to be capable of accommodating and installing X-ray equipment and could also be rendered safe by being appropriately screened with lead shields to avoid any health and safety hazards to the other operators in the mortuary. X-ray machines had to be found which were surplus to requirements in hospitals, packaged, crane lifted and delivered to the mortuary site and then installed therein. Trolleys on which the bodies could be placed for this purpose also had to be provided from hospitals. The specialised personnel required also had to be found and shifts of volunteer radiographers had to be recruited and transported over long distances at the beginning and the end of their hours of duty and their involvement in the investigation. Dark room facilities also had to be provided so that the exposed plates could be developed and dried and made available to the pathologist together with all the chemical agents essential for these purposes.

The pathologists during their autopsies had to look for and remove any 'foreign bodies' which could be identified radiologically as present within the bodies; each of these once retrieved, had to be appropriately labelled and sent away for the appropriate forensic scientific analysis. This retrieval proved quite difficult on occasions in that two-dimensional pictures could not provide an adeqate localisation of the object, and often films in other planes or with radio-opaque markers inserted at strategic sites had to be retaken. The assistance of expert radiologists was also required to assist with the interpretation of the radiological findings in that extraneous materials from the ground or the surroundings from which the bodies had been retrieved often contaminated the bodies. Storage space for the unexposed X-ray film cassettes, the developed radiological plates was another requirement.

It was initially decided that to cut down on time, radiological examinations would be restricted to all the main body cavities. It became soon clear that the bodies could be carrying vital information in their upper or lower limbs muscular compartments and some of the bodies which had already been embalmed had to be brought back, washed and their limbs re -X-rayed. For the benefit of the eight dental colleagues working on the odontological identification of the victims another X-ray machine which could provide them with dental data was made available.

Towards the latter part of this investigation given that quite a number of the bodies were unaccounted for, the attention of the pathologists turned towards the examination of all the other human remains which had been retrieved form the site - in all about 650 sackfuls each about two meters tall by one meter diameter. Each of these sacks had to be X-rayed and any items which were thought to be of significance retrieved.

Among the additional bonuses derived from such extensive radiological investigations were

a. identification was assisted by the finding of radio-opaque bony deformities and prostheses and other significant radiological findings which could be compared with antemortem data

b. items of jewellery was often found on X-rays having been displaced into the chest and abdominal cavities and this assisted further with personal identification

c. all the bony injuries and some of the soft tissue injuries were reliably , more fully, and permanently recorded by the radiological investigation.

d. reproduction on X-ray plate of the configuration of the frontal sinuses - enabling matching with pre-morbid radiological investigations.

The decision that radiological investigation is to form an integral part of a major disaster investigations cannot be taken lightly and has to take into account all the various aspects of the radiological investigation which have been outlined. Such a decision should be made in consultation with the investigators and is not one to be taken in isolation by the legal officials who are involved in such an investigation. Furthermore it has to be made clear that adequate financial resources would have to be earmarked to cover the major expenses in obtaining the materials for such an investigation. In the planning phase for emergencies caused by disasters the radiological aspects of the investigation must be fully thought about and some preliminary arrangements are to be carefully considered for such an eventuality.

# AIR CRASH VICTIMS IDENTIFICATION: SCENE, AUTOPSY ROOM AND LABORATORY INVESTIGATIONS IN AN ITALIAN CASE

Lucia CASARINO PhD, Armando MANNUCCI PhD, Marco SALVI MD, Nicoletta FADDA MD, Andrea LOMI MD, Gianlorenzo BRUNI MD and Francesco DE STEFANO MD

*Istituto di Medicina Legale e delle Assicurazioni dell' Università di Genova - Via De Toni 12 - 16132 GENOVA - ITALY*

In a dark and stormy night, on September the 30th, 1993, a Cessna twin-engine airplane, carrying four males and one female, crashed against a mountain in the Italian Riviera.

An accident in which only five people die, can hardly qualify as a mass disaster, but the difficulties coming from early sloppy and unskilled investigation, asked for a special approach and led to use advanced DNA techniques for victims identification.

First arrived on the scene were the Carabinieri, they secluded the area and were commanded by a muddy and soaked prosecutioner to spent the night guarding. The morning after a Medical Doctor from the local Public Health Department of the National Health Service, was called to perform the earlier medico-legal tasks but decided to pile up toghether the human remains found in a 30 x 40 mt. area, unstripping those body parts that were still secured to the broken seats by the seat belts.

We were summoned by the Prosecutioner to perform identification and autopsy on the bodies. So in the early afternoon of October the 1st two of us climbed the slippery hill to perform the scene investigations and were welcomed by the disgruntled MD,in a hurry to complete collecting of human bits and pieces, we were delaying with our presence.

As scene data were useless, we had to start gathering data examining the human remains in the autopsy room.

A positive visual identification was possible in four out of five passengers; in the last case we were unable to attribute any of the bits and pieces we had to the missing male crew member, with enough certainty. Furthermore, no dental data were available, as often happens in Italy, due to the habit of many dentists of destroying patients records to avoid taxes.
For that reason, the Forensic Haemogenetics Laboratory was charged to employ advanced DNA techniques to reach the positive identification.

Among the autopsy findings we collected ten hands. Three of them (two right and one left) were still joined with the body parts of identified passengers. The remaining three right hands, whose owner was unknown, were sampled. Muscular samples were drew out in the depth to avoid decomposition bacterial contamination. Then, The mother, the son and the wife of the fifth not recognized passenger were called out to give a blood sample. DNA was extracted by employing the usual protocols (1). Sex of the samples was checked employng amelogenin homologous sequences (2). All the right hands were from males. Then, we amplified a total of 11 loci, using about 10 ng of DNA for each reaction. Bovine Serum Albumine was added to samples from muscular extraction to enhance results. Commercial kits from Perkin Elmer were used for D1S80, HLA-DQA1 and Polymarker. Published sets of primers and conditions were applied for HUMFES/FPS, HUMCD4, HUMVWA31/A and HUMTH01 (3; 4; 5; 6). All the amplifications were carried out with controls for contaminations. Amplification products were analised by reverse dot-blot for Polymarker and HLA-DQA1, GeneAmp detection gel for D1S80, 8% denaturing polyacrilamide denaturing gel (PAGE) for HUMTH01, 8% PAGE for HUMCD4 and HUMVWA31/A and 12% PAGE for HUMFES/FPS.

Table 1 shows genotype profiles of the three sampled hands, the mother ( M ), the son ( S ) and the wife of the alleged crew member ( W ). D1S80, HLA-DQA1, HUMCD4 and LDR excluded hand n° 3. HUMVWA31/A excluded hand n° 2. No markers excluded hand n° 1. A paternity test was performed for that hand and the final casual allelic sharing was $4 \times 10^{-5}$.

## CONCLUSIONS

We can point out that this air-crash was not a major disaster, but a major screw-up, considering the "investigations" performed before our arrival at the scene. Inadequate medico-legal investigations can happen, due to the system provided by the law (7). In this case, the scientific investigation techniques we had to use led to the positive identification of the last passenger the law needs for declaration of death and execution of inheritance rights. However, we have to stress that a sloppy or unskilled scene investigation can cause an irreparable loss of data that no laboratory technique can mend. For example, in this case was not possible to know who was the pilot in the air-crash time for assurance needs.

**REFERENCES**

1) Sambrook, Fritsch, Maniatis (1989) Molecular Cloning, Cold Spring Laboratory Press. 3:E3-E4.
2) Mannucci A., Sullivan K.M., Ivanov P.L., Gill P. (1993) Forensic application of a rapid and quantitative DNA sex test by amplification of the X-Y homologous gene amelogenin. Int. J. Leg. Med. 106:190-193.
3) Polymeropoulos M.H., Rath D.S., Xiao H., Merril C.R. (1991) Tetranucleotide repeat polymorfism at the human c- fes/fps proto-oncogene (FES). NAR vol 19 n 14:4018.
4) Edwards M.C., Clemens P.R., Tristan M., Pizzuti A., Gibbs R.A. (1991) Pentanucleotide repeat lenght polymorphism at the Human CD4 locus. NAR vol 19 n17: 4791.
5) Kimpton C.P., Walton A., Gill P.: A fur4ther tetranucleotide repeat polymorphism in the vWF gene. Hum. Mol. Gen. 1, 287-289.
6) Polymeropoulos M.H., Xiao H., Rath D.S., Merril C.R. (1991) Tetranucleotide repeat polymorfism at the human tyrosine hydroxilase gene (TH). NAR vol 19 n 13:3753.
7) Gianelli Castiglione A., Lomi A. (1993) Forensic autopsies in Italy. J. Forensic Sci. 38, 3: 622-627.

# TEACHING DISASTER MEDICINE : TRAINING IN PRESERVATION OF EVIDENCE NECESSARY FOR IDENTIFICATION PURPOSES

AM DUGUET, M DISTEDORF, P COUGOT, CH VIRENQUE

The purpose of teaching disaster medicine is to supplement the training of accident and emergency specialists. The goal therein is not only a medical training in the sort of pathology encountered in disasters, but also a training connected with the organisation of aid after a disaster.

During a time span of approximately 100 hours, the theoretical side is completed by means of practical training on the site and an annual practice. Toulouse University has, since 1984, trained 570 doctors in first aid for mass disasters, in the organisation of a chain of help, and in the procuring of hospital spaces. With seven teaching centres in France, the notion of disaster medicine plays an integral role in all regional programmes of medical aid.

The teaching of forensic medicine deals with the problems raised by the deaths of victims following a disaster, and the specialised side involving forensic identification of disaster victims. Specialists must therefore be aware of the urgency of the demands which are necessary in order to preserve evidence used in identifications.

Classical forensic references about identification methods and the expected results are used, with particular reference to police techniques such as photographs, clothing, jewellery, fingerprints or tattoos, which are useful guides allowing one-third of all victims to be identified.

Elaborate protocols for the management of corpses are also presented, such as have been used in preceding practice exercises, where the quality improves according to the chosen topic, and extends to new targets.

**1. Practical teaching within the diploma of disaster medicine**

The organisation procedure used to aid injured victims is well codified for simulated disasters. However, the deceased only figure briefly, and are quickly dealt with by the person in charge at the end of the exercise, by saying : "all the victims have been identified and the corpses moved to a temporary morgue". The management of the dead requires a large amount of work and assessment at the location, which should be in place at an early stage in the proceedings.

The intervention of the first aid teams to help the living is of the utmost importance, but this must not hinder the chances of identifying the other victims through untimely actions. Therefore those concerned with the medical help must be put in position and, by keeping in touch with the identification specialists, can anticipate and thus integrate their constraints into the organisation of help.

**Aims of the identification team**

1. Inform the police officers of how a disaster exercise works.

2. Integrate the police officers with the early emergency teams.

3. Associate the police officers with the doctors in order to keep each other informed as to their own professional requirements.

4. Evaluate the possibilities of communication between those in charge of the first aid centres and the other groups which organise the help available.

The team is made up of five trainee doctors, a forensic specialist and six police officers. It uses specific materials, provisional identification forms and a camera in order to collect the information.

A medical co-ordinator establishes a link with the organiser of medical help, while a police officer does likewise with the administrative and judicial authorities. The person in charge of the help is told of all the orders necesary for preserving evidence :

* Objects and bodies must be left in place

* Clothes must not be lost

* Any body moved out of necessity must be numbered and its position marked

**2. In the operation of 2 June 1989**, a group specially designed for identification was installed for the first time, thus linking the police officers with the forensic specialists.

The theme of the disaster was an earthquake, with many victims scattered across a large area. There were several stations for the injured, which were directed towards three first aid centres ; then they were taken to a medical evacuation centre, before finally being taken to different hospitals. As in all simulations, dummies were needed to play a double role. Firstly they were the corpses at the scene of the disaster, and secondly, they were the seriously injured, who were liable to die either at the scene or in the later stages. Some of these dummies had been given identification cards - in real life, two out of three people in France carry their identity papers on them.

**The results**

According to a diagram of the exercise, there were 16 corpses at the scene of the accident, of which seven were still unidentified by the end of the operation. This corresponded exactly to the number of dummies. However, at the medical evacuation centre, 37 victims died from the first three aid centres. Only eight of these casualties had been provisionally identified, instead of the 24 which had identity papers on them. Those concerned were the unconscious casualties who had not been able to give their name during treatment. Therefore it would be essential to have someone in charge of an identification team at the medical evacuation centre.

**3. In a second exercise, the disaster was an aeroplane accident.** It was organised on a military field with the co-operation of both the army and the air force, who were also testing their own rescue and identification plan by joining the group. This co-operation worked perfectly. However, despite military checking at each level of the operation to remove the casualties, at the end of the count the list of the dead was incomplete. Following a check of the passenger list, it was shown that no victim had been forgotten on the site. Rather, several had been lost after their transportation from the scene of the accident, and it was not possible to determine whether they had been evacuated or whether they had died. In addition, for several victims who had died whilst receiving treatment, no time of death had been noted.

**4. In a third exercise, where a theatre had collapsed**, the measures used for the deceased had been applied for all the casualties. Therefore, every one, both conscious and unconscious, received an identification form, in order to produce a registered or numbered list at all stages in the relief operation.

Despite careful attention, the police officer present at the hospital admissions had to change the omissions from former stages three times.

**In conclusion**, this theoretical and practical teaching would seem to provide the necessary additional training for first aid doctors, with regard to the management of injured and dead victims. It works best through close co-operation with the police force, and with the aim of facilitating links with the forensic teams who will give definite identifications.

Doctors specialised in the field of disaster medicine who come in at the level of help for the casualties should know both the strategy and the logistics necessary in order to preserve all the evidence.

The identification team thus establishes the preliminaries, which must be confirmed at a later date in the medical identification centre by the forensic surgeons and police in charge of criminal identification.

Sincere thanks must go to Dr T Krompecher, who gave a copy of his film of the Lockerbie disaster to be shown to the students. It illustrated the teaching particularly well.

Bibliography by request : Anne Marie Duguet, Faculté de Médecine, 37 allées Jules Guesdes, 31000 Toulouse, France.

# IDENTIFICATION OF THE VICTIMS OF AIRCRAFT ACCIDENT AT THE OHRID AIRPORT

A.DUMA, K.STANKOVSKI, Z.CAKAR, K.BOSKOVSKI, M.BELOKAPOSKI, A.RAMADANI, Z.KOTEVSKI
INSTITUTE FOR FORENSIC MEDICINE - UNIVERSITY ' KIRIL I METODIJ ' - SKOPJE, REPUBLIC OF MACEDONIA

The aim of this expose is to give a real presentation of the way the Institute for Forensic Medicine is organized,, as well as all the forensic and medical service in the Republic of Macedonia during identification of casualties after the aircrash of the "JAK" plane that took place near Ohrid.

## INTRODUCTION

The air crash happened on 20 November 1993 at 11 p. m. in the vicinity of Ohrid, when the "JAK" plane of the AVIOIMPEX company hit the near-by mountains surrounding Ohrid, went on fire and burnt, and it was the second air crash in 1993 on the territories of the Republic of Macedonia.

This air crash , subsequent to the air crash of the PALAIR MACEDONIAN "Fokker 100," represented a second experience for the workers of the Institute for Forensic Medicine and Crinminalistic at the Faculty of Medicine in Skopje.

Just after the investigating team had informed about the details concerning the accident, the head of the Institute calculated the needed number of teams, the needed equipment for a successful implementation of the identification, and it also made an assessment about the possible methods to be used.

The medical team for the identification of the victims was composed of 9 individual teams. Each team was composed of a specialist in forensic medicine who headed the team, an assistant for autopsy, and an administrator.

## GOAL OF THE IDENTIFICATION PROCEDURE

The goal of the identification procedure was the following:

- to determine the exact number of the passengers in the plane according to the previously received passengers list;
- to determine the exact number of the disappeared after the air crash;
- to determine the number of the survivals;
- to determine the type of injuries with each casualty,
- to determine the personal identity of every one of the casualties, on the fundamental basis of the identification characteristics,
- to describe the parts of the clothing and personal belongings and to compare them with the obtained information on the preliminary description of the agnosticians (recognizers).

## METHODS OF WORK

After the assignments of the tasks and the goals, the medical identification teams approached the formation on the identification basis, composed of 4 separate rooms,. as follows:

- a room for preliminary discussions with the agnosticians
- a room where the personal belongings and documents found with the bodies.
- a room for dactyloscopic analysis
- a room in which the bodies and parts of the cadavers were placed, where the work of the aims was carried out.

On the basis of the afore mentioned the following methods were parallely applied:

- determination of sex, age, and length of the bodies.
- the determination of the possible identity according to the detected documents with each body;
- recognition of personal belongings, parts of the clothing, as well as recognition of documents by their families members, after a previous detailed description;
- recognition of the bodies by the agnosticians after a previous detailed description.
- dactyloscopic method,
- the odontologic method;
- during the identification procedure, after the accomplished autopsy of a number of female persons, the identity was confirmed also according to the autopsy findings, when it was concluded they were pregnant, thus the pregnancy stage of the fetus and the data were compared to the data received from the family members;

- we used the method of looking for special marks, anomalies, operations and protheses,
- we used the identification method of analysis for the inspection of the biological material by determining the blood group
- the DNA fingerprint method was not used due to financial difficulties.

The identification was considered accomplished only in those cases when all the applied methods mutually coincided.

With the greatest part of the victims, we found out that the injuries were of a mechanical character, mainly located on the head, the thorax, the upper and lower extremities, which had occurred in lifetime. We also found out other thermical injuries which had occurred in lifetime.

## RESULTS

According to the passengers list from the AVIOIMPEX company from Skopj, there were 108 passengers in the "JAK" plane flying from Zurich, as well as 8 members of the crew. Therefore, there were 116 persons on board.

On the spot of the accident there was only one survival, heavily injured, who was shortly transported to the Macedonian Army Hospital in Skopje, who died after a week.

With the successful implementation of the identification procedure by the previously determined methods, we identified 107 deceased and parts of the cadavers, 9 persons were taken as disappeared, while a body and the parts of a cadaver remained unidentified.

## CONCLUSIONS

Out of experience, knowledge ,and after the accomplished identification of the casualties in the two air crashes during 1993 in the Republic of Macedonia, particularly the air crash in Ohrid, we came to the conclusion that the following tasks have to be undertaken in order to accomplish the identification successfully:

1. Selection of representatives to the identification teams and organized transport of the teams to the spot of the accident.
2. Security of the accident spot and provision of rooms for the work of the identification teams.
3. Detection, dragging out, and markation of the victims on the accident spot.
4. Organized transport of the victims from the accident spot to the space of identification.
5. Plan for the implementation of the tasks to be undertaken in the identification process.
6. Composition of the forensic medical team formed of groups for identification of the victims and their personal security.
7. Formation of an identification base by the teams for identification. The identification base must be composed of four separate rooms in which the teams will perform their duties. It is necessary for them to be independent in their work in order to avoid the suggestiveness and subjective errors.
8. Security in the identification base by the Macedonian Army and interior Ministry representatives, so as to prevent pressure from the public.
9. Implementation of previously planned identification methods and the maximum engagement of the identification teams for their full realization.
10. The psychological preparation of the agnosticians is indispensable for the successful realization of the methods of identification of the casualties.
11. For the successful accomplishment of identification with this kind of accidents it is necessary to have a high level cooperation among the forensic medical services, the Interior Ministry bodies, and the transport and funeral services for the identification on the cadavers.

### *Literature:*


1. Gorkic S., Medical Criminalistic, Publishing House "Privredna stampa,: 1981.
2. Straziscar S., Lovsion J., Milcinski J., Zerjav C., Jancigaj T., Fourth Congress of the Association of Forensic Medicine - Yugoslavia, Ljubljana 1983.
3. Hunger., D. Leopold.,m IDENTIFICATION., Forensic inspection in civil catastrophes.
4. Milosevski P., Security - a Journal, 1986.
5. Popov V. L., Forensic medical Classification of Air trauma, Sudebno-medicinska ekspertiza N.1, Moscow, 1982.
6. A. Slolohin, Characteristically injuries in falls from great heights, Sudebno-medicinska ekspertiza, N. 4, Moscow, 1984.
7. S. Ogbuihi, T. Petkovic, and B. Brinkmann, International Journal of Legal Medicine, Springer-Verlag, 1991.
8. Pile, Rlc, Hill, I R Some legal and medical problems in aircraft accident investigations. Zentralblatt fur die gesamte Rechtsmedizin und ihre Grenzgebiete, Springer-Verlag, 1981.

# ODONTOLOGICAL IDENTIFICATION OF THE VICTIMS OF FLIGHT AI.IT 5148 AIR DISASTER LYON - STRASBOURG 20.01.1992

## Proposal of a new data classification

J.M. HUTT, B. LUDES, B. KAESS, A. TRACQUI, C. KAEMPF, P. KINTZ, H. PFITZINGER, F. FRIEDERICH, R. HAAG, M. DISTELDORF, F. LEVY, B. MEMHELD, M. EVENOT R. JULIEN, and P. MANGIN

Work was conducted by the multidisciplinary identification team, Institut de Médecine Légale, 11 rue Humann 67085 Strasbourg Cedex.

## INTRODUCTION

Odontological identification is an essential, accurate and rapid method with allows a body to be identified from its dental characteristics. This anthropometrical method of identification is included between the descriptive and the biological methods. The authors present their experience in performing a formal identification about the cases in less than 15 days. The identification techniques used are comparative. They compare a dental chart made on a body to the information given by the families and in particular by family doctors and dental surgeons.

## MATERIAL AND METHODS

The authors provide a report on the contribution of odontological identification of the flight AI.IT 5148 air disaster victims, which took place on January 20, 1992.
The choiced technique consisted of a bilateral temporo-mandibulary dislocation after a muscle and ligament desinsertion at the mandible or distal sectioning with the sawbone back of the wisdom teeth and a Lefort I type osteotomy at the upper jawbone. The second stage was to proceed with an extemporeous odontogram chart on files, at the same time trying to damage the flabby facial tissues as little as possible. Given the high number of major skull and face fractures noted, jawbones were often broken, scattered or incomplete, sometimes charred, sometimes burned, which made identification work more difficult.
The jawbones or the jawbone fragments were removed, cleaned, their characteristics recorded, photographs and X-ray photographs taken. The jawbones were then tagged and kept in cold storage.

The method, complemented with macro-photographs and X-ray photographs is quick, effective and accurate.
The examination of dental structures describes : anatomical characteristics (proalveoly, prognathism, retrognathia, etc.), the dental chart, the presence of fixed or removable prosthesis, implants, occlusion, diastema, misalignments, signs of abrasism.
For each tooth, the following criteria are recorded : position, colour, shape, fractures, the presence of caries, type of restoration.
The X-ray examination will show : the presence of an endodontic treatment, the persistence of roots.
Finally, it is necessary to look for dislocated teeth on the ground, in the throat and flabby tissues as well as the lost or swallowed prosthesis.

## RESULTS

We set up the following classification which seems simple, discriminant and in line with the work and comprehension of a pluridisciplinary team (Figures 1 and 2) :

CLASSIFICATION

GROUP A : *Perfect* correlation between ante- and post-mortem data allowing for the identification of the person concerned.
With a slight difference :
Aa : perfect correlation of sufficient ante and post-mortem data allowing for the identification of the person concerned.
Ab : perfect correlation of incomplete ante- and post-mortem data, but enough to allow for the identification of the person concerned.

GROUP B : *Partial* correlation of ante- and post-mortem data enabling the identification of the person concerned, providing that other non-odontological elements are present.
From this stage onward, we took into account the lack of ante- and (or) post-mortem information, and subdivided this group into 2 subgroups :
B1 : partial correlation, despite the relative lack of sufficient ante-mortem data, enabling the identification of the person concerned, providing that other non-odontological elements are present;
B2 : partial correlation, despite the relative lack of sufficient post-mortem data, enabling the identification of the person concerned, providing that other non-odontological elements are present.

GROUP C :*Possible* correlation of ante- and post-mortem odontological data, although not enabling the odontological identification of the person concerned given the number of possible points of comparison :

C1 : lack of ante-mortem information;
C2 : lack of post-mortem information;
C3 : lack of ante- and post-mortem information.

GROUP D :*Impossible* odontological identification on account of the absence of elements of comparison.

D1 : absence or serious lack of ante-mortem information;
D2 : absence or serious lack of post-mortem information;
D3 : absence or serious lack of ante- and post-mortem information or correlating elements.

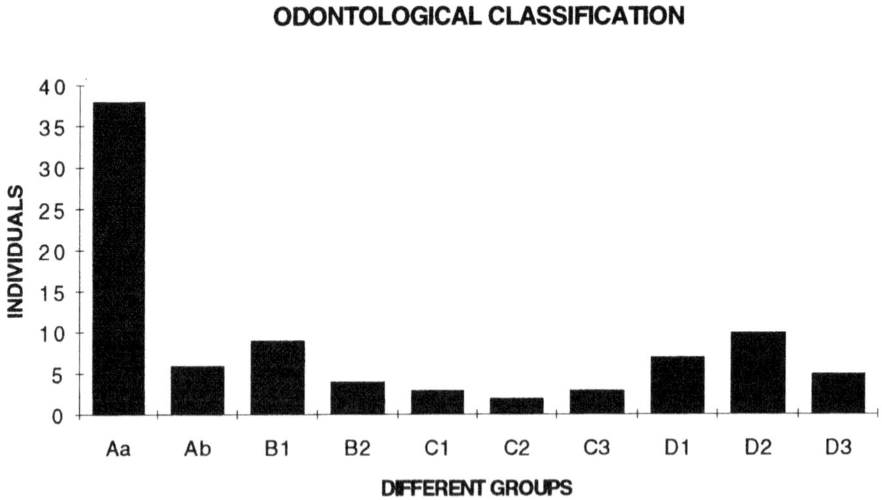

**DISTRIBUTION OF THE ODONTOLOGICAL CLASSES FOR IDENTIFICATION**

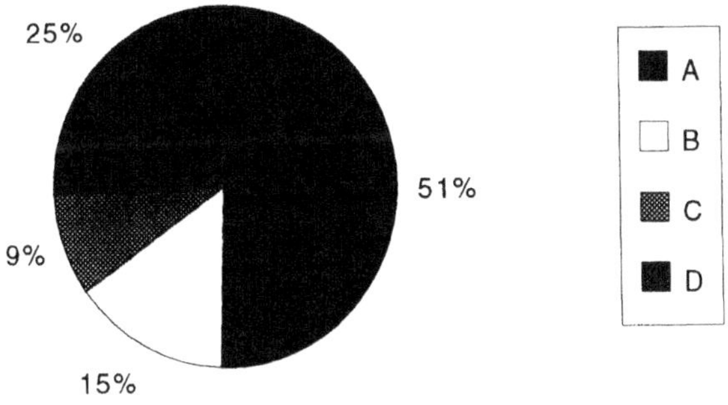


DISCUSSION AND CONCLUSION

The dental examinations alone enabled 16 victims to be identified and by including a morphological examination the figure reached 68 victims.
With regard to dental identification, in 44 cases perfect correlation between ante- and post-mortem data was achieved allowing for the identification of the person concerned (Group *A*). In 13 cases, partial correlation between ante- and post-mortem data was achieved, but nevertheless it allowed for the identification of the person concerned, providing that other non-odontological identification elements were present (Group *B*). In 28 cases, the insufficient or absent odontological data (Groups *C* and *D*) did not enable the victim to be identified.
By the end of the identification operations, 85 of the 87 victims were positively identified.

Forensic odontology, a product of dental art and forensic medicine, has produced renewed interest. Although this interest has not lead to its full integration or provided sufficient training structures in the profession as yet, the importance and the role of forensic odontology are now recognized by forensic pathologists and legal authorities.

# Forensic identifications of the victims of the Airbus A320 crash (20.1.1992)

B. Ludes, P. Mangin, A. Tracqui, H. Pfitzinger, P. Kintz, F. Levy, M. Disteldorf, R. Julien, J.M. Hutt, B. Kaess, C. Kaempf, F. Friederich, M. Evenot, R. Haag and B. Memheld

Institut de Médecine Légale, 11 rue Humann, 67085 Strasbourg Cédex, France.

The authors present the forensic identification investigations after the aircrash of the Airbus A320 upon the Mount Sainte-Odile (3400 feet), France. The airbus, non equipped with a ground proximity warning system and coming from Lyon airport (take off : 6.30 pm) with 96 occupants including the crew, was requested to delay its landing approach by flying over the mountains when it disappeared from the central tower radar at 7.30 pm. Four hours later the impact point was located at a wooded area close to the Mount Sainte-Odile and 30 km away from the Strasbourg airport. 85 fatalities and 9 survivors were found on the arrival of the rescue squads. The aircraft was completely fragmented with the cockpit and the tail separated. The bodies were dispersed all around the wreckage but no relation could be found between the situation of the bodies and the seats occupied by the victims during the flight. In fact, in domestic flights, there is no seat reservation. Most of the carbonized bodies were found in the region where the fuselage had caught fire and was destroyed.

The goals of the medico-legal team comprising investigators from the gendarmerie, forensic pathologists, odontologists and scientists were :

- to identify the victims
- to report the patterns of injuries
- to report the causes of death
- to look for the presence of intoxicants in the bodies of the crew members.

## Methods

Each victim or human remain were removed with their personal belongings without undressing the corpse. In the same time, a questionnaire was distributed to each family in order to know the clothing, the jewels as well as the medical antecedents, the name of the family doctor and dental surgeon. These forms were quickly returned to the I.D. team within the 24 or 48 hours. After transportation of the bodies to the Institute, the external examination included :

- the identification of personal properties
- the identification of the clothing
- the collection of fingerprints if possible.

The second step consisted in the examination of the bodies to look for morphological characteristics such as birth marks, scars, deformities or osteosynthesis material. The X-ray examination was performed only to confirm the medical information reported by the families. The odontological identifications

were positive when relevant coincidental features between ante and post mortem dental records were found.
In the third step, full autopsies of the corpses and human remains were performed in order to :

- describe the patterns of injuries
- identify the cause of death
- take biological samples for toxicological and genetic analyses.

The identification criteria were first preliminary criteria : personal effects, sex, height, colouring of hairs and eyes, and second conclusive criteria : at least two specific morphological features, odontological identification and DNA identification when the other methods failed.

The final identification was pronounced by the co-ordinator of the team (Professor Mangin) on the basis of classical or genetic data.

Results

The forensic investigations allowed to identify 85 victims out of 87 fatalities. 2 corpses were never found at the spot of the crash.

The identifications were performed by :

- morphological examination in 44 cases
- dental data in 9 cases
- morphological and dental criteria for 15 victims
- DNA typing for the last 17 victims.

**RESULTS OF THE IDENTIFICATION PROCEDURES**

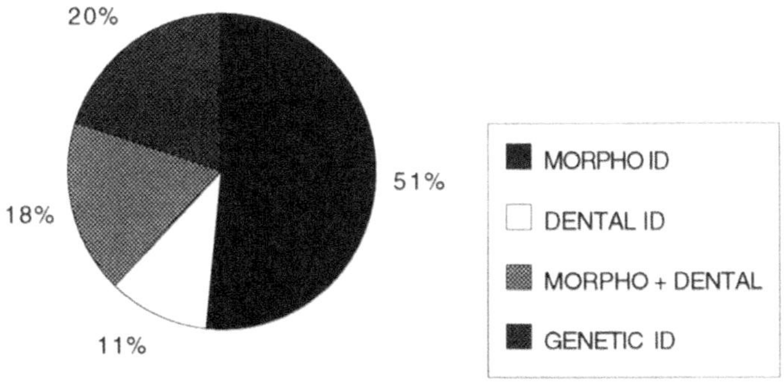

68 victims were identified within 2 weeks using the classical I.D. methods. The DNA reverse paternity testing took 12 more weeks.

The fragmentation of the bodies (60 cases) as well as the severe head injuries, including decapitation (2 cases), were due to the high speed of impact (350-400 km/h), leading to the widespread destruction of the aircraft. Mid trunk and low trunk sections (12 cases) were caused, during the deceleration, by the seat belt after rupture of the spine and dilasceration of the surrounding soft tissues. Amputations and fractures of arms (46 cases) and legs (68 cases) occurred by striking portions of the aircraft structures.

Incinerated bodies (27 cases) and burns have been considered as the results of a post crash fire. In fact, at autopsy, no smoke inhalation or evidence of explosion were found. Toxicological analyses restricted to the captain and co-pilot were negative for both drugs and alcohol in body fluids and tissues collected.

Discussion and conclusion :

This aircrash raised complex and unforeseeable forensic problems because of the number and the many mutilations of the victims as well as their different citizenships.

The identification of the victims was essential for the families to begin mourning, for the juridical authorities to establish the death certificate and for the investigators for the reconstruction process with legal and administrative investigations. We dare think that the efficiency of the identification operations of the victims after the aircrash was due to the use of accurated techniques such as recovery of the body, identification procedures, autopsies, biological investigations as well as a multidisciplinary team which associated pathologists, odontologists, radiologists and biologists.

The result of our experience stressed the following three major points :

- not to hurry in any way despite the pressures
- to perform the autopsies only after collecting the information given by the families
- the importance of DNA analyses when all conventional identification methods have failed.

The conventional identification procedures (morphological and dental examination) allowed to identify 68 victims while 17 others were identified by genetic methods by fingerprinting. No biological sample could be found on the spot of the crash for only two victims.

References

CAIRNS FY, HERDSON PB, HITCHCOCK GC, KOELMEYER TD, SMEETON WMI, SYNECK BYL (1981) Aircrash on Mount Erebus. Med Sci Law 21(3):184-188

ECKERT WE (1990) The Lockerbie disaster and other aircraft breakups in midair. Am J Forens Med Pathol 11(2):93-101

LECOMTE D (1991) Identification après catastrophe aérienne (DC10 au Niger). résultats et réflexions. J Méd Lég-Droit Méd 34(5):307-312

MC CARTY VO, SOHN AP, RITZLIN RS, GAUTHIER JH (1987) Scene investigation, identification and victim examination following the accident of Galaxy 203 : disaster preplanning does work. J Forens Sci 32(4):983-987

MOODY GH, BUSUTTIL A (1994) Identification in the Lockerbie Air Disaster. Am J Forens Med Pathol 15(1):63-69

STAHL CJ, MC MEEKIN RR, RUEHLE CJ, CANIK JJ (1988) The medical investigation of airship accidents. J Forens Sci 33(4):888-898

# DNA FINGERPRINTING FOR POST-MORTEM FORENSIC IDENTIFICATION : SUCCESSFUL APPLICATION TO THE IDENTIFICATION OF AIRCRASH VICTIMS

**H. PFITZINGER, B. LUDES, and P. MANGIN**
**Institut de Médecine Légale, Faculté de Médecine, 11 rue Humann, 67085 Strasbourg, France.**

## INTRODUCTION

On january 20, 1992 an Airbus A320 crashed in Strasbourg area with 90 passengers and 6 crew members on board : 87 persons died and 9 persons survived. Among the 87 victims, 68 victims were identified owing to conventional methods such as dental records, physical and X rays examinations. Nineteen other presumed victims remained unidentified after this first step using the conventional methods. Finally, 17 out of the 19 remaining victims were identified, in a second step, through DNA fingerprinting.
This paper describes briefly the strategy followed for the step of genetic identification as well as the techniques applied for the formal identification of the different victims but also for the reconstitution of the heavy mutilated bodies from the numerous human fragments.

## MATERIALS AND METHODS

A.- *Biological samples available for the extraction of DNA* : the forensic samples taken during the autopsies consisted mainly of muscle but also, though less often used, bone, brain , heart, kidney, skin and skalp. The post mortem period of these samples varied from 36 to 240 hours. Other biological samples were the blood samples given from the missing bodies relatives. The DNA was extracted from the forensic samples and from the blood samples as already described ( 1 ). Time and temperature of incubation were defined according to the origin of the biological sample.

B.- *Application of two different techniques*

a ) DNA fingerprinting or RFLPs ( Restriction Length Polymorphisms ) ( 2 ) :
The RFLPs are very informative systems and were therefore used in order to identify with certainty the 19 victims who could not be found after having used conventional morphological and odontological methods. The identification was possible using the DNA fingerprinting method by parentage testing with the members of the families missing bodies. However, the RFLP technique is expensive and time consuming ( results are obtained after 4 to 6 weeks ) and was thus applied to identify complete bodies or large body fragments only.

The bodies were identified by establishing the existence of a genetic filiation with the members of the families of the presumed victims. The filiations were determined by comparing the DNA fingerprints obtained with the blood samples taken from the available family members with the DNA fingerprints corresponding to the tissue samples taken from the unidentified bodies or human fragments. The family members implicated in the filiation tests were father, mother, children, brother, sister but also husband and wife.

42 forensic DNA samples ( muscle, bone, brain, heart, kidney, skin and skalp ) and 52 DNA samples purified from blood samples were digested with the restriction enzyme Hinf I, fractionated on 0.7% agarose gels and transfered by Southern blotting onto nylon membranes. Hybridizations were performed with the 5 non isotopic single locus NICE probes ( MS1, MS31, MS8, MS43A and g3 ) from ICI Cellmark Diagnostics.

b ) The DNA amplification or Polymerase Chain Reaction ( PCR ) ( 3 ) :
This second technique was used for the reconstitution of the heavy mutilated bodies from the numerous body fragments found on the aircrash site. The PCR technique has a great sensitivity ( 5-10 ng DNA are amplified per reaction ), is rapid ( results are obtained into 24 h ) and easily applied and therefore permitted us to process a large number of samples simultaneously.

Analysis of three different nuclear genomic regions :

* *HLA-DQα locus* ( 3 ) : 2 ng of DNA were amplified according to the protocol of the Perkin Elmer ( Cetus Corporation, USA ) " Amplitype$^{TM}$ HLA-DQα Forensic DNA Amplification and Typing " kit.

* *D1S80 locus* ( 4 ) : 10 ng of DNA were amplified using the instructions of the Perkin Elmer " D1S80 Forensic DNA Amplification Reagent Set ". Amplified D1S80 alleles were analysed on ethidium bromide stained 1.5% Seakem GTG agarose gels and were identified against the allelic ladder fournished in the kit.

* *sex determination* ( 5 ) : the sex was determined for some DNA samples by simultaneous amplification of X-specific and Y-specific DNA sequences. The conditions used were as already described ( 5 ).

The HLA-DQα and the D1S80 loci were analysed for each human fragment and each body in our possession whereas sex was determined for a restricted number of samples only.

## RESULTS AND DISCUSSION

The first step of identification of the victims using morphological and odontological conventional methods ( dental records, physical and X rays examinations ) covered a period of 2 weeks. This first step resulted in the identification of 68 victims out of the 87 presumed victims. The second step of genetic investigations ( DNA fingerprinting determined by the analysis of RFLPs, DNA PCR typing at the HLA-DQα and D1S80 loci and sex determination ) lasted 10 weeks and permitted to identify 17 additional victims.

During the genetic investigations 42 DNA fingerprints were obtained from forensic samples ( mutilated bodies and large human fragments ) and 52 DNA fingerprints were determined from the blood samples of the family members of the 19 unidentified victims. The comparison of the 94 DNA fingerprints was realized with the BioImage system from Millipore : each of the 42 forensic DNA profiles was compared to each of the 52 DNA profiles corresponding to the family members.

The reconstitution of the mutilated bodies was achieved by comparing the phenotypes resulting from the PCR analyses of 298 forensic samples and 52 blood samples : 350 DNA samples were therefore amplified at both HLA-DQ$\alpha$ and D1S80 loci and represented a total of 700 PCR tests. Furthermore, the sex was determined for 30 forensic samples. The attribution of the body fragments to the mutilated bodies was possible by the comparison of all the PCR results with the morphological and odontological data gathered during the first step.

## CONCLUSION

The medico-legal investigations, which lasted 12 weeks, allowed the identification of 85 victims among the 87 listed by the investigators. Two presumed victims could not be found. The mendelian inheritance was established for 17 of the 19 unidentified remaining victims using the DNA fingerprinting method. The reconstitution of the heavy mutilated bodies from the numerous body fragments was carried out owing to a detailed and close team work gathering all the experts for exploiting each information and result obtained from the morphological, odontological and genetic investigations.

## REFERENCES

1.- Ludes B, Mangin P, Chaumont AJ ( 1991 ) Stability of DNA in brain cortex after long post mortem periods. In : Berghaus G, Brinkmann B, Rittner C, Staak M (eds) DNA-technology and its forensic application. Springer, Berlin Heidelberg New York, pp 187-191

**2.-** Jeffreys AJ, Wilson V, Thein SL ( 1985 ) Hypervariable minisatellite regions in human DNA. Nature 47 : 515-523

3.- Saiki R, Bugawan T, Horn G, Mullis K, Erlich H ( 1986 ) Analysis of enzymatically amplified B-globin and HLA-DQ$\alpha$ DNA with allele specific oligonucleotide probe. Nature 324 : 163-166

4.- Budowle B, Chakraborty R, Giusti A, Eisenberg A, Allen R ( 1991 ) Analysis of the VNTR locus D1S80 by the PCR followed by high-resolution PAGE. Am J Hum Genet 48 : 137-144

5.- Pfitzinger H, Ludes B, Mangin P ( 1993 ) Sex determination of forensic samples : co-amplification and simultaneous detection of a Y-specific and an X-specific DNA sequence.Int J Leg Med 105 : 213-216

**IDENTIFICATION OF THE VICTIMS OF THE AIR CRASH OF KAFOUTINE (SENEGAL) WICH TOOK PLACE ON FEBRUARY 9 TH 1992**

**Authors :** SCHULIAR, Y., M.D., French military medical services
MASSELIN, P., French National Gendarmerie
SALON, J., French National Gendarmerie
MICHAUT, J.F., French National Gendarmerie
LAFARGUE, P., Professor Doctor, Director, French military medical services

**Adress** : I.R.C.G. - 1, bd Théophile Sueur 93111 ROSNY-SOUS-BOIS

**KEYS-WORDS** : Air crash, forensic inquiry, identification.

**Circumstances of the crash** :

On february 9th 1992, 140 tourists taken on by a tour operator and flying from Paris landed at Dakar'sYof airport (Senegal). Once the administrative formalities were completed, the group went on within three different planes to Ziguinchor in Casamance.

One of the aircraft, a Convair 640, from Air Gambia, left Dakar with 50 passengers (48 french and 2 belgian citizens) and 4 crew members on board. After a 3/4 of an hour flight, the plane crashed while he was starting on its landing procedure in the surroundings of Kafountine, in a semi-swampy area nearby the Gambian border. The rescue squads rapidly took action, 20 injured and 30 victims (26 passengers and 4 crew members were counted. The corpses of the pilot, copilot and mechanic were left to their national authorities. The other corpses were disposed into bags in a cold room of the freight zone of Dakar's airport.

**Action taken by the team of identification of disaster victims (DVI) of the criminal research institut of the national gendarmerie** :

On february 9th 1992, at the request of the senegalese authorities, the french authorities decided to bring in the team of identification of disaster victims (DVI). The team was composed of four members : one gendarmerie officer, one army medical officer and two technical assistants bringing with them identification equipment. They arrived in Dakar on february 10th 1992.

**Identification organization** :

The initial objective of DVI team was to make a survey of the situation and to define the scope of action. After examination of the corpses, identification operations on the spot did not seem to pose any problem and were performed at the mortuary of the Dakar Hospital, the civil security squads being in charge of the transfer of the corpses into small group from the airport to the hospital.

**Means and results** :

The corpses were separated into two groups according to sex : 11 male and 16 female victims.

Antermortem information along with identity documents were obtained. Before examination, the corpses were numbered, photographed, undressed by the medical team. Clothes and various objects were also examined.

The examination of corpses complied with the interpol identification form consisted of :

- An anthropometrical analysis and a careful account of the morphological features of the corpses,
- A research for congenital or acquired malformation, scar, tatto and neavus.
- An assessment of lesions and a research of the direct causes of death.
- The establishment of an odontogram.

The corpses were identified after 48 hours. The rest of the mission dealt with the technical management of the files.

**Conclusions** :

That was the first overseas mission of the national gendarmerie DVI team. The identification operations did not present any major difficulty and were managed on the spot within 6 days.

If a disaster of any kind happens to french citizens, even outside the national borders, a DVI team composed of forensic surgeons, odontologists and specialists in judiciary identity should go on the scene to evaluate the situation and the local identification capacities ; the presence on the scene of the DVI team 24 hours after the disaster occured, permitted to secure pieces of evidence.

This mission also demonstrated the importance of logistic support.

# THE DISASTER VICTIMS IDENTIFICATION TEAM OF THE FRENCH NATIONAL GENDARMERIE

**AUTHORS** : SCHULIAR ,Y., M.D., *French military medical services*
MASSELIN, P., *French National Gendarmerie*
SALON, J., *French National Gendarmerie*
MICHAUT, J.F. , *French National Gendarmerie*
LAFARGUE, P., *Professor Doctor, Director, French military medical services*

**Adress** : I.R.C.G.N.
1, bd Théophile Sueur
93111 ROSNY-SOUS-BOIS Cedex

**KEY-WORDS** : Forensic inquiry, victim identification, mass disasters.

The french national gendarmerie has at its disposal a team of identification of disasters victims (DVI team) that can be put into action by the general direction of the national gendarmerie at the legal, administrative, and military authorities request.

**Location and mission** :

The DVI team is located in Rosny-sous-Bois is part of the Institute of Forensic Sciences of the National Gendarmerie. Its mission is to intervene on disaster scenes of any kind (at home and abroad), 24 hours a day.

Its role is :
- to bring assistance to investigators for the search and collect of corpses,
- to provide help to forensic surgeons for the centralization and the exploitation of antemortem and postmorten information,
- to obtain contacts with the various contributors,
- to organize synthesis meeting,
- provide qualified technical assistance to help in victims identification.

## ORGANIZATION

DVI COMMANDER

| IDENTIFICATION SECTION | LOGISTIC SECTION |
|---|---|
| - Collection of antemortem and postmortem data<br>- Internal/external information<br>- Information analysis<br>- Filing of identification documents<br>- organisation of synthesis meeting | - Staff provision<br>- Supply corps<br>- Accomodation<br>- Means of transport<br>- Other needs |

TECHNICAL ORGANISATION OF IDENTIFICATION

| SCENE SECTION | EXAMINATION SECTION | FORENSIC SURGERY SECTION |
|---|---|---|
| - Protection of the scene<br>- Area covering<br>- Collection of the corpses<br>- Checking and storage of the corpses<br>- Conveying of the corpses | - Undressing corpses<br>- External examination<br>- Clothes and objects description<br>- Specific photographs<br>- Fingerprinting<br>- Putting on the seals | - X-rays screenings<br>- Autopsy<br>- Anthropology<br>- Dental records<br>- Post mortem records<br>- Photographs<br>- Seals |

**Equipement** :

The DVI team disposes of :

- Transport facilities,
- Kits of forensic surgery, forensic odontology, anthropology, criminal records, secretariat,
- Microcomputers,
- Telecommunication sets.

**Achievements** :

The DVI team participated to the identification of the victims in :

- Strasbourg (Airbus plane A 320 crash, 20.01.92),
- Dakar (Air Gambia plane crash, 09.02.92),
- Roissy (Lufthansa plane crash, 06.01.93),
- Bordeaux (heavy car-crash ont he A-10 highway, 10.11.93).

**Cooperation** :

It has been established with :

- Military disaster victim identification team (french military medical services),
- Interpol (permanent committee on the identification of disaster victims),
- Foreign DVI teams.

# Medical inspection after the earthquake in southwest off Hokkaido in Okushiri island

T.Tsukamoto, H.Mikami, K.Haga, K.Terazawa
Department of Legal Medicine, Hokkaido University School of Medicine
North 15 West 7, Kita-ku, Sapporo, 060, Japan
Correspondence to: T.Tsukamoto Tel:81-11-706-5063 Fax:81-11-706-7860

## Introduction

On July 12, 1993 at 22:17, the earthquake in southwest off Hokkaido occured at 60 km north undersea of 34 km in depth of Okushiri island which places at southwest of Hokkaido (Fig. 1). Okushiri island is about 20 km long north to south, 10 km wide east to west, where approximately 5000 people are living.

The total deaths were 199 who were recovered most from the sea, 29 are still missing, and approximately 300 people were injured. One of the victims was found dead about 300 km north from the island after translocation by an ocean current.

In Aonae district, the south end of Okushiri island, the most severe damage due to twice Tsunami attacks had taken place a few minutes after the onset of the earthquake, followed by fire, and approximately 350 houses were lost. Most of the victims died due to Tsunami, not the earthquake itself.

Tsunami is a transient and huge elevation of the tidal level, in short, an earthquake sea wave, caused by rapid volume change or generation of the energy in the sea, as a consequence of the earthquake occured at the sea bottom or the eruption of a volcano, and sometimes by an underground experiment of an atomic bomb. Eighty percent of Tsunamis in the world occured in Japan. A Tsunami also occured by the conduction of the energy generated at a distant place. The earthquake in Chile in 1960 conducted at the velocity of 700 km/h through the Pacific ocean and 140 Japanese were killed by the resulting Tsunami. Tsunami waves tend to concentrate on a promontory and disperse along a large gulf. That is why the Tsunami attacked most severely Aonae district in the island.

## Examination and identification procedures

We were engaged in medical examination of the victims for personal identification and for determination of cause of death of the each person at the request of Hokkaido Police Headquarters during July 16 to 22 at Aonae district. Two places for examination were settled independently and spontaneously at Aonae and Okushiri districts in the island. Okushiri district places at the center of the east coast of the island. The number of the victims recovered was at the maximum on the day after the earthquake, i.e., 38 % of the total cadavers. A leading cause of death was drowning which was diagnosed by a lot of thoracic fluid obtained by puncture. An autopsy on a burnt victim proved massive aspiration of sand into tracheal branches and the cause of death was drowning, not by the fire.

The important purpose of the medical inspection in such mass disasters is personal identification. Except a severely burnt body and a set of burnt skeletal remains, 197 bodies were successfully identified. The characteristics used for the identification were facial appearances, called "visual identification" for 68 % , dental features 43%, and so on.

The visual identifications were effective limitedly a few days after the disaster, whereas the identification based on the dental features was applicable for several days after. Identification using fingerprints was applicable if their posessions were available, and was of the limited use practically. In addition, visual identification by the family was useless in several cases where all of the families were killed simultaneously in the disaster. Those features for personal identification reported to be essential in non-natural disasters are not always useful in natural disasters, since antemortem records can also be lost by the disaster.

## Discussion

The medical inspection in a mass disaster would always be an unexpected task for most of the forensic pathologists. However, it is an event which all forensic institute should plan for (1). Most of the mass disasters in Japan are of natural, whereas non-natural disasters occur more frequently in Europe as aircraft crashes, railway accidents, sinking of ships and some of them are acts of terrorism (2).

Until July 16 when we arrived at the island, two thirds of the cadavers recovered had been inspected by five physicians belonging to the Self-Defence Forces who stayed there for a general practice, not inspection. The inspection activities over one hundred cadavers apparently bothered their practice. A similar trouble was recognized also in Okushiri district. One dentist living in the island took the priority of the inspection and was obliged to neglect his patients who had lost their dentures during the disaster. A chain of command from the police headquarter was inadequate, which can lead to serious organizational difficulties (3).

Furthermore, major disaster plans for the dead are always temporizing in Japan. Adequate mortuary facilities are not provided in most cases. Far from provision of refrigerated trailers for body storage (4), we had no water supply during examinations and the dental X-ray apparatus was our own. A body preservation using dry ice was practically beneficial, however an effect was unsettled. As emphasized by Besant-Matthews who was a co-author of a report on the Delta Airlines crash, refrigerated trucks or trailers are a must (5) to prevent unnecessary decomposition of the cadavers. We have failed to perform single-locus VNTR profiling for personal identification due to advanced decomposion of DNA.

The diagnostic procedure during inspection where full autopsy cannot be performed should be easy and require no special instruments. A positive thoracic fluid is relatively specific to drowning and the procedure is performed easily on the site, though it is, of course, not a substitution of autopsy (6). Although the necessity of an autopsy on the victims of mass disasters has been the subject of much controversy (7), we reconfirmed the importance of the autopsy in differential diagnosis through our experiences. The legal permissions for autopsies except criminal victims are released rather negatively in Japan and often delayed. Even if it was for the early sampling of a small piece of the muscle for DNA analysis, the same permission as full autopsy is necessary. This negative attitude might be a cause of increased number of unidentified bodies.

In most of the natural disasters, the number of the victims is unknown which is called "catastrophe ouverte" in French, means "opened disaster" (8). However, the people living in this island had been well acquainted with each other, and visitors to this island were very few in that period of time. If it had been two weeks later, the identification would have been more difficult. Therefore the disaster in this island, in which the names and the number of the victims were known from the beginning, being called as "catastrophe fermée" in French that means "closed disaster", was a special form of the natural disaster.

## References


1. Pounder DJ (1985) Natural disaster potential and counter disaster planning in Australia. Am J Forensic Med Pathol 6:347-357
2. Barbash GI, Yoeli N, Ruskin S, Moeller DW (1986) Airport preparedness for mass disaster: a proposed schematic plan. Aviat Space Environ Med 57:77-81
3. Doyle CT, Bolster MA (1992) The medico-legal organization of a mass disaster —the Air India crash 1985. Med Sci Law 32:5-8
4. Ritzliv R, Gauthier JH (1987) Scene investigation, identification and victim

examination following the accident of Galaxy 203: disaster preplanning does work. J Forensic Sci 32:983-987
5. Gilliland MGF, McDonough ET, Fossum RM, Dowling GP, Besant-Mattews PE, Petty CS (1986) Disaster planning for air crashes – a retrospective analysis of Delta Airlines flight 191. Am J Forensic Med Pathol 7:308-316
6. Terazawa K (1993) Drowning. In: Takatori T (ed) Essentials of Forensic Medicine. Ishiyaku Publishers, Tokyo, pp 134-141 (in Japanese)
7. Mason JK (1984) The importance of the autopsy examination in major disasters. Ann Acad Med Singapore 13:20-24
8. De Valck E (1990) Le dentiste, en tant qu´expert lors de catastrophes: Identification dentaire lors de la catastrophe du ferry à Zeebruges. Rev Belge Méd Dent 90:11-20

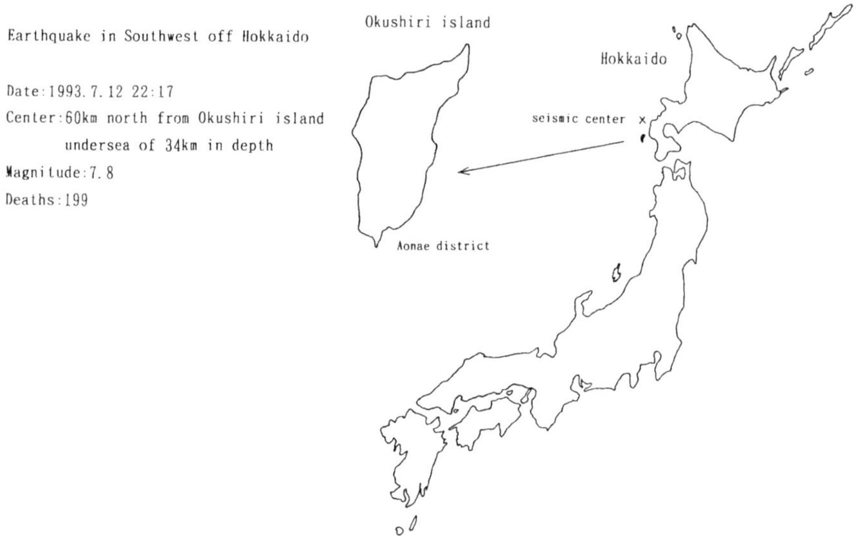


Fig. 1 The location of Okushiri island in Japan.
The cross on the map shows the seismic center.

# MASS ACCIDENTS ON MOTORWAYS: SOME BIOMECHANICAL AND MEDICOLEGAL CONSIDERATIONS UPON AN EPIDEMIOLOGICAL STUDY

**Franco Zuppichini, Mario Marigo**

Institute of Legal Medicine, University of Verona (Dir. Prof. M. Marigo)

*Key words:* Motorway; Mass accidents; Rescue organisation.

## BACKGROUND

The "Serenissima" motorway (A-4) is part of a longer lifeline that links Turin to Venice in Northern Italy, crossing the whole Po Valley. It is 142.1 km long, and it is run by around 55 million vehicles each year.

Among all motorway sinisters, it is possible to observe a subgroup of accidents that differ substantially from the average, both in number of involved cars and in number of casualties.

We shall refer to these accidents as "disasters", even if their dimensions are far smaller than natural catastrophes (or non-natural events such as an aeroplane collision or a shipwrecking), and if never a road accident has surged to such dimensions to enrol in the main catastrophes [3] in history.

This epidemiological, retrospective research is aimed to identify the collision patterns, risk factors and possible counter-measures in this kind of accidents [1,2,4,5].

## MATERIALS AND METHOD

There is not a clear line between an "accident" and a "disaster"; therefore, we have chosen as a threshold marker the impact on traffic flow and on rescue systems. According with this criteria, we have selected a group of accidents comprising 10 vehicles or more, with at least 5 casualties.

We performed a retrospective research, selecting all the accidents that satisfied the given criteria on the A-4 motorway "Serenissima" (from Brescia to Padua), in a period ranging from January 1983 to June 1992.

The following data were looked for: Day and hour of the accident; Weather and visibility; Site (km) of the accident; Number and type of involved vehicles; Direction and number of impacts; Number of casualties; Injury severity, according to the Abbreviated Injury Scale, 1990 Edition.

Further informations about condition of vehicles, modality of impact, patients clinical evolution, conditions and means of rescue were obtained from Police data, from Hospital data, or sometimes directly from witnesses.

## RESULTS

We analysed 12 motorways accidents, with 475 involved vehicles, 170 wounded and 21 dead motorvehicle users. Their main characteristics are summarised in Table I.

It is eye-catching how a few black spots, particularly in the outskirts of Verona, are associated to the majority of the disasters. Four accidents alone, occurred in a 8-km long tract, account for 15 deaths, that is 5.2% of the global mortality on the whole motorway in the whole decade.

The distribution by year and month shows a rather quiet period in 1986-1988, while a flourishing of disasters may be observed from Winter 1989. These accidents happen mostly in the first hours of the morning in working days. About seasonal distribution, disasters on this motorway are a fog-related, "winter" happening, even if in summertime strong flows of traffic are directed from the Brenner motorway towards the Adriatic sea and vice versa.

It is important to note that 10 out of 12 accidents happened with intense fog.

Cars represent around 69.2% of all vehicles, while light commercial vehicles represent around 9% of the specimen and heavy vehicles (>25 tons) set around 20% of vehicles. Trucks are more

| Date | Hour | Site | Weather | N. of vehicles | Casualties |
|---|---|---|---|---|---|
| 24 Jan. 83, Monday | 8.45 am | km 65.8 | Fog | 68 vehicles | 31 w., 9 dead |
| 30 Dec. 83, Friday | 4.30 pm | km 84.2 | Fog | 16 v. | 13 w. |
| 11 Jan. 85, Saturday | 8.45 pm | km 67.8 | Fog | 14 v. | 5 w., 1 d. |
| 25 Nov. 85, Monday | 7.40 am | km 53.3 | Fog | 12 v. | 4 w., 2 d. |
| 3 Jan. 87, Sunday | 7.40 am | km 23.6 | Fog | 15 v. | 5 w. |
| 24 Dec. 89, Sunday | 6.50 pm | km 50.7 | Fog | 10 v. | 7 w. |
| 18 Jan. 90, Thursday | 7.30 am | km 127.1 | Fog | 187 v. | 60 w., 3 d. |
| 10 Feb. 90, Saturday | 10.00 am | km 67.2 | Fog | 31 v. | 19 w., 2 d. |
| 3 March 90, Saturday | 2.20 pm | km 96.0 | Clear | 14 v. | 5 w. |
| 7 Oct. 90, Sunday | 5.00 pm | km 40.9 | Rain | 28 v. | 9 w., 1 d. |
| 6 Jan. 91, Sunday | 9.15 am | km 139.4 | Fog | 40 v. | 7 w. |
| 5 March 92, Thursday | 8.00 am | km 60.5 | Fog | 40 v. | 5 w., 3 d. |

*Table I: Main features of the selected mass accidents.*

heavily represented in accidents with fatalities. In a few cases toxic or inflammable goods were reported; however, no case of environmental pollution from wasting of chemicals was reported.

As one could expect, the lesions suffered by occupants are significantly more severe in cars than in heavy vehicles. All fatal cases regarded car occupants, except a passenger of a commercial vehicle that was downed when escaping. Also truck drivers are exposed to lesions, even near to fatal, and even without intrusion of the passenger compartment. Three pedestrians (escaping car occupants) are reported among the deaths.

**DISCUSSION**

Since the very first analysis of data, it is evident how some of the most severe cases happened with a repetitive pattern on the same 8 km of motorway around Verona. These four accidents alone account for 15 deaths, that is 5.2% of the global mortality on the whole motorway in the same decade.

The number of lightly wounded persons is surely underestimated. Under emotional distress, people often leave the scene and will eventually be cured in distant places, hours later.

A common finding in motorway disasters is a very critical level of visibility. Fog was present in 10 out of 12 cases; another case was associated to a cloud of smoke coming from a weed fire just outside the external border of the motorway.

For what concerns the global dynamics of the accidents, they appear to be divided into sub-units, that are separated by a certain number of cars that have been able to stop without colliding. The distance between each sub-unit may be as long as kilometres; for instance, in the worst case in our sample there were around 3.9 km between the first and the last group of vehicles.

Each group of impacted vehicles was composed by a minimum of 4 up to 53 vehicles; in the majority of cases, the vehicles in each sub-unit were from 10 to 15. Usually the worst consequences for road users are not in the "head" of the accidents, but rather in the middle or "tail" sub-units.

The sequential chain of interruption and replay of impacts is rather instructive, suggesting that a better management of the behaviour of oncoming drivers may prevent at least this "oscillation" between accident and accident-free zones.

Almost surely this pattern is due to differences in speed and braking spaces, that are enhanced not only by different vehicles, but also by different driving habits. In this situation, an impact causes a sharp deceleration or pushes a vehicle out of trajectory. If the flow of vehicles is suddenly locked, in conditions of poor visibility further collisions are rather immediate; at this point, the end of the collisions (with a dangerous permanent stop to oncoming traffic) or the precipitating of situation by a speedy and loaded truck is depending only by the local composition of traffic.

This mechanism may reproduce twice or more, at various distances, generating "impact waves" that may propagate as long as kilometers.

Of course, this division of the mass accident into sub-units affects substantially the effectiveness of rescue operations, because it is very difficult not only to access the different sites of the accident, but also to understand where there is need of urgent medical aid.

The narrow contact of deformed vehicles may allow a rapid development of flames, adding trouble and risk to rescue operators.

From a medicolegal point of view, there are often trouble in accident reconstruction and sometime in assessing the seat position inside cars. Personal identification is usually not difficult, and even in cases with destroyed plates and burned documents it was always possible to identify victims in a few hours. Responsibility problems concerning motorway structure are more difficult to discuss, although there is evidence of black spots in the examined tract.

The singularity of motorway "disasters" is not only in the crude number of vehicles and/or casualties, nor in worse deformation of single vehicles, but rather in the dynamic, in the number and sequence of offence to vehicles and, finally, in their risk factors: poor visibility, high kinetic energy, promiscuity of light and heavy traffic. To understand and master this singularity may lead to prevent a "normal" accident to grow up to this catastrophic level.

## Conclusions

Motorway "disasters" are rare events (less than 1% of all motorway accidents), but dramatically severe in their economic and human consequences. Normally they force rescue teams to close both the lanes, adding economical damage and causing overcrowding and sometimes other accidents on alternative paths.

There is evidence of a repetitive pattern in these accidents: a sharp reduction in speed ignites a first set of rear bumpings, that may completely stop the circulation. At this point, differences in braking spaces or openly wrong manoeuvres may "coagulate" the circulation in a mass of impacted vehicles. At this point, the chance of severe collisions is very high; a "trigger" is often given by exceedingly high speed of one or more oncoming heavy commercial vehicles.

The downing of pedestrians, as well as the occurrence of multiple impacts, suggests that the danger of casualties is extended far beyond the simple time of collisions.

Despite the occurrence of such "disasters", motorways offer theoretically the best environment for safe traffic. Some countermeasures of primary and secondary prevention may be suggested and regard both drivers, road and vehicles. A correct real-time information to drivers and a better separation of light and heavy vehicles, as well as a better control of truck speed, could reduce their prevalence and human cost. Moreover, rescue organisation must be accurately planned in order to overcome trouble in access to the scene and in triage of casualties.


1. Ernst G, Brühning E, Heuser W (1989): *Massen- und Serienunfällen auf BAB. Ergebnisse für die Jahre 1980–1985.* Straßenverkehrstechnik, Heft 1:13–20.
2. Ernst G, Brühning E, Heuser W (1989): *Häufungsstellen von Massen- und Serienunfällen auf BAB. Ergebnisse für die Jahre 1980–1985.* Straßenverkehrstechnik, Heft 6:213–222.
3. Skeet M (1977): *Manual for Disaster Relief Work.* Churchill Livingstone, Edinburgh, London and New York.
4. Zuppichini F, Simone B, Motton G, Orsi O, Poggi C (1991): *Risk factors and rescue patterns in motorway disasters: An epidemiologic study.* 1st Congress of Traffic Medicine, Alps-Adria. Zagreb, 29/31.5.1991, Abstracts:23–24.
5. Zuppichini F (1992): *Impact patterns and risk factors in motorway disasters: Some lessons from real cases.* 1992 Ircobi Conference, Verona, 9/11.9.1992, Proceedings.

# 14. Systematic Toxicological Analysis

# Toxicological Analysis of Drugs: GC-MS Screening and Confirmation

**Hans H. Maurer**

Department of Toxicology, University of Saarland, D-66421 Homburg / Saar, Germany

## Introduction

Gas chromatography-mass spectrometry (GC-MS) revolutionized the analysis of trace amounts of e.g. toxic compounds in complex matrices like body fluids. The relatively low costs for quadrupol or ion trap MS led to their wide distribution in the last few years. In clinical and forensic toxicology, a systematic toxicological analysis procedure is necessary that allows the simultaneous detection of as many toxicants as possible in biosamples. Unspecific chromatographic methods even if several were combined are not sufficient for these purposes, because the same chromatographic behavior is not evidential for the identity of two compounds. All chromatographic peaks or spots have to be identified because any of them may represent a potential poison. In the following, a GC-MS procedure is presented that allows the simultaneous and highly specific detection (screening and confirmation) of nearly all toxicologically relevant drugs in one single step.

## Materials and Methods

### *Apparatus*

A Hewlett-Packard (HP) series 5890 GC combined with a HP MSD series 5970 MS and a HP Vectra PC with HP G1034B software were used. GC conditions: splitless injection mode; column, HP capillary (12 m x 0.2 mm I.D.), cross-linked methylsilicone, 330 nm film thickness; injection port temperature, 270°C; carrier gas, helium; flow rate 1 ml/min; column temperature, 100 to 310°C in 30°C/min, initial time 3 min, final time 5 min; MS conditions: scan mode; ionization energy, 70 eV; ion-source temperature, 220°C; capillary direct interface heated at 260°C.

### *Hydrolysis, extraction and acetylation procedure*

A 10 ml volume of urine was refluxed with 3 ml 37% hydrochloric acid for 15 min. Following hydrolysis, 4 ml sodium hydroxide (10 mol/l) were added and the resulting solution was mixed with 10 ml 30% aqueous ammonium sulphate to obtain a pH between 8 and 9. This solution was extracted with 10-ml of a mixture of dichloromethane/2-propanol/ethyl acetate (1:1:3). After centrifugation the organic extract was carefully evaporated to dryness.

The residue was acetylated for 30 min at 60°C with 0.1 ml of a mixture of acetic acid anhydride/pyridine (3:2). The acetylation mixture was then carefully evaporated to dryness, the resultant residue dissolved in 0.1 ml methanol and 0.5-2 µl of this sample was injected into the gas chromatograph.

## Results and discussion

A systematic toxicological analysis procedure (so called "general unknown analysis") using GC-MS was developed that allows the simultaneous screening and confirmation in urine of the following categories of drugs: barbiturates and other sedative-hypnotics, anticonvulsants, benzodiazepines, antidepressants, phenothiazine and butyrophenone neuroleptics, opioid and other potent analgesics, non-opioid analgesics, antihistamines, antiparkinsonian drugs, beta-blockers, antiarrhythmics, diphenol laxatives and the metabolites of all of these (Maurer 1992a, 1992b). For sample preparation the urine samples are hydrolyzed by hydrochloric acid, extracted at pH 8-9 with a mixture of dichloromethane, isopropanol and ethyl acetate followed by acetylation. The screening is performed using reconstructed mass chromatograms which may indicate the presence of suspected mass spectra in the full mass spectra stored during GC analysis. Eight ions per category were individually selected from the mass spectra of the corresponding drugs and their metabolites identified in authentic urine samples (Maurer 1992a, 1992b). These groups of fragment ions were named *computer monitoring programs*. Since some fragment ions were selected from different categories, reduced monitoring programs were recommended for general unknown analysis. Using these programs for mass chromatography, the presence of the abovementioned drugs and/or their metabolites can be indicated. The identity of any of these compounds can be confirmed by computerized comparison of the peak underlying full mass spectra with reference spectra (Pfleger et al. 1993). This reference data base contains mass spectra, GC retention indices and further chemical and toxicological informations of more than 1500 drugs, 800 pesticides and pollutants as well as 2000 of their metabolites.

In the following, the procedure is illustrated by an example. A total ion chromatogram of an urine extract after acid hydrolysis and acetylation is shown in Fig. 1 (*top*) indicating series of unknown peaks. By clicking the corresponding pull down menu *(e.g. opioids)* the computer monitoring program for the desired drug class can be started. In the middle part of Fig. 1 the selected mass chromatograms are shown indicating the possible presence of opioids. In the lower part of Fig. 1 the peak underlying full mass spectrum and the reference mass spectrum given as result of the library search (Pfleger et al. 1993) are shown. The marked peak in the selected mass chromatogram can be identified as the hydrolysis product of the nor metabolite of the opioid methadone. The presented systematic toxicological analysis procedure allows fast and specific detection of most of the toxicologically relevant drugs in urine samples after therapeutic doses, and has proved to be suitable also for screening of abused medicaments in psychiatry.

For toxicological screening procedures in urine, quality criteria of the parent compound are of minor value, if the concentrations of the metabolites are much higher in urine than those of the parent drug and if the metabolites are detected by the procedure. Most of the toxicologically relevant drugs are lipophilic substances that undergo extensive metabolism. Since pure reference substances of the metabolites are usually not available, it is necessary to control the quality of the screening procedures using urine samples of volunteers or in-patients treated with a known dose of the drug. The procedure should be sufficiently sensitive to detect therapeutic concentrations at least over a 12-24h period after ingestion. Procedures are suitable for toxicological purposes if this prerequisite is met.

After unequivocal identification, quantification of the drugs can be performed by immunological or chromatographic methods favourably by GC-MS using stable isotopes as internal standards.

The drugs of abuse cannabinoids, cocaine and LSD cannot be detected by the general unknown procedure. Special procedures must be used for sample preparation (Maurer 1992a, 1992b). These extracts can also be analyzed by GC-MS. Diuretics and non-steroidal analgesics which are also misused can also be detected by GC-MS after suitable sample preparation (Maurer and Hausmann 1990, Maurer et al. 1994).

## Conclusions

The procedure presented allowed rapid screening and confirmation of most of the toxicologically relevant drugs in one single step. Since in clinical toxicology the prevalence of positive results is high, not only the confirmation but also the screening should be performed by GC-MS.

## References

Maurer HH (1992a) Systematic toxicological analysis of drugs by GC-MS. J Chromatogr 580: 3-41

Maurer HH (1992b) Methods for GC-MS. In: Pfleger K, Maurer HH, Weber A (eds) Mass spectral and GC Data of drugs, poisons, pesticides, pollutants and their metabolites, 2nd ed, part 1. VCH Publishers, Weinheim, P 3-32

Maurer HH, Hausmann E (1990) Identification of diuretics and their metabolites in urine using computerized gas chromatography-mass spectrometry. Bull. Soc. Sci. Med. Grand Duché Luxemb. 127 suppl.: 121-125

Maurer HH, Kraemer T, Weber A (1994) Toxicological detection of ibuprofen and its metabolites in urine using gas chromatography-mass spectrometry (GC-MS). Pharmazie 49: 148-150

Pfleger K, Maurer HH, Weber A (1993) Mass spectral library of drugs, poisons, pesticides, pollutants and their metabolites, 2nd rev. Hewlett Packard, Palo Alto, CA

**Fig. 1.** Total ion chromatogram of a urine sample after acid hydrolysis and acetylation. The given pull down menus of the detectable drug classes can be clicked by mouse to start the generation of the selected mass chromatograms using macros (*top*).
Mass chromatograms indicating opioids. The marked peak is the trace of ion *m/z* 69 (*middle*).
Result of the computer library search of the spectrum underlying the marked peak (*bottom*).

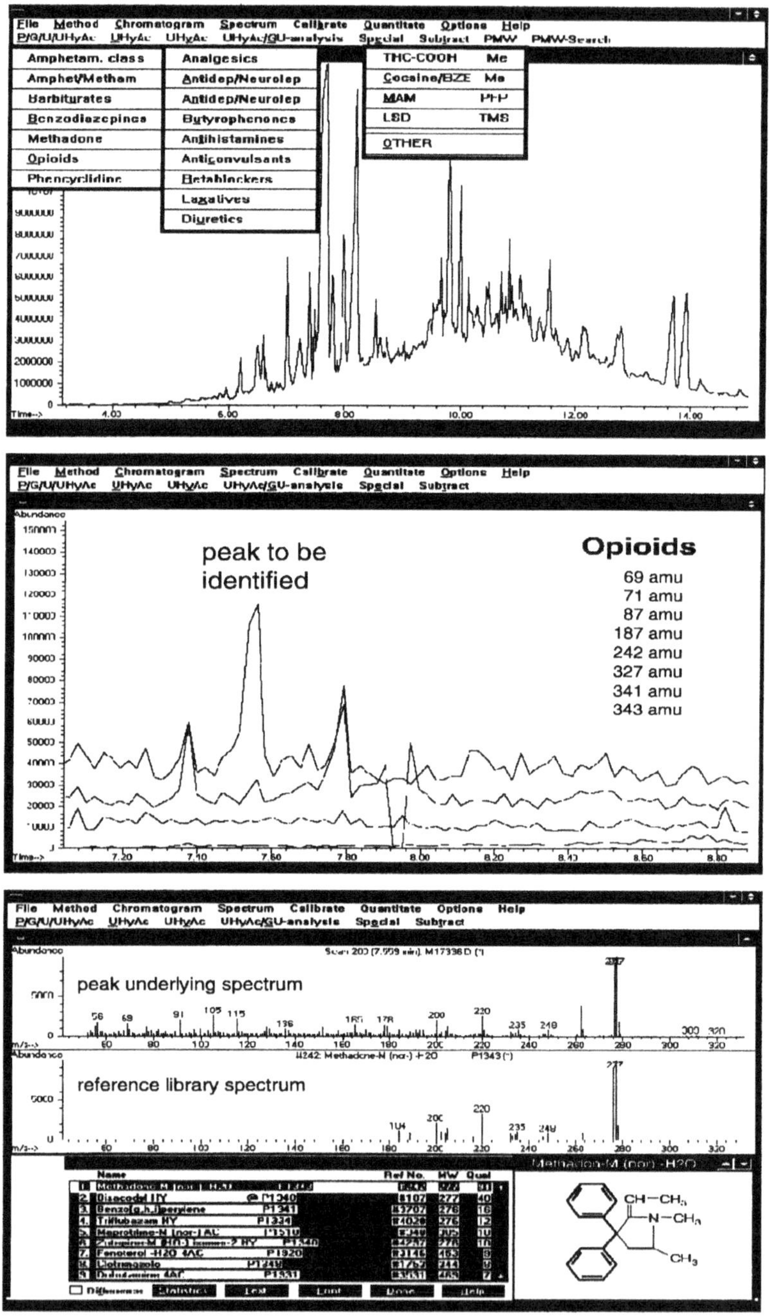

## General approach of Systematic Toxicological Analysis - Current status and future

R. Klaus Mueller, Institute of Forensic Medicine, Leipzig University,
and Institute of Doping Analysis, Kreischa near Dresden (Germany)

Systematic Toxicological Analysis (STA) is the logical, algorithmical analytical strategy for the general toxicological analysis, the "undirected" or "unconfined" search in questionable cases of poisoning. It is suggested to be the most promising way to solve "generalunknown" cases. Although having been considered necessary since more than a century by some, this concept remained to be more or less a philosophy or an illusion for many and for decades. The analytical tools of the past had hardly been suitable to detect any unsuspected poison without hints, and to identify detected substances beyond any doubt. The ever growing number of potentially harmful (mainly organic) compounds was an additional impediment, steadily and considerably increasing until our times.
The few who believed in the principal possibility of a final solution considered it to be approached only slowly and asymptotically by an optimised combination of objectively selected sets of analytical methods.
But proclaiming a philosophy in an area of natural science may be suspicious for the majority, - this leaves the solid ground of an experimental field like our analytical chemistry and toxicology. Therefore - and even more if one confesses that this concept is a kind of CREDO - it is crucial, to put such a philosophical concept into question from time to time. Is it still necessary, and does it still seem realistic?
At first - have not the modern instrumental analytical principles and techniques together with computerisation made superfluous any additional concept or strategy in this direction? GC/MS or the increasingly used HPLC/MS alone are so powerful, that some consider them as the only techniques of choice without any alternative. Undoubtedly, their performances - whether information capacities or detection limits - seem to be more than sufficient.
At second - the introduction of new pharmaceutical or other potentially toxic agents has slowed down considerably for well-known reasons, so that the number of toxicologically relevant compounds grow much slower than during the last decades. So should not any "general unknown" case be solved almost automatically, without basic problems in any well equipped modern laboratory - whether doing forensic toxicology in the narrow sense or analysing clinical poisonings as well?
As every experienced toxicological analyst will admit, there are still weaknesses and gaps, - there might easily be a latent number of undetected poisonings under the "general unknown" cases without directed hints. If this is accepted, what can be the reasons?
We have GC/MS with huge libraries and with automatic search programmes,

we have extensive files of GC Retention Indices, TLC Retention Factors. Colour Reactions, collections of UV or IR spectra. Each of these technical approaches in itself comprises hundreds or thousands of compounds, and altogether those principles should include almost any relevant substance.

And we have our TIAFT Guidelines for Toxicological Analysis, adopted quite recently, and hopefully followed within Europe by even more detailed EU Guidelines for the same purpose. Should not they provide also an optimal guidance for STA, making negligible any additional considerations about weaknesses or even failures of this category of toxicological analysis?

Independently from the subsequent combination of analytical techniques and procedures, the compounds encompassed in principle are the basis of this general approach.

A compound not encompassed cannot really become included into the systematic search, and if present in a sample, it would not be detected with certainty, - perhaps only by chance. At least any substance demanding special analytical precautions would be neglected, if not included into the schedule of STA.

There are two consequences.

The first one: If a certain substance would not be necessarily detected without directed suspicion, a "general unknown" case and a questionable poisoning will remain undetected, will contribute to the "dark number" of latent intoxications. Impossible? Perhaps not very frequent, perhaps even improbable, but not unthinkable. And how important should we consider one single case of unrecognised poisoning in our time of overwhelming analytical possibilities? Do we have a general register of toxicologically relevant compounds, compiled by rational means and approved by suitable consent, whether world-wide or at least for certain regions?

Of course we have lists of compounds of toxicological relevance, having been produced by various means. There are collections of substances having been identified as the causes of poisoning cases. But there is a principal weakness: They have been the source of <u>detected</u> poisonings. Substances not included into our analytical schedules would have little chance to be detected. Because they would hardly appear in corresponding statistical surveys, they will also not appear in those lists, apparently supporting the image of their irrelevance.

This is the second consequence of the "statistical" relevance mentioned above.

Another kind of relevance is certainly reflected by the numerous data collections, which partly have lead to the STA data files of our TIAFT STA Committee (books on GC RI, TLC RF). But they are strongly influenced by the outlined statistical approaches, necessarily including their weaknesses.

Are there other approaches to determine the toxicological relevance, and to limit by this measure a number of compounds to be reasonably encompassed for STA?

At this point, we can refer to own earlier proposals, which cannot be repeated here.

But although this step of STA has been discussed already at the e very beginning, it was considered to be of minor importance. Initially the number of problems of STA appeared to be overwhelming, enfacing the principal decisions among techniques, procedures, systems, conditions, or the selection of objective criteria for the performances of systems and procedures. In comparison, the consent about a possibly large list of toxicologically relevant compounds was not regarded to be crucial. But now, having access to much more powerful analytical means, we should again recognise this challenge. How high or how low must or dare a probability be to disregard a poisoning case? Could we accept a probability threshold of 0.001 or 0.00001, - one tenth or one thousandth of a percent? If assuming only one million of questionable poisoning cases world-wide per year, this could mean 1000 or 10 undetected cases. Acceptable? Negligible? We are challenged to decide and to draw our conclusions for the subsequent needs of our STA strategy.

Another neglected or side staffed step of STA is isolation.

Keeping aside the immunoassays, all instrumental techniques need extraction, purification, concentration steps. Confessed, that the higher importance of this step is associated with quantitation, which comes after STA. Confessed also, that the very low detection limits of modern analytical procedures have made the yield of extraction procedures a secondary aspect. But should not play the extraction some role even then?

Could one imagine, that a substance would be isolated below the detection limit due to improper conditions, thus mainly focusing on other compounds considered exclusively relevant? Isn't it true, that new proposals of extraction procedures - may they be liquid/liquid or solid phase extraction - are mostly checked by examples instead of a total number of substances considered relevant for STA?

But we have not yet any extensive collection of parameters for the extraction of toxicologically relevant organic compounds from aqueous phase - or even from biological material. And everybody knows, that the number of different extraction procedures for smaller or larger groups of compounds is vast, the data being hardly compatible and the performance remaining incomparable from this general standpoint.So we encounter still another challenge of an unsolved or at least insufficiently optimised step of STA.

Several further stages or steps of STA could or should be discussed in the same light, asking whether we have already reached a more or less ideal position, or whether we are still far away from this our target. But chromatography (GC, TLC, HPLC), spectrometry and further principles will be dealt with in subsequent papers in detail, so that the presented general comments to the situation of STA may be shortened.

Beyond all methodical advances and beyond theoretical considerations, Systematic Toxicological Analysis as a tool for "general unknown" cases will remain a challenge as well as a matter of believing in an analytical philosophy, - a credo.

(Literature references at the author)

# 15. Forensic Aspects of Drug Addiction

# THE IMPORTANCE OF STANDARDS AND REGULATIONS DERIVED FROM TOXICOLOGY FOR THE PROTECTION OF HUMAN HEALTH AND THE ENVIRONMENT BY THE PUBLIC HEALTH AUTHORITY

O. FEENSTRA

Amt der Kaerntner Landesregierung
Abteilung 12 - Umweltmedizin
A-9021 Klagenfurt

## SUMMARY

Legal medicine has been for a long time reluctant to introduce standards and regulations derived from toxicology into the public health aspects of chemicals present in air, food, water and other parts of the environment and has therefore neglected what should get a new subset of the discipline.
On the other hand public health authorities are often confronted with doubtful and inaccurate predictions, speculations and guesses about environmental impacts on human health.
Given this situation legal medicine as a discipline should not fail to support public health with sound facts based on toxicological science and should engage far more in these activities of governmental organizations as they share common interests.
An example of an environmental exposure to lead illustrates future possibilities of interdisciplinary answers to the challenge.

## KEY WORDS

Legal Medicine - Environmental Toxicology - Public Health

## INTRODUCTION

In all branches of toxicology, scientists explore the mechanisms by which chemicals produce adverse effects in biologic systems and that way participate in the development of standards designed to protect human health from the exposure to chemical agents possibly leading to both acute and chronic illness. Environmental toxicologists have expanded their studies to the effects of chemicals in flora and fauna.
Main support for toxicological health evaluation comes from appropriate investigations of the contaminating agent, its pollutant concentrations in air, soil and water and from uniform procedures when performing studies and comparing the results with generally accepted values. A still tolerable pollutant concentration is supposed to mark a threshold separating pollutant concentrations tolerable from the point of view of toxicology and environmental hygiene from those pollutant concentrations leading to undesired and negative health effects.
Metal contamination of the environment reflects both natural sources and contribution from industrial activity, metals being probably the oldest toxins known to humans, lead usage having begun prior to 2000 B.C..

## MATERIAL AND METHODS

Environmental exposure to toxic agents like lead most frequently is caused by chronic inhalation and oral exposure at industrial sites. Adverse health effects may occur as a result of long-term low-level exposure to lead.
As an example of the support to public health based on legal medicine the results of appropriate investigations from blood-lead-levels of 1251 inhabitants living around one industrial site where lead has been processed for decades and where families grew their vegetables in gardens reveiling severe heavy metal contaminations up to 5660 mg lead per kg of soil are presented. Development of sound analytical methods (AAS) made it possible to assess internal exposure by means of whole blood analysis.

## RESULTS

The influence of distance from an industrial site on the concentration in blood of a toxic agent is shown in table 1. The blood-lead-levels definitely correlate to the distance of individual homes from the industrial site, with children showing the highest mean value rates.

Table 1: *Influence of distance from the industrial site on the lead concentration in blood (µg Pb/100 mL)*

| Group | Distance | Cases | Blood-lead-concentration | |
|---|---|---|---|---|
| | | | Median | Mean value |
| Children | less 1 km<br>more 1 km | 169<br>69 | 8,72<br>5,27 | 10,27<br>6,36 |
| Adolescents | less 1 km<br>more 1 km | 125<br>57 | 6,61<br>4,31 | 7,64<br>4,68 |
| Adults, nonworkers | less 1 km<br>more 1 km | 431<br>216 | 6,51<br>5,66 | 7,34<br>6,49 |
| Adults, active workers | less 1 km<br>more 1 km | 52<br>21 | 26,54<br>22,06 | 29,58<br>36,60 |
| Adults, former workers | less 1 km<br>more 1 km | 89<br>22 | 17,07<br>15,95 | 18,22<br>17,19 |

The typical effect of lead accumulation in the food chain resulted in different blood-lead-levels depending on the distance from the industrial site on one hand **and** on the intake of food from vegetable origin out of the own garden, with children showing a fifty percent increase in the mean values when fed with vegetables grown on this lead-contaminated soil. These effects are shown in table 2.

Table 2: *Influence of food of vegetable origin grown at a defined distance from the industrial site on the blood-lead-level (µg Pb/100 mL blood)*

| Group | Distance | Mean value of blood-lead-levels due to intake of own garden vegetables when eaten | | |
|---|---|---|---|---|
| | | never | sometimes | ever |
| Children | less 1 km<br>more 1 km | 8,87<br>5,10 | 9,92<br>5,51 | 12,22<br>7,22 |
| Adults | less 1 km<br>more 1 km | 6,92<br>5,55 | 7,62<br>6,52 | 8,11<br>6,37 |
| active workers | | 34,85 | 42,75 | 24,15 |
| former workers | | 15,90 | 19,69 | 18,61 |

## DISCUSSION

Since low-level, long-term exposure is the most common way of exposure to environmental metals, in the general environment as well as in the work environment, the possible chronic effects of these agents are of great concern to toxicologists, regulatory officials and the general public. The basis to elucidate possible effects consists in the evaluation of heavy metals in body fluids or teeth in men corresponding to the contamination of soil and of food of vegetable origin from their surrounding environment. Lead is a non-essential metal whose toxicity is largely due to the inhibition of enzymes responsible for heme synthesis and competition for calcium in Ca-dependent reactions.

Children as a risk group for CNS effects have received particular attention in studies dealing with lead-induced neuropsychological deficits at Pb-blood-levels between 10 and 50 µg/100 mL. The results of this study have therefore been classified regarding possible toxicological effects induced by low-level chronic lead exposure as suggested by the advisory commitee to the German Federal Parliament shown in table 3.

Category I (less than 15µg/100mL) is classified as inconspicuous, category II (between 15 and 25 µg/100mL) as raised value without obvious negative health effects, category III (more than 25 µg/100mL) as distinctly raised value with possible negative health effects. As a conclusion all children ranging in group II and III and all adults ranging in group III were counseled to attend further clinical exploration.

Table 3: *Toxicological assessment of Pb-blood-levels*

| Group | Distance | Cases in categories | | |
|---|---|---|---|---|
| | | I | II | III |
| Children | less 1 km<br>more 1 km | 204<br>66 | 30<br>2 | 4<br>1 |
| Adolescents | less 1 km<br>more 1 km | 115<br>56 | 10<br>1 | 1<br>0 |
| Adults | less 1 km<br>more 1 km | 409<br>210 | 20<br>6 | 2<br>0 |
| Adults related to workers | | 116 | 8 | 5 |
| former workers | | 48 | 56 | 7 |

## REFERENCES


Alexander LM, Heaven A, Delves HT, Moreton J, Trenouth MJ (1993) Relative Exposure of Children to Lead from Dust and Drinking Water. Archives of Environmental Health 48: 392-400

Amdur MO, Doull J, Klaassen CD (ed) (1991) Casarett and Doull`s Toxicology. Pergamon Press, Oxford-New York-Toronto

Drasch G, Müller RK, Grasemann F, Adang M, Roider G, Wowra D(1994) Vergleich der Belastung der Bevölkerung im Leipziger und Münchner Raum mit den Schwermetallen Kadmium, Blei und Quecksilber - eine Untersuchung an menschlichem Organmaterial. In: Gesundh-Wes, vol 56. Georg Thieme Verlag Stuttgart· New York, P263-267

Glotzer DE, Bauchner H (1992) Management of Childhood Lead-poisoning: A Survey. Pediatrics 89:614-618

Merian E (1991) Metals and Their Compounds in the Environment. VCH Verlag, Weinheim

Rat von Sachverständigen für Umweltfragen für den Deutschen Bundestag (1990) Sondergutachten Altlasten. Bundestags-Drucksache 11/6191

# EVALUATION AND DEVELOPMENT OF NARCOTICS AFTER ANALYSIS OF SEIZED SAMPLES IN THE NORTH OF FRANCE 1989 - 1993

GHYSEL M-H. ; BERQUEZ N. ; BOUDJADA S. ; DERAMAUX C. ; DUPONT V. ; SALVADORE O. ; VILETTE V. ; HAGUENOER J-M.
Laboratoire de Police Scientifique - 7 Bd VAUBAN 59021 LILLE Cédex FRANCE

We have investigated about 600 narcotics samples each year. These represent only a small part of the national seizures but they are a fair indication of the trend in drug traffic. Analytical procedure and results are presented for heroin, cocaine, amphetamines, cannabis and LSD.

**General analytical procedure** : All solvents used are analytical grade. Qualitative analysis are carried out by Thin Layer Chromatography (T.L.C.) and Gas Chromatography-Mass Spectrometry (GC-MS). Gas Chromatography (GC) or High Performance Liquid Chromatography (HPLC) with UV detector were used for quantitative analysis.

**1. HEROIN** : Since 1989, number of seizures and weight has increased each year. Table 1 reports for each year the number of cases of heroin, the number of samples analysed, their weight and the percentage in relation to the National seizure.

| **HEROIN** | **1989** | **1990** | **1991** | **1992** | **1993** |
|---|---|---|---|---|---|
| number of cases | 31 | 28 | 35 | 50 | 65 |
| number of samples | 67 | 139 | 41 | 70 | 153 |
| weight (gr) | 7767 | 18642 | 9071 | 12226 | 18464 |
| % national | 2,6 | 4,6 | 1,6 | 3,73 | 4,78 |

**Table 1: Heroin : number and weight of seizures**

**Results** : Before 1990, a lot of products were used to cut powders : caffeine, paracetamol, phenobarbitone, acetylsalicylic acid, procaïne, methaqualone... and sugars like lactose, saccharose or polyol like mannitol. Since 1990, the tendency has, in most cases, been to cut heroin with a mixture of caffeine and paracetamol. We have already met on several occasions a package of beige powder looking like heroin samples, but containing only a mixture of caffeine and paracetamol. In a case, an antifungal, the griseofulvine, has been used. In a case of overdose, heroin was cut with xylazine. Xylazine is a short acting, nonopioid, sedative analgesic used in veterinary medicine. A dosage of 2-3 mg/kg IV is used for horses. In Dallas Texas USA, xylazine has already been found in Heroin exhibits.

**2. COCAINE** : In our experience, no real increment has been observed since 1989, but we have, in the North of France, very little cocaine in comparison to other areas (cf. table 2).

| **COCAINE** | **1989** | **1990** | **1991** | **1992** | **1993** |
|---|---|---|---|---|---|
| number of cases | 19 | 8 | 6 | 36 | 16 |
| number of samples | 40 | 111 | 6 | 45 | 18 |
| weight (gr) | 1255 | 1604 | 269 | 1808 | 688 |
| % national | 0,13 | 0,09 | 0,03 | 0,83 | 0,04 |
| **CRACK** | **1989** | **1990** | **1991** | **1992** | **1993** |
| number of cases | | | | 1 | 2 |
| number of samples | | | | 1 | 3 |
| weight (gr) | | | | 937 | 8 |

**Table 2 : cocaine : number and weight of seizures**

**Results** : We have very rarely met CRACK : cocaïne chlorhydrate transformed in base with sodium bicarbonate or ammonia. We have often seen cis and transcinnamoylcocaïnes alcaloïds present in illicit samples of cocaïne. Qualitative and quantitative data of these compounds provide information about the isolation and purification procedures to which the sample has been subjected (LE BELLE 1991). Sometimes, traces of tropacocaïne, ecgonine... are detected. Cocaïne is sometimes blended with other local anesthesic product like lidocaïne and often cut with polyol like mannitol or inositol. In some occasions, we have discovered lidocaïne in place of cocaïne.

**3. AMPHETAMINES** : Before 1990, we have analyzed several amphetamine powder samples, but since, we have found more amphetamine by-products in tablets (powder is rarer now ; our seizure of 18 kg in 1993 represents 42 % of the national seizure of amphetamine powder - cf table n° 3).

| **AMPHETAMINE POWDER** | **1989** | **1990** | **1991** | **1992** | **1993** |
|---|---|---|---|---|---|
| number of cases | 4 | | | | 1 |
| number of samples | 8 | | | | 10 |
| weight (gr) | 989 | | | | 18323 |
| % NATIONAL | 5 | | | | 42 |
| **TABLETS** | | | | | |
| number of cases | 8 | 8 | 3 | 8 | 4 |
| number of samples | 18 | 17 | 3 | 11 | 7 |
| quantity of tablets | 2789 | 3600 | 3410 | 543 | 5777 |
| % national | | | 5,5 | 3,9 | 4,8 |

**Table 3 : amphetamines : number and weight of seizures**

**Results** : There are about 15 by-products of amphetamines. Most important are :

- methylenedioxymethamphetamine or MDMA or Ecstasy or Adam
- methylenedioxyethamphetamine or MDEA or Eve
- methylenedioxyamphetamine or MDA
- methamphetamine or ICE...

Tablets are generally white or beige, sometimes pink, generally without inscription. Exceptionnaly, however they are marked with a heart, a spade, a rabbit-head, an elephant... Ecstasy is also sold in capsules (cf. photography 1).

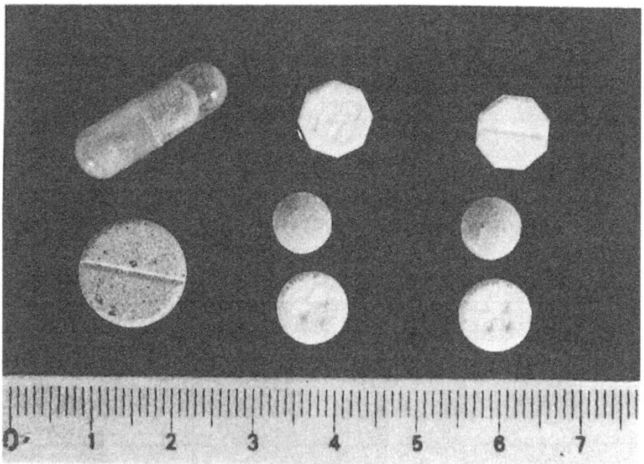


**Photography 1 : different kinds of « ECSTASY »**

When we analyse these tablets, we often find other products than amphetamine like caffeine, codeine, methadone, phenobarbitone, oxazepam, biperidene, ephedrine... and from 1994 heroine, monoacetylmorphine, acetylcodeine. In most cases, there is about 20% of MDMA per tablet, but sometimes we find only 0,5% , and sometimes nothing.

A new presentation of the drug recently appeared in Belgium, i.e. a small thin flask of 3 ml looking like perfume sample containing a clear slightly yellowish solution, called « PERFECTIL » or « DRACH ». The pH of this solution is 4, it contains caffeine, amphetamine and very little MDEA, diazepam and cocaïne.

**4. CANNABIS** : Drug-addicts continue to use haschisch and marijuana, but we have also seen the appearance of « SKUNK » : cf table 4.

| **CANNABIS** | **1989** | **1990** | **1991** | **1992** | **1993** |
|---|---|---|---|---|---|
| **HASCHISCH** | | | | | |
| number of samples | 20 | 26 | 51 | 49 | 35 |
| weight (gr) | 463250 | 22976 | 50521 | 36395 | 344437 |
| % national | 2,86 | 0,1 | 0,15 | 0,09 | 0,76 |
| **MARIJUANA** | | | | | |
| number of samples | 2 | 2 | 5 | 4 | 4 |
| weight (gr) | 521 | 3740 | 919 | 13758 | 794 |
| **« SKUNK »** | | | | | |
| number of samples | 3 | 6 | 13 | 10 | 8 |
| weight (gr) | 37 | 773 | 383 | 267 | 146 |
| **OIL** | | | | | |
| number of samples | | | | | 1 |
| weight (gr) | | | | | 998 |

**Table 4 : cannabis : number and weight of seizure**

« SKUNK » (cf. photography n° 2) is the flowering top of the female Cannabis, rich in tetrahydrocannabinolic acid (THCA) a precursor of psychotropic substance, the delta 9 tetrahydrocannabinol (THC).

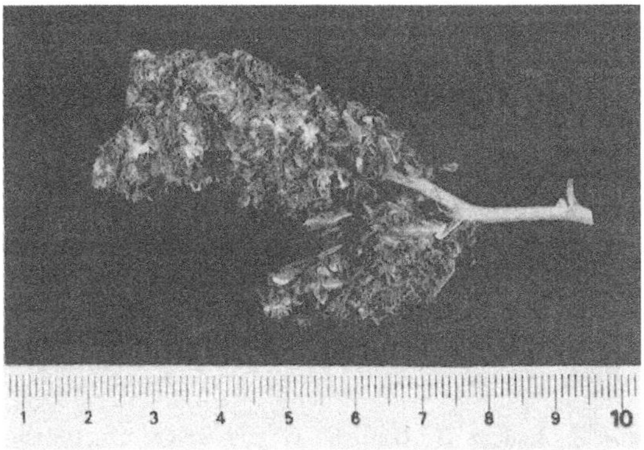


**Photography 2 : flower top of a female cannabis « SKUNK »**

In the North of France, this « SKUNK » or « NETHERWEED » comes from the greenhouse cultivation of hemp in the Netherlands (HUIZER 1992). The plants are not usually grown from seed but from cloning from a female plant. Pieces of the young stem are dipped into a special growth stimulating powder. The plants may grow on their own, but the use of special growing lamps as used in horticulture is common. The growth is enormously stimulated after the plants have been exposed to long periods of light exposure. The amounts of water and nutrition are regulated by pumps with time clocks or even with computerized systems. When using artificial light, the cycle is less than 3 months. This means that 4 harvests per year can be effected.

**Analytical procedure** : When we analyse this kind of cannabis by H.P.L.C., in these conditions : chromatograph Perkin-Elmer ; column Novapack Waters C18 ; mobil phase acetonitrile/methanol /sulfuric acid 0,02 M (37/34/19 v/v) flow 2 ml/mn, we see a large THCA peak and sometimes very few THC. So, we have to change our analytical procedure (GHYSEL and al. 1993). Now, we analyse samples by G.C. : apparatus Delsi Di 200 ; injector and detector temperatures are 260 and 280°C respectively ; oven temperature 150°C to 250°C (8°C/mn) ; detector FID. Docosane is used as internal standard.

**Results** :The injector temperature 260°C transforms Δ9THCA into Δ9THC. The same phenomenom happens when people smoke SKUNK cigarettes. Δ9THC values of 10 % are the most common but sometimes we have found 15 and 20 % Δ9THC values in some seizures.

**5. L.S.D.**
We have observed a slight decrease of the seizure in 1991 (cf. table n° 5).

| L.S.D. | 1989 | 1990 | 1991 | 1992 | 1993 |
|---|---|---|---|---|---|
| number of cases | 6 | 4 | 2 | 2 | 3 |
| units | 2116 | 1880 | 997 | 1086 | 1507 |
| % national | 17 | 6,13 | 3,6 | 0,85 | 0,35 |

**Table 5 : LSD number of seizures**

**Results** : usually 20 to 200 μg of LSD by units. Apart the emergence of new design, we haven't met modification in LSD exhibits.

**CONCLUSION**
The results of the analyses we have carried out indicate an evolution in the nature of drug abuse : new practises of cutting heroin exhibits, the appearance of designer drugs related to amphetamine [MDMA (ECSTASY) MDEA]... the new presentation of some narcotics like DRACH, the flower top of the female cannabis called « SKUNK » or « NETHERWEED » very rich in THCA, which is a precursor of a high concentration of Δ9THC.
The tendency since 1994 seems to be the emerging of tablets sold as « ECSTASY ».
The breakdown of Eastern European barries hasn't as yet brought with it, the introduction of drugs into Northern France, such as ephedrone, Jeff or Methcatinone but we have to remain vigilant. Unfortunately, the drug dealer's need for new markets is as great as the drug abuser's curiosity.

**References** :
- Ghysel M.-H. ; Salvadore O. ; Berquez N. ; Déramaux C. ; Vilette V. ; Haguenoer J.-M. (1993) Dosage chromatographique du delta 9 tétrahydrocannabinol dans les nouvelles présentations du cannabis. Analusis V21, n° 6, 31-33

- Huizer H (1992) About professional hemp cultivation in the Netherlands. Lecture SKL LINKOPING 16 June 1992

- Le Belle M., Callahan S., Latham D., Lauriault G. and Savard C. (1991) Comparison of Illicit Cocaine by Determination of Minor Components. J. For. Sci. 36:4 July 1102-1120

# QUANTITATIVE DETERMINATION IN A SUBSTITUTION PROGRAMME WITH LEVOMETHADONE

**H. Käferstein, M. Staak**

Institute of Legal Medicine, Melatengürtel 60,
D-50823 Köln Germany,

**INTRODUCTION**
In the USA, methadone has been used for the substitution of heroin addicts since 1964. (1) In European countries too - for example in Great Britain, Sweden, Switzerland and the Netherlands - methadone has long since become an established therapeutic means for helping heroin addicts survive or give up their addiction. However, in all countries the racemic form was or is being used, i.e. the mixture of the biologically active l-form and the practically inactive d-form. When a few years ago methadone substitution was also started in Germany, exclusively the active levomethadone was approved for use. Our experience has therefore been obtained with the levomethadone form. This gave rise to the question, for example, whether levomethadone produces better correlations between the concentration in serum and urine or between dose and concentration, and how additional drug consumption becomes manifest.

**METHODOLOGY**
Twenty volunteers who had been participating in the substitution program for several years already (long-term substitution) were enrolled in our study. These included 6 female and 14 male subjects with an average age of almost 34 (23-41) years. Another 8 patients of the same age group (5 male and 3 female subjects) were included in the study only after our analyses had already started. On average, the patients received daily 52 mg levomethadone in fruit juice, which is equivalent to a mean dose of 0.8 mg/kg body weight. Blood and urine samples taken without previous notice were subjected to HPLC-DAD testing. (Käferstein and Sticht, 1994) The urine samples were additionally tested with the EMIT - System for several drugs. 711 samples from 20 patients with long-term treatment and 193 samples from the 8 newly included patients were available for the quantitative assays in the blood. In 72 cases we could analyse blood and urine taken at the same time.

**RESULTS AND DISCUSSION**
There is no correlation between the amount of levo-methadone excreted with the urine and the corresponding blood levels. This applies also if the sum of levomethadone and its principal metabolite EDDP is measured instead of the levomethadone concentration in the urine alone. This means that the quantification of methadone in the urine does not permit any conclusions as to the corresponding serum concentrations. In urine, qualitative detection is therefore sufficient. Even if given in an adequately high dose, however, the levomethadone concentration may be below the threshold concentration of 0.3 mg/l urine usual in immunoassays. But it must not be concluded from such a negative immuno-

assay finding that the patient had not taken his/her methadone. In all cases of this kind, with very low methadone concentrations in the urine, the metabolite EDDP was identified chromatographically in considerably higher concentrations. Up to 96% EDDP appear in the urine. At a percentage of more than 90% EDDP, the levomethadone concentrations were generally under 0.3 mg/l urine. If more than 80% EDDP was excreted, the levomethadone concentrations were always under 3 mg/l, and in the presence of more than 60% EDDP they were always under 9 mg/l. This obviously indicates that metabolization has a great significance for the levomethadone concentrations appearing in the urine.

The average levo-methadone levels 24 hours after the last dose are around 0.1 mg/l serum. Under "steady state" conditions there is a correlation between daily dose and serum methadone concentration up to a dose of 0.7 mg/kg body weight. After that a plateau is reached. Similar results for d,l-methadone are published (Wolff et al, 1991).

The frequency of additional sedative consumption in relation to the mean serum levomethadone concentrations, subdivided into patients with long-term treatment and patients newly included in the substitution program was of special interest. The extent of additional drug consumption was independent of the methadone concentrations.

Only in 6 subjects additional drug consumption was not established at all or in less than 15% of the serum samples. None of these subjects consumed opiates in addition to the sedatives. In 17 patients additional consumption was detected in between 15 and 60% of the samples, with an accumulation at around 40%. Only 7 subjects restricted themselves to sedatives, 10 consumed, at least occasionally, also opiates. In 5 subjects additional use was established in more than 80% of the serum samples. Of these, 4 took additionally opiates - predominantly heroin and dihydrocodeine. Three of the subjects using sedatives and opiates regularly in addition to the methadone had been newly included in the program. Differentiation between long-term patients and newly included subjects exclusively under the aspect of additional opiate consumption shows that 8 of 20 long-term patients (40%) still take opiates, in contrast to 6 of 8 newly included subjects (75%). In the latter, there is furthermore an increased consumption of heroin and cocaine.

In our patient group, benzodiazepines and pentobarbital were detectable particularly frequently (table 1). Regarding flunitrazepam we recorded that the patients newly included in the program and with positive finding are considerably overrepresented. In both groups the median values, at 0.01 mg/l serum in each case, are equally high, but comparison of the concentration range in which 80% of all values are found - 10-90% range - there is a clear tendency toward altogether higher concentrations.

Apart from the general frequency of additional consumption of sedatives, the extent of consumption and the activity levels occurring are of particular interest.

Since diazepam is intravitally metabolized to nordiazepam, temazepam and oxazepam, the substances listed in the table have been comprised under the heading diazepam/nordiazepam for reasons of clarity. The median values of patients with long-term treatment and newly included patients do not differ to any appreciable extent. The tendencies toward very high concentrations, of over 1 mg/l serum in individual cases, however, are observed only in the long-term patients. This is the reason why 10% of the values lie even above 2.5 mg/l, with a maximal concentration of 6.6 mg/l.

Table 1: **CONCENTRATION OF SEDATIVES**

**BLOOD SAMPLES**
Long-term substitution (L): 711
Newly includet patients (N): 193

| Substance | positive n | % | Median mg/L | 10 % - 90 % mg/L | |
|---|---|---|---|---|---|
| Flunitrazepam | | | | | |
| 20 L | 90 | 12.7 | 0.01 | 0.003 | 0.020 |
| 8 N | 59 | 30.6 | 0.01 | 0.005 | 0.037 |
| Diazepam/ Nordiazepam | | | | | |
| 20 L | 71 | 10.0 | 0.15 | 0.02 | 2.45 |
| 8 N | 22 | 11.4 | 0.13 | 0.02 | 0.29 |
| Bromazepam | | | | | |
| 20 L | 17 | 2.4 | 0.33 | 0.06 | 1.18 |
| 8 N | 3 | 1.6 | 0.13 | - | - |
| Pentobarbitone | | | | | |
| 20 L | 51 | 7.2 | 1.47 | 0.17 | 4.70 |
| 8 N | 12 | 6.2 | 0.55 | 0.22 | 2.75 |

Bromazepam is determined only infrequently. Comparatively high - toxic - concentrations are observed, as in the case of diazepam, only in patients with long-term substitution.

For pentobarbitone, the median value after long-term substitution is almost 3 times as high as in the comparative group. In contrast, the relative incidence does not show any relevant differences between the two groups, as was also the case with diazepam/nordiazepam and bromazepam.

The concentration pattern over a longer period in two of the patients with long-term substitution should be discussed some more detailed. In the first two weeks patient 21 obviously took pentobarbital twice and oxazepam once, with an oxazepam concentration of almost 3 mg/l serum. After that, the patient took regularly flunitrazepam, first together with pentobarbital, later with oxazepam. Then the active substances named were not detectable any more. Instead the patient then took high doses of clomethiazole for about 3 months. When apparently he was not able to obtain clomethiazole anymore, there was a massive relapse with consumption of heroin, cocaine, pentobarbitone and benzodiazepines. This led to the exclusion of the patient from the program.

First, the patient 15 took repeatedly high doses of diazepam and bromazepam. After not having taken any detectable additional drugs for about 3 weeks, the patient consumed high doses of pentobarbitone, and then bromazepam again. Subsequently, this patient apparently did not take any additional drugs for almost 4 months, after which another relapse occurred with consumption of dihydrocodeine and benzodiazepines. This was followed by several months in which he did not consume any additional drugs, and another few weeks of benzodiazepine intake in low doses. Altogether, this patient showed a clear tendency toward stabilization with relapses becoming less frequent and involving lower concentrations.

The results indicate that patients are stabilized by long-term substitution with levo-methadone only to the extent of consuming flunitrazepam considerably less frequently and in lower doses than at the start of therapy. In contrast, tendencies in the opposite direction become evident for the other benzodiazepines and pentobarbital, at least with respect to the dosage.

Compared with newly included patients, patients with long-term substitution also clearly tend to reduce additional consumption of opiates in conjunction with cocaine. In patients substituted with methadone this combination constitutes the best way to achieve intoxication - a kick. Hence, additional consumption of opiates does in these cases not serve to compensate withdrawal symptoms in subjectively experienced underdosage, but is due to the addiction to further intoxication experiences.

In our opinion the detection of additional consumption via quantitative determinations in the serum is of considerable significance in a substitution program. Only this method provides data on the dosage and in the case of active substances with a long half-life also on the frequency of consumption, and thus objective data about current abuse.

**LITERATURE**


1. Dole V P, Nyswander M (1965) A medical treatment for diacetylmorphine (heroin) addiction. A clinical trial with methadone hydrochloride. JAMA 193:646-650

2. Käferstein H, Sticht G (1994) Quantitative Determination of methadone in urine with FPIA and HPLC. In: Contributions to forensic toxicology, Ed. R.K. Mueller, Molinapress, Leipzig, P 304-308

3. Wolff K, Sanderson M, Hay A W M, Raistrick D (1991) Methadone concentrations in plasma and their relationship to drug dosage. ClinChem 37:205-209

# THYMUS ALTERATIONS RELATED TO INTRA-VENOUS DRUG ABUSE OR EARLY HIV INFECTION

*C. PADONOU, *F. PARAIRE, **M. RAPHAEL, ***P. GRENOT, *** P. DEBRE, *M. DURIGON and *** B. AUTRAN

* Service d'anatomie Pathologie et Medecine légale.
Hôpital Raymond Poincare, Garches, FRANCE.
** Laboratoire d'Hématologie, Hôpital Avicenne, Bobigny, FRANCE.
*** Laboratoire d'Immunologie, Hôpital de la Pitié-Salpétrière, Paris, FRANCE.

## INTRODUCTION

The thymus is the primary lymphoïd organ for differentiation of CD4+ and CD8+ lymphoid T cells. Bone marrow T cell precursors colonize the cortex where they differentiate into immature CD1+CD4+CD8+ and CD3+ T cells representing 80% of thymocytes, then migrate to the medulla where they loss CD1 and either CD4 or CD8 expression, and definitively leave the thymus as mature CD3+CD4+ or CD3+CD8+ lymphocytes for peripheral compartment.

During the first years of live, thymus crucial importance for T-cell differentiation is now clearly admitted and contrast with its uncertain role during adult life because of organ involution. The mean thymic weight is modulated as a function of age and differs from one author to another. Thymus is involved during HIV infection and some secondary alterations are already documented in patients deceased from AIDS such as profound CD4+ T cell depletion.

In mice, Arora et al have demonstrated the existence of morphine-induced thymic alterations. Drug addict patients are, in France as elsewhere, a population at risk for HIV infection. The aim of our study was to characterize the existence or not of drug-induced thymic alterations of thymus in man and to know whether this hypothetical thymic involvement was related to the development and the progression of HIV infection.

## MATERIALS AND METHODS

***Thymus selection.*** Four groups of individuals (mean age from 12 to 41 years) were analyzed. Group 1:15 thymus from HIV seronegative drug abusing patients group 2:3 thymus from HIV seropositive drug abusing patients without autopsy criterion of AIDS such as cutaneomucous Kaposi, opportunistic diseases and lymphocytic depletion of spleen and lymph nodes. Group 3:3 thymus from HIV seropositive patients without drug abuse nor AIDS criterion as described above. Group 4:7 thymus from violently dead patients (seronegative for HIV, no drug abuse). After dissection, perithymic fat tissue was removed and thymus weight was calculated. The organ was then divided into three parts. The first part was fixed with 10% formaldehyde for histological methods. The second part was fixed for 1 minute in liquid nitrogen and then frozen at -80°C before analysis. Cells from the third part were teased out in RPMI medium. The lymphoid cells were then separated by Ficoll Hypaque gradient. The cell viability was assessed by trypan blue exclusion. A threshold of 60% viable cells was selected to perform immunofluorescence analysis.

***Histologic study.*** Fixed thymus were included into paraffin. Microsections were stained with Safran Eosin Haematoxylin (SEH) and GIEMSA. Three parameters were studied, in blind assay, for each thymus sample : (a) thymus structure (corticomedullar index) (b) presence or not of Hassal's bodies (c) cellular density.

***Immunologic study on tissue sections.*** The thymus were frozen and microsections 5µm) were fixed with acetone. The whole T-lymphocyte population was studied with monoclonal antibodies (mAbs) directed against CD1a,CD2,CD3,CD4,CD7 and CD8. The thymus microenvironment was studied with KL1 antibody (anti-epithelial cell), KP1 and KiM7 mAbs (anti-macrophage). Immunostaining with the peroxydase technique was used for 15 samples (8 from group 1,2 from group 2 and 5 from group 4).

***Flow cytometric analysis.*** The flow cytometric analysis was done on 10 thymus; 4 from group 1; 2 from group 2 and 3 from group 4. Unfortunately, the thymus of the third group were not analyzed. T-lymphocytes were studied with the following mAbs; anti-CD1a,CD3,CD4 and CD8 using a standard staining method. Ten samples were studied, as mentioned above. Flow cytometry was performed on a Fascan flow cytometer (Becton-Dickinson, Sunnyvale, CA).

## RESULTS

***Patients characteristics.*** The patients were subdivided as mentioned above into 4 groups according to their HIV and drug addiction status. The post-mortem delay before autopsy was from 24 to more than 72 hours. This delay was unknown for 5 cases. Of note, the post-mortem delay was short (24-48 hours) for the majority of the patients (18 out of 28).

***Thymus weights.*** Just after autopsy, the thymus weight was appreciated, in relationship to the patients's age and compared with control patients. As shown in Table 1, the thymus weight in HIV and/or drug abuse did not significantly differ from that observed in the control group.

**TABLE 1 :**
**THYMUS WEIGHT AS A FUNCTION OF AGE AND DRUG USAGE**

| AGE | CONTROL | | IVDA | |
|---|---|---|---|---|
| | Number | Mean Weight | Number | Mean Weight |
| 12-17 | 2 | 65 | 1 | 30 |
| 18-24 | 1 | 40 | 6 | 42 |
| 25-29 | 2 | 36 | 7 | 35.1 |
| 30-41 | 2 | 33 | 4 | 25.25 |

***Thymus histological analysis.*** This study was performed for all samples (28 thymus) and allowed the subdivision of patients into 2 groups: (a) subject with normal histologic structure (b) patients with cortical depletion. Thymic cell depletion was preferentially observed in the drug addicted patients from group 1 (p 0.05 versus normal control). No significant correlations could be found between patient groups and the other histologic. Features because of the small sample sizes. Results are summarized in Table 2.

**TABLE 2 :**
**THYMUS HISTOLOGICAL ANALYSIS**

| HISTOPATHOLOGY | Group I HIV- TOX+ | Group II HIV+ TOX+ | Group III HIV+ TOX- | Group IV HIV- TOX- |
|---|---|---|---|---|
| Normal architecture | 4 | 3 | 0 | 6 |
| Thymic cell depletion | 11 | 0 | 3 | 1 |
| Hassal Bodies | | | | |
| - Calcified | 6 | 1 | 2 | 5 |
| - Necrotic | 4 | 0 | 1 | 2 |

***Immunological analysis of thymus samples.***

1. Immunohistological analysis: patients from group 1,2 and 4 were tested. The results are expressed as less than 20% positive cells(+), 20 to 80% positive cells (++) and more than 80% (+++). Interestingly, the number of cortical epithelial cells (KL1+) increased in drug abuse group 1. In the same group, we could observe an increase of the CD8+ lymphocyte population, in the cortex as well as in the medulla. Group 2 (HIV+) shared the same immunohistological abnormalities and we did not observe any CD4+ T cell depletion. Of note, results for CD1a were similar for the three groups.
2. Flow cytometric analysis of thymocytes: could be performed on group 1,2 and 4 only. We observed an increase of CD4+ and CD8+ lymphoid cells in group 1 and mainly in group 2 as compared to control group. In the samples from group 2, there was a major decrease of CD1a+ and double positive CD4+ CD8+ cells but no depletion in mature CD4+ T cells.

## TABLE 3 : THYMUS IMMUNOHISTOLOGICAL ANALYSIS

| | Epitheli al Cells | Macrophages | | lymphocytes | | | | |
|---|---|---|---|---|---|---|---|---|
| Patients | KL1 | KP1 | KIM7 | CD1a | CD2 | CD3 | CD4 | CD8 |
| GroupI(n=8) | | | | | | | | |
| HIV- TOX+ | | | | | | | | |
| Cortex | +++ | + | + | +++ | +++ | +/- | ++ | ++(+) |
| Medulla | + | ++(+) | ++ | +/- | +++ | +++ | +++ | ++(+) |
| GroupII(n=2) | | | | | | | | |
| HIV+ TOX+ | +++ | + | +/- | +++ | +++ | - | +++ | ++ |
| Medulla | ++ | +++ | + | +/- | +++ | +++ | ++(+) | +(+) |
| GroupIV(n=5) | | | | | | | | |
| HIV-TOX- | | | | | | | | |
| Cortex | ++ | + | + | +++ | +++ | +/- | +++ | ++ |
| Medulla | + | ++(+) | ++ | - | +++ | +++ | +++ | + |

## TABLE 4: FLOW CYTOMETRY ANALYSIS OF THYMOCYTES

| Patients | | | Cell Surface Antigens | | | | | |
|---|---|---|---|---|---|---|---|---|
| Group | UPN | Post Mortem Delay | CD1a | CD4+CD8+ | CD4+ | CD8+ | CD3+ | CD4/CD8 |
| GroupI | 4865 | 48-72 | NT | 39 | 25 | 36 | 65 | 0.7 |
| HIV- | 4894 | 24-48 | 85 | 55 | 27 | 16 | 90 | 1.7 |
| TOX+ | 4916 | 24-48 | 77 | 64 | 18 | 12 | 99 | 1.5 |
| | 4961 | 24-48 | 44 | 56 | 19 | 17 | 82 | 1.1 |
| | | **Mean** | **75** | **53** | **22** | **20** | **84** | |
| GroupII | 4895 | 48-72 | 35 | 14 | 38 | 44 | 98 | 0.86 |
| HIV+ | 4913 | >72 | 23 | 9 | 43 | 42 | 91 | 1 |
| TOX+ | | | | | | | | |
| | | **Mean** | **29** | **11** | **40** | **43** | **94** | |
| GroupIV | 4833 | 24-48 | 65 | 53 | 10 | 10 | 74 | 1 |
| HIV- | 4857 | 24-48 | 51 | 74 | 12 | 13 | 85 | 1 |
| TOX- | 4874 | 24-48 | 51 | 58 | 21 | 13 | 85 | 1 |
| | 4878 | 24-48 | 79 | 79 | 9 | 7 | 73 | 1.23 |
| | | **Mean** | **61** | **66** | **13** | **11** | **79** | |

Flow cytometry analysis performed on a suspension of thymocytes teased out from thymus.
Results expressed as percent of positive thymocytes.

## CONCLUSION

No thymic hypertrophy was detectable in the case of chronic drug addicts, whether they were HIV positive or not. This result corroborates the experimental observations made on mice implanted with morphine pellets which presented at first a thymic hypertrophy and then a normalisation of thymic weight during the chronic phase. Significative thymic alterations were observed in drug addicts patients died from overdose as characterized by a clear depletion of the thymic cortex and an increase of epithelial KP1+ cortical cells. In contrast, in HIV infected monkeys a cortical depletion has been reported at the onset of the disease, which as accompanied by a diminution of epithelial cells. The epithelial cells display CD4 molecules on their cell surface and are infectable in-vitro by HIV. Their increase in HIV-infected thymus might therefore participate to the local amplification of HIV infection in drug addicts and to the abnormalities of thymus differentiation. The main modification observed in the thymus of HIV positive subjects not suffering from AIDS is a sharp decrease of immature double-positive CD4+CD8+ and CD1a cells, constrasting with the persistance of mature CD4+ T cells. These aspects might represent early phases of thymus abnormalities in HIV infection.

## BIBLIOGRAPHIE


1. **ARORA P.K.** Morphine-Induced Immune Modulation: Does it predispose to HIV infection. NIDA. Res. Monogr., 1990,96,150-165.

2. **DE ROSSI A., CALABRO M.L., PANOZZO M. ET AL.** In vitro studies of HIV 1 infection in thymic lymphocytes : a putative role of the thymus in AIDS pathogenesis. AIDS research and human retroviruses, 1990,6,3,287-298.

3. **GRODY W.W., FLIGIEL S., NAEIM F.** Thymus involution in the acquired immunodeficiency syndrome. Am.J.Clin. Pathol.,1985,84,85-95.

4. **JOSHI V.V., OLESKE J.M., SAAD S. et al.** Thymus biopsy in children with acquired immunodeficiency syndrome. Arch.pathol.Lab.Med.,1986,110,837-842.

5. **MULLER J.G., KRENN V. et al.** Alterations of thymus cortical epithelium and interdigitating dentritic cells but no increase of thymocyte cell death in the early course of Simian Immunodeficiency Virus Infection. Am.J.Pathol.,1993,143,3,699-713.

6. **NUMAZAKI K., BAI X.Q., GOLDMAN H. et al.** Infection of cultured human thymic epithelial cells by human immunodeficiency syndrome. Clin. Immuno. Immunopathol., 1989,51,185-195.

7. **PAPIERNIK M., BROSSARD Y., MULLIEZ N. et al.** Thymic abnormalities in foetuses aborted from human immunodeficiency virus type I seropositive women. Ped.,1992,89,2,197-201.

8. **PREVOT S., AUDOIN J., ANDRE-BOURGARAN J. et al.** Thymic pseudotumorous enlargement due to follicular hyperplasia in human immunodeficiency virus seropositive patient. Immunohistochemical and molecular biological study of viral infected cells. Anat.Pathol.,1992,97,3,420-425.

9. **SCHUURMAN H.J., KRONE W.J.A., BROEKHUIZEN J.et al.** The thymus in acquired immune deficiency syndrome. Comparison with other types of immunodeficiency diseases, and presence of components of human immunodeficiency virus type I.Am.J.Pathol.,1989,134,6,1329-1338.

# DRIVER FITNESS OF HEROIN ADDICTS SUBSTITUTED WITH METHADONE

**Staak, M and G. Berghaus**

Institute for Legal Medicine, University at Cologne, Melatengürtel 60, D-50823 Köln

## Introduction

At the moment some methadone substitution programms are performed in Germany to evaluate benefits to heroin addiction problems. The fact that within this project in Cologne patients were treated on a trial basis offered the possibility of complementing previous studies concerning driver fitness of substituted patients.
At the ICADTS-Congress in Cologne two years ago we presented first results (1). In the meantime the study is finished giving the chance to present the final results.

## Subjects and methods

Our experimental study comprised overall 47 subjects. 24 substitutes looked after by the Public Health Department of the City of Cologne, 10 substituted by a doctor's practice and 13 control subjects beeing non-users of drugs.

Apart from the usual procedure as for example the welcome and the informed consent the first afternoon of the investigation consisted of answering to personality questionnaires including traffic specific questions:
The 8-personality questionnaire:, an adapted form of the 16 personality questionnaire of CATTELL evaluating traits such as among other things emotional stability, dominance, expressivity, social conscientiousness and anxiety. Derived are scales to measure proneness to accidents and physical health for example.
A questionnaire to evaluate risk-taking factors (FRF): 49 Items differentiated among other things in two scales measuring physical and social risk-taking.
The Freiburger personality inventory: comprising traits such as contentedness with life, social orientation, achievement orientation, inhibitedness, sensitivity, aggressive behavior
The MMPI (Minnesota Multhiphasic Personality Inventory) analysing among other things depression, hysteria, psychopathological traits, masculinity/femininity, paranoia, psychasthenia.
An inventory of the 'study-group for methodology and documentation of psychiatry' (AMDP) was diagnosed by the doctors of the probands. It is part of a documentation system which describes psychopathologic characteristics concerning endogeneous and physically caused psychosis.
Finishing the first day the subjects practised the psychophysical test devices to get accustomed to it. We used the Act-and-React-Apparatus developed by the Austrian Road Safety Board, Vienna, which consists of several later mentioned tests.

The 2nd day started in the morning with the administration of polamidone followed by questions about performance influencing factors such as sleeplessness or labor the night before. Afterwards a self-rating scale concerning performance, a mood scale (von ZERSSEN) and a traffic-specific-questionnaire was completed by the subjects. The traffic specific item pool consists of 49 questions differentiated in 4 dimensions registering the critical feeling of one's own value, agressive interaction, emotional feeling for the vehicle and for driving and

orientation towards requests of the society. (In this place we would like to thank the 'Kuratorium für Verkehrssicherheit' Vienna for kindly providing us with the 8-personality-, the risk-taking- and the traffic-specific-questionnaire and permitting to use it with our research.)
The psychophysical tests were conducted, as mentioned before, using the Act-and-React-Test-System. This apparatus is controled by a personal computer and allows an automatic and standardized presentation of tests. In particular we tested the following performance areas: short term memory, tracking, decision and reaction behavior, perception, sustained attention, speed estimation, peripheral attention with simultaneous central task, reactive loading. The test battery was interrupted by taking a blood sample. After conducting the tests we begged the subjects for an urine sample and rewarded them.
The blood and urine specimens were toxicologically analysed for drugs (see contribution by KÄFERSTEIN and STAAK in this volume).
As usual all data have been stored on a PC and have been analysed by statitical procedures.

## Results

Overall 22 men and 12 women were tested. Their age varied between 26 and 42 years with a mean of 33 years for patients looked after at the Public Health Department and 31.5 years for patients looked after at the doctor's practice. Methadone dosage levels administered: 50 mg on an average, between 17.5 and 80 mg; the duration of methadone treatment varied between a few months and 6 years, on an average two and a half years for Public Health Department patients and a half year for doctor's practice patients. The period of addiction varied between 2 and 23 years, overall 5 patients were HIV positive.

**In a first step** those patients were selected
- (A) who, at the time the tests were conducted, had been under the influence of at least one psychotropic substance above defined levels,
- (B) who at prior blood tests within 3 months had at least twice been found to be under the effect of drugs or who were known as concomitant drug users,

11 patients met the criteria (A) and (B), 6 the criteria (A) only and 3 the criteria (B) only. One further patient had to be excluded due to a BAC of 0.06% during the test. In all 21 patients had to be excluded that means 13 substitution subjects remained after this selection and can thus be considered as a positive selection from the total population of methadone patients checked.

In **the second step** the 13 remaining methadone patients were matched with 13 control subjects of the same sex, education and--within a range of $\pm$ 2 years--also the same age. All 26 subjects were tested using the Act-and-React-Testsystem.
Compared with the control group, the methadone substitution patients yielded poorer results in all psychophysical performance tests. In our further presentation we would like to confine ourselves to the items with significant differences between these two groups.
In the tracking test the time needed showed significant differences: the methadone patients required more time on average than the control group. Furthermore, the methadone group drove less steady, applying the brakes and accelerating more frequently.
In the tachystoscopic perception test--15 slides showing traffic situations were displayed--the substitution group identified less traffic stimuli correctly (31.5%) than the control group (35.2%). The patients also needed more time to register what they had seen.
The complex task of peripheral perception combined with the central task of tracking again revealed clear differences between the two groups. In both cases, not only when stimuli approached the field of vision from the left-hand side but also when they approached from the right-hand side, the average reaction time of the test group was clearly longer than that of the control group. The test on reaction to stress--the subjects were required to differentiate between

and correctly react to colours, sounds and a radiant field--yielded significant differences in the simplest version of the test (38 signals per minute). The methadone group not only showed less correct reactions, but also skipped a larger number of signals. The reactions of the substitution group occurred less often within the time required and with a corresponding delay.
Based on the psychophysical performance tests, it can thus on the whole be said that the performance of the substitution group was clearly poorer than that of the control group. Deficiencies were noted mainly in the more complicated tasks. It must be considered as typical in this context that the performance in the tests most characteristically describing driver fitness, such as tracking, perception of traffic situations, peripheral perception while concentrating on the central task at the same time and multiple choice reactions, turned out to be much poorer than in the other tests.

Concerning personality traits we found the following resülts: The Minnesota Multiphasic Personality Inventory reveals relevant differences in the validity scales 'validity' and 'correction' and in the scales depression, conversion hysteria, psychopathic deviate, paranoia and hypomania. The differences in the validity scales make it evident that the substitution patients filled in the questionnaire more cursory or could not understand the items as good as the control subjects. The members of the control group seem to be more inclined to admit psychic weakness. The personality traits describing the other scales in which the substitution patients differ from the control group are according to (2) typical of addictive persons beeing asthenic-sentimental, sensitiv-reserved personal characters who incline to emotional internal stress and feelings of insufficiency due to a discrepancy between ambition and efficiency.
In line with these traits the Freiburger Personality Inventory reveals the substituted patients beeing more sensitive, more aggressive and more emotional compared to the control subjects.
Overall 4 dimensions yielded significant differences between the groups examined by the 8 Personality Questionnaire. The methadone substituted patients revealed a higher degree of anxiety, a poorer degree of check on oneself and of accident avoidance and a poorer degree of psychic healthiness as well compared to the matched group, characteristics of the methadone patients which were verified too by the physicians caring for the patients. The traffic specific item pool showed the control subjects as above average uncritical against themselves.

In **a third step** we selected 6 patients of whom the physicians decided that they are optimal patients especially taking no other drugs apart from methadone and beeing resocialized. In a matched pairs design we compared these patients with 6 healthy subjects of the same age, gender and school education. Concerning the psychophysical performance there were no significant differences left but relating to personality traits and the psychopathological results some differences still remained.

## Discussion

In summary we conclude: In our study there are only a few substituted patients left who are not taking other drugs simultaneously to the prescribed methadone. Depending on the selection criteria at least 21 subjects are from the first unfit to drive according to several reasons. Due to psychophysical performance, personality traits and the psychopathological results only very few subjects of the patients remained can be decided as fit to drive.
Compared to other international studies on driver fitness of patients in methadone maintainance programms the result of our study is very bad. The reason , we think, is to be seen in the prerequisites of getting substituted: it was only some years ago that the substitution programms started in Germany and only patients are substituted with a very long history of addiction or with a very bad state of health. In contrary in other countries, like for example Switzerland, people who are taking heroin for about half a year can be substituted. Hence the chance of

patients in Germany to get resocialized seems to take up more time. Liberalizing the admittance to substitution programms probably will improve the situation concerning driver fitness.

## Literature

(1) Berghaus G.,. Staak M,. Glazinski R, Höher K, Joó S, Friedel B (1993) Complementary empirical study on the driver fitness of methadone substitution patients. In: Utzelmann HD, Berghaus G, Kroj G(eds) Alcohol, Drugs and Traffic Safety, TÜV Rheinland, Köln, P 120

(2) Huber G (1987) Psychiatrie. Systematischer Lehrtext für Ärzte und Studenten. Schattauer, Stuttgart, 4. Aufl.

(3) Berghaus G, Staak M, Glazinski R, Höher K (1993) Methadonsubstitution und Verkehrssicherheit. Berichte der Bundesanstalt für Straßenwesen, Heft M 18, Wirtschaftsverlag NW, Bremerhaven

# THE SCIENCE AND POLITICS OF DRUG TESTING IN THE USA

J. Michael Walsh, Ph.D.
The Walsh Group, PA
6701 Democracy Boulevard,
Suite 300, Bethesda, Maryland 20854 USA

Over the last 14 years "employee drug testing" has become common business practice in the American workplace. A recent survey conducted by the American Management Association (1) [the 7th annual survey on "Workplace Drug Testing and Drug Abuse Policies" (Jan. 1993)] indicates nearly 85% of surveyed firms test employees for drugs. Since 1987, the date of the AMA's initial survey, company drug testing in the United States has increased by 300%. It is estimated that more than 25 million American workers will be tested for illicit drugs this year.

This phenomenon of workplace drug testing has not occurred overnight, but rather has evolved slowly over more than a decade (2). Over the last twenty years there has been a significant increase in the impact of drug abuse on the daily living of the average American. One can't pick up a newspaper or watch a television newscast without being reminded of the tragic consequences of drug abuse. Drug-related crime, disease (HIV-AIDS), accidents, injuries, deaths, and associated sordid details have become daily reminders of the limited effectiveness of police interdiction efforts to reduce the supply of illegal drugs.

Currently there is a clear mandate from all segments of society to develop a change in focus in the "drug war" and to concentrate efforts on reducing the demand for drugs. During the Reagan and Bush administrations the political drug strategy argued that the key to reducing the demand for drugs is to hold the individual drug user responsible for his/her behavior: that is, to develop societal contingencies which censure and penalize the individual user with stiff sanctions (e.g., seizing assets, withholding the opportunity for employment). The environment in which this technique has been most effectively used is in the workplace. Beginning with the military experience in the early 1980's, workplace programs have been developed which send a straight-forward message that drug use by employees will not be tolerated (3). Clearly, one of the key elements of such policies has been the use of drug detection technology to identify drug users.

The basic philosophy of why to test and what to do with the results of testing has changed dramatically over the last ten years. Initially, the rationale for testing was to identify drug users and fire them without addressing the problem. In the last 10 years a more positive "helping-hand" philosophy has evolved. The basic purpose of today's model workplace anti-drug policy is to help those who want to be helped and get the substance abusing employee into treatment, afford the opportunity to get help, and get the individual back on the job.

The question of whether or not to utilize drug testing technology evokes a complex array of moral, social, ethical, medical, scientific, and legal dilemmas for many Americans.

Although most citizens do not condone drug abuse, their concerns about the erosion of civil liberties generate feelings of uncertainty as to whether the end justifies the means.

Many people view the drug testing process (i.e., collection of urine) as degrading and dehumanizing. Government employees, employee unions, and civil libertarians argue strongly that drug testing is an invasion of privacy, that it constitutes an illegal search and seizure (i.e., of body fluids) and therefore violates individual rights guaranteed by the U.S. Constitution. In general, the Constitutional protections apply only to testing conducted by government (Federal, State, and local). Government mandated drug testing of private sector employees, for example in the Federally regulated transportation and nuclear power industries, must pass Constitutional muster. In the early years (1982-1986) a legal uncertainty, whether testing would be upheld legally and programs go forward, or would testing be found unconstitutional and therefore be stopped, created a great deal of confusion for policy makers as well as for employees and unions. Most of the legal issues have now been resolved and case law has defined the parameters under which testing can be legally conducted.

Medical and scientific questions about the accuracy and reliability of drug testing were continually raised by those who opposed testing. Concerns were voiced that many laboratories engaged in offering drug testing services did not have the expertise or capability to perform the assays required. In addition, many employers were thought to be using inappropriate technology and falsely accusing employees of drug use. Congressional support for these concerns was manifested by the passage of Federal law (4) which requires stringent technical and scientific procedures for Federal workplace drug testing programs, as well as standards for the certification of laboratories engaged in drug testing for Federal agencies. Similar legislation has been introduced in both the U.S. Senate (5) and House of Representatives (6) which would require such standards and lab certification for the private sector.

In response to concerns about the accuracy and reliability of drug testing, the U.S. Department of Health and Human Services (HHS) issued "Technical and Scientific Guidelines for Federal Drug Testing Programs" (7). These "Guidelines" are mandatory for Federal programs and have rapidly become the gold standard for private sector programs as well. The rigor of the Federal standards has virtually dispensed with concerns regarding accuracy and reliability. The issue of the quality of laboratories has also been addressed by HHS through the establishment of a National Laboratory Certification Program which assures quality, accuracy and reliability of laboratory assays through a system of proficiency testing and semiannual inspections. The use of a "certified lab" has become the standard by which company programs are being measured (8).

Clearly, employee drug testing in America is here to stay. The question of how much more the testing phenomenon will grow depends to a great extent on how businessmen assess the cost-effectiveness of a drug-free-workplace program. The cost of testing has been reduced considerably in recent years. Employers are beginning to realize the cost-savings produced by "Drug-free Workplace Programs" (9, 10), for example, reduced accident rates, reduced insurance rates, reduced theft and workplace crime, less absenteeism, and apparent higher productivity. The availability of testing and employeecounseling services through business consortiums have made these programs more accessible and affordable to small businesses. All of these factors suggest that workplace anti-drug efforts will continue to grow in the United States at a rapid rate. Based on the last ten years' experience, employers in the United States have concluded that drug free workplace programs are good for employees, good for business, and good for the national interest.

References

(1) Greenberg, Eric Rolfe, American Management Association, New York, New York, 1994.

(2) Walsh, J.M. and Trumble, J.G., The Politics of Drug Testing, Drug Testing: Issues & Options, (R.H.Coombs, LJ West, Eds.), Oxford University Press, New York, 1991, pp. 22-49.

(3) Mulloy, P.J., Winning the War on Drugs in the Military, Drug Testing: Issues & Options, (R.H. Coombs, LJ West, Eds.), Oxford University Press, New York, 1991, pp. 92-112.

(4) Public Law 100-71, section 503, July 11, 1987.

(5) H.R. 33, 102nd Cong., lst Sess., Senators John D. Dingell and Thomas J. Bliley, Drug Testing Quality Act, January 3, 1991.

(6) S. 1903, (now S. 2008), 101st Cong., 2nd Sess., Senator Orrin Hatch, The Quality Assurance in the Private Section, Drug Testing Act of 1991.

(7) Mandatory Guidelines for Federal Workplace Drug Testing Programs; Notice, Federal Register, Part V, DHHS, SAMHSA, June 9, 1994.

(8) Technical, Scientific and Procedural Issues of Employee Drug Testing: Consensus Report, (B.S. Finkle, R.V. Blanke, J.M. Walsh, Eds.), DHHS, ADAMHA, 1990.

(9) Normand, J., Salyards, S. and Mahony, J.J., The evaluation of pre-employment drug testing, Journal of applied Psychology, 1990, 75:629-639.

(10) Under the Influence? Drugs and the American Work Force, National Research Council, Institute of Medicine, (J. Normand, R.O. Lempert, and C.P. O'Brien, (Eds.) National Academy Press, Washington, D.C., 1994.

# 16. Entomology

# APPLICATION DE L'ENTOMOLOGIE A LA PRATIQUE MEDICO-LEGALE : PRELEVEMENTS SUR LE CADAVRE

par P. DODINVAL (Institut médico-légal de l'Université de Liège, Belgique)

## RESUME
Se basant sur l'expérience acquise par les collaborateurs de l'Institut médico-légal de l'Université de Liège depuis 1947, l'auteur propose un certain nombre de conseils pour le prélèvement des insectes et acariens sur le cadavre en décomposition, de manière à fournir à l'entomologiste un matériel adéquat, à la fois sur le plan quantitatif et qualitatif. L'approximation la plus exacte possible du moment de la mort en dépend.

## INTRODUCTION
Dès que la rigidité d'un cadavre humain a disparu, la dégradation progressive du corps, variable en fonction de diverses circonstances extérieures, ne permet de déterminer, que de façon très imprécise, le laps de temps écoulé depuis le décès. La méthode entomologique peut alors être d'un précieux secours (Leclercq, 1978; Leclercq et Verstraeten, 1993).
Il importe que le médecin légiste praticien connaisse les rudiments de la méthode entomologique, qui permettra le plus souvent à un entomologiste spécialisé d'apprécier le moment de la mort. Une telle expertise ne pourra aboutir à des conclusions valables que si le légiste effectue des prélèvements corrects et dès lors, une collaboration étroite entre médecin légiste et entomologiste est requise.
La méthode entomologique est basée sur un principe fondamental : les insectes et les acariens, dits bio-indicateurs, sont dotés d'un système sensoriel très perfectionné, adapté à la détection rapide d'un cadavre, qui est pour eux une ressource alimentaire et un endroit propice pour la ponte des oeufs. Ils réagissent de façon assez spécifique aux conditions météorologiques, surtout aux températures ambiantes en ce qui concerne leurs déplacements (diurnes, le plus souvent : rythme circadien) que pour la durée des métamorphoses et de leur cycle biologique complet (ponte, incubation des oeufs, croissance des stades larvaires, transformation en nymphes, pupes ou chrysalides et éclosion des adultes).

## PRELEVEMENTS SUR LE CADAVRE ET LEUR CONSERVATION
(Voir aussi Lord et Burger, 1983; Erzinclioglu, 1989).

### *A) Cadavre "frais"*
Dès le décès, on assiste très précocement à la ponte de "mouches", représentant la 1ère escouade, et ce, pour autant que les conditions d'environnement s'y prêtent : pas de pluie, clarté diurne (avec exception), température supérieure à 12 - 14 degrés centigrades, mais variable selon les espèces).

Cette ponte va se faire d'abord sur les endroits ensanglantés : sang frais de plaies ou de taches, même sur les vêtements, puis au niveau des orifices naturels ou des régions humides (bouche, nez, yeux, anus).
Ces oeufs, très nombreux, prennent un aspect que l'on compare à de la sciure de bois. Chaque oeuf a une longueur d'environ 1 à 1, 5 mm et un diamètre de 0,1 à 0,2 mm.
Après quelques heures (8 à 24 h; durée variable selon la température), l'éclosion des oeufs survient et parmi les masses d'oeufs sur un cadavre frais, on découvrira quelquefois, des petites larves très courtes.
Sur de tels cadavres, l'intervalle post-mortem est en général déterminé à l'aide des critères thanatologiques habituels (lividités, rigidité, température du corps) .
Toutefois, il faut savoir que la température conditionne, avec précision, l'incubation des oeufs, si bien qu'il est possible de fixer la date du moment de la mort, parfois uniquement avec des oeufs. Ce prélèvement peut servir de confirmation aux autres constatations thanatologiques.

***B)Cadavre altéré***

Lorsque la rigidité aura disparu, l'altération du cadavre va se poursuivre plus ou moins rapidement : c'est alors que le prélèvement entomologique prend toute sa valeur. En effet, dans le décours de la putréfaction, différentes escouades d'insectes ou d'acariens vont se suivre au cours du temps. On observera des oeufs, des larves de mouches, ainsi que leurs pupes, pleines ou vides, des larves d'autres insectes ou leurs nymphes, ainsi que divers insectes adultes (diptères, coléoptères, acariens...).
Les larves de mouches (asticots) sont parfois de longueurs différentes : il importe de mesurer leur longueur, leur croissance se faisant à raison de 1 à 3 mm / jour (la mesure est facilitée si les larves sont ralenties par un séjour préalable de quelques heures au frigo (+ 4 à 8 ° C).
La colonisation d'un tel cadavre est souvent extrêmement abondante et on n'a que le choix pour les prélèvements. A l'opposé, sur un cadavre situé à l'extérieur et réduit à l'état de squelette depuis un certain nombre de mois, il y a relativement peu d'insectes indicateurs (Dodinval et al., 1990 a et b) et souvent les pupes de mouches sont très peu nombreuses; souvent, elles auront été emportées par des insectes nécrophiles, par des oiseaux ou des animaux. Sur ces cadavres, on trouvera des insectes banals, tels que fourmis, cloportes, sans intérêt pour la datation de la mort.
Dans ces conditions, il sera utile de revoir, après quelques heures les ossements transportés au laboratoire, car l'éclosion d'un oeuf ou d'une pupe, favorisée par l'élévation de la température pourra faire apparaître une larve ou un insecte adulte que l'observateur n'aurait pas pu apercevoir sur les lieux de la découverte des restes cadavériques.
C'est sur ces cadavres altérés, que les **prélèvements** devront être particulièrement soigneux, réalisant un échantillonnage complet, à la fois qualitatif et quantitatif, de manière à ramener le plus grand nombre d'espèces possibles dans leurs divers stades de développement.

Les prélèvements auront lieu à la fois sur le cadavre lui-même et en dehors de lui.

***1) Sur le cadavre*** :
A l'aide d'une pince fine ou des doigts gantés, on prélèvera larves, pupes et insectes adultes à différents endroits du corps, parfois en incisant le tégument pour y découvrir des niches plus abondantes.
- a) Les exemplaires vivants destinés à l'élevage seront disposés dans un récipient (tube, flacon) avec un peu de muscle du cadavre (si un envoi ultérieur doit être effectué à distance) et avec un volume d'air suffisant ou une aération assurée, par de petits orifices ou un couvercle en gaze serrée.
On veillera à disposer, autant que faire se peut, les insectes adultes d'espèces différentes séparément, car certains insectes nécrophiles peuvent détruire des nécrophages.
- b) des exemplaires de larves ou d'adultes seront fixés. La méthode habituelle utilisée par les entomologistes consiste à plonger les prélèvements dans de l'alcool éthylique à 70 % . Toutefois, une étude récente (Tantawi et Greenberg, 1993) a montré que cette façon de faire provoque une rétraction tissulaire conduisant à une légère diminution de la longueur des larves de mouches. On commet alors une erreur dans l'estimation de la durée de vie de ces larves (considérée alors comme trop courte).
Les auteurs conseillent actuellement d'utiliser de l'eau bouillante ou très chaude pour tuer les larves, pendant 2 à 3 minutes, puis alors seulement de les plonger dans l'éthanol. Cette procédure peut encore être effectuée après quelques heures, dès le retour au laboratoire.
L'utilisation de l'eau bouillante a l'intérêt de détruire des enzymes digestifs et la flore intestinale. Elle n'altère pas la longueur des larves et évite leur mélanisation, facilitant ainsi l'identification.
En général, le formol est déconseillé, mais peut être utilisé provisoirement en attendant de déposer les insectes dans l'alcool. Ni l'un ni l'autre n'ont d'effet sur les opiacés, la cocaïne ou les barbituriques présents dans les larves (Tantawi et Greenberg, 1993).

***2) En dehors du cadavre*** :
On prélèvera également larves et insectes se trouvant à la surface du sol, sous le cadavre, ainsi que des fragments de sol où les larves vont parfois s'enterrer sous le cadavre pour faire leur pupaison. Ne pas oublier non plus les vêtements qui peuvent contenir des insectes adultes et des larves ou des nymphes.
La capture d'insectes volant autour du cadavre rend nécessaire l'utilisation d'un filet.

## MODALITES D'ENVOI A L'ENTOMOLOGISTE

Les prélèvements effectués doivent être adressés le plus rapidement possible au spécialiste, par porteur de préférence. Toutefois, si cela n'est pas possible, l'envoi est réalisable par voie postale dans des emballages adéquats, en protégeant de manière convenable les flacons contenant les prélèvements.
Il sera indispensable de communiquer à l'entomologiste, différents renseignements relatifs au cadavre : température environnante, température du cadavre, situation (à l'extérieur ou à l'intérieur), conditions climatiques, cause de la mort, utilisation d'insecticide ou de produit répulsif, susceptible de modifier le développement des insectes ou de l'empêcher, altérations post-mortem du cadavre.
Il est parfois utile de transmettre à l'entomologiste des macrophotographies des insectes sur le corps (Leclercq, 1993).

## CONCLUSIONS

L'expertise entomologique médico-légale s'avère particulièrement utile pour déterminer l'intervalle post-mortem, particulièrement lorsque le cadavre est altéré. C'est le plus souvent le médecin légiste appelé sur place qui sera amené à faire les prélèvements et le présent travail a pour but de lui donner quelques conseils à ce sujet.

Il s'agit d'une procédure qui peut être longue et difficile dans les conditions où l'on est amené à travailler. Aussi est-il souhaitable que la trousse du médecin légiste prévoie un nombre suffisant de flacons qui pourraient servir à des prélèvements de ce type.

C'est à partir de ces prélèvements et des renseignements fournis, que, après un bilan de la récolte, l'entomologiste pourra apprécier en fonction des conditions ambiantes, les laps de temps nécessaires au développement de chaque espèce d'insectes depuis l'éclosion de la larve jusqu'à l'émergence de l'adulte.

Il déterminera aussi les étapes de la colonisation du cadavre par les insectes bio-indicateurs. Puis, il en déduira une approximation, la plus précise possible, du moment de la mort.

## REFERENCES

Dodinval, P., Leclercq, M., Piette, P. et Verstraeten, C. : Identification of a skeleton and timing of death after months. Cooperation between forensic scientist, odontologist and entomologists, in Forensic entomology for pathologists and crime scene examiners. Abstracts of the 12th meeting of the International Association of Forensic Sciences, Adelaide, South Australia, 24 -29 oct. 1990 (a).

Dodinval, P., Leclercq, M., Piette, P. et Verstraeten, C. : Identification of a skeleton and timing of death months later. Acta Medicinae Legalis et Socialis, 50, 167 - 169, 1990 (b).

Erzinclioglu, Y. Z. : Protocol for collecting entomological evidence. Forensic Sci. Intern., 43, 211 - 213, 1989.

Leclercq, M. : Entomologie et médecine légale. Datation de la mort. Ed.Masson, Paris, 1978, 100 pages.

Leclercq, M.: Entomologie et médecine légale. Datation de la mort sur des documents photographiques. Rev. Med. Liège, 48, 279 - 284, 1993.

Leclercq, M. et Verstraeten, C. : Entomologie et médecine légale. L'entomofaune des cadavres humains; sa succession par son interprétation, ses résultats, ses perspectives. J. Med. leg., 36, 205 - 222, 1993.

Lord, W. D. et Burger, J. F. : Collection and preservation of forensically important entomological materials. J. Forensic Sci., 28, 936 - 944, 1983.

Tantawi, T. I. et Greenberg, B. : The effect of killing and preservative solutions on estimates of maggot age in forensic cases. J. Forensic Sc., 38, 702 -707, 1993.

# L'expertise entomologique médico-légale et ses résultats

M. LECLERCQ

Institut Médico-Légal, B 4020 Liège (Belgique)

L'expertise entomologique, technique d'identification ancienne, est reconnue actuellement comme essentielle en médecine légale (Leclercq et Brahy, 1990 ; Miras et al., 1991). Depuis 1947, elle est pratiquée à l'Institut Médico-Légal de Liège, en association avec les médecins légistes. Sans pareille association pluridisciplinaire, l'expertise entomologique risque en effet de n'être pas valable.

L'entomologiste responsable doit suivre la procédure suivante :
1) Tout d'abord, il s'assure que l'échantillonnage complet des insectes et des acariens, à tous les stades de développement, a bien été effectué au niveau du cadavre. Aucun chaînon ne peut être oublié. Une vérification devrait encore être faite après l'autopsie sur les scellés, car des insectes inapparents au début peuvent souvent se manifester ultérieurement.
2) Préparation du matériel : adultes avec des épingles entomologiques et fixation d'un échantillonnage sélectif des stades larvaires, indicateurs potentiels (eau bouillante pour éviter la mélanisation, puis conservation dans de l'alcool dénaturé à 70% ; le reste des larves et des nymphes, pupes, chrysalides sera mis en élévage...
3) Identification des espèces de l'entomofaune : travail précis systématique pouvant nécessiter la compétence d'un ou de plusieurs entomologistes spécialisés dans certaines familles.
4) La liste systématique complète des insectes et des acariens retrouvés sur le cadavre.
5) Bilan de la succession des escouades et des 4 groupes écologiques :
a.- les nécrophages se nourrissant du cadavre, arrivant en premier lieu, parfois très rapidement et se succédant selon le stade biochimique de la décomposition,
b.- les nécrophiles : prédateurs ou parasites des nécrophages,
c.- les omnivores dont le cadavre et ses habitants (nécrophages et nécrophiles) sont la nourriture,
d.- les opportunistes qui s'amènent pour s'abriter ou hiberner et parfois se nourrir.

Généralement, les meilleurs indicateurs sont les nécrophages. Cependant les autres ne peuvent être exclus. Omalium rivulare seul (coléoptère Staphylinide nécrophile) a permis par exemple de préciser : datation de la mort, endroit du crime (ne correspondant pas à celui de la découverte des ossements de la victime), manipulation et transport du cadavre dans une affaire compliquée, où l'intervalle postmortem était très long (environ 8 mois) (Leclercq et al., 1991).

6) Graphique des températures journalières (maximale, minimale, moyenne) établi depuis le jour de la disparition de la victime (s'il est connu) jusqu'au jour de la découverte du cadavre ou alors, pendant une période déterminée par l'état du cadavre et les données de l'enquête. L'étude de pareil graphique permet de préciser les périodes d'activité et d'inactivité non seulement des insectes récoltés, mais

aussi de ceux qui n'ont pas été retrouvés et auraient pu arriver sur le cadavre. Cette éventualité nécessite l'analyse de toutes les hypothèses susceptibles de pouvoir justifier leur absence, celle-ci pouvant être due à l'action des coupables. Dans ce cas, il en résulte que l'endroit de la découverte du cadavre n'est pas celui de la mort de la victime. Une comparaison entre les températures enregistrées par l'observatoire météorologique le plus proche de l'endroit de la découverte du cadavre est parfois nécessaire pour identifier le microclimat. Si le jour du crime a pu être précisé, un graphique des températures notées toutes les quatres heures avec le lever et le coucher du soleil, permet d'évaluer le moment d'exposition du cadavre.

7) Estimation de l'intervalle postmortem : elle pose plusieurs problèmes (Catts, 1992). Nous ne pouvons pas les discuter tous dans ce texte limité. Voici nos réflexions :
a.- la connaissance des données météorologiques conditionnant le rythme circadien des espèces permet d'évaluer le moment de l'arrivée et de la ponte des oeufs pour les premières mouches nécrophages sur le cadavre (Grösse, 1993). Si les conditions sont optimales, c'est très rapide, puisqu'elles sont notamment attirées par le sang frais coagulé, même au niveau des vêtement, avant d'aller au niveau des orifices naturels de la victime.
b.- estimation de l'âge des larves : il ne suffit pas de mesurer uniquement leur longueur en tenant compte seulement des températures ambiantes. D'autres facteurs influencent la durée de leur nutrition et de leur croissance :
- la période ou les périodes d'arrêt de nutrition, repérables sur le graphique des températures. La progéniture des *Calliphora vicina* montre par exemple, une influence maternelle à l'induction de la diapause larvaire : exposées aux jours courts, elles ont une progéniture entrant en diapause si la température larvaire est de 15° C ou en dessous et exposées aux jours longs (ou les larves) à des températures supérieures à 15° C mènent à la non diapause.
- bien que l'induction photopériodique soit maternelle, Vaznunes et Saunders (1989) ont démontré que les larves sont légèrement sensibles à la photopériode et, en outre, les oeufs pour l'éclosion des larves. Ce n'est qu'une donnée particulière intervenant dans le calcul de la durée de la croissance des larves. Il est bien évident que le progrès des connaissances sur la physiologie et la biochimie de ces mouches permettra d'améliorer les résultats de l'expertise entomologique (Leclercq et Verstraeten, 1993).
- nymphes ou pupes vides (dont l'adulte est sorti) : témoignage d'une ou de plusieurs générations avec cycle biologique complet.

## Un exemple d'expertise entomologique (Leclercq, 1993)

En l'absence de prélèvement entomologique sur le cadavre, l'expertise a pu être réalisée en disposant de documents photographiques très précis fournis par les enquêteurs et les médecins légistes :
1) Le 6 septembre 1988, vers 8 heures 45, découverte dans un bois, d'un cadavre partiellement carbonisé.
2) Constatations des médecins légistes (autopsie le 7.09.1988) : victime jeune, sexe féminin-carbonisation-larves d'insectes grouillant dans le thorax, sinus frontaux, mâchoires...
3) identification de la victime, portée disparue depuis le 26 août 1988, très tard dans la soirée et à une vingtaine de kilomètres de l'endroit de la découverte du cadavre.

4) Identification des larves : environ 18 mm pour les plus âgées. Calliphora : vicina ou vomitaria? Non précisées sur photographies.
5) Graphique des températures maximales, moyennes, minimales : 26 août au 7 septembre 1988 : on repère un pic des températures le 27 août (25 ; 21,15 ; 17,30 °) ; puis une descente du 28/8 au 3/9, à des températures maximales entre 15,5-19,4° ; moyennes entre 13,25-16,4 ° ; minimales entre 10,8-14,7 ° ; puis la température remontera du 4/9 au 6/9 atteignant des valeurs de 24,2 ; 18,6 et 13 °.
6) Calcul des températures moyennes (en degré Celsius) : successivement : Minimales - Maximales - Moyennes : 26 au 31/8 : 12,91, 19,38, 16,15, et 1 au 6/9 : 12,73, 19,10, 15,91 et 7/9 : le cadavre a été mis en chambre froide.
7) Durée du développement des Calliphora spp. : plusieurs publications citent les données d'interprétation (Smith, 1986 ; Leclercq et Brahy, 1990 ; Leclercq, 1993) : incubation des oeufs - vie larvaire - vie des pupes - éclosion des adultes...

Dans ce texte limité, il n'est pas possible d'analyser tous les facteurs. Nous présentons un résumé des résultats obtenus :
- L'arrivée des premières mouches Calliphora sp. sur le cadavre paraît bien être limitée au 27 août 1988, après le lever du jour.
- Aucune ponte nocturne n'est envisageable ici. La durée probable de l'incubation des oeufs est d'environ 24 heures.
- L'âge des larves les plus âgées : pas moins de 9 jours.
- Aucune pupe n'est visible sur les documents photographiques.
- L'intervalle entre la disparition de la victime et la découverte de son cadavre est de 10 jours plus environ 10 heures.

La datation de la mort de la victime peut logiquement être estimée durant la dizaine d'heures qui ont suivi son enlèvement le 26 août 1988 vers 23 heures. Il faut nécessairement en déduire la succession des évènements : enlèvement, manipulation, transport à une vingtaine de kilomètres de distance, déroulement de l'affaire criminelle, carbonisation partielle (preuve d'utilisation d'un carburant très volatil et de courte durée, comme par exemple l'essence), puis feu éteint permettant l'attirance et l'arrivée des mouches. Dès lors, la datation de la mort de la victime peut être fixée très tard dans un délai très court.

L'enquête judiciaire a suivi son cours. La conclusion de cette expertise a été confirmée par les aveux de l'accusé qui a été reconnu coupable d'homicide volontaire avec préméditation et condamné à la plus lourde peine en Cour d'Assises.

## Conclusion

Les résultats actuels des expertises entomologiques ne sont plus limités à l'estimation de l'intervalle postmortem (Leclercq et Verstraeten, 1993). En effet, la littérature internationale conduit à des conclusions concernant : endroit du crime - manipulation, dissimulation, transport du cadavre - identification du coupable d'un homicide (acariens) - utilisation de répulsif sur le cadavre - correction d'une erreur judiciaire - enfants maltraités et manque d'hygiène - indicateurs d'abus sexuels : présence de morpions (Phthirus pubis) sur des enfants de sexe féminin - identification de l'origine de cannabis (insectes accompagnant cette drogue) - identification de médicaments, de substances toxiques, de drogues dans les stades

larvaires d'insectes nécrophages quand il est impossible de le faire à partir de cadavre putréfié (Kintz et al., 1990 ; Goff et Lord, 1991 ; Goff et al., 1991 ; Nolte et al., 1992).
Chaque expertise entomologique médico-légale est plus ou moins spécifique ; elle est pluridisciplinaire. Sous certaines conditions, les insectes et les acariens peuvent être de précieux témoins en médecine légale. Ils n'ont pas fini d'être correctement exploités.

## Références

Catts EP (1992) Problems in estimating the postmortem interval in death investigations. J Agric Entomol 9:245-255
Goff ML, Lord WD (Correspondence no date) Entomotoxicology : a new area for forensic investigations. Dept of Entomology University of Hawaii at Manoa Honolulu Hawaii 96822 & Forensic Sciences Research and Training Center FBI Academy Quantico Virginia 22135:1-18
Goff ML, Lord WD, Hewadikaram KA, Omori AI (1991) Effect of heroin in decomposing tissues on the development rate of Boettscherisca peregrina (Diptera Sarcophagidae) and its implications of this effect in estimation of postmortem intervals using Arthropod development patterns. J Forensic Sci 36:537-542
Grösse WR (19983) Zur Flugaktivität von Calliphora vicina RD in Freiland. Wiss Z Univ Halle 32:23-29
Kintz P, Godelar B, Tracqui A, Mangin M, Lugnier AA, Chaumont AJ (1990) Fly larvae a new toxicological method of investigation in forensic medicine. J. Forensic Sci 35:201-207
Leclercq M (1993) Entomologie et médecine légale, datation de la mort sur des documents photographiques. Rev Méd Liège 48:279-284
Leclercq M, Brahy G (1990) Entomologie et médecine légale, origines evolution actualisation. Rev Méd Liège 45:348-358
Leclercq M, Dodinval P, Piette P, Verstraeten Ch (1991) Exemple d'une coopération entre médecin légiste ondontologiste et entomologistes, identification d'ossements humains, datation de la mort et fixation du lieu d'un crime. Rev Méd Liège 46:583-591
Leclercq M, Verstraeten Ch (1993) Entomologie et médecine légale, l'entomofaune des cadavres humains sa succession par son interprétation, ses résultats, ses perspectives. J Méd Lég Droit Méd 36:205-222
Miras A, Mali M, Malicier D (1991) L'identification en médecine légale. Lacassagne A (éd) Lyon:1-202
Nolte KB, Pinder RD, Lord WD (1992) Insect larvae used to detect cocain poisoning in a decomposed body. J Forensic Sci 37:1179-1185
Smith KGV (1986) A manual of forensic entomology. British Museum Natural History London:1-205
Vaznunes M, Saunders DS (1989) The effect of larval temperature and photoperiod in blowfly Calliphora vicina. Physiological Entomol 14:471-474

# ENTOMOLOGY APPLICATION TO TIME OF DEATH DETERMINATION

PH. MASSELIN, J. SALON, B. CECCALDI, B. CHAUVET

INSTITUT DE RECHERCHE CRIMINELLE DE LA GENDARMERIE NATIONALE, département ENTOMOLOGIE
(Institute of Forensic Sciences of the French Gendarmerie, forensic entomology department).
1, Bd Théophile SUEUR 93111 ROSNY-sous-BOIS, FRANCE.

Key-Words : Forensic entomology, carrion, postmortem interval.

On July the 15th 1992, the decaying corpse of a woman is discovered undergrowth in the outer suburbs of Paris. The forensic observations allow to estimate the maximal postmortem interval to six months.

The entomological takings made at the death scene and during the postmortem examination bring to light a very important presence of insects (Diptera and Coleoptera) at various stages of development. These are divided in necrophagous :

- *Calliphora vomitoria* (Linné, 1758) : larval and pupal stage,
- *Ophyra* sp. : larval stage,
- Silphinae sp. : larval stage and exuviae,
- *Muscina pabulorum* Fallen (= *Muscina prolapsa* Harris) : mature stage,
- *Necrodes littoralis* (Linné, 1761) : mature stage,

and necrophilous :

- *Nicrophorus humator* (Olivier, 1791) : mature stage,
- *Creophilus maxillosus* (Linné, 1758) : larval and mature stage,
- Staphylinidae sp. : mature stage,
- *Saprinus semistriatus* (Scriba, 1790) : mature stage.

These species identified at the laboratory match a coherent entomological ecosystem which was present during the decay of a necromass and was consistent with a rural dwelling.

The study of insect's biology mainly focused on *Calliphora vomitoria*, *Ophyra* sp. and *Creophilus maxillosus* compared to local weather data allows to determinate a first entomological activity between June the 13th and June the 24th with a more favorable period on June the 14th to June the 16th.

The dental examination allowed to identify the victim. The various witnesses'examinations have established that the deceased person had been seen alive for the last time on June 10th, 1994.

Thus, the inquiry provided confirmation of the postmortem delay obtained through entomological analysis.

---

1 - DAJOZ R. et CAUSSANEL Ch. (1968) *Creophilus maxillosus* (L.) (Staphylinidae). In : Cahier des Naturalistes, T.24, Fasc.3.

2 - ERZINCLIOGLU Y.Z. (1985) Immature stages of british Calliphora and Cynomya, with a re-evaluation of the taxonomic characters of larval Calliphoridae (Diptera) . In : J.N.H. 19 : 69-96.

3 - LECLERCQ M. (1978) Entomologie et médecine légale, datation de la mort. In : Masson (ed) Collection de Médecine Légale et de Toxicologie Médicale N° 108.

4 - SMITH K.G.V. (1986) Manual of Forensic Entomology. In : The Trustees of the British Museum (Natural History).

# Springer-Verlag and the Environment

We at Springer-Verlag firmly believe that an international science publisher has a special obligation to the environment, and our corporate policies consistently reflect this conviction.

We also expect our business partners – paper mills, printers, packaging manufacturers, etc. – to commit themselves to using environmentally friendly materials and production processes.

The paper in this book is made from low- or no-chlorine pulp and is acid free, in conformance with international standards for paper permanency.

GPSR Compliance

*The European Union's (EU) General Product Safety Regulation (GPSR) is a set of rules that requires consumer products to be safe and our obligations to ensure this.*

*If you have any concerns about our products, you can contact us on ProductSafety@springernature.com*

In case Publisher is established outside the EU, the EU authorized representative is:

Springer Nature Customer Service Center GmbH
Europaplatz 3
69115 Heidelberg, Germany

**Batch number: 10844669**

Printed by Printforce, the Netherlands